Contents

W9-CBE-387

Germany: the "Länder"

Principal sights

Worth a journey ★★★

Worth a detour ★★

Interesting ★

The names of sights described in the guide appear in black on the map. See the index for the page number.

De	in Deutsch
En	in English
Es	en Español
Fr	en Français
It	in Italiano
Ne	in het Nederlands
Po	em Português

0   60 km

DANMARK

NEDERLAND

Nederland	
En	
Fr	
Ne	

OSTSEE

Kap Arkona
Stubbenkammer
Granitz
RÜGEN
Putbus
Zingst
Darß
Fischland
Stralsund
Greifswald
Warnemünde
Kühlungsborn
Bad Doberan
ROSTOCK
Wismar
Güstrow
Schwerin
Ludwigslust
Ratzeburg
LÜBECK
Travemünde
Laboe
KIEL
Holsteinische Schweiz
Schleswig
Flensburg
Nolde-Museum
Husum
Eider
Eidersperrwerk
Nordfriesische Inseln
Halligen
Sylt
Westerland
Helgoland
NORDSEE
Ostfriesische Inseln
Frise
Emden
GRONINGEN
Oldenburg
Bremerhaven
BREMEN
Steindenkmäler
Stade
Altes Land
HAMBURG
Lüneburger Heide
Wilseder Berg
Lüneburg
Gedenkstätte Bergen-Belsen
Celle
Wienhausen
HANNOVER
BRAUNSCHWEIG
Königslutter
Stendal
Tangermünde
Havelberg
Brandenburg
Lehnin
POTSDAM
BERLIN
Oranienburg
Rheinsberg
Ravensbrück
Neubrandenburg
Chorin
SZCZECIN
POLSKA
Spreewald
MECKLENBURGISCHE SEENPLATTE
Peene
USEDOM
Kap Arkona
WESER
ELBE
Aller
Havel
Warnow
ODER / ODRA
WARTA

Touring programmes

Places of interest with a selection
of hotel accommodation for an overnight
stop are indicated by ▣

★★★ MOSELTAL — Name under which a route
is described. See the index for
the page number.

Baden-Württemberg
and Bavaria :
2 000km – 1 240 miles

Palatinate, Rhineland
and the Moselle :
1 200km – 750 miles

Saxony, Thuringia
and Franconia :
1 350km – 840 miles

Northern Germany
and the Baltic Coast :
1 700km – 1 060 miles

OSTSEE

POLSKA

ODRA
ODER

Warta

BERLIN ★★★

Chorin ★★

SZCZECIN ★★

T 198

A 11

A 10

A 20

Peene

A 24

Havel

Kap Arkona ★

RÜGEN ★

Greifswald ★

Stralsund ★

Neubrandenburg

96

109

105

104

Warnow

ROSTOCK ★

A 19

Warnemünde ★

Bad
Doberan ★

501

Kühlungsborn ★

Wismar ★

Schwerin ★★★

104

A 24

ELBE

DANMARK

Westerland ★★★

Sylt ★

Flensburg ★

199

5

Husum

76

Schleswig ★

Eider

A 7

A 215

KIEL ★

78

Travemünde ★

LÜBECK ★★★

A 1

A 23

HAMBURG ★★★

A 7

Stade

71

BREMEN ★★

A 27

Bremerhaven ★

A 28

A 1

A 7

NORDSEE

GRONINGEN

10

Introduction

11

Description of the country

In the heart of Europe, bordered by the Alps to the south and by the Baltic Sea to the north, Germany is virtually without natural frontiers to the east and the west. Such a lack of barriers, and the subsequent accessibility to outside influences has had a profound effect on the country's history and civilization.

Modern Germany covers an area of 356 000km^2 - 139 000sq miles. Geologically and geographically, this vast area is divided into three separate regions. In the **north**, the immense **Germano-Polish Plain**, formed by the glaciation of the Quaternary era, owes the fact that it was scarcely touched by the Hercynian and Alpine mountain-building movements to the resistance of its crystalline bedrock.

In the **centre**, during the Primary era, the formidable **Hercynian folding** created a complex of minor massifs – now smoothed by erosion and for the most part wooded – separated by geographic depressions. The most important of these Hercynian massifs are the Black Forest, the Rhenish schist massif, and – encircling Bohemia – the Böhmerwald, the Bavarian Forest, the Erzgebirge (or metal-bearing mountains) and the Sudeten Mountains. On the edges of this Hercynian zone accumulated the coal-bearing deposits of the Ruhr and Silesia which led to the industrial expansion of the 19C. The sedimentary basin of Swabia-Franconia, its vast area drained by the Main and the Neckar, offers a less dramatic landscape; abutting the Black Forest on the west and the Swabian Jura to the south, the limestone plateau is patterned with lines of hills sculpted according to the resistance of the varied strata.

In the **south**, the Alpine portion of Germany is delimited by the **Pre-Alps**, where the debris torn up and crushed during the final exertions of Quaternary glaciation formed the Bavarian plateau – a huge area stretching in a gentle slope as far as the Danube.

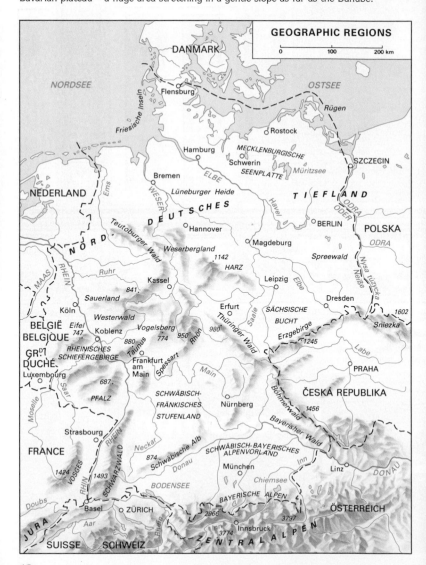

THE SCENERY
Northern Germany

Lower Rhine Valley and Westphalia – Lush, green and flat, protected from flooding, the plain of the Lower Rhine, with its cosy houses, brings to mind the landscape of the neighbouring Netherlands. There is similar scenery around Münster on the Westphalian plain, where the farmlands patterned by hedges and trees offer the additional attraction of many moated castles (Wasserburgen).

Great Northern Plain – Despite its apparent monotony, this enormous area (which extends eastwards into Poland but is confined, so far as Germany is concerned, between the Ems and the Oder) does offer a certain variety of landscapes.

In the south, below the Weser and Harz foothills, the Börde country lies between the Weser and the Elbe – a region covered by an alluvial topsoil whose fertility is legendary. Farms and market gardens flourish in this densely populated zone, which is favoured also with mineral deposits rich in iron and potassium.

Further north, on either side of the Elbe, is the Geest – a region with little to recommend it geographically, since it was covered by the Scandinavian glaciers right up to Palaeolithic times. This has resulted in poor drainage and soils that are too sandy; between Berlin and the Baltic, the Mecklenburg plateau is scattered with shallow lakes interspersed with morainic deposits that bear witness to the prolonged glacial presence. The Baltic coast has been little affected by erosion, thanks to the relatively shallow depth of the sea, and local currents have been strong enough to link up the rocky islets at Rügen with the mainland to form the Darß peninsula.

The Spree and the Havel, meandering through the flatlands, supply the lakeland regions of the Spreewald and Potsdam.

West of the Lower Weser, and in the Worpswede neighbourhood north of Bremen, peat bogs (Moore) alternate with very wet pastureland. Most of the peat moors are now under cultivation, after drainage using Dutch methods.

The nature reserve south of Lüneburg, however, has preserved for all time a typical stretch of the original moorland.

Loop of the Saar at Cloef

North Sea Coast – Huge areas of cultivation have been reclaimed from the vast mudflats once uncovered here at low tide. Germany's two largest seaports, Hamburg and Bremen, lie at the inner ends of the Elbe and Weser estuaries.

Schleswig-Holstein – There is a striking contrast between Germany's North Sea coast, scoured by the ocean winds and constantly threatened by storms, and the Baltic shoreline, where the flat, wooded countryside is deeply penetrated by arms of the sea (Förde), and calm waters lap peacefully against picturesque fishing villages and sandy beaches. Naturally the principal towns are built on this eastern side of the peninsula – with the exception of Husum. Inland, the many lakes and woods make up Holstein's enticing "Little Switzerland", while further west – towards the harsh Atlantic weather – there is an alternation of dunes, marshes and moorland.

Central Germany

The Rhenish Schist Massif – This ancient geological mass, cut through by the Rhine – the only real channel of communication between the north and south of the country – the Lahn and the Moselle, comprises the highlands known as the Eifel, the Westerwald, the Taunus and the Hunsrück. They share the same inhospitable climate and the same evidence of volcanic activity, witness the crater lakes, known as the Maare *(qv)*, of the Eifel plateau.

The Eifel will be familiar to motoring enthusiasts as the home of the Nürburgring Grand Prix race circuit. The Upper Sauerland, a thickly wooded, mountainous region (alt 841m - 2 760ft), with its many dams, acts as a water reserve for the Ruhr industrial area.

Mountains of Upper Hessen and the Weser – Between the Rhenish schist massif and the forest of Thuringia (Thüringer Wald) lies a confused amalgam of heights, some of them volcanic (Vogelsberg, Rhön), and depressions which have been used as a highway linking north and south by German invaders throughout the ages. Between Westphalia and the north, the Weser Mountains – extended westwards by the Teutoburger Wald – form a barrier that is breached at the Porta Westfalica, near Minden. Further to the east, the Erzgebirge (metal-bearing mountains) form a natural frontier with the Czech Republic.

Harz Mountains – This relatively high range (alt 1 142m - 3 747ft at the Brocken) has a typical mountain climate, characterized by heavy snowfalls in winter.

Southern Germany

Plain of the Upper Rhine – Between Basle and the Bingen Gap, a soil of exceptionally fertile loess, accompanied by a climate which combines light rainfall, an early spring and a very hot summer, has produced a rich agricultural yield (hops, corn and tobacco) and a terrain highly suitable for the cultivation of vines. The whole of this low-lying, productive tract has become a crossroads for the rest of Europe, which is why certain towns – Frankfurt, for instance – have profited internationally from their development.

Black Forest – This crystalline massif (alt 1 493m - 4 899ft at the Feldberg), which overlooks the Rhine gap, is relatively well populated. The region's healthy climate and many thermal springs, with their attendant, highly reputed spa resorts, draw large numbers of tourists here every year.

Swabian-Franconian Basin – Franconia, formed by vast, gently indulating plateaux, is bordered on the southeast by the small limestone massif of the Franconian Jura which produces Germany's finest building stone, and to the north and northeast by the heavily wooded crystalline ranges flanking Bohemia and Thuringia.

Swabia, once ruled by the kings of Württemberg, offers a great variety of landscapes – barred to the south by the blue line of the Swabian Jura, which rises to 874m - 2 867ft. Small valleys, enlivened by orchards and vineyards, alternate here with the gentle slopes of wooded hillsides.

The Alps and the Bavarian Plateau – The Bavarian Alps and the Alps of Allgäu offer impressive contrasts between the sombre green of their forests and the shades of grey-colouring their rocks and escarpments, which make an impressive sight when seen against the backdrop of a brilliant blue sky. The Zugspitze, the highest point in Germany, reaches an altitude of 2 962m - 9 720ft.

Torrents such as the Isar, the Lech and the Iller, gushing down from the mountains throughout the ages, have carved out wide corridors with broad, flat floors suitable for the cultivation of the land and the development of towns (Ulm, Augsburg and Munich).

Garmisch-Partenkirchen with the Zugspitze range

NATURE AND CONSERVATION

The preservation of natural assets, particularly of trees, is of prime concern to Germans.

The Forest – The colossal forests of the old Germania are of course no more than a memory, but the long survival of feudal customs and the difficulties of adapting undergrowth to the establishment of pastureland have resulted over the centuries in a remarkable preservation of wooded countryside. Such regions, gravely threatened today by pollution, are now the subject of protective measures greatly supported in their application by the ecological conscience of the great majority of the German people. Forests of deciduous trees flourish above all in the centre of the country, in the zone of the Hercynian massifs. In the Westerwald, the Thüringer Wald, the Weser Mountains and the land around Kassel, there are still magnificent beechwoods. Clumps of beech and spruce predominate in the Swabian Jura, the Harz and the heights of the Black Forest. Superb oaks cover the Spessart and the Reinhardswald, while the homogeneous carpet of conifers is found mainly in the Alps.

> The **lime tree**, symbol of poetic inspiration and of youth, is widely prevalent throughout Germany, growing with its fellows around a village square or giving welcome shade along urban thoroughfares. Numerous solitary lime trees can be found standing in silent commemoration of the poetic reverie of great writers such as Goethe or Schiller, or the musings of statesmen such as Bismarck.

The Parks – Whether it be a municipal park or the grounds of a spa, an English garden at Munich or one in the formal French style at Brühl, a Romantic fantasy like Linderhof or a contemporary design such as can be found in the Ruhr, all German parks have one thing in common: the impeccable standard of their upkeep. Every other year, one of these great parks hosts the National Horticultural Exhibition or Bundesgartenschau.

In Germany there are many **natural parks** (Naturpark), the details and extent of which can be found in Michelin maps 415 to 420. These must not be confused with the great number of **nature reserves** (Naturschutzgebiet), which are less extensive and frequently play a scientific role justifying certain restrictions of access. The natural parks are kept, especially in forest regions, specifically for the pleasure of walkers. The biggest are in the Altmühl Valley, in Swiss Franconia and the Bergstraße-Odenwald. The Pfälzer Wald is limited in the south by France's North Vosges Regional Park; that of the southern Eifel (Südeifel), which also straddles a frontier, includes the Grand Duchy of Luxembourg's "Little Switzerland". Between Berlin and the Oder lies the Märkische Schweiz.

There are also National Parks in Germany. Among them are the Watten-Meer on the North Sea coast, the Bavarian Forest in the southeast, Swiss Saxony (Sächsische Schweiz) in the east and the Hochharz in the north centre.

Apart from these official parks, all mountain ranges of any importance and most woods near holiday resorts are crisscrossed with public footpaths, well sign-posted and – if they qualify as a *Waldlehrpfad* – posted with information on local flora and fauna.

Four seasons

Continuous interaction between oceanic and continental air masses determines the atmospheric conditions over Germany, producing a climate notable for its instability – even turbulence – especially in the north of the country. The months which are the least cloudy, although not necessarily the warmest, are normally April and May in coastal regions, June and September in the interior.

Throughout the year, the climate is bracing and breezy on the North Sea coast, a little milder on the Baltic. But beach life tends to be active because of the prevailing west winds. From April onwards, the Rhine Valley and southern Germany as a whole enjoy calm, mild weather brightened with the blossom of fruit trees and orchards. On the shores of Lake Constance, in the valleys of the Inn and the Salzach, the arrival of the Föhn – a cool, dry south wind blowing violently down from the Alps – hastens the approach of springtime.

Summer in the centre of the country is marked by a rapid rise in temperature, particularly in the sheltered depressions of the Hercynian massifs (the plains of the Upper Rhine for instance), where the heat can become heavy and thundery. At such times holidaymakers are especially glad of the bathing facilities and the various opportunities for forest walks. In the Alps, the climate at this time of the year is very variable, depending on the orientation of valleys, the direction of local winds, which way the slopes face, etc.

Often enough in late October and mid-November the sun reappears in a kind of Indian summer, known locally as the *Altweibersommer* (old women's summer), which enhances autumn tints marvellously, particularly in southern Germany. But night falls fast. From the first chill days of winter, the Bavarian Alps, the Allgäu, the Black Forest, the Sauerland and the Harz begin to be hidden beneath a carpet of snow.

Overview of modern Germany

A Federal State – Subdivided throughout history into different regions that were largely autonomous, owing allegiance to no single capital (prior to 1945 Berlin was only capital of the Reich for just over 70 years), Germany has naturally gravitated towards a governmental structure that is federal in origin.

The **Fundamental Law** established in 1949 guarantees the liberty of the individual and defines the principles underlying the institutions of the Republic. The Federal Parliament is composed of two chambers: the **Bundestag**, a national assembly of 500 members elected by universal suffrage, is invested with legislative power, chooses the Chancellor, and controls the government; the **Bundesrat**, a federal council comprising 41 members drawn from the local governments administering the Länder, or provinces, is concerned with certain aspects of legislative power, particularly when they affect the Länder.

At the head of the Federal government, the Chancellor, who is invested with wide-ranging powers, defines the broad lines of policy. The Federal President (Bundespräsident) is elected by a Federal Assembly. It is he who concludes treaties with foreign states, decides upon or revokes the appointment of judges and Federal functionaries as well as Federal ministers suggested by the Chancellor, and verifies that the laws of the Constitution are respected.

The Federal Republic comprises 16 **Länder** (eleven of which formed the old West Germany plus the five added in 1990 which were re-constituted from the 15 districts of the former East German Democratic Republic - *see opposite*). Each Land organizes its constitution within the terms of the Fundamental Law. Apart from questions concerning the Federal authority – foreign affairs, defence matters, financial policy – each enjoys wide powers, notably in the spheres of education, culture and professional training. They are responsible, in addition, for the application of Federal laws and numerous administrative functions.

Industrial Dynamism – Despite the devastation inflicted during the final years of the Second World War and the dismantling of industrial potential demanded by the Allies after the capitulation of Hitler's Reich, the Federal Republic has raised itself to the position of the world's fourth industrial power and the second biggest exporter. This success is the result of a **social market economy**, linking private enterprise to social progress, in which unions and management work together as partners.

The decline of Germany's traditional iron and steel industry has been compensated by dynamic advances in the fields of mechanics (machine-tools, electro-technology) and automobile construction (the world's third largest producer). Numerous smaller businesses maintain the reputation of the country's optical industry and its talent for the manufacture of precision machinery. Craftwork too occupies an important place in the economy, as exemplified in the annual Munich International Fair, the largest in the world.

Progressive Cities – The political disintegration of the old Germany raised many provincial cities to the status of local capital. The absence, for almost a half-century, of a single national capital dealing in both political and economic matters, as well as the federal character of institutions in West Germany in general, permitted a certain number of cities to develop an unexpected industrial and cultural influence.

Major centres such as Cologne, Düsseldorf, Hanover, Frankfurt and Munich, not to mention also Dresden and Leipzig, each with its own university, theatre and symphony orchestra, organize a packed annual programme of festivals, congresses and commercial fairs which confirms their position as trail-blazers in modern cultural affairs, as well as winning them international acclaim.

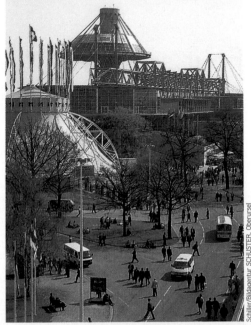

Hanover Trade Fair Centre

Schiller/Bildagentur SCHUSTER, Oberursel

THE LÄNDER

	AREA	POPULATION	CAPITAL
Baden-Württemberg	35 751 km² 13 530sq miles	9 400 000	Stuttgart
Bayern (Bavaria)	70 555 km² 27 213sq miles	11 000 000	München (Munich)
Berlin	883 km² 341sq miles	3 400 000	Berlin
Brandenburg	26 000 km² 10 036sq miles	2 700 000	Potsdam
Bremen	404 km² 156sq miles	682 000	Bremen
Hamburg	755 km² 292sq miles	1 600 000	Hamburg
Hessen	21 114 km² 8 106sq miles	5 600 000	Wiesbaden
Mecklenburg-Vorpommern (Mecklenburg-West Pomerania)	22 500 km² 8 685sq miles	2 100 000	Schwerin
Niedersachsen (Lower Saxony)	47 344 km² 18 258sq miles	7 200 00	Hannover (Hanover)
Nordrhein-Westfalen (Rhineland-Westfalia)	34 070 km² 13 124sq miles	16 900 000	Düsseldorf
Rheinland-Pfalz (Rhineland-Palatinate)	19 849 km² 7 662sq miles	3 700 000	Mainz
Saarland (Saar)	2 570 km² 065sq miles	1 100 000	Saarbrücken
Sachsen (Saxony)	17 000 km² 6 562sq miles	4 900 000	Dresden
Sachsen-Anhalt (Saxony-Anhalt)	25 000 km² 9 650sq miles	3 000 000	Magdeburg
Schleswig-Holstein	15 729 km² 6 060sq miles	2 600 000	Kiel
Thüringen (Thuringia)	15 209 km² 5 867sq miles	2 500 000	Erfurt

Traditional Costumes – These have tended to be less common since the Second World War. Nevertheless, men in Upper Bavaria still wear leather shorts, a Loden cloth jacket with horn buttons, and the famous "Tyrolean hat" adorned with a tuft of chamois beard or badger's tail, an outfit which makes a tremendous impression on tourists. In the Schwalm region (Alsfeld, Ziegenhain and Marburg), women still sometimes wear the traditional short, flared skirt and white stockings. At festivals such as the Schwalm Salad Fair, young women wear heavy, tight-fitting ceremonial costumes embroidered in brilliant colours and crowned with a tiny red hood – as in the well-known Grimms' fairy tale.

To see other regional costumes – for example, those of the Black Forest, the Kleinwalsertal or the region of Forchheim – it is usually necessary to attend a carnival, pageant or local fête.

The **Dirndl**, worn by women in Bavaria, is not in fact attached to any specific folklore or tradition. But the charm of the gathered skirt, the puff-sleeved bodice, and the colourful pinafore ensures a demand for the costume as a souvenir.

Young girl from the Schwalm region

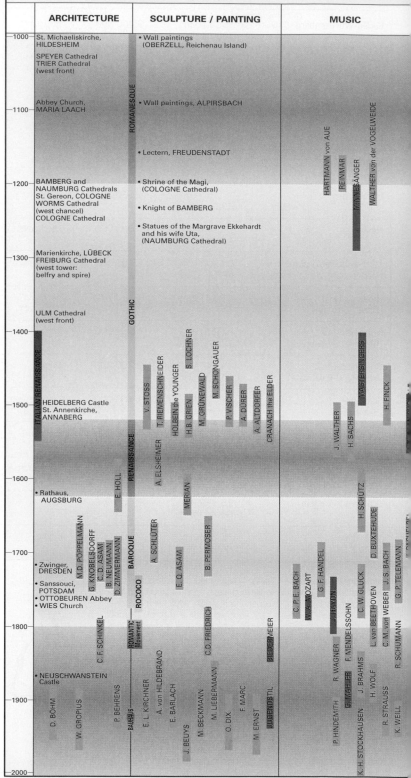

FROM THE MIDDLE AGES

After the Treaty of Verdun in AD 843, Germany united from the Baltic Sea to the Alps all those peoples sharing a common language and culture. Faced with constant incursions from the barbarians, a number of powerful princes asserted their authority, and it was from among these that eventual kings of Germany were elected. It was Otto I, who was finally created "Emperor" by the Pope.

	ARCHITECTURE	SCULPTURE / PAINTING	MUSIC
1000	St. Michaeliskirche, HILDESHEIM SPEYER Cathedral TRIER Cathedral (west front)	• Wall paintings (OBERZELL, Reichenau Island)	
1100	Abbey Church, MARIA LAACH	• Wall paintings, ALPIRSBACH	
		• Lectern, FREUDENSTADT	
1200	BAMBERG and NAUMBURG Cathedrals St. Gereon, COLOGNE WORMS Cathedral (west chancel) COLOGNE Cathedral	• Shrine of the Magi, (COLOGNE Cathedral) • Knight of BAMBERG • Statues of the Margrave Ekkehardt and his wife Uta, (NAUMBURG Cathedral)	HARTMANN von AUE REINMAR MINNESÄNGER WALTHER von der VOGELWEIDE
1300	Marienkirche, LÜBECK FREIBURG Cathedral (west tower: belfry and spire)		
1400	ULM Cathedral (west front)		MASTERSINGERS H. FINCK
1500	HEIDELBERG Castle St. Annenkirche, ANNABERG	V. STOSS — T. RIEMENSCHNEIDER — HOLBEIN the YOUNGER — H.B. GRIEN — M. GRÜNEWALD — M. SCHONGAUER — S. LOCHNER — P. VISCHER — A. DÜRER — A. ALTDORFER — CRANACH the ELDER	J. WALTHER H. SACHS
1600	• Rathaus, AUGSBURG	E. HOLL — A. ELSHEIMER — MERIAN	H. SCHÜTZ
1700	• Zwinger, DRESDEN • Sanssouci, POTSDAM • OTTOBEUREN Abbey • WIES Church	M.D. POPPELMANN — G. KNOBELSDORFF — C.D. ASAM — B. NEUMANN — D. ZIMMERMANN — A. SCHLÜTER — E.Q. ASAM — B. PERMOSER	C.P.E. BACH — W.A. MOZART — J. HAYDN — G.F. HÄNDEL — C.W. GLUCK — D. BUXTEHUDE — J.S. BACH — G.P. TELEMANN
1800	• NEUSCHWANSTEIN Castle	C.F. SCHINKEL — C.D. FRIEDRICH — BIEDERMEIER	
1900	D. BÖHM — W. GROPIUS — P. BEHRENS — BAUHAUS — J. BEUYS	E.L. KIRCHNER — A. von HILDEBRAND — E. BARLACH — M. BECKMANN — M. LIEBERMANN — O. DIX — F. MARC — M. ERNST — JUGENDSTIL	P. HINDEMITH — R. WAGNER — G. MAHLER — F. MENDELSSOHN — L. van BEETHOVEN — C.M. von WEBER — J. BRAHMS — H. WOLF — R. STRAUSS — R. SCHUMANN — K.H. STOCKHAUSEN — K. WEILL
2000			

TO THE PRESENT

Otto I became the founder of the Holy Roman Empire. For a long time after that, the control of the Papacy itself was the Empire's principal objective, but when this policy failed and the organization was reduced just to Germany, the different territorial principalities grew stronger and the "Empire" shrank in fact to what in time developed into an elective monarchy.

LITERATURE	RELIGION AND PHILOSOPHY	HISTORY	ECONOMY, SCIENCE AND TECHNOLOGY	
SONG OF THE NIBELUNGEN		SAXON DYNASTY / Ottonian Emperors / SALIAN DYNASTY	Growth of trade / Founding of the monasteries	1000
	POPE GREGORY VII. / • CANOSSA 1077 (Investiture Controversy)	Henry IV		
HEINRICH von VELDEKE				1100
GOTTFRIED von STRASSBURG	Concordat of Worms (1122)		• Demographic growth	
WOLFRAM von ESCHENBACH		House of HOHENSTAUFEN / Conrad III / Emperor Frederick I Barbarossa	• Expansion towards the East	
	ALEXANDER III / TEUTONIC ORDER 1190 / Third Crusade		• Working of the mineral deposits in Silesia and Thuringia	1200
Master ECKHART	ALBERTUS MAGNUS / Sixth Crusade	Frederick II (King of Sicily) / Rudolph I of Habsburg	• HANSEATIC LEAGUE: growth of Baltic trade / • Growth of towns	
H. SUSO / J. TAULER		House of LUXEMBOURG		1300
		Charles IV / The Golden Bull	• Famines / • BLACK DEATH 1349 / • Demographic decline	
	Council of Constance / The Hussite Controversy	Sigismund		1400
		House of HABSBURG	• GUTENBERG	
H.J.C. von GRIMMELSHAUSEN / A. GRYPHIUS / M. OPITZ / D.C. von LOHENSTEIN / M. LUTHER / PARACELSUS / H. SACHS / F. FISCHART	1517: Luther exhibits his 95 "theses" on the door of the church at Wittenberg / 1521: Luther is excommunicated / 1530: Confession of Augsburg / 1546: death of Luther (Counter-Reformation)	Maximilian I (1493-1519) acquires the duchy of Burgundy and the rich Netherlands by marriage / Maximilian I / Emperor Charles V / • Peace of AUGSBURG 1555 / Rudolf II	Powerful Merchant Families (The FUGGERS and the WELSERS) / • Rapid urban expansion	1500
		Matthias II / • THIRTY YEARS WAR	• KEPLER: astronomical telescope	1600
		• Peace of WESTPHALIA 1648 / Revocation of the Edict of Nantes / French Huguenots arrive	• LEIBNIZ: differential and integral calculus	
J.C. GOTTSCHED / F.G. KLOPSTOCK / G.E. LESSING / C. WIELAND / J. von EICHENDORFF / J.W. von GOETHE / NOVALIS / H. von KLEIST / E.T.A. HOFFMANN / F. von SCHILLER / J. and W. GRIMM / H. HEINE	W.G. LEIBNIZ / J.G. von HERDER / E. KANT / J.G. FICHTE / G.W.F. HEGEL / A. SCHOPENHAUER (AUFKLÄRUNG)	Rise of BRANDENBURG and PRUSSIAN Rulers / THE HOHENZOLLERN / • Seven Years War	• BÖTTGER: Saxon porcelain / • FAHRENHEIT: mercury thermometer	1700
		• Confederation of the Rhine / • Chancellor Otto von Bismarck / • North German Confederation	• DRAIS: draisienne (prototype of the bicycle) / • HAHNEMANN: homeopathy	1800
K. MARX / F. ENGELS / G. HAUPTMANN / T. MANN / H. HESSE / B. BRECHT	K. MARX / F. ENGELS / E. HUSSERL / M. HEIDEGGER / K. JASPERS / F. NIETZSCHE	• SECOND REICH	• G. DAIMLER and K. BENZ: internal combustion engine / • DIESEL engine / • RÖNTGEN: X-rays / • PLANCK: quantum theory	
H. BÖLL / G. GRASS		FIRST WORLD WAR / • Weimar Republic / • THIRD REICH / SECOND WORLD WAR	• EINSTEIN: theory of relativity / • O. HAHN: nuclear fission	1900
		• TREATY OF GERMAN REUNIFICATION		2000

(HANSEATIC LEAGUE — economy column, spanning c. 1300–1500)

Historical table and notes

The Origins

The first human occupation of the territories which lie between the Rhine and the Elbe is thought to have been at the time of Neanderthal Man *(qv)*, during the final stages of the Ice Age about 60 000 years ago. From the 10C to the 6C BC, Germans arrived from the north and east. Looking to expand their territory and being under pressure themselves from both Slav and Asiatic invaders, they crossed the Rhine to invade Celtic countries before being contained and then forced to retreat by the Romans.

Romans and Germans

1C AD	In the year 9, annihilation of 3 Roman legions under the command of Varus by Arminius *(see DETMOLD)*, the leader of the Germans. Demarcation of the limit of Roman colonization by a fortified wall linking the Rhine and the Danube, known as the Limes.
314	Foundation of the first Christian bishopric in Germania at Trier.
c375	Pursued by the Huns, the Goths cross the Elbe.

The Frankish Empire

Early 6C	Conversion of Clovis, king of the Franks (a tribe originally based on the Rhine estuary), to Christianity. Overcoming the Alemanni in the east, he colonizes the territory later to become Franconia.
785	Charlemagne conquers the Saxons (west of the Elbe) and the Bavarians.
800	Crowning of Charlemagne by the Pope in Rome. The Emperor thus legally assumes sovereignty, on behalf of the Roman Empire, in ancient Gaul and Germania.
911	The Franks in the east choose one of their own men as King of Germania and start to quarrel with the western Franks, the nation later to become France.
929	Colonization and conversion to Christianity of the Slav peoples east of the Elbe.

The Battle between the Priesthood and the Holy Roman Empire

962	In Rome, Otto I revives the imperial title as ruler of the Holy Roman Empire in the West, comprising the kingdoms of Germania, Italy and – after 1032 – the kingdom of Burgundy.
1073	Beginning of the reign of Pope Gregory VII, the Church's great reformer, who disputes the imperial supervision of the Papacy. A period of strife between the rival powers (Investiture Controversy) weakens the empire and threatens the unity of Christendom.
1152-1190	Frederick I ("Barbarossa") strives to reinforce the imperial power (deposition of Henry the Lion *(qv)* and dismemberment of the states of the Guelph) and to limit pontifical influence to spiritual matters. The title Holy Roman Empire derives from the reign of Frederick Barbarossa and signifies, constitutionally, that the Emperor is heir to the Caesars; that the imperial power is based on legal ties of a feudal nature.
1356	The Golden Bull, fundamental law of the Empire, inaugurates the election of the King of Germania by a college of three ecclesiastics (the archbishops of Mainz, Cologne and Trier) and four lay electors (the Duke of Saxony, the Margrave of Brandenburg, the Count of the Palatinate and the King of Bohemia).

Trade and Humanism

1358	Organization of the maritime and commercial Hanseatic League, linking more than 200 towns to guarantee the prosperity of northern Germany, and establishing Lübeck as the capital *(qv)*.
1386	Foundation of Heidelberg University, the oldest in Germany.
cl450	The invention of movable type by the printer Johann Gutenberg in Mainz. The flowering of Humanism.

The Reformation and the Thirty Years War

Luther (1483-1546) – In 1503, Martin Luther enters the Augustinian monastery of Erfurt. A dedicated cleric, he is tormented by the problem of salvation. Appointed Professor of Theology, he finds in the Holy Scriptures (c1512-13) his answer: "Man justifies himself by his Faith, not through the workings of the Law." Man's salvation, therefore – Luther argues – lies entirely within the gift, or Grace, of God. And to this, since he plays no part in that salvation himself, Man responds with Faith. This concept leads him to attack the Roman traffic in Indulgences and, on 31 October 1517, he exhibits on the doors of Wittenberg church 95 "theses" condemning such practices and reminding the Faithful of the primordial

Martin Luther – a 16C coloured picture

Lausat/ EXPLORER, Paris

importance of the sacrifice on the Cross and the Grace of God. Luther is denounced in the court of Rome, refuses to retract, and in 1521 burns the Papal Bull threatening him with excommunication. Subsequently he criticizes the institutions and hierarchy of the Church and opposes to the primacy of the clergy in spiritual matters the universal priesthood of Christians conferred by baptism.

Refusing to retract once more before the Diet of Worms (1521), he is summoned before the young Charles V and banished to the outer confines of the Empire. His works are condemned to be burned.

The patronage of Frederick the Wise, Duke of Saxony, enables him to work on a translation of the Bible considered to be the first literary work in modern German.

The Edict of Worms having been confirmed in 1529 – and the controversy aggravated by an official ruling forbidding all and any religious innovations – six Princes and the representatives of 14 free towns meet in Speyer to "protest" against these decisions. From this support of the Lutheran cause, the term Protestant derives.

| 1530 | Invited by Charles V to meet in Augsburg, theologians of the opposing faiths fail to agree, and Melanchthon draws up in the name of the Lutherans the "Confession of Augsburg" which becomes the charter of the new Protestantism. |
| 1555 | The Peace of Augsburg (*Cujus regio ejus religio* – to each state the religious faith of its people) establishes a compromise, and Protestantism is officially recognized in the states of northern Germany. |

Thirty Years War – The revival of Roman Catholicism brought about by the Council of Trent (1545-1563), the Counter-Reformation supported by the Emperor and certain internal differences among the Protestants, added to a quarrel between Rudolf II and his brother Matthias, disrupt this balance of power. The "Protestant Union", under the Elector Palatinate, gathers its forces to oppose the "Catholic League" supported by Bavaria.

The war, sparked off by a revolt in Bohemia in May 1618, is at first limited to the states ruled by the House of Austria; it spreads to become a generalized German conflict, localized physically to the west and north of the country; then finally degenerates into a European war devoid more and more of religious justification.

After the intervention of Sweden and Denmark, Protestant countries concerned at the threat menacing their national religion, Richelieu's France joins in with the intention of expelling the Habsburgs from the Franche-Comté and the Low Countries, at that time possessions of Spain. Fought almost entirely on German soil, the campaigns lay waste to the countryside, sack most of the major towns and ruin the economy. The Peace of Westphalia *(qv)* in 1648 re-establishes the rights in Germany of both faiths.

| 1689 | Provoked by the designs of Louis XIV on the west bank of the Rhine, the "War of the House of Orleans" breaks out. French troops commanded by the Marquis of Louvois devastate the Palatinate. |

The Rise of Prussia

In the 17C the German Empire is weakened by internal squabbling and the sovereign pretensions of its princes. One state alone stands out through the efficiency of its organization: Prussia, fief of the Hohenzollerns. Friedrich-Wilhelm of Brandenburg, "The Great Elector" (1640-1688), and to a greater extent his son's successor, the second King of Prussia, Friedrich-Wilhelm I – known as "The King Sergeant" – were the true founders of this Prussian strength, based on a permanent army, centralized administration and national pride.

Frederick the Great (1740-1786) – Inheriting on his accession this model state with its standing army, Frederick II soon raises Prussia to the status of second power within the Empire. He challenges Austria first of all. His success during the War of Austrian Succession wins him the alliance of Silesia – and Silesia's participation in the dismemberment of Poland enables him to reinforce his eastern provinces.

Correspondant and friend of Voltaire, lover of literature and music (he was an accomplished flautist), Frederick the Great is revered as a model of "the enlightened despot", enjoying the respect of intellectuals all over Europe. The greatness of Prussia is strengthened by his reign, marked by a meticulous administration and the renewed links forged between royalty and the nobility.

1792	Beginning of the Revolutionary Wars. Prussians defeated at Valmy.
1806	Napoleon enters Berlin. The Emperor Francis I of Austria renounces the crown of the German Holy Roman Empire, which is thereby dissolved. Creation of the Confederation of the Rhine, under the protection of France.
1813	Prussia is the bulwark of resistance to the French invader and leading force in the "War of Liberation", which ends, after "The Battle of Nations", in victory at Leipzig.

Towards German Unity

The dissolution of the Holy Roman Empire and the Napoleonic onslaught simplify the political map of Germany, breaking up the princeling states and secularizing the domains of the Church. The status of most of the so-called Free Imperial Cities is abolished and a number of principalities, most of them very small, are amalgamated to form medium-sized states.

German Confederation – The Congress of Vienna establishes, in place of the Holy Roman Empire, a German Confederation of 35 autonomous states and free cities, represented by a Diet of 11 members appointed by the state and town governments, sitting at Frankfurt-am-Main and presided over by Austria. A decisive role in the German Confederation is played by Prince Metternich from the Rhineland, once he has become Chancellor. However, his antiquated constitution clashes with the ideas of those liberal Germans dreaming of an independent nationhood.

The creation of a customs union (Zollverein), suggested by Prussia in 1834, goes some way towards unification through a common economic policy, but the meeting of a National German parliament at Frankfurt in 1848-49, following a revolutionary flare-up, produces no result.

Bismarck Era (1862-1890) – Bismarck, appointed Minister-President of Prussia in 1862, takes no more than eight years to impose "by fire and the sword" the unification of a "Lesser Germany" under his own rule. He thus dismisses Austrian attempts to create a "Greater Germany" extending from the North Sea to the Adriatic. Confident in the loyalty

FORMATION OF GERMAN UNITY
(1866-1871)

0   300 km

Kingdom of Prussia in 1865
Prussian annexations in 1866
Limits of German Empire in 1871

K = Kingdom   GD = Grand Duchy
D = Duchy   ● = Free City

of an elite bourgeoisie born through the advance of industrialisation – and also in the neutrality of Napoleon III – he manipulates events so as to make war inevitable. He defeats the Austrians at Sadowa in the lightning campaign of 1866, thus leaving himself free to organize Germany's Northern Federation. This attaches Hanover, Hessen and Schleswig-Holstein to Prussia and unites the group with all other states north of the Main. Then, profiting from the mistrust arising in southern Germany from the crude demands of Napoleon III – who sought the Palatinate and Luxembourg as the price of his neutrality – Bismarck works up throughout the whole of Germany a violent anti-French reaction. Finally, after the Hohenzollern candidature affair *(see LAHNTAL: Bad Ems)* has unwisely been exaggerated by the French government, he succeeds in inflaming national pride on both sides of the frontier and France declares war. The southern states unite in defence, and the whole of Germany stands shoulder-to-shoulder with Prussia.

Second Reich (1871-1918)

1870	After the victory of Sedan (2 September), the southern states open negotiations with Prussia to strengthen federal ties.
1871	On 18 January, the German Empire is proclaimed at Versailles with Wilhelm I at its head. Imperial Germany, enlarged by the acquisition of Alsace-Lorraine, remains in theory a federation – but it is in fact under Prussian domination.
1888	Wilhelm II succeeds his father.
1890	The Emperor, disliking the "Iron Chancellor"'s authoritarian approach, forces Bismarck's resignation. The Kaiser finds himself in the middle of a growth crisis: the demographic explosion, added to an over-rapid industrial development, has created a need for expansion that the "pan-Germanists" elevate to a creed. The Kaiser's dubious foreign policy provokes the enmity of England, Russia and France.

First World War – Erupting into an international atmosphere crackling with tension, the assassination of the Austrian Archduke Ferdinand at Sarajevo on 28 June 1914 unleashes the cataclysm. Austria's declaration of war against Serbia mobilises the armies of Europe.

1914	On 3 August, Germany declares war on France and Russia. German invasion of Belgium. Great Britain declares war on Germany on 4 August. German offensive halted on the Marne; the "war of attrition" begins.
1917	Russia, shaken by the Bolshevik revolution, asks for an armistice. In the West the United States, whose merchant marine has been attacked by German U boats, declares war on the Reich.
1918	In October, an all-out counterattack by the Allies throws back the German armies, while behind their lines revolution breaks out. Wilhelm II abdicates on 9 November. It is therefore a Socialist Council of People's Representatives which signs on 11 November the armistice at Réthondes.

Weimar Republic

Spartacists who formed and led the military and workingmen's Soviets behind the revolution fail to gain the support of the popular masses. Ebert, the Social Democrat head of the provisional government, summons the army and suppresses the revolution before the activists can consolidate their power.

On 11 August 1919, Germany adopts a Republican Constitution, virtually imposed by the victors. The Kaiser goes into exile. This "Republic without republicans" shoulders the heavy task of assuming the obligations of the Treaty of Versailles (28 June 1919): territorial concessions, loss of colonies, limitation of army and armaments, and crippling reparations. Very quickly, the economic crisis provoked by the impossibility of reestablishing an efficient industry, plus the country's general indebtedness, results in an insane cycle of inflation; the middle classes are ruined.

In 1923 the French, angry at the delay in the payment of reparations, occupy the Ruhr. The passive resistance of the German people aggravates the economic situation, and extremists come to the fore once more. On the Right, they unite around the "German National Socialist Worker's Party", which Adolf Hitler joins in 1919. Once leader of the party, he attempts to seize power in a putsch at Munich (8-9 November 1923). It fails and he is imprisoned. Freed in 1924, he waits for ten years before his next, successful, attempt.

From 1923 to 1929, Germany enjoys six years of relative calm. There is a spectacular reestablishment of the economy, encouraged by the spreading out of reparations, the French evacuation of the Ruhr and massive injections of American capital. On the international scene, Foreign Minister Gustav Stresemann recognizes the western frontiers imposed at Versailles and makes Germany a member of the League of Nations. But the worldwide financial crash of 1929 hits the German recovery hard: there is a recurrence of inflation and unemployment increases dramatically. Profiting from the general discontent, and with the cynical use of paramilitary organizations (SA and SS) prepared to resort to political violence, the National-Socialists win more than 38% of the suffrage in 1932. Management and the governing classes, seeing in Hitler a rampart against the spreading flood of Communism, allow him to accede to the post of Chancellor on 30 January 1933.

Hitler and the Third Reich

The Dictatorship – Very quickly, Hitler organizes a totalitarian state. After the Reichstag fire, in fact secretly set up by the SA on 27 February 1933, he orders the arrest of 4 000 Communist leaders and assumes total power. On 1 December, the Nazis (the word is an abbreviation of the German for National Socialist German Workers' Party) become the sole political party in the country, and this coup receives "popular approval" in a plebiscite (12 December) organized in a climate of terror. The death of President Hindenburg in August 1934 leaves Hitler absolute master of Germany – the Führer (Guide or Leader). He is now free to put into operation his blueprint for "a thousand-year Reich".

Reabsorption of the workless is achieved through a programme of public works (motorways, drainage schemes), a policy of rearmament, and the regimentation of the young. The population is subjected to a barrage of propaganda, and all forms of resistance are ruthlessly suppressed: opponents, tracked down by the Gestapo, are interned in so-called concentration camps from 1933 onwards. Persecution of the Jews becomes, with the racial laws of Nuremberg (September 1935), a radical and systematic official policy: pogroms, bans and mass arrests are the instruments of this antisemitic ideology. The arts and literature are subject to control and all works judged "decadent" forbidden. A majority of Germany's most creative artists choose exile. To familiarize the German public with the "rights" and "wrongs" encompassed by Hitler's artistic credo, an exhibition of *Entartete Kunst* – degenerate art – is held in Munich in 1937. Among the "outcasts" whose work is pilloried are Max Ernst, Oskar Kokoschka, Marc Chagall, Ernst Ludwig Kirchner and Otto Dix – artists considered today as major influences on the modern art scene. Their work is contrasted with paintings approved by the Nazis – mainly over-life-size Aryan warriors and their buxom, blonde Brünhildes. Hitler's foreign policy encounters little resistance on the part of the democracies. Without raising more than offended protests, he violates the Locarno Treaty by the military occupation of the Rhineland (1936), annexes Austria in the Anschluß of 1938, and browbeats Britain and France at the Munich Conference that year into accepting the return of the Sudetenland from then Czechoslovakia to Germany. The progress towards war accelerates: Czechoslovakia itself is demolished in March 1939, and the unprovoked aggression against Poland on the following 1 September obliges the Allies at last to honour their commitments.

Second World War – Germany, Mussolini's Italy and Japan are on one side, Britain, France, the United States and the Soviet Union (after an initial period of alliance with the Reich) on the other.

1940	A lightning offensive allows the Germans to invade the greater part of Western Europe. Only Britain, retreating to her island base, holds out thanks to the heroic resistance of her air force.
1941	On 22 June, Hitler attacks Russia while the Balkans are overrun and Rommel expands his offensive in North Africa. In 1942, the Third Reich is at the height of its power.
1943	Soviet counter-offensive, initiated by the victory of Stalingrad. The Americans, involved in the conflict since the Japanese attack on Pearl Harbour (December 1941), land in Sicily in July.
1944	Allied landings in Normandy (June). On 20 July, Hitler narrowly escapes a bomb attack planned by his opponents.
1945	After the suicide of the Führer (20 April), the Reich capitulates on 8 May. Germany is nothing but a wasteland of ruins. The liberation of the death camps reveals to a horrified world the reality of the Nazis' "final solution" policy of exterminating Jews and other "impure" races on a European scale (6 million dead).

Germany Today

1945	The "Big Three" (Britain, USA and USSR) meet in Potsdam for the division of Germany into four zones of Occupation (France administering the fourth zone).
1946/7	Beginning of the Cold War with the confrontation of the USA and the USSR over occupation policies.
1948	Soviet blockade of the western sectors of Berlin. The Berlin Airlift.
1949	Creation (23 May) of the **Federal Republic**, comprising the three western zones. The Soviet zone becomes (7 October) the **German Democratic Republic**. Under the leadership of Konrad Adenauer, Chancellor until 1963, the Federal Republic enjoys a spectacular economic rebirth and re-establishes normal international relations.
1961	At the crisis point of the Cold War, construction (13 August) of the "Berlin Wall".

INTER NATIONES, Bonn

Konrad Adenauer.

1972	Signature of a treaty between the two Germanys confirms Chancellor Willy Brandt's policy of openness towards the East (Ostpolitik).
1989	Under pressure from its citizens, the government of East Germany decides (10 November) to open the frontier between the two states. The Berlin wall comes tumbling down.
1990	Free elections (May) in East Germany; ratification of the Treaty of Reunification on 3 October by Parliament sitting in the Reichstag, Berlin; eventual re-establishment of Berlin as capital of united Germany. Germany's national day is transferred from 17 June to 3 October.
1991	The Bundestag votes for Berlin to become capital of a reunited Germany.
1994	By September, Soviet troops have been withdrawn from all the provinces of the old East Germany, and the last Allied troops have left Berlin. The government body (Treuhandanstalt) set up since 1990 for the dismantling and privatisation of the ex-Democratic Republic's state-owned industry and property finally completes its task.

Art

Germany's geographical situation and eventful history have favoured the intrusion of artistic currents from the rest of Europe – mainly French in the Gothic period and Italian in the Renaissance. The originality of German art manifests itself above all in the sumptuous decoration of the Baroque abbeys in Bavaria.

ROMANESQUE ARCHITECTURE (9-12C)

Pre-Romanesque Architecture In Germany, as elsewhere in the Christian West, religious architecture developed from the adaptation of Roman lay basilicas, the long halls of worship now oriented towards the east and terminated by an apse. The central portion is raised above two or four side aisles and the whole covered with a plain wooden ceiling. The Carolingian period is marked by the building of churches with two chancels. The western chancel sometimes forms part of another characteristic feature: the **Westwerk**, a tall square tower of military appearance onto which the nave is securely anchored. The Westwerk – at Corvey for instance – frequently constitutes almost a church in itself. Such large, tall chapels, opening on the nave via galleries sometimes several storeys high, were traditionally reserved for the Emperor.

Ottonian Architecture (10C and early 11C) – The restoration of imperial dignity by Otto I in 962 was accompanied by a revival of religious architecture in Saxony and in the regions of the Meuse and Lower Rhine. The huge churches erected at this period were characterized by deeply projecting transepts and wide aisles. As yet, they had no stone vaulting. An alternation of piers and columns broke up the uniformity of the aisles, which were not yet divided by bays. The churches of St. Michaelis at Hildesheim and St. Cyriacus at Gernrode are the best examples of buildings of this period.

Rhineland Romanesque Style – At Cologne and in the surrounding countryside, several churches share in their plan a triple apse designed in the form of a cloverleaf. These tri-lobed extensions are adorned on the outside with blind arcades and a "dwarf gallery" (Zwerggalerie) – a motif of Lombard origin. In the Middle Rhine region, the style achieves its full splendour in the majestic "imperial" cathedrals of Speyer, Mainz and Worms. These are characterized in their floor plans by a double chancel with neither ambulatory nor apsidal chapels, and sometimes by a double transept; in their elevation by a multiplicity of towers; in their exterior decoration by the use of galleries of blind arcades and Lombard bands (vertical motifs in low relief with small blind arcades linking them at the top). Typically, the roofs of these Rhineland towers are in the form of a bishop's mitre, the base decorated with a lozenge pattern. Towards the end of the 11C, the architects of the cathedral at Speyer boldly projected groined stone vaulting over the nave. Marking the transition from Romanesque to Gothic are the churches of Limburg and Andernach and the cathedral at Naumburg, which were built with pointed vaulting early in the 13C.

GOTHIC ARCHITECTURE (13-16C)

For its great interior width, the slenderness of the two tall towers built on either side of the façade in the French style, and the height of its pointed vaulting, Cologne cathedral is famous throughout the world. Equally inspired by the French Gothic style are the cathedrals of Regensburg, Freiburg-im-Breisgau, Magdeburg and Halberstadt.

French influence, too, may be seen in the Cistercian monasteries built in such profusion between 1150 and 1250. Their churches, usually without towers or belfries, often modified subsequently in the Baroque manner, were habitually designed with squared-off chancels flanked by rectangular chapels. The abbey of Maulbronn, one of the most complete monastic ensembles remaining in Europe, is an example.

East of the Elbe, the most imposing edifices were brick-built, complete with buttresses and flying buttresses. Typical of this brick Gothic style (known in German as Backsteingotik) are the Nikolaikirche at Stralsund, the Marienkirche in Lübeck, the town halls of those two cities, Schwerin cathedral and the abbey church at Bad Doberan.

Late Gothic Architecture (Spätgotik) – This long period (14, 15 and 16C) is marked in Germany by the widespread building of hall-churches, usually with vaulting divided by purely decorative ribs that form stars or groining in contrast to the bareness of the walls.

St. Annenkirche at Annaberg-Buchholz is exemplary of a style that allows the artists involved to express their virtuosity freed from all architectural constraint. These **hall-churches** are completely different from those constructed on the basilical plan at the end of the Romanesque period. The aisles are now the same height as the nave, separated from it only

Münster, Bad Doberan

by tall columns. The most famous examples – extra-tall buildings erected at the end of the Gothic period – are the Frauenkirche in Munich and the Georgskirche, Dinkelsbühl.

Civil Architecture in the Late Middle Ages – Commercial prosperity among merchants and skilled craftsmen in the 14C and 15C led to the development in town centres of impressive town halls and half-timbered private houses, frequently adorned with painting and sculpture. Examples of such civil projects may be seen today in Regensburg, Goslar, Rothenburg ob der Tauber and Tübingen.

THE RENAISSANCE (c1520-1620)

The Renaissance, eclipsed by the troubles of the Reformation, is no more than an episode in the history of German architecture. Italian influence in this period is restricted to southern Germany: elegant Florentine arcading, for instance, was used by Fugger the Rich as decoration for his funerary chapel at Augsburg (1518); the Jesuits, building the Michaelskirche in Munich (1589), were clearly inspired by their own Sanctuary of Jesus (Gesù) in Rome. Northern Germany was influenced by Flemish and Dutch design. In the rich merchants' quarters, many-storeyed gables such as those of the Gewandhaus in Brunswick were loaded with ornamentation in the form of obelisks, scrollwork, statues, pilasters, etc. The castle at Güstrow and the old town of Görlitz are important examples of Renaissance influence, while Celle, Wolfenbüttel, Bückeburg and Hamelin are saturated with the particular charm of the so-called "Weser Renaissance" *(qv)*.

BAROQUE ARCHITECTURE (17C and 18C)

Characterized by an irregularity of contour and a multiplicity of form, the Baroque seeks above all the effect of movement and contrast. Taken to its extreme, the style degenerates into Rococo, where the fantasy element is employed mainly as decoration. From the middle of the 17C, Baroque influence was most marked in Roman Catholic southern Germany, encouraged by the Counter-Reformation's exaltation of dogmatic belief in the Real Presence, the cult of the Virgin Mary and the saints, and in general all manifestations of popular piety.

A hall-church
St. Georgskirche, Dinkelsbühl
1) Central nave – 2) Side aisle
3) Network vaulting

Enterprising abbots set about rebuilding their abbeys to plans so ambitious that, today, they would seem stupefying. Masons, painters, sculptors ans stucco-workers were thus offred extraordinary opportunities. Stucco designs – worked with an amalgam of lime, plaster and wet sand that could be modelled to give a three-dimensional effect – covered every available surface.

The Masters of German and Danubian Baroque – The blossoming of the Baroque style owes much to the **Vorarlberg School** (1680-1750), of which the masters remain largely anonymous, so great was the group's corporative spirit. These architects, working chiefly in Swabia but also in Bavaria, Switzerland and even Alsace, lavished a great deal of care on the lines and perspectives of their single naves.

But, in Bavaria especially, there were also brilliant individuals, rarely specializing in a single technique, who produced designs of great subtlety – in ground plans,

The west front at Ottobeuren abbey church

for example, using as a focal point a round or oval bay. Johann Michael Fischer (Dießen, Zwiefalten and Ottobeuren), the Asam brothers (Weltenburg and the Asamkirche in Munich) and Dominikus Zimmermann (Steinhausen and Wies) were the virtuosi of this Bavarian school.

The Baroque movement in Franconia, patronized by the prince-bishops of the Schönborn family, who owned residences in Mainz, Würzburg, Speyer and Bamberg, was closely linked with the spread of similar ideas in Bohemia. The Dientzenhofer brothers decorated the palaces in Prague as well as the one in Bamberg.

Balthazar Neumann, who worked for the same prelates, dominated his contemporaries by the breadth of a culture enriched by contact with the French, Viennese and Italian masters he encountered.

In Saxony, the Zwinger Palace in Dresden, joint masterpiece of the architect Pöppelmann and the sculptor Permoser, brilliantly illustrates this German Baroque with Italian roots; the refinement of the Rococo décor in the Schloß Sanssouci at Potsdam is even more astonishing, given the Prussian reputation for austerity – but is explained by the studies in France and Italy followed by the architect Knobelsdorff.

Vaulting at Vierzehnheiligen

Churches – A sinuous movement, generally convex in line, animates the façades, while the superimposition of two pediments, different in design, adds vitality to the whole. The façades are additionally adorned with twin domed towers (a single tower in the case of pilgrimage churches). The later the church, the more detached are the towers.

Huge galleries stand above the lateral chapels, at the height of pilaster capitals with jutting abaci. Chapels and galleries stop at the level of the transept, giving it a much

greater depth. Clerestory windows, pierced at gallery height, allow plenty of light to enter. Bohemian and Franconian Baroque is typified by **complex vaulting**, round or oval bays being covered by complicated structures in which the transverse arches bow out in horse-shoe shape, only to meet in their keystones.

The **altarpiece** or reredos, focal point of the church furnishing, is treated monumentally, its design architecturally that of a triumphal arch. The arch, in carved wood or stucco, frames either a large painting or a group of statuary. Columns twisted into spiral form accentuate the concept of movement distinguishing Baroque art, and back lighting from a hidden source, with its contrasts of brightness and shadow, is equally typical.

An ornamentation that is both exaggerated and asymmetric characterizes the **Rococo** style.

Palaces – The one-storey construction of these country residences was often lent additional importance when built on a raised foundation. The focal point was a circular central bloc whose convexity was evident only from the garden front. Monumental stairways with several flights and considerable theatrical effect are often the centrepieces of the larger German castles and palaces built in the 18C. The staircase, embellished with arcaded galleries and a painted ceiling, leads to the first floor state room whose elevation rises majestically to the roof level of the second storey. Such pompous – almost pretentious – arrangements characterize many of the great abbeys of this period, often complemented by that other ceremonial room, the library.

State staircase at
Schloß Pommersfelden

THE ARRIVAL OF NEO-CLASSICISM

The example of Versailles inspired in Germany a new style of court life, particularly in the Rhineland and the Berlin of Frederick II. Many French architects were employed by the Electors of the Palatinate, of Mainz, of Trier and of Cologne; mainly, they produced plans for country mansions with names such as Monrepos (my rest) or Solitude.

Unadorned pediments, balustrades at the base of the roofs, columned porticoes at the main entrance, all indicate a desire for unobtrusive elegance outside, while the interior decoration, carried out with a lighter touch, confined itself to cornucopiae of flowers mingled with Rococo motifs that were now a little more discreet. From 1750 on, Winckelmann's work on the art of antiquity, and the excavations taking place at Pompeii, threw a new light on Greco-Roman architecture. A new fashion arose, in which architects favoured the Doric style, the coldest of all, and a preference for the colossal – pilasters and columns of a single "order" no longer stood one storey high but always two. Symmetrical balance and a purely static line became the ideal to such an extent that, in some churches, a false pulpit was added to balance the genuine preacher's eyrie. As well as churches, abbeys and castles, skilled craftsmen now turned their attention to commemorative monuments and museums – a new sign of their interest in the past – especially in Berlin where Schinkel, the master of the colonnade, was working. Interior decoration showed a preference for sculptured motifs such as garlands, urns, vases and friezes of pearls.

By 1830, the Neo-Classical movement had become sterile; it was superseded, except in Munich, by a renewed interest in the Gothic which became, for the Romantics, emblematic of "the old Germany". The **Biedermeier** taste – lightweight, cushioned furniture with flowing lines, glass-fronted cabinets for the display of knick-knacks – corresponded perhaps with the later Edwardian style in England.

The year 1850 marks the beginning of the **Gründerzeit** (Founders' Period), when wealthy industrialists fell for pretentious reproductions of medieval or Renaissance furniture. Similiar pieces were to be found also in public buildings such as the Reichstag in Berlin.

MODERN AND CONTEMPORARY MOVEMENTS

At the beginning of the 20C, **Jugendstil** ("Style 1900") or Art Nouveau became the vogue in Germany, largely due to mass-production of well-made furniture. Of far greater importance to Germany was the growth of the idea that there could be an aesthetic for industrial design, promoted by such pioneers as Peter Behrens, Mies van der Rohe and Walter Gropius. After the First World War, Gropius was appointed head of the **Bauhaus**.

Urban growth and the reparation of war damage after the Second World War called for the building or rebuilding of many churches, and architects such as Dominikus Böhm and Rudolf Schwartz were among the craftsmen who brought to light by this renewal of interest in sacred work, many of their designs being markedly austere. New concepts, too, characterized the construction of municipal and cultural enterprises such as Hans Scharoun's Philharmonia in Berlin and the Staatsgalerie in Stuttgart by British architect James Stirling – buildings of an architectural audacity only made possible by the development of materials and construction techniques that were entirely new.

GERMANY'S GREAT ARTISTS

Architects and Sculptors *(blue lettering)* – **Painters and Engravers** *(1)*

15th Century

Stefan LOCHNER (d 1451) – At the head of the School of Cologne: golden backgrounds, sweetness of expression, freshness of colours (**Adoration of the Magi**, Cologne cathedral; **Virgin and Rose Bush**, Wallraf-Richartz-Museum/Museum Ludwig, Cologne).

Veit STOSS (c1445-1533) – Artist and tormented genius, admirable when working in wood (**Angel's Greeting**, Lorenzkirche, Nuremberg; **Reredos of the Nativity**, Bamberg cathedral).

Tilman RIEMENSCHNEIDER (1460-1531) – Sculptor whose works, delicately modelled, are rich in expression, intensely felt (**Tomb of Henry II the Saint**, Bamberg cathedral; **Adam and Eve**, Mainfränkisches Museum, Würzburg; **Altarpiece to the Virgin**, Herrgottskirche, Creglingen).

The Master of St Severinus (late 15C) – His sense of intimacy and his iridescent colours display Dutch influence (**Christ before Pilate**, Wallraf-Richartz-Museum/Museum Ludwig, Cologne).

The Master of THE LIFE OF THE VIRGIN (late 15C) – Delightful, anecdotal artist much influenced by Van der Weyden (**Vision of St Bernard**, Wallraf-Richartz-Museum/Museum Ludwig, Cologne).

Friedrich HERLIN (d 1500) – Picturesque and precise realist (**Almswomen at Prayer**, Stadt-museum, Nördlingen).

---

(1) Artists in the 16C were, as a rule, both painters and engravers.

16th Century

Matthias GRÜNEWALD (c1460-1528) — A powerful genius, producing works of a tragic intensity (**Crucifixion**, Staatliche Kunsthalle, Karlsruhe; **Virgin and Child**, Stuppach parish church).

Albrecht DÜRER (1471-1528) — A humanist, the most famous artist of the German Renaissance school; religious scenes and portraits of extraordinary intensity; a profusion of wonderful drawings and engravings (**The Four Apostles, Self-Portrait with Cloak**, Alte Pinakothek, Munich; **Charlemagne**, Germanisches Nationalmuseum, Nuremberg).

Lucas CRANACH THE ELDER (1472-1553) — Master of an important studio; portraitist of the most eminent men of the Reformation.
His sense of the wonders of nature allied him to the painters of the Danube school (**Portrait of Martin Luther**, Germanisches Nationalmuseum, Nuremberg).

Albrecht ALTDORFER (1480-1538) — Member of the Danube school *(qv)* and one of the earliest landscape painters. His use of chiaroscuro has a moving effect (**Battle of Alexander at Issus**, Alte Pinakothek, Munich).

Venus in a landscape, by Lucas Cranach

Hans BALDUNG GRIEN (c1485-1545) — Artist achieving his effects by the use of unusual colours and dramatic lighting (**Altarpiece: The Coronation of the Virgin**, Freiburg cathedral).

Hans HOLBEIN THE YOUNGER (1497-1543) — Author of religious compositions and portraits of a striking realism (**The Nativity and the Adoration of the Magi**, Freiburg cathedral, **Portrait of the Merchant Georg Gisze**, Museum Dahlem, Berlin).

17th Century

Adam ELSHEIMER (1578-1610) — Elsheimer's mythological and Biblical paintings were often small scale but exquisitely worked and his influence is apparent in the work of numerous French and Italian artists (**The Flight into Egypt**, Alte Pinakothek, Munich).

Elias HOLL (1573-1646) — Architect responsible for the most important buildings of the Renaissance in Germany (**Rathaus**, Augsburg).

Andreas SCHLÜTER (c1660-1714) — Master of Baroque sculpture in northern Germany. A most vigorous talent (**Statue of the Great Elector**, Schloß Charlottenburg, Berlin; **Masks of Dying Warriors**, Zeughaus, Berlin).

The MERIANS (17C) — A family of engravers specializing in plates illustrating German towns.

18th Century

Balthazar PERMOSER (1651-1732) — Sculptor to the Court of Dresden. After studying in Rome, Florence and Venice, he transplanted with great virtuosity the exuberance of Italian Baroque (**Wallpavillon** and **Nymphenbad**, Zwinger, Dresden).

Matthäus Daniel PÖPPELMANN (1662-1736) — Architect-in-Chief to Augustus the Strong, he worked in Prague, in Vienna and in Italy before designing his masterpiece, the **Zwinger**, in Dresden, an epitome of the Late Baroque style.

Antoine PESNE (1683-1757) — A French painter who emigrated to the Court of Friedrich II, much favoured for his use of brilliant colours (**Portraits of Friedrich II and his Sister Wilhelmina**, Private Apartments, Charlottenburg, Berlin).

Dominikus ZIMMERMANN (1685-1766) — Architect of the most successful churches in the Bavarian Rococo style (**Churches of Wies and of Steinhausen**).

Balthazar NEUMANN (1687-1753) — An architect and engineer. Technical virtuosity and the inbuilt harmony of his compositions made him master of the Baroque style (**Vierzehnheiligen Church**).

The **ASAM BROTHERS** – The sculptor Egid Quirin (1692-1750) and his brother, the painter and architect Cosmas Damian Asam (1686-1739) provide a splendid example of the collaboration existing between artists in the Baroque period (**Asamkirche**, Munich).

Georg Wenzeslaus von KNOBELSDORFF **(1699-1753)** – Official architect – and friend – of Frederick the Great; master of the Rococo (**Berlin Opera House; Schloß Sanssouci**, Potsdam).

19th Century

Caspar David FRIEDRICH (1774-1840) – Artist of the Romantic school; he developed the tragic in landscape painting (**The Monk by the Sea, The Cross on the Mountain**, Private Apartments, Charlottenburg, Berlin; **Rambler Above a Sea of Clouds**, Kunsthalle, Hamburg).

Carl-Friedrich SCHINKEL **(1781-1841)** – Architect whose long, elegant colonnades typify the cityscape of central Berlin (**Neue Wache, Altes Museum** and **Schauspielhaus**).

Wilhelm LEIBL (1844-1900) – Master of the Realist school (**Three Women in Church**, Kunsthalle, Hamburg; **Portrait of Frau Gedon**, Neue Pinakothek, Munich).

Adolf von HILDEBRAND **(1847-1921)** – As a monumental sculptor, his sureness of taste is in contrast to the excesses of most 19C artists (**Wittelsbach Fountain**, Munich).

Max LIEBERMANN (1847-1935) – Leading German Impressionist painter (**Jewish Street in Amsterdam**, Wallraf-Richartz-Museum/Museum Ludwig, Cologne).

20th Century

Ernst BARLACH **(1870-1938)** – His massive, tormented sculptures in wood and bronze are characteristic examples of the Expressionist school (**The Angel**, Antoniterkirche, Cologne; **Frieze of the Listeners**, Ernst-Barlach-Haus, Hamburg; **The Singer**, Ratzeburg).

Dominikus BÖHM **(1880-1955)** – Pioneer of a new type of religious architecture **(Church of Maria Königin**, Cologne; **Church of St. Wolfgang**, Regensburg).

The BAUHAUS – Architectural school founded in Weimar then transferred to Dessau where it was directed from 1925 to 1928 by Walter Gropius (1883-1969). The marriage of all plastic arts with architecture in prime position was the fundamental theme uniting the members of this school, which soon attracted a galaxy of brilliant avant-garde painters and sculptors (Bauhaus-Archiv, Berlin).

The **EXPRESSIONISTS** – German Expressionism introduced a distorted, violent and tragic vision of the world to modern painting. The movement owed much to Van Gogh and the Norwegian painter Edvard Munch (1863-1944), whose work had a marked influence in Germany. See the works of **Emil Nolde** (1867-1956) at Seebüll; and of Expressionism in general at the Brücke-Museum, Berlin. The **Brücke** (Bridge) Group united from 1905 to 1913 such painters as Erich Heckel, Ernst Ludwig Kirchner, Karl Schmidt-Rottluff – whose work, with its passion for pure colour, recalls that of the Fauvists in France.

Der BLAUE REITER (The BLUE RIDER MOVEMENT) – An artistic group founded in Munich in 1911 by Kandinsky and Marc, later to be joined by Macke and Klee. Their aim was to free art from the constraint of reality, thus opening the way to abstraction (**Deer in the Forest**, by **Franz Marc**, Orangerie Staatliche Kunsthalle, Karlsruhe; **The Dress Shop**, by **August Macke**, Folkwang-Museum, Essen)

The **NEW OBJECTIVITY (NEUE SACHLICHKEIT)** – An artistic current affecting all the arts around 1923, based on a realistic illustration of social facts and phenomena (**War**, by **Otto Dix**, 1932, Albertinum in Dresden).

Second half of the 20C – After the Second World War, abstract art was advocated by West German artists such as Willi Baumeister, and Julius Bissier and Ernst Wilhelm Nay (who formed the Zen group), not least because it was far removed from the style of art favoured by the Nazi regime. In the early 1950s, Otto Greis, Bernhard Schultze, Hans Kreutz and Karl-Otto Götz formed the Quadriga group, representing German **Art Informel** (linked with Tachisme), while the members of **Gruppe Zero** (Heinz Mack, Otto Piene, Günther Uecker), formed in 1957, concentrated on light, movement and material objects in their work. A high point of abstract painting in Germany was the Documenta II exhibition held in Kassel in 1959 (the **Documenta** exhibition dedicated to contemporary art takes place every 4 or 5 years in Kassel, and is just one of the initiatives of the German art scene to "demystify" modern art).

The 1960s saw a turning point in German artistic creativity. **Gruppe Zebra** (Dieter Asmus, Nikolaus Störtenbecker, Dietmar Ullrich), took up the credo of New Objectivity against Abstract Expressionism. Konrad Klapheck used a hyperrealistic style to depict objects from everyday life and machines in his cool, almost clinical paintings.

A giant of the German art scene was **Joseph Beuys**. In the 1960s and 1970s, together with the artists of his entourage (school of Constructivist Sculpture in Düsseldorf), he strove to create a direct relationship between the artist and the viewing public in his Happenings and Performances, and to redefine the role of art and the artist in contemporary society (works by Beuys can be found in the Kunsthalle in Hamburg, the Neue Nationalgalerie in Berlin, the Hessisches Landesmuseum in Darmstadt and the Staatsgalerie in Stuttgart).

At the end of the 1970s, the term "**Neue Wilde**" (New Savages) was coined for a group of neo-Expressionist painters as diverse as their subject matter, who included **Georg Baselitz, Jörg Immendorff, Anselm Kiefer,** Markus Lüpertz, A R Penck, **Sigmar Polke** and Gerhard Richter. This new generation of German artists managed to break through onto the international scene, examining the theme of Germany stripped of all illusions and using their art to step back from the age in which they lived.

Social Realism dominated art in **East Germany** until well into the 1960s and 1970s, although there have been signs of growing experimentation since 1970. Artistic creativity on the whole took ideologically sound themes as its subjects (workers, historical themes).

Deer in the Forest, by Franz Marc

The painters of Leipzig in particular won international acclaim. Among the most prominent painters of this new variation of social realism are Bernhard Heisig, Wolfgang Mattheuer, Willi Sitte and Werner Tübke, whose enormous panoramic paintings of the German Peasant's War (at Bad Frankenhausen) belong to the most monumental creations in painting. In East Germany in the years leading up to reunification, non-conformist artists were also given the opportunity to express themselves.

Literature

Great philosophers' names appear in bold type.

Middle Ages

9C	The Lay of Hildebrand.
Late 12C	National folk saga of Niebelungen.
13C	Wolfram von Eschenbach writes the epic poem *Parsifal* – the knight in quest of the Holy Grail (chalice said to have contained the blood of Christ).
1170-1228	Walther van der Vogelweide, the troubadour knight, raises medieval lyric poetry to its greatest heights.
Early 16C	Chronicle of the picaresque adventures of the buffoon Till Eulenspiegel.

The Reformation and the Thirty Years War

Only at the end of the Reformation and after the disastrous Thirty Years War was German literature in a position to develop freely.

1534	Luther finishes his translation of the Bible, the first literary work written in modern German.
1669	Grimmelshausen publishes his cautionary account of the fortunes and misfortunes of picaresque Simplicissimus.

"Aufklärung" (Age of Enlightenment)

1646-1716	**Leibniz** writes his *Theodicy* in French and in Latin; he invents differential calculus.
1729-1781	Lessing establishes the principles of the new German theatre *(Hamburg Theory of Drama)*; in defiance of Aristotle, he writes the first German tragedies in domestic, "non-aristocratic" settings (Bürgerliches Trauerspiel, eg *Emilia Galotti*).
1724-1804	**Kant** defines the balance between liberty and morality: man finds liberty in submission to "the categorical imperative".

"Sturm und Drang" and Classicism

In reaction against the stark rationalism of the Aufklärung, the "Sturm und Drang" movement exalts emotion, sentimentality, nature and a titanic liberty. Goethe (1749-1832), a universal genius (science, poetry, philosophy, theatre) tempers this fashionable enthusiasm with a proposal for a classical ideal of a triumphant and harmonious humanity.

1759-1805	Schiller, poet and dramatist, writes historical dramas (*Don Carlos, Wallenstein, Maria Stuart* and *Wilhelm Tell*) which are in fact hymns to liberty.
1774	*The Sorrows of Young Werther*, the novel in the form of correspondence (Part One), which traces the doomed passion of a young man increasingly unable to identify with the world around him, makes the young Goethe's reputation.
1788	Returning from Italy, Goethe publishes his great classical dramas: *Iphigenie auf Tauris, Egmont* and *Torquato Tasso*.
1796 and 1821	Goethe's *Wilhelm Meister* – a Bildungsroman (novel of educational development) in two parts.
1808 and 1832	*Faust*, the quintessence of Goethe's message to mankind.

Lausat/EXPLORER, Paris

Johann Wolfgang von Goethe

The Romantic Movement (1790-1850)

This movement, reflecting an essential element in the German character, charts the individual soul's quest for the infinite in all its forms. It is the movement of Me. Besides literature, it influences the fine arts, philosophy and even politics and religion. Heidelberg, Jena and Berlin are centres from which the movement blossoms. The Romantic can create his own world from reality or from fancy and he is able to turn whatever he likes into poetry. The subconscious becomes a subject for serious study and the supernatural comes into vogue, while in religion Romantic subjectivism leads to mysticism.

1770-1831	**Hegel** defines the historical conscience and dialectic.
1772-1801	Novalis, poet and mystic, exalts the art and the religion of the Middle Ages; his "Blue Flower symbol" *(Heinrich von Ofterdingen)* comes to represent the Absolute, or object of Romantic longing.
1805	Publication of *The Child with the Magic Horn (Des Knaben Wunderhorn)*, a collection of popular folk poems.
1810	Heinrich von Kleist writes *The Prince of Homburg*, a play about a man of action led away by his dreams. Von Kleist also publishes (1804) *The Marquise of O...*, one of a collection of 8 powerful novellae.
1812	First publication of *Grimms' Fairy Tales*.
1776-1822	E T A Hoffmann explores the world of fantasy and the supernatural in his vivid tales.

Naturalism and political realism

The disillusioned idealism of the Romantic Movement is succeeded by a search for realism and, after 1848, by philosophic materialism and social-critical literature.

1797-1856	Heinrich Heine, the "defrocked Romantic", poet of the *Loreley*, mingles a bitter irony with the heated emotions of a liberal "Young Germany".
1788-1860	**Arthur Schopenhauer**, pessimistic theorist of the human will as slave-master, propound pity as the only antidote to life's suffering.
1813-1863	Hebbel composes forceful tragedies *(Maria Magdalena, Agnes Bernauer)*.
1848	**Karl Marx** and **Friedrich Engels** publish their Communist *Manifesto*.
1862-1946	Gerhart Hauptmann develops Naturalist, social-critical drama *(The Weavers)*.

The modern period

1844-1900	**Friedrich Nietzsche** denounces, in lyrical language, the decadence of humanity, praising a future "super-man" freed from slavish, accepted (especially Christian) morality *(Thus Spoke Zarathustra)*.
1868-1933	Stefan George publishes poems which, in their formal perfection, ally him with the French Symbolists.

1875-1955	Thomas Mann, novelist (*Buddenbrooks*, *Dr Faustus*, *The Magic Mountain* and *Death in Venice*).
1877-1962	Hermann Hesse's preoccupation with psychoanalytical issues and most particularly the conflicting sides of man's nature produces some masterly novels (*Der Steppenwolf*, *Narziß und Goldmund*, *The Glass Bead Game*).
1883-1924	Franz Kafka, symbolic novelist of the absurd (*The Trial*, *Metamorphosis*, *The Castle* and *America*).
1898-1956	Bertolt Brecht, social-critical dramatist who experimented with radical new forms of theatre (*The Threepenny Opera*, *Mother Courage*, *Galileo* and *Caucasian Chalk Circle*).
c1900-1930	The Austrians Rainer Maria Rilke and Hugo von Hoffmannsthal attain the peak of poetic impressionism.
1900-1983	Anna Seghers, exiled since 1933, returns to East Germany after the war and questions the relationship between art and reality.
1920-1950	The Existentialist movement **(Husserl, Heidegger, Jaspers).**

National Socialism forced numerous poets and writers into exile (Walter Benjamin, Alfred Döblin, Lion Feuchtwanger, Else Lasker-Schüler, Thomas and Heinrich Mann, Carl Zuckmayer, Stefan Zweig). The "inward emigration" undertaken by dissenting authors, who rather than expressing their disapproval of the Nazi regime imposed silence on themselves to avoid being penalised, was the option chosen by Gottfried Benn (1886–1956) and Ernst Jünger (1895-) among others.

Post-1945 literature

Twelve years under National Socialist rule had broken the flow of literary creation in Germany, necessitating repair work in this domain too. The association of authors known as **Gruppe 47** (after the year of its founding), which centred around Hans Werner Richter and Alfred Andersch, was instrumental in putting Germany back onto the map as far as world literature was concerned. This loosely associated group of writers served as a forum for reading, discussion and criticism, until its last conference in 1967, exerting a lasting and formative influence on the contemporary German literary scene. Authors associated with Gruppe 47 included Paul Celan, Heinrich Böll (Nobel Prize winner in 1972), Günter Grass, Siegfried Lenz, Peter Weiss and Hans Magnus Enzensberger. By the end of the 1950s, works of international standing were being produced: Günter Grass's masterpiece *The Tin Drum*; Uwe Johnson's *Speculations about Jakob*; Heinrich Böll's *Billiards at Half Past Nine*, and Martin Walser's first novel *Marriages in Philippsburg*.

Increasing politicisation was what finally put an end to Gruppe 47's activities.

Authors not associated with Gruppe 47 were hard at work also; Arno Schmidt developed a highly original and well-received body of work, while Wolfgang Koeppen produced some wickedly satirical novels on contemporary society. The literature of the 1960s was characterised by a wave of social criticism, but by the 1970s German literary concerns were withdrawing to a newly discovered "inner contemplation". A particularly prolific amount of good writing was produced by women during the 1970s and 1980s (Gabriele Wohmann, Karin Struck, Verena Stefan).

In the world of **theatre**, dominated initially by the dramatic theory of Bertolt Brecht, a new band of writers began to make their presence felt, with works by Tankred Dorst (*Toller*, 1968), Peter Weiss (*Hölderlin*, 1971) and Heinar Kipphardt. Rolf Hochhuth was particularly successful with his "documentary dramas" in which he examines contemporary moral issues (*The Representative*, 1963), and Botho Strauß, the most widely performed modern German dramatist, has won international acclaim with plays such as *The Hypochondriac* (1972), *The Park* (1983) and *Final Chorus* (1991).

The division of Germany was naturally reflected in German literature. In the old **East German Republic**, literature was supposed to contribute to a socialist programme for educating the masses. The Bitterfelder Weg, the East German Republic's cultural programme inaugurated in 1959, was intended to unite art and everyday life under such slogans as "Take up your pen, comrade" and its opposite number "Poets into the workplace". This, however, rapidly proved to be a pipe dream. Poetry was the literary form least easily subject to the censorship of the Communist Party and the State, and poets such as Peter Huchel, Johannes Bobrowski and Erich Arendt produced some remarkable work. During the 1970s, Günter Kunert, Reiner Kunze, Sarah Kirsch and Wolf Biermann all made a name for themselves. Biermann's expatriation from the DDR in 1976 provoked a storm of protest and hundreds of expulsions and emigrations. From the early 1960s the prose work of Günter de Bruyn, Stefan Heym and Erwin Strittmacher was widely appreciated, and Christa Wolf became the new Anna Seghers, winning equal approbation in both Germanys. Important contributions to the theatre were made by playwrights Ulrich Plenzdorf, Peter Hacks and above all Heiner Müller (*The Hamlet Machine*, 1978).

Any overview of German literature since the Second World War must of course acknowledge the enormous contribution made by Max Frisch and Friedrich Dürrenmatt, of Switzerland, and Ilse Aichinger, Inge Bachmann, Thomas Berhard and Peter Handke, of Austria.

Music

Middle Ages

12C and 13C	The Minnesänger (musical narrative poets), minstrels and troubadours who included in their number noble knights such as **Wolfram von Eschenbach** and **Walther von der Vogelweide**, draw inspiration from French lyric poetry for their songs (Minnesang = love song).
14C and 15C	The Mastersingers (Meistersinger) organize themselves into guilds. They introduce polyphony to German music (**Heinrich von Meißen** and **Hans Sachs**).

Luther (1483-1546) and the precursors of Bach

The Lutheran Reformation brings independence to German music. The new liturgy requires a new musical form: the chorale. Sung in the common tongue, this leads, later, to the German cantata and oratorio.

1529	Chorale *Eine Feste Burg* (words by Luther, music by **Johann Walther**).
1645	*The Seven Words of Christ*, by **Heinrich Schütz**, shows Italian influence **(Monteverdi)**.
1637-1707	**Dietrich Buxtehude** organizes the first concerts of sacred music.

Johann Sebastian Bach (1685-1750)

His compositional expertise, his genius for invention and his total mastery of counterpoint enable Bach to excel in every branch of music he writes.

Johann Sebastian Bach

Eichhorn/EXPLORER, Paris

1717-1723	Kapellmeister at Court of Cöthen. *The Brandenburg Concertos.*
1723	Following his appointment as "Cantor" at St Thomas School, Leipzig, Bach's duties include the composition of a cantata every week, to be sung at the Sunday service. He has, in addition, to supervise the services at four other churches, teach Latin and singing, and find the time to compose innumerable instrumental and vocal works.
1722-1744	*The Well-Tempered Clavier.*

Music of the Baroque period

1685-1759	Georg Friedrich Handel, inspired and prolific Composer to the Courts of Hannover and St James, excels in both opera and oratorio (*The Messiah*, 1742).
1681-1767	**Georg Philipp Telemann**, influenced by French and Italian composers, forsakes counterpoint for melody. He originates public concerts.
Middle of 18C	Musicians of the **School of Mannheim** help establish the form of the modern symphony. **Carl Philipp Emmanuel Bach** (1714-1788) popularizes the sonata in its classic form. Appearance in Germany of the **Singspiel**, a type of popular operetta in which dialogue is interspersed with songs in the form of Lieder.
1743	Berlin's first Opera House is built.
1714-1787	**Christoph Willibald Gluck** provokes the enthusiasm of the innovators – and the horror of fans of traditional, Italian-inspired opera – by staging, in Paris, his *Iphigenia in Aulis* and *Orpheus*.

The Viennese School – Haydn and Mozart

At the height of the classical period, **Haydn** (1732-1809) establishes the definitive form of the symphony and the string quartet. **Mozart** (1756-1791) perfects both forms and creates operas that become immortal.

Beethoven (1770-1827)

Transforming the existing forms of music, Beethoven introduces new harmonies presaging the Romantic movement. The profundity of his reflection, varying from pure introspection to a wider belief in the force and universality of his art, shines out with extraordinary power. This is particularly true of the symphonies, moving and majestic, considered to be the major expression of his genius – and certainly the most popular.

1824 | First performance of the *Ninth Symphony*.

The Romantics

1797-1826 | **Franz Schubert** helps revive the Lied, blending folk and classical music in his unique style.

1786-1826 | **Carl Maria von Weber** creates Germany's first Romantic opera, *Freischütz* (1821), paving the way for the characters of Wagnerian drama.

1810-1856 | **Robert Schumann**, passionate and lyrical in turn, but brought up in the Germanic tradition, strives to reconcile a classical heritage with personal expression.

1833-1897 | **Johannes Brahms** exemplifies a more introverted style of German Romanticism.

Richard Wagner (1813-1883)

Wagner revolutionizes German opera. Music, he insists, should serve the dramatic action; it must therefore create "atmosphere", the décor of sound without which the opera's message could not be conveyed. Orchestration thus becomes of paramount importance. The singing, like the plot, is continuous, to correspond with dramatic truth. Wagnerian "leitmotivs" – musical phrases used recurrently to denote specific characters, moods or situations – are essential to the continuity of the action.

1848 | *Lohengrin*.
1876 | Inauguration of the Bayreuth Festival Theatre with *The Ring*.
1882 | *Parsifal*.

EXPLORER, Paris

Richard Wagner.

Late 19C

At the end of the 19C, **Gustav Mahler** (1860-1911), creator of the symphonic Lied, and **Hugo Wolf** (1850-1903) develop a new musical language which forms a bridge between Romanticism and Dodecaphony. **Richard Strauss** (1864-1949) unites at the same time a certain harmonic audacity with the sumptuous talent of a colourist.

Contemporary Music

Contemporary musical experimentation is derived principally from the Austrian school of atonal, or serial (especially twelve-note systems) music (**Schönberg, Berg, Webern**), with **Paul Hindemith** (1893-1963) remaining faithful to a national, traditional style.

1895-1982 | **Carl Orff**'s innovative ideas about music education (Orffsches Schulwerk, 1930-1933) win him international recognition. His theatrical compositions combine drama, speech and song in a fascinating rhythmic framework (*Carmina Burana*).

1921 | **Alban Berg**'s *Wozzeck*.

1900-1950 | **Kurt Weill**, influenced at the beginning of his career by the atonal composers, returns under the impact of jazz to tonal music, and composes *The Threepenny Opera* (1928).

1901-1983 | The compositions – mainly opera and ballet music – of **Werner Egk**, a student of Carl Orff, reveal the influence of Igor Stravinsky and Richard Strauss.

If **Wolfgang Fortner** (1907-1987) is influenced initially by Hindemith, he nonetheless turns to modal twelve-note serial music later on. His mature works introduce electronic elements into his musical compositions.

Bernd Alois Zimmermann (1918-1970) perceived past, present and future as one, and the multiple layers of reality are reflected in his composition technique. Quotations and collage are particularly important to him. His major work is the opera *The Soldiers*.

From 1950, a younger generation of musicians developed the potential of electronic music under the aegis of **Karlheinz Stockhausen** (b1920). **Hans Werner Henze** (b1926) created expressive operas, in which modernity and tradition, and atonality and tonality are combined. **Wolfgang Rihm** (b1952), like Henze, a student of Fortner, also mixes traditional stylistic elements with new techniques in his extremely complex musical language.

Stage and screen

Few countries can boast a cultural life so intense, so decentralized and involving so great a proportion of the population as modern Germany.

Music and the Theatre – Amateur orchestras as well as highly-regarded professional organizations proliferate all over the country: the Berlin Philharmonic, the Gewandhaus Orchestra of Leipzig, the Bamberg Symphony Orchestra and resident radio station orchestras (Südwestfunk, Norddeutsche Rundfunk 3, Westdeutsche Rundfunk 3), and thus perpetuate a strong musical tradition.

This decentralization is equally characteristic of drama and the lyric arts. It is due to the founding of theatres by the sovereigns of the 17C and 18C and, subsequently, by the wealthier classes living in the big towns in the 19C.

Among the most important centres concentrating on music and the lyric arts, Bayreuth is celebrated for performances of the works of Wagner; Berlin, Hamburg, Dresden, Leipzig and Stuttgart for opera and ballet; and Nuremberg for organ music. Stuttgart again is renowned for choral singing, and Munich for the music of Bach and Richard Strauss. Donaueschingen, Darmstadt and Kassel are noted for performances of works by contemporary composers.

Cinema

The creation in 1917 of UFA (Universum Film Aktiengesellschaft) a production company of considerable means, plus the emergence of an expressionist movement linked with the troubled post-war political and social scene, produced the golden age of German cinema. Aside from the more lavish productions, the period is marked by the work of directors Robert Wiene (*The Cabinet of Dr Caligari*, 1919), Fritz Lang (*Dr Mabuse*, 1922; **Metropolis**, 1925) and Friedrich Wilhelm Murnau (*Nosferatu the Vampire*, 1922; *Faust*, 1926). Georg Wilhelm Pabst's *Lulu* (1929) and *The Blue Angel* of Josef von Sternberg (1930), with Marlene Dietrich, marked a change of direction towards realism. This adventurous spirit was quenched with the arrival of the Third Reich, in which the cinema became no more than a tool in the service of an ideology. *The Gods of the Stadium* (Leni Riefensthal, 1938) – a glorification of the 1936 Berlin Olympics – and *Jud Süß* (Veit Harlan, 1940) remain the most striking examples. The period immediately after the Second World War was a cultural desert for the German cinema.

In the 1960s and 1970s makers of "New German cinema" rose up against the prevailing influence of the French "nouvelle vague", seeking to distance themselves from "daddy's films". Films made by Werner Herzog (*Young Törless*, 1966) and Alexander Kluge (*Artists at the Top of the Big Top: Disorientated*, 1968) quickly met with success. It was not long – the mid-1970s – before this younger generation had reestablished German cinema on an international scale. Volker Schlöndorff shot *The Lost Honour of Katharina Blum* (in collaboration with Margarethe von Trotta, 1975), and *The Tin Drum* (1979). Werner Herzog explored a fantastic, often quite exotic world in *Aguirre, Wrath of God* (1972), *Nosferatu the Vampire* (1979), and *Fitzcarraldo* (1982), A prominent figure in the Munich School of film-making was Rainer Werner Fassbinder (1945-1982), who also worked in television, and who was responsible for a considerable number of excellent films: *Fear the Eats Soul (Angst essen Seele auf)* (1973), *The Marriage of Maria Braun* (1978), *Berlin Alexanderplatz* (a fourteen-part television series, 1980), to name but a few. Other Munich film-makers included Wim Wenders: *The American Friend* (1977), *Paris, Texas* (1984) and *Wings of Desire* (1987). Important and innovative women film directors, besides Margarethe von Trotta (*Rosa Luxemburg*, 1986; *Das Versprechen*, 1995), include Elfi Mikesch (*Ich denke oft an Hawaii*, 1978) and Ulrike Ottinger (*Johanna d'Arc of Mongolia*, 1988). Doris Dörrie has created refreshing films with a humourous side: *Men... (Männer)* (1985) and *Ich und Er* (1987). Wolfgang Peterson's fantasy world in *The Neverending Story* (1984) was a resounding commercial success. Edgar Reitz won international acclaim with his film epic *Heimat* (1984) and its sequel *Heimat II* (1993). However, West German cinema was, and still is, characterised by a strongly individual narrative feel which perhaps makes it less approachable to outsiders.

It is difficult to summarize East German cinema, since like all other art forms it was compelled by the state to fulfil a didactic function. Thus a number of films were made taking literary classics as their theme, since directors felt unable to confront issues relevant to contemporary East Germany. Konrad Wolf made his mark on three decades of East German film-making, with films such as *Sterne* (1958), which won him recognition world-wide. In *Solo Sunny* (1979), he put the case for individualism, thus paving the way for a breakthrough in the East German film industry. Egon Günther made the highly successful *Der Dritte* (1971), while the greatest hit of the East German Film Industry Cooperative (DEFA) was Heiner Carow with *Die Legende von Paul und Paula* (1973). 1984 was a particularly fruitful year, with Hermann Zschoche's *Hälfte des Lebens*, Iris Gusner's *Kaskade Rückwärts*, and Helmut Dzuiba's *Erscheinen Pflicht*. One of the leading East German film-makers of the 1970s and 1980s was Rainer Simon (*Das Luftschiff*, 1982, *Die Frau und der Fremde*, 1985). Finally, Lothar Warneke studied the problems of everyday life and of dismantling rigid ideological points of view (*Bear Ye One Another's Burdens (Einer trage des Anderen Last)*, 1988). In contrast to the West German film industry, East German film-makers produced a number of delightful, well directed children's films (*Ottokar der Weltverbesserer*, 1976).

Fairy tales and legends

Snow White and the Seven Dwarfs – In the original story, written by the Brothers Grimm, the traditional costume worn by the dwarfs is in fact that used by miners in the Middle Ages.

Rübezahl – A giant with a red beard, a righter of wrongs. Sometimes he appears in the form of a rich merchant, sometimes as a collier in rags.

The Witches of Brocken – On the first night of May (Walpurgisnacht), they assemble for a Sabbath on the summit of the Brocken, in the Harz – a legend immortalized by a scene in Goethe's *Faust*.

Pöppele of Hohenkrähen – From his castle perched high on a rock he surveys the highway and plots the downfall of travellers – preferably nobles or important officials.

The Heinzelmännchen – Elves who helped the craftsmen of Cologne with their secret night work – but fled forever when discovered through the curiosity of a woman.

The Seven Swabians – An unfair caricature of the people of Swabia: they aimed to conquer the world, but scattered and ran when confronted by a hare.

Baron Münchhausen – Perhaps the most famous of the extravagant literary fantasists. His fanciful adventures and exploits include a journey to the centre of the earth, a moon safari, and absurdly exaggerated deeds of heroism on the high seas. There was a real Baron Münchhausen (1720-1797) who fought with the Russian army against the Turks and is said to have wildly overstated his military prowess. It was the Hanoverian Raspe (in England at the end of the 18C) and De Crac (in France in the 19C) who grossly inflated these stories into the realms of the unreal.

Till Eulenspiegel *(see BRAUNSCHWEIG)*, the **Pied Piper of Hamelin** *(see HAMELN)*, the **Nibelungen** and the **Loreley** *(see RHEINTAL)* are the principal characters of other, no less celebrated, legends.

Books to read

HISTORY AND BIOGRAPHY

A History of Germany 1815-1985. W Carr (Edward Arnold)
Exploring the Roman World: Roman Gaul and Germany. A King (British Museum Press)
Frederick the Great: Absolutism and Administration. W Hubatsch (Thames & Hudson)
The Concise German History: A Survey of the Development of German History Since 1815. AJP Taylor (Routledge)
The Last Days of Hitler. H Trevor-Roper
The Past is Myself. C Bielenberg

THE ARTS

An Outline of European Architecture. N Pevsner (Penguin)
Art in Germany: 1990-1939 From Expressionism to Resistance. R Heller (Prestel Art Books)
Baroque Art and Architecture in Central Europe. E Hempel (Pelican)
Bauhaus. F Whitford (Thames & Hudson)
Caspar David Friedrich. H Börsch-Supan (Prestel Art Books)
Early Medieval Art – Carolingian, Ottonian and Romanesque. J Beckwith (Thames & Hudson)
German Architecture and the Classical Ideal 1740-1840. D Watkin and T Mellinghoff (Thames & Hudson)
German Cathedrals. J Baum (Thames & Hudson)
The Expressionists. W-D Dube (Thames & Hudson)
The Weimar Years: A Culture Cut Short. J Willett (Thames & Hudson)

LITERATURE

Heinrich **Böll** *The Lost Honour of Katharina Blum*
Bertolt **Brecht** *The Caucasian Chalk Circle; Threepenny Novel; Mother Courage*
Elias **Canetti** *Auto da Fé*
Erskine **Childers** *The Riddle of the Sands*
Gunter **Grass** *The Tin Drum; The Flounder; From the Diary of a Snail*
Hermann **Hesse** *The Glass Bead Game; Narcissus and Goldmund; Steppenwolf*
Ernst Theodor Amadeus **Hoffmann** *Tales of Hoffmann*
Thomas **Mann** *Buddenbrooks; The Magic Mountain*
Rudolph Erich **Raspe** *The Adventures of Baron Münchhausen*
Erich Maria **Remarque** *All Quiet on the Western Front*

TRAVEL AND MODERN GERMAN SOCIETY

A Time of Gifts. P Leigh Fermor (Penguin)
Atlas of German Wines. H Johnson (M Beazley)
A Tramp Abroad. M Twain
Berlin: Coming in from the Cold. K Smith
Berlin: The Dispossessed City. M Simmons (Hamish Hamilton)
Deutschland: A Winter's Tale. H Heine
Germany and the Germans. J Ardagh (Penguin)
Goodbye to Berlin. C Isherwood (Penguin)
Guide to the Wines of Germany. I Jamieson (Reed International)
The Germans. G A Craig
The New Germany. D Marsch (Random Century Group)
The Origins of Modern Germany. G Barraclough (Blackwell Publishers)
The Rhine. J Bentley (George Philip)
To the End of the Rhine. B Levin
Vanishing Borders. M Farr
Winter - A Berlin Family 1899-1945. L Deighton (Random Century Group)

Principal museums

Antiquities

Berlin: Pergamon-Museum★★★
   (Museumsinsel)

Cologne: Römisch-Germanisches Museum★★★
Trier: Rheinisches Landesmuseum★★

Painting and Sculpture: 13C to 18C

Cologne: Wallraf-Richartz-Museum★★★
Dresden: Gemäldegalerie Alte Meister★★★
   (Zwinger)
Kassel: Staatliche Kunstsammlungen★★★
   (Schloß)
Munich: Alte Pinakothek★★★
Nuremberg: Germanisches
   Nationalmuseum★★★
Berlin: Gemäldegalerie★★ (Dahlem)

Frankfurt: Städelsches Kunstinstitut★★
Hamburg: Kunsthalle★★
Karlsruhe: Collection of German Primitives★★
   (Kunsthalle)
Leipzig: Museum der Bildenden Künste★★
Stuttgart: Old Masters Section★★
   (Staatsgalerie)
Würzburg: Mainfränkisches Museum★★

Painting and Sculpture: 19C and 20C

Cologne: Museum Ludwig★★★
Dresden: Gallery of 19C and
   20C Painters★★★ (Albertinum)
Berlin: Gallery of Romanticism★★
   (Nationalgalerie, Charlottenburg)
Berlin: Nationalgalerie★★
   (Museumsinsel)

Essen: Museum Folkwang★★
Frankfurt: Städelsches Kunstinstitut★★
Halle: Galerie Moritzburg★★
Hamburg: Kunsthalle★★
Leipzig: Museum der Bildenden Künste★★
Mannheim: Kunsthalle★★

Decorative Arts and Applied Arts

Dresden: Green Vault Collections★★★
   (Albertinum)
Nuremberg: Germanisches
   Nationalmuseum★★★

Dresden: Porcelain Collection★★
   (Zwinger)
Munich: Bayerisches Nationalmuseum★★

Science

Bremerhaven: Deutsches
   Schiffahrtsmuseum★★★
Munich: Deutsches Museum★★★

Dresden: Salon of Mathematics
   and Physics★★ (Zwinger)
Idar-Oberstein: Deutsches Edelsteinmuseum★★

Open-Air Museums

Gutach: Schwarzwälder Freilichtmuseum
   Vogtsbauernhof★★

Kiel: Schleswig-Holsteinisches
   Freilichtmuseum★★

Food and drink

German food is more varied and better balanced than is generally supposed, and the composition and presentation of meals are in themselves original.

Breakfast **(Frühstück)** – there is plenty of it – includes cold meats and cheese, and there is invariably a soft-boiled egg. Lunch **(Mittagessen)** generally begins with soup, followed by a fish or meat main course always accompanied by a portion of salad (lettuce, cucumber, shredded cabbage). For the evening meal **(Abendessen)**, there will be a choice of cold meats **(Aufschnitt)**, delicatessen and cheeses, usually with a selection of different types of bread and/or rolls.

Certain dishes are served all over the country: **Wiener Schnitzel** (veal escalope fried in breadcrumbs), **Eisbein** (salted knuckle or shin of pork), **Sauerbraten** (beef in a brown sauce) and **Gulasch** (either in the form of soup or as a stew) are the most popular.

Beer and Wine – Germans are justifiably proud of their national beverage, produced by nearly 1 200 breweries throughout the country. Brewing techniques respect a purity law *(Reinheitsgebot)* decreed in 1516, whereby nothing but barley, hops and plain water may be used in the fabrication of **beer** (with the addition, today, of yeast).

German vineyards cover 69 000ha - 170 500 acres, extending from Lake Constance to the Siebengebirge, from Trier to Würzburg. The growers produce a great variety of wines from a wide range of grapes – as the visitor may discover in most bars and restaurants, sampling them by the glass *(offene Weine)*.

Notable among the **white wines** – 80% of production – are the vigorous Rieslings of the Middle Rhine and those of the Moselle, Saar and Ruwer rivers, aromatic and refreshing; the noble and delicate wines of the Rheingau; full-bodied and elegant Nahe wines; those of Franconia, potent, sometimes almost bitter; and the numerous and varied wines of Baden and Württemberg. Among the **red wines**, particularly choice examples come from Rheinhessen and Württemberg, not forgetting the ardent and thoroughbred reds of the Palatinate and, above all, the red wines of the Ahr, paradise of the Spätburgunder.

SOME REGIONAL SPECIALITIES

Bavaria and Franconia

Leberknödel: Large dumplings of liver, bread and chopped onion, served in a clear soup.
Leberkäs: Minced beef, pork and liver, cooked as a galantine.
Knödel: Dumplings of potato or soaked bread.
Haxen: Veal or pork trotters.
Schlachtschüssel: Breast of pork, liver sausage and black pudding, served with pickled cabbage and dumplings.
Rostbratwürste: Small sausages grilled over beechwood charcoal.

Baden-Württemberg

Schneckensuppe: Soup with snails.
Spätzle: Egg-based pasta in long strips.
Maultaschen: Pasta stuffed with a mixture of meat and spinach.
Geschnetzeltes: Slices of veal in a cream sauce.

Rhineland-Palatinate

Sauerbraten: Beef marinated in wine vinegar, served with potato dumplings.
Reibekuchen: Small potato pancakes with apple or blueberry sauce.
Hämchen: Pork trotters with pickled cabbage and mashed potato.
Saumagen: Stuffed pork belly with pickled cabbage.
Schweinepfeffer: Highly seasoned, spicy pork in the form of a ragout, thickened with blood.
Federweißer: Partially fermented new wine, customarily accompanied by an onion tart.

Hessen and Westphalia

Sulperknochen: Ears, trotters and tail of pork, served with pickled cabbage and pease pudding.
Töttchen: Ragout of brains and calf's head, cooked with herbs.
Pickert: Sweet potato cakes with raisins.

Thuringia

Linsensuppe mit Thüringer Rotwurst: Lentil soup with Thuringian sausages.

Saxony

Rinderzunge in Rosinen-Sauce: Calf's tongue in a grape sauce.
Dresdener Stollen: Raisin cake.

Lower Saxony and Schleswig-Holstein

Aalsuppe: Sweet-and-sour soup, made of eels, prunes, pears, vegetables, bacon and seasoning.
Labskaus: Favourite sailor's dish, basically beef, pork and salted herrings with potatoes and beetroot, the whole topped with cucumber and fried egg.
Buntes Huhn: Salt beef on a bed of diced vegetables.

Schloß Neuschwanstein

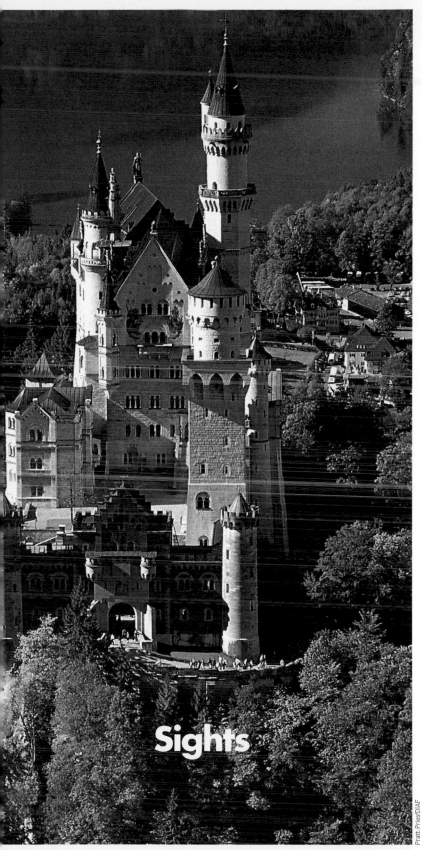

Sights

AACHEN

AIX-LA-CHAPELLE – Nordrhein-Westfalen – Population 253 000
Michelin map 417 N 2

Aachen, situated among the northern foothills of the Ardennes, is the most westerly town in Germany. Its hot springs, already famous in the time of the Celts, were transformed into thermal baths by the Romans ("Aquae Grani"). Under Charlemagne, Aachen became the capital of the Frankish Empire.

Coal seams and rich veins of lignite in the vicinity allowed the town to develop into an important industrial centre with a renowned college of technology.

Charlemagne (747-814) – King of the Franks from the year 768, Charlemagne chose Aachen as a permanent site for the Frankish Court – which had previously been held, as it was in the time of his ancestors, wherever war or the chase led him. In AD 800, Charlemagne was crowned Holy Roman Emperor. He then conquered the Saxons and the Bavarians, consolidating his frontiers north of the Pyrenees to resist invasions by Moors, Slavs and Danes.

The Court became a fountain-head of wisdom, culture and Christianity, which spread throughout his realm. Charlemagne brought to the West the treasures of Latin civilization and culture as well as the advantages of a centralized government.

The sovereign was buried at Aachen, in the Octagon of the Palatine chapel (Pfalzkapelle).

The Imperial City – Between 936 and 1531, thirty princes were crowned King of Germania in the cathedral at Aachen. In 1562 the town lost the status of Coronation City to Frankfurt.

SIGHTS

⋆⋆**Dom (Cathedral)** ⊙ – Shortly before the year 800, Charlemagne organized the building of a domed octagonal basilica (the **Pfalzkapelle**) on the lines of the churches in the Eastern Roman Empire – the first time this type of construction had been seen north of the Alps. The Gothic chancel, started in 1355, was consecrated in 1414, on the 600th anniversary of the Emperor's death.

Exterior – *Starting at the Katschhof (north side), walk around the cathedral.* Successively, the chapel of St Nicholas, the chapel of Charlemagne with its Flamboyant portal, and finally the chancel (19C statues between the clerestory windows) come into view.

From the Münsterplatz *(south side)*, there is a good view of the original Carolingian octagon, crowned now with a 16-sided cupola dating from the 17C.

On this side are the Gothic chapels of St Matthias and St Anne, together with the Hungarian chapel. The Carolingian porch on the cathedral courtyard is closed by **bronze doors** embellished with lions' heads (c800).

Interior – The octagon is surrounded by a two-storey ambulatory with bronze grilles of the Carolingian period closing the openings on the upper level. Rich mosaics decorate the dome. From the centre hangs a magnificent **chandelier**★★ (Radleuchter – *currently being restored*) in copper, the gift of Frederick Barbarossa (12C). To the right of the two octagon piers in front of the chancel is the 14C statue of the Virgin of Aachen. Modern stained-glass windows light the chancel. On the right, above the door leading to the sacristy, the **ambo of Henry II**★★★ – a small pulpit in gilded copper, decorated with precious stones – can be seen (early 11C). The Carolingian high altar is adorned with a **Pala d'Oro**★★★ – a gorgeous, gold-faced frontal illustrated with scenes from the Passion and Christ in Majesty (c1020). Behind the altar is the **Charlemagne Shrine**★★★ (Karlsschrein: 1200-1215), a reliquary where the Emperor's bones are preserved. This marvellously hand-worked silver shrine is gilded and embossed.

On the upper floor of the octagonal ambulatory *(west side)* is the **Throne**★ of Charlemagne *(only visible during the guided tour)*. Made of simple, close-fitting marble slabs, this royal seat was where the German sovereigns installed themselves after their coronation to receive the homage of their subject princes. After the canonisation of Charlemagne in 1165, pilgrims were permitted to slip through the narrow passage below the throne.

★★★ Domschatzkammer (Treasury) ☉ –
Access via Klostergasse.
Aachen cathedral treasury is one of the richest in Germany.

Basement: the gold **Cross of Lothair** (Lotharkreuz) (990), encrusted with precious stones and set with a fine Roman cameo of the Emperor Augustus, is on display here. Note also a 2C marble sarcophagus with a bas-relief illustrating the abduction of Proserpine, which contained the bones of Charlemagne while the Karlsschrein reliquary was being completed.

Ground floor: among other ecclesiastical reliquaries is a **Bust of Charlemagne** (1350) in silver and gold, which was presented by Karl IV together with the crown worn by the Emperor when he reigned. A blue velvet chasuble embroidered with pearls recalls the visit of St Bernard de Clairvaux to Aachen in 1147.

Rathaus (Town Hall) (R) ☉ – The town hall was built in the 14C, on the site of Charlemagne's palace, of which the squat Granus tower may still be seen on the corner of the Krämerstraße.

Cross of Lothair, from the Cathedral Treasure, Aachen

HUBER, Garmisch-Partenkirchen

The façade of the tower, decorated with statues of the kings and emperors crowned at Aachen, overlooks the market place, with its **fountain** and statue of Charlemagne.

The Peace Treaty of 1748, which ended the War of Austrian Succession, was signed in the **White Room** (Weißer Saal), embellished with Italian stuccowork (c1725), on the right of the entrance. On the left, the **Council Chamber** (Ratssaal) is clad with panelling executed in 1727 by a master woodworker of Liège. From the staircase, there is a fine view of the cathedral.

On the upper floor, the Coronation Chamber (Reichssaal), with its ogive vaulting, was used for the royal banquets when kings were crowned. Of the eight 19C **frescoes of Charlemagne** by the local painter Alfred Rethel, only five remain. In a showcase on the eastern side of the chamber, **copies of the crown jewels** can be seen, along with valuable Gospels and Charlemagne's crown, weapons and accoutrements; the originals have been kept at the Hofburg in Vienna since the French Revolution.

Each year in this chamber, the International Charlemagne Prize is awarded to those who have worked best for the unification of Europe.

★ Couven-Museum ☉ –
On the site of the medieval public weigh-house Aachen architect Couven built this bourgeois mansion for the pharmacist Andreas Monheim. The museum displays exhibits of a century's worth of middle-class domestic life in Aachen. There is remakable variety and quality of furniture on show, as well as some magnificent chimney-pieces and Italian stuccowork. Besides a collection of tiles, the museum houses a pharmacy – the Adler-Apotheke – in which chocolate was made for the first time ever in Aachen in 1857.

★ Suermondt-Ludwig-Museum ☉ – *Wilhelmstraße.*
The tour of this museum follows a different chronological order from the norm – from present to past. First, the ground floor exhibits a collection of **contemporary art** ranging back to the 19C and 18C and Neoclassicism. On the first floor, the display focuses on Dutch, German, Spanish and Italian painting from the 17C back to the 15C. The collection of **Late Gothic sculpture** is particularly highly prized. The second floor contains displays of **stained glass** and craftwork.

Ludwig Forum für Internationale Kunst (Ludwig International Art Forum) ☉ – *Jülicherstraße 97-109. Leave via the Peterstraße.*
A former umbrella factory, in its time the biggest in Europe, is the unexpected site for this remarkable collection of modern art. The handsome brick building (1928) is, moreover, a splendid example of the Bauhaus style, which has lost nothing of its original character despite its change in role. Founded by a local industrialist named Ludwig and his wife, both connoisseurs and patrons of the arts, the exhibition includes works by Nam June Paik and Horst Antes *(The Seven Monuments of Desire)*. Also represented are Duane Hanson *(Supermarket Lady)*, Roy Lichtenstein, Georg Baselitz, Jonathan Borowsky *(Ballerina Clown)* and Jörg Immendorf *(Brandenburger Tor)*. Theatrical performances (events also include dance, music, film and video) and a park displaying sculptures add to the interest of the Forum, opened in 1991 with the intention of creating a cultural meeting place.

EXCURSION

Kornelimünster – *10km - 6 miles to the southeast.*
This suburb of Aachen in the valley of the Inde is typical of small towns in the Eifel, with its slate-roofed, blue and grey stone houses. In the centre is the old abbey church of **Kornelimünster★**, an unusual construction with five naves (14-16C), which dates back to a Benedictine church of the Carolingian period. The galleries above the chancel *(east side)* were added in the 17C, the octagonal Kornelius chapel in the early 18C. The Gothic interior (ogive vaulting, painted ceilings) is essentially Baroque; note particularly the Baroque **high altar**, subsequently modified (c1750) by J J Couven in the Rococo style. On the left there is a stone statue of St Kornelius (c1460).
The richness of the relics belonging to the church (valuable ancient cloths, a 1360 bust of the saint in embossed silver, etc) attract a large number of pilgrims in September of each year. There is a fine **view** of the church, the abbey and the town from the Romanesque-Gothic church of St. Stephanus (in a burial ground on a height to the north).

Deutsche ALPENSTRASSE★★★

German ALPINE ROAD – Bayern
Michelin maps 419 X 13-18/420 X 14-22

From Lindau to Berchtesgaden, from Lake Constance (Bodensee) to the Königssee, this splendid scenic route runs through the foothills of the Allgäu and the Bavarian Alps, passing on the way such heights as the Zugspitze (2 962m - 9 718ft) and the Watzmann (2 712m - 8 898ft). One of the attractions of the trip is the fact that it allows the traveller both to enjoy the splendours of mountain scenery and visit such renowned monuments as the Wieskirche and the castles of Ludwig II of Bavaria, near Füssen. To cover the whole itinerary, allow three days.

① THE ALLGÄU

From Lindau to Füssen *112km - 70 miles – half a day*

The landscape at this stage of the tour is not so much Bavarian as Allemannian. The farmers of the region have made their mountain countryside into the great cheese manufacturing area of Germany.

★★ Lindau – *See LINDAU.*

Paradies – Between Oberreute and Oberstaufen, engineers have given this name to a viewpoint built halfway around a sweeping curve, from which, far off to the southwest, the distant Appenzell Alps in Switzerland (Säntis and Altmann) can be seen.

Oberstaufen – This charming resort, at the foot of the Hochgrat massif (1 834 m - 6 017ft), has some interesting ski slopes.
The route continues up the Alpine valley of the Iller river, which is dominated by the Grünten, "Guardian of the Allgäu".

* **Hindelang** – Together with its neighbour, Bad Oberdorf, this flower-decked village is a holiday centre and spa (sulphur waters) from which mountain walks can be enjoyed in summer, and skiing on the slopes of the Oberjoch in winter.

Above Hindelang, the climb of the **Jochstraße★** affords a variety of views over the jagged limestone summits of the Allgäu Alps. From the **Kanzel★** viewpoint, almost at the summit, admire the panorama embracing the Ostrach valley and the surrounding mountains.

Descending on the far side, the road crosses the valley of the Wertach, skirts the Grüntensee and passes near the large Pfronten ski resort before it arrives at Füssen.

* **Füssen** – See FÜSSEN.

★ 2 THE AMMERGAU

From Füssen to Garmisch-Partenkirchen

95km - 59 miles – half a day

★★★ **Königsschlösser von Hohenschwangau und Neuschwanstein (Royal Castles of Bavaria)** – *About 3 hours walking and sightseeing. See KÖNIGSSCHLÖSSER.*

This itinerary bypasses to the north the salient of the Ammergau Alps and then crosses a stretch of country that is seamed and broken up by the moraines deposited when the ancient Lech glacier withdrew. The "onion" domes crowning the belfries of village churches punctuate this rolling countryside.

Steingaden – The former Abbey of the Steingaden Premonstratensians, founded in the 12C, still retains its remarkable minster, though this **abbey church★** was modified in the 18C in the Baroque style. Only the outside, with its massive towers and Lombardy arcading, has preserved the original thick-set Romanesque appearance.

The Gothic entrance is enriched with a painted genealogy of the House of Welf, the original founders of the Abbey. The sobriety of the stucco-work embellishing the whole of the chancel is in sharp contrast to the lightness of that in the wide nave, which is enhanced by finely painted motifs. Furnishings in both the Baroque and Rococo style – pulpit, organ loft, altarpieces, statues – lend the ensemble a certain theatrical quality, symbolizing the triumph of decoration over architecture.

★★ **Wieskirche** – See WIESKIRCHE.

Rottenbuch – First built as an Augustinian monastery, the **Mariä-Geburts-Kirche★** (Church of the Nativity of the Virgin) was entirely remodelled in the Baroque and Rococo styles in the 18C. The stuccowork here exemplifies the virtuosity of the School of Wessobrunn, of which Joseph and Franz Schmuzer were among the masters. Frescoes by Matthäus Günther harmonize perfectly with this exuberantly sculpted decor. The pulpit, organ loft and altars are overburdened with statues and giltwork in the pure Rococo tradition.

* **Echelsbacher Brücke (Echelsbacher Bridge)** – Since 1929, this audacious reinforced concrete structure has spanned the Ammer gorge, which at this point is 76m - 250ft deep. Walk on foot to the middle of the bridge to get the most impressive view of the gorge.

* **Oberammergau** – This small town of peasants and craftsmen, hemmed in by the wooded foothills of the Ammergau, owes its fame to the internationally-known **Passion Play**, which is performed only once every ten years (next performance: AD 2000). The play, involving 1 100 amateur actors drawn from the local population, lasts an entire summer's day. The tradition derives from a vow made by the inhabitants in 1633, after a plague epidemic had miraculously been cut short.

★★ **Linderhof** – See Schloß LINDERHOF.

Ettal – A blossoming of the Benedictine tradition, added to local veneration of a statue of the Virgin attributed to Giovanni Pisano, explain the vast dimensions of Ettal Abbey, founded by the Emperor Ludwig of Bavaria in 1330.

The sole example in Germany, the abbey church was based on a Gothic building with a polygonal floor-plan, the present elevation being due to the Baroque architect Enrico Zucalli, who built the façade and the chancel (1710-1726). Joseph Schmuzer of the school of Wessobrunn *(see above)* added the dome after the church was gutted by a fire in 1774. The painted decorations on the inside of this dome are the work of Johann Jakob Zeiller.

The road now rejoins the Loisach valley. In the south, the Wetterstein range appears, with the summits of the Zugspitze, the Dreitorspitze and the pyramid peak of the Alpspitze. Continue to Garmisch-Partenkirchen.

★★★ **Garmisch-Partenkirchen** – See GARMISCH-PARTENKIRCHEN.

★ ③ THE LAKE DISTRICT AND THE UPPER ISAR VALLEY

From Garmisch-Partenkirchen to Schliersee

105km - 66 miles – one day

★ **Mittenwald** – *See GARMISCH-PARTENKIRCHEN: Excursions.*

At Wallgau, the route joins the upper valley of the Isar *(toll road as far as Vorderriß)*, a wild, bleak stretch of open country.

Sylvenstein-Staudamm (Sylvenstein Dam) – Controlling the excessive flooding of the Isar, this earthwork dam with its waterproof core has created a huge artificial lake whose waters power an underground power station.
The road crosses the wooded Achenpaß *(going 2km - 1.2 miles into Austria)* and then plunges down towards the Tegernsee.

★ **Bad Wiessee** – An elegant resort, both a fashionable holiday centre and a major spa (iodized sulphur springs), Bad Wiessee is admirably placed on the shores of the Tegernsee lake in cultivated, green semi-Alpine surroundings.

★ **Schliersee** – Beside the lake of the same name, this small town – together with the neighbouring municipalities of Fischhausen, Neuhaus and Spitzingsee *(see itinerary below)* – offers interesting possibilities for a short stay. The **Parish Church**★ (Pfarrkirche) is a former Collegiate of the Chapter of Our Lady in Munich, rebuilt in the Baroque style between 1712 and 1714. Both the painted vaulting and the delicate stuccowork were executed by Johann-Baptist Zimmermann (1680-1758), brother of the architect of the Wieskirche *(qv)*.

★ ④ THE SUDELFELD AND THE CHIEMGAU MOUNTAINS

From Schliersee to Berchtesgaden

172km - 107 miles – one day

Spitzingsee – A little less than a mile from the summit, the steeply-climbing access road offers a fine **overall view**★ of the Fischhausen-Neuhaus plain and the Schliersee lake. Soon afterwards, the road ends by the Spitzingsee, a small lake around which a mountain resort is developing.
3km - 1 3/4 miles before Bayrischzell, the route passes the lower terminal of a cableway leading to the summit of the Wendelstein *(the climb can also be made by train, starting from Brannenburg-Waching – description below)*.

Tatzelwurm-Wasserfall – *1/4 hour Rtn on foot.*
From the "Naturdenkmal Tatzelwurm" car park, a footpath leads to this impressive cascade.

★★ **Wendelstein** ⊙ – *5 hours Rtn, of which 2 hours on a funicular railway and 3/4 hour on foot. Leave from the lower station at Brannenburg-Waching.*
Boldly forcing a passage up increasingly steep slopes, the little train finally reaches an altitude of 1 738m - 5 702ft. The rest of the climb is via a footpath carved out of the bedrock. The summit (1 838m - 6 030ft) is crowned by a solar observatory and a chapel built in 1718.

The **panorama**★★ visible from there encompasses, from east to west, the mountains of the Chiemgau, the Loferer and the Leoberger Steinberge, the Kaisergebirge range with its jagged peaks, and the glacial crests of the Hohe Tauern.

The road winds down the valley of the Inn and then follows the Munich-Salzburg motorway, which skirts the southern shore of the **Chiemsee**★ *(qv)*. After Marquartstein, the route lies through a succession of tortuous, steep-sided valleys, running out finally above the Reit Basin, at the foot of the Zahmer Kaiser.

Turning back towards the east, the Alpine itinerary traverses a long corridor which passes near a series of shallow, dark lagoons.

★ **Ruhpolding** – The locality, very popular with holiday-makers, is well known for upholding local traditions, crafts and folklore. The life of the town centres around the parish church of St George, where there is a Romanesque Virgin.

Gletschergarten – *1/4 hour on foot.*

Opened up by the building of the road, this "garden of glaciers" forms a natural museum of glacial erosion. A prolongation of the Tauern glacier, moving along the Saalach valley *(see Michelin Green Guide Austria)*, once transported huge blocks of crystalline rock which striated or excavated the rolling, rocky surface of the land.

After the Schwarzbachwacht pass (alt 868m - 2 848ft) there is a sharp contrast between the severe, wooded valley of the Schwarzbach river and the open pastureland on the Ramsau side. At a number of places, the descent offers an opportunity to appreciate fine **panoramas**★★, revealing the "teeth" of the Hochkalter biting into the white surface of the Blauois (along with the Höllentalferner, in the Zugspitze massif, the only glacier in Germany) and the bulk of the Watzmann.

The German Alpine Road ends at Berchtesgaden.

★★ **Berchtesgaden** – *See BERCHTESGADEN.*

Passion Plays

These religious dramas date from the Middle Ages, originally focussing purely on Christ's suffering, death and Resurrection. The early passion plays were in Latin, but included Gospel readings and poetical interludes in the vernacular, on related subjects such as the Last Supper. Increasingly, the plays were performed in the vernacular, until eventually an independent tradition of passion play was established, the earliest examples of which were in German. Initially, the play's main emphasis was the Resurrection story, but gradually, the additional episodes included led to the evolution of play cycles, including episodes as early as the fall of Lucifer and of Man.

By the 16C, secular influences had led to many passion play cycles becoming so debased that they were banned by the Church. More still were banned after the Reformation.

Besides in Oberammergau, passion plays are performed in the Austrian Tirol, in northern Spain (in Catalan) during Lent and Holy Week, and in the Netherlands (modern version by Jacques Scheurs).

ALSFELD★

Hessen – Population 17 100
Michelin map 417 N 11

A situation on the main route linking Hessen and Thuringia – in which, until the middle of the 13C, the town was administratively incorporated – brought prosperity to Alsfeld in olden times. Today the charm of the town lies in the half-timbered houses grouped around the picturesque old market place.

SIGHTS

★ **Marktplatz** – The northeast corner of this square, where the Rathaus and the Weinhaus (recognizable by its stepped gable) are overlooked by the church tower, is quite delightful. Twin, spired turrets surmount the façade of the 1516 **Rathaus**★ (Town Hall), half-timbered above stone arcades that once served as a covered market. Diagonally opposite stands a solid stone house with a two-storey oriel window at one corner. Known as "the Wedding House" (Hochzeitshaus), this interesting building dates from 1565. Its two gables, set at right angles, are embellished with festoons and scroll-work typical of the First Renaissance in Germany.

The Marktplatz, Alsfeld

Nach Foto Erich Müller

Rittergasse – This street, leaving the square on the side opposite the Rathaus, has two of the most interesting **old houses**★ in Alsfeld. The Neurathhaus at No 3 is a particularly fine example of projecting half-timbering in the Baroque style, while the Minnigerode-Haus at No 5, which is built of stone, conserves its original spiral staircase within. This masterpiece of carpentry rises without any support from the walls around a tall, twisted tree trunk.

Stadtkirche – The church is early Gothic, still with its original furnishings. Note the wooden galleries and, behind the altar on the left, a fine carved and painted panel of the Crucifixion between four scenes from the life of Jesus.

In the small square to the north of the church there is a house adorned with modern graffiti and a fountain presided over by a goose-girl in Schwalm costume. Noticed in the neighbourhood of Alsfeld by the Brothers Grimm *(qv)*, a costume of this type was used by them as a model for the clothes worn by Little Red Riding Hood.

ALTENBURG

Thüringen – Population 48 000
Michelin map 418 N 21

An Altenburg was recorded for the first time in the year 976. It was expanded to become an imperial palace under the Hohenstaufen emperors – Kaiser Friedrich Barbarossa stayed there on many occasions – and the settlement raised to the status of a free imperial city. In 1328, it fell into the hands of the Margraves of Meißen, and from 1603 to 1672 and again from 1826 to 1918 Altenburg was the residence of the Dukes of Saxe-Altenburg. During the intervening period, it was the residence of the Dukes of Saxe-Gotha. The town was one of the few to escape relatively unscathed from the damages wrought during the Second World War. However, in the decades after the war a good many streets and houses were demolished or fell into disrepair. Projects are afoot to put a stop to this process. The town's hillside location, with steep streets running up and down hill, lends Altenburg a certain charm and affords visitors some pretty views.

The home of the playing card – Altenburg is well known among the card-playing fraternity, since playing cards have been manufactured here since 1832. The town is also birthplace of the popular German card game Skat, which evolved from other card games between 1810 and 1818.

Altenburg can also be proud of the fact that the first ever Brockhaus encyclopædia was printed here in 1836.

SIGHTS

Rathaus and Markt (Town Hall and Market Square) – The elongated market square with its handsome town houses is dominated by the town hall. This was built between 1562 and 1564 by Weimar architect **Nikolaus Grohmann**, and is one of the most remarkable Renaissance buildings in Germany. An eight-storey staircase tower with an onion-domed roof crowns the edifice, which is further adorned by a wealth of sculpted decoration on the round oriel windows and doorways. Note the so-called "Gaffköpfe" (gaping heads), which are most probably representations of the aldermen at the time the town hall was built. On the west side of the market square stands the **Brüderkirche**, with charming Jugendstil (Art Nouveau) mosaic work on the church façade.

Brühl – *Northeast of the market square.*
The Brühl, the oldest square in the town, is located at the foot of the **Bartholomäuskirche**. The square features an ornate Baroque building, the **Seckendorffsche Palais**, dating from 1724, and opposite this, the **Alte Amtshaus**. In between the two stands a fountain, the **Skatbrunnen**, which was erected in 1903.

Schloß (Castle) – High above the town, perched on a rocky outcrop, stands the castle, which is particularly imposing when seen from the southwest. The various castle buildings, arranged in a semi-circle around a great courtyard, represent nine centuries of architectural evolution. Note especially the **Schloßkirche★**, a Late Gothic church dating from 1444. The chancel is roofed with stellar-vaulting. The richly decorated Baroque interior contains an interesting organ built by **Gottfried Heinrich Trost** in 1738. The castle, which was the scene of the legendary kidnapping of the Prince of Saxony in 1455, now houses the **Schloß- und Spielkartenmuseum** ⊙. Walk through the extensive castle grounds (Schloßpark) to the north to get to the Lindenau-Museum.

★★ Lindenau-Museum ⊙ – The Saxon statesman, astronomer and art collector **Bernhard August von Lindenau** (1779-1854) bequeathed a valuable collection to his native town which is housed in a building dating from 1873. The bequest has earned Altenburg its reputation among connoisseurs of art. In particular the remarkable collection of **antique ceramic ware** (7-2C BC) testifies to Von Lindenau's excellent artistic judgment.
The jewel of the exhibition is perhaps the collection of **Italian Primitive painting**, which is the most comprehensive of its kind outside Italy, including 180 canvases dating from the 13-16C, principally by the schools of Florence and Siena. The variety, quality and range of paintings in this section are astounding.
One or two examples of European painting from the 16-18C, most notably German painting from the 19C (charming *Girl with Basket of Flowers* by **Ferdinand von Rayski**) and the present, lend a note of contrast to the exhibition as a whole.

AMBERG

Bayern – Population 42 000
Michelin map 420 R 19
Town plan in the current Michelin Red Guide Deutschland

In the 14C and 15C, Amberg had an important role to play as a commercial centre on the route from Nuremberg to Prague. The large number of rich burghers' houses, tightly packed between the ramparts, testify today to that prosperity. A modern town has evolved around that ancient, picturesque nucleus, still very well preserved in its green setting.
The twin arches of the old fortified bridge, reflected in the water of the river below, form two perfect circles – reminiscent of a pair of spectacles. This image, which can be appreciated best from the Ring Bridge, in the south, and the footpath skirting the Arsenal (Zeughaus) to the north, is known as the **"Stadtbrille"** (Town Spectacles) and has come to stand as a symbol for Amberg.

Marktplatz – Closing off this square, the **Rathaus** (14C and 16C town hall) displays a Gothic gable above a charming Renaissance balustrade. Opposite is the **St. Martinskirche**, a powerful 15C Gothic construction to which a tower of almost 100m - 328ft was added in the 18C. Three huge naves, supported by elegant columns, make this the largest church in the Upper Palatinate.

★ Deutsche Schulkirche (Salesian Church) – This small church, built at the end of the 17C by Wolfgang Dientzenhofer *(qv)*, is covered by graceful Rococo decorations, most of them the work of Amberg's own master craftsmen (1738-58). Original features include the curious position of the altar niches flanking the triumphal arch, and an organ loft in the form of a shell.

Wallfahrtskirche Maria-Hilf (Chapel of Mary-the-Helper) – This votive chapel was built as a thanksgiving gesture at the end of a plague epidemic which ravaged the region in 1634 *(see also Oberammergau Passion Play)*. Vault **frescoes★**, painted by C D Asam in his youth, illustrate this tragic event and the subsequent pilgrimages.

ANNABERG-BUCHHOLZ★

Sachsen − Population 26 500
Michelin map 418/420 O 23 - Local map under ERZGEBIRGE

This locality on the eastern slopes of the Erzgebirge was blessed with a sudden prosperity after the discovery, in 1492, of rich mineral lodes (silver and tin) in the mountain of Schreckenberg. When the seams ran out several decades later, Annaberg turned to the production of fine lace – a craft for which the town is still famous today.

JÜRGENS OSTEUROPA, Köln

Vaulting in St. Annenkirche, Annaberg-Buchholz

★★**St. Annenkirche** − Built in a relatively short time (1499-1519), this church with three naves is one of the most successful and impressive examples of Saxony's Flamboyant Gothic style. Twelve tall pillars soar into the ribs of the vaulting so effortlessly, with such elegance, that they seem not to support it but merely to link it with the ground − perhaps only to anchor it there. The parapets of the galleries on the side walls are embellished with scenes from the Old and New Testaments.

At the far end of the church, in the left-hand wall, is the "**Schöne Pforte**"★★ (beautiful door), a brilliantly multicoloured portal originally designed for another church. It was made by Hans Witten in 1512. The **pulpit**★★ (1516) is the work of the sculptor F Maidburg. Note the relief figure representing a miner. A similar reference to Annaberg's old activity lies in the painted panels to be found behind the **Miners' Reredos**★ (Bergmannsaltar, c1520). Placed in the left-hand chapel of the chancel, these depict the various stages of work in a mine of that period.

Technisches Museum Frohnauer Hammer (Frohnau Forge) ⊙ − Once a flour mill, this old building was turned into a workshop for the striking of coins when silver was discovered in the region; it was subsequently transformed into a blacksmith's forge. Hydraulically-operated bellows and power-hammers (100, 200 and 300kg - 220, 440, 660lb) can be seen there today.

EXCURSION

★ **Erzgebirge** − See ERZGEBIRGE.

*If you intend combining a tour of Germany
with a visit to one of the neighbouring countries,
remember to take the appropriate Michelin Green Guide
to Scandinavia-Finland, Netherlands, Belgium and Luxembourg, France,
Switzerland, Austria or Europe (forthcoming).*

ANSBACH

Bayern — Population 40 000
Michelin map 419/420 S 15

Ansbach, half medieval, half Baroque, is a peaceful Franconian town which owes its fame to the Hohenzollerns. The Margraves of the House of Hohenzollern's Frankish line settled in Ansbach and Bayreuth as early as the 13C. Since then the two towns have often been associated in history — the Ansbach-Bayreuth Dragoons, for example, fought under Frederick the Great.

On the feminine side, the cultivated Margravines of the 18C, one of whom — Friederike Luise — was a sister of Queen Wilhelmina (qv), made the life of the Ansbach Court almost as brilliant as that of Bayreuth.

SIGHTS

★ **Residenz (Castle)** ⊙ — This 14C fortress was enlarged and transformed in the Franconian Baroque style by Gabrieli, architect to the Court of Vienna, and Retti, at the behest of the Margraves of Brandenburg-Ansbach (1705-1750). The façade, with its sober lines and simple decoration, is imposing. The interior — symmetrical like the inside of most German Baroque palaces — is especially remarkable for: the princes' apartments (Fürstenzimmer); the **Porcelain Gallery ★★** (Gekachelter Saal), which displays some 2 800 Ansbach pottery tiles, lightly and delicately designed with rural motifs; the **Hall of Mirrors ★** (Spiegelkabinett) and its unbelievable profusion of china ornaments and gilded woodwork; the Family Gallery (Familienzimmer), exhibiting portraits of the Hohenzollerns; and the Gobelins Gallery, with three tapestries woven after cartoons by Charles Le Brun.

On the far side of the esplanade, the castle park extends away to the site of the Baroque Orangery, which contains a monument to the rather enigmatic Kaspar Hauser, thought to have been the son of Karl Ludwig Friedrich, Grand Duke of Baden, fatally wounded here in 1833.

St. Gumbertus-Kirche — This church, with its 15C Gothic chancel, was transformed in the 18C into a huge preaching hall. The salient feature today is the Chapel of the Order of the Knights of the Swan (St. Georgskapelle des Schwanenritterordens), a lay order founded by the Elector of Brandenburg in 1440. Through the glass door (on the left, behind the altar), emblems and funerary monuments of the Knights can be seen, along with a fine late 15C altarpiece of the Virgin in Glory.

ASCHAFFENBURG

Bayern — Population 65 000
Michelin map 417 Q 11
Town plan in the current Michelin Red Guide Deutschland

Aschaffenburg, which has grown up at the foot of the wooded Spessart hills above a broad sweep of the River Main, has enchantingly beautiful parks — which makes it easy to understand why the **Prince-Electors and the Archbishops of Mainz** made it their second home in the 13C. The castle and the Schönbusch park are reminders of this illustrious past. The town was re-attached to Bavaria in 1814. The proximity of Frankfurt's urban and industrial centres is largely responsible for the changing face of Aschaffenburg today.

SIGHTS

★ **Schloß Johannisburg (Castle)** — Built on the site of a medieval fortress destroyed in the mid-16C, this huge red sandstone castle is in the form of a hollow square quartered by lantern towers. The architect commissioned by the Bishops to design it was Georg Ridinger of Strasbourg. Constructed between 1605 and 1614, the castle was the pioneer example of the charmingly decorated style that came to be known as German Renaissance. Inside the walls, the steeply sloping roofs of the three-storey wings are dominated by the massive square towers and the 14C keep, retained from the old fort. The central portion of the three façades is topped by dormers adorned with shell niches, pilasters and obelisks — a typical Renaissance concept.

The **State gallery** (Staatsgalerie) ⊙ is on the first floor of the castle, in the wing nearest the river. Apart from 17C Dutch masters (Aert de Gelder), paintings are exhibited by — among others — Hans Baldung Grien (Golgotha) and members of the school of Lucas Cranach the Elder (qv). In the **Paramentenkammer**, vestments and liturgical objects used during the 17C and 18C in the Archdiocese of Mainz may be viewed. Between the West Tower and the old keep is the **chapel** (Schloßkirche). The Franconian sculptor Hans Juncker was responsible for the splendid altar, richly decorated with motifs in relief and alabaster figurines.

On the second floor is a **collection of architectural models** of ancient buildings, made in cork. These formed part of the "Collection of Corkery" amassed by Archbishop K T von Dalberg between 1802 and 1806. The **Royal Apartments** in the riverside wing contain late 18C and early 19C furniture, landscape paintings and portraits of the princes who lived there. Finally the **Municipal Museum** (Städtisches Schloßmuseum) ☉ displays examples of religious art and craftwork from the 15C to the present day, and several collections illustrating the history of Aschaffenburg.

Walk through the castle grounds (Schloßgarten) to reach the **Pompeianum**. This is a reconstruction of the house of Castor and Pollux at Pompeii, built by Ludwig I of Bavaria on the bank overlooking the river.

Stiftskirche – Well situated at the top of a monumental Baroque stairway, this Romano-Gothic church has an oddly asymmetric appearance from the outside, owing to the overshadowing peristyle which flanks the west front and the northern aisle. The oldest part is the long 12C nave (the tower was not completed until c1490). The Romanesque west door (early 13C) has an interesting decoration with plant motifs; on the tympanum above, Christ in Majesty.

Inside, the major interest lies in the works of art. **Grünewald's The Lamentation** (1525), the praedella of an altarpiece now lost, is on display in a glass case: the artist-architect was Court Painter to the Prince-Electors at Aschaffenburg from 1516 until the Peasants' Revolt. The south transept contains a Resurrection (1520) by Lucas Cranach the Elder, that on the north a Romanesque Crucifixion (12C). In the **Maria-Schnee-Kapelle** (Chapel of Our Lady of the Snow) is a copy of Grünewald's famous painting of the Virgin Mary, which was taken from the church in the 16C and is now at Stuppach *(qv)*. The late Romanesque **cloister** is supported on 64 columns whose capitals are as varied as they are original.

EXCURSION

Park Schönbusch – *3km - 2 miles to the west.*
In the middle of this shady 18C park, which is laid out with ornamental ponds, canals, islets and follies (Temple of Friendship), there is a small and delightful **country house** (Lustschlößchen) built for the Archbishops of Mainz in 1780 and decorated in the Empire style.

From the Hall of Mirrors on the first floor, there is a fine **view** of the castle, with the wooded heights of the Spessart massif in the background.

AUGSBURG★★

Bayern – Population 250 000
Michelin map 419/420 U 16
Plan of the conurbation in the current Michelin Red Guide Deutschland

Tacitus wrote of Augsburg that it was "the most brilliant colony in all the province of Rhaetia". Situated on the Romantic Road (Romantische Straße – *qv*), the town today is both a busy industrial and commercial centre and an attractive reminder of life in the Renaissance period.

HISTORICAL NOTES

Roman origins – Founded in 15 BC by a kinsman of the Emperor Augustus, Augsburg is, along with Trier and Cologne, one of the oldest cities in Germany. It became a trading centre on the highway to Italy and, at the fall of the Roman Empire, an episcopal see. By the end of the 13C it was a Free Imperial City and the seat of the Diet.

The Fuggers – At the end of the 15C, Augsburg – which already had a population of 50 000 – became a centre of high finance and banking. This was due to the Fuggers and the Welsers, two local dynastic families who – so it was said – shared the known world between them so far as money and trade were concerned. History has preserved the name of Jakob Fugger the Rich (1459-1529), renowned as the Empire's banker and even better known as the financier of the Habsburgs. Charles V himself once received from this powerful man the rebuke: "It is well known that, without my help, Your Majesty would no longer wear the crown of the Holy Roman Empire." The debt of the Habsburgs to their Augsburg bankers, never settled, has been estimated at 4 million ducats.

The Augsburg Confession – In 1530 Charles V, disturbed by the growing strength of the Reformation in many states of the Empire, called an Imperial Diet at Augsburg with the hope of dissipating the religious troubles. The Protestants, inspired by Luther, thereupon proclaimed in a celebrated "Confession" the basic tenets of their belief. The statement was rejected, and it was not until the Peace of Augsburg in 1555 that Protestants in Germany won the freedom of worship.

The name of the town was once more inscribed in the history books in 1686 with the creation of the Augsburg League – directed by Austria and Prussia against Louis XIV following the Revocation of the Edict of Nantes.

The Pine Cone – This emblem, an ancient fertility symbol, appears on the city's arms, and indeed through the years Augsburg has flowered with the ideas and talents of artists and humanists. They include Holbein the Elder (d 1525), Hans Burkmair (1473-1541), and Martin Schongauer, son of Augsburg goldsmith Konrad Peutinger. Augsburg's emergence as "the city of the German Renaissance" is due to the architect Elias Holl (1573-1646). Mozart's father was born in Augsburg, and some of the great composer's glory, too, has been reflected on the town. The famous playwright and poet Bertolt Brecht was born in Augsburg in 1898.

By the 18C, the textile manufacturing industry was flourishing. The 19C was marked by the production (1893-7) of the first diesel engine.

SIGHTS

★ **Fuggerei** (**Y**) – This name was bestowed in 1519 on the quarter founded by Fugger the Rich to house the town's poor. The eight streets in the Fuggerei are lined by 53 gabled houses. The district has its own church and its own administration. Each evening the four gateways to the quarter are closed, as they always have been. The social settlement, the first of its kind in the world, still welcomes citizens in need as it did in the 16C, charging them only a token rent but placing on them the moral obligation of praying for the souls of the founders.

★ **Maximilianstraße** (**Z**) – Lined by mansions and private houses built by the wealthier burghers of Augsburg during the Renaissance, this street offers today one of the most majestic vistas of Old Germany. Many façades have been extensively restored. Three bronze Renaissance fountains adorn the street.

AUGSBURG

Annastraße	**Y**	Karlstraße	**Y**	Leonhardsberg	**Y** 24
Bahnhofstraße	**YZ**	Karolinenstraße	**Y** 22	Margaretenstraße	**Z** 25
Bürgermeister		Maximilianstraße	**Z**	Mittlerer Graben	**Y** 27
Fisher Str.	**Y** 5	Dominikanergasse	**Z** 8	Porlachberg	**Z** 32
Grottenau	**Y** 17	Frauentorstraße	**Y** 12	Predigerberg	**Z** 33
Hoher Weg	**Y**	Fuggerstraße	**Y** 13	Rathausplatz	**Y** 34
		Haunstetter Str.	**Z** 18	Unterer Graben	**Y** 39
		Lechhauser Str.	**Y** 23	Vorderer Lech	**Z** 43
				Wintergasse	**Y** 44

B	St. Anna-Kirche	**M³**	Maximilianmuseum
D	Heilig-Kreuz-Kirchen	**M⁴**	Staatsgalerie
M¹	Deutsche Barockgalerie		in der Kunsthalle
M²	Staatsgalerie Augsburg	**R**	Rathaus

★ Münster St. Ulrich und St. Afra (Z) – This former Benedictine abbey-church, founded c1500 by Maximilian, lies adjacent to a Protestant church of the same name. The core of the building, high and impressive, is separated from the three aisles by a fine Baroque screen. The ribbed vaulting is well lit by the clerestory windows and at the far end are three Baroque altars: in the choir, the Altar of the Nativity, to the right, the Altar of the Resurrection and to the left the Pentecostal Altar. At the transept crossing is a bronze group of the Crucifixion dating from 1607.

Among the chapels on the north side, St Simpert's is furnished with a Gothic baldachin and a balcony surmounted by terracotta **Statues of the Saints★**. Note also, above the pulpit, the sounding-board supported by two angels.

The juxtaposition of the two churches, one Catholic, one Protestant, each with the same name, is characteristic of Augsburg. The two **Heilig-Kreuz-Kirchen (Y D)** are another example.

Städtische Kunstsammlungen (Municipal Art Gallery) (Z M¹) ☉ – *Entrance: Maximilianstraße 46.*

The **Schaezler-Palais** galleries (1767) are the first to be passed through (Deutsche Barockgalerie). Paintings by masters of German Baroque are on display here. The enormous **banqueting hall★★** (Festsaal) is noteworthy for a ceiling lavishly decorated with Rococo frescoes and stucco-work, and wall panelling adorned in the same style. Beyond this, a second gallery, the Staatsgalerie Alter Kunst (**Z M²**) exhibits paintings by 15C and 16C Augsburgan and Swabian masters, including a votive portrait of *The Schwarz Family* by Hans Holbein the Elder and the famous *Portrait of Jakob Fugger the Rich* by Albrecht Dürer.

Works by Van Dyck, Tiepolo and Veronese can be seen on the second floor.

Rathaus (Town Hall) (Y R) – This vast Renaissance building is by Elias Holl. Two onion-domed towers frame a pediment adorned with the traditional pine cone. The **Perlachturm (Y)**, on the left, was originally a Romanesque watchtower. It was re-modelled in the 17C. When the Alps can be seen from the top of it, a yellow flag is flown.

Inside, the Town Hall's Golden Room (Goldener Saal), with its restored coffered ceiling, can be visited.

St. Anna-Kirche (Y B) – This church was formerly part of a Carmelite convent where Martin Luther found sanctuary when he arrived in Augsburg in 1518. The Late Gothic architecture contrasts with the Rococo stucco-work and frescoes.

Städt. Kunstsammlungen Augsburg

Banqueting Hall in the Schaezler-Palais, Augsburg

The **Fugger Funeral Chapel**★ (Fuggerkapelle) is considered to be the first example of the Italian Renaissance style in Germany. It dates from 1518. Blind arcades at the back of the chapel frame four sculptured scenes: centre, above the recumbent figures, The Resurrection, and Samson Wrestling with the Philistines after Dürer, at each side, the arms of the House of Fugger, from which the fleur-de-lys is reproduced on the pavement.
In the church there are paintings by Lucas Cranach the Elder: *Jesus, the Friend of Little Children (at the high altar in the main chancel)*, a Portrait of Martin Luther and the Prince-Elector Johann-Friedrich of Saxony.
The Goldsmiths' Chapel (Goldschmiedekapelle), on the north side of the chancel, dating from the 15C, has retained its original Gothic structure and murals.

Maximilianmuseum (Y M³) ⊙ – This museum contains evidence of life in Augsburg in days gone by; examples of Swabian sculpture; work by local goldsmiths and silversmiths.

Dom (Cathedral) (Y) – The church was rebuilt in Gothic style in the 14C. Outside, note the Gothic south door to the chancel (Südportal des Chores) or **Virgin's Door**★★ (Jungfrauen-portal), and also the bronze Romanesque **panels**★ (Türflügel) embellished with 32 bas-reliefs illustrating scenes and characters from the Old Testament and from mythology. Inside the church, the tall nave is flanked by double side aisles. The chancel, at its eastern extremity, has a double ambulatory with Gothic chapels added. The four altars in the nave are adorned with **paintings**★ (Tafelgemälden) by Holbein the Elder (on the left: *Birth of the Virgin Mary and Entry Into the Temple*; on the right, *The Offering Refused* and *The Presentation*). The clerestory windows on the south side of the nave contain stained glass **Windows of the Prophets**★ (Prophetenfenster - 12C) which are very rigid in style. The alabaster panes surrounding them are modern.

Mozarthaus (Mozart Family House) (Y) ⊙ – *Leave by Frauentorstraße.*
Documents and other exhibits emphasize the Swabian origins of the Mozart family and the life and work of father and son.
From this house, by way of the Stephingerberg and the Müllerstraße, the tree-lined promenade bordering the moats which follow the line of the ancient ramparts can be reached.

Rotes Tor (Red Gate) (Z) – This is a group of 16C fortified buildings with two vaults and a central courtyard, remodelled by Elias Holl in 1622. The tower overlooking the town is circled by bands of decoration between the engaged pillars. At the foot of the tower is an open-air theatre *(operatic performances late June to late July)*.

★ **Staatsgalerie in der Kunsthalle (State Gallery)** (M⁴) ⊙ – *Leave by Imhofstraße* (Z).
German painters of the 19C and 20C for the most part fill this museum. Among some 200 works displayed, the visitor will remember those of the New Landscape school (*Mills by Moonlight*, 1874, by Schleich the Elder – Room 2), the Post-Impressionists (Corinth's *Three Graces*, 1904, and canvases by Slevogt – Room 3), the Expressionists of the Brücke Group (Kirchner's *Cows in the Forest* – Room 7) and the members of the Blauer Reiter movement *(qv)* who were precursors of modern art (Paul Klee's *Dance of the Sad Child*, Gabrielle Münter's *Man in an Armchair*). Enthusiasts of modern painting will linger by works that characterize the movements of the 1920s: Surrealism (*The Mathematics Room*, by Zimmermann – Room 12), Abstract and Concrete Art (Room 14), Art Informel and New Figuration (Rooms 15, 16 and 17).

Alphabetical order...?
In the German alphabet, ä = ae, ö = oe and ü = ue.

BAD HERSFELD (etc.)

See Bad HERSFELD (etc.)

MICHELIN GUIDES

The Red Guides (hotels and restaurants)
Benelux – Deutschland – España Portugal – Europe – France – Great Britain and Ireland – Italia – Switzerland

The Green Guides (fine art, historic monuments, scenic routes)
Austria – Belgium and Luxembourg – Brussels – California – Canada – England: The West Country – France – Germany – Great Britain – Greece – Ireland – Italy – London – Mexico – Netherlands – New England – New York – Portugal – Quebec – Rome – Scandinavia-Finland – Scotland – Spain – Switzerland – Tuscany – Venice – Wales – Washington DC

and the collection of regional guides to France.

BADEN-BADEN★★

Baden-Württemberg — Population 50 000
Michelin map 419 T 8 - Local map under SCHWARZWALD
Plan of the conurbation in the current Michelin Red Guide Deutschland

Sheltered between the Black Forest and the Baden vineyards, Baden-Baden is one of the most luxurious German health resorts, of which the latest asset is the "Caracalla-Therme" establishment (**CY**) *(premises open to the public)*.

Spa and Casino – In Roman times the Emperor Caracalla came frequently to Baden-Baden to cure his rheumatism.

In the 12C, the town became the seat of the Zähringer branch of the Margraves of Baden. In the 16C, the great Paracelsus, one of the founders of modern pharmacy, came to take care of the Margrave.

By the 19C, a casino launched by the Frenchman Jacques Bénazet, a theatre and opera house (opened in 1862), and a racecourse organized by the Paris Jockey Club had transformed the town into the summer capital of Europe.

In the gardens of the spa park, behind the white Corinthian columns of the **Kurhaus** (**BZ**), glittering balls and concerts are held, and the gaming rooms are always crowded. Nearby in the same park (Kurgarten) is the Pump Room **(Trinkhalle)** (**BY**), embellished with murals illustrating the legends of the Baden countryside.

SIGHTS

★★**Lichtentaler Allee** (**BZ**) – This, the most beautiful promenade in Baden-Baden, runs beside the Oos river, flowing here over an artificial bed, and recalls irresistibly the 19C parades of carriages, complete with crinolines, parasols and gentlemen in tall hats. The esplanade has been the scene of many historical and political encounters. Queen Victoria rode along it; Napoleon III and Eugénie strolled beside the river; Bismarck was pursued by diplomats; the attempt on the life of the King of Prussia in 1861 was made in the shade of its trees.

Originally these were oaks, planted more than 300 years ago, but exotic species – azaleas, magnolias, silver poplars, tulip trees – have been added since. On the left, beyond the swimming-pool, is the **Gönneranlage** (**BZ**), a pretty park with fountains and pergolas flanking a rose garden.

BADEN-BADEN

Gernsbacher Straße	**BCY** 8
Kreuzstraße	**BZ** 23
Lange Str	**BY** 25
Lichtentaler Str	**CZ** 28
Luisenstraße	**BY**

Sophienstraße	**CY**
Burgstraße	**BY** 3
Eichstraße	**CZ** 6
Hirschstraße	**BY** 18
Kaiser-Wilhelm-Straße	**BZ** 19
Ludwig-Wilhelm-Platz	**CZ** 30
Markgrafenstraße	**CZ** 32

Marktplatz	**CY** 33
Merkurstraße	**CZ** 35
Prinz-Weimar-Straße	**CY** 38
Sonnenplatz	**CY** 42
Steinstraße	**CY** 43

M Stadtmuseum « Im Baldreit »

Neues Schloß (New Castle) (CY) ☉ – Built by the Margraves of Baden at the time of the Renaissance, the castle has been partly transformed into the **Zähringer Museum**, where local history can be traced through exhibits in the state rooms and salons. From the terrace, there is a fine **view** of the town, with the Stiftskirche in the foreground.

Stiftskirche (CY) – 1754 funerary monument of Ludwig the Turk in the chancel.

Römische Badruinen (Roman Baths) ☉ – Beneath the **Römerplatz (CY)**, excavations have unearthed the ruins of a Roman bath house (note particularly the hypocaust under-floor heating system).

EXCURSIONS

★ **Yburg Ruins** – *6km - 3 1/2 miles to the southwest. Leave by Friedrichstraße (BZ).* From the tower *(110 steps)* there is a **vast panorama★★** over the Rhine plain, with the Baden vineyards in the foreground.

★ **Autobahnkirche (Motorway Church)** – *8km - 5 miles to the west. Leave by Langestraße.* Placed under the patronage of St Christopher, patron saint of travellers, this modernistic church is the work (1976-78) of the architect F Zwingmann and the painter-sculptor F Wachter. The design presents a harmonious blend of the plastic arts and architecture. Sculptures and stained glass panels are devoted to Biblical and symbolic themes.

Merkur – *2km - 1.2 miles to the east. Leave by Markgrafenstraße (CZ).* From the upper terminal of the funicular, take the lift to the top of the panoramic tower (Aussichtsturm); the immense **view★** takes in the site of Baden-Baden, the Rhine valley to the west, the Murg valley to the east and (on a clear day) the Vosges.

Altes Schloß Hohenbaden (Ruins); Ebersteinburg – *Round tour of 13km - 8 miles: about 1 1/2 hours. Leave Baden-Baden by the Schloßstraße (CY).* The parapet walk of the old castle of Hohenbaden commands a view over the town and valley. Afterwards, climb to the top of the Ebersteinburg keep, from which the foothills of the Black Forest can be seen.

★ **Baden Vineyards** – *30km - 19 miles: 1 1/2 hours. Leave by the Kaiser-Wilhelm-Straße and then the Fremersbergstraße. Once outside the town, follow the signposts "Badische Weinstraße".* The **Badische Weinstraße★★★** twists sinuously from village to village as it winds through the vineyards on the lower slopes of the Black Forest.

Leave the Weinstraße at Altschweir and return to Altwindeck.

★ **Burg Altwindeck** – This ancient castle, built on a circular plan, has been transformed into a restaurant with panoramic views. From its precincts there is a wide **view★** of the plain.

Sasbach – *1/4 hour on foot Rtn. Leave the car opposite the Hotel Linde and walk into the park surrounding the Turenne monument.* An obelisk and plinth with inscriptions in German, French and Latin mark the spot where, in 1675, a fatal cannon-ball ended the glorious career of Turenne – the French hero charged by Louis XIV with the defence of Alsace against the Imperial forces, during the conquest of Franche-Comté.

★★★ **Schwarzwald-Hochstraße (Black Forest Crest Road)** – *See SCHWARZWALD.*

BADENWEILER★

Baden-Württemberg – Population 3 400
Michelin map 419 W 7

In the southern foothills of the Black Forest, Badenweiler lies on a slope at the mouth of a valley with a view both of the Rhine Plain and the Vosges. The spa, noted for its curative treatments of rheumatism and disorders of the respiratory and circulatory systems, is surrounded by orchards and vineyards. Despite its limited population, Badenweiler boasts more than a score of good hotels.

★★ **Kurpark (Spa Park)** – The rolling parkland abounds in tropical plants and splendid trees. Beside the lake, cedars and cypresses mingle with enormous sequoias. The park also includes extensive remains of Roman baths and a ruined castle from which there is a fine **view★** of the resort, the Rhine Plain and the Vosges.

EXCURSIONS

★ **Blauen** – *8km - 5 miles to the southeast, then 1/4 hour on foot Rtn.* From the viewing tower, rising above the woods at the top of a hill, there is a remarkable **panorama★★** over the plain – the parallel ribbons of the Rhine and the Grand Canal of Alsace can easily be distinguished – and the tree-covered humps of the Vosges. The bare summit to the northeast is the Belchen. The Swiss Alps are also visible.

★ **Schloß Bürgeln** ☉ – *10km - 6.2 miles to the south.*

This gentleman's residence, set in beautifully kept, terraced gardens, was built in 1762 for the Abbots of St Blasien. The property overlooks the last undulations of the Black Forest, several reaches of the Rhine, and part of the city of Basle. Inside, there are beautiful examples of stucco-work in the Rococo style.

★ **Burg Rötteln** – *27km - 17 miles to the south*

The Oberburg, defensive nucleus of this fortress, is reached by a series of ramps and a drawbridge. The Green Tower (Grüner Turm), which overlooks the whole complex, has been restored and modified into a lookout tower.

From the tower, the view includes the Wiese valley (eventually lost among the outskirts of Basle), the wooded massif of the Blauen in the Basle Jura, the gentler slopes of the Black Forest and, far off on the horizon, the Swiss Alps.

BAMBERG ★★

Bayern – Population 70 000
Michelin map 419/420 Q 16

It was Emperor Henry II the Saint (1002-1024) who transformed this Imperial residence into a flourishing episcopal city.

From the 12C onwards, as was the case with all episcopal towns, the clergy, installed in the higher part, traded on their authority and came into conflict with the burghers who had settled in the valley, on the island, around the Grüner Markt and in the Sand quarter. The quarrel ended in the 16C with the ecclesiastics prevailing. Then gradually the schism healed and the 18C found all parts of town being equally endowed with prestigious buildings in the new Baroque style under the Schönborn bishops.

The sculptor **Tilman Riemenschneider** (1460-1531) and the **Dientzenhofer** family, architects of distinction, were the most brilliant of those responsible for the creation of this beautiful cathedral city whose art treasures have been spared by war.

Among Bamberg's many gastronomic specialities visitors should sample carp (Karpfen) prepared to a traditional local recipe, small Franconian sausages (Bratwürstchen), and "smoked beer" (Rauchbier).

BAMBERG

Grüner Markt	**CZ**	13
Hauptwachstraße	**CZ**	15
Lange Str	**CZ**	
Luitpoldstraße	**CY**	
Maximiliansplatz	**CY**	
Obere Königstraße	**CY**	34
Untere Königstraße	**CY**	55
Äußere Löwenstraße	**CY**	2

Am Kranen	**BZ**	3
Bischofsmühlbrücke	**BCZ**	5
Dominikanerstraße	**BZ**	8
Domstraße	**BZ**	9
Geyerswörthstraße	**CZ**	12
Herrenstraße	**BZ**	18
Judenstraße	**BZ**	20
Karolinenstraße	**BZ**	23
Luitpoldbrücke	**CY**	26
Mittlerer Kaulberg	**BZ**	30
Nonnenbrücke	**CZ**	32
Obere Karolinenstraße	**BZ**	33

Obere Sandstraße	**BZ**	36
Residenzstraße	**BZ**	40
Richard-Wagner-Str	**CZ**	44
St-Getreu-Str	**BZ**	45
Schillerplatz	**CZ**	47
Schönleinsplatz	**CZ**	48
Untere Brücke	**BZ**	52
Unterer Kaulberg	**BZ**	54

D E.T.A. Hoffmann-Haus
M Diözesanmuseum

CATHEDRAL PRECINCTS *time: 1 hour*

The Domplatz is surrounded by the cathedral itself, the Neue Residenz (18C) and the Alte Hofhaltung, which houses the Historical Museum.

★★ Dom (Cathedral) (BZ)

Transitional Gothic in style, the cathedral is characterized by its two apses. That to the east, the Georgenchor, the older, stands raised upon a terrace with a fine balustrade, its cornices worked in a chequered pattern; that to the west, the Peterschor, is entirely Gothic. Four towers quarter the two choirs. The design, inherited from the original Ottonian edifice, exemplifies the reticence of the Empire's powerful ecclesiastical institutions when faced with the innovations of French Gothic.

The finest of the cathedral entrances is the Fürstenportal (Princes' Doorway), on the Domplatz. It comprises ten recessed arches supported on fluted, ribbed or chevroned columns which alternate with statue columns representing prophets with apostles on their shoulders.

Enter the church through the Adamspforte, decorated with diamond and dogtooth carving (the statues are in the Diocesan museum). From east to west, the progression from Romanesque to Gothic is at once apparent. Two choirs, noticeably raised because of the crypts built beneath them, enclose a single nave whose walls – with neither triforium nor galleries – attest to the conservatism of the prevailing style. Underneath the eastern choir, the crypt is huge: three Romanesque naves with heavily ribbed vaulting supported on stout piers. The western choir is furnished with tall windows beneath diagonal rib vaulting.

Masterpieces of early German Gothic sculpture are on view in the cathedral.

1) Equestrian statue of **The Knight of Bamberg★★★** (Bamberger Reiter), a 13C representation of a non-identified king (possibly St Stephen, first King of Hungary and brother-in-law of Henry II), symbolizing an idealized view of the Middle Ages – much as Bayard, the "blameless and fearless knight" of France stands for the same chivalrous ideals.

2) Celebrated statuary group, The Visitation (note the features of St Elizabeth). The group, and the Knight on his horse, are the work of an artist strongly influenced by the French School, particularly that of Reims.

3) The **tomb★★★** of Henry II the Saint and Cunegunda (St. Heinrichs-Grab) stands in the centre of the nave, at the entrance to the eastern choir. It took Tilman Riemenschneider *(qv)* fourteen years to complete the tomb. The following scenes can be identified, circling the tomb: Cunegunda's ordeal by fire under suspicion of adultery; Cunegunda's dismissal of dishonest workmen; death of Henry II the Saint; the weighing of the Emperor's soul before St Lawrence; St Benedict miraculously operating on the Emperor for gallstones.

4) Reredos of The Nativity (1523) by Veit Stoß *(qv)*.

5) Funerary statue of a bishop (Friedrich von Hohenlohe).

6) Statue representing The Church.

7) Remarkable statue symbolizing The Synagogue, in the form of a blindfolded woman.

The Knight of Bamberg

★ **Diözesanmuseum** (Diocesan Museum) (**BZ M**) ⊙ – *Access through the cathedral.*
The collections displayed include lapidary remains, among them statues of Adam and Eve, the former giving his name to one of the cathedral doorways *(see above)*, and the cathedral treasury, rich in imperial and pontifical vestments.

Alte Hofhaltung (Old Residence) (**BZ**) – *The courtyard is open until dusk.*
This was formerly the episcopal and imperial palace (10C-11C). Its façade, with carved gables, oriel window and corner turret date, along with the doorway, from the Renaissance. The delightful **inner courtyard**★★ (Innenhof) is bordered by half-timbered Gothic buildings with steeply sloping roofs and picturesque, flower-decked wooden galleries. Opposite the entrance, take a covered alleyway which leads to a small square surrounded by houses once inhabited by the canons.

Follow Domstraße back to the Domplatz.

Neue Residenz (New Residence) (**BZ**) ⊙ – This palace, the largest building in Bamberg, comprises four main blocks: two, bordering the Obere Karolinenstraße, were constructed in the early 17C and are Renaissance in style; the two wings on the Domplatz are Baroque. They were started in 1695 by the architect Leonard Dientzenhofer, on the orders of Lothar Franz von Schönborn, Prince-Elector of Mainz and Bishop of Bamberg. (The palace boasts its own mystery. One morning in 1815, a corpse was found beneath the windows. It was the body of Marshal Berthier, retired to Bavaria after the return of Napoleon from the Isle of Elba. Accident, murder or suicide? The question has never been answered.)
On the first floor, works of the German masters are on **view**★ (Master of the Life of the Virgin, Hans Baldung Grien, etc). The Imperial Apartments on the second floor are among the finest in the Residenz, with beautiful parquet floors, Baroque furniture and authentic Gobelins tapestries. The Emperors' Hall is outstanding for its portraits and its allegorical frescoes. From the palace rose garden, there is a **fine view**★ of the town and the former Benedictine abbey of St. Michael.
Follow the Karolinenstraße to the lay quarter of the old town, built on the banks of the Regnitz river (note the statues of the Virgin Mary on the house corners).

★ **Altes Rathaus** (Old Town Hall) (**BZ**) – Standing alone on an islet in the river, this unusual building was remodelled in the 18C. In addition to the town hall proper, with its façades painted in trompe-l'oeil, there is a monumental Rococo gateway and a small half-timbered house, known as the Häuslein, balanced on a pierhead of the bridge leading to the islet. From the Untere Brücke – the bridge at the lower end of the isle – there is a good view of the old fishermen's cottages along the river bank.

E.T.A. Hoffmann-Haus (Hoffmann's House) (**CZ D**) ⊙ – This tiny house in the Schillerplatz occupies a special place in the memory of the poet ETA Hoffmann (1776-1822), whose tales, set to music by the Franco-German composer Jacques Offenbach *(The Tales of Hoffmann)*, made him a celebrity worldwide. Hoffmann lived here from 1809 to 1813, in three small rooms. The poet dreamed up the first few of his fantastic tales and some of his poems in the "Poetenstübchen". A museum contains information on Hoffmann's activities as writer, musician and caricaturist.

The Bamberg Christmas Crib Circuit

It is not only during summer that Bamberg has something to offer tourists. An increasing number of people choose to visit the town in winter, during the Advent period (and up to 6 January) to take advantage of a particularly seasonal attraction on offer here – the **Bamberg Christmas Crib Circuit** (Bamberger Krippenweg), which takes in 30 or so churches, museums and squares featuring highly original, decoratives crib scenes.

The circuit begins in the cathedral with the altar to the Virgin Mary by Nürnberg master Veit Stoß, and continues to the Maternkapelle and the Obere Pfarre, in which the scenes portrayed include events from the Annunciation to the Wedding at Cana. The Bamberg cribs come in all shapes and sizes – from the enormous crib in Schönleinsplatz with life-size figures in traditional local costume, to the tiny peepshow crib in the church of St. Gandolf. There is an astonishing variety of cribs on display – encompassing the modern crib scene in St. Stephan's, the lovingly arranged figures (over 200 of them) in the crib scene at St. Martin's and the marvellous 18C crib in the Siechenkapelle – each with its own unique charm to commend it.

Bamberg crib scenes are largely set against backgrounds featuring some aspect of the local environment, such as half-timbered Franconian houses, the outline of the town of Bamberg itself, or a grotto in Franconian Switzerland, which lends them a distinctive "local flavour". The 400 year old tradition of crib-making is carefully nurtured and handed on to future generations in a special training college, the Bamberger Krippenbauschule.

NB Leaflets on the Bamberg Christmas Crib Circuit are available from the tourist office (Fremdenverkehrsamt).

EXCURSIONS

★ **Ebrach** – *35km - 22 miles to the west.*
The **Old Abbey** (Ehemaliges Kloster - currently used as a prison), founded in 1127 and not completed until the end of the 13C, was extensively remodelled in the Baroque fashion, first by J L Dientzenhofer and then by Balthazar Neumann *(qv)*.
The design of the **abbey church★**, with its flat-ended chancel and square ambulatory, is directly inspired by that of Cîteaux. A rose window 7.6m - 25ft in diameter illuminates the façade. Inside, there are fine Rococo railings, a Baroque organ in the choir, and a Renaissance altarpiece *(north transept)* illustrating the Vision of St. Bernard.

★ **Schloß Pommersfelden (or Schloß Weißenstein)** ⊘ – *21km - 12 miles to the south.*
Designed by Dientzenhofer and Hildebrandt and built for Bishop Lothar Franz von Schönborn between 1711 and 1718, this castle is one of the most outstanding examples in Germany of a Baroque palace.
A rapid tour permits the visitor to admire the galleried **state staircase★** *(illustration p 27).* The paintings on the ceiling represent the Olympian gods and the four quarters of the globe. On the ground floor, an artificial grotto opening onto the garden perpetuates a Renaissance tradition. The marble hall on the first floor, lined with stucco pilasters, is decorated with frescoes by Rottmayr.
A longer visit would include the Elector's apartments with their small painting gallery and a hall of mirrors.

Forchheim – *25km - 15.5 miles to the south.*

St. Martins-Pfarrkirche here stands amidst an imposing group of half-timbered houses. Inside are eight **paintings★** (15C), once part of an altarpiece. Seven of them illustrate on one side the legend of St Martin – commemorated with a procession each year on the 11 November – and on the other side scenes from the Passion. The **palace** (Pfalz), a crude Gothic edifice dating from the 14C, was built on the site of a former Carolingian castle.

BAUTZEN ★

Sachsen – Population 50 000
Michelin map 418 M 27

Bautzen owes much to a situation from which one can see as far as the horizon in three different directions – it is built on a rock outcrop skirted by the winding course of the Spree. There is an especially picturesque view of the town from the bridge (Friedensbrücke), combining the cathedral (Dom St. Peter), the castle (Ortenburg), a network of narrow streets and an ancient fountain which serves as an emblem for the municipality.

City of the Sorbians – There are many Sorbian families in Bautzen – descendants of a western Slav people settling between the Elbe and the Neisse (mainly in south Brandenburg and east Saxony) after the migrations of the 6C. The Sorbian language is still taught in local schools and numerous folk traditions – the decoration of eggs at Easter, the wearing of tall embroidered headdresses, the use of Sorbian national costume for festivals and holidays – perpetuate the identity of this ethnic minority.

SIGHTS

Hauptmarkt – The old market square is surrounded by fine burghers' houses and a three-storey town hall which had Baroque features added to it in 1732. There is a tourist information bureau on the Fleischmarkt, behind the town hall.

★ **Dom St. Peter** – This hall-church with three naves (1213-1497) is the sole place of worship in the region to be used both by Roman Catholics and by Protestants (Catholic Masses in the chancel; Protestant services in the main nave).
The floor plan is distinguished by an "elbow" bending the central axis. In the middle of the 15C the southern part of the structure was enlarged, and the Late Gothic windows date from this period. In 1664, the 85m - 279ft tower was crowned with a Baroque cupola.
Inside the cathedral, note the large wood Crucifix (1714) by Balthazar Permoser, and the Princes' Loggia (1674) in the Protestant section. The Baroque (1724) high altar in the chancel (St Peter Receiving the Keys) is the work of G A Pellegrini.
Follow the road that runs past the cathedral as far as the monastery.

Those parts of the **monastery** that remain standing date from 1683. The southern façade with its imposing portal (1753-55) is particularly fine. The armorial bearings of the monastery are displayed between the rounded pediments.
Now follow the Schloßstraße.

Ortenburg – The construction of this fortress, built by the Margraves of Meissen to defend the frontier of the province of Upper Lusatia, was started in 1144. Originally known as Burg Budusin, it was remodelled between 1483 and 1486, then extensively damaged during the Thirty Years War. The tower of the north wing (1486) of that building is still standing. It is embellished with a bas-relief representing Matthias Curvinus, King of Hungary (Lusatia was a Hungarian province from 1469 to 1490). The later part of the castle, dating from the end of the Gothic period and subsequently transformed in the Baroque style, was garnished in 1698 with three Renaissance gables – already anachronistic for that period.

Serbski Muzej (Sorbian Museum) ⊘ – *In a building adjoining Ortenburg castle.* Numerous exhibits, including the distinctive traditional costume with its large elaborate headdress, illustrate the history, culture and way of life of the Sorbians.

A walk around the town's ramparts gives the visitor an idea of what it must have been like in the Middle Ages. Note particularly the **old fountain** (Alte Wasserkunst) and, in the cemetery beside the northern sector of the city wall, the ruins of the **Nikolaikirche**.

BAYERISCHER WALD ★

BAVARIAN FOREST – Bayern
Michelin map 420 S 20-T 23

On the borders of Bavaria and Bohemia (Czech Republic), the crystalline massif of the Bavarian Forest, dark beneath its carpet of fir and spruce, reaches a height of 1 456m - 4 777ft at the Großer Arber. A number of villages in the region have been developed as holiday centres which offer a variety of different excursions.

ROUND TOUR STARTING FROM BODENMAIS

66km - 41 miles – allow 4 hours

★ **Bodenmais** – The town lies in a pastureland depression at the foot of the Arber. A subsoil rich in sulphur and magnetic rock has been exploited since the 15C. From Kötzting onwards, the road mounts the pastoral Weißer Regen valley within sight of the peaks of the Osser.

Motorists continue climbing as far as the Lamer Winkel, a hollow of woods and upland meadows at the head of the valley. A panoramic drive across the mountainside, enlivened by a closer view of the Großer Arber, terminates this part of the journey (highest point: Brennes-Sattel, alt 1 030m - 3 380ft).

★ **Hindenburg-Kanzel** – A **lookout point** ★ offers a fine view of the Lamer Winkel and the Arber.

★★ **Großer Arber** ⊘ – *From the lower chairlift terminal, 1 hour Rtn, of which 20min chairlift and 1/2 hour Rtn on foot.*

From the upper terminal, continue to climb on foot. At the top there are two rocky crags. That on the left (above a small chapel) overlooks the Schwarzer Regen depression, with an extended **view** ★★ of the frontier region of the southeast. The right-hand rock (surmounted by a cross) affords a splendid view of the Lamer Winkel and the wooded undulations of the forest to the north.

The **Großer Arbersee** ★, a dark, romantic lake surrounded by pines, is passed on the right as the road goes down, winding through the tree-covered foothills on the southern slopes of the Arber. On the way, there are several magnificent **viewpoints** ★ commanding the Zwiesel basin, the Falkenstein and the Großer Rachel.

Lam – A most attractive small resort, at the bottom of a wide, open valley.

BAYREUTH ★

Bayern – Population 72 000
Michelin map 420 Q 18

Bayreuth is the town of Wagner. Built between the wooded heights of the Fichtelgebirge and the curious, desolate landscape of Swiss Franconia, it existed peacefully for hundreds of years before a series of events starting in the 18C placed it once and for all on the world map. First of all, it was chosen as a residence for the Margraves of Brandenburg-Bayreuth, with all the prominence attached to the life of the Court; later it became one of Europe's architectural capitals of Baroque and Rococo; and today the town is the goal of Wagnerian pilgrims from the four corners of the globe.

HISTORICAL NOTES

Princess Wilhelmina – The Margravine Wilhelmina, daughter of the King-Sergeant *(qv)*, sister of Frederick the Great and lifelong friend of Voltaire, was one of the most cultivated women of the 18C. She could have been in line for the Prussian throne, but decided instead to marry the Margrave Friedrich of Brandenburg-Bayreuth. Finding him in fact rather a dull man, she allowed her talents to flower among the more cultivated members of her entourage.

Her life (1709-1758) marked the most brilliant period in Bayreuth's history. A gifted artist, writer, composer, architect and decorator, dilettante and patroness of the fine arts, the Princess was responsible for the blossoming of "Bayreuth Rococo" – a highly personal style whose garlands and flowers differed markedly from the more rustic French Rococo then in vogue.

Wagner and Liszt – It is often said that many of Wagner's masterworks would never have seen the light of day if it had not been for the influence of Liszt. The two innovators of musical expression, stimulated by mutual admiration and drawn closer by family ties (Wagner married Liszt's daughter Cosima in 1870), were united again even in death: the tomb of Liszt, who died during one of the first festivals in 1886, is in the Bayreuth cemetery (Stadtfriedhof via Erlanger Straße - **Y**), while the remains of Wagner, who died three years earlier in Venice, repose in the gardens of the Villa Wahnfried.

The Festival – Creator of a new musical form, Richard Wagner searched on his many wanderings for the ideal place to present his works. He chose Bayreuth in 1872. With the support of Ludwig II of Bavaria, he had the Festival Theatre (Festspielhaus) built to his own design. It was inaugurated in 1876 with a performance of *The Ring*.
The festival tradition established by the maestro was continued after his death, thanks to the tenacity of Cosima and, subsequently, his son Siegfried, his grandson Wieland (d 1966) and Wolfgang Wagner today. Each year the world's greatest exponents of the Wagnerian ethos re-transmit the immortal message to an audience of spellbound enthusiasts.

SIGHTS

★ **Markgräfliches Opernhaus** (Margraves' Opera House) **(Y)** ☉ – The Margravine Wilhelmina was responsible for the building of this theatre between 1745 and 1748. The austere façade, hemmed in between 18C burghers' houses, is designed with a projecting centre-section, divided into three parts on its upper floors by four columns that stand on a balcony.

The interior, constructed entirely of wood, attains with the stage and apron an astonishing depth of 72m - 236ft. There used to be no seats in the stalls, as that part of the auditorium was reserved for dancing. The three galleries are subdivided into boxes, the most luxurious – beneath a canopy bearing the crown of Prussia and the arms of the local Margraves – being the Royal Box. The decoration, by Giuseppe and Carlo Galli-Bibiena, brilliant artists from Bologna, is of an exuberant richness. Their reds, greens and browns harmonize perfectly with the abundance of gilded stucco-work which winds around the columns, frames medallions and festoons the candelabra hanging over each box. This Baroque Court theatre is one of the best preserved in Germany.

Schloßkirche (Castle Church) **(Y A)** – The single aisle, painted rose-pink and decorated with stucco-work by Pedrozzi (1756), is a visual delight. A closed oratory beneath the organ contains the tombs of the Margrave Friedrich, the Margravine Wilhelmina and their daughter.

Neues Schloß (New Castle) **(Z)** ☉ – Wishing to make Bayreuth into a second Potsdam, Wilhelmina created this palace between 1753 and 1754, unifying and remodelling a number of existing buildings.

The **interior decoration**, of a fascinating elegance, was executed by the stucco-master Pedrozzi, greatly influenced by the Princess, whose delight in the airy, flowered Rococo style is everywhere in evidence. Wilhelmina, whose private apartments were on the first floor of the north wing, concerned herself particularly with the decor of the Mirror Room, the Japanese Room and the old Music Room.

The solemnity of her husband's apartments in the south wing is alleviated by the decorative fantasy of the Palm Chamber, whose panels are carved to resemble exotic trees, and of another room designed to look like an arbour. On the ground floor of the north wing is a **museum of Bayreuth porcelain**.

★ **Haus Wahnfried-Richard-Wagner-Museum** (**Z M'**) ☉ – The Villa Wahnfried (Supreme Peace), which the composer lived in from 1874 onwards, and which was owned by his family until 1966 is still one of the main centres of Wagnerian pilgrimage. The only remaining original feature of the house is the façade. Collections on display in the museum evoke the maestro's life and work (furniture, manuscripts, pianos and death mask) as well as the history of the Bayreuth Festival (construction of the Festival Theatre, costumes and scenery). At the end of the garden, in front of a rotunda, Richard and Cosima lie beneath a simple plaque on the edge of the Hofgarten.

Festspielhaus (Festival Theatre) ☉ – *Leave by Karl-Marx-Straße* (**Y 18**).
The theatre is intended to concentrate all the attention on the dramatic action.
Even the music, rising from a camouflaged orchestra pit, is no more than a fluid complement to the story. The acoustics have been worked out to the point where even the fabric of the seats (padding is forbidden) and the density of the human audience is taken into account.

★ **Schloß Eremitage** (Hermitage Castle) ☉ – *4km - 2 1/2 miles to the east by ② on the town plan.*
The **Schloßpark★**, in which the unexpected and the fantastic manifest themselves in the manner of an English garden, is suffused with memories of Princess Wilhelmina. The **old castle** (Altes Schloß), surrounded by geometric flower beds, was built in 1715 and remodelled by the Margravine, who was given it as a gift by her husband, in 1736. There is a particularly interesting, if only for its somewhat original decoration, **Chinese Mirror Cabinet** (Chinesisches Spiegelkabinett) in which Wilhelmina wrote her memoirs. Note the curious lower grotto opening onto the inner courtyard, and the hermitage of the Margrave Friedrich. Nearby is the artificial ruin of a theatre constructed in 1743. The **new castle** (Neues Schloß), designed on a semicircular plan, was rebuilt after 1945. In the centre, the Temple of the Sun contains an image of Apollo in his golden chariot.

EXCURSIONS

★★ **1 Swiss Franconia** (Fränkische Schweiz) **and Sanspareil** – *Round tour of 125km - 78 miles – allow one day*

Southwest of Bayreuth, far from the main road and rail arteries, an undulating plateau gashed by deep valleys forms the northern extremity of the Franconian Jura. Heavy erosion of this porous limestone shelf has resulted in a landscape of dolomitic relief, pitted with many caves.

Tüchersfeld – The houses of this village are dispersed among an astonishing series of rocky pinnacles.

Pottenstein – The castle, a former residence of the Elector-Bishops of Bamberg, overlooks the town. There are many natural curiosities (gorges, caves, etc) in the neighbourhood.

Teufelshöhle ⊙ – The most famous karst cave of Swiss Franconia is adorned with impressive stalactites and stalagmites. The exit through a maze of towering Jura cliffs is most picturesque.

★ **Gößweinstein** – The Circuit of **Marienfelsen** *(about 3/4 hour Rtn on foot, leaving the castle to follow the signposts: Marienfels-Schmitt-Anlagen)* leads, through undergrowth strewn with picturesque rocks, to several fine **viewpoints**★★ above the deep valley of the Wiesent.
In the town, the **Pilgrimage Church** (Wallfahrtskirche), built between 1730 and 1739 by Balthazar Neumann, contains on the upper part of the high altar an early 16C Gothic group of the Trinity.

★ **Sanspareil and Burg Zwernitz** ⊙ – After the completion of the hermitage in Bayreuth, Margravine Wihelmina and Margrave Friedrich turned their attention to an old hunting estate, converting it into an impressive **rock garden**★ which they named Sanspareil (Without equal). At the edge of the grove stands an **Oriental building**, fitted out in the Bayreuth Rococo style making it an example of Frankish court art. Further architectonic features of this 17ha - 42 acre park include caves, grottoes and ruined theatres.
The earliest documentary evidence of **Burg Zwernitz** (of which there is a good view from the keep) dates from 1156. From 1338, the fortress was the property of the Hohenzollern, then in 1810 it fell to Bavaria. It contains furnishings, and a selection of cutting and stabbing weapons from the 16-18C.

The towns and sights described in this Guide
are shown in black on the maps.

★ **2** **The Franconian Mountains** (Frankenwald) – *Round tour of 104km - 65 miles – allow 5 hours*

★ **Döbraberg** – *3/4 hour Rtn on foot.* Climb to the lookout tower (795m - 2 608ft). The majestic **panorama★** extends as far as the mysterious depths of the Thuringian Mountains in the north, and the Fichtelgebirge in the south, which enclose the Hof Basin.

Kronach – **Festung Rosenberg**, one of the largest medieval fortresses in Germany, towers over the small town of Kronach and the wooded heights of the Frankenwald. Star-shaped bastions surround the nobly designed 16-18C fortress buildings.

Kulmbach – *Town plan in the current Michelin Red Guide Deutschland.* This industrial town, once the seat of the Hohenzollern Margraves of Franconia, is famous today for its strong beers (Echt Kulmbacher, Bayrisch Gfrorns).

The **Plassenburg★** ⊙, an impressive medieval fortress in an excellent state of preservation, surprises the visitor with the contrast between the crudeness of its original buildings and the delightful elegance of its **Renaissance courtyard★★** surrounded on three sides by tiered galleries. Various collections are on display in the refurnished apartments, the most attractive being that of **tin soldiers★** ⊙ (Deutsches Zinnfigurenmuseum), with more than 300 000 pieces grouped in dioramas. The battle scenes are the most successful.

★ **3** **The Fichtelgebirge** – *Round tour of 92km - 57 miles – allow about 5 hours*

The route follows the Steinach valley, penetrating deeply into the pine-covered granite massif of the Fichtelgebirge. Above Fleckl, a cable car mounts to the **Ochsenkopf** (1 024m - 3 360ft), one of the highest peaks in the massif, which is crowned by a television tower.

★★ **Luisenburg** – This labyrinth of enormous granite boulders, in situ or fallen, eroded into round shapes or piled on top of each other, can be walked through along a pine-shaded, hilly path *(blue arrows indicate the way up, red the way down).* Several lookout points along the way afford varying views of the Fichtelgebirge.

Return to Bayreuth on the B303, which passes through the small spa of Bad Berneck.

BERCHTESGADEN★★

Bayern – Population 8 200
Michelin map 420 X 22 - Local map under Deutsche ALPENSTRASSE

The basin of Berchtesgaden is enclosed on three sides by the mountain chains of the Watzmann, the Steinernes Meer and the Hagengebirge, the whole complex forming a salient that penetrates deeply into Austria. Apart from these natural barriers, a number of historical events explain the unusual frontier situation. The development of the area, and of the small town of Berchtesgaden itself, is linked with the importance of a priory of Augustinian monks, which became a pivot of the Bavarian political machine at a time when the grasping Archbishops of Salzburg were becoming too demanding. Secularized in 1803, the priory and its lands were definitively incorporated into the kingdom of Bavaria six years later. Berchtesgaden was chosen as a holiday retreat by Adolf Hitler, who built his notorious "Eagle's Nest" sanctuary on the Kehlstein.

Journey's end on the German Alpine Road *(Deutsche Alpenstraße – qv)* and departure point for many other tourist excursions, Berchtesgaden is intensely busy throughout the summer. The town is dominated by the bulk of the Watzmann (2 712m - 8 900ft).

SIGHTS

★ **Schloßplatz** – This square – it is in fact triangular in shape – is the heart of the old village. On the western side are the granary and a tax collector's office, remodelled and furnished with an arcaded gallery in the 16C. The church front and the façade of the old priory, now known as the castle, complete the picture.

Stiftskirche St. Peter und Johannes – The church, whose foundations are Romanesque, is interesting because of the comparison with St Zeno's at Bad Reichenhall *(qv)*, for it too was originally built for Augustinian monks. A Lombard influence manifests itself in the façade, where an alternation of stone in different colours makes a decorative pattern. The towers were rebuilt in the last century after a fire. The interior of the building is distinguished by early 16C network vaulting in the nave, and by a chancel some 200 years older, much higher and of a purer Gothic style.

Schloß (Castle) ⊙ – At the time of the commendatory prelates, the monks' priory did indeed become a sumptuous palace. From 1923 onwards, it was the home of the Crown Prince Rupert, former commander-in-chief of the Bavarian forces during the First World War and head of the House of Wittelsbach until his death in 1955. The Prince embellished the palace with furniture and art treasures, opening to the public his collections of weapons, French tapestries and Nymphenburg porcelain. German wood sculptures of the 15C and 16C, and examples of oriental art are also on view.

Cloister – Conserving its Romanesque galleries on three sides, the 13C cloister has a variety of columns – circular, polygonal or twisted, garnished with latticework, plant designs and capitals with foliated scrolls.

★ **Dormitory** (Dormitorium) – A fine Gothic hall with two aisles. Note among other examples of religious art, twelve magnificent busts from the stalls of Weingarten basilica (1487).

Museum – Worth special attention here are the two Renaissance rooms on the first floor (Italian furniture of the 15C and 16C), and the row of eight interconnected Seigneurs' rooms (Herrenzimmer) which offer an attractive glimpse into the 19C and its Biedermeier style *(qv)*.

Salzbergwerk (Salt Mines) ⊘ – Exploitation of the Berchtesgaden salt mines, started in 1517, brought prosperity to a region formerly very poor. The salt rock is washed by fresh water and the resulting brine (Sole), containing 27% of salt, is piped to Bad Reichenhall to be refined.

The tour, in miner's overalls, includes a trip through the galleries in a small train, a vertiginous 34m-112ft scramble down (luckily there are steps for those who prefer) to the salt caves, the crossing by raft of an illuminated underground lake, and a documentary film show on salt extraction.

A room arranged as a salt museum exhibits the machinery, based on the hydraulic pump, invented by the engineer Georg von Reichenbach for raising the brine to the pipeline.

EXCURSIONS

★★ **Obersalzberg and the Kehlstein** ⊘ – *4km - 2 1/2 miles, there is a shuttle service by bus between Obersalzberg and the Kehlstein.*

After the abortive putsch of 1923 and the end of his prison sentence, Hitler, linked by friendships and family ties to the region, settled in Obersalzberg. When the Nazis seized power in 1934, the new Chancellor started an increasingly ambitious plan to enlarge and enhance the chalet (Berghof) which he had acquired. Subsequently, the sanctuary of "the lonely man of Berchtesgaden" became the stage for a number of expertly manipulated diplomatic receptions, notably that for the Austrian Chancellor, Dr. Schuschnigg, on 12 February, 1938, and that for British Prime Minister Neville Chamberlain on 15 September the same year.

The greater part of the Berghof buildings were destroyed in an American air raid on 25 April, 1945, prior to their capture on 4 May by a detachment of the French 2nd Armoured Division operating with the 101st U S Airborne Division.

Obersalzberg – With the exception of the Platterhof – a "People's Hotel" where the faithful could be lodged, at Hitler's behest, for the nominal sum of a single mark – the ruins of all the other buildings comprising the Nazi sanctuary have been razed. Only a few basement walls mark the site of the Führer's Berghof.

★★ **The Kehlstein** – The bus climbs an impressive **road** ★★★ blasted from the bedrock on the craggy spur of the Kehlstein. At the end of the road *(reserve seats for the return journey)*, a lift ascends the final 100m - 328ft. On the summit there is now a tea-room (Teehaus) on the premises of the old Eagle's Eyrie (Adlernest) – which, despite its name, was never a security refuge; Hitler himself only went there half a dozen times.

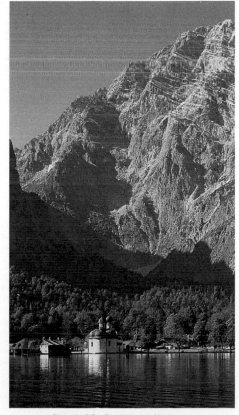

Chapel of St. Bartholomä, Königssee

U. Wazmann/ZEFA, Paris

The **panorama★★** *(climb a little higher up the crest)* extends over the neighbouring peaks and, on the far side of Salzburg, the rolling, rounded Pre-Alps of Salz-kammergut, hard against the massif of Dachstein, glittering with small glaciers.

★★ **Königssee** ◷ – *5km - 3 miles to the south, then about 2 hours in a boat.*
This long, narrow lake, with its dark waters and steep banks, is one of the most romantic sites in Bavaria. Dominated on the west by the giant escarpments of the Watzmann, and the rocky base of the Steinernes Meer to the south, the lake narrows at St. Bartholomä, making a **picturesque scene★**, where visitors can go ashore to admire the pretty **chapel of St. Bartholomä** with its triple apse and explore the interesting old houses nestling in a dense thicket of maples *(photograph previous page)*.
From the landing stage at Salet, a 15-minute walk brings the visitor to the Obersee, below the Teufelshörner at the circular end of the valley. From here the Röthbach falls, hurtling down from a height of 400m - 1 312ft, can be seen.

★★ **Roßfeld-Höhenringstraße** ◷ – *Round tour of 29km - 18 miles (to be followed in an anticlockwise direction) to the east of Berchtesgaden – about 1 1/2 hours.*
The Roßfeld road reaches the lip of the crest and runs above the Austrian valley of the Salzach.
It overlooks the Golling Basin, hollowed out at the foot of the Tennengebirge, and the steep ridge linking the Hoher Göll to the Kleiner Göll. The Dachstein, still recognizable by its glaciers, fills in the background. On the other side of the ridge there is a wonderful view of the countryside around Berchtesgaden and Salzburg.
From the Hennenkopf car park, it is only a few minutes' climb to the beacon and the Hennenkopf Cross at 1 551m - 5 089ft. The road plunges down from the crest after the Roßfeldhütte (Inn) and winds through the charming, wooded valleys of the Oberau region.

★ **Hintersee** – *12km - 7 1/2 miles to the west.*
The road climbs the narrow Ramsau valley to reach this lake framed by the steep-sided domes of the Reiteralpe and the Teeth of Hochkalter. The eastern shore, and the "enchanted forest" (Zauberwald) bordering it, together with the shady banks of the rapids feeding the lake, are greatly appreciated by ramblers.

BERGSTRASSE

Baden-Württemberg and Hessen
Michelin map 417 R 10

This old road running at the foot of the low, scrub-covered mountains of the Odenwald *(qv)* has given its name to a strip of sunny hillsides sloping towards the Rhine valley. Orchards flourish on this fertile tract, and its ideal position assures the marketing of fruit earlier than anywhere else in the region. The old villages and small towns of the Bergstraße are surrounded by typical Rhineland scenery.

FROM HEIDELBERG TO DARMSTADT

58km - 36 miles – about 3 hours

Weinheim – At the foot of the town, the picturesque half-timbered cottages of the tanners' quarter cluster around the Stadtmühlegasse. Take the Wachenbergstraße to the **Wachenburg** (castle completely restored at the beginning of the 20C). There is a good view of the Rhine plain from the terrace. The **gardens★** of the castle in Weinheim itself, above the perched houses of the upper town, are planted with rare shrubs and trees.

Heppenheim an der Bergstraße – The **Marktplatz★**, or Großer Markt, owes its charm to two wooden buildings with corner oriel windows: the Liebig pharmacy and the 16C town hall. The square is dominated by a vast Neo-Gothic church, nicknamed "the Bergstraße Cathedral".

Lorsch – Of the great abbey founded in 774, there now exist at the east end of the town only the church narthex and the **Torhalle★** ◷, a triumphal arch in Carolingian style. Above the columns with their composite capitals is an impressive wall adorned with blind, cowled bays and sandstone marquetry in red and white. Behind the church, there is a wide view of the Rhine plain in the direction of the Odenwald.

Bensheim-Auerbach – This "town of flowers and wine" is justly proud of its pretty **old town** (Altstadt). Beautiful half-timbered houses are to be found principally in the Marktplatz, and along the Haupstraße and the Wambolterhofstraße. In a sheltered valley is the **Fürstenlager★★**, once the summer residence of the Landgraves of Hessen. The park surrounding the building (Herrenhaus) is planted with tropical trees and studded with pavilions and symbolical monuments in the late 18C style. A little further north, **Auerbacher Schloß** ◷ commands a view over the whole region.

Berlin, for so long a symbol of the world's division into two opposing camps, owes its economic and cultural dynamism today to the fact that both the Federal Republic and what used to be called East Germany have for thirty years been determined to use the city as a shop window for their respective ways of life.

HISTORICAL NOTES

In the 13C Cölln and Berlin were small towns built respectively on a sandy island and on the east bank of the River Spree, each inhabited by fishermen and travelling merchants. The first castle to be constructed on Cölln was completed in 1451. Nineteen years later it became the permanent residence of the Hohenzollern family – and it was the Hohenzollern Electors of Brandenburg who were politically responsible for the evolution of Berlin as a capital city.

The Great Elector (1640-1688) – Friedrich-Wilhelm of Brandenburg found Berlin largely deserted at the end of the Thirty Years War. The great commander, who had in 1675 succeeded in beating the Swedish army at Fehrbellin, was also a very capable administrator. Emulating the Dutch (he had spent his youth in Holland), he constructed quays along the banks of the Spree and established many laws making Berlin a healthy and well-governed town.

The construction of a canal between the Spree and the Oder stimulated commerce, but Friedrich Wilhelm's most important contribution was to open Berlin to the French Huguenots after the Revocation of the Edict of Nantes in 1685. The arrival of a massive contingent – approximately one Huguenot for every five Berliners – transformed the city, strengthening its influence on its neighbours through the increased number of craftsmen, theologians, doctors, scholars and others now living there.

Berlin In the Age of Enlightenment (18C) – The first King of Prussia, Friedrich I, built the palace of Charlottenburg for his wife, Sophie-Charlotte. He entrusted the work to Andreas Schlüter, a sculptor of genius (c1660-1714) who had worked mainly at the Royal Palace and the Arsenal.

Friedrich was succeeded by **Friedrich-Wilhelm I** (1713-40), known to history as the **King-Sergeant** because of his punctilious administration and a policy of systematic recruitment which laid the foundations of Prussian military power. He was less interested in the embellishment of Berlin than in making it more powerful. He ordered a new town, Friedrichstadt, to be laid out beyond the old city bastions. Commanding access to this were three monumental squares: the Quarré (Pariser Platz), the Oktogon (Leipziger Platz near Potsdamer Platz - **GY**) and the Rondell (Belle Alliance, later Mehringplatz - **GY**). Draconian measures accelerated the development and peopling of the district, which is cut by such wide arteries as the Leipziger Straße, the most lively street of pre-war Berlin, the Friedrichstraße and the Wilhelmstraße (now the Toleranzstraße), the Whitehall of the Reich.

Frederick II the Great (1740-86) continued this civic effort, adding monuments along the famous Unter den Linden and the Forum Fredericianum (Bebelplatz). To fulfil his ambitions, he enlisted the aid of Knobelsdorff (1699-1753), an architect as much inspired by the Rococo tradition (Sanssouci) as by the Antique (Opera).

The evolution towards Neo-Classicism continued until 1835. The monuments of Berlin were finally completed by the Brandenburg Gate (1789) and the Neue Wache (1818), among others.

Towards Bismarck's Berlin – Berlin found its soul for the first time when the high patriotism inaugurated by the professors of the University, founded in 1810 by Wilhelm von Humboldt, was allied to the King of Prussia's call to arms in 1813 when he joined the Allies against Napoleon.

The city benefited from the growing prestige of the Prussian Reich and, as a favoured subject, developed its industrial life under the forceful direction of such great advisers as August Borsig, "the locomotive king", Werner von Siemens (1816-92), the pioneer electrical engineer and Emil Rathenau, the founder of the giant AEG. Although official projects like the Reichstag were pretentious, the number of open spaces increased as the residential suburbs moved westwards towards Grunewald forest. By 1871, Berlin had become the capital of the Empire and numbered almost one million inhabitants.

Greater Berlin – In 1920 the city united, under a single administration, six urban suburbs, seven towns, 59 villages and 27 demesnes to form a unit of four million inhabitants. Despite the upheavals from which Germany was still suffering, "The Twenties" was an exciting period in Berlin, intellectually and artistically in particular. Berlin newspapers set the tone for newspapers all over Germany.

Films made in Berlin won international acclaim thanks to such directors as Ernst Lübitsch, Fritz Lang, Carl Mayer, Georg-Wilhelm Pabst and the actors Emil Jannings and Marlene Dietrich (*The Blue Angel, Maidens in Uniform*, etc.).

The theatre, rejuvenated by Max Reinhardt (1873-1943), also flourished brilliantly. In 1928 Bertolt Brecht produced his famous Threepenny Opera *(Die Dreigroschenoper)*. The blossoming of this talent was interrupted by the advent of the Hitler regime, when, along with the persecution of the Jews, a wealth of the country's artistic and literary heritage was forbidden or destroyed in the name of the campaign against "degenerate art" – that is to say all schools of writing, painting and sculpture judged by the Nazis as "decadent".

M¹⁵ Brücke-Museum   **M¹⁶** Jagdschloß Grunewald

The Taking of Berlin – The final communiqué of the Yalta Conference in February 1945 announced that Berlin would be occupied after the war by the major powers.

From 21 April to 3 May, Berlin was a battlefield: the Red Army commanded by Generals Zhukov and Koniev against the remnants of the German army. The Soviet troops advanced through the defence lines, destroying everything above ground, including 120 of Berlin's 248 bridges. At last able to crawl out of their hiding places, the inhabitants learned of the final capture of the Reichstag and the suicide of Hitler (30 April 1945).

Berlin divided – After the German capitulation had been signed in Berlin on 8 May, the four victorious allies (Great Britain, the United States, France and the Soviet Union) took over the administration of Greater Berlin.

The political evolution of the (eastern) Soviet Sector, visualised by the occupants as the potential kernel of a future People's Democratic Republic, nevertheless hindered very rapidly the municipal administration as a whole.

Political pressures, vetoes, and various incidents built up an increasing tension. Municipal Councillors unaligned with the concept of State Socialism walked out of the City Hall and formed a rival Council at Schöneberg. The Soviet representatives on the Allied Control Commission no longer took their seats. From 1948 onwards, the eastern sector found itself isolated.

The Berlin Blockade, provoked by Russian opposition to a currency reform introduced in the Western sectors, was beaten by the Berlin Airlift (26 June 1948 - 12 May 1949). The split was aggravated by the proclamation in 1949, in the east, of the German Democratic Republic, the popular uprising of 17 June 1953 and its suppression, the influx of refugees into West Berlin, and numerous other incidents.

On 13 August 1961 the eastern authorities ruled out all communication between the two parts of Berlin. A few days later the construction of the "Wall" began – following with implacable exactitude the theoretical borderline of the Soviet zone marked on the maps.

From then on, on either side of a concrete barrier 160km - 99.4 miles long and 4m - 13ft high, augmented by barbed wire, watchtowers and sentry posts, the two parts of the city evolved separately, each motivated by an ideological pattern opposed to the other. Attempts to pass from East to West through this hermetically sealed cordon ended more often than not in tragedy.

The "fall" of the Wall – A night of wild celebration, especially around the Brandenburg Gate, followed the official "opening" of the Berlin Wall during the evening of 9 November 1989: the eastern authorities, bowing to increased pressure from public protest movements, had finally agreed to re-establish the right of free passage between the two Germanys.

In June 1991, the Bundestag voted in favour that Berlin should become capital of the united Germany.

For a certain time, nevertheless, the two halves of the once-divided city will preserve certain particularities: "socialist" town-planning, for instance, with its broad avenues and grandiose residential units, is a constant reminder of the political climate and community which produced it. And the traces of the wall, in the mind as much as on the ground, will only fade slowly, as a scar that remains too long unhealed.

LIFE IN BERLIN

An outdoor city – Berlin, the biggest city in Germany, occupies an area eight times greater than Paris. Devastated in the last months of the war, the capital lost much of its historical heritage.

But thanks to the famous architects (Le Corbusier, Scharoun and others) involved in its reconstruction, a modernistic town, served by broad arteries linking different quarters separated by vast green belts, has emerged from the ruins of 1945.

The River Havel has been widened in its course through the woods to form lakes (Tegeler See, Stössensee, Großer Wannsee). More than one third of the city's surface is covered by forests, parks and waterways.

A lively cultural scene – Before the Second World War, the centre of the city's life was concentrated around the Potsdamer Platz and the Friedrichstraße. Today the liveliest part of Berlin is around the Kurfürstendamm, the Gedächtniskirche (memorial church) and the Alexanderplatz complex. Nightlife centred on the **Kreuzberg hill** (**GZ**) has more of a cosmopolitan, anti-establishment flavour.

Deservedly, the city enjoys a worldwide reputation for the quality and diversity of entertainment it offers, particularly during the annual festivals of music, theatre and cinema.

During the past 300 years, Berlin has welcomed a large number of immigrants (French Huguenots after the Revocation of the Edict of Nantes, refugees from Poland, and Bohemia), all of whom have contributed to the emergence of a "typical" Berliner, lively, tolerant, with a sardonic sense of humour directed against the world around him.

After Theodore Hosemann in the Biedermeier period, Heinrich Zille (1858-1923) caught this character exactly in a series of spicy sketches satirising the everyday life of Berlin's "little people".

Because of this intermixture of populations, Berlin restaurants offer – along with such Brandenburger specialities as pig's feet (Eisbein) with sauerkraut and pease-pudding – a great variety of dishes from the international cuisine. Berliners term a tankard of lager beer a "Berliner Molle", and a dark beer with a dash of raspberry syrup a "Berliner Weiße mit Schuß".

★★HISTORIC CENTRE *See plan below*

An ambitious programme for the reorganization of Berlin's museums will entail the regrouping and relocation of many of the collections.
The descriptions and sometimes even the names of the museums are accordingly subject to change.

The itinerary starts from the Reichstag and then follows the celebrated Unter den Linden, which until the war was the capital's busiest, most lively avenue.

Reichstag – This massive Neo-Renaissance style palace was inaugurated in 1894 and has housed the sessions of the new Diet of the Empire (an Assembly elected through universal suffrage) ever since.
Gutted by a fire in 1933 and heavily damaged in 1945 during the Battle of Berlin, the building has now been restored. On 4 October 1990, it housed the inaugural session of the Parliament of reunified Germany.

★★**Brandenburger Tor (Brandenburg Gate)** – *Photograph overleaf.* This triumphal arch, the very emblem of Berlin, was nevertheless for almost three decades the symbol of the city's division: the structure was integrated into the Wall, which followed a north-south axis here towards the Potsdamer Platz.
There is a vast perspective westward towards Straße des 17 Juni and the Victory Monument (Siegessäule), and eastward towards the Unter den Linden.
Six Doric columns, incorporated into the stonework of the arch, support an antique-style entablature. Inspired by the Propylaea of the Parthenon, the gate was built by Carl Gotthard Langhans in 1789 and surmounted by the famous Victory Quadriga of Gottfried Schadow (1793).
The original group, reconstructed post-war, was removed to Paris after one of Napoleon's campaigns and returned to Berlin in 1814.

★ **Unter den Linden** – The famous avenue "under the lime trees", conceived by the Great Elector Friedrich-Wilhelm in 1647, is bordered from the Friedrichstraße onwards by monuments of the 17C and 19C.

Lustgarten	102	Münzstraße	124	Rosa-Luxemburg-Str.	158
Memhardstraße	115	Rathausstraße	150	Weinmeisterstr.	199
Mühlendamm	122	Reinhardtstraße	153	Werderstraße	203

M¹	Alte Nationalgalerie		**M³**	Altes Museum		**R**	Rathaus
M²	Bode-Museum		**M¹²**	Märkisches Museum		**U¹**	Humboldt-Universität

Alte Bibliothek (Old Library)

(A) – Designed by GF Boumann the Younger in the Viennese Baroque style for the royal book collection, this library was inaugurated in 1780.

On the right, take the Charlottenstraße to rejoin the Gendarmenmarkt.

★ **Gendarmenmarkt** – This is undoubtedly the most beautiful square in Berlin, named after the King-Sergeant Friedrich Wilhelm I's "Gens d'Armes" regiment, which had stables here. In this square, the Schauspielhaus, an elegant theatre built by Schinkel in 1821, is bounded on the south side by the German cathedral (Deut-

Berlin's Brandenburg Gate

scher Dom), and on the north by the French cathedral (Französischer Dom), both early 18C churches decorated by Karl Gontard during the reign of Frederick the Great. Once it has been restored, the German cathedral will house the exhibition "Fragen an die deutsche Geschichte" (German History in Question), which was to be found in the Reichstag.

St. Hedwigs-Kathedrale – Situated behind the Opera House, this Catholic church (1747-1773) was modelled on the Pantheon in Rome by the architects JL Leguay and J Boumann the Elder.

★ **Staatsoper (State Opera House)** – Built by Knobelsdorff between 1740 and 1743 on the site of the "Forum Fredericianum", the Opera House burnt down a century later. Langhans' reconstruction follows the original plans.

Humboldt University (U¹) – The palace of Frederick II's brother, Prince Heinrich, built by J Boumann the Elder in 1753, was transformed into a university in 1810. On the left side of the entrance, a statue of one of its founders, Wilhelm von Humboldt, faces that of his brother, the geographer Alexander von Humboldt, on the other. An **equestrian statue** of Frederick the Great stands in the centre of the avenue.

★ **Neue Wache (New Guardhouse)** – This small, exquisitely proportioned memorial, designed by Schinkel in 1818, is in the form of a temple with Doric columns, wedged between two massive pillars. It was consecrated in 1966 as a Monument to the Victims of Fascism and Militarism.

Since 1993, it has been designated the leading memorial for Germany, a "place of remembrance for the victims of war and violence". The interior houses a larger than life sculpture by Käthe Kollwitz: *Mother with Dead Son.*

★★ **Zeughaus (Arsenal)** – Berlin's most important Baroque edifice, erected between 1695 and 1706. It houses the **German Historical Museum** ⊙.

Masks of dying warriors, sculpted by Andreas Schlüter, can be seen in the inner courtyard.

Friedrichswerdersche Kirche – *Werderstraße.*

This impressive brick church was built in 1824-1830 following the designs of Karl Friedrich Schinkel. it houses the **Schinkelmuseum**, with sculptures by this multi-talented artist, who left his mark on the city-scape in a way that none other has. There is also various literature on Schinkel's work.

Cross the Spree and carry on to the Museumsinsel (described below). On the left stands Berlin cathedral.

Berliner Dom – This imposing building in the Italian Renaissance style was constructed between 1894 and 1905. Its overriding effect of might and power can be felt inside as well as out; the cathedral can seat congregations of 1 500. Part of the **cathedral crypt** is open to the public. it contains over 90 sarcophagi with the remains of five centuries of the Prussian-Brandenburg Hohenzollern family.

At this point it is possible to prolong your walk to take a look at the modern districts around the Alexanderplatz.

Alexanderplatz – The name of this square derives from Tsar Alexander's visit to Berlin in 1805. An important public transport junction and immense commercial centre, the square – known as "Alex" by locals – acts as a focus of city life in the eastern sector of Berlin. The **Marienkirche** (end of the 14C: 15C Danse Macabre fresco in the tower; Baroque pulpit by Schlüter) looks flimsy indeed at the foot of the 365m - 1 198ft **Fernsehturm** (Television Tower). The revolving sphere at the top of the tower houses a restaurant and a panoramic viewing platform.

South of the square, the **Rathaus** (Town Hall) **(R)**, built from 1861 to 1869 entirely of bricks, raises the red openwork of its tower 74m - 243ft above the surrounding roofs.

★★ **Nikolaiviertel** – With its narrow cobbled streets and its old taverns, this quarter of restored period houses between the Rathaus and the Spree, and between the Rathausstraße and Mühlendamm, seems like a country town transported to the heart of the city. The quarter is dominated by the Neo-Gothic bell-towers of the **Nikolaikirche** **(B)**, the oldest church in Berlin.

The old Romanesque basilica, with its Gothic chancel (1379), was transformed into a brick-built Gothic hall-church after the great fire which ravaged the city in 1380. Inside, there is a **permanent exhibition** ⊙ from the Märkisches Museum *(see Additional Sights section below)* outlining the history of Berlin from the city's foundation to the end of the Thirty Years War (models of Berlin and Cölln in 1440, weapons, jewels, domestic articles, manuscripts, letters patent). Polychrome statues in carved wood, gravestones and bells from the church (15C and 16C) can also be seen.

The Museums of Berlin

The Altes Museum, the first museum to grace Berlin, was built in 1822 by Schinkel. It was followed during the rule of Friedrich Wilhelm IV by the Neues Museum and Nationalgalerie on the Museumsinsel. Wilhelm von Bode, director of the Berlin museums from 1916 onward, made a major contribution to the further organisation of the city's collections, using his energy and far-sightedness to bring them to the attention of connoisseurs world-wide. After the Second World War, with the most important museums being situated on the Museumsinsel now part of East Berlin, plans got under way to build a new set of museums in the West sector. Thus many of the city's museums were duplicated. After reunification, the authorities were faced with the enormous challenge of merging Berlin's two sets of museums. The first stage of this gigantic project, which is set to run far into the next century, was the unification of the museums' administrations into a single body: the **Staatliche Museen zu Berlin – Preußischer Kulturbesitz**, founded in 1992.

To clarify the current situation (at the time of going to press), there follows a brief outline of the individual museums regrouped under the Staatliche Museen zu Berlin:

---

in Charlottenburg

Gallery of Romanticism
(Nationalgalerie)
Schloß Charlottenburg,
Knobelsdorff-Flügel
Ⓤ Sophie-Charlotte-Platz
and Richard-Wagner-Platz,
⊕ X 26, 109, 110, 145

Museum of Pre- and Proto-History
Schloß Charlottenburg, Langhansbau
Ⓤ Sophie-Charlotte-Platz
and Richard-Wagner-Platz,
⊕ X 26, 109, 110, 145

Egyptian Museum and Papyrus Collection
Schloßstraße 70
Ⓤ Sophie-Charlotte-Platz
and Richard-Wagner-Platz,
⊕ X 26, 109, 110, 145

Collection of Antiquities
Schloßstraße 1
Ⓤ Sophie-Charlotte-Platz
and Richard-Wagner-Platz,
⊕ X 26, 109, 110, 145

Reproductions workshop
Sophie-Charlotten-Str. 17-18
⊕ X 26, 110, 145, 149

in Berlin city centre

Museumsinsel:
Pergamonmuseum with
■ Middle East Museum
■ Collection of Antiquities
■ Museum of Islamic Art
Entrance Kupfergraben
■ Art Library
Library in Pergamonmuseum
Bodemuseum with
■ Egyptian Museum
and Papyrus Collection
■ Museum of Late Antique
and Byzantine Art
■ Sculpture Collection
■ Paintings Gallery (Gemäldegalerie)
■ Numismatic Collection
■ Children's Gallery
Entrance Monbijoubrücke

Alte Nationalgalerie
Entrance Bodestraße

Altes Museum with rotating exhibitions
Entrance Lustgarten
Ⓤ and Ⓢ Friedrichstraße,
Ⓢ Hackescher Markt,
▦ 1, 2, 3, 5, 15, 53
⊕ 100, 147, 157, 257, 348

Friedrichswerdersche Kirche
Schinkelmuseum (Nationalgalerie)
Werderstraße
Ⓤ Hausvogteiplatz,
⊕ 100, 142, 147, 257, 348

in Dahlem

Entrance Arnimallee 23/27
■ Paintings Gallery (Gemäldegalerie)

Entrance Lansstraße 8
■ Sculpture Collection and
Museum of Late Antique
and Byzantine Art
■ Museum of Indian Art
■ Museum of Far Eastern Art
■ Museum of Islamic Art
■ Museum of Ethnography
Ⓤ Dahlem-Dorf
🚌 X 11, 101, 110, 180

German Folk Museum
Im Winkel 6/8
Ⓤ Dahlem-Dorf,
🚌 X 11, 101, 110, 180

in Tiergarten

Museum of Decorative Arts
Matthäikirchplatz

Neue Nationalgalerie
Potsdamer Straße 50

Prints and Drawings Collection
Matthäikirchplatz

Art Library
Matthäikirchplatz
Ⓤ Kurfürstenstraße,
Ⓤ and Ⓢ Potsdamer Platz
🚌 129, 142, 148, 248, 348

in Schloß Köpenick

Museum of Decorative Arts
Schloß Köpenick, Schloßinsel
Ⓢ Spindlersfeld und Köpenick,
🚌 168, 169,
🚋 26, 60, 62, 67, 68

Besides these great National Museums there is a wealth of other buildings which contribute to the outstanding variety of museum collections which Berlin has to offer.

Future outlook for the National Museums of Berlin

An art gallery is being built in the Kulturforum of the Tiergarten, which from 1998 will house the paintings currently being kept in Dahlem. The museum complex at Dahlem will then become a centre for non-European art and culture, with its museums of ethnography and Indian, Islamic and Far Eastern art.

The Gallery of Romanticism is to be moved from Schloß Charlottenburg to the Alte Nationalgalerie on the Museumsinsel, so that this gallery will become the centre for 19C art. The Neue Nationalgalerie in the Kulturforum will be the backdrop for modern art from Expressionism to the mid 20C. Furthermore, plans are afoot to exhibit contemporary art from the mid 20C onwards in the Hamburger Bahnhof, which is currently being converted for this purpose.

A competition has been launched for the redesign of the Museumsinsel. This project will include the reconstruction of the Neues Museum which was destroyed during the Second World War.

★★MUSEUMSINSEL

Created at the instigation of Friedrich-Wilhelm III at the beginning of the 19C, this huge museum complex was the home until the Second World War of the fabulously rich collections of the National Museums of Berlin.

★★★Pergamonmuseum ☉ – *Entrance Kupfergraben.*
The museum building, completed in 1930, is divided into three sections (we indicate, for each one, the main centres of interest; plan at the entrance).

– **Collection of Antiquities** (Antikensammlung): altar of Pergamon, a masterpiece of Hellenistic art, dedicated to Zeus (2C BC); richly ornate gateway to the Milet market (AD 2C); Greek and Roman sculptures; objets d'art and mosaics.

– **Middle East Museum** (Vorderasiatisches Museum): Processional Way and Gate of Ishtar from ancient Babylon, 580BC (Rooms 8 and 9); Plinth of Asachadon, 7C BC (Room 3); brick façade of the Temple of the Goddess Irmin at Uruk (Sumerian period); bas-reliefs of the Temple of Assurnasirpal II at Kalchu, 9C BC (Rooms 10 and 11).

– **Museum of Islamic Art** (Museum für Islamische Kunst): façade of Omayyade Castle, Mchatta (8C), east Jordan; painted and lacquered panelling from a house in Aleppo (early 17C); miniatures (15-17C).

The Babylonian Processional Way (detail)
in the Pergamonmuseum

R. Truchot/EXPLORER, Paris

* **Alte Nationalgalerie (National Gallery) (M¹)** ⊘ – *Entrance Bodestraße.*
This building (1867-1876), designed by Friedrich A Stüler *(qv)*, a pupil of Schinkel's, houses paintings and sculptures from the 19C. Large canvases by **Adolf von Menzel** depicting life at the Court of Frederick II *(Flute Concert)*, but also the world of industry *(Iron Rolling Mill)*. The Prussian Army discovered its chronicler in **Franz Krüger** (paintings of parades). **Max Liebermann** distinguishes himself as a portraitist and observer of the life of the poor *(The Flax Weavers)*. French painting from this period is represented by the fore-runners of the Impressionists, the Barbizon school (Rousseau, Corot) and Gustave Courbet. The highlight of the exhibition is the Impressionist paintings by Edouard Manet *(Winter Garden)*, Claude Monet *(St-Germain-l'Auxerrois)*, Auguste Renoir *(Summer)*, Camille Pissarro and Paul Cézanne. German "Idealist" painting, by a group of artists nicknamed the **Deutsch-Römer**, as they modelled themselves on the art of Classical Antiquity, can also be studied here, with impressive works by Hans von Marées *(The Rowers)*, Anselm von Feuerbach and Arnold Böcklin *(The Island of the Dead)*. In the field of statuary, **Johann Gottfried Schadow** and **Christian Daniel Rauch** are especially to be noted. Here also are sculptures by Hildebrand, Kolbe *(The Dancer)*, Degas, Rodin and Maillol.

** **Bodemuseum (M²)** ⊘ – *Entrance Monbijoubrücke.*
At the tip of Museumsinsel, the old Kaiser-Friedrich-Museum now houses five separate sections (see below for the most interesting exhibits in each).

  – **Egyptian Museum and Papyrus Collection** (Ägyptisches Museum und Papyrussammlung): in the course of reorganization.

  – **Museum of Late Antique and Byzantine Art** (Museum für Spätantike und Byzantinische Kunst): mosaic (6C) from San Michele Church, Ravenna; Coptic art.

  – **Sculpture Collection** (Skulpturensammlung): Medieval religious sculpture (Naumburg Crucifix, 13C); Italian Renaissance sculpture.

  – **Paintings Gallery** (Gemäldegalerie): 13-18C. Collections of works by Italian (Lippi), German (Cranach the Elder), Dutch Renaissance and Baroque artists.

  – **Numismatic Collection** (Münzkabinett): three galleries trace the history and evolution of the art of medals in Europe from the Renaissance to the present. *During the reorganisation of the Bodemuseum, this exhibition may be temporarily closed.*

* **Altes Museum (Old Museum) (M³)** ⊘ – *Entrance Lustgarten.*
Berlin's first public museum, built by Schinkel between 1824 and 1830. The **colonnade** of the main façade (pleasure garden), 87m - 285ft long, is a masterpiece of Neo-Classical art. Inside, note particularly the frescoes decorating the cupola (rotunda). The building, severely damaged during the war, was reconstructed between 1951 and 1966; the granite basin (7m - 23ft diameter) in front of the museum was originally intended for the inside of the rotunda. Nowadays, the Altes Museum houses large exhibitions on special themes from the National Museums of Berlin.

* TIERGARTEN DISTRICT

The oldest park in the city stretches almost 3km - 1 3/4 miles from Ernst Reuter Platz to the Brandenburg Gate. Originally a royal hunting reserve, it was transformed – thanks to the celebrated landscape architect Peter Joseph Lenné (1789-1866) – into a delightful park in the English style. The Hanse residential quarter (**FY**), a model of town-planning which lies to the north, was reconstructed in 1957 by 14 world-famous architects.

Siegessäule (Victory Column) (FY) ⊘ – Sixty-seven metres - 222ft high, this landmark monument, surmounted by a Victory, commemorates the campaigns of 1864, 1866 and 1870. From the top *(285 steps)*, there is an aerial **view★** of the Spree, the Hanse complex, the Tiergarten, the Brandenburg Gate, Unter den Linden, the Berlin Rathaus and the 12km - 7 1/2-mile perspective that extends to the shores of the Havel.

Schloß Bellevue (FY) – Built in the Neo-Classical style by Boumann in 1785, this was the summer palace of Frederick the Great's younger brother, Prince Augustus-Ferdinand. Today it is the official residence of the President of the Republic. The ground floor and first floor can be visited.
Behind the castle there is a 20ha - 50-acre park, the western sector laid out in the English fashion.

** **Zoologischer Garten (Zoological Gardens) (FY)** ⊘ – *Main entrance: Hardenbergplatz.* Situated in the heart of Berlin, this zoo, gathering together 14 000 creatures from more than 1 400 species, is one of the largest in the world.
The **Aquarium** ⊘ *(entry via the zoo or directly from Budapester Straße)* displays an important collection of approximately 650 species. On the first floor are the widely renowned crocodile hall and the terrarium.

Berliner Allee	**HX** 13	Friedrich-List-Ufer	**GY** 41	Königin-Elisabeth-Str	**EY** 85
Blissestraße	**FZ** 16	Fürstenbrunner Weg	**EY** 43	Kolonnenstraße	**FZ** 87
Brandenburgische		Hallesches Ufer	**GY** 48	Konstanzer Straße	**EZ** 90
Straße	**EZ** 18	Heinrich-Heine-Str.	**HY** 51	Kurfürstenstraße	**FY** 92
Cauerstraße	**KX** 24	Holtzendorffstraße	**EY** 62	Lichtenberger Straße	**HY** 95
Dominicusstraße	**FZ** 29	Jakob-Kaiser-Platz	**EX** 69	Lindenstraße	
Entlastungsstraße	**GY** 33	Katzbachstraße	**GZ** 79	(KREUZBERG)	**GY** 97
Franklinstraße	**FY** 38	Klingelhöferstraße	**FX** 83	Loewenhardtdamm	**GZ** 99

C	Gipsformerei	**F**	Kupferstichkabinett	**M⁵**	Neue Nationalgalerie
D	Staatsbibliothek	**L**	Gedenkstätte Deutscher	**M⁶**	Nebengebäude
E	Kaiser-Wilhelm-		Widerstand	**M⁷**	Postmuseum
	Gedächtniskirche	**M⁴**	Kunstgewerbemuseum		Berlin

★★**Kunstgewerbemuseum (Museum of Decorative Arts)** (GY M⁴) ⊘ – *Matthäikirchplatz.*
This new three-storey building by the architect Rolf Gutbrod offers a broad survey of decorative art from the Middle Ages to contemporary industrial design.

Gallery I *(ground floor)* is devoted to the Middle Ages. Just inside the entrance, the Enger-Herford (Westphalia) **Treasure of Dionyslus★** is displayed. This includes a remarquable reliquary-purse encrusted with precious stones (second half of the 8C).

In the centre of the gallery, the **Guelph Treasure**★★ is displayed. The reliquary here is in the form of a Byzantine church with a dome (Cologne *c* 75).

It is thought to have held the head of St Gregory, brought back from Constantinople in 1173. The portable St Elbertus altar dates from the same period. The Guelph Cross (11C) almost certainly came from northern Italy.

Gallery II *(ground floor)*: Italian majolica from the 14C to the 16C, Venetian glassware from the 16C to the 17C; Gallery III *(ground floor)*: Lüneburg's **municipal plate**★ (Late Gothic and Renaissance) and jewellery from Nuremburg; Gallery IV *(first floor)*: the splendid **Pommern Cabinet**★ and its contents (card games, draughts, measuring instruments, articles of toiletry from the 15C to the 17C); Gallery V *(first floor)*: porcelain from China and Germany (Meissen, Berlin), 17C and 18C, Chinese lacquer cabinets; Gallery VI *(first floor)*: Biedermeier and Jugendstil objets d'art, panelled glass from Schloß Wiesentheid in Franconia (1724); Gallery VII (first floor): porcelain, earthenware (glazed) and glass from the Jugendstil (Art Nouveau) and Art Deco periods. Galleries IX and X (basement) exhibit the largest existing permanent collection of international design in Germany (furniture, domestic appliances etc.).

A second exhibition of decorative arts is to be found in Schloß Köpenick.

★ **Kupferstichkabinett und Sammlung der Zeichnungen und Druckgraphik (Prints and Drawings Collection)** (**GY F**) ⊙ – *Matthäikirchplatz.*
About 80 000 drawings and 520 000 prints from the Middle Ages to the present make up this collection, which is one of the most significant of its kind in the world.

Representative of the Old Masters of the 14-18C are **Dürer**, **Brueghel the Elder**, **Rembrandt** and **Botticelli**; of the 19-20C, Goya, Daumier, Menzel, Kollwitz and Picasso. The collection includes medieval manuscripts and illuminations, incunabula and illustrated books from the 15-20C, as well as sketch books (Knobelsdorff). By far the largest part of the collection is held in reserve, but it is possible to consult works from this in the reading room.

Since 1994, the Matthäikirchplatz has been home to the **Kunstbibliothek** (**GY F**), a particularly richly-stocked art library. Part of its function as a public reference library includes hosting special exhibitions.

★ **Neue Nationalgalerie (New National Gallery)** (**GY M⁵**) ⊙ – *Potsdamer Straße 50.*
This steel and glass structure, designed in 1968 by **Mies van der Rohe** *(qv)*, houses paintings and sculptures from the 20C.

The collections include important work from the classic European Modern art movements and the American art of the 1960s and 1970s. The exhibition begins with the heralds of German **Expressionism** (Gauguin, Munch, Holder) and the impressive gallery of work by artists of the **Brücke** (Kirchner, Schmidt-Rottluff, Heckel, Otto Müller) provides the first of many highlights. There follow numerous works by Lovis Corinth, Oscar Kokoschka, Wilhelm Lehmbruck and Ernst Barlach. French Cubism is represented by Picasso and Juan Gris. Other artists with work on display include members of the **Bauhaus** (Schlemmer, Kandinsky), Georges Grosz *(The Crutches of Society)*, **Paul Klee** *(Boats Leaving)* and the Surrealist **Max Ernst**. Group Zero, the New Realists, and American painters provide the high points of contemporary art.

Among the sculptures gracing the interior of the gallery or the terrace, note *The Washerwoman* by Renoir, Calder's *Heads and Tails*, and the elegant statue of *Maja* by Gerhard Marcks.

★★★ **Philharmonie** (**GY**) ⊙ – *Matthäikirchstraße 1.*
The roof of this boldly asymmetrical building by Hans Scharoun (1963) is in the form of a giant wave. The Berlin Philharmonic Orchestra, directed from 1954 to 1989 by Herbert von Karajan, plays here – the musicians in the middle of the auditorium, surrounded by tiered rows of seats that can accommodate up to 2 200 people. Von Karajan's successor is Claudio Abbadio who, like him, is appointed for life.

The **Chamber Music Hall** (1988), built beside the Philharmonia by Scharoun and his pupil Edgar Wisniewski, can seat an audience of 1 150. Here, the roof is shaped like a tent.

The **Musical Instruments Museum**★ ⊙ is housed in an annexe *(Tiergartenstraße 1)*, also designed by Scharoun and Wisniewski. Keyboard instruments, strings and percussion dating back to the 16C can be seen in this museum.

The massive **National Library** (Staatsbibliothek), which faces the Neue Nationalgalerie and houses some 3.7 million volumes, is also the work of Scharoun.

Gedenkstätte Deutscher Widerstand (Monument to German Resistance) (**GY L**) ⊙ – *Stauffenbergstraße 13-14.*
The monument stands inside the former army headquarters. This is where Claus Schenk, Count of Stauffenberg, had his office, which served as the planning centre for the attempted overthrow of Hitler of 20 July 1944. An exhibition describes German resistance to the Nazis.

★KURFÜRSTENDAMM DISTRICT

★ **Kurfürstendamm** (**EFY**) – In the 16C, the Kurfürstendamm was no more than a simple path allowing the Prince Electors to reach the Grunewald hunting lodge *(qv)*. It was Bismarck who transformed it, between 1882 and 1886, into the prestigious thoroughfare known to Berliners today as the "Ku'damm". Along its 3.5km - 2-mile expanse, the boulevard unites the cafés, restaurants, theatres, cinemas, art galleries, luxury hotels, nightclubs and fashionable boutiques that make this area the centre of cosmopolitan high-life in the capital.

Kaiser-Wilhelm-Gedächtniskirche (**FY E**) – This Neo-Romanesque church was built between 1891 and 1895 as a memorial to the Emperor Wilhelm I. It was badly damaged during the Second World War, but the ruins were preserved – and have indeed become a symbol of Berlin – as a reminder of the horrors of conflict. The shattered tower has been incorporated in a modernistic complex (1959-61) of pierced concrete modules in polygonal form, lit by 20 000 blue glass windows designed by Gabriel Loire and made in Chartres.
The old entrance beneath the tower has been arranged as a **Memorial Hall**. An exhibition traces the history of the church, recalls the victims of the war, and pleads for reconciliation.
On the ceiling and walls, **mosaics★** (1906) to the glory of the Hohenzollerns and the Empire are in a good state of preservation.

Tauentzienstraße (**FY**) – This is the fashionable shopping street where the "KaDeWe", said to be the largest department store in Europe, is situated. The abbreviation stands for Kaufhaus des Westens: Big Store of the West. Behind the Gedächtniskirche at the beginning of the street is the **Europa-Center**, a shopping and business complex which also offers restaurants, cinemas and the famous cabaret "Die Stachelschweine" (The Porcupines).
The water-clock on the Blumenhof is by the Frenchman Bernard Gitton. From the roof of this building, 100m - 328ft above the street *(lift to the 20th floor then staircase for the last two storeys)* there is a fine **view★** over the centre of the city.
The fountain in the square between the Gedächtniskirche and the Europa-Center, with its bronze sculptures and exotic figures, symbolizes the terrestrial globe. Berliners call it simply "**Wasserklops**".

★★CHARLOTTENBURG (**EY**) ⏱ *time: one day*

Charlottenburg was the favourite retreat of Queen Sophie-Charlotte, wife of Frederick I. With the philosopher-mathematician Leibniz she founded, in 1700, a scientific society which later became the Royal Academy of Science and Fine Arts.
Building started in 1695. The original castle was small, but it was soon enlarged, and a dome was added in 1710. The modern, gilded figure of fortune on top of this cupola serves as a weather-vane.

K. Kerth/ZEFA, Paris

Charlottenburg

Charlottenburg was abandoned by the King-Sergeant, but Frederick II had a new east wing (Neuer Flügel) added by Knobelsdorff, whose peristyled forefront was the sole decorative motif allowed the addition. Later, Queen Louise, the wife of Friedrich-Wilhelm III, lived in the castle.

In the Court of Honour stands the **equestrian statue★★ of the Great Elector**, the masterpiece of Andreas Schlüter (1703).

Central Block – Built between 1695 and 1713 by the architects Arnold Nering and Eosander Göthe for Queen Sophie-Charlotte.

★ **Apartments of Frederick I and Sophie-Charlotte** (Historische Räume) (**1**) – *Guided tour: 1 hour.* The itinerary traverses several sombre galleries adorned with portraits of the Royal Family by **Antoine Pesne** (1683-1757), a French painter summoned to the Court by Frederick I, who remained its official portraitist for 46 years. Note particularly, in the apartments of Frederick I, his study, with the portrait of King Stanislas Leszczynski of Poland by Pesne. The room is decorated in red damask. See also the huge courtroom. In the apartments of Sophie-Charlotte, tapestries woven by Charles Vigne in Berlin and richly carved furniture (consoles, mirrors, fire screens with Chinese motifs) evoke the memory of the "Philosopher-Queen".

★★ **Porcelain Room** (Porzellankabinett) (**2**) – The visitor cannot fail to be impressed by the richness and beauty of the vases, figurines and plates on view here, most of them Chinese.

Chapel (**3**) – *Public access only during concerts.* Restored. Facing the altar, the enormous Royal baldaquin (canopy). Decorated pilasters frame medallions on the side walls.

1st floor – Take the elegant staircase by Eosander Göthe. The salons on this floor contain several tapestries by Philippe Mercier of Berlin, views of the city by the painters Fechhelm and Gaertner, and large decorative vases. In the southeast arcade of the Oval Salon, a plate-glass window reveals the Insignia of the Prussian Crown (sceptres, globes) together with the swords of the Elector Princes (15C and 16C). To the north, there is a view over the park.

Knobelsdorff Wing – The eastern or new wing (Neuer Flügel) was built between 1740 and 1748 as a counterpart to the Orangery.

Summer Apartments (**4**) – *Ground floor.* The two Chinese rooms and the Etruscan room on the garden front were used by Friedrich-Wilhelm II. On the street side, Friedrich-Wilhelm III's apartments contain works dating from the Napoleonic Wars (Jacques Louis David: *Napoleon Traversing the Great St Bernard Pass*; Ludwig Elsholz: scenes from the wars of liberation) in addition to Royal portraits and the death mask of Queen Louise.

★★ **Gallery of Romanticism** (Nationalgalerie) (**5**) ⊙ – *Ground floor.* Works by the great Romantic painters of the early 19C can be seen to the right of the entrance hall. The collection of works by **Caspar David Friedrich** *(qv)* is the most significant in the world (23 canvases). Works such as *The Abbey in the Oak Forest, Woman at her Window,* or *The Watzmann* mark important stages in the development of this chief representative of German Romanticism. Important landscapes by the painter-architect **Karl Friedrich Schinkel** *(qv)* and by **Carl Blechen** can also be seen. One room is reserved for the Nazarenes (scenes from the Bible).

In the Biedermeier section on the left of the entrance, pictures by **Carl Spitzweg,** Moritz von Schwind and Ferdinand Georg Waldmüller are on display.

Royal Apartments and Banqueting Halls – *First floor.* The result of a collaboration between Knobelsdorff and the sculptor and interior decorator Johann August Nahl, these still present today the impact of "Frederician Rococo" manifested in equally grandiose style at Sanssouci *(qv)*. The galleries exhibit masterpieces, essentially by **French painters of the 18C★★**, collected by Frederick II.

Principal Apartment of Frederick II (**6**) – Some idea of the private life of a monarch can be gleaned from these rooms. A medallion portrait of Frederick the Great himself hangs in the study. It was executed by Knobelsdorff.

In the **library**, display cupboards contain works from Potsdam; in a glass case there is a selection from the King's priceless collection of snuffboxes. One room is embellished with Italian landscapes, another with Beauvais tapestries (cartoon motifs by François Boucher). In **Queen Louise's Bedchamber** the pearwood sideboard for flowers and the bed itself were designed by Schinkel.

★ **White Room** (Weißer Saal) (**7**) – This huge salon in the central portion of the wing served as a banqueting hall and throne-room. The walls are clad with pink marble. The ceiling frescoes, painted by Hans Trier in 1973, express in abstract fashion the ethereal atmosphere of Pesne's original (destroyed) design: *The Marriage of Peleus* and *Thetis*.

★★ **Golden Gallery** (**8**) – In this superb example of Prussian Rococo, Knobelsdorff renounces the severe, purely architectural approach in favour of decoration.

The pink vaulting and spring green walls of the 42m - 138ft-long gallery recall the palette of Watteau, one of Frederick II's favourite painters. The Rococo ornamentation impresses above all in the gilded stucco surrounding the mirrors, along the walls and around the embrasures, above the doors and on the ceiling. Here, representations of cherubs, the elements and the four seasons are entwined with the decorative scrolls, garlands, foliage and cornucopia above.

BERLIN

CHARLOTTENBURG

CENTRAL BLOCK

FIRST FLOOR

ORANGERY

Temporary Exhibitions

WEST WING

★★ Great Elector

KNOBELSDORFF WING

Spandauer Damm

Apartments and salons   Museums

Second Apartment of Frederick II (9) – Frederick the Great appears to have had a preference for this series of rooms at the eastern extremity of the wing. It is here that the most remarkable examples of his collection of paintings are hung. **Watteau's** *Shop Sign* (painted for his friend, the art dealer Gersaint, in 1720) was acquired by the King in 1745 to decorate the **concert hall**, where it remains today.

Also in the concert hall are two celebrated works by Jean-Baptiste Chardin: *The Letter Sealer* and *The Supplier (Die Köchin)*. The adjoining room contains one of Watteau's versions of the *Embarcation for Cythera* series.

West Wing (Orangery) – This Orangery wing was built by Eosander Göthe between 1701 and 1707. The theatre at the far end is later; it was built by Langhans (1788-91).

Museum of Pre- and Proto-History (Museum für Vor- und Frühgeschichte) (**A**) – Excellent dioramas and exhibits from archaeological digs give an overview of the pre- and proto-history of Europe and Asia Minor.

★ **Schloßpark (EY)** – Landscaped in the English fashion under Friedrich-Wilhelm II, this green space is an oasis of tranquillity amidst the bustle of the city. To the west, at the end of a yew and cypress walk, is a small mausoleum in the form of a temple, built in 1810 by Heinrich Gentz. It contains the tombs of Friedrich-Wilhelm III, Queen Louise, the Emperor Wilhelm I and Queen Augusta.

The **Schinkel Pavilion** (*between the east end of the Knobelsdorff Wing and the castle bridge*) was built by Schinkel in 1824 as a personal residence for Friedrich-Wilhelm III. It is carried out in the Pompeian style very popular in Berlin at that time. Almost all the interior decoration was also designed by Schinkel. The pavilion is a splendid setting for the two biscuit porcelain statuettes of Queen Louise and her sister Frederika (1796) and Queen Louise of Prussia (1802), by **Johann Gottfried Schadow.**

North of the lake, in the direction of the Spree, is a **Belvedere** designed by Langhans. It houses an **historic exhibition★** of the Royal Berlin Porcelain Manufactory founded in 1751 (Rococo tableware). Start the tour on the 3rd floor – view of the castle.

Auxiliary Buildings (EY M⁶) – The two blocks facing the Court of Honour, built by Stüler between 1851 and 1859, once lodged the Royal bodyguards. The building which adjoins the south side of the left-hand pavilion (1893) was once an infantry barracks.

★ **Collection of Antiquities** (Antikensammlung) ⊙ – Ceramics, bronzes, weapons and the usual artefacts from Crete, Greece and the Etruscan regions.

The treasury (in the basement) contains a fabulous collection of antique **objects in gold and silver★★★**: thousand-year-old gems from the Mediterranean basin, superbly engraved Scythian jewellery (including a gold fish weighing more than 600gm - 1.3lbs), the fantastic Roman silverware unearthed near Hildesheim in 1868, extraordinary portraits painted on wood found with Egyptian mummies at the time when the country was a Roman colony, a multicoloured cameo depicting the triumph of Hadrian, insignia of Roman legionnaires, etc.

The Collection of Antiquities is housed in two locations; the other part of it is in the Pergamonmuseum (on the Museumsinsel).

★ **Egyptian Museum and Papyrus Collection** (Ägyptisches Museum und Papyrussammlung) ⊙ – The collections here retrace, in the main, the historical and artistic evolution of Egypt during the time of the Pharaohs. Quality takes precedence over quantity, with the result that only works of particular beauty and value are on show, in a well-appointed display. The highlights of the exhibition are the impressive ebony head of the Queen Teje (18th Dynasty), the unusually expressive head of a priest (*c*300 BC), and the world-famous **Bust of Queen Nefertiti★★** (painted plaster over limestone - 1350 BC), exerting the magical fascination on the onlooker that has won the bust its reputation as the best known work of Egyptian art.

The Egyptian Museum and Papyrus Collection are housed in two locations; the other part is in the Bodemuseum (on the Museumsinsel).

★ **Bröhan-Museum** ⊙ – This exhibition, based on a private collection, presents arts, crafts and industrial design from the Paris World Fair of 1889 until the 1930s (Jugendstil, Art Deco). Note particularly furniture from the French cabinet-makers in the 1920s

Bröhan-Museum

Bröhan-Museum

(J E Ruhlmann), the art of French glass-makers (Marinot and Gallé), and the porcelain (Berlin, Meissen, Copenhagen and Sèvres). Do not miss, either, the paintings of the Berlin Secession (Hans Baluscheck, Karl Hagemeister and W Jaeckel) or the paintings and sculpture of the Franco-Polish Cubist, Jean Lambert-Rucki.

Those interested in Jugendstil and Art Deco should be sure to visit this excellent exhibition, well laid out in spacious galleries.

Not far from the Charlottenburg, at 17-18 Sophie-Charlotten-Straße, is the **Reproductions Workshop (EY C)** (Gipsformerei) of the National Museums of Berlin, which contains 6 500 figures. These make it one of the largest in the world, alongside those of the British Museum and Louvre. An impressive selection of busts, masks and figures are on sale in the salesroom.

***DAHLEM MUSEUMS (BV)

Before the tour it is advisable to obtain a map of the museum at the entry.

** **Gemäldegalerie (Paintings Gallery)** – *Arnimallee entrance. The Department of Paintings occupies two floors in the right wing and one in the left wing of the old building.*
This important collection gives an overall view of European painting from its beginning in the 13C to the 18C.

Ground floor – All the schools, up to the end of the 16C, are represented.

The section devoted to **German painting** begins on the right with the 14C *Madonna of Glatz*, from the School of Bohemia *(large gallery)*. In the side galleries, German Renaissance paintings are exhibited. Note especially: the portraits of Jakob Muffel and Hieronymous Holzschuher, two masterpieces from **Albrecht Dürer's** final period; the admirable portrait of the merchant Georg Gisze by **Hans Holbein the Younger**; the luminous *Rest During the Flight into Egypt* by Albrecht Altdorfer, founder of the Danube School; and *Portrait of the Wife of Doctor Johann Reuss* by Lucas Cranach the Elder.

The section on Dutch and Flemish Primitives includes: Van Eyck's celebrated *Virgin in Church*; the delicate *Portrait of a Young Girl* by Petrus Christus; **A Sturdy Man** by the Master of Flemalle, and his pupil Rogier van der Weyden's **Woman in a Wimple**. Equally remarkable are the tumultuously animated *Adoration of the Shepherds* by Hugo van der Goes, and the phantasmagoric figures peopling **Brueghel the Elder's** *Proverbs*. *St John the Baptist (Geertgen tot Sint Jans)*, and *St John at Patmos* by **Hieronymus Bosch** testify to the religious fervour experienced by the Dutch Primitives. Jean Fouquet represents French art of the 15C with his splendid *Portrait of Estienne Chevalier*.

The French School of the 18C is represented in another room, with Watteau's graceful *Dance*, Antoine Pesne's *Frederick the Great as Crown Prince* and *The Designer*, by Chardin.

On the left, at the entrance, are some magnificent **Italian works** from the 13C to the 16C. The Florentines include **Giotto's** *Entombment of Mary* and *Virgin with Choir of Angels* by **Botticelli**.

The School of Padua (early Renaissance) is illustrated by Mantegna's moving *Virgin and Child Sleeping*. To be admired also are Raphael's *Colonna Madonna* and *Young Girl with a Basket of Fruit* by Titian.

1st floor – Flemish and Dutch painting of the 17C. In the Rubens Room *Portraits (separate) of a Genoese Couple* by Van Dyck and **Rubens'** own *Andromeda Chained to the Rock* are on display. Side galleries, on the right, exhibit landscape and genre paintings: *Man and Woman Beside a Pitcher of Wine* by Vermeer, Pieter de Hooch's *The Mother* and works by Van Goyen, Ruysdel and Jan Steen *(The Inn Garden)*. The *Portrait of Malle Babbe* by Frans Hals impresses by the force of character it reveals.

Two other rooms are devoted to **Rembrandt** and his studio, notably the master's *Portrait of Hendrickje Stoffel* and the splendid *Man with the Golden Helmet*. The strong impression of power emanating from this canvas derives from the contrast between the rich, warm gold of the helmet and the menacing expression of the face, half hidden in the obscurity.

On the staircase leading to the gallery: 17C and 18C French and Italian paintings; note first of all Georges de la Tour's *Peasant Couple Eating*. Here, too, are such masters of Baroque in the Italian style as Caravaggio and **Annibale Carracci**. The 18C School of Venice is represented by Tiepolo, Canaletto and Guardi (views of Venice).

Finally, the visitor can enjoy works by those two great masters of classical landscapes, the Frenchmen **Poussin** and **Claude Lorrain**.

A second collection is housed in the Bodemuseum on the Museumsinsel. Plans are afoot to bring the two collections together in the Kulturforum in the Berlin-Tiergarten in 1998.

★★ **Sculpture Collection (Skulpturensammlung)** – *Lansstraße entrance.*
Masterpieces of Byzantine and European sculpture from the 3C to the 19C.
Exceptional works such as the 4C *Pyxidus of Berlin* in ivory, and the glass mosaic Christ of Mercy (12C) garnish the section of primitive Christian and Byzantine art.

German medieval statuary is represented by work that is equally exceptional, in particular wooden sculptures from Swabia, Franconia and the Upper Rhine: the *Ravensburg Virgin with Mantle*, the *St John group, The Virgin of Dangolsheim*. Two superb works by **Tilman Riemenschneider**, *The Four Evangelists* and *Choir of Angels*, show the artist at the height of his powers. French Gothic is represented by a life-size Virgin as the Queen of Heaven (14C).

The Italian Renaissance section contains figures typical of the Quattrocento: the gracious *Pazzi Madonna* by **Donatello**, terracotta Virgin Marys by Luca and Andrea della Robbia, small bronzes from the studio of Giovanni Bologna. Baroque and Rococo sculpture is well represented, including statues by the German masters of the 18C: Martin Zürn's *St Sebastian* and *St Florian*; Feuchtmayer's *Assumption*.

Here too, a second part of this collection is on display in the Bodemuseum on the Museumsinsel.

★★ **Museum für Völkerkunde (Museum of Ethnography)** – *Lansstraße entrance.*
Important collections from all over the world.

Central America and South America – Stone sculptures and **steles** from the Mayan civilization (Cozumalhuapa, Guatemala); **sacred and secular Aztec statuary** (human sacrifice cup); anthropomorphic ceramics and pre-Inca cloths in multicoloured designs from Peru. The **Gold Room**★ displays magnificent jewels and exquisitely engraved cult objects dating from the 7C BC to the AD 11C.

Oceania Section (Südsee) – Among exhibits assembled since the end of the 18C – many of them due to the expeditions of Captain Cook – note the **painted masks** and **wooden sculptures** from New Guinea, the **Oceanian boats**, and the magnificent ochre and red feathered cloak of the King of Hawaii *(1st floor)*.

Africa, Southern Asia, the Far East – The most interesting objects in this collection include **terracottas** from Ife (Nigeria), **bronzes** from the ancient kingdom of Benin, and carved and painted wood from Bali.

★ **Museum für Indische Kunst (Museum of Indian Art)** – *Lansstraße entrance.*
Extensive archaeological collections from India, Nepal, Tibet and southeast Asia. The art of Central Asia is represented by the unusual **Turfan collection**★, named after an oasis in Chinese Turkestan (on the Silk Road).

★ **Museum für Islamische Kunst (Museum of Islamic Art)** – *Lansstraße entrance.*
This exhibition gives a good introduction to Islamic art: antique Oriental carpets (16-18C), glassware and glazed earthenware made using a variety of techniques (8-18C), exceptional bronzes (12-14C) and miniatures (16C).
A second collection of Islamic Art, including important architectural monuments, is on display in the Pergamonmuseum on the Museumsinsel.

★ **Museum für Ostasiatische Kunst (Museum of far-Eastern Art)** – *Lansstraße entrance.*
Archaeological exhibits, art and decorative arts from China, Japan and Korea. The display includes items made of bronze, stone, wood, ivory, lacquer and ceramic dating from the 3C BC to the present. highlights of the exhibition are Chinese and Japanese painting and calligraphy, and Oriental woodcuts.

★ **Museum für Deutsche Volkskunde (German Folk Museum)** – *Im Winkel 6-8.*
Everyday household objects dating from the 16C onwards, predominantly from Germanic countries.

Ground floor – This floor gives an insight into the various aspects of daily rural life and work. The historical evolution and regional variation in the shape and ornamentation of objects can be traced in the furniture, costume, jewellery, kitchen utensils and tools on display from all over Germany. Besides these, the exhibition includes toys, wall decoration and tableware arranged according to function and the material of which they are made.

1st floor – One or two tools illustrate technical processes used in the cultivation, harvesting, and processing of foodstuffs and natural fibres used in the textile industry, such as wool and linen (threshing, milling, backing, spinning, weaving, embroidering, dyeing, blue-printing).
This floor also houses temporary exhibitions on European folk issues of historical or topical interest.

2nd floor – Evidence of the religious devoutness and the annual traditions of everyday folk.

ADDITIONAL SIGHTS

Postmuseum Berlin (Berlin Museum of Post and Telecommunications) **(FY M⁷)** ⊘ – *An der Urania 15.*
Documents, models and uniforms trace the evolution of Berlin's postal service during the past three centuries. Vintage machinery, explanatory diagrams and graphs explain the introduction and function of telegraphy, the telephone, radio and television.

★ **Museum für Verkehr und Technik** (Transport and Technical Museum) **(GZ M⁸)** ⊘ – *Trebbinerstraße 9.*
The very setting of this museum merits a visit, as it was once the main Anhalt goods depot. The now disused buildings and station land have been converted into a transport and technical museum. Technical progress is presented as part of the cultural evolution of mankind in a series of vivid displays. Air and space travel, road traffic and maritime transport are all represented, along with the application of technology to the media, photography and energy production. The **Railway Section★★** – particularly well represented – includes a selection of locomotives, some of them dating back to the very earliest rail transport. In the **Spectrum** over 200 experiments demonstrate scientific phenomena to visitors.

★ **Käthe-Kollwitz-Museum (FY M⁹)** ⊘ – *Fasanenstraße 24.*
A broad survey of the works of the talented graphic artist and sculptress Käthe Kollwitz (1867-1945), in which – to quote Romain Rolland – "the trials and tribulations of simple folk are reflected". Her series of engravings *The Weavers' Revolt* (1893-1897) and *The Peasants' War* (1903-1908), the wood engravings titled *War* (1922-1923) and *The Proletariat* (1925), as well as the self-portraits and the late series of lithographs labelled *Death*, all mark milestones in the Kollwitz career.

Open-air section of the Transport and Technical museum

MVT, Berlin

Well-known posters from the 1920s such as *Nie wieder Krieg (No More War)* underline the artist's political and humanistic commitment. The sculptures are exhibited on the upper floor, among them the *Muttergruppe (Mother Group)* in bronze (1924-1937). Also on display is a large bronze seated statue of the artist herself, by Gustav Seitz (1957). One of the museum's concerns is also to shown the – much less well-known – brighter side of this artist.

★ **Martin-Gropius-Bau (GY M¹⁰)** ☉ – *Stresemannstraße 110.*
This building in the form of a cube (1881) was originally conceived by Martin Gropius and Heino Schmieden as a home for the Royal Museum of Decorative Arts. Its reconstruction, after heavy war damage, was begun in 1978. The Neo-Classical style shows the inflence of Schinkel. The interior, with its majestic columned hall, is a living proof of the expertise of Prussian designers during the Founders' Period or Gründerzeit *(qv)*. There are several museums in the building.

Berlin Gallery (Berlinische Galerie) – *First floor*. Paintings and sculptures by Berlin artists of the 1920s can be seen here. But the highlights of the collection as a whole, from the turn of the century to the start of the 1930s, consist of works by **The New Secession** (Arthur Segal), **The November Group** (Walter Kampmann), founded in 1919, and the **Dadaists** (Hanna Höh, *The Journalists*).
One room is devoted to the Russian Constructivist working in Berlin, Naum Gabo. Special attention is paid to paintings concerned with emigration (Felix Nussbaum, *Prisoners' Camp*). The accent is placed also on the art of the immediately post-war period, notably the work of Carl Hofer *(qv)*, and that of the circle of artists centred on the Rosen Gallery (Alexander Camaro, Hans Uhlmann). The years 1960-1980 are represented by the Critical Realists, Tachistes and Abstract Expressionists (Fred Thieler), by the Junge Wilde (Young Savages), by Wolf Vorstell (collages) and by George Rickey's Kinetic Sculpture.

Jewish Section, Berlin Museum (Jüdische Abteilung) – *Second floor*. Collections illustrating the history of Berlin Jews until their persecution by the National Socialists. By the end of the 1920s, 170 000 Jews lived in Berlin and there were 100 synagogues in the city. Documents stored in the museum retrace the activities of numerous Jewish organizations. The **Judaica Collection** exhibits tombstones from the old Jewish cemetery at Spandau, together with numerous religious cult items, mainly from Poland and Germany (18C and 19C): scrolls from the Torah, curtains, Sabbath lamps, Chanukka candelabra, Hawdala plates, etc.

"Topographie des Terrors" ("Topography of Terror") ☉ – Adjacent to the Gropius building lies an area known as the **Prinz-Albrecht-Gelände** (after the old Prinz-Albrecht-Straße). From 1939 on, this was the Reich security and secret police centre, grouping together the headquarters of the SS, the Gestapo and the SD (Sicherheitsdienst: Security Service). In the 1980s, on what had been considered just a stretch of wasteland, the foundations of the centre's prison building were unearthed. They have been left exactly as they are, silent witness to a **"Topography of Terror"**. Beside them, a documentation bureau explains the Nazis' power structure, the persecution of their opponents and the planned extermination of the Jews.
In the middle of this district is **Viktoria Park**, the highest "natural" piece of ground (66m - 216ft) in the city. The hillock is surmounted by Schinkel's monument to the "Wars of Liberation". There is a panoramic view of Berlin from the terrace.

Luftbrückendenkmal (Airlift Memorial) (GZ) – The three west-facing arcs of this structure symbolize the three air corridors still open to the Allies during the Berlin Blockade.

★ **Berlin-Museum (GY)** – The exterior portions of this one-time administration building have been restored in the original Baroque style. On the pediment, allegorical figures representing Justice and Misery surmount the Prussian coat of arms. The permanent exhibition is closed as the Berlin-Museum is currently being restructured.
It is planned to build an extension to the museum by the end of 1997, in which the Jewish section of the Berlin-Museum, currently in the Martin-Gropius-Bau, will be housed.
The Berlin-Museum and the Märkisches Museum will be merged to form the "Stadtmuseum", or city museum, without however losing their original premises, which will continue to be known by their present names. The Märkisches Museum will handle the history of Berlin from its origins to about 1820, while the Berlin-Museum will contain displays on the city's history since 1820.
At the time of going to press, the precise use to which these two buildings and their contents are to be put had not been decided.

Museum Haus am Checkpoint Charlie (Berlin Wall Museum) (GY M¹¹) ☉ – Documentation on the building of the Berlin Wall and attempts to cross it, and also on the movements for human and civil rights. Display of works of art on these themes.

Märkisches Museum (March Museum) ☉ – *See plan of city centre, p. 73* (**M¹²**).
Art and craftwork produced by the artists of Berlin from the 17C to the present, and a display on the history of Berlin theatre.
See also Berlin-Museum above.

Volkspark Friedrichshain (**HY**) – Rubble from the battle-scarred city has enabled two artificial hills to be constructed in this leisure park. Homely characters from German folklore surround the fountains playing in the "Fairy Basin" (Märchenbrunnen).

★ **Sowjetisches Ehrenmal (Soviet Memorial)** (**CU**) – This monument in Treptower Park was erected in memory of the Red Army soldiers who fell during the Battle of Berlin.

★ **Kunstgewerbemuseum (Museum of Decorative Arts)** (**DV M**[15]) ⊙ – *In Schloß Köpenick (Schloßinsel)*.

A visit to this museum takes the visitor into the old-world provincial charm of the Köpenick suburb, southeast of the city centre and far from the hectic bustle of international tourism.

The museum is situated in a Baroque mansion built by the Dutch architect Rutger von Langerfeld. The **furniture** is specially interesting (chests, cabinets, writing desks and tables, many of them inlaid with marquetry: 16C-19C). Note also the **panelled room**★ from Haldenstein castle (Switzerland, 16C) and the **writing desk**★ by David Roentger (Neuwied, 1779), on which the marquetry represents the Seven Liberal Arts of Frederick II.

The **Treasury**★ (*ground floor, on the left*) contains jewellery and 16C gold plate and Baroque silverware. In the Heraldry Room *(Wappensaal, second floor, on the right)* 18C porcelain – including Frederick II's breakfast service – is on display. In the room behind is the great **silver sideboard**★ from the Knights' Room in the old Castle of Berlin (made by J Ludwig and A Biller, the famous silversmiths of Augsburg, between 1695 and 1698). Beside this is a **cask** (Münzfaß, 1719) decorated with 688 talers (old German coins) and 46 medals.

Großer Müggelsee – *Leave by the Köpenicker Landstraße* (**DV**).
The largest of the Berlin lakes. From the terrace at the top of the tower: broad view of the surrounding lakes and woods.

★★**Botanischer Garten (Botanical Gardens)** (**BV**) ⊙ – *Königin-Luise-Straße 6-8.*
Vegetation from the temperate zone of the northern hemisphere, planted out geographically from mountains to plains. There are rare species (trees and shrubs) in the Arboretum, while 16 greenhouses contain tropical and subtropical plants.

Botanical Museum (Botanisches Museum) (**M**[14]) ⊙ – The museum shows the evolution of flora in all its diversity. In addition to the "useful" plants, there are specimens of decorative species (offerings) discovered in Ancient Egyptian tombs. At the entrance, there is a cutting from an 800-year-old Sequoia tree.

Brücke-Museum (**BV M**[15]) ⊙ – *Bussardsteig 9.*
This museum contains works by members of the Brücke, the most important school of German Expressionists.

The movement was founded in Dresden in 1905, by a group of students who wished to create an expressive art by the deformation of lines and the use of violent colours.

In 1911, the group moved to Berlin, where it disbanded two years later. The greater part of the oil paintings, water-colours, sculptures and drawings on display is the work of **Karl Schmidt-Rottluff** and Erich Heckel. Max Pechstein, Otto Mueller, Ernst Ludwig Kirchner and Emil Nolde are also represented.

★ **Grunewald** (**AUV**) – A hunting reserve of the Prince-Electors in the 16C, this forest of oak, pine and silver birch covers an area of 3 100ha - 745 acres. Wild boar, stags and deer still roam freely here.

The Grunewald is bounded on the east by a chain of small lakes, interspersed with residential areas. Beside one of these lakes, the Lake of Grunewald, is the elegant **Jagdschloß Grunewald**★ ("Haus zum gruenen Walde" – **BV M**[16]) ⊙, a hunting pavilion built in 1542 by Caspar Theyss for the Elector Prince Joachim II. The building overlooks a courtyard surrounded on three sides by outbuildings (**Jagdzeugmagazin**) and bordered by 100-year-old beech trees. All that remains of the Renaissance original is the two-storey front and a hexagonal staircase tower. Among the paintings on view, note the nine gripping scenes of The Passion from the studio of Lucas Cranach the Elder, as well as Flemish and Dutch work of the 17C (Jordaens, Jan Steen, *Portrait of Caesar* by Rubens).

The western boundary of the Grunewald abords the **Havel lake**★. Beside this runs the picturesque Havelchaussee road, which leads, a little further south, to the beaches of the **Wannsee**★★ (**AV**), a favourite place for Berlin bathers in the summer.

★ **Pfaueninsel (Peacock Island)** (**AV**) – *Access by boat, leaving from the landing stage at the end of Nikolskoer Weg (service on demand).*
Landscaped gardens studded with small, picturesque buildings offer a perfect example of late 18C taste on this isle on the Havel.

The **castle** ⊙ (1794-1797), left incomplete in accordance with the taste for false "ruins" at the beginning of the Romantic period, displays souvenirs of Queen Louise in a number of salons panelled and floored with exotic woods.

Funkturm (Radio Tower) (EY)
⊙ – This 150m - 492ft structure, known to Berliners as the "Beanpole", is indissolubly linked to the city and has become its mascot. At a height of 126m - 413ft, reached by a lift which travels at 4m/s - 13ft/s, there is a viewing platform offering a **panorama**★ of Berlin. At the foot of the tower is the **German Radio Museum** (Deutsches Rundfunk-Museum) ⊙, which traces the evolution of the medium since its inception.

★ **Olympia-Stadion (AU)** – From the top of the campanile (77m - 286ft) *(lift)* there is a view of the former 132ha - 316-acre Reich Sports Ground. The stadium, built for the 1936 Olympic Games, was used for propaganda reasons by the Hitler regime.

Pfaueninsel

Verwalt. d. Staatl. Schlösser u. Gärten Berlin

Bauhaus-Archiv (Museum für Gestaltung) (FY M¹⁷) ⊙ – *Klingelhöfersstraße 14.*
The building housing this museum was constructed in 1979 after the original designs of **Walter Groplus**, the founder of the Bauhaus *(qv)*.
The Bauhaus School is known predominantly for its work in the field of architecture (Walter Gropius, Mies van der Rohe), but it exerted a strong influence too on the plastic arts; through the everyday objects it designed (furniture, the first tubular steel chairs by Marcel Breuer, tapestries, ceramics), it was the precursor of contemporary design. Attempting to make art a component of day to day life through the uses of technology, the Bauhaus called into question the traditional function of art itself.
In this museum, apart from industrial products and craftwork, one can see sculptures and paintings (including montages) by Schlemmer, Moholy-Nagy, Feininger, Kandinsky and Klee, as well as models, experimental typography for posters and adverts, and drawings from the Bauhaus school.

Kirche Maria Regina Martyrum (EX) – Built in 1963 by Hans Schädel and Friedrich Ebert as a memorial to the victims of National Socialism, this church is entered via a Ceremonial Courtyard whose sombre walls of grey basalt evoke captivity and death. One of them is embellished by the Stations of the Cross, by O H Hajek. Passing below *The Woman of the Apocalypse*, a sculpture by F König, one reaches the crypt, which is shrouded in half-light: only the front wall emerges from the dark, with a warm golden tint. Beneath König's *Pietà* is engraved the epitaph: "To all the Martyrs refused a grave – to all the Martyrs whose graves are unknown." Go to the upper part of the church. A soft light indirectly illuminates one part or another of an immense coloured fresco by Georg Meistermann, representing the passage of night (death, evil) into day (the Redemption). To the right of the altar, there is a Gothic Madonna dating from 1320.

Gedenkstätte Plötzensee (Memorial) (FX) ⊙ – The memorial to victims of the Nazi regime occupies the old execution chamber in Plötzensee prison. Between 1933 and 1945 over 2 500 political prisoners were murdered here, dying under the guillotine or by hanging. Following the failed coup against Hitler on 20 July 1944, over one hundred victims were hanged here.

Schloß Tegel (Humboldt-Schloß) (BT) ⊙ – *Abelheidallee 19-20.*
A 16C manor house transformed by Schinkel for Wilhelm von Humboldt into a small Neo-Classical mansion (1821-1824). Bas-reliefs on the four corner towers represent the gods of the four winds. Inside: Antique sculptures and family souvenirs.

Spandauer Zitadelle (AU) ⊙ – The Spandau citadel was built in the second half of the 16C on the site of a medieval castle (12C) at the confluence of the Havel and the Spree. Right-angled bastions occupy the four corners of the square, brick-built keep – a break with tradition in comparison with the old, round bastions used until that time. Spandau is the sole example north of the Alps of this so-called "Italian" system of fortification. In the course of its turbulent history, the citadel has been assaulted successively by Swedish, Austrian, French, Russian and Prussian troops, but it is best known as a state prison.
A drawbridge leads to the gateway. Armorial bearings painted on the pediment represent the different provinces of Prussia.

Julius Tower (Juliusturm) – *Skirt the right-hand side of the building.* Sole remnant of the original castle, this 32m - 105ft keep has become the emblem of Spandau. It was here, in 1874, that the authorities stored the 120 million marks in gold demanded from France as war reparations after the defeat of 1870. The entrance is guarded by an impressive system of bolts. Inside the tower, 145 steps lead to a lookout point with a panoramic view. The external walls on the southern side of the citadel are studded with Jewish gravestones bearing 13C and 14C Hebraic inscriptions. They were salvaged from the Spandau Jewish cemetery sacked in 1510. A **Museum of Local History** has been installed inside the citadel *(entrance via the footbridge).*

* **Nikolaikirche (AU)** – This hall-church is one of the last Gothic buildings in brick to remain in Berlin. The piers support ribbed barrel vaulting over the naves and star vaults above the choir. The entrance to the north chapel in the polygonal choir is surmounted by a handsome **Crucifixion Group** (1540) in polychrome carved wood. The magnificent **Renaissance altar★** (painted limestone and stucco) was a gift from the military architect, Count Rochus de Lynar. The central panel represents The Last Supper. Above it is a striking version of The Last Judgement. On either side there are likenesses of the donor's family. Note the gilded Baroque pulpit, which is finely carved, and the baptismal font cast in bronze (1398).

EXCURSIONS

★★★**Potsdam** – *19km - 12 miles to the west. See POTSDAM.*

Oranienburg ⊙ – *31km - 19 miles to the north by* ⑨ *on the plan.*
The **Concentration Camp of Sachsenhausen** (Gedenkstätte und Museum Sachsenhausen) dates from 1936. More than half the 200 000 victims imprisoned there perished. A museum traces the resistance of European peoples to Hitlerism. A tour of the camp (*follow the plan distributed at the entrance*) gives some idea of the implacable organization of the Nazi concentration system, whose cynical approach is exemplified by the slogan still above the entrance gates: "Arbeit macht frei" (Work brings Freedom).
The camp inspectorate ("Inspektion der KZ"), a feature common to all the concentration camps within the German Reich, contains a display on the National Socialists' various crimes against humanity, such as medical experimentation on prisoners and their planned "final solution" for the extermination of the Jews.
After the camp had been liberated in August 1945, the Soviets set up "No 7" forced-labour camp here; a commemorative stone to the victims of this stands in the main courtyard.

★★**Kloster Chorin** ⊙ – *58km - 36 miles to the northeast by the Bundesstraße no 2* (**DT**). Constructed from 1273 onward by the Cistercian monks of Lehnin *(qv),* the ruins of this **abbey** convey a fairly precise picture of primitive Gothic building in brick. The church is designed on the basilica principle with three naves, each preceded by a pedimented façade.

BERNKASTEL-KUES★

Rheinland-Pfalz – Population 7 200
Michelin map 417 Q 5 - Local map under MOSELTAL

Bernkastel-Kues is in fact two towns, one on each side of the Moselle, at the confluence of the main river and a stream which has gouged a ravine through the Hunsrück schist. This is a famous wine-growing area, gay and animated during the first week in September, when the Wine Festival is held. Apart from the wine, which may be tasted in many specialized cellars, the local delicacy is smoked eel from the Moselle.

The Vineyards – Bernkastel-Kues boasts the largest single vineyard in Germany, spread over the slopes flanking a wide **bend in the Moselle** (Moselschleife) and continuing as far as Graach and Zeltingen. The grapes – 95% of the Riesling variety – produce a dry white wine of which the most sought-after is the fruity Bernkasteler Doktor.

SIGHTS

* **Markt** – Colour-washed houses, most of them half-timbered, surround this small, sloping square in the middle of which is the 17C **St Michael fountain** (Michaelsbrunnen).

St. Nikolaus-Hospital (Cusanusstift) ⊙ – *On the Kues side of the river.*
Founded in 1447 by **Cardinal Nicholas of Kues** (or Nikolaus Cusanus) (1401-1464), a humanist and theologian, the hospice was built to house people in need. The number of lodgers was restricted to a symbolic 33 – the age of Christ at his death – a tradition still respected today.
Admire the late Gothic cloister, the chapel with its fine 15C reredos, and the copy in bronze of the Cardinal's tombstone (the original is in Rome, at San Pietro in Vincoli). On the left, entering the chapel, note the fresco depicting The Last Judgement – and, on the right, **the tombstone of Clara Cryftz**, the prelate's sister.
The **library** houses almost 400 manuscripts and early printed works, in addition to astronomical instruments used by the founder.

EXCURSION

Burg Landshut – *3km - 1 3/4 miles to the southeast towards Longkamp and uphill to the right.*
The castle, built on a rocky promontory, was from the 11C the property of the Archbishops of Trier. It has been in ruins ever since the War of the Orléans Succession *(qv)*. From the ruin there is a fine **panoramic view★★** over the bend in the Moselle, above which even the steepest slopes are planted with vines.

BLACK FOREST★★★

See SCHWARZWALD

Going Skiing?
Germany's Winter Sports Resorts are listed in the Practical Information section at the back of the Guide.

BODENSEE★★

LAKE CONSTANCE – Baden-Württemberg and Bayern
Michelin map 419 W 10-X 13

With the immensity of its horizons, sometimes lost in the summer haze, and a climate mild enough to permit tropical vegetation in the more favoured sites, Lake Constance, or the Bodensee as it is known to German speakers, attracts a multitude of German holidaymakers, who regard it as their local "Riviera".
With an area of 53 000ha - 210sq miles, the lake is only marginally smaller than Lake Geneva, biggest of the Alpine waterways. A wide choice of boat services provides many possibilities for cruises and excursions; the most frequent of these services run from the ports of Constance, Überlingen, Meersburg, Friedrichshafen, Lindau and Bregenz *(see Michelin Green Guide Austria)*. The lakeside roads offer numerous vistas of the lake with the Alps, in clear weather, as an impressive background.
The islands of **Reichenau★**, *on the Untersee, and* **Mainau★★**, *on the Überlingersee, are described under KONSTANZ: Excursions.*

FROM ÜBERLINGEN TO LINDAU
56km - 35 miles – allow 4 hours

★ **Überlingen** – *See ÜBERLINGEN.*

★ **Birnau** – The present church *(illustration overleaf)* was built between 1746 and 1750 on a terrace overlooking the lake, the Cistercians of Salem *(qv)* having entrusted the work to Peter Thumb, Master of the Vorarlberg school.
The building's Rococo charm is most evident in the architectural design, the painted decoration of the interpenetrating oval spaces and curved surfaces over the single aisle, the flattened dome above the chancel, and the cupola surmounting the apse.
Halfway up the walls, an elegant gallery is supported on corbels, the bosses of which are embellished with Rococo cartouches. Pilgrims venerate the early 15C Virgin above the tabernacle on the high altar.

* **Meersburg** – Birthplace of the painter Stefan Lochner *(qv)*, Meersburg is an attractive town perched above the lake shore. The stylish upper town (Oberstadt) is centred on the **Marktplatz★**, from which the **Steigstraße★**, bordered by half-timbered old houses, offers delightful views of the lake.

Apartments in the Old Castle where the great poet Annette von Droste-Hülshoff (1797-1848) spent the last years of her life may be viewed. From the terrace of the New Castle there is a **panorama★** of Lake Constance and the Säntis massif.

Birnau – The Church

Nach Foto Lauterwasser

Friedrichshafen – The lakeside areas have been furnished with attractive, wide promenade-quays. The town's **municipal museum** (Städtisches Bodensee-Museum) includes a section devoted to the history of Count Zeppelin's dirigibles, which were built here.

Wasserburg – This much-visited village is squeezed onto a narrow tongue of land jutting out into the lake. Appreciate it on foot, walking to the tip of the promontory.

★★ **Lindau im Bodensee** – *See LINDAU IM BODENSEE.*

BONN★

Nordrhein-Westfalen – Population 296 000
Michelin map 417 N 5
Plan of the conurbation in the current Michelin Red Guide Deutschland

This city is placed at a point where the Rhine flows out across Germany's great northern plain. The site has been inhabited since it was a camp for Roman legionaries, but it was not until the 16C that the town subsequently built there had any importance. At that time it became the fortified capital of the see of Cologne. In the 18C, the fortifications were transformed into a Baroque residence.

In 1949, what had grown into a peaceful, medium-size, riverside town was transformed again: Bonn was chosen as the "provisional" capital of the new West German Federal Republic – which earned it the nickname of "Bundesdorf" ("Federal Village"), but set it firmly on the road to civic advancement. As the national seat of parliamentary and diplomatic activity, Bonn drew on a cloak of industriousness and international style, whilst never quite managing to shake off its essentially provincial air. The parliamentary buildings are located in a well-off residential area on the banks of the Rhine, to the southeast of town. The **Villa Hammerschmidt** (which housed the Bundespräsident) and the **Palais Schaumburg** (which housed the Bundeskanzler) are set in well-tended parkland. The neighbouring offices of the old Bundeskanzler were purpose-built in 1976. The two chambers of the ex-West German Federal parliament sat in the **Bundeshaus**, while the government administrators had their offices in the office block nearby.

Bonn, whose status as German capital could never be more than provisional, nevertheless fulfilled that role for forty years and became in the process a true seat of government. It is sure to continue in this role for some time yet, as the transferral of the seat of national government to Berlin cannot be made overnight. In any case, some government ministries will remain in Bonn.

The whole town, including the Rhine and the surrounding countryside, can be seen from the **Alter Zoll** (**CZ**). The **view★** of the river and the Siebengebirge range *(see below)* is particularly attractive in late afternoon and early evening. From the foot of the bastion, riverside promenades beckon those with time for a leisurely stroll *(this is the departure point also for boat trips)*.

The Youth of Beethoven – Precursor of the great stream of Romantic music, **Ludwig van Beethoven** (1770-1827) was born and grew up in the quarter around the **church of St. Remigius** (**CYZ**). At 13, Beethoven was already an accomplished musician, playing violin, viola and harpsichord in the orchestra attached to the brilliant Court of the Elector. When he was 22, a fervent admirer of Mozart and Haydn, he left Bonn for good, arriving in Vienna with only his virtuosity at the piano as an asset.

The **Beethovenhalle** (**CY**), a bold example of modern architecture, is the impressive setting for Bonn's triennial Beethoven Festival. The architect was Siegfried Wolske.

BONN

D Beethovenhaus   M Rheinisches Landesmuseum   R Rathaus   U Kurfürstliche Residenz

SIGHTS

Rheinisches Landesmuseum (BZ M) ⊙ – The history, culture and art of the Middle and Lower Rhinelands, from prehistory to the present day, is traced on three floors.

The **Prehistoric Section** (Urgeschichtliche Abteilung) *(1st floor)* shows, besides the skull of the celebrated Neanderthal Man *(see DÜSSELDORF: Excursions)*, interesting artefacts from the Stone and Bronze Ages and La Tène culture (weapons, metalwork, jewellery found in tumuli, etc.).

In the department of **Roman Antiquities★** (Römische Abteilung) *(also on the 1st floor)*, note the **Altars to the Matrones**, a cult popular with Roman soldiers stationed in the Rhinelands. The fine votive stone (AD 164), discovered beneath Bonn Cathedral in 1928, clearly shows the distinguishing characteristic of these benevolent deities: a huge round headdress. A masterpiece of Roman craft is the **Sun God Mosaic** (c250 AD), which shows the Sun God in his chariot, surrounded by the circle of the Zodiac. Large **memorial stones**, such as that for Marcus Caelius found at Xanten (early 1C AD) and that for Firmus of Andernach (middle of 1C AD), illustrate funerary cults. Among the treasures of this particularly rich collection, admire also the delightful **bronze statuettes** (Venus, Diana, Hercules, etc.) and the **glassware**, often decorated with chased or spun motifs. Explanatory panels, illuminated illustrations and dioramas bring to life such facets of the Roman civilization as military service, building, water supply, traffic control and day-to-day existence in that period.

Pride of place in the **Frankish Section** *(2nd floor)* is reserved for a reconstruction of a chieftain's tomb (c600 AD). Gold pieces on display are decorated with serpents and the heads of birds. The two adjacent rooms are devoted to **medieval archaeology**. Among the exhibits are two 12C oakwood pirogues (canoes).

The section from the **Middle Ages to the Present Day** *(2nd floor)* displays arts and crafts from the Romanesque era to the 19C. Worth special attention: Romanesque sculpture (chancel parclose from Gustorf, 1130-1140); sculptures carved from wood; and above all the **Gothic paintings** (Master of the Life of St Ursula, Master of St Severin, Bartholomäus Bruyn the Elder, Derick Baegert, etc.).

93

Dutch painting of the 16C and 17C is represented by Pieter Brueghel the Younger and Joos de Momper. Note also the selection of 19C **views of the Rhine**. The third floor galleries show art of the 20C. There is an interesting **numismatic collection** (Münzkabinett).

★ **Münster (Collegiate Church) (BCZ)** – This was originally a triple-aisle basilica, built on the site of a Roman necropolis. The present edifice – an excellent example of Late Rhineland Romanesque – was constructed after the fire of 1239.

Two rounded apses close off a transept surmounted by an octagonal tower. Tall, openwork flying buttresses support the nave. The eastern apse, flanked by two square towers, is circled by a miniature gallery topped by an upright gable.

Inside, the height of the nave at once proclaims a Gothic influence. The furnishing is essentially Baroque. Note the **lateral altars** at the entrance to the choir (1735), and the bronze statue of St Helen at the end of the nave. A fine Romanesque **cloister★**, the arcades supported by small columns, adjoins the southern part of the church.

Beethovenhaus (Beethoven's Birthplace) (CY D) ☉ – Beethoven passed the first years of his childhood in this house in the old town. A genealogical tree of the family is displayed in the entrance. The bronze statue of the famous composer, at the foot of the small garden, is the work of N Aranson, a pupil of Rodin's.

The room in which Beethoven was born contains a simple marble bust. The larger room beside it houses souvenirs of the great man: a grand piano, an ear trumpet, a cast of his face at the age of 42. In the small rooms on the first floor one can see the organ on which Beethoven played when he was 10 years old, his violin, some original scores, a few pieces of furniture and mementoes of his friends, admirers and great interpreters.

In the house next door *(entrance two numbers further on)* are the **Beethoven archives**.

Rathaus (Town Hall) (CZ R) – A charming Rococo building (1738) with a pink and grey façade and a fine outside staircase with two flights.

Kurfürstliche Residenz (Electors' Residence) (CZ U) – The lawns of the **Hofgarten** park make a fine setting for this long Baroque building (1697-1725). Since 1818 the palace has housed the university.

★ **Haus der Geschichte der Bundesrepublik Deutschland** ☉ – *Adenauerallee 250.*

This is the first museum of contemporary history to be opened in Germany. Great efforts have been made to present recent history in an interesting way – with displays making full use of modern audiovisual technology such as video screens, interactive control panels and electronic buttons. Older visitors will be able to retrace the historical events of their youth, while the younger generations, for whom this museum already seems to be a popular attraction, watch fascinated as the past unfolds before their eyes. Economic and social history are just as interestingly portrayed as recent cultural and political evolution. From Konrad Adenauer's official Mercedes, to an ice-cream parlour or a cinema from the 1950s, no item of potential historical interest is left out. Even the rough wooden seats used by Mikhail Gorbachev and Helmut Kohl during their summit meeting in the Kaukasus Platz in 1990 are to be seen here. The evolution of the former East German Republic (DDR) is unfolded at the same time as that of the former West German Republic (BDR).

During construction work, a **Roman cellar** was uncovered, which was forthwith incorporated into the museum *(basement level)*. Should visitors find that the two labourers standing on the balcony in front of the library do not look exactly enthusiastic about setting to work, then they should not be surprised as the sculpture group is the work of contemporary realist artist **Duane Hansen**.

★ **Kunstmuseum Bonn (Bonn Museum of Art)** – *Friedrich-Ebert-Allee 2.*

The charm of Axel Schulter's exciting architecture lies not so much in the façade as in the interior of this spacious building, adorned with a particularly elegant circular staircase. The ground floor houses works by the Expressionists, with particular emphasis on the œuvre of **August Macke**, who lived in Bonn. In the adjoining rooms are exhibitions of German art since 1945 (Nay, Emil Schumacher, Günther Uecker). On the first floor each room is devoted to a particular artist, among others Gerhard Richter, Anselm Kiefer, Georg Baselitz, A.R. Penck, Marcus Lüpertz. Three rooms are devoted to the constructions of Joseph Beuys alone. From room 15, which contains the work of Sigmar Polkes, there is a delightful **view** of the neighbouring **national art gallery and exhibition hall** ☉ (Bundeskunst- und Ausstellungshalle) by Viennese architect Gustav Peichl with three spires representing science, art and technology.

Poppelsdorfer Schloß (BZ) – The design of this building was entrusted to the French architect **Robert de Cotte**. It was built between 1715 and 1753. A splendid dual carriageway avenue, bordered by chestnut trees and divided by a broad grass strip (the **Poppelsdorfer Allee, BZ 32**), links it to the electoral castle.

The outer façade, with its three wings, reflects a classical French influence, while the inner courtyard, bordered by a semicircular colonnade, is more Italian in style. At the back, on level ground where a moat once flowed, are the university's **Botanical Gardens**.

Alter Friedhof (Old Cemetery) (BZ) – Artists, scholars and celebrities are buried here. One can visit the graves of Robert and Clara Schumann, Beethoven's mother, Ernst Moritz Arndt, August Wilhelm von Schlegel, and others.

THE OUTSKIRTS

★ **Schwarz-Rheindorf** – *Leave by the Kennedy bridge* (**CY**).
This **two-storey church**★ in the Romanesque style was consecrated in 1151. The upper part, communicating directly with the palace, was reserved for the Elector and his immediate circle; the Archbishop's suite occupied the ground floor – where the walls are decorated with expressive frescoes illustrating the Book of Ezekiel.

Bad Godesberg – *Town plan in the current Michelin Red Guide Deutschland.*
With its comfortable villas and many parks (Redoute, Draitschbrunnen), this rich residential suburb south of the city is the seat of embassies, ministries and international organizations. The **riverside walk** between the Rhine ferry landing-stages is very popular. The Petersberg Hotel and the Drachenfels ruins overlook the heavy flow of traffic on the river.
The ruins of **Godesburg castle** ☉, built in the 13C by the Prince-Electors of Cologne, stand on a basalt outcrop in the town centre. From the keep, there is a fine **panoramic view**★ of Godesberg, the Bonn depression northwards as far as Cologne, and the Siebengebirge massif.

EXCURSIONS

★ **Siebengebirge (The Seven Mountains)** – This volcanic massif with an average height of 400m - 1 312ft rises opposite Bad Godesberg on the eastern bank of the Rhine. The whole range is classed as a national park with traffic circulation strictly controlled. Each of the seven summits, now heavily wooded, was once crowned by a castle. The slopes of the Siebengebirge form the most northerly point in Germany where vines are cultivated. The best known local wine is the Drachenblut (Dragon's Blood - *see below*).
At the foot of the range, bordering the Rhine, are the localities of **Bad Honnef-Rhöndorf** (house of Konrad Adenauer) and **Königswinter**, from where a **funicular** ☉ rises to the jagged **Drachenfels**★ ruins. It was here, so the legend has it, that Siegfried, the hero of the *Nibelungen (qv)*, slew the dragon and then bathed in its blood to render himself invulnerable.
From the terrace, near the ruins of the castle tower, the visitor can admire a vast **panorama**★★ comprising (from left to right) the Weserwald and Eifel plateaux, Bad Godesberg, Bonn, and finally Cologne.

Remagen – *23km - 14 miles to the south. Leave by the Adenauerallee* (**CZ**).
Passing Mehlem, one sees on the right the ivy-covered ruins of **Rolandsbogen**, and, on the left, the island of **Nonnenwerth**, linked to it by legend.
The origin of the small town of Remagen goes back to a Roman fortified camp. It became famous because of its **bridge** across the Rhine, which fell into American hands almost intact on 7 March 1945 – the first time they had been able to establish a bridgehead east of the river. Then days later, the bridge collapsed under the weight of armoured vehicles. The remaining towers are today the site of a **Peace Museum** (Friedensmuseum) ☉, tracing the history of the bridge and the battles of March 1945. In the town itself, see the **parish church**: its outer wall is furnished with **double Romanesque doors** – a carriage entrance and one for pedestrians. The reliefs which embellish the arches represent sirens and fantastic beasts.

BRAUNSCHWEIG

BRUNSWICK – Niedersachsen – Population 260 000
Michelin map 416/418 J 15
Town plan in the current Michelin Red Guide Deutschland

Brunswick's prosperity today is linked to the development of modern industries (electronics, optics, office equipment) and to the fact that the town is a centre of scientific research. The monuments to its illustrious past have nevertheless been restored.

HISTORICAL NOTES

Till Eulenspiegel Country – Memories of the famous jester and buffoon, Till Eulenspiegel, spread far and wide from the beginning of the 16C by storytellers and minstrels, are especially cherished in his native Brunswick. He was born *c*1300 in **Schöppenstedt**, 23km - 14 miles southeast of the city, where there is a small museum in his honour.

A Cultured Court – Brunswick ceased being a princely residence after the fall of Henry the Lion, but the Court was reinstated in 1753 by a younger branch of the House of Brunswick. In 1807, after its conquest by Napoleon, the region was added to the ephemeral kingdom of West phalia. The young Stendhal (Henri Beyle) spent almost two years in Brunswick at this time, first as Commissioner for War, and subsequently as Steward of the Emperor's Domains.
Patrons of the arts were numbered among the later Brunswick princes: it was Karl II who invited Goethe to stage the first performance of *Faust* in the city in 1828.

The Lion of Brunswick – In 1166, having boosted the House of Guelph to the summit of political power in Germany, Henry the Lion, Duke of Bavaria and Saxony, settled permanently in Brunswick. Frederick Barbarossa, offended at Henry's meteoric rise, summoned him before the Diet. When "the Lion" refused to appear, he stripped him of everything except his personal properties between the Upper Weser and the Lower Elbe. Henry the Lion died in 1195.

The Lion of Brunswick

Stadt Braunschweig

SIGHTS

* **Dom (Cathedral)** – The Westwerk *(qv)* supports two octagonal towers, linked the whole way up by a Gothic bell gable (1275) which acts as a campanile. This general design was later copied by other churches in the city. The original Romanesque church built by Henry the Lion has groined vaulting with the weight reduced by sizeable cut-outs. The aisles were replaced in the Gothic period by four naves – those on the north side, in late or Flamboyant style, having spiral columns turned in alternate directions. The choir and transept are decorated with 13C painted murals. Note especially: the massive **candelabrum★** (Bronzeleuchter) in the choir; an impressive mid-12C **Christ Clothed★** by Imervard, in one of the north aisles; and, in the nave, the recumbent effigies of Henry the Lion and his second wife, Matilda of England, the daughter of Henry II Plantagenet. In the main crypt are the tombs of the Guelph princes.

Altstadtmarkt – One steps back in time when visiting this district, where the old municipal institutions of Brunswick's merchant quarter can be seen. The old **town hall** (Altstadtrathaus) is built with stepped gables, the two wings set at right angles to one another (13C-15C). The buttresses of buildings facing the square support statues of the Princes of Saxony and the House of Guelph. In the middle of the Poststraße is the **Drapers' Hall** (Gewandhaus), the building with the town's most decorated gable (late Renaissance). Four principal floors rise above the street, and these are surmounted by four further pediment levels. The divisions of the gable are softened by inverted consoles, statuettes and globes topped by stone spikes.

Martinikirche – Strongly influenced by the design of the cathedral, this church was built in the mid-13C. In the 14C, the transept gables were adorned with statuary: on the north, the Resurrection of Christ in Glory, on the south, the Virgin, the Magi and the Saints. Inside, the first chapel on the south aisle (statues of St Anne and the Virgin) has a bronze Gothic baptismal font with a Baroque cover. St Martin, in the uniform of a 17C officer, rides on horseback at the foot of the pulpit.

Herzog Anton-Ulrich-Museum ⊙ – The painting gallery is mainly devoted to Flemish and Dutch Masters of the 17C: Rembrandt *(Family Portrait, Stormy Landscape)*, Rubens, Vermeer, Ruysdael. Worth attention also are the 16C German painters (Cranach, Holbein the Younger, Adam Elsheimer), and the 15C Italians (Palma Vecchio, Giorgione).
Works ranging from the time of Dürer to the present day are on display in a gallery of drawings and engravings (Kupferstichkabinett). A department of Baroque and Renaissance decorative arts completes the museum collections (furniture, bronze statuettes, ivories and watches in the first case; majolica and Limoges enamels in the second).

* **Medieval Art Collection in the Burg Dankwarderode** ⊙ – This collection of church plate, on display in the ducal castle, includes a reliquary of the arm of St Blaise (patron saint of the cathedral and protector of the Guelphs), the imperial robes of King Otto IV, and the Gospels from the church of St. Ägidius.

EXCURSION

Königslutter am Elm – *20km - 12 miles to the east.*
On the fringe of the lovely beech forests of the Elm, Königslutter is renowned for its ancient **abbey★** (Abteikirche). This is a Romanesque basilica with three naves and five apses, of which the principal is embellished with a fine, Lombard-inspired, **carved decoration★★**. The north doorway is original: it comprises three lobes upheld by twisted columns, each supported by a grimacing lion. The north gallery of the **cloister★** consists of two Romanesque naves with groined vaulting resting on elaborate fluted, trellised and chevroned columns.

BREMEN★★

Bremen – Population 530 000
Michelin map 415 G 10
Plan of conurbation in the current Michelin Red Guide Deutschland
and on Michelin map 415

Bremen, at the inner end of the long Weser estuary, and Bremerhaven, its outer harbour 59km - 37 miles downstream, together form a remarkable port system. Bremen itself is Germany's oldest maritime city. It had market rights from 965; in 1358 it joined the Hanseatic League; in 1646 it was declared a Free Imperial city; and direct trading with America began as early as 1783. By tradition it is a cotton and coffee town, its Cotton Exchange ranks with Liverpool as a world authority.

Bremen is also a town of culture, where the Weser Renaissance architectural style *(qv)* blossomed. For those interested in food, the city specialities are chicken ragout (Kükenragout), Vegesack herring (Vegesacker Matjeshering), and black pudding with cabbage (Braunkohl mit Pinkelwurst).

The Port ⊘ – The port of Bremen ranks second only to Hamburg in Germany and provides employment for twenty-five percent of the city's population. Bremen specializes in the importation of raw materials: timber, copper ore, wool, cotton, coffee, tobacco, cereals and cocoa. By far the most important of its activities is however the handling of container transport and automobiles – to the tune of 850 000 containers and 780 000 vehicles in 1993, making Bremen Europe's leading port for the turn-around of vehicles.

OLD BREMEN *time: 2 1/2 hours*

★★**Marktplatz (Z)** – The market square, its wide expanse surrounded by the finest buildings in the city, lies in the heart of the old town. The centre is marked by a giant 10m - 33ft **statue of Roland** beneath a Gothic canopy (1404). The knight bears the sword of justice and a shield adorned with the imperial eagle.

The **Schütting (A)**, a restrained but elegant 16C building, used to house Bremen's Guild of Merchants. The decoration of its façade shows a Flemish influence.

★ **Rathaus (Town Hall) (Z R)** ⊘ – The main building is Gothic, its upper floors crowned by decorative gables – part of a 17C transformation made in the Weser Renaissance style. The three-storey principal façade rises from an arcaded gallery emphasized by a richly carved balustrade. Above this, tall windows alternate with statues of Charlemagne and the Seven Electors (copies: the Gothic originals are in the Focke-Museum). Three Renaissance gables embellish the top floor.

At the corner of the west wing is a bronze group by the modern sculptor Gerhard Marcks representing the *Animal Musicians of Bremen* (a pyramid formed by an ass, a dog, a cat, and a cockerel) – characters from a popular fairy tale by the Brothers Grimm.

Interior – A splendid **spiral staircase**★★ (Wendeltreppe) in carved wood (1620) adorns the first floor Council Chamber. The room's Renaissance decoration recalls connections with the law courts *(The Judgement of Solomon)* and with the sea (models of boats). The **Guildhall** (Güldenkammer) – a small adjoining chamber renovated in 1905 – is noteworthy for its sumptuous leather wall hangings enriched with gold. *(It is open to groups of less than 12 people.)*

The Ratskeller (wine cellar) serves exclusively German wines from 600 different vineyards.

★ **St. Petri-Dom (Z)** – In general, the cathedral presents much the same massive appearance as it did in the 11C, but traces of the 16C and 19C rebuilding are clearly evident in the exterior detail.

Inside, against the first left-hand pillar of the raised chancel, stands a fine 16C **Virgin and Child**★. Among the 16C carvings on the organ balustrade can be seen, in the middle, the figures of Charlemagne and Willehad, the first Bishop of Bremen, who carries a small replica of the cathedral (16C). Beneath the organ loft, an 11C crypt houses Romanesque capitals and a magnificent bronze **baptismal font**★★ (Taufbecken - 13C).

At the end of the right-hand aisle, a gallery from the **cathedral museum** (Dom-Museum) displays items recovered from tombs beneath the nave – in particular, medieval vestments and a priceless 13C bishop's crozier.

Liebfrauenkirche (Church of Our Lady) (Z B) – The bare interior of this church is relieved by 13C rounded ogive vaulting. The stained glass windows, on Biblical themes, were executed between 1966 and 1979 by Alfred Manessier.

Stadtwaage (Weigh-House) (Z D) – A lovely 16C building constructed with alternating layers of brick and embossed stone.

★ **Böttcherstraße (Z)** – This narrow street, running from the Marktplatz to the river Weser, was built between 1923 and 1933 by the industrialist Ludwig Roselius, who had become wealthy through the coffee trade. While architects Runge and Scotland took the local building style as their inspiration, Bernhard Hoetger gave free rein to

BREMEN

A Der Schütting
B Liebfrauenkirche
D Stadtwaage

E Roselius-Haus
   und Paula Becker-Modersohn-Haus
F Atlantishaus

M³ Focke-Museum
R   Rathaus

his imagination, drawing on the Expressionist style with Jugendstil (Art Nouveau) and Art Deco overtones. The tall, gabled buildings of this highly original street house art galleries, museums, a theatre, bookshops and taverns. Between two of the gables, a porcelain carillon chimes at 12noon, 3pm and 6pm.

★ **Roselius-Haus (No 6) and Paula Becker-Modersohn-Haus (No 8)** ⊘ **(Z E)** – The Roselius-Haus, a merchant's mansion dating from 1588, contains examples of domestic decor, luxurious furnishings and furniture, paintings and craftwork from the 12C to 19C. Works from Cranach the Elder's studio and a Lamentation group by Tilman Riemenschneider are the high points of this collection built up by Roselius.

The Paula Becker-Modersohn-Haus was built by Bernhard Hoetger and provides the ideal setting for the display of paintings, drawings and graphic work by Becker-Modersohn (1876-1907), one of the pioneers of modern art. The first and second floors of the house are given over to the varied work of Bernhard Hoetger himself, who made a name for himself as a sculptor.

Atlantishaus (No 2) (Z F) – This 1931 block, decorated with the signs of the zodiac, has an unusual spiral staircase made of concrete and glass.

Not far from there, beyond the Martinistraße, on the banks of the Weser, is the 13-14C **hall-church of St. Martini** ⊘.

ADDITIONAL SIGHTS

* **Wallanlagen (Rampart Promenade) (YZ)** – The walk includes a delightful green belt where the ancient bastions used to be. There is also a working windmill.

* **The Schnoor (Z)** – The cottages in this quarter, once the homes of fisherfolk, are all that remains of Old Bremen. In styles ranging from the 15C to the 19C, they have all been restored and are now used as art galleries, antique shops, restaurants and craft boutiques. The narrow streets of the quarter, popular with tourists, are very busy after dark.

* **Kunsthalle (Art Gallery) (Z)** ⊙ – An outstanding collection of 19C and 20C French and German art is the main attraction here. On display are works by: Courbet, Delacroix and the Barbizon School; Menzel, Leibl, Beckmann; the French Impressionists and their German counterparts, in particular Liebermann and Corinth; artists of the Worpswede School *(see below)*, notably Paula Becker-Modersohn and her husband Otto Modersohn. Earlier periods of European art are illustrated by 15C Old Masters, and by Rubens, Terborch, Rembrandt, Tiepolo, Maulbertsch, etc., up to Picasso. In the print room (Kupferstichkabinett) are over 230 000 prints and drawings of exceptional quality from Dürer's day to the present.

Übersee-Museum (Overseas Museum) (Y) ⊙ – Well-displayed exhibits in this museum are devoted to Oceania, Japan, Southeast Asia, India, Africa, China and Australia. The best items, either original or in the form of scale models, relate to living conditions (a Papuan village, a Chinese house completely furnished), to occupations (fishing boats), and to customs and beliefs (legendary masks, effigies of ancestors, objects of worship). There is even a miniature Shinto temple and a Zen garden.
On the first floor there is a collection of masks from Black Africa. The second floor is concerned with the economic life of Bremen and in particular its port activities.

** **Focke-Museum (Y M³)** ⊙ – *Leave via the Rembertiring (Y). See the plan of the conurbation in the Michelin Red Guide Deutschland.*
This regional museum set amidst parkland covers the artistic and cultural evolution of Bremen and its surroundings. The quality of the exhibits, which include archaeological finds and maritime displays, and the well-organised layout of their presentation combine to make the visit a particularly rewarding one.
In the main gallery, the power and wealth of Bremen in the Middle Ages and during the Renaissance are evoked through the original statues from the town hall façade, church furnishings, tableware and works of art from aristocratic houses.
On the first floor *(staircase on the right, at the far end of the gallery)*, the 17C and 18C are illustrated by engraved goblets, portraits of merchants, stained glass windows, ceramics and the work of goldsmiths and silversmiths.
Return to the ground floor.
The first gallery here contains a chronological display on the 19C, the most notable feature of which is the remarkable collection of locally crafted silverware. the second gallery retraces the local history of navigation and economic activities from the Middle Ages to the present. Other examples of a city whose history is indissolubly linked with the sea include exhibits on whaling (harpoons, carved whalebone), on the transport of emigrants to the United States, on the famous steamers of the Norddeutscher Lloyd line, and on Bremen's shipbuilding yards.
The archaeological collection is on display in a thatched barn. An old manor house houses a large collection of furniture providing a glimpse of domestic decor in the merchant classes from the Middle Ages to the 20C completed by a display of toys and glassware.
In the park outside, do not miss the typical Lower Saxony thatched farmhouse (Haus Mittelsbüren), with its barn (Tarmstedter Scheune) and well.
Haus Riensberg – *To the right of the lane leading to the Focke-Museum.*
Once a farmhouse, this building was enlarged in 1768 for a noble family. Today it has been transformed into a museum showing mainly furniture from the 16C to the Jugendstil *(qv)* and 19C toys. One gallery is devoted to 19C women's fashions.

EXCURSION

Worpswede 24km 15 miles – about 1 1/2 hours. *Leave Bremen by the Rembertiring (Y).*
Isolated at one time in a desolate landscape of peat moors, the village of Worpswede attracted at the end of the 19C a colony of artists, notable among whom were Paula Becker-Modersohn, her husband and the poet Rainer Maria Rilke. Since then, galleries, studios and craft workshops have multiplied. Odd, asymmetrical buildings such as the Worpswede Café and the Niedersachsenstein First World War Memorial illustrate the avant-garde ideas and innovations of the architects allied to the group.

BREMERHAVEN*

Bremen – Population 133 300
Michelin map 415 F 9
Town plan in the current Michelin Red Guide Deutschland

Bremerhaven, founded at the mouth of the Weser estuary in 1827, is Bremen's deep-sea port and one of Europe's major gateways to the ocean.

The **Columbuskaje ship terminal**, once the home of transatlantic luxury liners, now handles ferries and cruise ships, while north of the town there is an immense specialized basin (Kaiser Wilhelm Container Terminal), protected from the tides, designed for the rapid turnaround of ore freighters and container ships.

The **fishing port** (Fischereihafen), in the southern part of Bremerhaven, harbours half Germany's trawler fleet.

Visit the famous fish auction, held in the Fischauktionshallen sheds from 7am, Mondays to Fridays.

Deutsches Schiffahrtsmuseum, Bremerhaven

***Deutsches Schiffahrtsmuseum** (National Maritime Museum) ⊙ – Facing the sea and designed by the architect Scharoun, this museum traces the history of the German merchant marine since olden times, and the navy since 1848. It was opened in 1975.

Basement – Liners after 1900; bridge and controls of the nuclear-powered ship Otto Hahn, built in 1968; modern German port activities; maritime developments since 1945; miniature harbour with remote-controlled model ships.

Ground floor – The age of the great sailing ships (from the 18C to 1918); different types of fishing; naval shipyards.

First floor – European fleets in antiquity (models); yachts and pleasure boats; navigation in the Elbe and Weser estuaries; cutaway display of a 1944 pocket submarine. At the back of the museum is a special chamber **(Koggehalle)** where a mixture of water and polyethylene-glycol assures the preservation of a medieval cog excavated in Bremen in 1962. This ancient craft, common in the Middle Ages, was able to serve the smallest of ports because of its shallow draught.

In the adjoining galleries: pre-12C German navigation; flat-bottomed Rhine skiff; Roman bireme; Viking drakkars; reconstitution, based on rock carvings, of the world's earliest ship (9 000 BC).

Technikmuseum U-Boot Wilhelm Bauer (Submarine Museum) ⊙ – Launched in January 1945, this submarine (U 2450) was scuttled on 4 May, shortly before the German capitulation.

It was refloated in 1957 to serve as an experimental unit. A visit to the museum gives some idea of the technical complexity of a submarine as well as the way of life aboard one.

Freilichtmuseum (Open-Air Museum) ⊙ – Eight historic craft are preserved in the Old Port. Moored in the dock basin are: the sailing ship Grönland, which accompanied the first German polar (Arctic) expedition in 1868; the three-master *Seute Deern* (Germany's last wooden sailing ship, 1919); the lightship *Elbe III* (1909); the ocean going tug *Seefalke*; the small Antarctic whaler *Rau IX*; the tug *Stier* with Voith-Schneider propulsion; the high-speed patrol launch *Kranich*; and an experimental (1953) "sea spider" craft said to be a hydroplane prototype.

Deichpromenade – From the top of the breakwater (converted into a promenade) on the south side of the Geeste estuary, it is possible to see the mouth of the Weser and watch the cargo ships waiting their turn to pass up- or downstream.

Zoo am Meer (Aquarium) ⊙ – The aquarium makes a special feature of edible North Sea fish. Open-air grottoes in the outer Weser dike house polar bears, seals, sea-gulls, monkeys, etc.

EXCURSION

Cuxhaven – *39km - 24 miles to the north. Town plan in current Michelin Red Guide Deutschland.*
At the mouth of the Elbe, Cuxhaven is not only Germany's second fishing port but also a control point for navigation in the estuary and a seaside resort. There is an excellent **observation point★** on the **Alte Liebe** (Old Love) Pier (the name derives from a mispronunciation of *Olivia* – the name of a ship that sank close inshore in 1732, whose wreck was for a time used as a primitive landing stage). At the far end of the breakwater marking the geographic – if not the hydrographic – limits of the Elbe estuary stands the **Kugelbake**, a huge beacon no longer used but known to sailors the world over. From here there is a splendid **view★** of the river mouth and the open sea.
The **Wreck Museum** (Wrackmuseum) ⊙ vividly retraces maritime losses and the hazards of navigation in the dangerous waters of the German bight and the Elbe, Weser and Ems estuaries.

Schloß BRUCHSAL★★
Baden-Württemberg
Michelin map 419 S 9 – 17km - 11 miles north of Karlsruhe

Bruchsal, residence of the last four prince-bishops of Speyer, is blessed with a pretentious **Baroque palace** ⊙ comprising something like 50 dwellings or annexes (reconstructed after the total destruction of 1945). Maximilian von Welsch was the architect of this vast complex, begun in 1720 on the orders of the Prince-Bishop Damian Hugo von Schönborn. The main road from Karlsruhe to Heidelberg runs through the extensive palace grounds.

Central Block ⊙ – Pride of place here is held by a magnificent **staircase★★** with an oval well designed by Balthazar Neumann in 1731. Rococo stucco decorates the dome above it. The state apartments **(Regional Museum)** have items from the original furnishings on display. Apart from silver and porcelain tableware, portraits of the prelates can be seen and, above all, **tapestries** from the 16C to the 18C. These, fabricated in the renowned workshops of Holland and France (Beauvais), include a series representing scenes from ancient Greece.
At the west end of the castle's main block, the Gartensaal – a vaulted room with a marble floor – opens onto the **park** (Hofgarten). When they were at their best, blazing with formal flowerbeds in the French manner, the gardens boasted a broadwalk that extended as far as the river, ten miles away.

★★ **Museum Mechanischer Musikinstrumente (Mechanical Musical Instruments Museum)** ⊙ – *In the main building Guided tour of about an hour, with demonstration of instruments.*
This department of the Regional Museum derives from a private collection and includes about 200 instruments ranging from the 18C to the present day, most of them worked by cylinders, by pricked-out metal or cardboard, or rolls of paper. Cinema organs, "Barbary organs", and pianolas (mechanical pianos operated by perforated "piano-rolls") are also represented. Note particularly the "household" **organs** and **orchestrions** (in 19C England Aeolian Orchestrelles – machines resembling an oversize upright piano, complete with manual keyboard and stops for different "voices" – wind-operated by means of pedals). Orchestrions were often conceived as two-part instruments, imitating both piano and violin via their organ pipes. Before the arrival of the phonograph, such machines usually provided the music in taverns and at fairs. Examples from Leipzig and the Black Forest are well represented here. Many of the instruments were decorated with mechanical figures. The philharmonic organ by Freiburg manufacturer Welte was intended for the *Titanic*, but was not delivered in time for the fateful voyage.

Städtisches Museum (Municipal Museum) ⊙ – *Southern part of the main block, on the attic floor.*

Apart from a palaeontology section and a collection of coins and medals (struck in Baden, the Palatinate and the see of Speyer), the museum houses a department of archaeology. Interesting exhibits include a finely-worked flint dagger (*c*1800 BC) from the centre of France, evidently brought this far north by way of trade, and 51 iron bars or rods excavated from riverside gravel beds – part of the cargo of a boat which foundered in the Rhine in the late La Tène period.

BRUNSWICK

See BRAUNSCHWEIG

BÜCKEBURG

Niedersachsen – Population 19 400
Michelin map 417 J 11 – 10km - 6 miles southeast of Minden

Bückeburg retains certain Renaissance buildings, traces of the period when the town was a princely seat. The Schaumburg-Lippe princes ruled, until 1918, over a small but extremely well administered state in the Bückeburg region.

Schloß (Castle) ⊙ – Before visiting the castle proper, visitors are advised to walk into the park, on the right of the state entrance. From here, across velvet lawns beyond the moat, a splendid example of German First Renaissance architecture is visible in the gabled **façade★** with its semicircular pediments. The overall effect is majestic.

Pass through the early 17C monumental gateway, then to the main courtyard – and beyond that to a small inner courtyard surrounded on three sides by a Renaissance balcony. This is the earliest (16C) part of the castle.

During the tour, visitors see some of the rooms, decorated with luxurious furniture, tapestries and Old Master paintings, and the castle chapel, adorned with fine late Renaissance woodwork. An arcaded framework with decorative pediments supports the pulpit – placed, in accordance with Lutheran traditions, in the middle of the nave, facing the sumptuous Princes' Gallery. The highlight of the tour is undoubtedly the Golden Room (Goldener Saal) with the famous "Doorway of the Gods" (Götterpforte) made in 1604. The White Room features a beautiful stucco ceiling adorned with weapon and trophy motifs.

Stadtkirche (Church) – This was one of the first great religious buildings to be designed expressly for the Lutheran sect (1615). The massive façade is symmetrically divided, in Renaissance style, by an alternation of cornices and vertical elements, but several features – the false bull's-eye windows, for example – hint already at the Baroque. There is a fine 17C font inside.

★ Hubschraubermuseum (Helicopter Museum) ⊙ – *Sableplatz.*

From Leonardo da Vinci to the present day, first in theory and then in practice, the evolution of this flight technique is illustrated by numerous models and no less than 40 actual helicopters. Some, like the BO-46, designed to fly at more than 400kmph - 249 miles per hour, have yet to go beyond the experimental stage.

EXCURSION

Besucherbergwerk (Mining Museum) ⊙ – *At Kleinenbremen, 3km - 1 3/4 miles to the south. Be sure to wear warm clothing.*

Worked from 1883 to 1982, this mine had produced a million tons of iron ore by 1952. Visitors go through enormous excavations, supported by huge pillars, before being shown the different systems of extraction which were utilized.

BURGHAUSEN★★

Bayern – Population 17 500
Michelin map 420 V 22

The town, whose centre still retains its medieval aspect, lies within a curve of the Salzach river, where it forms the frontier between Bavaria and Austria. Above the old town is the castle, built on a quite exceptional **site★★** – a long, narrow, rocky spur separating the Salzach from the Wöhrsee.

The Dukes of Bavaria, seigneurs since the 12C, made Burghausen into the biggest fortress in Germany: the defence system, reinforced at the beginning of the 16C in the face of a threatened invasion by the Turks, stretches for more than half a mile.

★★ Burg (Castle) – *Allow about 2 1/2 hours walking and sightseeing.*
Leaving the car in the Stadtplatz, follow the road which circles the cliff at the southern extremity of the spur and pass beneath the **Wöhrenseeturm**. Beyond the lake, a steep path leads to the outer line of fortifications. From here, the ramparts stepped up the Eggenberg hill, on the far side, are visible. A wooden footbridge – fine view of the old town below, and the Salzach – carries the path across a moat to arrive at the **Georgstor**, or St. George's Gate. This is set in the innermost ring of battlements, which protect the last small courtyard at the castle's centre.
The full strategic value of Burghausen becomes apparent: the lower town with its main square lined with brilliantly coloured house facades, onion-domed churches and the fortifications linking the castle with the Eggenberg, and, as far as the eye can see, the Salzach valley winding through the hills.
There are two museums in the main block.

Burgmuseum und Gemäldegalerie (Castle Museum and Painting Gallery) ⊙ – The former ducal apartments (furniture from the 15C to the 17C) house an interesting collection of paintings from the Bavarian School. On the first floor are works by, among others, the Master of the Passion of Freising (*c*1500). Battle scenes painted by Hans Werl (*c*1600) are noteworthy on the second floor – especially a huge canvas depicting the Battle of Ampfing (1322), at which the Emperor Ludwig of Bavaria vanquished his rival Frederick the Handsome of Habsburg. From the **observation platform** *(62 steps higher up)*, there is a splendid panoramic **view★** of Burghausen, the Salzach and the surrounding hills.
The Gothic **chapel** *(in the same wing)* has elegant star vaulting.

Stadtmuseum (Municipal Museum) ⊙ – This is installed in the apartments once reserved for the Duchess *(west side of the main block)*. The main exhibit traces the history of Burghausen. It includes a scale model of the town and castle in the 16C. Also on display are examples of local folk art, craftwork and peasant furniture.
Returning directly to the Stadtplatz via the **Burgsteig** *(a ramp between the castle entrance and the Georgstor)*, there is a particularly fine view of the old town: the onion-domed church towers rising above brilliantly coloured house façades are typical of the regions watered by the Inn and the Salzach.
It is also possible to reach the castle by car: there is a parking space on the flat area to the north of the spur.

EXCURSIONS

Marienberg – *4km - 2 1/2 miles to the south.*
Here there is a Rococo pilgrims' church (1764) almost square in plan. Inside, the dome over the central part of the building is adorned with a fresco painted by Martin Heigel: a boat (symbol of the Church) lies beneath the Holy Trinity, surrounded by celebrated members of the Founding Fathers. In the centre of the ornate high altar is an early Baroque Virgin Mary in Glory.

★ Raitenhaslach – *6km - 3 1/2 miles to the south.*
Red marble tombstones enshrining the memory of abbots from the 15C to the 18C can be seen in this 12C Cistercian church, which was modified in the Baroque style in the late 17C. The life of St Bernard of Clairvaux is illustrated in the fine **ceiling paintings★** (1739) by Johannes Zick of Lachen, near Ottobeuren (1702-1762). The same artist executed the paintings on the sumptuous high altar (Assumption of the Virgin Mary). The Austrian Baroque artist J M Rottmayr painted the pictures in the first two side chapels. The stucco work is by M Zick; the abundant bright blue stucco decoration on the chancel arch is particularly striking.

Tittmoning – *16km - 10 miles to the south.*
On the west bank of the Salzach, across the water from Austria, Tittmoning preserves the remains of its medieval fortifications and a castle which was once the residence of the Prince-Bishops of Salzburg. Two old fortified gateways give access to the wide **Stadtplatz**, which is bordered by houses with ridge roofs masked by perpendicular copings *(qv)*. Brightly painted façades, some decorated with gilded figures, wrought iron signs, oriel windows and emblazoned fountains add considerable style to the ensemble.

Altötting – *21km - 13 miles to the northwest.*
This pilgrimage centre consecrated to the Virgin is one of the oldest in Bavaria and draws more than 700 000 people to the town each year. The Miraculous Virgin stands in a silver niche on the altar of the octagonal **Holy Chapel** (Heilige Kapelle).
In the Late Gothic **Parish Church** (Stiftskirche), there are two fine pieces in the Treasury (Schatzkammer): a splendid Flemish ivory crucifix dating from 1580, and a masterpiece of goldsmith's work (*c*1400) – a small gold horse given to Charles VI of France by his wife, Isabella of Bavaria, which he subsequently pledged against a loan from his brother-in-law, Ludwig the Bearded, Duke of Bavaria-Ingolstadt. Johann Tzerklaes, Count of Tilly (1559-1632), a famous general on the side of the Catholic League in the Thirty Years War *(qv)*, is buried in the crypt *(entrance through the cloisters)*.

CELLE ★★

Niedersachsen — Population 71 500
Michelin map 415/416/418 I 14
Town plan in the current Michelin Red Guide Deutschland

From 1378 to 1705, Celle was the official residence of the Lüneburg branch of the Dukes of Guelph *(qv)*, who had been banished from their original ducal seat by liberated burghers. With its carefully preserved centre of 16-18C half-timbered houses, Celle retains today the air of an aristocratic retreat.

The Three Ladies of Celle – Eléonore d'Olbreuse, a beautiful Huguenot from the old French province of Poitou, seduced Georg-Wilhelm, last of the Guelph Dukes to live in Celle, and became the town's chatelaine in 1676. As Duchess, she opened the Court to influences from her own country. The beautiful French-style garden (Französischer Garten) in the southern part of the town stands as her memorial.

Sophia-Dorothy, Eléonore's daughter (1666-1726), was married for reasons of state to her cousin, the future George I of England *(qv)* – a union which produced, first, George II, and subsequently a daughter who became the mother of Frederick the Great. Sophia's love affair with Count Philip of Königsmark was discovered, and she was banished for the rest of her life to Ahlden Castle.

From 1772 to 1775, a third doomed adventuress, **Caroline Matilda of England**, wife of the eccentric Christian VII of Denmark, expiated in Celle castle her ill-advised affair with Struensee, the all-powerful minister and King's favourite. There is a monument to her in the French Garden.

★★OLD TOWN *time: about 1 hour*

The half-timbered houses of Celle are distinguished by a superpositioning of crow-stepped gables. Well-preserved buildings of this type can be seen in the Rabengasse, the Zöllnerstraße and the Poststraße (note the richly carved **Hoppenerhaus**, which dates from 1532). A recess widening the narrow Kalandgasse allows more space for the 1602 **old college** (Lateinschule), remarkable for the luxuriant ornamentation of its posts and wooden beams engraved with Biblical slogans.

Rathaus (Town Hall) – Roughcast in a pale colour, this building pleasingly blends several different Renaissance styles. The north gable, built in 1579 by craftsmen who came from the banks of the Weser, is heavily scrolled and bristles with fantastic pinnacles (The Weser Renaissance *qv*).

ADDITIONAL SIGHTS

Schloß (Castle) ⊙ – This rectangular fortress, flanked by massive corner towers, boasts roofs in the shape of ribbed helmets. The eastern façade, overlooking the town, is designed with dormer windows topped by rounded pediments – a characteristic of the Weser Renaissance style.

The castle **chapel★** (Hofkapelle) is Renaissance in origin; the ogive vaulting dates from the late 15C. The chapel was modified in the late 16C by the Flemish painter Martin de Vos, whose Crucifixion adorns the altar. With galleries that are both open and glassed-in, colourful frescoes, and curious decorations hanging from the ceiling, the chapel is a strange mixture. Nearby is the **Schloßtheater**, built in 1674 to an Italian design and said to be the oldest court theatre in Germany.

Bomannmuseum ⊙ – *Schloßplatz.*
The permanent exhibitions in this museum cover the folklore of Lower Saxony and the history of the town of Celle. In the centre of the local history section is a display on the history of the former kingdom of Hanover.

Stadtkirche (Church) – This dark and originally Gothic church was considerably renovated in the Baroque style by Italian stucco-workers between 1676 and 1698. The remains of dukes from the Celle branch of the House of Guelph lie in the princes' vault beneath the chancel. The commemorative stones are above in the chancel itself.

EXCURSION

★ Kloster Wienhausen ⊙ – *10km - 6 miles to the south.*
This Cistercian abbey, founded in 1233 by Henry the Lion's daughter-in-law, has been occupied since the Reformation by a small community of Protestant canonesses. Among the piously preserved relics are a stone statue (1280) of the founder, and 13C wooden figures of the Virgin of Wienhausen and Christ Resurrected. The **Nuns' Choir** is embellished with fine early 14C **mural paintings**. During restoration work in 1953, a collection of trinkets was discovered beneath the floor of the choir – penknives, spectacles, small notebooks, etc., hidden there by the nuns five hundred years before to keep them from the hands of the Reformers *(the trinkets are on display in a small museum)*.
Once a year, for 11 days only, starting on the Friday after Whitsun, the Convent holds an exhibition of its famous tapestries, woven by the nuns in medieval times *(the museum is closed during this period)*.

CHEMNITZ

Sachsen – Population 300 000
Michelin map 418 N 22

Situated on the edge of the Erzgebirge mountain range *(qv)*, Chemnitz has been an industrial town since the Middle Ages, when it became a centre of textile production – a role it still fills today. Since the early 19C it has also developed an important engineering and heavy industry sector. Between 1800 and 1900, the population increased from 10 000 to 200 000 inhabitants, the great majority of them belonging to the working class.

From Fritz Heckert to Karl Marx – With such a history, it is hardly surprising that Chemnitz became one of the most militant centres of the German workers' movement.

Fritz Heckert, born in Chemnitz in 1884 and co-founder of the German Communist Party after the failed revolution of November 1918, was one of the driving forces behind this movement. From 1953 to 1990, the town was known as Karl-Marx-Stadt.

SIGHTS

Brückenstraße – With the Straße der Nationen (Avenue of Nations), which it crosses, this fine street is one of the two main arteries around which the new city centre was conceived. It is in this quarter that the impressive apartment blocks and such modern buildings as the Hotel Kongreß, the Kongreßhalle (Conference Palace) and the central post office can be found.

The imposing **Karl Marx Monument** (12.5m - 40ft high), designed by Lew Kerbel in 1971, stands in front of a huge plaque bearing in several languages the last words of the Communist Manifesto: "Workers of the world, unite!"

Returning in a southerly direction, the visitor passes a series of panels decorated with bas-reliefs illustrating the history of the workers' movement.

Altes Rathaus (Old Town Hall) – *Located right at the southern end of the Düsseldorfer Straße.*

Painstakingly rebuilt after 1945, this building has a fine Gothic façade, remodelled at the beginning of the 17C. There is a Renaissance doorway at the foot of the tower.

Museum für Naturkunde (Natural History Museum) ⊙ – The main exhibit here is a "Petrified Forest"★, in the open air, formed by the trunks of trees geologically turned to stone some 250 million years ago. The museum itself is currently undergoing reorganisation. The insectarium and section on the nature and landscape of the Chemnitz region are open to the public.

Städtische Kunstsammlungen (Fine Arts Museum) ⊙ – German painting and sculpture of the 19C and 20C (Dresden Romantic school, German Impressionism and Expressionism). The artist most prominently represented is Karl Schmidt-Rottluff, born in Chemnitz in 1884 and a member from 1905 to 1913 of the Die Brücke movement *(qv)*. The textile and arts and crafts collections include furniture and handicrafts by Jugendstil (Henry van de Velde, Vienna Workshops), Art Deco and contemporary artists.

Schloßkirche (Castle Church) – Approach via the northern part of the Düsseldorfer Straße, then the Müllerstraße on the left. Once part of a Benedictine abbey founded in 1136, this building was transformed into a hall-church at the beginning of the 16C.

There is an elegantly carved Late Gothic doorway (now transferred to the interior, on the south wall). In the chancel is a moving painted wood **Flagellation Group**★ by Hans Witten (1515), that is more than 3m - 10ft high.

EXCURSION

★ **Schloß Augustusburg** – *15km - 9 miles to the east, via Erdmannsdorf.*
The Elector of Saxony Augustus I built this hunting lodge (c1570) on top of Schellenberg hill (515m - 1 690ft). In the chapel, the high altar is adorned with a painting by Lucas Cranach the Younger (1571), showing the Elector surrounded by his 14 children.

The **Museum of Game and Ornithology**★ (Museum für Jagdtier und Vogelkunde) ⊙ presents the fauna of the nearby mountains in reconstitutions of their natural habitat (dioramas). A series of paintings (16C) in the "Hasensaal" illustrate *The Victory of the Hares over the Hunters*.

The castle also houses a **Motorcycle Museum**★★ (Motorradmuseum) ⊙ which gives an overview of more than a century of motorcycle history. The large collection of motorcycles is one of the most comprehensive in Europe, placing particular emphasis on illustrating the technical evolution of this means of transport.

CHIEMSEE★

Bayern

Michelin map 420 W 21 – Local map under Deutsche ALPENSTRASSE

Known as the "Bavarian Sea", the Chiemsee (pronounced Keem-zay) is the largest of the province's lakes, with a surface area of 82km - 32 square miles. Its calm waters lie between gently sloping, rush-covered banks on one side, and the foothills of the Bavarian Alps, clearly visible to the south, on the other. Two islands, not far from the west bank, are worth a visit. They are named the Herreninsel (gentlemen's isle) and Fraueninsel (ladies' isle). On the former is an extraordinary castle, which took Versailles for inspiration; on the latter, an abbey.

Summer resorts popular with water sports enthusiasts line the banks of the lake, in particular **Prien**, the busiest, and **Seebruck**.

The Salzburg-Munich motorway runs close to the Chiemsee's flat, marshy southern extremity, but it is from the northern bank, between Rimsting and Seebruck, that the most interesting vistas – with the Alpine peaks as a colourful backdrop – can be seen.

THE ISLANDS

From the motorway (Bernau exit), approach the lake from the west, and make for the **Prien-Stock landing-stage** ⊙. *Allow 1/4 hour for the trip to the Herreninsel, 1/2 hour for that to the Fraueninsel.*

Herreninsel – The island, for the most part wooded, is famous for its castle.

★★ **Schloß Herrenchiemsee** ⊙ – The young King Ludwig II of Bavaria bought the whole of this island in 1873 to save it from a systematic deforestation, but also because he wanted to build a sumptuous palace there. His visit to Versailles in 1867 had greatly strengthened his admiration for Louis XIV, "the Sun King", and his Court; the castle on his island would be a replica of Versailles. Building started in 1878 and continued until 1886 – by which time 20 million marks had already been spent and the royal coffers were empty. The death of the King, who had spent only one week in the castle, put an end to the dream.

The resemblance between the original and the copy is striking: the Latona fountain stands in the middle of formal French-style gardens; the huge façade is adorned with columns and crowned by a flat roof with balustrade in the Italian style; the apartments include a State Room and a Hall of Mirrors, both of which are magnificent.

Fraueninsel – Although it is small, this islet boasts a charming fishing village and an ancient Benedictine monastery whose 13C church was rebuilt in the Gothic style in the 15C.

COBURG★

Bayern – Population 44 000

Michelin map 418/420 P 16 – Town plan in the current Michelin Red Guide Deutschland

The town centre, lying between the Marktplatz, the Moritzkirche and Ehrenburg castle, still bears the Renaissance imprint given to it c1600 by the Duke Johann Casimir, most enterprising of the Saxe-Coburg dynasty, which married into half the illustrious courts of Europe (Albert of Saxe-Coburg was the husband of Queen Victoria).

VESTE COBURG (FORTRESS) *time: 1 hour*

This complex, which can be seen from afar, is one of the largest fortresses in Germany with a double ring of fortified walls. The original castle dated from the 12C, but the present structure is 16C, the epoch of Johann Casimir. The buildings, with high roofs punctuated by dormer windows, enclose an inner garden.

Fürstenbau (Princes' Palace) ⊙ – The palace contains the royal apartments of the Saxe-Coburg-Gotha family, fitted with magnificent furnishings, including some paintings by Lucas Cranach the Elder. The castle chapel commemorates Martin Luther, who visited the palace in 1530.

Kunstsammlungen (Art Collections) ⊙ – The art collections consist mainly of the possessions of the dukes of Coburg and are a particularly fine example of their kind in Germany. In the **central wing** (Carl-Eduard-Bau), there is a display of 16-19C decorative arts on the ground floor, glassware on the first floor, and prints on the second. The **Steinerne Kemenate** wing houses Luther's room and the great hall (Große Hofstube) which was used for jousting tournaments. On the second floor is one of the castle's best known features, a 1632 room decorated with marquetry (Old German Master paintings).

On the ground floor of the **Duchess's Building** (Herzoginbau), there is an interesting display of gilded carriages frome the 16C and 17-18C tournament sledges. A collection of weapons occupies the first and second floors.

ADDITIONAL SIGHTS

★ **Gymnasium Casimirianum** – Opposite the Moritzkirche, this high school building, with its Baroque turret and lantern (1605), is the finest example of Renaissance civil architecture in Coburg.

Schloß Ehrenburg ⊘ – This castle was the official residence of the Dukes of Coburg from 1547 to 1918. Only the south wing facing the Steinstraße dates from the original Renaissance palace built between 1586 and 1633. After a fire in 1690 the castle was rebuilt. Its present appearance thus features elements of the Baroque, although the façade facing the Schloßplatz was remodelled in the early 19C in the English neo-Gothic manner.
The castle rooms are adorned with sumptous furniture in the Empire and Biedermeier styles. Visitors should not miss Queen Victoria's apartments, the rich stucco ornamentation in the Gobelins Room (French tapestries), the Red Room and the Great Hall, and also in the castle chapel. There is a paintings gallery with works by German and Dutch Masters.

Schloß Rosenau ⊘ – *7km - 4 miles east of Corburg, in Rödental.*
This castle in its picturesque setting is a fine example of neo-Gothic architecture. Duke Ernst I of Saxony, who had the medieval fortress rebuilt in 1808 following the designs of Karl Friedrich Schinkel, is also responsible for the English-style landscaped gardens. Prince Albert, the future husband of Queen Victoria of Great Britain and Ireland, was born in this castle in 1840. The ducal apartments and reception rooms are open to the public (neo-Gothic mural paintings and tracery, fine Viennese Biedermeier style furniture). The **orangery** houses a museum of modern glassware.

EXCURSION

Kloster Banz – *26km - 16 miles to the south.*
Banz is the holy mountain of Franconia. In the 6C, the Franks, having subdued the tribes of Thuringia, settled in the region and introduced the Cult of St Denis, protector of the Merovingian dynasty. In 1120 Bishop Otto of Bamberg declared the martyr saint patron of this abbey.
The **abbey church**, completed in 1719 according to plans by Johann Dientzenhofer, has interior roofing of bewildering complexity. The principal dome breaks down into a series of niches that frame a central, tapering space; the wide supporting arches, themselves out of true and springing from keys, emphasize the virtuosity of this layout. The Baroque abbey towers, looking out over the valley of the Main, are balanced by the silhouette of **Vierzehnheiligen church** *(qv)*, built on the opposite slope. There is a fine **view**★ from the terrace.

COLOGNE★★★
See KÖLN

CONSTANCE★
See KONSTANZ

Lake CONSTANCE★★
See BODENSEE

DARMSTADT

Hessen — Population 139 000
Michelin map 417/419 Q 9
Town plan in the current Michelin Red Guide Deutschland

The former capital of the Grand Duchy of Hesse-Darmstadt, now a thriving industrial centre (machine tools, armoured glass, electronic equipment and chemicals) lies close to the Odenwald massif. It has long been renowned also as a cultural centre, thanks to the endeavours of a succession of enlightened princes who were lovers of art — of Jugendstil notably, at the end of the last century.

Numerous institutions continue the tradition today, in particular the German Academy of Language and Poetry (Deutsche Akademie für Sprache und Dichtung), and the Institute of Industrial Design (Rat für Formgebung).

SIGHTS

★ **Hessisches Landesmuseum** ⊙ — *Plan to different museum sections available at the entrance.*

Main block — *Ground floor, right:* excellent choice of **medieval altar paintings** (Ortenberg and Reidberg), with works by Stefan Lochner and Lucas Cranach the Elder.

Ground floor, left: craftwork and religious sculptures. Note especially the liturgical accessories, medieval enamels, and **sculptured ivory** from Syria, Byzantium, Holland, Italy and Germany itself (of particular interest: the marquetry room from Chiavenna, Lombardy — *c*1580).

Second level: Flemish and Dutch painting (Brueghel, Rembrandt, Rubens), 19C German painting (Schwind, Böcklin, Stuck), and the famous **Werkkomplex of Beuys**.

Basement: religious art (stained glass) and Jugendstil (ceramics, silver, glassware, furniture).

In the main building are the zoological and geological-palaeontological sections and the graphics collection.

Annexe — *Ground floor:* representative collection of Expressionist painting.

Basement: German Impressionism, French "New Realism", art of the 1980s.

Mathildenhöhe — This is the site on which the Grand Duke Ernst Ludwig founded in 1899 the colony of Darmstadt artists known as the Künstlerkolonie. It united painters, sculptors and architects anxious to work together in search of a "total art" corresponding to the Jugendstil *(qv)* ideals of Art Nouveau. Outstanding were the architects Joseph Olbrich and Peter Behrens and the sculptor Bernhard Hoetger.

The dwellings and workshops grouped near the Russian chapel formed in 1901 the centre of an exhibition titled "A Document on German Art". The ensemble, with its terraces and pergolas, is typical of this movement seeking new forms of expression.

The **Wedding Tower** (Hochzeitsturm), built in 1908 to celebrate the marriage of the Grand Duke, overlooks the whole site. Inside are two mosaics (allegories on the subject of Love).

Darmstadt — Mathildenhöhe

Schloß (Castle) ⊙ – The former residence of the Landgraves, in the town centre, comprises two separate buildings: the New Castle (Neuschloß, 18C), a Rémy Delafosse design with its symmetrical façade fronting the market place; and the Old Castle (Altschloß), an edifice with voluted gables and the family coat of arms on the gateway which leads to an inner courtyard.

In the Castle Museum (Schloßmuseum), family collections on view include carriages, furniture, silver and, in the picture gallery, Holbein the Younger's *Darmstadt Madonna*.

Prinz-Georg-Palais ⊙ – This onetime summer residence of the Landgraves (built in 1710) houses the Grand Dukes' **porcelain collection★**. The table services and ornaments belong to the ducal family and constitute one of the largest collections of porcelain from the ducal factory at Kelsterbach, as well as from other German and Russian factories. Almost all the pieces were gifts from the royal and imperial families of Europe. *(During restoration of the building, the porcelain collection is being stored at the royal warehouse in Bensheim-Auerbach.)*

The **Prinz-Georg-Garten** has been preserved as a work of art of landscape gardening. It is a unique example in Hessen of a historical garden laid out in formal geometric patterns following late 18C principles of landscape gardening. The garden is roughly 2ha – 5 acres in area and contains both useful and decorative plants arranged in formal flowerbeds divided by clipped yew broders. It features a number of charming ornamental elements (summer house, tea pavilion, ponds etc.) and an orangery.

EXCURSION

Jagdschloß Kranichstein ⊙ – *5km - 3 miles to the northeast.*
The **hunting museum★** in this small hunting-lodge has assembled an interesting collection of weapons, trophies and pictures.

For a pleasant hotel in peaceful surroundings look in the current
Michelin Red Guide Deutschland

DETMOLD

Nordrhein-Westfalen – Population 68 000
Michelin map 417 K 10
Town plan in the current Michelin Red Guide Deutschland

Until 1918, Detmold was the capital of the Lippe principality. It is a pleasant town, on the edge of the wooded heights of the Teutoburger Wald.

Residenzschloß (Castle) ⊙ – Dormer windows with semicircular pediments in the First Renaissance style adorn the façade of this fine 16C rectangular building. The interior courtyard is noteworthy for a corbelled gallery which links the corner towers. Souvenirs, the gifts of foreign royalty, enrich the apartments inside. Note particularly an outstanding porcelain service presented by the Empress Josephine, and fine 17C tapestries illustrating, after cartoons by Charles Le Brun, the life of Alexander the Great.

★ **Westfälisches Freilichtmuseum (Westphalian Open-Air Museum)** ⊙ – Over 95 peasant dwellings in which families lived together with their beasts have been reconstituted, along with their outbuildings, furniture, etc., in this 80ha - 200-acre park which recreates rural life in Westphalia from the 15C to the 19C.

★ **Hermannsdenkmal (Arminius Monument)** ⊙ – This commemorates the victory in the year AD 9 of the local hero Arminius over the Roman legions, after he had united the tribes living in what are now Westphalia and Hessen. There is a **view★** of the surrounding forest, the town of Detmold and the Weser hills from the gallery *(75 steps)*.

EXCURSION

★ **Externsteine** ⊙ – In a forest setting beside a lake, this curious group of eroded sandstone rocks was once a place of worship for Germanic peoples, and subsequently, in the Middle Ages, a Christian pilgrimage. In the 11C a replica of the Holy Places of Jerusalem was constructed for the pilgrims. The most extraordinary sight is a **bas-relief★** of the Descent from the Cross, carved in the 12C from the living rock. Rare in Germany, this work is an example of Romanesque sculpture with a Byzantine influence.

DONAUESCHINGEN★

Baden-Württemberg – Population 19 600
Michelin map 419 W 9

This small town in the middle of the Baar, a fertile basin between the Black Forest and the Swabian Jura, stands at the confluence of two streams, the Breg and the Brigach. From this fact stems the German proverb "Brigach und Breg bringen die Donau zuweg" – roughly, "from small streams great rivers flow". This is because after the confluence the united streams are known as the Danube.

Source of the Danube – Its site on the confluence has earned Donaueschingen official recognition as the source of Europe's second-longest river (2 826km - 1 756 miles; the longest is the Volga, 3 895km - 2 292 miles), marked by the monumental fountain (**Donauquelle**) built in the castle park in the 19C. The geographical source of the Danube is in fact the source of the Breg, near Furtwangen *(qv)*.

Leading the way in music – The annual Festival of Contemporary Music, founded in 1921, soon became famous worldwide, thanks to the participation of such musicians as Richard Strauss, Arnold Schönberg and Anton von Webern. The concerts, relayed by the Südwestfunk radio station, gained a much wider public for composers like Pierre Boulez, Iannis Xenakis and Karlheinz Stockhausen.

SIGHTS

Fürstenberg-Sammlungen (Princely Collections) ⊙ – These are on display in the Karlsbau building *(on the Karlsplatz)*. The **picture gallery★** (Gemäldegalerie) on the second floor is the most interesting. In the large room on the right are works by 15C and 16C Swabian masters such as Bartholomäus Zeitblom and, above all, the very fine **Altarpiece of The Passion★★** (Passionsaltar) by Hans Holbein the Elder (note the pose of the Saviour). The gallery on the left is devoted to other Swabian painters, including the Master of Sigmaringen. Adjacent rooms exhibit pictures by Cranach the Elder and Younger, Kulmbach, the Master of Meßkirch, etc.

Schloß (Castle) ⊙ – Remodelled in the 19C, the home of the Fürstenberg princes retains the luxurious amenities of the period, enriched now with gold and silver plate, porcelain and fine Beauvais and Brussels tapestries.

Pfarrkirche (Parish Church) – This was built in the Baroque style between 1724 and 1747. In the first (south) bay is the 1522 Madonna of Donaueschingen.

MICHELIN

Donaueschingen – Donauquelle

The Blue Danube

On its course to the Black Sea, from its source in the Black Forest, the Danube flows through or along the border of ten different countries: Germany, Austria, the Slovak Republic, Hungary, Croatia, Yugoslavia, Bulgaria, Romania, Moldavia and the Ukraine. The beauty of the river and some of the countryside through which it flows has inspired many a poet, musician and artist.

Perhaps the most famous tribute to the Danube, however, is *The Blue Danube* waltz composed in 1867 by Viennese maestro Johann Strauss the Younger (1825-99) – just one of over 400 waltzes he composed during his lifetime.

DORTMUND

Nordrhein-Westfalen – Population 570 000
Michelin map 417 L 6
Town plan in the current Michelin Red Guide Deutschland
Local map under RUHRGEBIET

Dortmund, an old Hanseatic town, is the most easterly industrial centre of the Ruhr. Producing 10% of the raw steel used by the former Federal Republic, it is also a thriving supplier of machine tools and electronics. But, for the visitor, it is above all the beer capital. The city's six breweries are responsible for more than 7% of the country's total output.

SIGHTS

★ **Westfalenpark** ⊘ – The two main centres of attraction in this 70ha - 173-acre park are the **Television Tower** (Fernsehturm "Florian") and the **Rose Garden** (Deutsches Rosarium), which cultivates some 3 200 varieties from all over the world. The tower is 220m - 722ft high (102ft higher than the Telecom Tower in London). At a height of 450ft there is a revolving platform with a restaurant and a terrace from which there is a superb **panorama★** of the Ruhr and the Sauerland.

★ **Reinoldikirche** – *In the Ostenhellweg, near the market.*
This triple-aisle basilica dating from the early Gothic period has interesting furnishings, which include a 15C sculpted reredos that represents the Crucifixion. Note the 14C wood statue of St Reynold, patron saint of the town, on the north side of the chancel, and a 15C statue of Charlemagne on the south.

Marienkirche – *Opposite the Reinoldikirche.*
A Romanesque basilica with a Gothic chancel. The **Altarpiece of Our Lady★**, one of the finest works of Konrad von Soest, dates from 1420. The Madonna's face and hands are superbly expressive.

Petrikirche – *In the Westenhellweg.*
This 14C hall-church is famous for its **carved reredos★**, created in 1521 by members of the Guild of St Luke of Antwerp. Including the high altar itself, the work measures 6 x 7.5m - 20 x 25ft. It incorporates 633 carved and gilded figures and 54 paintings.

Propsteikirche – *Entrance from the Westenhellweg, via Mönchenwordt.*
Another hall-church. This one, restored after the Second World War, contains a **triptych** by Derick and Jan Baegert (*c*1490). Open, this reveals, from left to right, the Holy Family, the Adoration of the Magi and the Crucifixion.

Brauereimuseum (Brewery Museum) ⊘ – *In the Dortmunder Kronen brewery, at no 85, Märkische Straße (entrance on the corner of Landgrafenstraße).*
Alongside a permanent exhibition on 5 000 years of beer-related history, this museum presents a survey of the evolution of breweries during the 100 years from the middle of the 19C to the middle of the 20C. Two complete **brewing installations** (1928 and 1936) can be viewed at work on the ground floor.

Museum für Kunst und Kulturgeschichte (Museum of Art and Civilization) ⊘ – *At no 3, Hansastraße.*
The exhibits here, displayed chronologically, cover such diverse subjects as the history of Dortmund (many items from archaeological digs); religious art at the end of the Middle Ages; houses and furniture in different periods; and 19C painting (Berlin Secession, C D Friedrich). The section devoted to the Romanesque epoch contains the **Dortmund Treasure★** (Dortmunder Goldschatz) - a collection of 444 gold coins, dating for the most part from the AD 4C.

Ostwall-Museum ⊘ – *At no 7, Ostwall.*
Works by the greatest exponents of German Expressionism are on view here: paintings by Paula Becker-Modersohn, Jawlensky, Macke, Nolde, Müller and Rohlfs; sculptures by Barlach, Kolbe and Kollwitz. There is also a big display of international art from the years 1960-1980, in particular the installations of Wolf Vostell, Robert Filliou, Milan Knizak and Joseph Beuys.

Help us in our constant task of keeping up to date.
Send your comments and suggestions to
Michelin Tyre PLC
Tourism Department
The Edward Hyde Building
38 Clarendon Road
WATFORD Herts WD1 1SX
UK
Fax: 01923 415250

DRESDEN ★★★

Thanks to an exceptional artistic and architectural heritage and its position in the heart of Saxony, on the banks of the Elbe at and the gates of "Swiss Saxony" *(Sächsische Schweiz – qv)*, Dresden has become one of the most popular and important tourist centres in Germany.

"The Florence of the Elbe" – Originally a Slav town, germanized in the 12C by the Margraves of Meißen, Dresden remained a possession of the Albertine succession from the partition of Saxony in 1485 until 1918.

The major development of the city took place during the first half of the 18C, in the reigns of the Electors Augustus II the Strong (Frederick-Augustus I) and Augustus III (Frederick-Augustus II). To them we owe the magnificent Baroque ensemble of the Zwinger, the Japanese Palace and the Hofkirche (the Court church), as well as outstanding collections of paintings and objets d'art. These, completed by the work of 19C and 20C German painters – Dresden was the cradle of German Expressionism – make the city one of Europe's most prestigious artistic centres. On the cultural side, the Staatskapelle and the Staatsoper orchestras enjoy a worldwide reputation.

The Night of the Apocalypse – A few months before the end of the Second World War, on the night of February 13-14, 1945, Dresden was the target of one of the Allies' most destructive air raids, designed to break the morale of the population. Three successive waves of heavy bombers left the blackened skeletons of the city's principal monuments emerging from a waste of smoking ruins, and a death-toll of over 100 000. 75% of the city was destroyed.

Restoration of Dresden's historic patrimony – in particular the miraculous reconstitution of the Zwinger – and the rebuilding of residential quarters traversed by wide new thoroughfares have given the town a special quality marrying modern urbanism with this ancient heritage. The **Prager Straße** (**Z**), linking the old town with the quarter around the railway station, is the most striking example of this contemporary town-planning, with imposing modern blocks en each side of a broad pedestrian mall.

HISTORIC CENTRE

★★★ **Zwinger** – T*he best view of the whole complex is gained if you go in via the Glockenspielpavillon on Sophienstraße.*

Augustus the Strong's original idea was to build, on the side of a former fortress, a simple orangery. But his architect, **Matthäus Daniel Pöppelmann** (1662-1736), brought such breadth of vision to the project that its conception changed in the course of construction and it ended up as an enormous esplanade surrounded by galleries and pavilions. On every side, an impressive succession of windows and arcades with rounded arches lends the composition as a whole its rhythmic unity.

The main appeal of this jewel of German Baroque lies in the harmonization of archi-tectural work with sculp-tures from the studio of **Balthazar Permoser** (1651-1732), a Bavarian artist strongly influenced by his visits to Italy.

The huge rectangular court-yard has two semi-ellipti-cal extensions which include the **Wallpavillon**★★ (Rampart Pavilion) and the **Glockenspiel-pavillon** (Carillon Pavilion). It is in the former that the intimate relationship bet-ween sculpture and archi-tecture most admirably expresses itself. Not a single transverse wall breaks up the soaring lines of these verticals animated by the exuberance and vigour of atlantes with the face of Hermes, drowned in a sea of vegetation. Crowning the pavilion, **Hercules Carrying the World** is the only work personally signed by Permoser.

Glockenspielpavillon, Zwinger

Jogschies/EXPLORER, Paris

Steps from the Wallpa-villon lead to the terrace on which Pöppel-mann's **Nymphenbad★★** (Bath of the Nymphs) can be seen. It was undoub-tedly in Italy that the artist found inspi-ration for this marvel-lous set-piece, in which a subtle blend between the inor-ganic representation of nature – grotto work and fountains – and the grace of feminine forms creates an atmosphere that is irresistibly sensual. The southwest side of the complex is closed off by the elegant **Zwinger Gallery**, best seen from the outside, passing beneath the **Kronentor** (Crown Gate).

This latter, embellished with statues repre-senting the four seasons, comprises two superim-posed arcades surmoun-ted by an onionshaped dome, which terminates in four eagles supporting the Polish crown.

ZWINGER

0 ___ 30 m

WALLPAVILLON ★★

NYMPHENBAD ★★

★★ **Salon of Mathematics and Physics**

Allee

graben

Zoological Museum

Old Masters Gallery ★★★

ZWINGER

SEMPER

Theaterplatz

Ostra

KRONENTOR

GALLERY

GALLERY

Zwinger-

Armoury

★★ **Porcelain Collection**

N

GLOCKENSPIEL-PAVILLON

Sophienstr.

The **Semper Gallery**, built in 1847 by **Gottfried Semper** (1803-1879), occupies the northeast side of the Zwinger reserved since 1728 for the exhibition of the royal collections. Of the Baroque ensemble as a whole – two-storey pavilions linked by one-storey galleries – the Anglo-German critic Sir Nikolaus Pevsner wrote: "What exulta-tion in these rocking curves, and yet what grace! It is joyful but never vulgar; vigo-rous, boisterous per-haps, but never crude... of an inexhaustible crea-tive power, with ever new combinations and varia-tions of Italian Baroque forms placed against each other and piled above one another."

★★★**Old Masters Gallery** (Gemäldegalerie Alter Meister) ☉ – *Semper Gallery.*

This collection of paintings built up by Augustus II the Strong and his successor Augustus III is one of the best of its kind in the world. The most important Old Masters of their age are represented by masterpieces:

Ground floor:

Gallery 1: Tapestries after cartoons by Raphaël.

Galleries 2-4: Numerous "vedute" (townscapes which are detailed and realistic enough for the town in question to be identified) by Bernardo Bellotto, otherwise known as Canaletto Belotto, who painted Dresden and Pirna with extraordinary precision of detail in the middle of the 18C, to the extent that many of his paintings were used as a guideline during the reconstruction of Dresden after the Second World War. This makes an ideal introduction to a visit to Dresden.

Galleries 5-6: Paintings by Dresden masters Johann Alexander Thiele, a landscape painter and etcher who is credited with the invention of pastel painting in colours across the spectrum, rather than the black, white and red tones that had been used until then, and Christian Wilhelm Ernst Dietrich, a painter and etcher who produced an extraordinary variety of work, mainly in the style of 17C masters.

1st floor:

Galleries 101-102: Works by Silvestre and Canaletto Belotto.

Galleries 104-106 and 108-111: Flemish and Dutch painting from the 16-17C. Note in particular Rembrandt's *Self-portrait with Saskia* (Gallery 106), Rubens' *Bathsheba*, and Vermeer's *Girl Reading a Letter by the Window* (Gallery 108).

Gallery 107: Paintings by the Early Netherlandish (Jan van Eyck is represented by a marvellous triptych) and Early German (masterpieces by Holbein, Cranach the Elder and Dürer) schools.

Gallery 112: 17C French painting (Claude Lorrain, Nicolas Poussin).

Galleries 113-121: 16C Italian painting. Works by Veronese, Tintoretto, Giorgione *(Sleeping Venus)*, Titian and Correggio, are on display in galleries 117-119 which are lit from above. A highlight of the collection is Raphaël's most famous portrayal of the Virgin and Child, the *Sistine Madonna*, in gallery 117.

Gallery 116: Paintings by Botticelli, Mantegna and Pintoricchio *(Portrait of a Boy).*

OLD MASTERS GALLERY (Gemäldegalerie)

Flemish and Dutch painting
German painting
Italian painting
French painting
Spanish painting
♦ Lift

2nd floor

1st floor

2nd floor:

Gallery 201: pastel painting. Jean-Étienne Liotard's *Chocolate Girl* is particularly captivating. World's largest collection of works by Rosalba Carrieras (75 pastels).
Gallery 202: 18C French painting (Rigaud, Silvestre, Watteau).
Galleries 203-207: 18C Italian painting with works by Tiepolo and Crespi.
Galleries 208-210: Spanish painting (El Greco, Ribera, Murillo, Zurbarán, Velázquez).
Galleries 211-216: 17C and 18C German painting (Elsheimer's *Jupiter and Mercury with Philemon and Baucis*, small in scale but exquisitely executed, in gallery 211). The exhibition reaches the threshold of the 19C in gallery 216, which contains works by Angelica Kauffmann and Anton Graff.

To help you get your bearings: Italian paintings are hung on a red background, Dutch and Flemish on a green background, and Spanish and French on a grey background.

★★**Armoury** (Rüstkammer) ⊙ – *Semper Gallery.*
Even those not particularly interested in armour will appreciate this fascinating exhibition of what must be among the finest hand-crafted armour in the world. The **suits of armour** are most impressive, and include the work of one of the most famous Augsburg armourers Anton Peffenhauser. The ceremonial suit of armour for King Erik XIV of Sweden, the work of Libaert of Antwerp, is particularly ornate, and includes an equally sumptuous set of armour for the king's horse. There is also a unique display of children's armour, worn by the little princes during children's jousting tournaments at the Saxon court. Other parts of the exhibition not to be missed include the collections of **jousting tournament weapons, guns** and **pistols**.

★★**Porcelain Collection** (Porzellansammlung) ⊙ – *Entrance on Sophienstraße.*
This gallery displays not only the products of the famous factory at Meißen *(qv)*, but also porcelain acquired by Augustus the Strong from Japan and China (from the best period in the 19C). Do not miss the "giant animal room" on the upper floor, including characters by Kirchner and Kändler of Meißen (first half of the 18C). There is also space devoted to **Johann Friedrich Böttger**, a potter who profited from the discovery of kaolin deposits nearby to create (1708) in Europe a porcelain modelled on that of the Far East. His first attempts to colour glazes are particularly interesting. The largest room displays Meissen tableware of the 18C and a carillon of 52 porcelain bells.

★★**Salon of Mathematics and Physics** (Mathematisch-Physikalischer Salon) ⊙ – *Northwest corner pavilion* – A visit to this gallery recalls the inventive genius of scientists in past ages, with special reference to measuring instruments (thermometers, clocks, barometers), cartography (globes), and methods of observation. A collection of clocks on the first floor unites the most representative models since the 16C.

On the way to the **Theaterplatz (Y 52)** – note the equestrian statue of King John (1854-1873) in the centre of the square – the road passes the **Old Town Watchtower** (Altstädter Wache), which was designed by Schinkel.

★★ **Semperoper (Opera)** – Built between 1871 and 1878 by Manfred Semper based on plans designed by his father Gottfried – Professor of Architecture at Dresden responsible for the previous edifice, destroyed by fire in 1869 – the present opera house owes its form to the Italian Renaissance.

The tiered façade, in plan a wide arc, comprises two storeys of arcades, surmounted by a third in recess. Each side wall is furnished with twin niches, occupied on the left by statues of Shakespeare and Sophocles, on the right Molière and Euripides.

★★ **Katholische Hofkirche (Cathedral)** – This enormous basilican edifice was built between 1738 and 1755 following the conversion of the Albertines to Roman Catholicism, the condition of their accession to the Polish throne. Its 5 000m^2 - 53 820sq ft floor area make it the largest church in Saxony. The building, strongly influenced by Italian Baroque, is dominated by an 85m - 279ft bell tower and decorated with statues of the saints and apostles, mainly on the attics.

The nave is separated from the side aisles by a semicircular ambulatory opening on to four oval chapels. Above the high altar, a fine painting (1750) by Anton Raphael Mengs depicts the Ascension. The pulpit was executed by Permoser in 1722, while the organ was the last work (1750-1753) of the master craftsman Gottfried Silbermann. The tombs of several kings and princes of Saxony can be seen in the crypt.

Schloß (Castle) – Most of this Renaissance-style building, once the official residence of the Court, is in the process of being restored.

That part of the exterior façade linking the west wing to the Johanneum is covered by a colossal mosaic, **The Procession of Dukes★** (Fürstenzug, 1906). Composed in tiles of Meissen porcelain, the work represents a parade, in chronological order, of all the ducal members of the house of Saxe-Wettin. It measures 102m x 957m - 335ft x 3 140ft. The inner façade is formed by the **Langer Gang★**, a series of 22 Tuscan arcades enclosing the stable courtyard.

The **Johanneum (M¹)** (left of the Schöne Pforte entrance, a gateway in the Renaissance style) was itself once used as the stables. It now houses a **Transport Museum** (Verkehrsmuseum), where collections of vintage cars and motor cycles join a display outlining the evolution of public transport.

Leaving the Johanneum, cross the Neumarkt towards the ruins of the **Frauenkirche**, preserved as a spine-chilling reminder of the destruction of the city in 1945. Visit the **Brühlsche Terrasse (Y 6)**, laid out on the site of ancient fortifications, where there is a **view★** of the Elbe and the Neustadt quarter, on the river's east bank.

Albertinum – This one-time arsenal was transformed, in 1884-1885, into a museum

★★★**Gallery of 19C and 20C Painters** (Gemäldegalerie Neuer Meister) ☉ – A visit to these rooms permits the visitor to gauge the richness and diversity of German art from the Romantics (**Casper David Friedrich**, *Two Men Contemplate the Moon*; **A L Richter**, *The Crossing of the Elbe*) to the Biedermeier (**Carl Spitzweg**, *The Hook and Line Fisherman*); from the Bourgeois Realists (**Adolf von Menzel**, *Sermon in the Old Church of the Berlin Monastery*) to the so-called "Deutsch-Römer" (**Arnold Böcklin**, *A Summer's Day*; **Wilhelm Leibl**, *Portrait of the Baron von Stauffenberg*) and the painters of Jugendstil (**Fritz von Uhde**, *The Nativity*). The Impressionists are represented by their leading lights: **Max Slevogt**, *Scenes of Egyptian Life*; **Max Liebermann**, *Portrait of Alfred von Berger*; **Lovis Corinth**, *The Painter's Model*.

The Brücke movement, spearhead of German Expressionism, was born in Dresden at the beginning of this century. The group, a spin-off from Fauvism, is notably represented by **Karl Schmidt Rottluff**, *After the Bath*; and **Max Pechstein**, *A Baltic Landscape*.

Two triptyches illustrate in a gripping way the "revolutionary" German school operating between the wars: *War* (1929-1932) by **Otto Dix**, a denunciation without concession of the cruelty and folly of the warlike mentality; and *The Thousand-Year Reich* (1935-1938), a vision both ironic and prophetic of the new National Socialist regime by **Hans Grundig**.

The remaining rooms are devoted to painters from the former East Germany.

★★★**Green Vault Collections** (Grünes Gewölbe) ☉ – To visit this exhibition is to enter a real "Ali Baba's Cave", for here is the artistic treasury collected by the sovereigns of Saxony, in particular Augustus the Strong. Centred around *The Court of Delhi on the Birthday of the Grand Mogul* – an extraordinary composition comprising more than 130 gilded and enamelled figurines – there is a display of marvels worked by goldsmiths, silversmiths and jewellers from different parts of the world.

★ **Stadtmuseum Dresden (Y M⁴)** ☉ – Installed in the Landhaus, an elegant palazzo built from 1770 to 1775 in the classical and late Baroque styles, with elements of Rococo, this exhibition retraces the stages of Dresden's development and the principal facts of its history.

DRESDEN

★ **Kreuzkirche** – The original church, the city's oldest (early 13C), was remodelled in the Baroque style after its destruction (1760) during the Seven Years War. The damage inflicted during the Second World War has been repaired on the outside of the church, but the inside strikes visitors with quite a shock since it has so far only been roughly plastered over. The Kreuzkirche is home to the Kreuzchor, a famous choir.

DRESDEN

E	Reiterstatue
M¹	Johanneum
M²	Museum für Sächsische Volkskunst
M³	Deutsches Hygiene-Museum
M⁴	Museum für Geschichte der Stadt Dresden

NEUSTADT QUARTER (EAST BANK)

The **Hauptstraße** (**X 19**), which links the Albertplatz and the Neustädter Markt – dominated by the gilded **equestrian statue★** (**X E**) of Augustus the Strong – was the object after the catastrophe of 1945 of a tasteful restoration scheme which managed to preserve several 18C dwellings.

★ **Japanisches Palais (Japanese Palace)** (**X**) – Built between 1715 and 1737 under the direction of Pöppelmann, this huge quadrilateral was designed to display Augustus the Strong's collection of Meissen tableware. The oriental-style roofs of the corner pavilions lend the place its Asiatic character. On the side nearest the Elbe, there is a pleasant garden with a **view** of the river's west bank.

★ **Museum für Sächsische Volkskunst (Museum of Saxon Arts and Crafts)** (**X M²**) ⊙ – All the skill and taste of Saxon workmanship is apparent in the numerous exhibits displayed in this pretty Renaissance building (multicoloured furniture in painted wood, toys, ironwork, etc.).

ADDITIONAL SIGHTS

★ **Großer Garten** (**Z**) – This huge public park is traversed by a broad walk leading to a Palace (1678-1683) in the Baroque style. On either side there are groups of statuary, a zoo, botanical gardens and an open-air theatre, all in a pleasant sylvan setting.

★ **Russisch-orthodoxe Kirche** (**Z**) – *Leave to the south, left of the railway station.*
The designers of this colourful church, built in 1874, were inspired by Russian architecture of the 17C.

Deutsches Hygiene-Museum (**Z M³**) ⊙ – *Lingnerplatz 1.*
Karl August Lingner, who invented Odol mouthwash and became in his time the richest man in Saxony, was instrumental in the founding of this highly original museum in 1912. The main focus of the exhibition is the human body. In the current climate of awareness about health and ecology, the clearly displayed information on a range of fundamental and contemporary issues seems more than ever relevant. One of the main features of the permanent exhibition is the "glass person" (Gläserner Mensch), giving an insight into the structure and functioning of the human body. The section on "Our Senses" (Unsere Sinne) gives the opportunity to test out your senses at first hand. In short, this unusual museum stimulates both young and old alike to experiment and find out more about how their bodies work.

EXCURSIONS

Schloß Moritzburg ⊙ – *14km - 9 miles to the northwest, via Hansastraße* (**X**).
Built by the Duke Moritz on one of the Royal Saxon Hunting Reserves in 1542-1546, this was originally designed to be no more than a simple hunting lodge in the Renaissance style. But it was considerably refashioned between 1723 and 1736 by Matthäus Daniel Pöppelmann, at the request of Frederick-Augustus I (1670-1733), who had wanted to transform it into a Baroque château. Adjoining the present striking edifice, with four wings and imposing ochre and white corner towers (the colours of the Baroque in Saxony), are an artificial lake and a large park. The stone sculptures (urns, cupids and statues of hunters) on the balustrades of the entrance drive and on the terrace are the work of JC Kirchner and B Thomae. Inside the castle there is a **Baroque Museum** (Barockmuseum) displaying furniture of the period, and three main galleries containing an impressive collection of trophies. The castle chapel was built between 1661 and 1672 by WC von Klengel (1630-1691) and integrated by Pöppelmann into the remodelled building. The small **Pheasantry Pavilion** (Fasanerieschlößchen) – *a 30 min walk away* – houses a museum of ornithology. It was built between 1769 and 1782.

★ **Schloß Pillnitz** ⊙ – *15km - 9 1/2 miles to the southeast, via the Bautznerstraße* (**X**).
Pöppelmann, favourite architect of the Electors, was responsible for this pleasure palace too. Designed between 1720 and 1724, the **Riverside Palace** (Wasserpalais) was originally built on the east bank of the Elbe. The Late Baroque predilection for Chinese motifs is apparent in the roof treatment. A new castle, between the waterside structure and the **Upper Palace** (Bergpalais) was built between 1818 and 1826 under the architect Schuricht, following a fire which gutted the Renaissance building.
There is a **Decorative Arts Museum** (Museum für Kunstgewerbe) in the upper and riverside palaces. Furniture, gilded bronzes, Baroque faience, silverware, glassware and Asiatic porcelain are on display.
The park was transformed into an English-style garden in 1778. A lagoon was added, a circular pavilion or gazebo a year later, and then a Chinese pavilion (one of the most perfect copies of Chinese architecture in Europe) in 1804. The banks of the Elbe offer attractive riverside walks. The islet opposite the gardens is a bird reserve, inhabited by grey herons.

★★★ **Swiss Saxony** – *See SÄCHSISCHE SCHWEIZ.*

★ **Meißen** – *See MEISSEN.*

DÜSSELDORF★

Nordrhein-Westfalen – Population 570 000
Michelin map 417 M 14
Plan of the conurbation in the current Michelin Red Guide Deutschland

Once a fishing village on the east bank of the Rhine, Düsseldorf today is one of the most important economic centres of Germany. The development of the city, which lies at the confluence of the Rhine and the Düssel, has been given an added administrative importance since it was established, in 1946, as the capital of the Rhineland-Westphalia Land.

HISTORICAL NOTES

Düsseldorf first acquired city status in the 13C when it was chosen as the official residence of the Dukes of Berg. Four centuries later, the family of the Electors of the Neuburg-Palatinate settled there and the fame of the city spread. This was largely due to the energy and intelligence of the family's most famous member, Johann Wilhelm (Elector from 1690 to 1715). Patron and apostle of the Baroque, **Jan Wellem** as he was known surrounded himself with a brilliant Court of musicians, painters and architects who transformed Düsseldorf into a true city of the arts.
After the French Revolution, Napoleon created the town capital of the Grand Duchy of Berg, and it became a minor Paris. Murat, and then Jerome Bonaparte were its first rulers. In 1815 it seceded to Prussia.

Heinrich Heine (1797-1856) – Heine, son of a Bolkerstraße merchant, lived in Düsseldorf throughout his youth, deeply impressed by the presence of the French and the personality of Napoleon. In his *Memories of Childhood* he expressed his admiration of France with characteristic verve, at once biting and melancholic. A poet who was also a willing pamphleteer, eternal traveller, defender of liberalism, a Francophile and a genuine European, Heine once described himself as "a German nightingale which would have liked to make its nest in Voltaire's wig".

A Musical City – Among the musicians who have given Düsseldorf its enviable reputation as an artistic centre are Robert Schumann and Felix Mendelssohn. **Schumann** (1810-1856) was appointed conductor of the municipal orchestra in 1850. Living for four years in a house in the Bilker Straße (**DZ**), he was already seriously ill mentally, attempting to drown himself in the Rhine in 1854. His friend **Mendelssohn** (1809-1847) brilliantly directed the city's Rhine Festival. He made his first journey to England in 1829, conducting his own *Symphony in C Minor* at the London Philharmonic Society.

LIFE IN DÜSSELDORF

The Head Office of the Ruhr – Seat of one of Germany's most important stock exchanges, Düsseldorf is not only the country's second banking and financial centre but also administrative capital for most of the Rhineland industries. All these functions are exemplified in the **Dreischeibenhaus** (the Thyssen Building) (**EY E**). Practically all business and commercial transactions concerning the Ruhr and surrounding cities are negotiated in an area between the Kasernenstraße (**DZ**) and the Berliner Allee (**EZ**).

The World of Fashion – Exhibitions, fairs and collections of haute couture several times a year maintain Düsseldorf's reputation as a "minor Paris" and fashion capital of Germany. A walk along the **Königsallee★** (**EZ**) (popularly known as "the Kö") demonstrates that the reputation is deserved. Everything that is elegant in the town centres on this graceful promenade. With its boutiques and arcades, its cafés and restaurants, built on either side of the old moat.

Food – It is in the taverns typical of the old town that regional specialities can best be appreciated: Blutwurst mit Zwiebeln (black pudding with onions); Halve Hahn (caraway cheese eaten with strong local mustard); and Röggelchen (small rye bread rolls). On Friday evenings, there is a tradition of eating Reibekuchen, a kind of savoury potato cake. **Altbier**, the still, dark, brown ale of the region, is brewed in Düsseldorf.

The Way Ahead – Düsseldorf plays an increasingly important role in economic relations linking Germany with the Far East. Japanese firms alone have 300 branches in the city. This strong Oriental presence is reinforced by the existence of the **Japanese Cultural Center** in the Immermannstraße (**EYZ**) and the Taiwan Trade Center, near the central station.

SIGHTS

Old Town (**DEY**) – This riverside quarter, with its taverns and bars jam-packed from the earliest hours of the evening, is known as "**the biggest boozer in Europe**". It is here that the "**Radschläger**" – local street urchins and buskers who perform outdoor acrobatics for a few pennies – can be found.
The **Bolkerstraße** (**DY 8**), birthplace of Heine (no 53), is the busiest and liveliest of the city's pedestrian precincts. The neighbourhood is equally linked with the story of the tailor Wibbel, who attended his own funeral after switching identities to escape a prison sentence. This folklore legend is recalled by the figures of the Schneider-Wibbel-Gasse carillon clock (**DY 95**), which operates at 11am, 1pm, 3pm, 6pm and 9pm.

DÜSSELDORF

A St. Lambertus-Basilika	**M⁴** Deutsches Keramikmuseum
E Dreischeibenhaus	**M⁵** Landesmuseum Volk und Wirtschaft
M¹ Goethe-Museum	
M² Kunstmuseum	**M⁶** Löbbecke-Museum und Aquazoo
M³ Kunstsammlung Nordrhein-Westfalen	**R** Alte Rathaus

Marktplatz (DY 68) – Separated from the Rhine only by the **Altes Rathaus (DY R)** (late 16C town hall), this square is embellished with the bronze equestrian statue (early 18C) of the famous Jan Willem. There is a good view of the river from the Burgplatz adjoining this square to the north, in the shadow of the **Schloßturm**, a free-standing tower.

Lambertuskirche (DY A) – This huge 14C Gothic hall-church is distinguished by a spire that is both leaning and twisted. The interior decoration is basically Baroque. A finely-worked late Gothic ciborium – a canopy or baldachin above the altar – can be seen in the northern part of the chancel. The remains of 15C wall paintings are visible on the south wall.

At the far end of the nave there is a Pietà (c1420) in a modern (1975) setting. The bronze entrance door is by Ewald Mataré.

★ **Schloß Jägerhof and the Hofgarten** (**DEY**) – The Hofgarten park forms a shady continuation of the Königsallee, northwest towards the riverside museum quarter and east as far as **Schloß Jägerhof**. This delightful building, one-time home of the Electors Master of the Hunt, dates from the 18C. The French architect Nicolas de Pigage contributed to the plans. Today the mansion houses the **Goethe-Museum★** (**EY M¹**), which displays the author's manuscripts, autographs, drawings and engravings, as well as busts and first editions of his works. On the second floor, a sumptuous apartment provides a perfect setting for the **Dr. Schneider Private Collection**: note especially the Augsburg gold and silver plate and the Meissen porcelain. Napoleon Hill, in the park, is crowned with a small Maillol bronze entitled *Harmony* – in fact a modest monument to Heine.

★ **Kunstmuseum (Fine Arts Museum)** (**DY M²**) ☉ – Romantics of the Düsseldorf School (Cornelius, Schirmer, Achenbach, Rethel) dominate the important painting gallery in this museum. There is equal exposure for Impressionists and members of the German Expressionist movement (Corinth, Kandinsky, Jawlensky, Macke, Klee, Kirchner and Nolde). Space is also devoted to contemporary art (painting, sculpture and objets d'art), in particular that of the 1960s. The museum is also home to an interesting collection of medieval sculpture, and an outstanding collection of

Les Glycines
by Emil Gallé,
Kunstmuseum, Düsseldorf

glassware★★ which includes glass from Roman times to the present from both Europe and the Far East, and a large amount of Jugendstil glassware. Other museum departments incude an **Oriental section** (with textiles) and a **graphics collection** (80 000 prints and original engravings from the 15-20C; works not display can be viewed in the reading room).

★ **Kunstsammlung Nordrhein-Westfalen** (**Rhineland-Westphalia Art Collection**) (**DY M³**) ☉ – Designed by the Danish architects Dissing and Weitling, this modern building houses a 20C art collection including works by Picasso, Braque, Léger, Chagall, Ernst, Beuys and **Paul Klee** – who was Fine Arts Professor in Düsseldorf from 1930 to 1933. Ninety-two of the artist's pictures are exhibited in rotation.

★ **Hetjens-Museum (Deutsches Keramik-Museum)** (**DZ M⁴**) ☉ – This collection of 12 000 ceramic objects from all over the world covers a time span of 8 000 years.

★ **Landesmuseum Volk und Wirtschaft (Land Economics Museum)** (**DY M⁵**) ☉ – Photographs, charts, comparative tables, graphs, maps and animated models illustrate in lively fashion the precepts of the science of economics. The process of extraction in a coal mine is demonstrated by means of a **diorama**.

★ **Löbbecke-Museum und Aquazoo** ☉ – *Kaiserwerther Straße 380, in the North Park, via the Hofgartenufer* (**DY M⁶**).
This building houses under a single roof the Löbbecke Natural History Museum (insects, molluscs, reptiles) and an aquatic zoo. No less than 69 aquariums, and 62 terrariums, display aquatic creatures of every sort, including sharks and seals. Instructive explanations familiarize the visitor with all kinds of life in a marine element, and its ecological importance. A **Tropical Hall** in the middle of the building (crocodiles) can be crossed by means of a footbridge.

EXCURSIONS

Neuss – *10km - 6 miles to the southwest. Leave Düsseldorf via the Elisabethstraße. Town plan in the current Michelin Red Guide Deutschland.*
The 13C **Quirinuskirche★** with its trefoil apse is one of the last Rhenish Romanesque constructions of importance. The octagonal tower above the transept crossing is flanked by four small square turrets with pointed diamond-shaped roofs. The shell form of the church's clerestory windows, as well as unusual mingling of round and pointed arches, marks the transition in Germany to the Gothic style. From the raised chancel there is a good view of the aisles.

Schloß Benrath ☉ – *10km - 6 miles to the southeast. Plan of the conurbation in the Michelin Red Guide Deutschland.*
This exemplary late Baroque building was designed by Nicolas de Pigage from 1755 to 1770 as a country palace for Carl Theodor Prince Elector of the Palatinate.

Two subsidary wings and two gatehouses flank a central pavilion. The interior is decorated in a style which is transitional between Rococo and early Classicism, and fitted with elegant late 18C furniture.

The **park**★ was also designed by Pigage and laid out in the formal French style. It extends west as far as the Rhine. The deer garden contains century-old trees and is criss-crossed by avenues which intersect to form star patterns. Other parts of the park feature large lakes and flowerbeds.

Neandertal – *14km - 9 miles to the east, via Am Wehrhahn.*

The deep and steep-sided valley of the Düssel owes its name to the Calvinist poet Joachim Neander (1650-1680), who liked to use it as a retreat. It was here, in a grotto since destroyed, that the famous skeleton of **Neanderthal Man**, 60 000 years old, was discovered in 1856. A plaque on a triangular rock *(on the right-hand side of the road, two miles beyond the motorway underpass)* marks the site of the cave.

Leave the car near the Neanderhöhle restaurant.

The **Neandertal-Museum** ⊙ gives an idea of the everyday life and the culture of prehistoric man. The cast of Neanderthal Man's skull is on display here (the original skull is in the Rheinisches Landesmuseum in Bonn). Nearby the museum is a wild animal reserve which contains the sorts of animals that lived at the time of Neanderthal Man: aurochs, bison, etc.

EICHSTÄTT★★

Bayern – Population 13 100
Michelin map 419/420 T 17

Eichstätt is a small episcopal city embraced within a curve of the Altmühl river, in Germany's biggest natural park. It owes its Baroque character to the reconstruction following the sack of the town by the Swedes in 1634. Many of the roofs are covered with limestone slabs (Solnhofen) peculiar to the region.

★EPISCOPAL QUARTER (BISCHÖFLICHER RESIDENZBEZIRK) *time: 1 1/2 hours*

Dom (Cathedral) – The building as a whole dates from the 14C, though parts of it are Romanesque, and others Gothic or Baroque. On the north side, facing the Domplatz, a sober Romanesque door opens into the transept, but the main entrance is via a Gothic door decorated with multicoloured statues. The west face is Baroque.

Inside, the most fascinating feature is the late 15C **Pappenheim Reredos★★**, almost 30ft high, in the north aisle. The representation of the Crucifixion with its attendant figures is a masterpiece of religious sculpture. In the west chancel is a seated statue of **St Willibald** (Bishop of Eichstätt in the 8C) as an old man, the major work of local sculptor Loy Hering (1514).

Go through the south transept to the Mortuarium.

EICHSTÄTT

Domplatz
Gabrielistraße 4
Luitpoldstraße
Marktgasse 12
Marktplatz
Westenstraße
Ostenstraße

Freiwasserstraße 3
Herzoggasse 5
Kapuzinergasse 8
Loy-Hering-Gasse 10
Pater-Philipp-
  Jeningen-Platz 13
Spitalbrücke 17
Walburgiber 20
Weißenburgerstraße 23
Widmanngasse 25

A Kreuzgang
B Fürstbischöfliche
    Residenz
D Muschelpavillon

* **Mortuarium** – This funerary chapel, forming the west wing of the cloister, is a late 15C Gothic hall with two naves. Handsome tombstones pave the floor. A twisted column ends each line of pillars supporting the groined vaulting. The so-called "Beautiful Column" is very finely worked. Four **stained glass windows** in the east wall are by Hans Holbein the Elder (c1500). There is a 16C Crucifixion on the south wall.

Diocesan Museum (Diözesanmuseum) ⊙ – *Upper floor, above the Mortuarium.*
The long history of the Diocese is illustrated by means of pictures, maps, vestments, liturgical accessories and statues in stone and wood. In the Bishop's Room, note **St Willibald's Chasuble**, the oldest liturgical vestment in the See – a Byzantine work dating probably from the 12C.
Reliquaries, chalices, monstrances and other examples of religious art are on view in the **treasury.**

* **Cloister** (**A**) – This element was a 15C addition to the cathedral. The stone tracery of the windows is richly decorated.

* **Residenzplatz** – The southeast corner is the best place from which to obtain a general view of this irregularly shaped square which nevertheless displays a striking unity. Lawns carpet the centre; Rococo palaces surround it. The south side is bordered by four imposing houses with decorated gables and entrances guarded by atlantes. Facing them is the southern wing of the Residence and, on the west side, the former Vicar-General's mansion. The **Virgin's Column** in the immediate foreground (Mariensäule) rises from a fountain surrounded by cherubs.

Fürstbischöfliche Residenz (Former Episcopal Residence) (**B**) ⊙ – (Local administration office). The main entrance opens on a magnificent staircase with a Baroque banister and painted ceiling.

ADDITIONAL SIGHTS

Hofgarten – This park was designed in the style of an English garden by Eugene de Beauharnais, the son-in-law of Napoleon created Duke of Leuchtenberg and Prince of Eichstätt by King Maximilian of Bavaria. It extends in front of the summer residence of the Prince-Bishops. Three delightful pavilions adjoin the south wall. In the centre, the **Shell Pavilion**★ (Muschelpavillon) (**D**), with its fountain and stuccowork, is a true shrine to the Rococo style.

Kapuzinerkirche – One of the chapels in this 17C church contains a 12C copy of the Holy Sepulchre in Jerusalem.

St. Walburg – The interior of this Benedictine monastery church (built 1626-1631) is discreetly decorated with Wessobrunn stuccoes. From the balcony outside the main doorway there is an attractive view over the roofs of the old town to the Altmühl valley.

Willibaldsburg – *Access via route B13 and the Burgstraße.*
This 14C castle, unfinished until the beginning of the 17C, occupies a dominant position on a height overlooking the river in the western part of the town. Inside the castle, note the **well** (Tiefer Brunnen), 75m - 246ft deep *(access through the courtyard).* From the top of the crenellated tower *(98 steps)* there is a **view** of the fortifications, the town and the river.

* **Jura-Museum** ⊙ – The geological history of the Franconian Jura is traced in this museum. Most of the fossils on display (ammonites, crustaceans, fish, reptiles and dragonflies) were discovered in the limestone beds of Solnhofen. An interesting comparison can be made between these fossil fish and those to be found in an aquarium. The museum's prize exhibit is the complete fossilized skeleton of an Archaeopteryx (prehistoric ancestor of birds). Halfway between the reptile and the bird in the evolution of species, this extremely rare example was found in 1951 near Workerzell, northwest of Eichstätt.

Museum of Early History (Museum für Ur- und Frühgeschichte) ⊙ – The exhibits here chart the history of settlers and settlements in the valley of the Altmühl from the epoch of hunters and crop-gatherers to the Middle Ages. Note especially the objects found in archaeological digs which relate to iron-working during the Hallstatt civilization, the collection of Ancient Roman artefacts and a double grave from the Merovingian period.

EXCURSIONS

Weißenburg – *24km - 15 miles to the northwest.*
At the limit of the ancient Roman province of Rhaetia, Weißenburg was an important garrison town. The **Roman Baths**★ (Römische Thermen) ⊙, discovered in 1977, a **Roman Museum**★ (Römermuseum) ⊙ – note particularly the fine collection of bronze, and the "Porta decumana", a perfectly reconstructed fortified gateway, in the Kastell Biriciana testify to this significant past. Wießenburg's historical old town centre is worth a visit for the 15C Gothic town hall, the market square and the wooden market with elegant merchants' houses around it.

The **Ellinger Tor**, to the north of the town, is an interesting gateway once part of the surrounding 14C ramparts. The **Andreaskirche** has an elegant Late Gothic chancel built at the beginning of the 15C.

Ellingen – *3km - 1 3/4 miles to the north of Weißenburg.*
This locality owes its fame to the Teutonic Knights *(qv)*, whose Commander for Franconia was based in this small town from the 13C until Napoleon's dissolution of the Order in 1809.
The **castle** (Schloß) ⊙ (1708-1721) comprises an inner courtyard framed by four imposing wings, one of which is entirely occupied by the church.
The huge twin-flight **main staircase★** links the different apartments with a frigid solemnity.

EIFEL★

Nordrhein-Westfalen and Rheinland-Pfalz
Michelin map 417 O-P 4

The Eifel, geographically an eastward extension of the Ardennes, is the largest and most complex of the four Rhineland schist massifs. An undulating plateau at an average altitude of 600m - 1970ft, the region is deeply gashed by the Ahr, the Rur and the Kyll rivers, which meander through picturesque wooded valleys.
The **Upper Eifel** (Hocheifel), in the centre, shows traces of ancient volcanic activity, with basalt crests (Hohe Acht: 747m - 2 450ft), tufa deposits, hot springs and lakes (Maare).
The **Schnee Eifel**, the most rugged and isolated of the four, forms a sombre barrier along the Belgian frontier, northwest of Prum. Much of it rises to 700m - 2 300ft.
The **North Eifel**, a landscape of moors and forests cut by deep valleys, is romantic and attractive. The touristic Seven Lakes sector extends in the northwest to the Upper Fagnes (Hohes Venn), a marshy tableland belonging more to the Ardennes than the Eifel.
The **South Eifel**, bordering Luxembourg's "Little Switzerland", is a region of picturesque valleys with small villages among the trees.

Ahr Wines – The vineyards bordering this river, planted with Burgundian stock on schistous slopes, produce dark red wines late in the season, which are at their best when drunk almost warm.

FROM BAD MÜNSTEREIFEL TO MANDERSCHEID
145km - 90 miles – one day

This excursion follows the busy valley of the Ahr, climbs to the rolling, forested immensity of the Upper Eifel, and then snakes between the volcanic lakes of the Maare.

★ **Bad Münstereifel** – Surrounded by massive **ramparts★** (Stadtbefestigung), the town still boasts a quantity of old houses and monuments. The **Stiftskirche St. Chrysanthus und Daria** is an outstanding abbey church recalling St Pantaleon in Cologne because of the two towers flanking its 11C Romanesque west front.
A few miles east of Münstereifel, the road leaves on the left a giant **radio-telescope**, rejoins the Ahr at Kreuzberg and continues along the winding valley. The telescope is 100m - 328ft in diameter and its parabolic depth is 21m - 69ft.

Altenahr – On a site between two bends in the river, Altenahr is an excursion centre dominated by the scattered ruins of the 12C **Burg Are**. There is an attractive view from the upper terminal of the chairlift.
The valley, in which vineyards now alternate with rock outcrops, plays host to a number of wine producing villages: **Rech**, on either side of its Roman bridge; **Dernau** with its "wine fountain"; **Marienthal** and its ruined convent.

Bad Neuenahr-Ahrweiler – The old town of **Ahrweiler★** still retains its medieval gates and its fortifications. Half-timbered houses line the narrow, pedestrians-only streets of the town centre.
The spa at Bad Neuenahr, much favoured by diabetics, produces *(as you leave the town, on the east)* the celebrated "Apollinaris" sparkling mineral water.
Leaving Ahrweiler, the road climbs swiftly towards the forest before it runs out over a rolling highland area.

★ **Hohe Acht** – *1/2 hour on foot Rtn.*
From the viewpoint at the top of the tower *(75 steps)* erected at the highest point of the Eifel (747m - 2 451ft), there is a superb **panorama★★** to delight the eye – a vast landscape slashed by deep valleys above which the only prominent points are Nürburg castle to the southwest and, in the opposite direction, the ruins of Olbrück In front of the distant Siebengebirge (Seven Mountains).

Nürburg – *1/2 hour on foot Rtn.*
A much-restored ruin in the middle of a rugged **landscape★** which can be admired to the best advantage from the top of the keep.

★ **Nürburgring** – *See NÜRBURGRING.*

Ulmen – A pretty volcanic crater lake between the village and a ruined castle.

★ **The Maare** – The ancient volcanic region of the Maare starts at Daun. The lakes which distinguish it, of modest dimensions, mark the upheavals which occurred in the volcanic areas of the Upper Eifel in the Tertiary era. Gas pressure produced explosions, creating craters with neither cone nor lava but only a surrounding circle of cinders. The water which has gathered within these craters has formed lakes that are both deep and calm. *Follow the green signposts with the word "Maare".*

Gemündener Maar – A small, sombre green lake at the bottom of a wooded funnel, very popular in summer with bathers and canoe enthusiasts.

Weinfelder Maar and Schalkenmehrener Maar – These two lakes fill craters well clear of the road, one on either side.

★ **Pulver Maar** – A perfect circle in form, this is the most beautiful lake in the area.
After the motorway underpass, the route leaves the plateau to follow the pretty, steep-sided valley that leads to Manderscheid.

★ **Manderscheid** – Arriving from Daun, stop at Niedermanderscheid and climb up to the **Niederburg★** ruins. From the top of the castle keep, there is a fine **view★** over the village to the Oberburg ruins and the Lieser valley. Return to the car and drive as far as the Pension Talblick. From here, take the footpath which leads to the **viewpoint★★** overlooking the Oberburg and Niederburg ruins.

EINBECK ★

Niedersachsen – Population 29 400
Michelin map 417/418 K 13

In the Middle Ages, no less than 700 small breweries in this former Hanseatic town supplied the whole of Germany with "Einpöckisches Bier" (from which the modern name Bockbier is derived). Situated between the Harz mountains and the Weser, Einbeck still retains part of its medieval fortifications, but a more attractive heritage is a collection of almost 120 half-timbered 16C houses, richly decorated with multicoloured carvings.

★★ **Half-timbered Houses** – *Time: 1 hour.*
Most of these half-timbered dwellings are near the old market place.

★★ **Marktplatz** – Note first of all the two houses on the corner of the Münsterstraße: the Brodhaus (1552), and especially the Ratsapotheke (1590), an impressive building which has – like most of the old houses – ventilated attics which served as lofts for hops and barley. Opposite is the town hall (Rathaus), its three projecting fronts crowned with unusual pointed roofs.

★ **Ratswaage (Weigh-House)** – The well preserved façade of this ancient weigh-bridge exhibits an embellishment typical of the burghers' houses in Einbeck: fan-shaped, palm-leaf motifs, beaded and twisted mouldings to frame doors and traverses, friezes festooned with garlands.

★★ **Tiedexerstraße** – *Start behind the church tower (Marktkirche).*
The gables and façades on either side of this street offer an especially pleasing perspective.

Marktstraße – Note particularly the **Eickesches Haus**★ (*No 13 in the street, on the corner of the Knochenhauerstraße*). Erected between 1612 and 1614, this wood-built construction ignores the traditional local style and imitates the stone mansions of the Renaissance. Carved panels represent the virtues and the artistic muses in an allegorical cycle; statues and expressive masks adorn the uprights and the beam-ends.

EXCURSIONS

Bad Gandersheim – *22km - 14 miles to the northeast.*
The birthplace of Roswitha von Gandersheim, Germany's first (10C) poetess, is today an appreciated hot spring and salt-water spa. The twin octagonal towers of the **cathedral**★, buttressing the 11C central façade, overlook the historic town centre. Inside are two very fine **altars**, one 15C and the other 16C. Around the market place are many well-preserved half-timbered houses (especially those dating from the 16C) and the **Renaissance town hall**, which adjoins the Moritzkirche.

Alfeld – *24km - 15 miles to the north.*
It is above all the **Alte Lateinschule** (*photograph pp 10-11*) which makes a detour to this town on the banks of the Leine worthwhile.
Today this half-timbered old school building, which dates from 1610 and is adorned with carved figures, is the site of a **local museum** (Stadtmuseum) ⊘.

Four new Michelin Green Guides:
Brussels, Scandinavia-Finland, Tuscany and Venice

EISENACH ★

Thüringen – Population 45 000
Michelin map 418 N 14 – Local map under THÜRINGER WALD

Eisenach was founded at the end of the 12C by Ludwig I, first of the Landgraves of Thuringia. The town, on the northwestern edge of the Forest of Thuringia, is indissolubly linked with the Fortress of **Wartburg**, which not only symbolizes but also externalizes the very spirit of German civilization.

At the Heart of Germany – At the beginning of the 13C, the Minnesänger (troubadours) took part in the famous jousts at Wartburg – a custom which inspired the theme of Wagner's opera *Tannhäuser*. It was at Eisenach that Luther studied before embarking on his translation of the New Testament under the patronage of the Duke of Saxony. **Johann Sebastian Bach** was born there in 1685, when the town was the seat of the Dukes of Saxe-Eisenach, who were obliged to relinquish it in 1741 to the house of Saxe-Weimar.
In 1817, the Wartburg fortress was the site of a manifestation by student corporations designed to stimulate patriotism and progressive ideas. Fifty years later (1869) the "Eisenach Declaration" marked the creation by August Bebel and Wilhelm Liebknecht of the German Social Democrat Party.

MARKT

Schloß – The sober Baroque façade of the castle seals off the northern side of the market place. This former residence of the Dukes of Saxe-Weimar now houses the **Thuringian Museum** ⊘ (porcelain, faience and regional glassware of the 18C and 19C; Rococo banqueting hall).

During the lengthy restoration work on the castle, the Thuringian Museum is closed. The interesting exhibition on Medieval Art in Thuringia is on display in the Predigerkirche during this period.

Rathaus – The town hall is a three-storey 16C building in both Baroque and Renaissance styles, restored after a disastrous fire in 1636. Note the (slightly) leaning tower.

Pfarrkirche St. Georg – This triple-aisle 16C hall-church contains the tombs of several Landgraves of Thuringia. Luther preached here on 2 May 1521, despite the fact that he was officially banned from the Holy Roman Empire *(qv)*, and Johann Sebastian Bach was baptized in this church on 26 March 1685.

Predigerkirche – The church, an Early Gothic (late 13C building), now houses the wooden **sculpture collection★** formerly in the Thuringian Museum (*see above*). The carvings date from the 12C to the 16C.

Lutherhaus ⊘ – It was in this fine late 14C house that Luther lived between 1498 and 1501, while he was a student at the School of Latin. The display includes historical rooms, paintings and literature retracing the history of the Reformation.

OTHER SIGHTS

Bachhaus ⊘ – *From the Lutherhaus, return along the Lutherstraße as far as the Frauenplan.*
Ambrose Bach, himself a musician and an eminent citizen of Eisenach, owned the house at no 21 Frauenplan, which is believed to have been the birthplace of the great composer. The interior of the house provides fascinating insights into the life-style of a late 17C burgher. Manuscripts, scores and portraits recall not only Johann Sebastian Bach but several other members of the family, all of them composers. The music room contains instruments dating from Bach's day.

Automobil-Ausstellungspavillon ⊘ – The entire range of motor cars made in Eisenach is on display here, from vintage models like the Wartburg-Motorwagen, via "Dixi"s and BMWs, to the Wartburg model with a two-stroke engine which was so popular in the former East German Republic.

Fritz-Reuter-und-Richard-Wagner-Museum ⊘ – *Follow the Wartburgallee southwards as far as the Reuterweg.*
The apartment in which Fritz Reuter lived from 1863 to 1874 can be viewed. It was while he was living here that the poet, most of whose work is written in "Plattdeutsch" (Low German), excited the wrath of the Prussian authorities by participating in the Liberal Students' Movement.
The Richard-Wagner-Museum illustrates the life and work of the composer.

★★WARTBURG

time: 2 hours

Leave the car in the car park halfway up the hill, from where it is a 15 min walk up to the fortress.

Perched on a rocky spur, the fortress shows clearly that it combines elements from several different periods. The visitor passes first beneath the porch of an entrance lodge, the oldest parts of which date from the 12C. Beyond this, the **outer courtyard** (Erster Burghof) is framed by half-timbered buildings erected in the 15C and 16C.

The Wartburg fortress, Eisenach

Jogschies/EXPLORER, Paris

A second, inner courtyard leads to the most interesting parts of the fortified complex. On the left, the **Palais★**, where the Landgraves lived, piles three storeys one upon the other, the whole garnished with early 13C arcading.

The fortified wall and south tower give a panoramic **view★** of Eisenach, the Forest of Thuringia and the Rhön foothills.

Interior ⊘ – *Guided tour 1 hour.*
Successively, one passes through: the **Knights' Hall** (Rittersaal), where the vaulting is supported by an outsize central pillar; the **dining room**, with 11C capitals; **Elizabeth's boudoir and gallery**, with mosaics (1902-1906) and frescoes (Moritz von Schwind, 1854) recalling the life of the King of Hungary's daughter; the **Hall of the Troubadours**, with Von Schwind's huge fresco illustrating episodes from the epic jousts of the Minnesänger on the Wartburg; the **Landgraves' Courtroom**, with a central capital illustrating the plunging flight of eagles; the **Great Banqueting Hall**, decorated in a style popular in the middle of the 19C.

Finally, the tour ends in the **Wartburg Museum**, which displays selected works from the Wartburg foundation's collections. There are several paintings by Lucas Cranach the Elder.

Following the watchpath, the last thing to see is **Luther's Room** (Lutherstube).

EXCURSION

★★ Forest of Thuringia – *See THÜRINGER WALD.*

EMDEN

Niedersachsen – Population 50 000
Michelin map 415 F 5
Town plan in the current Michelin Red Guide Deutschland

The silting up of the Ems estuary in the 16C struck the port of Emden a fatal blow. The subsequent construction of dykes, however, together with the opening of the Dortmund-Ems and the Ems-Jade canals, have enabled the town to regain its position as the chief maritime port of Lower Saxony, specializing in shipbuilding and the export of new cars. Large freighters sail into the inner harbour to tranship iron ore destined for the Ruhr, and there are now installations for the processing of North Sea gas.

Emden is the departure point for a daily service to the Isle of Borkum, and for tours of the East Frisian Islands *(see FRIESLAND).*

★ Ostfriesisches Landesmuseum (East Frisian Museum) ⊘ – *In the former town hall.*
Items excavated in peat bog digs, models of the port and fishing boats (Emden was the principal base of the German herring fleet), and paintings by the Dutch School evoke the colourful history of the town. Pride of place is given to the **Rüstkammer★★**, the old burghers' arsenal, which contains a splendid collection of 16-18C side-arms and armour, together with old reproductions illustrating the evolution of the arsenal.

From the bell tower, there is a view of the harbour and surrounding country-side.

Fifteen kilometres - 9 miles to the north is the picturesque fishing port of **Greetsiel**, a colourful sight when the boats are in.

★ Kunsthalle – Stiftung Henri Nannen (Art Gallery) ⊘ – *Hinter dem Rahmen 13; to the northwest of town.*
The post-modern red-brick building houses the sizeable collection of works of art by the German Expressionists and Neue Sachlichkeit *(qv)*, gathered together during his lifetime by founder of *Stern* magazine Henri Nannen, who was born in Emden. The exhibition includes contemporary painting and sculpture.

GERMANY: *the Michelin Map Series at 1:300 000*
When choosing a lunchtime or overnight stop
use the above maps as all towns listed in
the Red Guide Deutschland are underlined in red.

When driving into or through a town
use the map as it also indicates all places with
a town plan in the Red Guide Deutschland.

Common reference numbers make the transfer
from map to plan easier.

ERFURT ★

In the year 742, Wynfrith, a missionary arriving from England who was later canonized as St Boniface *(qv)*, created a bishopric at Erfurt which was soon joined to that of Mainz.

From the Middle Ages onward, the town's position on the important trade route linking the Rhine with Russia lent it such commercial consequence that it was incorporated into the Hanseatic League in the 15C. Erfurt thus became an essential part of the connection uniting Central Europe with the powerful ports of the north.

Spirituality and Humanism – The numerous steeples and bell towers rising above the roofs of the town bear witness to the religious activity in Erfurt under the influence of the Archbishop-Electors of Mainz.

After the Dominican **Master Eckhart**, established in Erfurt from 1303 as Provincial of Saxony, the town was host two centuries later to the young **Martin Luther**. Eckhart was the instigator of what developed into the Rhineland spiritual mystique. Luther studied philosophy at the university – considered to be the cradle of German Humanism – entered the Augustine monastery in 1505 and left six years later to establish himself in Wittenberg *(qv)*.

The Congress of Erfurt – With the aim of persuading the Tzar Alexander I to "neutralize" Austria while he pursued his Spanish campaign, Napoleon received the Russian ruler in Erfurt with great pomp and ceremony from 27 September to 14 October 1808. His plan, backed up with a demonstration of force, was only partly successful: all he could get was a promise of Russian military aid in the case of Austrian aggression. During the 17-day conference, Napoleon met Goethe several times, the two men sharing a mutual admiration, and sub-sequently created him a Che-valier de la Légion d'Honneur.

SIGHTS

★★ **Dom (Cathedral)** – The original Romanesque basilica, built in 1154 on a hill occupied by the citadel, was added to in the middle of the 14C – a porch at the entrance to the north transept; a soaring Gothic chancel at the east end. A century later, the Romanesque nave was replaced by a nave in the Flamboyant Gothic style, with broad side aisles.

★★ **North Entrance** – The porch embodies two doors set obliquely and supporting elegant statuary groups – on the northwest side, the Wise and Foolish Virgins; on the northeast the Apostles at work, a group recalling the French master-masons.

Interior – There are several works of art worthy of attention: the Romanesque Altar of the Virgin (1160); the **statue-candelabra★** known as "the Wolfram" (1160); the tombstone of the Count of Gleichen and his two wives; the intricately worked choir stalls (14C). Some of the **stained glass windows★** above the choir (*c*1370-1420) show scenes of everyday life in the latter part of the Middle Ages.

★ **Severi-Kirche** – Formerly the Augustinian monks' abbey-church, this Early Gothic building is of the hall type, with five naves. The **sarcophagus★** of the saint (*c*1365) is in the southern-most aisle.

Cross the Domplatz and take the Marktstraße.

Northwest door of the cathedral, Erfurt

Jogschies/EXPLORER, Paris

Fischmarkt – Inside the imposing neo-Gothic Rathaus are **frescoes**★ which illustrate the legends and the history of Thuringia. On the north side of the square (nos 13-16) there is a fine three-storey Renaissance building, "Zum Breiten Herd".

★ **Krämerbrücke** – Each side of this bridge, known as "the Grocer's Bridge", there are houses dating from the 17C to the 19C.

Augustinerkloster ⊘ – *Entrance at Augustinerstraße 10.*
The monastery church, founded by hermits in the mid-13C, has a window (*c*1340) illustrating the life of St Augustine. The Gothic cloister leads to the abbey buildings where Luther lived and worked.

★ **Angermuseum** ⊘ – *Anger 18.*
This museum is located in a Baroque building dating from 1706. The focal point of the museum is the exhibition of medieval art from Thuringia (14C and 15C **altarpieces**★★, including the Augustineraltar; a **Pietà**★★ by the Master of St. Severin's sarcophagus; paintings by Hans Baldung Grien depicting the Creation). In the paintings gallery is a collection of 18-19C German landscape painting. Porcelain and faïence produced in the workshops of Thuringia are a prominent feature of the craftwork on display. Note the gem of the museum – a mural by Erich Heckel (1923-4), entitled *Life of Man.*

Barfüßerkirche (Franciscan Church) ⊘ – The nave of this triple-aisle church has been left in a state of ruin since 1944. The reconstructed chancel (consecrated 1316) serves as an extension to the Angermuseum, housing the remaining furnishings (stained glass from 1235-40; the earliest depiction of the Legend of St Francis north of the Alps; altars and impressive tombstones) and temporary exhibitions.

EXCURSIONS

Arnstadt – *16km - 10 miles to the south.*
A small Thuringian town dating from the 8C, but known above all for the fact that JS Bach stayed there from 1703 to 1707, when he was organist at the parish church, which todays bears his name. There is a **Local History Museum** (Museum für Stadtgeschichte) ⊘ outlining the history of the town and displaying mementoes of the composer and literary exhibits in the house named "Zum Palmbaum" on one side of the market place (Am Markt).
In the old cemetery (Alter Friedhof, Bahnhofstraße) are the graves of more than 20 members of the Bach family.
In the **New Palace** (Neues Palais, *August-Bebel-Straße*) ⊘, see the **collection of marionettes and dolls**★ (Mon Plaisir Puppensammlung), the Brussels tapestries of the Renaissance period, and the **porcelain**★ from Meissen and the Far East.

Gotha *25km - 16 miles west.*
This town, first mentioned in 775, flourished in the 15C and 16C thanks to its far-reaching commercial contacts. From 1640 to 1918, the town was the residence of the dukes of Saxe-Gotha. It won world-wide renown through the publication of the Gotha Almanac on the genealogy of the aristocracy. The market square, surrounded by beautiful town houses dating from a variety of periods, stretches as far as the ducal palace. In the lower part of the town, on the Hauptmarkt, stands the **Rathaus**, an elegant Renaissance building (1567-1574), with an eye-catching, richly ornate north façade and beautiful doorway. The massive of the Friedenstein palace, set back slightly from the main line of sight, dominates the town.

★ **Schloß Friedenstein** ⊘ – This austere early Baroque palace, which has three wings, was begun in 1643 under Ernst I the Pious, and finished in 1655. An arcaded gallery around the inner courtyard is the only decorative feature apart from the differently shaped roofs of the corner turrets. However, the visitor is amply compensated for this by the palace interior, which consists of more than thirty rooms decorated in the Baroque, Rococo and Classical styles, with fittings that verge in part on the absolutely sumptous. Note in particular the original stucco ceilings (late 17C), the beautiful marquetry flooring, and the fine quality furniture (from the workshop of Abraham Roentgen among others).
The palace houses numerous collections built up over the centuries by the Gotha dynasty with some later additions.
The **art collection** includes 17C Dutch and Flemish painting, while specialising in 15C and 16C German works. Note especially the **paintings by Lucas Cranach the Elder** and the charming **Gotha Lovers**★, painted by the Master of the Housebook in 1484 and the first ever separate double portrait in German painting. The Gotha altarpiece is also a magnificent work, comprising 157 panels depicting the Life of Christ, making it one of the most heavily illustrated of its kind in German art.
The collection of **Egyptian and Antique art** testifies to the enthusiasm of its founder. Finally, the visitor to the palace should not miss the **Ekhoftheater** (1774).

Schloßpark – The extensive palace gardens, landscaped in the English style, with a number of beautiful old trees and an orangery built from 1747-1767, make a pleasant place for a stroll.

ERZGEBIRGE ★

Sachsen
Michelin map 418/420 ○ 21-22

Known as the Ore Mountains, this medium-height massif owes its name to the many veins
and deposits of silver, tin, cobalt, nickel and iron distributed among its strata – a natural
wealth which has brought prosperity to a number of small towns such as Zwickau *(qv)*,
Annaberg *(qv)*, and Schneeberg.

The crest of the range marking the frontier with the Czech Republic reaches a modest
750m - 2 461ft, and the relatively high altitude of the valley floors frequently gives
the impression more of an upland plateau than a mountain range. The most impressive
single summit on the German side is the **Fichtelberg**, at 1 214m - 3 950ft. Landscapes
that are both open and wooded, reservoir lakes, forests criss-crossed by footpaths
and picturesque holiday villages combine to make the region particularly attractive to
visitors.

The itinerary described below, which explores the western part of the range, follows the
Czech frontier to start with.

FROM ANNABERG-BUCHHOLZ TO KLINGENTHAL

81km - 50 miles (93km - 58 miles via Schwarzenberg) – time: 3 hours

★ **Annaberg-Buchholz** – *See ANNABERG-BUCHHOLZ.*

Leave Annaberg-Buchholz by road no 95 in the direction of Oberwiesenthal.

★ **Fichtelberg** – Towering above the health and winter sports resort of Oberwiesenthal,
this peak is identifiable from far off by the meteorological equipment adorning its
summit. The top is reached by ski-lift or on foot (*1/2 hour Rtn. Leave the car in the
car park 500 yards after the lower ski-lift terminal*). A vast **panorama★** opens out when
the top is reached, showing all of the surrounding country and, away in the south, the
silhouette of Mount Klinovec in the Czech Republic. At 1 244m - 4 800ft, this is the
highest peak of the Erzgebirge.

*From Oberwiesenthal to Ehrenzipfel there is a pretty forest road which follows the
course of a river. At Rittersgrün, one can either take the detour via Schwarzenberg or
continue along the direct route.*

Schwarzenberg – Beside a castle, built on the ruins of ancient fortress at the
beginning of the 15C, stands the **Pfarrkirche St. Georg★**. This Baroque church (1690-
1699) has a wide, very attractively decorated nave. Note the elegant pulpit, apparently supported by a statue, the wrought-iron chancel screen, and the cherubs on
the ceiling.

Sosa Talsperre – *From the car park, walk to the kiosk and then the promontory.* This
small lake and its dam are in an idyllic forest setting.

*The road follows the northern bank of the reservoir formed by the Eibenstock barrage
and then (Route 283) climbs the winding valley of the Zwickauer Mulde before it runs
into* **Klingenthal**.

*Michelin Maps, Red Guides and Green Guides
are complementary publications to be used together.*

ESSEN★

Nordrhein-Westfalen – Population 620 000
Michelin map 417 L 5 – Local map under RUHRGEBIET

Essen is by no means the smoke-blackened industrial complex that many people imagine. On the contrary, the capital of the Ruhr has the air of a residential town, with attractive pedestrian precincts bordered by elegant shops, a lovely art gallery and pleasant suburbs in green surroundings (**Grugapark**, **RS**). Woods, extending southwards, border the tranquil Baldeneysee. Neither steelworks nor blast furnace has resumed activity since the end of the Second World War. The main industry is now the manufacture of machine tools, and there is a permanent exhibition of industrial design at the **Industrial Design Centre** (Design Zentrum Nordrhein-Westfalen) (**DZ B**) ⊙ in the centre of this altogether surprising town.

SIGHTS

★★**Museum Folkwang** (**R**) ⊙ – *Museumszentrum.*
This museum houses a major collection of 19C and 20C painting, sculpture, graphic art and photography, particularly rich in works of art from Germany and France: German Romantics (Carus, C D Friedrich, Koch) and 19C Realists (Böcklin, Feuerbach, Leibl), French Realists (Corot, Courbet, Daumier) and Impressionists, and French Cubists (Braque, Delaunay, Léger, Picasso) and Surrealists (Dalí, Ernst, Magritte).

ESSEN

A Johanniskirche
B Design Zentrum
  Nordrhein-Westfalen
M' Domschatzkammer

Works by the artists of the Brücke group (Heckel, Kirchner, Nolde, Pechstein), the Blauer Reiter (Kandinsky, Macke, Marc) and the Bauhaus (Feininger, Klee) demonstrate the tremendous variety of German Impressionism and art of the 20C. Note also sculptures by Rodin, Barlach, Lehmbruck and Archipenko, and the collection of post-1945 art, the Paris School and Art Informel, and works by Baselitz, Kiefer, Lüpertz, Penck and Richter, as well as Americans Pollock, Newman and Stella.

Münster (Cathedral) (DZ) – The 10C **west chancel★**, with three angled side walls, is the oldest part of the building. It was directly influenced by that in the cathedral at Aachen. The nave, a Gothic hall with ogive vaulting, dates from the end of the 13C; the Ottonian crypt now has stained glass windows by Manessier. Off the northern aisle, there is a lateral chapel housing a priceless work: **The Golden Madonna★★★**, said to be the oldest (980AD) statue of the Virgin in the West. In the western part of the church there is a gigantic seven-branch candelabra (c1000) decorated with geometric motifs. The **cathedral treasury★★** (Domschatzkammer) **(DZ M')** ☉ holds four splendid **processional crosses★★★** (10 and 11C), the Golden Madonna's crown, monstrances, gospels, and the sword of the martyr-saints Cosmas and Damian.

Johanniskirche (DZ A) – Originally a baptistry of the cathedral chapter – from which it is separated by an 11C atrium – this meditation chapel was transformed into a hall-church c1470. In the south aisle, an **altarpiece★** painted by Bartholomäus Bruyn the Elder (16C) represents scenes from the life of Jesus.

★ Villa Hügel (S) – This mansion stands in an attractive park on the north shore of the Baldeney lake. It was built in 1872, after designs by Alfred Krupp. The complex included a residential wing and a guest wing, connected by a lobby, and could boast 269 bedrooms, 103 of which merit being classified as suites. Until 1945, the Villa Hügel was home to three successive generations of the Krupp family. Since 1953, it has been open to the public. The construction and fittings of the great house date from 1915. The 15C-18C tapestries are one of the main features to have survived from the mansion's earlier magnificent décor. The Villa now houses temporary exhibitions. The **Krupp Collections★★** (Historische Sammlung Krupp) ☉ themselves are housed in the smaller house. They offer an insight into the extraordinary success story of this family business, which started in 1811 with Friedrich Krupp's construction of the first steel-casting crucible and subsequently reflected the entire growth and development of heavy industry in Germany.

Abteikirche St. Ludger (S) – The structure of this building is Romanesque (12C), but hints of early Gothic design are already evident, particularly in the ogive vaulting of the nave. The transept crossing is surmounted by a **dome on pendentives★**. In the treasury, note an 11C bronze **crucifix★** with a particularly pure line, as well as a 5C ivory pyx. In the crypt is one of the rare pierced galleries in Germany, from which pilgrims praying could at the same time venerate the tomb of St Ludger, lying in a central vault.

ESSLINGEN AM NECKAR

Baden Württemberg – Population 91 000
Michelin map 419 T 11
Town plan in the current Michelin Red Guide Deutschland

The old Swabian town of Esslingen, at the foot of the vine-covered banks of the Neckar, retains, especially on the east bank of the river, all the atmosphere of a one-time free imperial city. Visually, the town is distinguished by belfries, the Burg tower, and ruins of the 13C fortifications.

SIGHTS

Marktplatz – The finest ornament to this picturesque, irregularly shaped square, which dates only from the 19C, is the Kielmeyer house. All the streets leading into the market are interesting, most of them bordered by old houses decorated with wood carvings.

★ **Altes Rathaus** – This 15C and 16C building combines the severe charm of old half-timbering with the gracefulness of decorated Renaissance façades. The curvilinear stepped gable overlooking the Rathausplatz is surmounted by a double lantern (carillon) and vibrant with colour. But it is the south gable above all which must be seen – an outstanding feature typical of Swabian half-timbering, with heavy corbels and obliquely crossed beams.

St. Dionysius-Kirche – A Gothic building, its towers oddly linked by a footbridge, which overlooks the Marktplatz. The name of its patron saint recalls the fact that Esslingen, originally a hermitage, was given in the 8C to the great Frankish Abbey of St Denis.
Inside the church, a rood screen divides the nave. Beyond this, a 15C Pietà adorns the lintel of a door on the south side. Fine 13C and 14C stained glass illuminates the chancel.

Frauenkirche – A pleasing architectural unity distinguishes this Gothic church, which stands on a hillside and can be reached from the Marktplatz via the Untere Beutau rise. From the west there is a fine view of the ornate church tower flanked by twin staircase turrets. The interior is richly decorated. The doorways are especially noteworthy – in the southeast, the Life of the Virgin (1350); in the southwest a 15C Last Judgement. Note the stained glass windows (1330) in the chancel.

FLENSBURG★

Schleswig-Holstein – Population 87 000
Michelin map 415 B 12
Town plan in the current Michelin Red Guide Deutschland

The port of Flensburg lies at the head of a sinuous arm of the sea, the **Flensburger Förde**★, appreciated by holidaymakers who can sail pleasure craft up numerous inlets shaded by beech trees. A glance at shop signs and newspaper kiosks along the quays or on the Holm, the town's principal artery, will confirm the immediate proximity of the **Danish border** ☉. Germany's most northern town, Flensburg lives mainly from its naval shipyards and its rum and spirit trade.

SIGHTS

★ **Städtisches Museum (Municipal Museum)** ☉ – There is an attractive choice of antiques offering a perspective on the art and culture of Schleswig-Holstein (including that part of Schleswig that is now Danish). The **furniture and household items** on display include cupboards, trunks and marvellous wedding chests from the Gothic and Renaissance periods. Brass and copper gleam from the carefully reconstructed peasant and bourgeois interiors in the lower rooms. Note especially the room containing works by the painter Emil Nolde.

Commercial and Warehouse Quarter – Maritime trade with Norway, the Baltic and the East Indies, inseparable from Flensburg's prosperous past, is recalled by these buildings (**Kaufmannshöfe und Speicherhäuser**), mainly of the 18C, restored as part of an old town rehabilitation project. Note particularly the **Handelshof** (at no 86 Norderstraße), the **Künstlerhof** (no 22 in the same street), and the **Westindienspeicher** at Große Straße 24 (in the courtyard).

Nikolaikirche – Overlooking the bustling Südermarkt, this massively proportioned brick church dates from the Gothic period (late 14C). There is a fine **Renaissance organ**★ (1609) inside.

Nordertor (North Gate) – This simply designed late 16C structure, with stepped gables over its brick façade, has become the symbol of the town.

EXCURSION

Glücksburg – *9km - 5 miles to the north.*
The road offers glimpses of the Flensburger Förde, and then suddenly the **Wasserschloß Glücksburg** ⊙ swims into view, apparently floating on the waters of its own lake. Four corner towers link the three wings of the 1585 building, said to have been inspired by the French Château de Chambord, on the Loire. The castle is distinguished by a simplicity of decoration typical of northern Renaissance architecture.
A visit recalls memories of the House of Oldenburg-Schleswig-Holstein, to which the Danish Royal Family is related. Do not miss the great **banqueting hall** (Roter Saal) on the first floor. The heavy vaulting is delicately embellished with coffering, between which stars, rosettes and miniature busts are inserted. Note also the unusual **leather hangings**, embossed with designs in silver and gold, which were crafted in Mechelen (Belgium) in 1703.

FRANKFURT AM MAIN★★

Hessen – Population 627 500
Michelin map 417 P 10
Plan of the conurbation in the current Michelin Red Guide Deutschland

At the crossroads of the country's north-south and east-west communications, a truly cosmopolitan city rich in traditions, Frankfurt is the commercial capital of Germany. Owing to its central position, numerous government organizations, including the Federal Bank, are based there. Research institutes, the university founded in 1914, the opera, theatres and an ever increasing number of museums have made the city the scientific and cultural metropolis of the Hessen Land.

HISTORICAL NOTES

The historic centre of the town is the **cathedral hill** (Domhügel), on which there were already fortifications and a palace in Roman and Carolingian times.

When the Emperors Ruled – In 1152, Frederick Barbarossa engineered his election as King of Germania at Frankfurt, thus inaugurating a tradition which was to be ratified by the Golden Bull *(qv)* of the Emperor Charles IV in 1356. Two centuries later, in 1562, the town replaced Aachen as the **coronation place** of the rulers of the Holy Roman Empire – a privilege it retained until the dissolution of the Reich in 1806. In Poetry and Truth *("Dichtung und Wahrheit")*, Goethe describes in great detail the sumptuous ceremonies and popular enthusiasm he witnessed as a boy when Josef II was crowned in 1764.

The Young Goethe – Johann Wolfgang von Goethe was born in Frankfurt in 1749, the son of a worthy Imperial Counsellor and a lively, charming, much younger woman. The great writer frequently described his debt to his parents, especially in his memoirs (*Aus meinem Leben*). To his father he owed his serious attitude to life, to his mother a happy temperament and a love of telling stories.
At the age of 15 he fell in love for the first time, with a girl called Gretchen – who was later to serve as a model for the the character of Gretchen in **Faust**. After the tragic love affair at Wetzlar *(qv)*, where he was studying to be a young lawyer, Goethe returned to Frankfurt where, between 1772 and 1775 he enjoyed his most prolific period as a writer. It was during this period that **Werther**, based on the Wetzlar tragedy, was completed in four weeks.

Finance and Economy – In the 16C Frankfurt was granted the right to mint money. The money market rapidly flourished and the **stock exchange** was founded.
German banks dominated the economy in the 18C; in the 19C they acquired a worldwide reputation thanks to financiers such as **Bethmann** and above all **Rothschild** (1744-1812) whose sons, "the Five Frankfurters", established branches in Paris, London, Vienna and Naples. Profiting from such an economic climate, industries were not long to establish themselves in the city. Chemicals and pharmaceuticals (Hoechst) remain the most active today.
The first Autumn Fair was held in 1240. The Spring Fair was added in 1330. Since the war the Fur Fair (Pelzmesse), the Motor Show (Automobilausstellung) and the famous **Book Fair** (Buchmesse) have confirmed Frankfurt as the country's commercial capital.

FRANKFURT TODAY

City Life – Despite its cosmopolitan character (one inhabitant in four is foreign), this "metropolis on the Main" has managed to preserve a typical Hessian atmosphere. It is around the **Hauptwache** (**GY**), a square dating from 1729 at the junction of the Roßmarkt and the **Zeil** (**HY**), that the life of Frankfurt is at its busiest. The Zeil is said to be the most shopped-in street in Germany.
To the north, the quarter known as the Westend, a tranquil, shady residential area from the Bismarck era, fights to stave off the encroaching office blocks of the commercial centre.

Cafés, cabarets, bars, and restaurants, often exotic, are grouped around the central station, while the taverns of the Alt Sachsenhausen quarter, on the south bank of the Main, specialize in the celebrated **Äppelwoi** (a very dry cider), and Handkäs mit Musik (small yellow cheeses in an onion sauce).

A General View – The old town, almost entirely destroyed in 1943-1944, lay within a green belt on the site of former fortifications razed in 1805. The **Eschenheimer Turm** (**GHY**) still stands however as a well-preserved example of the medieval defence system. The tower dates from 1428.

After 1945, a small kernel of the **old town** was reconstructed around the Römerberg. The contrast between its modest silhouettes and those of the business quarter skyscrapers is at its most striking when seen from the southern end of the **Untermainbrücke** (**GZ**) river bridge. Between the apse of the old Carmelite church and the cathedral, one can see (from left to right) the dome of the Paulskirche, the sharply pointed roofs of the Römer, the Leonhardskirche on the riverside, the soaring steeple of the Nikolaikirche and finally, at the end of the Eiserner Steg (a metal bridge), the Saalhof, a one-time Imperial Palace of which only the Gothic corner tower remains. The most imposing skyscrapers are the Fair Tower, the Deutsche Bank and the Dresdener Bank.

From the 120m - 394ft **Henninger Turm** (**HZ**) ⊙, *(leave by the Paradiesgasse)* in the Sachsenhausen quarter, there is a **panorama**★ taking in the town, the river, the sprawling forest of the Stadtwald and the wooded massif of the Taunus *(qv)*.

OLD TOWN *time: one half day*

Römer and Römerberg (**HZ R**) – The **Römer** is a disparate collection of (reconstructed) medieval burghers' houses. From 1405 the block served as a town hall, and subsequently as the banquet hall for the election and coronation of the Emperors. The most characteristic façade, with three stepped Gothic gables, overlooks the Römerberg. The name applied to the whole complex derives from the **Haus Zum Römer**, the centre of three houses and also the oldest and most richly decorated. The four statues of Emperors, above a balcony with a carved balustrade and beneath imperial eagles, are 19C additions. A graceful pierced Renaissance stairway adorns the small inner courtyard. In the 19C, to celebrate the thousand-year history of the Holy Empire, 52 statues of Emperors, from Charlemagne to Franz II (1806) were installed in niches hollowed from the walls of the **Imperial Hall** (Kaisersaal) ⊙.

The southern side of the **Römerberg** is closed off by the **Alte Nikolaikirche** (**A**), built in the 13C from the local red sandstone. The building is crowned by a gallery with four corner turrets, from which the city officials and their families would observe the lively popular fairs and fêtes. In the southwest corner is the **Haus Wertheim** (**B**), a fine half-timbered mansion in Late Renaissance (1600) style.

On the north side of the square, the 1464 **Steinernes Haus** (**C**) was clearly built in imitation of an Italian city mansion. A row of half-timbered houses dating from the 15C to the 18C (all reconstructed) flank the Römerberg to the east. In the centre of the square is the **Gerechtigkeitsbrunnen** (Fountain of Justice) (1543).

The restored sector of old Frankfurt is right next door to the post-modern **Kunsthalle Schirn** (**D**) – a long, low, domed cultural centre, stark and uncompromising, where exhibitions of contemporary art are organized.

★ **Dom (Bartholomäuskirche)** (**HZ**) – This church was designated a cathedral after it had been chosen first as the election and subsequently the coronation site of the Emperors (1356 and 1562 - *see above*). A Gothic hall-church with three naves and a wide transept, it was built between the 13C and the 15C on a hill previously occupied by a Carolingian edifice. Its outstanding feature is the tall **west tower**★★ (Westturm), ornamented with a gabled polygonal crown topped by a dome and lantern, although this was not in fact completed until 1877, following the plans of the cathedral's original architect, Madern Gerthener.

In the columned peristyle erected in front of the tower in neo-Gothic style after the fire of 1867, note the outstanding grey sandstone sculpture of **The Crucifixion** (1509) – the work of the Mainz artist Hans Backoffen.

Inside, the finely worked **choir stalls**★ are due to a master-craftsman from the Upper Rhine (*c*1350). The (restored) **mural paintings**, which date from 1427, are the work of a Master of the Cologne School *(qv)*. They illustrate the legend of St Bartholomew. In a niche on the south side of the chancel is the tombstone (1352) of Count Günther von Schwarzburg, unsuccessful rival to the Emperor Charles IV for the title of King of Germania. A door alongside leads to the chapel (Wahlkapelle: early 15C) where the seven Electors of the Holy Roman Empire in Germany *(qv)* made their final choice.

In the opposing chapel (north chancel) is the **Altar of Mary Sleeping** (Maria-Schlaf), which dates from 1434. Sole remaining altar from the church's original interior furnishings, this too is the work of the Cologne School. It represents the twelve Apostles grouped around the bed of the dying Mary. The large **Descent from the Cross** hanging on the west wall of the north chancel was painted by Anthony van Dyck in 1627.

★ **Cathedral Museum** (Dommuseum) ◷ – This has been installed in what remains of the Gothic cloister. Note the sumptuous **ornaments** worn by the ecclesiastic Electors at the coronation ceremonies. The oldest vestments date from the 15C.

West of the cathedral is an **Archaeological Garden** (Historischer Garten), where the remains of Roman and Carolingian fortifications can be seen.

Historisches Museum (**HZ M¹**) ◷ – This museum retraces the history of the city of Frankfurt from the time of its earliest settlers to the present. Exhibits include sculpture, glassware, porcelain, items illustrating technological evolution, a numismatic collection and a display of graphics.

Three models of the city *(on the ground floor)* represent Frankfurt in the Middle Ages, at the end of the Second World War and as it is at present. Behind this display, a passage leads off to a 12C chapel, the **Saalhofkapelle**, which is the oldest building in the city – in fact all that remains of the old Emperors' Palace.

Museum für Moderne Kunst (**Modern Art Museum**) (**HY M¹⁰**) ◷ – The Viennese architect, Hans Hollein, has achieved a spacious custom-built gallery in spite of the rather cramped and awkwardly-shaped site. The building in the form of a boat makes an interesting landmark in the cathedral quarter. The imaginatively designed interior is surprisingly large and makes an ideal setting for the mainly contemporary art collection. The New York school is represented by George Segal *(Jazz Combo)*, Roy Lichtenstein *(Brush-stroke)*, Claes Oldenburg and Andy Warhol. On the ground floor there is a work by Katharina Frische *(Tischgesellschaft)* remarkable in its disproportion. Also represented are Joseph Beuys with a monumental bronze installation, Mario Merz and one of his famous Igloos and Gerhard Richter and his oppressive *Stammhein Cycle (Stammhein Zyklus)*.

Rudolf Nagel/Museum für Moderne Kunst

Museum für Moderne Kunst

The modern art collection is complemented by a collection of photographs by Thomas Ruff (monumental portraits), the husband and wife team Becher and Blume and Jeff Wall.

Leonardskirche (**HZ**) – The outer aspect of this 15C Gothic church denies its Romanesque basilican origins. Two octagonal towers remain at the east end, along with the fine carvings of **Master Engelbert's Doorway** – although these can only be seen from inside (north aisle) now, as aisles were subsequently added on either side. The central nave, almost square, is surrounded on three sides by a gallery. Fine stained glass windows illuminate the chancel. Left of the chancel are a superbly carved reredos representing scenes from the life of the Virgin, and a painting by Holbein the Elder depicting the **Last Supper**. The baptismal chapel of the north aisle displays a very large hanging keystone.

Paulskirche (**HZ**) – It was in this circular building dating from the beginning of the classic era (again, reconstructed) that the German National Assembly elected after the revolution of March sat from 1848 to 1849. The church houses an exhibition devoted to the history of the German democratic movement.

Liebfrauenkirche (**HY E**) – The church, today a Capuchin monastery, was built as a Gothic hall-church in the 14C. The interior was remodelled in the Rococo style in the 18C.

The early 15C tympanum of the south doorway (the Adoration of the Magi, inside) is attributed to the architect and sculptor Gerthener (*see above*).

★ **Goethe-Haus and Goethe-Museum** (**GZ**) ◷ – "The house is spacious, light and tranquil, with freestanding staircases, large vestibules and several windows with pleasant views of the garden" – it was thus that Goethe described the paternal home. An atmosphere lingers in these rooms today of ease and serenity, of a taste for the good things of life, of a love of Italy transmitted from the father to the son. Paintings on the walls evoke memories of family friends, while details of the Goethes' day to day life are recalled by the pots and pans in the kitchen.

The room in which the poet wrote – reconstructed like the rest of the house after the war – is as it was in his lifetime, haunted by memories of the object of his youthful passion, Charlotte Buff. Even his old marionette theatre is in its place in the next room.

The **Museum** adjoining Goethe's birthplace displays documents and manuscripts relating to his life and work, as well as paintings by such artists as Tischbein, Fuseli and Hackert (note especially Fuseli's *The Nightmare*, 1781). The museum also houses temporary exhibitions devoted to contemporary artistic and literary life.

Jüdisches Museum (Jewish Museum) (**GZ M³**) ⊘ – In the Rothschild-Palais (1821). Organized according to the most modern of museographic procedures, the exhibits trace the history of Frankfurt's Jewish community – one of the largest in Germany – from the Middle Ages to the present day.

SOUTH BANK OF THE MAIN

The south bank of the river, between the Eiserner Steg and the Friedensbrücke, is known to Frankfurters as the **Museumsufer**. An impressive series of museums does in fact stretch the length of the Schaumainkai in a middle-class residential area attractively interspersed with green spaces. The creation and development of projects such as the Museum of Applied Arts and the Museum of Architecture, started in the 1980s and now enjoying worldwide renown, has been skilfully integrated within this area of well-kept gardens and quiet streets.

★★ **Städelsches Kunstinstitut and Städtische Galerie (GZ)** ⊘ – On the second floor there is an important collection of **Flemish Primitives** and **16C German Masters**.

Room A: Van der Weyden, Hieronymus Bosch (Ecce Homo), Hans Memling (Man in a Red Cap), Jan van Eyck (the famous Lucca Madonna); **Room B:** Altdorfer (Adoration of the Magi); **Room D:** H Baldung Grien (Birth and Baptism of Chirst). There are also remarkable altarpieces, most of them from Frankfurt churches, including the main reredos of the Dominican church which embodies The Genealogy of Christ by Hans Holbein the Elder. In **Cabinets 19 and 20** there are several interesting works by Brueghel the Elder.

Added to this collection are early Renaissance paintings from Italy (Fra Angelico, Botticelli), including the Mannerists (Tintoretto, Veronese); **17C Flemish work** with the Masters **Rubens** and **Rembrandt** (The Blinding of Samson, 1636); **French Baroque Painting** (Poussin, Lorrain, Watteau, Chardin); and the masterworks of **Adam Elsheimer**, an early Baroque painter born in Frankfurt, who settled in Rome from 1600 (the Holy Cross altarpiece).

German works from the 18C and 19C dominate the first floor, among them the memorable meditation of Goethe in the Roman Countryside, painted by **JHW Tischbein** in 1787. French Impressionism is represented by **Renoir** and **Monet** (The Breakfast Party).

German Expressionists exhibited include Beckmann, Kirchner and Marc. Matisse, Picasso and Braque represent that part of the modern movement influenced by Fauvism and the Cubists. Max Ernst, Paul Klee and Feininger introduce Surrealism and the art of the Bauhaus. Contemporary art is represented by Dubuffet, Bacon, Tapiès and Yves Klein. Part of the museum display is also given over to an extensive **graphics collection**.

★ **Museum für Kunsthandwerk (Museum of Applied Arts) (HZ)** ⊘ – The museum building (1985) was designed by the New York architect Richard Meier, a pupil of Marcel Breuer at the Bauhaus (qv). Integrated within the design is the classically-styled Villa Metzler (1803).

Purity of line, richness of material and colour are all enhanced by the flood of light entering this airy, spacious building from every side. This is especially true of the furniture: medieval, 16C folding chairs, carved Renaissance and Baroque cupboards and chests, jewel-encrusted commodes and cabinets as well as Jugendstil items. The **glassware collection** (15C and 16C Venetian work) is particularly interesting; and plenty of space is given to German stoneware from the 15C to the 19C, and faience from Delft, Hanau and Berlin.

The **Islamic department** (second floor) contains carpets from Persia and Anatolia, furniture and weapons, and above all glassware and faience from 9C to the 15C.

The **Far East department** (also on the second floor) displays bronze statues (14C to 17C) from China and Tibet; Chinese porcelain from the Ming and Ch'ing periods, including the white and the blue porcelain from the 17C and 18C; and a fine collection of lacquer.

Objects from the Rococo and Classical periods are exhibited in the former Villa Metzler.

It is here that there is another remarkable **porcelain collection** assembled from the major European manufacturers in Meißen, Berlin, Fürstenberg, Nymphenburg, Vienna, Höchst and Sèvres.

The **book and calligraphy section** (in the new building) has temporary exhibitions of selected highlights from its rich collection of material.

★ **Deutsches Filmmuseum (German Cinema Museum) (GZ M⁷)** ⊘ – Here, the film buff may examine (first floor) the different inventions relating to the discovery of animation: stroboscopic discs, Emile Reynaud's 1882 Praxinoscope, a Thaumatrope, Edison's Kineto-scope (1889), and a copy of the Lumière Brother's Cinematograph (1894). A reconstruction of the Meliès studio recalls the first film director. Daguerreotypes, a magic lantern and a dark room conjure up the beginnings of cinema.

On the second floor, visitors – introduced backstage, as it were, in both silent and talking studios faithfully reconstructed – can amuse themselves composing different shots. Designs, drawings and models illustrate the techniques of special effects (King Kong, for instance). A small working cinema shows newsreels, publicity shots and shorts several times a day.

On the premises are also a **film and video library** and the local cinema.

Städtische Galerie Liebieghaus (Liebieg Museum of Sculpture) (GZ M⁴) ⊘ – Here there are fine examples of sculpture and statuary from different civilizations, from **ancient Egypt** to the **Classical era**. Egypt: head of a dignitary (Middle Kingdom). Greece and Rome: statuettes; small bronze horse (8C BC); woman's head (2C BC); Tanagra figurines.

There are also Roman copies of the great Greek sculptures: Myron's Athena, the Torso of Polycletus, and the famous Praxiteles Satyr.

Equally interesting is the section devoted to the Middle Ages. A Virgin and Child (Trier, 11C), the Head of Bärbel von Ottenheim (NG van Leyden, 1463), the Rimini Reredos (c1430), another Virgin and Child (French, 14C) and a Madonna by Riemenschneider – all these convey an idea of the wealth of talent working in that period. The genius of the Renaissance is exemplified by Andrea della Robbia's altarpiece of The Madonna of the Girdle (c 1500) and a small Black Venus with Mirror (16C).

Deutsches Postmuseum (German Postal Museum) (GZ M⁵) ⊘ – The history of communications systems from the earliest prototypes to state-of-the-art modern technological developments, displayed in appropriate historical contexts.

Deutsches Architektur-Museum (German Architectural Museum) (GZ M⁶) ⊘ – For this museum, inaugurated in 1984, the architect Oswald Mathias Ungers designed an original and extremely controversial complex incorporating a magnificent villa of the Bismarck period into an ultra-modern construction.

Examples of modern architecture from all over the world are on display, as well as the best of interior design. A collection of architects' **plans and models** (19C and 20C) is on display.

A series of tableaux illustrates the evolution of human settlement with different types of houses from various civilizations.

Museum für Völkerkunde (Museum of Ethnography) (GZ M⁸) ⊘ – This museum puts on special exhibitions only, on themes to do with either comparative ethnography or individual ethnic groups. The museum collections are particularly well-endowed with exhibits from South America, especially Bolivia, Sumatra, Flores and East Indonesia, Central Africa and Ethiopia, and the Sepik river basin in Papua-New Guinea.

ADDITIONAL SIGHTS

★★★**Zoo** ⊘ – Leave by Zeil **(HY)**.

The Frankfurt zoo is famous for its rare species (over 5 000 examples of 600 species), which are encouraged, successfully, to reproduce. The animals live in their natural habitat. The bird section, with its huge free-flight aviary, is particularly colourful, the occupants at liberty to fly around the visitors.

Penguins, reptiles, fish and insects inhabit the Exotarium. There is an amazing beehive with thousands of bees busily at work. In the **Grzimek-Haus**, darkened by day, nocturnal animals such as the desert fox can be observed.

★ **Naturmuseum Senckenberg (Senckenberg Natural History Museum)** ⊘ – Leave by the Bockenheimer Landstraße **(GY M⁹)**.

Opened in 1821, this museum is distinguished by its remarkable **Department of Palaeontology**★★ (ground floor). Fossils from the Lower Jurassic (Lias) are on display in the entrance hall, most discovered near Holzmaden, in Württemberg. They include ichthyosaurus, sea crocodiles and crinoids – which despite their vegetal appearance were in fact marine animals.

In the **Hall of Dinosaurs** (Room 5), the skeletons of huge beasts from the Secondary Era are on view: diplodocus, iguanodon, triceratops, stegosaurus and plateosaurus (both original and in the form of mouldings). In Room 6 there are impressive fossils including sea crocodiles, ichthyosaurus and the reptile with enormous teeth – placodus, which fed on whole crustaceans. In Room 8 there are turtles, tortoises, whales and an anaconda in the act of swallowing a sea pig. Room 9 (at the foot of the staircase) displays objects found in **Jurassic digs** – most of them near Solnhofen, on the banks of the Altmühl, where the archeopteryx was found.

Naturmuseum Senckenberg

See also an even older ancestor of the bird, the pterodactyl; a fish with circular teeth; and a dinosaur with a beak (tracodon), which lived in North America.

The great land and sea mammals (elephants, whales) are in Room 10. Nos 12 and 13 trace the evolution of the human race (numerous implements, weapons, etc., found in digs). In the rooms opposite, a geological display gives an insight into the dramatic forming of the Earth's crust and an overview of the evolution of life on Earth. A window into the geographical past is provided by the perfectly preserved fossils from the archaeological dig at Messel near Darmstadt. An interesting collection of stuffed animals (armadillo, apes), reptiles (python with 377 vertebrae) and birds can be seen on the first floor. On the second are insects, and marine vertebrates and invertebrates. Dioramas show mammals in their natural habitat. Tanks house both freshwater and marine fish.

★ **Palmengarten (Tropical Gardens)** ⊙ – *Leave by the Bockenheimer Landstraße* (**GY**).
These botanical gardens include a large area given over to various **greenhouses**, containing tropical plants, palms, Alpine plants, etc., and also exotic plants such as orchids, cacti and bromeliaceae (pineapples). The park itself is home many beautiful old trees and features various types of specialised garden (herbaceous borders, rock gardens, rhododendrons, rose gardens).

EXCURSIONS

Offenbach – *7km - 4 1/2 miles to the east. Leave on the Deutschherrn-Ufer* (**HZ**). *Town plan in the current Michelin Red Guide Deutschland.*
This town on the south bank of the Main is the centre of the German leather industry (International Leather Fair twice a year).

★★ **Deutsches Ledermuseum** (Leather Museum) ⊙ – *At Frankfurter Straße 86.*
The museum contains some interesting collections of articles made from leather, especially vellum and hides. There is an exhibition on tanning on the ground floor. On the first floor, the display covers the use of leather in various domains such as sport, travel and leisure, within Europe. the second floor looks at the use of leather in non-European countries (cowboys and Indians, Eskimos, shadow theatres). There is an interesting collection of handbags and suitcases, as well as some more unusual exhibits (such as one of Napoleon's portfolios). The **Shoe Museum** in the same building presents a history of foot fashion in all its variety, from Ancient Egyptian and Roman sandals to modern footwear. The section on shoes as works of art is particularly interesting.

★ **Friedberg** – *28km - 17 miles to the north on the Friedberger Landstraße* (**HY**).
This is an attractive example of a medieval community with two distinct centres: the town enclosed within the imperial castle and the bourgeois town grouped at the foot of the church, at either end of the main street (Kaiserstraße).
The **castle** (Stauferburg) erected by Frederick Barbarossa in 1180 together with its outbuildings still has the air of a small, self-sufficient town. The ramparts, now a promenade, have been made even more attractive with bays of greenery and lookout points. **Adolf's Tower★** (Adolphsturm, 1347) overlooks the assembled buildings.
The **Jewish Baths** (Judenbad, 13C) – at Judengasse 20, in the bourgeois sector – is a deep, square well with a dome, which served originally for ritual ablutions required by Jewish law. Columns with Gothic capitals support the arches over the stairway *(74 difficult steps)* leading 25m - 80ft to the water.
The **church** (Stadtkirche) is a 13-14C building with a typically Hessian exterior – transverse attics with separate gables jutting from the roof above the aisles. The façade is unusual, its towers resting on Gothic arches. Inside, an unusually tall **ciborium★** (1482) stands in the chancel. On the left of the rood-screen is the **Friedberg Madonna** (c1280).

★ **The Taunus** – *Round tour of 62km - 39 miles – 4 hours.*
The Taunus is limited in extent, but reaches at the Großer Feldberg a greater height (880m - 2 997ft) than any of the other Rhineland schist massifs *(qv)*. The area is covered by magnificent forests, and there are many mineral springs which have been developed into spas.

★ **Konigstein im Taunus** – The fortress here, on a height isolated from the main Taunus slopes, is a **feudal ruin** (Burgruine) ⊙ with impressive foundations: round 16C bastions and 17C projecting defences. Climb the keep (*166 steps*) for a **bird's eye view** of the small town and the surrounding woods.

★ **Großer Feldberg** ⊙ – The tower and antennae of an important telecommunications centre top this height. From the tower's observation platform visitors can enjoy an immense **panorama★★** including the Westerwald tableland to the northwest, the Wetterau depression to the northeast and, in the southeast, the plain of the Lower Main invaded by the outskirts of Frankfurt.

Saalburg – This is a complete Roman fortress camp in the middle of the forest, reconstituted on the orders of Kaiser Wilhelm II on the Limes (fortified lines marking the northern limit of Roman occupation). Note the external trenches and, in the inner courtyard, buildings which now house a Roman museum.

★ **Bad Homburg vor der Höhe** – *Town plan in the current Michelin Red Guide Deutschland.*
In 1840, the opening of a casino by the **Blanc Brothers** transformed this little spa into one of Europe's gaming capitals. But the establishment was obliged to close its doors in 1872.

Today the life of most visitors centres on the **Spa Park★** (Kurpark), where pavilions containing the health-giving springs are dispersed over shady lawns.

The **castle**, dominated by the tall White Tower – a survival of the original fortress – was successively the residence of the Landgraves of Hesse-Homburg, then the summer palace of the Prussian Kings (who became, after Wilhelm I in 1871, the Emperors of Germany).

A well-known exhibit in the castle is the artificial limb of Friedrich II (1633-1708), known locally as "the silver leg" because the joints of the wooden limb are fashioned from the precious metal.

FREIBURG IM BREISGAU★★

Baden-Württemberg – Population 179 000
Michelin map 419 V 7 – Local map under Der SCHWARZWALD

One of the most attractive cities in southern Germany, Freiburg was founded in the 12C by the Dukes of Zähringen, who conferred upon it a number of special privileges (Freiburg or "free town"). When the dynasty died out in 1388, the town passed under Habsburg rule. It was here, in May 1770, that the Archduchess Marie-Antoinette said farewell to Austrian territory and set out for Strasbourg, where she was greeted in the name of France by Cardinal Rohan as the bride of the future Louis XVI – and foredoomed victim of the guillotine in 1793.

Five centuries of Austrian rule, which was only ended by Napoleon, left the city with an agreeable, easygoing life-style appreciated by young and old alike. The climate can be hot, but a refreshing breeze blows gently from the Upper Black Forest at nightfall and, streams ("Bächle") from the nearby mountains sweeten the air – many running in open gullies beside the ancient streets between the cathedral and the Schwabentor.

SIGHTS

★★**Münster (Cathedral) (Y)** – Of the original Romanesque building, started c1200, only the transept crossing and the two "Cockerel Towers" flanking it remain. The octagonal towers are surmounted by Gothic superstructures. The technical progress characterizing the Gothic period was reflected as building continued westwards culminating in the erection of the splendid tower which crowns the west façade. This feature, with its multiplicity of planes interesting at sharp angles, is one of the few church towers in Germany to be wholly completed in the Middle Ages.

In 1354, work started on the construction of a new chancel, but the grandeur of the design and the severity of the times were such that this huge addition was not finished and consecrated until 1513. The ambulatory, typically German in concept, has fan vaulting in keeping with its Late Gothic style.

North Side – Above the door which leads to the chancel, the tympanum, carved c1350, illustrates the theme of Original Sin, while the archivolt concerns itself with the Creation of the World according to Genesis. On the right of this, note the rare representation of the Creator resting on the seventh day.

★★★**West Tower** – On the plain, square base of this stands a pierced octagonal belfry surmounted by a delicate openwork spire of stone. Four sharply jutting projections in the form of a star at the foot of the tower house the Sterngalerie. The gargoyles here are worth a second glance.

South Side – Statues of the Apostles and the Old Testament kings stand on the buttresses of this richly ornate façade. A Renaissance porch shelters the south door.

MÜNSTER

0   20 m

141

A	Erzbischöfliches Palais	**F**	Adelhauser Neukloster
B	Historisches Kaufhaus	**M¹**	Augustinermuseum
D	Wentzingerhaus	**M²**	Colombischlößle
E	Haus Zum Walfisch	**R¹**	Neues Rathaus

West Porch and Doorway (Vorhalle) – Late 13C figures crowd this main entrance. On the left wall, facing the door, Satan, beguilingly disguised as "the Prince of this world", leads a procession. He is followed by his victim, sparsely clothed in a goat-skin, the Wise Virgins, and a number of Biblical characters. The Foolish Virgins, their expressions bitter, decorate the right wall. Behind them are statues of the liberal arts (painting and sculpture), St Margaret and St Catherine, the patronesses of Christian wisdom.

The doorway itself, flanked by statues representing the Church (left) and the Synagogue (with eyes covered; right) is entirely occupied by the mystery of the Redemption. The tympanum is unusual in that it portrays scenes from Christ's earthly life and an interesting Last Judgement.

Nave – Moderately tall, the nave is embellished with graceful galleries, their blind, trefoil arcades decorating the aisle walls from end to end. Furnishings and statuary of particular interest include:

1) The Virgin at the pillar (1270-1280), worshipped by two angels (art from Ile-de-France);

2) A Late Gothic pulpit with rustic themes (1560); the sculptor himself is represented in a window beneath the stairway;

3) A statue (originally recumbent, remodelled in the 17C) of Berthold V, last of the Dukes of Zähringen, who founded the town;

4) The Holy Sepulchre, dating from 1340, behind a delicate Gothic grille;

5) In the three windows of the south transept, 13C stained glass medallions, the oldest in the cathedral, which were probably originally in the old Romanesque chancel;

6) A 1505 group sculpture, the Adoration of the Magi.

Chancel ⊘ – Very well lit, the chancel invites appreciation of the skilful design of the ambulatory vaulting combined with that of the widely-spaced side chapels. Among the many works of art note:

the **altarpiece★★** (Hochaltar) by Hans Baldung Grien (1512-16), which portrays the Coronation of the Virgin on the central panel;

a) a Rococo baptismal font by JC Wenzinger in the Stürzel chapel;

b) the Oberried altarpiece (1521) in the Universität chapel. The two side panels, the Nativity and the Adoration of the Magi, are by Hans Holbein the Younger;

c) in the Second Kaiser chapel: an altarpiece from Schnewlin depicting Rest during the Flight to Egypt by Hans Wydyz. The paintings are from the Baldung Grien studio;

d) reverse of the large Baldung Grien altarpiece: a painting of the Crucifixion;

e) the Böcklin chapel: the Romanesque Locherer Crucifix in beaten silver by Böcklin;

f) an altarpiece in the Locherer chapel by Sixt von Staufen (1521-24). The carved part depicts the Virgin, with her cloak – held up by cherubim – shielding humanity.

Ascent of the West Tower (Turmbesteigung) ◷ – The first section of stairway leads to the star-shaped gallery, and then, after a further climb, visitors reach the upper platform beneath the beautiful perforated spire. From here there are **views**★ over the city, with distant perspectives of the Kaiserstuhl and the Vosges.

Münsterplatz (Y) – Facing the cathedral's south front across this square stand buildings whose ostentation declares them to have been designed for municipal or ecclesiastical prestige. They comprise:

Erzbischöfliches Palais (Y A) – A fine wrought-iron balcony decorates the façade of the archi-episcopal palace (1756).

★ **Historiches Kaufhaus (YZ B)** – A picturesque medieval atmosphere is lent to the square by this roughcast red structure. The watchtowers on either side have pointed roofs; covered with glazed tiles and supported by an arcaded gallery, the Gothic façade shelters statues of the Habsburg emperors (1530) on the first floor. The building is still used for official receptions and other city functions.

Wentzingerhaus (Y D) – Built for himself in 1761 by the famous local painter and sculptor Christian Wentzinger, this mansion completes the layout of the square. A magnificent Baroque staircase adorns the interior which now houses the museum of the local history (Museum für Stadtgeschichte).

★ **Rathausplatz (Y)** – The town hall square is a pleasant sight, with its flowered balconies and its scented chestnut trees surrounding the statue of Berthold Schwarz, a Franciscan said to have invented gunpowder in 1350.

★ **Neues Rathaus (New Town Hall) (Y R¹)** – Two 16C burghers' houses, once the heart of the old university, were linked in 1901 by a central arcaded portion to form the present town hall.
The oriel window at the Eisenbahnstraße corner is decorated with carvings illustrating the *Lady and the Unicorn*.

Haus zum Walfisch (Whale House) (Y E) – Of the original 1516 construction, there remains today an oriel which forms a canopy above a richly ornamented Late Gothic doorway.

★★ **Augustinermuseum (Z M¹)** ◷ – The most interesting part of this museum is the **Medieval Art Section**★★ (Mittelalterliche Kunst), housed in the church of an old Augustinian monastery and adjacent ground-floor galleries. The works, destined originally for churches and abbeys in the Upper Rhine districts, came from Alsace, the Baden region and the country around Lake Constance. The statuary, in particular, includes admirable 14C and 15C pieces. Among the museum's treasures are a Grünewald altarpiece panel (once at Aschaffenburg – *qv*) depicting the miracle of the Snow, and an impressive 14C **Crucifix**★ (Adelhauser Kreuz).

Schwabentor (Swabian Gate) (Z) – From this remnant of the town's medieval fortifications, sightseers can walk down through the picturesque but poor Insel quarter to the quays bordering the Gewerbekanal, once the preserve of Freiburg's fishermen and tanners. A small bridge spanning the canal offers a view of the cathedral spire.

★ **Schloßberg (Z)** – A wooded walk climbs this last foothill of the Black Forest. The pathway, which starts from the Schwabentor, also offers fine views of the cathedral. A **cable-car** ◷ operates from the Stadtgarten (**Y**).

EXCURSIONS

★ **The Kaiserstuhl** – *Round tour of 73km - 45 miles – allow 3 hours. Leave Freiburg by the Lessingstraße (Z) and go to Breisach via Gottenheim.*
A small volcanic massif rising in the Baden plain, the Kaiserstuhl (the Emperor's Throne: 538m - 1 765ft) enjoys on its lower slopes a warm, dry climate particularly suitable for orchards and vineyards. The wines of Ihringen, Bickensohl and Oberrotweil are considered among the finest in the region.

★ **Breisach** – Breisach and its rock, crowned by a large church, tower above the Rhine, facing the twin town of Neuf-Brisach in France. The rock was the heart of one of the most redoubtable systems of fortification in Europe, the site serving at times as a French bridgehead, at times as an imperial advance post. French revolutionary troops sacked the town in 1793, and it was largely destroyed by the Allied armies in 1945.

As at Freiburg, the **Münster★** has a Romanesque nave, transept and two smaller twin towers, together with a Gothic chancel. The most important work of art is a carved **reredos★★** (1526) with an extraordinarily complex decoration of leaves, flowing hair and billowing draperies from which emerge a crowd of cherubim and the figures of the Eternal Father and Christ crowning the Virgin. Murals depicting the Last Judgement (in the first bay on the west side) were painted in the late 15C by Martin Schongauer of Colmar.

From the cathedral hill (Münsterberg) there is a good **view★** of the heights of the Black Forest to the south, the Sundgau and Lomont peaks, the Vosges from the Grand Ballon to Upper Königsburg Castle and, quite close, the Kaiserstuhl.

★ **Burkheim** – A village of wine growers, Burkheim is built on a gentle slope, rising in tiers above the roadway with three parallel streets giving access to the houses at different levels. The lowest of these, the Marktstraße, is delightful. Among the half-timbered buildings are a red, bow-windowed mansion and a town hall with a fine emblazoned doorway (1604).

★ **Endingen** – The Marktplatz in this village is surrounded by fine public buildings. The new Rathaus, a modified 18C burgher's dwelling, boasts a balconied frontage and an elegant mansard roof. The old (16C) Rathaus, in the northeast corner of the square, has impressive scrolled gables, while the gables of the long, low Kornhaus (the former granary), also dating from the 16C, are stepped.

Ettenheim – *33km - 20 miles to the north.*
Part of the Strasbourg bishopric until 1803, Ettenheim is worth seeing for the old residential quarter of Kirchberg, separated from the rest of the town by two 18C gates and clustered at the foot of the large parish church.

Facing the outer stairway of the Rathaus is the gable of the palace once owned by Cardinal Rohan, where the notorious "hero" of the celebrated affair of the diamond necklace lived out his eventful exile from 1790 to 1803. Higher up, where the Rohanstraße bends towards the church, is the house owned by the Duke of Enghien, complete with coat of arms above the door. The Duke, fiancé of the Cardinal's niece Charlotte, was arrested on the orders of Napoleon in violation of the sovereignty of the State of Baden on the night of the 14-15 March 1804 and executed by firing squad six nights later in the castle moat at Vincennes.

Cardinal Rohan's tomb lies beneath the chancel in the church.

★★★ **Upper Black Forest** – *See SCHWARZWALD* ③.

FRIESLAND★

Niedersachsen and Schleswig-Holstein
Michelin map 415 A-C 8-9 and E-F 4-7

Scoured by the wind, scattered with stunted trees, with sea-birds crying overhead, Friesland forms the old Zuyder Zee to the Danish border; a single flat landscape crosshatched with dykes and canals. Offshore, the Frisian Islands, following the wide curve of the coastline, have existed since tempests destroyed the band of protective coastal dunes in the 5C BC. Twice since then, in 1362 and 1634, unusually catastrophic ocean assaults have laid waste the lowlands between the estuaries of the Weser and the Scheldt, reducing sizeable tracts of land to a string of tiny islets, as in the case of the Halligens.

Agriculturally, the consolidated silt deposits known as the **Marschen** have proved more fertile than the areas of **Geest**, which are slightly higher, with a sandy soil.

The Frisian people, tall and fairskinned, with blond hair and blue eyes, speak a language related to ancient Anglo-Saxon. Fishermen and farmers – especially noted for their fine cattle – they fight the weather relentlessly for the preservation of their livelihood.

FRISIAN ISLANDS

Ostfriesische Inseln (Eastern Frisians) ⊘ – Formed of dunes sometimes 20m to 30m - 66ft to 98ft high, these islands between the estuaries of the Ems and the Weser are constantly being re-shaped by winds and coastal currents. Their form, indented on the west, tapering to the east, is symptomatic of this process. An extensive system of dykes preserves them from too rapid an erosion.

These islands now are oriented towards seaside holidaymaking. In the summertime, the beaches of fine sand blossom with brightly-coloured bathing tents, pitched in sandy gullies out of the wind. The area is a paradise for bird-watchers, and large colonies of seals live in the shallows, particularly between Borkum and Sylt.

Borkum, the largest, most westerly island, and **Norderney**, the nearest to the mainland, are the most popular vacation centres in the summer. **Wangerooge**, **Langeoog** and **Juist** (where motor cars are not permitted) are equally well equipped for restful holidays. A favourite activity, on the islands as well as the coast, is the lowtide ramble, on foot or on horseback (a local guide is indispensable). The immense stretches of hardened silt glitter with huge banks of shellfish and are scattered with colourful seaweeds and starfish.

Nordfriesische Inseln (Northern Frisians) ☉ – These are divided into two geologically different groups. Sylt *(qv)*, **Föhr** and **Amrum**, the three most northerly islands, are blocks of Geest which escaped drowning when the sea-level rose after the melting of Europe's Quaternary glaciers; the **Halligen archipelago★** *(qv)*, on the other hand, is all that remains of an area of Marschen inundated and destroyed during the storms of 1634.

As in the Eastern Frisians, the pleasures of the beach abound. But an atmosphere rich in iodine and the opportunities for nudism, mud baths, sulphur inhalations and sea-water therapy have led to the installation of successful climatic and thermal cures such as at those as **St. Peter-Ording** (on the mainland coast) and **Wyk**.

FRITZLAR★

Hessen – Population 15 000
Michelin map 417 M 11

The placid waters of the Eder reflect the medieval towers and belfries of this small town.

A General View – From the end of the bridge that leads to the station on the south bank of the river's main stream, there is a fine view of the old town, its fortified walls overlooked by the towers of the collegiate church. The **ramparts** (Stadtmauer) retain almost all their ancient defence towers, in particular the impressive 13C spur structure, known locally as the **Grauer Turm★** (Grey Tower).

SIGHTS

★ **Marktplatz** – The original half-timbered gables, some faced with wooden shingles, have been preserved in all their variety. Note especially the small, elongated, 15C Kaufhaus (now the Reformhaus store), which is crowned with a turret.
The stem of the fountain (1564) supports a statue of Roland – here, as in Bremen, the symbol of public liberty.

★ **Dom (Collegiate Church)** ☉ – The present building was constructed in the 13C on the site of an earlier church of which only the west face, the lower parts of the towers and the crypt remained. A typical Rhineland feature is the dwarf gallery, adorned with blind arcades, which encircles the apse. The church's individuality lies in the interplay of the many gable roofs and the graceful half-timbered design of the chapter house, built onto the north side of the apse.
Enter the church by the main door on the west side. The interior is noteworthy for an outstanding Gothic ciborium, and, on either side of the chancel opening, two Romanesque statues carved in wood. One of these represents the Virgin, the other St John. Below ground, the crypts are vast. The most important, with three aisles, has fine, Romanesque cushion capitals with a simple, ribbed decoration. It houses the tomb of St Wigbert, the first abbot of Fritzlar.

Museum and Treasury (Domschatz und Dommuseum) ☉ – *Enter via the cloister on the right of the chancel.*
Among the ritual objects, liturgical vestments and statues, the treasury displays the pearl-encrusted Cross of the Kaiser Heinrich II (1020), as well as cameos, precious stones and a 12C Romanesque reliquary plaque.

FÜSSEN★

Bayern – Population 16 500
Michelin map 419/420 X 16 – Local map under Deutsche ALPENSTRASSE
Town plan in the current Michelin Red Guide Deutschland

The importance of Füssen as a tourist centre lies in its position – at the foot of the gorge where the Lech river cascades down from the Alps, the town serves as a gateway to the Tyrol and departure point for trips to the Royal Castles *(qv)* built by Ludwig II of Bavaria. A number of small lakes downstream, as well as the **Forggensee** reservoir, offer opportunities for boating, bathing and sailing.

Below the **castle** (Hohes Schloß), which rises high above the roofs of the old town, are the remains of ancient fortifications and defensive towers.

SIGHTS

Ehemaliges Kloster St. Mang – A Benedictine foundation set up by the followers of St Gall, this abbey was built on the site where St Magnus (St. Mang), the Apostle of the Allgäu, died in his hermitage in 750. It was rebuilt in the Baroque style during the 18C and secularized in 1803, when the abbey church was given to the parish.

Parish Church (Stadtpfarrkirche) – Rebuilt between 1701 and 1717, this church displays a remarkable unity, for Johann-Jacob Herkomer, born in the parish, was not only the architect but also the painter and stucco-worker. The Romanesque crypt was remodelled in 1971.

St Anne's Chapel (St. Anna-Kapelle) – *The last door on the left before the church porch.* Within the chapel, there is a curious **Dance of Death**★ (Totentanz, c1600) by a local painter. There is also a group in the Gothic style portraying the Holy Family.

Abbey Buildings – The abbey buildings, which are also attributed to Herkomer, are a fine example of Baroque architecture with their three ante-chapels decorated with scrolled gables. The **Museum der Stadt Füssen** ⊙, reached across the main quadrangle, is housed in the former state apartments of the abbey (princes' hall, refectory, library, etc.) and contains displays on the history of the abbey itself. There is also an interesting exhibition of string instruments, illustrating the evolution of the manufacture of violins and lutes locally.

Hohes Schloß – The ramp leading up to the castle entrance starts behind the parish church.

In the late 15C, the castle was the summer residence of the Prince-Bishops of Augsburg. The surrounding property has been transformed into a **public park** (Baumgarten), picturesque and peaceful, affording unexpected views of the Säuling escarpment. The apartments housing the local museum, in particular the Knight's Hall (Rittersaal) with its sumptuous octagonally-coffered ceiling, display a collection of Swabian painting from the 15C to the 18C.

Lechfall – *0.5km - a quarter of a mile to the south.*
The river hurls itself tumultuously over a ledge in a small, rocky gorge. The site, 500 yards north of the Austrian frontier, is known as the **Magnustritt** (step of St Magnus). The falls are spanned by a footbridge which allows sightseers to return to Füssen by another route.

FULDA

Hessen – Population 56 500
Michelin map 417/418 ⊙ 13
Town plan in the current Michelin Red Guide Deutschland

Baroque palaces, towers, monumental doorways, balustrades and flights of stairs in the heart of Fulda bear witness today to the town's religious past, from the time of the prince-bishops who were guardians of the tomb of St Boniface. An overall view can be enjoyed from the top of the steps leading to the Frauenberg church.

St Boniface, the Apostle of Germany – Wynfrith, an English missionary from a monastery in Exeter, was sent in the 8C to preach the gospel in Germany. In 751, anointing Pepin the Short as king, he confirmed the union of the Church with the Frankish monarchy, a bond that was to last for centuries. Wynfrith, who had changed his name to Boniface, was on a mission to Friesland when he was murdered at Dokkum in 754. He lies buried in a monastery, founded on his orders, at Fulda. The Benedictine abbey, especially under the rule of Abbot Raban Maur (822-842), subsequently became a centre of religious devotion, art and scholarship. The abbey in fact was responsible for the production of Germany's earliest literary works (*The Lay of Hildebrand* was copied by two monks c820).

SIGHTS

Dom (Cathedral) – From the beginning of 1704, this church was rebuilt in a style inspired by Italian Baroque by the architect Johann Dientzenhofer. Pilgrims still worship the tomb of St Boniface, which lies in a crypt (Bonifatiusgruft) beneath the high altar. At the base of the **funerary monument**★, an 18C alabaster bas-relief represents Boniface, in his priestly vestments, raising the lid of his tomb on Judgement Day.
The reliquaries of the saint, the head reliquary and his sword, are conserved in the **Museum** (Dommuseum – *access to the left of the cathedral*) ⊙, which also displays an important collection of liturgical vestments from the Baroque period. Baroque art is also represented by a splendid silver altar. There is a good collection of medieval artefacts.

★ **Michaelskirche** – This church, built around an early 9C rotunda, with a stout, square tower, overlooks the cathedral forecourt. The crypt, in which the vaulting rests on a single pillar, is Carolingian. The rotunda itself is supported on eight columns marking the outline of an impressive well-head.

Schloß – Here, only the castle outbuildings and dependencies are of interest. It is however pleasant to walk through the park (Schloßgarten), surrounded by terraces and balustraded walls, to the main staircase leading to the Orangery (1724). Halfway up there is a monumental **"Flora-vase"**, a superb Baroque masterpiece by Humbach dating from 1728, depicting the plant goddess Flora atop a basket overflowing with flowers, garlands and cherubs.

EXCURSIONS

Probsteikirche St. Petersberg – *4km - 2 1/2 miles, plus 1/2 hour walking and sightseeing. Leave Fulda by the Petersberger Straße and road no 458, on the east of the town plan. Follow the Petersberg signposts to the foot of the rock on which the church is built, and leave the car there.*

A vast **panorama★** is commanded from the summit: to the east is the Rhön massif *(see below)*, the Milseburg spur and the rounded dome of the Wasserkuppe; southwest, behind Fulda, lies the Vogelsberg.

The Romanesque sanctuary built on this impressive **site★** was largely remodelled in the 15C. It contains five 12C **bas-reliefs★★** – Christ in Glory and the Virgin on either side of a triumphal arch; St Boniface, Carloman and Pepin the Short on the walls. Mural paintings from the 9C decorate three niches in the Carolingian crypt.

Schloß Fasanerie or Adolphseck ⊘ – *6km - 4 miles to the south.*
Constructed between 1739 and 1754 by Prince-Bishop Amand von Buseck, this Baroque mansion owes to the Landgraves and Electoral Princes of Hesse its interior style, decoration and furnishing. The museum offers visitors a good overview of the evolution in interior design between 1740 and 1860 and houses a fine collection of antiques, as well as porcelain from Europe and the Far East.

Schloß Fasanerie – Music room

★ **The Rhön** – *Round tour of 104km - 65 miles to the southwest of Fulda – allow 4 hours.*
The remnants of an enormous extinct volcano, the Rhön massif's craggy summits tower above the bleak moorlands clothing it up to a height of 1 000m - 328ft. These heights, swept by strong winds, have made the area a favourite among the organizers of gliding clubs.

Gersfeld – The most central resort in the Rhön district, Gersfeld has a Protestant **church** (1785) with interestingly placed furnishings: the grouping of organ, altar and pulpit in a single compact ensemble symbolizes liturgically the Lutheran reform.

★ **Kreuzberg** – From the Calvary – at 928m - 3 044ft after a steep uphill climb – there is a splendid **view★** of the massif. The Wasserkuppe can be seen to the north.

★★ **Wasserkuppe** – From the gliding centre, climb to the summit (950m - 3 116ft), following the fencing on the left. The **panorama★★** extends as far as Fulda and the Vogelsberg.

The Michelin Green Guide Austria,
an informative travel guide,
aims to make touring more enjoyable
by highlighting the country's
natural features, historic sites
and other outstanding attractions.

GARMISCH-PARTENKIRCHEN★★★

Bayern − Population 26 500

Michelin map 419/420 X 17 - Local map under Deutsche ALPENSTRASSE
Plan of the conurbation in the current Michelin Red Guide Deutschland

This is Germany's great winter sports resort, famed as the site of the fourth Winter Olympics in 1936 and the World Alpine Ski Championships in 1978. Worthy of its reputation internationally, the resort lies in an open mountain basin at the foot of the Wetterstein range, from which two massive silhouettes stand out. These are the Alpspitze and the axe-shaped Waxenstein, itself masking the Zugspitze.

Despite its modest altitude (720m - 2 362ft), favourable meteoric conditions assure the resort of a regular winter snowfall − from 12 to 20 inches in January and February, anything up to six feet in the areas served by the ski-lifts. This is complemented by the Zugspitzplatt snowfield, accessible in autumn and springtime via a rack railway.

Summer visitors are offered numerous mountain walks (Höhenwege), crisscrossing the lower slopes of the Wank and the Kramerspitze. Although more lively and sophisticated than the twin town of Partenkirchen, Garmisch nevertheless maintains certain customs and traditions. Thus, every evening around 6pm, there is the communal Return of the Herds − with cattle frisking through the streets and bringing traffic to a standstill.

The name of Richard Strauss is closely associated with Garmisch-Partenkirchen, as he lived here until his death in 1949. There is an annual Richard Strauss festival here in June.

SIGHTS

Olympia-Eisstadion (Ice Stadium) − *Garmisch.* Open all the year round, this comprises three separate skating rinks with a total surface of 6 500m² - 7 800sq yds. The covered stands allow 12 000 spectators to watch skating competitions and ice hockey matches.

Skistadion (Ski stadium) − *Partenkirchen.* A ski-jump and a slalom course here are equipped for 80 000 spectators.

Alte Kirche − *Garmisch.* The parish church stands on the west bank of the Loisach river, in a picturesque neighbourhood where the old chalets have been carefully preserved. The interior embraces two equal naves, where a single central column supports 16C Gothic vaulting with liernes and tiercerons (ancillary ribs). A large number of 15C and 16C murals have been uncovered and restored as far as possible (note especially a huge representation of St Christopher and scenes from the Passion).

Wallfahrtskirche St. Anton − *Partenkirchen.* To the octagonal nave of this 1708 pilgrim's sanctuary, a second nave, oval in shape, was added in 1738. The dome above this is decorated with frescoes by JE Holzer.

Philosophenweg (Philosophers' Way) − *Partenkirchen.* The park of **St. Anton-Anlagen** is the departure point for this panoramic walk which offers fine, clear **views★** of the surrounding massifs − with the Zugspitze visible this time behind the Waxenstein.

GARMISCH-PARTENKIRCHEN			
Bahnhofstraße	**X** 10		
Ferdinand-Bath-Straße	**X** 15	Parkstraße	**X** 32
Hindenburgstraße	**X** 18	Promenadestraße	**X** 35
Mittenwalder Str.	**X** 27	Rießerseestraße	**X** 37
Münchner Str.	**X** 30	Von-Brug-Str.	**X** 46
		Wildenauer Str	**X** 48

EXCURSIONS

★★★ Zugspitze – *For access and description, see ZUGSPITZE.*

★★ Wank ⊙ – *20 minutes in a cable car. Leave from the Schützenhaus inn, on the northern fringe of Partenkirchen.*
From the summit (1 780m - 5 840ft) there is a comprehensive view of the Wetterstein chain – and a vertiginous appreciation of the Garmisch-Partenkirchen basin far below. A panorama of the surrounding mountains can be enjoyed from many of the footpaths crossing the Alpine meadows and skirting the forest.

★★ Partnachklamm – *About 1 1/2 hours Rtn, of which 5 minutes are in a cable car. (Remember to take rainwear).*
From the Partenkirchen ski stadium, go to the lower terminus of the Graseck cable car. The upper station is at the Forsthaus Graseck hotel, and from here a footpath leads up to the **gorges**. The route, carved from the solid rock, passes two spectacular bottlenecks amid the thunder of falling water and clouds of spray. At the Partnachklamm inn, the path rejoins the upward route. It is possible to make the same trip in wintertime, when the route will be decorated with a huge frieze of icicles.

★ Eibsee – *8km - 5 miles to the west.*
The calm waters of this lake occupy a superb forest site. It lies at the foot of the Zugspitze, at an altitude of 1 000m - 3 881ft. A footpath *(2 hours' walk)* circles the lake.

★ Mittenwald – *20km - 12 1/2 miles to the east.*
An old frontier town on the Augsburg-Verona trade route, Mittenwald still suffers from heavy traffic today. This due to the large number of excursions possible in the nearby Kranzberg and Karwendel massifs, and to the beauty of the town itself. The **painted houses★★** lining the pavements of the main street are especially noteworthy.
If Mittenwald, as Goethe said, is "a living picture-book", a monument outside the church recalls that the town also has a place in the world of music. The memorial honours Matthias Klotz (1653-1743), who returned from Cremona in 1684 with a lute and, as an ex-pupil of Stradivarius, introduced the manufacture of stringed instruments to Bavaria despite the fact that it was then in the midst of an economic depression. A dozen artisans, a technical school, and a museum, the **Geigenbau-und-Heimatmuseum** ⊙, carry on that tradition today.

GELNHAUSEN

Hessen – Population 19 000
Michelin map 417 P 11

On the sunny slope of the Kinzig valley, Gelnhausen was built as a military installation by the Emperor Frederick Barbarossa, and is encircled to this day with fortifications. The most noticeable building is the Marienkirche, whose towers overlook the rural Untermarkt at the highest point of the town.

★ Marienkirche – Enter via the small south door that looks out over the valley. This solid, red sandstone building, with its spires and gables, is typical of the Rhineland Romanesque style *(see Introduction)*. The **choir★★** (Chorraum), adorned with trilobed blind arcades and heavily worked consoles, is considered to be one of the masterpieces of 13C religious architecture.

Kaiserpfalz (Imperial Palace Ruins) ⊙ – The ruins stand amidst the greenery of an island in the river. They comprise an entrance hall with two aisles, a colonnade with sculptured capitals, traces of the old perimeter wall, the chapel, and a watch-tower – all remarkable for the perfection of their Romanesque decoration.

EXCURSIONS

Büdingen – *17km - 10 1/2 miles to the north.*
The 15C and 16C **fortified perimeter★** (Stadtmauer) has fine decorative details. Arriving via the Bahnhofsstraße, note the 1503 Jerusalem gate, with its squat towers and Gothic embellishments.
The **castle** ⊙ of the Ysenburg Princes is one of the few Staufen residences which is still inhabited. From the entrance arch, moving in a clockwise direction, the buildings around the inner courtyard decrease in age from the 12C to the 15C. The **choir stalls★** of the 15C chapel are decorated with saints' effigies and coats of arms.

Steinau – *25km - 15 1/2 miles to the northeast.*
The Brothers Grimm *(qv)*, sons of a magistrate, grew up in this small town. They lived from 1791 to 1796 in the massive **Tribunal House** (Hanauisches Amtshaus), which stands back behind a courtyard at No 80, Brüder-Grimm-Straße. There is a **memorial** ⊙ to them in the castle, a fortified Renaissance ensemble with defensive towers and a square keep.

GÖRLITZ★

Sachsen – Population 82 400
Michelin map 418 M 28

Founded in the middle of the 13C and incorporated in Bohemia a century later, Görlitz has spread out along the west bank of the Neiße, which has formed, since 1945, the frontier with Poland. A busy town, famous for its mechanical and optical industries, it boasts many excellent Renaissance and Baroque buildings, recently renovated and displayed to their best advantage around the Obermarkt and Untermarkt.

SIGHTS

Obermarkt – On the north side of this square, fine Baroque houses have been preserved between the **Reichenbacher Turm**, a fortified 14-15C gateway to the west, and the **Dreifaltigkeitskirche** on the east. Flamboyant Gothic **stalls★** are worth looking at inside the church. At **no 29** (the tourist information centre), the façade, including an entrance framed by sculpted columns, is adorned with impressive stuccowork.

★ **Untermarkt** – Formerly the town's chief trading centre, the market place is overlooked by the tower (1378) of the **Rathaus** (town hall). Note, on the corner of the Brüderstraße, the outside staircase (1537-38) encircling an elegant statue (a copy) representing Justice. To the right of the building's Renaissance doorway, a Late Gothic (1488) sculptured plaque displays the arms of Matthias Corvinus, King of Hungary. The central part of the town hall dates from Renaissance times, while the neo-Gothic additions are less than a century old.
In the middle of the market, the **Alte Börse** (former money exchange), with its entrance surrounded by allegorical figures, is the oldest Baroque monument in the town. Dating from 1706, the exchange is adjacent to the **Alte Waage** (Weigh-house), which combines three Renaissance upper storeys with a Baroque base at street level.
Arcaded houses bordering the southern side of the Untermarkt evoke the lives of the gentry and eminent burghers living there in the past.

Städtische Kunstsammlungen (Municipal Art Museum) ⊙ – *At Neißstraße 30.*
This imposing Baroque mansion (1727-1729) at the southeastern corner of the square houses an interesting collection of art, 16C to 19C decorative arts and beautiful Renaissance and Baroque furniture. There is a particularly fine collection of glassware on display. A collection of 18C **rustic cupboards and cabinets★** on the second floor is distinguished by the interesting painted decoration of the exhibits. The print room containts prints and graphic work from the 16C to the 20C.

Kaisertrutz (Imperial Shelter) ⊙ – *Demianiplatz.*
This solid-looking circular keep, 19m - 62ft in diameter, was built as part of the town's fortifications between 1490 and 1541. It now houses the **Museum für Stadtgeschichte** ⊙ (local history museum).

GÖTTINGEN

Niedersachsen – Population 131 600
Michelin map 417/418 L 13
Town plan in the current Michelin Red Guide Deutschland

Along with Heidelberg, Tübingen and Marburg, Göttingen is one of the four German towns most deeply imbued with the university tradition. Student life, often noisy and highly coloured, lends a particular vivacity to the scene, especially at examination time and on Foundation Days (Stiftungsfeste). The streets of the old town, with their Gothic churches and neo-Classical university buildings, are frequently bustling with squads of students cycling to dispersed lecture halls and libraries.

Two Centuries of University Life – The university was founded in 1737 by George II of England in his capacity as Elector of Hannover. At first it tended to be an aristocratic institution, frequented by the sons of important English and Russian families and Hanoverian gentry. While lawyers and philologists studied, champion horsemen exercised their skills at the enormous riding school. In 1807, however, the nomination of **Carl Friedrich Gauß** (1777-1855) as Director of the Observatory and Professor of Astronomy ushered in a period of great learning and scientific achievement.
A mathematical genius even more precocious than Pascal, Gauß had, at the age of 16, envisaged the possibility of a non-Euclidian geometry. His name was later given to the international unit used in the measurement of magnetic field intensity, and to a society of learned researchers. Members of this body even today are still trying to distil the quintessence of Gauß's scientific testament, embodied in 145 enigmatic pronouncements which are condensed into only 19 pages.
Since the end of the Second World War, Göttingen has become the headquarters of the Max Planck Society (successor to the Kaiser-Wilhelm-Gesellschaft), which groups together some 50 scientific research organizations in Germany. Author in 1900 of the revolutionary Quantum Theory, Max Planck himself (1858-1947) is buried in Göttingen.

SIGHTS

Rathaus (Town Hall) – Students, tourists and citizens combine to make the market place and the wine cellars (Ratskeller) beneath the town hall the animated centre of social life in Göttingen. The 14-15C building is constructed on the classic medieval pattern *(see Introduction)*. In front of it is the modern **Goosegirl Fountain** (Gänseliesel-brunnen), end goal of student processions after the annual examinations.

Vierkirchenblick – A church is visible at each point of the compass from the south-east corner of the market: east, the countrified dome of St. Albanikirche; south, St. Michaelskirche; west, the octagonal towers of St. Johannis; and north, the lofty belfry of St. Jakobi – at 72m - 236ft the tallest tower in town.

Half-timbered Houses (Fachwerkhäuser) – Most of these are in the eastern part of the old town. Note particularly the ancient **Junkernschänke inn★** (near the Rathaus, at the junction of the Barfüßerstraße and the Judenstraße). Medallions with portrait heads adorning this half-timbered Renaissance building are surmounted by biblical characters such as Adam and Eve, Samson and Delilah, etc. The master and mistress of the house when it was built are depicted on the corner-post.

Städtisches Museum (Municipal Museum) ⊙ – This museum, which is housed in a Renaissance building, is devoted to the historical and cultural development of Göttingen, both town and university, and the surrounding area. It also exhibits an interesting collection of religious art.

EXCURSION

★ Duderstadt – *31km - 19 miles to the east.*
Once known as "the Nuremberg of the Eichsfeld", Duderstadt retains from its colourful past more than 500 half-timbered houses, most of them displaying sculpturing of the exposed beams. Overlooking the Marktstraße are the pointed turrets of the **Rathaus**, built at the beginning of the 13C and enlarged between 1432 and 1533.
Not far away is **St. Cyriakus-Kirche**, an enormous eight-bay hall-church built in the 15C. Among the works of religious art inside are 15 Baroque statues – including the twelve Apostles – joined to the supporting columns.

GOSLAR★★

Niedersachsen – Population 46 000
Michelin map 418 K 15 – Local map under HARZ

This town, built around an 11C imperial palace on the northern fringe of the Harz mountains, retains a singular grouping of half-timbered houses and important monuments around its medieval centre.

A Mining Town – A former Free Imperial City, Goslar owed its prosperity to the mineral wealth of the Harz, and particularly to the Rammelsberg mines, worked during the Middle Ages for lead and silver. The city's commercial importance reached its height in the 15C and 16C, when profit accrued also from the vast surrounding forests which provided timber to fire the metal refineries. It was during this period that the fine houses of the city guilds were built.
Religious controversy between the Free City and the Dukes of Brunswick, who owned the mines, brought an economic decline in the mid-16C. Today, although the Rammelsberg mines are still worked, tourism is Goslar's principal industry. The fact that the old town and the Ramelsberg silver mines have been designated a World Heritage Site by UNESCO has also given the local economy a boost.
From the terrace of the **Georgenberg (Y)** there is a fine view of the town packed tightly against the mountain slope.

★★★OLD TOWN (ALTSTADT) *time: 3 hours*

★ Marktplatz (Z) – The market square, dignified and austere in appearance, is surrounded by houses protected by slate cladding. Its architectural prestige derives from two Gothic buildings: the Kaiserworth and the Rathaus, behind which soar the spires of the 12C **Marktkirche**. In the centre of the square there is a **fountain** (Marktbrunnen) with two bronze basins (1230) surmounted by the crowned imperial eagle with outstretched wings. On the gable of a house opposite the Rathaus there is a **chiming clock** which animates four different scenes *(at 9am, noon, 3 and 6pm)* representing the history of mining in the Harz mountains from the Middle Ages to the present day.

Rathaus, Goslar

★ **Rathaus (Town Hall)** (**YZ R**) – Following the medieval custom, this 15C building was designed with an open hall at street level, an arcaded gallery opening onto the Marktplatz.

On the south side, an exterior staircase leads to the first floor **State Room** (Diele). The lower part of the roof is masked by an ornate balustrade alternating with decorative gabling.

★★ **Chamber of Allegiance** (Huldigungssaal) ⊘ – This room, transformed into the **Municipal Council Chamber** in 1450, was magnificently decorated *c*1510. Along the walls, beneath delicately carved upper panelling, Roman emperors alternate with sybils in Renaissance costume; on the ceiling, scenes from the childhood of Christ are surrounded by figures of the prophets and Evangelists. Concealed behind a door is a tiny chapel containing paintings of the Passion and an arm-reliquary (*c*1300) of St Margaret.

Kaiserworth (**Z S**) – Built in 1494, this Gothic edifice, now a hotel, is embellished with a turreted oriel and Baroque statues of emperors beneath baldachins. On a gable ridge, at the foot of an allegorical statue of Abundance, a grotesque figurine of **The Ducat Man** (Dukatenmännchen) vividly illustrates Goslar's ancient right to mint coins.

★★ **Carved half-timbered houses** (Fachwerkhäuser) – The **Schuhhof** (**Y 76**), a small square to the northwest of the Rathaus, is entirely surrounded by half-timbered buildings, those on the right resting on arcades.

Further on, a passageway on the left leads to the narrow Münzstraße, which in turn passes an old staging inn, **Am Weißen Schwan** (**Y A**) and then the **Alte Münze** (Old Mint) (**Y Z**). Transformed today into a restaurant, this timbered building dates from 1500.

The fine house on the corner of the Münzstraße and the Marktstraße (**Z V**), with its splendid two-storey oriel, was constructed in 1526.

Facing the Marktkirche is the huge pointed roof of the **Brusttuch** (**Z B**), also dating from 1526, which was built for a rich mineowner and decorated, according to Renaissance taste, with a host of biblical, mythological and legendary characters and motifs. Not far away, the tall gable of the **Bäckergildehaus** (Bakers' Guild Hall) (**Z Y**), built between 1501 and 1557, rises into view.

The **Renaissance Houses** at the Marktstraße-Bäckerstraße crossroads are adorned with friezes of the fan motif so often found in Lower Saxony *(no 2 Bäckerstraße)* or a row of blind arcades *(no 3 Bäckerstraße)* (**YZ W**).

Siemenshaus (**Z C**) ⊘ – An impressive half-timbered house built in 1693 by Hans Siemens, ancestor of the founder of the celebrated industrial firm of the same name. There is a particularly fine entrance hall (Däle), floored with small tiles, which serves as a living-room in summer.

Stift zum Großen Heiligen Kreuz (**Z K**) – This former almshouse, founded in 1254, is on the banks of the Gose river, which has given its name to the delicious local beer (Gosebier).

The Gothic gable, beneath overhanging eaves, overlooks the Hoher Weg. Inside, the galleried **Great Hall** (Diele) communicates with an unadorned chapel.

ADDITIONAL SIGHTS

★ **Klosterkirche Neuwerk (Y)** – This former Cistercian church (12-13C) stands alone in what was the convent garden. The tall **polygonal towers** are among the most elegant ever built for a Romanesque church. The exterior decoration of the apse is exceptionally elaborate.

Heavily ribbed, pointed vaulting characterizes the interior. In the central bay, the columns carrying the transverse arches, two of which have a stone ring, are hollowed in their upper parts to form a curious handle. The balustrade of the organ is decorated with six bas-reliefs (Christ, the Virgin, the four Apostles) which came from the original rood-screen and are already manifestly, elegantly Gothic.

★ **Pfarrkirche Peter und Paul (Z F)** – *Entrance on the Frankenberger Plan.*

The Plan, a square originally inhabited by miners, lends its name to the whole tranquil quarter. The 12C church was extensively remodelled, and in the 18C a Baroque roof and a lantern tower were added to it. Inside, note the **Nonnenempore** (nuns' gallery), where the blind arcades rest on capitals adorned with acanthus leaves and small columns with a plaited decoration borrowed from those at Königslutter *(qv)*. On the north and south walls are traces of huge murals painted in the early 13C.

★ **Kaiserpfalz (Imperial Palace) (Z)** ⊙ – The castle, originally built for Kaiser Heinrich III in the 11C and reduced to ruins with the passage of years, was rebuilt and restored between 1868 and 1879. The impressive proportions of the whole give some idea of the power and prestige enjoyed by the imperial rulers. Ambitious historical paintings in the gigantic **Reichssaal** *(on the first floor)* chart the significant events affecting Saxony when Goslar was still an imperial residence. Beyond the Reichssaal is the early 12C **Palatine Chapel of St Ulrich**, where the plan passes, in elevation, from that of a Greek cross to that of an octagon. Inside the chapel is the tomb of Heinrich III, whose heart is preserved in the plinth. The recumbent effigy of the ruler dates from the 13C.

Domvorhalle (Z) – Of the cathedral built in the 11C by Heinrich III and demolished in 1822, all that remains is this deconsecrated chapel in the Romanesque style, which houses the late 11C imperial throne.

GOSLAR

Rosentorstraße	**Y** 66	Münzstraße	**Y** 52
		Obere Kirchstraße	**Y** 58
Astfelder Straße	**Y** 2	Rammelsberger Straße	**Z** 63
Broite Straße	**Y**	Brüggemannstraße	**Y** 8	St-Annenhöhe	**Z** 09
Fischermäkerstraße	**Y** 19	Fleischscharren	**Y** 23	Schließenstraße	**Z** 71
Hokenstraße	**Z**	Hoher Weg	**Z** 37	Schreiberstraße	**Z** 74
Marktstraße	**Y**	Kaiserbleek	**Z** 42	Schuhhof	**Z** 76
Petersilienstraße	**Y** 61	Königstraße	**Z** 45	Worthstraße	**Z** 82

Rammelsberger Bergbaumuseum

A Alte Gasthof Am Weißen Schwan	**K** Stift zum Großen Heiligen Kreuz	**V** Ecklhaus Münz-Marktstraße
B Brusttuch	**M¹** Mönchehaus	**W** Renaissancehäuser
C Siemenshaus	**M²** Goslarer Museum	**Y** Bäckergildehaus
F Pfarrkirche Peter und Paul	**R** Rathaus	**Z** Alte Münze
	S Kaiserworth	

* **Breites Tor (Wide Gate) (Y)** – This massive construction with its round towers, its barrack quarters and its two huge doors (only the inner one remains) is in fact a fortress in the form of a gateway. It was built c1500.

* **Mönchehaus (Monks' House) (Y M¹)** – A **museum of modern art**, housed in an ancient half-timbered house, displays works by Beuys, Hundertwasser, Serra and de Kooning. In the garden are sculptures by Ernst and Rennertz, and an interesting Calder mobile.

Goslarer Museum (Z M²) ⊘ – This museum outlines the history of the town, with particular focus on domestic life (furniture from the 17C to the 19C), as well as examples of local arts and crafts. There is a fine collection of works of art from the Old Goslar cathedral, such as the **Krodoaltar**, a large bronze reliquary altar dating from the 11C, from which the jewelled decorations and precious stones have unfortunately been stolen. Note also the Goslar Gospel, a 13C manuscript, and a 16C Crucifixion.

The Zwinger (Z) – Built in 1517 as part of a defence ring, this fortified tower stands on the **ramparts** (Wallanlagen) south of the city centre. From the top of the tower, there is a fine view of the old town.

Rammelsberger Bergbaumusuem (Rammelsberg Mining Museum) ⊘ – *To the south-west of town, via Clausthaler Straße and Rammelsberger Straße.*
Over the centuries the Rammelsberg mines with their rich deposits of non-ferrous metals – lead, zinc, copper, silver – have been largely responsible for Goslar's prosperity. The mines were worked continuously for at least 1 000 years, if not longer, giving up almost 30 million tons of ore during this period. During the museum visit, the Roeder galery and other parts of the mine can be explored on foot or in a mining train.

EXCURSIONS

** **Harz Mountains** – *See HARZ.*

* **Grauhofer Kirche** – *3km - 1 3/4 miles. Leave Goslar by the Okerstraße (Y).*
Augustinian friars from Grauhof monastery (founded in 1527) employed an Italian architect to build this church in 1701. It was completed in 1717. The interior is remarkable both for its huge size and the restrained use of colour. Of particular interest are: a pulpit in the form of a boat (1721); the splendid organ case, which dates from 1737; and the **choir stalls** in exotic woods, where 56 separate scenes represent the life and philosophy of St Augustine.

GREIFSWALD *

Mecklenburg-Vorpommern – Population 70 000
Michelin map 416 D 23

Greifswald dates from the foundation of Eldena abbey. There is documentary evidence of the town's existence as early as 1248. Once it had joined the Hanseatic League *(qv)* in 1281, the town appears to have flourished. The construction at this time of three large parish churches, whose silhouettes still grace the town's skyline, provides evidence of its prosperity. In fact, Greifswald was to continue to expand and prosper for the next four centuries.

Swedish rule – Following the peace treaty of Osnabrück, which brought the Thirty Years War to an end, West Pomerania, and thus also Greifswald, passed into Swedish hands. The Swedes proved not to be oppressive rulers, exercising leniency for nigh on two hundred years and granting the town an unusual degree of autonomy for the age, if not exactly furthering any particular economic growth. From 1815, when West Pomerania became part of Prussia, a busy period of construction began, to which the numerous well-preserved burghers' houses still testify.

The greatest German Romantic painter – Caspar David Friedrich, the epitome of the German Romantic painter and a revolutionary landscape painter, was born in Greifswald in 1774 (his place of birth at no 57 lange Straße was destroyed by fire in 1901). Although he left Greifswald at the age of twenty (to settle in Dresden), he remained deeply attached to the town of his birth; Greifswald, and especially the ruins of Eldena abbey, feature in many of his works. Friedrich's paintings are suffused with symbolism of the transitory nature of human existence and reflect intense and subjective emotions to a degree never before committed to canvas. Many of his very spiritual works evoke mankind's isolation in the face of nature and destiny. His austere compositions appeal strongly to modern viewers.

Present and future outlook – Greifswald's geographical location near a national frontier has its advantages and disadvantages; a significant upturn in the town's economic fortunes is hardly to be expected this close to the Polish border. The town does however still have a large number of its original buildings, since it escaped any destruction during the Second World War. Its charming appearance, in which a faint suggestion of Scandinavian influence can be detected, and its tranquil atmosphere will certainly stand it in good stead for future growth as a holiday destination.

OLD TOWN (ALTSTADT)

★ **Marktplatz** – To the west of this square stands the **Rathaus** (1738) with its distinctive curved, Renaissance style gables; the roof turret is nonetheless in the Baroque style. The medieval arcades along the east gable were uncovered in 1936. Around the square stand a number of art-historically interesting houses, the most noticeable of which is **no 11★**: this early 15C building with its ornately decorated crow-stepped gable is one of the most beautiful examples of north German Gothic architecture in brick.

★ **Marienkirche** ⊙ – Typically for the architecture of the region, this hall-church with three naves has no chancel. the elegantly structured east gable with its ornate tracery alleviates the somewhat heavy, stocky appearance of the rest of the brick church, which is known affectionately as "podgy Mary" by locals. Construction of the church was begun in 1280 and lasted into the 14C. Inside there is a beautiful carved **pulpit★** dating from 1587, the work of Joachim Mekelenborg from Rostock. During the last phase of restoration work, late Gothic frecoes from the 14C were uncovered, including one which depicts a whale caught in the fishing village of Wieck in 1545.

★ **Dom St. Nikolai** ⊙ – The cathedral is dwarfed by its tower, which is almost 100m - 328ft in height and takes the form of a square base flanked by four small round towers, supporting a two-storey octagonal tower with blind double windows decorated with white plaster tracery. The crowning glory is a Dutch Baroque steeple dating from 1653. In the 14C the original hall-church was elevated to the rank of basilica, and the spaces between the flying buttresses were filled in to make a ring of 21 radiating chapels. In the 19C two students of Schinkel, Gottlieb Giese and Joachim Christian Friedrich (brother of Caspar David), undertook to remodel the church in the neo-Gothic style in the true spirit of Romanticism. The fruits of their labours are most apparent in the central nave, while the side chapels retain their medieval and Baroque features. Numerous oil paintings (16C-19C) and tombstones, including that of Heinrich Rubenow, founder of Greifswald University who was assassinated by his political opponents in 1462, are of interest. Note also the frescoes dating from c1430.

St. Jakobikirche ⊙ – This is the smallest of the town's three medieval churches. The west door features a remarkable sandstone frieze and has an alternating pattern of dark glazing and natural stone around the door jambs. The last set of restoration work reproduced the medieval coloured decoration of the church interior. Note the 13C granite font.

Ehemaliges Hospital St. Spiritus – *Lange Straße.*
The old hospital complex consisting of carefully restored 18C half-timbered single-storey buildings *(towards the courtyard)* and Classical town houses *(towards the street)* is now used a community meeting centre. The charming inner courtyard is a pleasant place to linger.

Universität – *Rubenowplatz.*
The university of Greifswald is the second oldest in northern Europe after that at Rostock. It was founded in 1456 by local mayor Heinrich Rubenow, who was its first vice-chancellor. The university's most famous student is the poet **Ernst Moritz Arndt**, after whom the university is named, who went on to hold the university chair in history. He was also instrumental in the abolition of the feudal serf system in West Pomerania. The various university faculties are scattered all over town. The university's elongated main building, decorated in red and white plasterwork, stands on Rubenowplatz and was built in the mid 18C by Andreas Meyer from Augsburg. The triangular gable above the central façade bears the coats of arms of the Swedish royal family on the side facing the street, and of Pomerania on the side facing the courtyard.

Museum Greifswald ⊙ – *Theodor-Pyl-Straße 1.*
The local museum occupies the porter's lodge (Guardianshaus) of the old Franciscan abbey. Besides the exhibition on local history, there are displays on Caspar David Friedrich and Ernst Moritz Arndt.

ADDITIONAL SIGHTS

★ **Botanischer Garten** ⊙ – *Grimmer Straße 88/Münsterstraße 1, either side of the railway line.*
The pretty, well laid-out botanical gardens, which are affiliated with the university, offer 1ha-2.5 acres of plants, shrubs and trees, as well as a garden of herbs and medicinal plants. The **greenhouses** full of exotic flora are particularly well worth a visit.

★ **Klosterruine Eldena (Abbey Ruins)** ⊙ – *Wolgaster Landstraße.*
The original Cistercian abbey was founded in 1199, and it appears to have reached the height of its wealth and power around the mid 14C. The Thirty Years War spelled large-scale destruction for it, and the remains were later used as a source of building materials by local people. Of the once splendid building, only fragments of the church, the cloisters and the east abbey building remain.

Swing bridge at Wieck

They are nonetheless still as picturesque a scene as they were in the days of Caspar David Friedrich, who not only committed them to canvas, but campaigned for their preservation. The red brick of the buildings contrasts with the greenery of the surrounding park, landscaped by Lenné.

★ **Wieck** – *Can easily be reached on foot from the Eldena abbey ruins.*
This little fishing village, now officially classified as a historical site, lies as the mouth of the river Ryck as it flows into Greifswald bay. The shipsmasters' and fishermen's cottages, the latter thatched with reeds, the idyllic little harbour and the wooden **swing bridge★** make a delightful scene. The bridge, based on a Dutch design, is a technical monument in itself, dating from 1887. If you are lucky, you may get the chance to see it in action, being raised by a hand-wound winch.

GÜSTROW ★

Mecklenburg-Vorpommern – Population 39 000
Michelin map 416 E 20

Güstrow was granted the civic charter in 1228 and went on from this promising start to become the residence of the dukes of Mecklenburg-Güstrow between 1556 and 1695. The wealth that accompanied this status continued to accumulate over the next few centuries, as can be seen from the elegant burghers' houses which line the cathedral and market squares and the streets surrounding them (Mühlenstraße nos 17 and 48, Grüner Winkel no 10). The **Rathaus** on the market square is an architectural oddity, comprising four gabled houses to which a decorative Classical façade was added in 1797.

Ernst Barlach – The name of this great Expressionist sculptor is linked with the town where he lived for nearly thirty years until his death in 1938. Barlach came to Güstrow in 1910, with the intention of settling, and produced some of his major life's work here.

SIGHTS

★ **Renaissanceschloß** – This Renaissance palace is one of the most important examples of its type in north Germany, combining Italian, French and German stylistic features. It was built from 1558 onwards for Duke Ulrich first by the north Italian architect Franziskus Parr, who completed the south and west wings, and then by his successor, Philipp Brandin from the Netherlands, who built the north wing (1587-1588). The gatehouse in front of the palace was built in the Dutch Baroque style in 1671, following designs by Charles Philipp Dieussart. The building's exterior is clearly divided by horizontal ledges and has distinctively patterned plasterwork, tapering up towards the level of the roof. Although the west façade with its corner turrets and the striking entrance pavilion is undoubtedly the main decorative façade, the side of the south wing facing the courtyard is also charming with its staircase tower and three-storey colonnaded gallery. Several rooms have been set aside to house the **Schloßmuseum** ⊙. The banqueting hall is decorated with remarkable **stuccowork** depicting exotic hunting and battle scenes. The museum also exhibits some paintings by Lucas Cranach the Elder and members of his studio.

★ Dom (Cathedral) ☉ – The massive shape of this Gothic brick basilica, consecrated in 1335, is a distinctive feature on the town's skyline. Inside it is plain to see that the nave and chancel are set at an angle to each other, rather than being in alignment. Having been the court church of the dukes of Mecklenburg, the basilica is richly endowed with works of art. The **triumphal cross** (c1370) in the south transept is portayed as the tree of life. The altarpiece was produced by the workshop of Henrik Bornemann of Hamburg in about 1500 and depicts a Cucifixion scene on the central panel. The elaborately designed **Renaissance tombs★** on the north side of the choir are the work of Philipp Brandin. A particular highlight among the cathedral's collection of art treasures are the **Güstrow apostles★**, 12 almost life-size oak figures made by Claus Berg of Lübeck in c1530.
A stark contrast to these is Ernst Barlach's *Der Schwebende* (a recast, as the original was branded "degenerate art" and destroyed in 1937), an expressive figure with the features of Käthe Kollwitz in an attitude of meditation, above an ornate early 18C wrought iron grille.

Pfarrkirche St. Marien ☉ – The Gothic parish church has undergone many alterations over the centuries. The present building is a hall-church with three naves and a tower topped with a bulbous cupola in the Baroque style. The original **high altar★**, a fine example of wood carving from the Brabant, is the work of Jan Bormann of Brussels, who created it in 1522. He depicts Christ's Passion in 13 masterly crafted oak reliefs. The altarpiece has three different views and can be positioned in two different ways. The paintings on the wings are a masterpiece by Bernard van Orley. A Late Gothic **triumphal Crucifixion group** dating from 1516 unusually depicts Adam and Eve next to the Virgin Mary and St John.

★ Ernst-Barlach-Gedenkstätte (Barlach Museum) ☉ – This museum in honour of Barlach is located in the Late Gothic Gertrudenkapelle, which the artist had always longed in vain to use as a studio. The old chapel now houses some of his most important works. The "Barlachweg" leads to Barlach's **Heidberg studio**, on the shores of the Inselsee just south of town.

The Michelin Maps which accompany this Guide are shown on the back cover.

HAIGERLOCH ★

Baden-Württemberg – Population 10 100
Michelin map 419 U 10

The **site★★** of this tiny town on the northern fringe of the Swabian Jura is extremely attractive. It lies cradled between two steeply enclosed and wooded horse-shoe bends of the Eyach river. When the lilac is in flower at Whitsun it looks delightful.

SIGHTS

Start at the Marktplatz in the lower town. Climb the slope or stairway, both of which rise to the castle, built along the clifflike promontory on the downstream bend of the Eyach.

Schloßkirche – Built on the end of the spur, this early 17C church is impressive with the splendour of its Baroque furnishings, which date from 1748.

Continue up the rise, cross the castle courtyard diagonally, and follow the signposted path to the Kapf.

Kapf – From the lookout point there is a view of the upstream river bend where it hugs the upper town, overlooked by the Roman Tower (Römerturm).
Return to the Marktplatz and take the Pfluggasse, on the left.

Atommuseum Haigerloch ☉ – This small museum explains, with the help of display panels and three-dimensional material, how Professor Heisenberg and his colleagues constructed, deep inside the cliff beneath the Schloßkirche in the closing months of the Second World War, Germany's first experimental nuclear reactor.
Return once more to the Marktplatz and the car. Take the Oberstadtstraße and park opposite the church at the top of the hill.

★ St. Anna-Kirche – At the end of a shady avenue, this church looks across the Eyach gorge at the Schloßkirche, high up on the far side of the river. To get a clear **view★**, walk back a little down the approach road.
A pilgrims' sanctuary built by Johann Michael Fischer in 1755, St. Anna-Kirche, together with its chaplain's house (Kaplaneihaus), forms a remarkably elegant Baroque site. Inside, note on each side of the altar the enveloping reredos by Johann Michael Feuchtmayer.

HALBERSTADT

Seat of a bishopric as early as the 8C and later a member of the Hanseatic League, Halberstadt was for hundreds of years one of northern Germany's most active commercial centres, trading mainly in linen and woollen goods. Sadly, a large part of the town's architectural heritage was destroyed in 1945, but the cathedral, despite the tremendous amount of restoration necessary after the war, remains one of the most interesting Gothic buildings in the country.

SIGHTS

★★ **Dom St. Stephanus** ☉ – In its opulence and the spirit of its design, this church recalls the Gothic cathedrals of France. Building began in 1240 with the base of each tower and the western bays. A second stage of the work extended from 1354 to 1402. During this period, the chancel was erected, prolonged by the small chapel of St Mary (Marienkapelle) and the ambulatory, where the High Gothic influence resulted in lower walls and the installation of stained glass windows in the space thus freed. The nave, completed towards the end of the 15C, has no triforium. Owing to the size of the chancel, the transept occupies an almost central position on the cathedral floor-plan.

The **rood-screen★** is finely worked in the High Gothic style (c1510). Above it, a group representing the **Triumphal Cross★** is a splendid example of late Romanesque sculpture. Dating from c1220, it is a relic from the Ottonian cathedral which once occupied the site of the present building. The figures of the Virgin Mary and St John, together with two seraphim, are represented on either side of the Saviour. The 15C choir columns are adorned with 14 statues of saints and the Apostles. A cloister decorated with 13C Stations of the Cross opens off the southern part of the nave.

★★ **Domschatz (Treasury)** ☉ – Rare liturgical vestments and religious vessels from the 12C to the 16C are displayed here with a precious collection of 12C tapestries, in particular the Abraham Tapestry, which is more than 10m - 33ft long.

Liebfrauenkirche – *To the west of the cathedral, at the far end of the square.*
The choir screen of this 12C Romanesque basilica is embellished with **high-reliefs★** representing Christ, the Virgin Mary and the Apostles. The workmanship, once again, rates them among the finest examples of late 12C Romanesque art.

Städtisches Museum (Municipal Museum) ☉ – *At no 36 Domplatz.*
Local furniture, craftwork and sacred statuary can be seen here. The museum covers the history of the town and the surrounding region. The display includes a model of medieval Halberstadt and reconstructions of an old-fashioned pharmacy and a glove-maker's workshop. In an adjacent building is the "Heineanum", where there is a splendid ornithological display.

Marktkirche St. Martini – The saint is represented in a bas-relief on the south door of this 13-14C church. A bronze baptismal font inside, dating from the beginning of the 14C, is decorated with scenes from the life of Christ.

HALLE★

Halle, on the banks of the Saale between the great northern plain and the first heights of central Germany, is a town with a dual identity: on the one hand it is an important industrial centre specializing in mechanical engineering and chemical manufacture; on the other hand, an intellectual enclave whose university traditions go back to the 17C.

The Salt City – As early as 806 a fortress was built to safeguard the sources of salt extraction which formed the base of Halle's prosperity. The high-point of this era was between the 14C and the 16C, after which – especially during the Industrial Revolution – local lignite mines formed the commercial base on which the town's commercial development relied. Halle never, however, attained the status of an Imperial City. Halle received a further boost to its economy from the mining of local seams of brown coal during the Industrial Revolution.

A Musical Tradition – The creation at the end of the 13C of the Brotherhood of Musicians and Fife Players (Spylleuten und Pfeiffern), and the foundation of an opera in 1654 by the Duke Augustus, illustrate the age-old support of music shown by the municipality. George Frederick Handel was born in Halle in 1685. Organist at the cathedral in 1702, he composed many sonatas and cantatas before moving, after a period in Italy, to north Germany and then, in 1710, to London, where he set up residence. His compositions quickly won him an enthusiastic reception from the general public, more importantly, royal favour and patronage.

In 1726, he took British citizenship, after which he was appointed composer of the Chapel Royal. One of his major interests was the composition of large-scale choral works, of which perhaps the most famous example is the oratorio *Messiah*.

In 1713 Johann Sebastian Bach attempted – unsuccessfuly – to obtain the post of organist at Halle's Marktkirche (a position, ironically enough, that went to his son Friedmann 30 years later). The city pays a tribute to the master of German Baroque music in the annual **Handel Festival**.

SIGHTS

* **Marktplatz** – This huge square is dominated by the belfries of the Marktkirche and by the **Roter Turm** (red tower), built in the 15C and almost 80m - 262ft high. An 1859 statue of Handel surveys the square from the centre. The market and the tramway junction there make this the most animated part of the town.

* **Marktkirche** – A triple-aisle hall-church with no chancel, this building was constructed during the first half of the 16C on the site of two ruined Romanesque churches of which nothing but the towers remains. Inside, admire the delicate interlacing of ribs beneath the barrel vaulting, unusual in the absence of transverse arches corresponding to the bays – a feature which seems to confer on the vaulting its own existence independent of the columns supporting it. The side aisles are fitted with stone galleries. The **reredos★** of the high altar carries a Virgin and Child painted by a pupil of the Cranach school (1529).

Moritzkirche – *On the Hallorenring*. This, another triple-aisle hall-church, built between 1388 and 1511, displays a network of star-vaulting characteristic of the Flamboyant Gothic style. **Works★** by the sculptor Conrad of Einbeck are on view in the church, masterpieces distinguished at the same time by a naive realism and a great power of expression. Note in particular *The Man of Sorrows*, a statue (1411) of St Maurice, and a *Pietà* (1416).

* **Händel-Haus** ⊘ – *Große Nikolaistraße 5*. The great composer's birthplace has been transformed into a museum outlining both his life and his work. One section of the museum exhibits period musical instruments, including several harpsichords dating from the 16C and 17C.

Dom (Cathedral) – *Am Domplatz*. The original, simple edifice (early 14C) was modified *c*1520 by Cardinal Albert of Brandenburg, who transformed it into a Gothic hall-church with three naves. The interior columns are decorated with statues of Christ, the Apostles and the saints, executed in the studios of Peter Schroh, one of the most talented sculptors of the time. Along with the pulpit (*c*1525), they show signs already of a Renaissance influence.

Technisches Halloren- und Salinenmuseum (Saltworks Museum) ⊘ – *Mansfelder Straße 52*. The history of the exploitation of the local salt mines and the cultural development of the "Halloren" – the Halle salt miners guild.

ᴀ ᴀ **Staatliche Galerie Moritzburg (Moritzburg National Gallery)** ⊘ – *Friedermann-Bach-Platz* In 1484, building began on the Moritzburg, a fortress complex with four wings. Until 1541, it was the preferred residence of the Archbishops of Magdeburg and Mainz. Having been destroyed during the Thirty Years War, part of the fortress was restored and converted into a museum at the beginning of the 20C. It now houses the most significant art collection in Sachsen-Anhalt.

Halle Cathedral by Lionel Feininger, Galerie Moritzburg

There is an excellent collection of **19C and 20C German painting**. The fine works on display embrace the periods of **Romanticism** (Hans von Marées, Caspar David Friedrich), **Impressionism** (Slevogt, Corinth, Liebermann) and **Expressionism**. Works by the artists of the **Brücke** group, as well as by Kandinsky and Feininger, are on display.

The department of **German sculpture of the 19C and 20C** includes works by, among others, Wilhelm Lehmbruck and Ernst Barlach. Numismatists will enjoy a fine collection of moneys and medals in the fortress tower. The museum also displays interesting collections of glassware and ceramics dating from the Middle Ages to the present, and also porcelain and gold ware.

EXCURSION

Eisleben – *34km - 21 miles to the west.*
Martin Luther was born – and died – in this small mining town within sight of the lower ranges of the Harz Mountains. Memories of the religious reformer are evoked in his **birthplace** (Luther Geburtshaus, *Lutherstraße 16*) and the house where he died (Luther-Sterbehaus, *Andreaskirchplatz 7*).

For sweet-toothed visitors to Hamburg, "Rote Grütze" is a local speciality dessert made of red fruit served with vanilla sauce or cream.

HAMBURG★★★

Hamburg – Population 1 650 000
Michelin map 415/416 F 14
Plan of the conurbation in the current Michelin Red Guide Deutschland

Hamburg, Germany's second largest city after Berlin, is one of the most important ports in Europe. Its old title of "Free and Hanseatic Town" and its status as a "City State" (Stadtstaat) testify to its eminence and influence through the centuries.

Each year, on May 7, there is an anniversary celebration (Hafengeburtstag) in the port of Hamburg, commemorating Frederick Barbarossa's concession in 1189 of the right to free navigation on the lower Elbe. The exercise of this right, menaced by piracy and the feudal pretensions of neighbour states – especially Denmark – demanded a continual watch by the city authorities which could not be relaxed until the 17C.

The Hanseatic Town (13C-15C) – Originally a modest settlement on the banks of the Alster, a small tributary of the Elbe, Hamburg enjoyed its first taste of prosperity when it became a member of the Hanseatic League *(qv)*, headed at that time by Lübeck. It was then that merchants started to organize the banks of the Elbe itself for warehousing and the berthing of ships. The town profited from the particular conditions then of Baltic-North Sea trade: in those days only heavy cargoes of grain and timber took the long sea passage through the Kattegat and the Skagerrak; more valuable material was landed at Lübeck, transported overland to Hamburg, then re-embarked.

General view of Hamburg

Liberty and Neutrality – The great geographic discoveries of the 16C, and the new sea routes they opened up, destroyed existing trade patterns and dislocated the Hanseatic monopoly. Hamburg traders were thus forced to become intermediaries in warehousing and distribution. The foundation of the first German Stock Exchange in 1558 reflected the intense business activity which resulted – a situation in no way worsened by the city's policy of strict neutrality, which kept it out of the Thirty Years War.

In 1618 Hamburg became a Free Imperial City. One year later the Bank of Hamburg was founded. From 1806 to 1814 French troops occupied the town. In 1842 it was ravaged by a disastrous fire.

But American independence and the emergence of Latin America lent an added impetus to the extraordinary expansion of the later 19C. By 1913, the Hamburg-Amerika steamship line was the largest in the world, and shipbuilding was the city's key industry. Today, port traffic in Hamburg has reached an annual turnover of 57 million tons.

LIFE IN HAMBURG

Business and Leisure – Like so many big ports, Hamburg has a reputation for night-life. This is mainly centred on the St. Pauli quarter, to the west of the city centre, where in the side streets flanking the **Reeperbahn** (**EZ 70**) and the Große Freiheit, in the gaudy illumination of multicoloured neon signs, bars, discothèques, exotic restaurants, clubs and the Eros Centre function day and night.

Many Hamburg residents are a little diffident about the fact that their city is known worldwide for the garish Reeperbahn district. They point to the elegance and attraction of the residential area around the northern end, and the business quarter around the southern part, and of the Alster lake which lies like a jewel in the heart of the city. Between the Staatsoper (Opera House) (**FY**) and the Rathaus (Town Hall), pedestrian precincts and covered malls form an almost uninterrupted labyrinth of art galleries, fashion shops, boutiques, jewellery stores and restaurants.

The Mönckebergstraße (**GHY**), which links the Rathaus with the railway station, is the city's other commercial artery. Antique shops around the Gänsemarkt (**FY**) specialize in oriental art. Between the Rathaus and the station, an impressive variety of old maps, prints, travel works and tourist guides can be found in a number of different booksellers', while philatelists and tobacco lovers will go to the small shops in the printing and counting-house quarter.

The people of Hamburg are said to be very "British" Germans, as they tend to be more reserved and serious than their lively southern copatriots. For visitors, Hamburg is among the most welcoming of German cities, and English is spoken in many of the restaurants, stores and wine cellars.

Culinary Specialities – These often mix local produce with Eastern spices, sometimes combining in one dish meat, fruit and sweet-and-sour sauces. Typical are Aalsuppe – eel soup – and Labskaus, a seamen's dish of minced meat, herring, chopped gherkins and mashed potato, topped with fried eggs.

CITY CENTRE *time: one day*

★★★ **Außenalster** (**GHXY**) ⊘ – This beautiful stretch of water offers sailing and canoeing in the centre of the city. A fleet of Alsterschiffahrt motorboats ferries passengers regularly between a series of landing stages.

A **boat trip**★★★ (Alsterrundfahrt) on the lake allows the visitor to get far enough away to appreciate the city skyline punctuated by Hamburg's famous five towers, all of them over 100m - 328ft high. They stand above the four main churches and the Rathaus.

It is equally pleasant to make a circuit of the Alster by car, driving clockwise around the long shaded avenues with blocks of luxury flats on one side and immaculate stretches of greensward between the water and the roadway on the other. Their use as **viewpoints** has conferred names on such quays as the **Fernsicht** (View. *Leave by the Alsterufer* - **GX**) and **Schöne Aussicht** (Beautiful Vista. *Leave by An der Alster* - **HX**).

★ **Jungfernstieg** (**GY**) – Bordering the southern end of the Binnenalster (inner) basin, this famous street is perhaps the city's most cosmopolitan thoroughfare: the crowded terraces of the waterfront Alsterpavillon café-restaurant, the craft busily crossing and recrossing the basin, the presence nearby of one of the world's most famous hotels, and the imposing new office blocks lining the Ballindamm above the eastern quay all contribute to the general animation.

Rathausmarkt (**GYZ**) – This square, replanned after the fire of 1842, is dominated by the high campanile of the **Rathaus** (**R**), built in the neo-Renaissance style in 1887 and supported by no less than 4 000 piles.

The bridge (Schleusenbrücke), which forms part of the lock controlling the level of the Alster, crosses the Alsterfleet, a final relic of the complex canal system once characteristic of the city. The monument at the end of the bridge with a plinth carving by Barlach is the First World War memorial. On the far bank the colonnade of the Alsterarkaden shelters elegant shops.

| M¹ | Kunsthalle | M² | Museum für Kunst und Gewerbe | M³ | Museum für Hamburgische Geschichte |

St. Jakobikirche (GZ) – Among the numerous treasures of this 14-15C hall-church are the reredos of St Luke and the Fishers' Guild; a triptych of the Coopers' Guild on the high altar; Georg Bauman's alabaster and marble pulpit (1610); and finally the famous 1693 organ by Arp Schnitger.

Kontorhäuser (Counting House Buildings) (GHZ) – Massively constructed of sombre brick, these stand in the printing, press and business quarter around the Burchardplatz.

The **Chilehaus**, built in 1924, stands against the sky like the prow of a ship. The **Sprinkenhof** (1930) is a town within the town, an office complex complete with roadways that can be used by motor cars.

HAMBURG

Alsterarkaden	**GY** 3		Adenauerallee	**HY** 2
Bergstraße	**GY**		Bei dem Neuen Krahn	**FZ** 9
Colonnaden	**FY**		Bei den St Pauli-Landungsbrücken	**EZ** 10
Dammtorstraße	**FY**		Böhmkenstraße	**EZ** 16
Gerhofstraße	**FY** 29		Börsenbrücke	**GZ** 18
Große Bleichen	**FY** 33		Cremon	**FZ** 21
Große Burstah	**FZ** 35		Dammtordamm	**FX** 23
Jungfernstieg	**GY**		Graskeller	**FZ** 31
Mönckebergstraße	**GHY**		Große Johannisstr.	**GZ** 34
Neuer Wall	**FYZ**		Große Reichenstr.	**GZ** 37
Poststraße	**FY**		Hachmannplatz	**HY** 39
Spitalerstraße	**GHY**		Helgoländer allee	**EZ** 43

Holstenglacis	**EY** 46		Reesendamm	**GY** 71
Kleine Reichenstraße	**GZ** 50		Rothenbaumchaussee	**FX** 72
Klingberg	**GZ** 51		Schleusenbrücke	**GY** 75
Krayenkamp	**FZ** 54		Schmiedestraße	**GZ** 76
Millerntordamm	**EZ** 63		Stadthausbrücke	**FY** 77
Pumpen	**HZ** 68		Steintordamm	**HY** 79
Rathausstraße	**GZ** 69		Steintorplatz	**HY** 80
Reeperbahn	**EZ** 70		Zippelhaus	**GZ** 88

M⁴ Postmuseum	**M⁵** Hamburgisches Museum für Völkerkunde	**R** Rathaus

To the south, the squat **Speicherstadt** (**GZ**) warehouses rise above the Zoll (customs) Canal and its secondary channels. The severity of these dark brick masses is relieved only by an upper decoration of stepped gables and turrets. Built in the late 19C for the free trade zone, they store in their 373 000m² - 447 000sq yds of floor space such valuable merchandise as coffee, tobacco, spices, raw silk and oriental carpets.

Altstadt (**FGZ**) – The old town is bounded by the Nikolaifleet, the Binnenhafen (docks reserved for river craft and tugboats) and the Zoll Canal.

Deichstraße (**FZ**) – 17C and 18C merchants' houses have today been converted mainly into bars and taverns. It was in the Deichstraße that the great fire of 1842 started.

The restored façades of warehouses opposite, lining the curve of the Nikolaifleet Canal, recall the Hamburg of yesteryear.

The best view is from the **Hohe Brücke**, which crosses the Nikolaifleet and lies parallel with the Binnenhafen. Pulleys once used for the transhipment of cargoes from ship to shore and vice versa can still be seen on the warehouse gables. Traces of the severe floods of 1962 and 1976 are visible on the walls.

Cremon (FZ 21) – From no 33 to no 36, this street is lined by warehouses and former lodging houses, each with dual entrances – one from the street, one from the canal.

St. Katharinen-Kirche (GZ) – This Gothic church, built of brick during the 14C and 15C, features a bulbous openwork tower that rises above the narrow streets of the old port.

★ **Hauptkirche St. Michaelis (EFZ)** – Another brick church, designed in 1762 by the architect Sonnin, this is one of the finest examples of the Baroque tradition in northern Germany. Intended for the Lutheran sect, the church is surprisingly spacious, well proportioned and well lit.

Its famous **tower** (1786), rising high above the Elbe with a lantern turret in the form of a rotunda, is known by local people simply as "Michel" and has become the emblem of the city.

The **view★** from the **platform** ⊘ takes in all of the town centre, but most particularly the river, zebra-striped with the wake of ships, and its docks, basins, warehouses and wharves.

Near the east end of the church, pass through the porch at no 10 Am Krayenkamp **(FZ 54)**. The blind alley beyond is lined with astonishing brick and timber houses built in 1670 as almshouses **(Krameramtswohnungen)** and today transformed into art galleries.

★★ **Kunsthalle (Fine Arts Museum) (HY M¹)** ⊘ – This museum houses one of the largest art collections in Germany. The galleries have correspondingly been recently refitted and the paintings rehung to create a most attractive exhibition. A large extension by arhitect Oswald Mathias Ungers is due to be opened in 1997, and it will house contemporay art.

The exhibition opens with medieval works. The **Grabow altarpiece** created in 1379 for St. Petri, Hamburg, by Master Bertram of Minden is one of the largest and most touching examples of primitive painting in north Germany. Its 24 separate panels are related to the concept of Salvation and comprise a variety of scenes from the naive to the animated. It is fascinating to compare this altarpiece with the polyptych of St Thomas of Canterbury by Master Francke.

The 17C Dutch school is represented by an early Rembrandt *(Simeon in the Temple)*, and by land- and sea-scapes by Avercamp, Van Goyen, the Ruysdaels and Van de Velde. Genre paintings by Jan Steen and Pieter de Hooch are also exhibited.

A particular strength of the exhibition is the section of 19C German painting. Prominently displayed are works by the Romantics Caspar David Friedrich *(Ice Field, Rambler above a Sea of Clouds)* and Philipp Otto Runge *(The Children of Hülsenbeck, Morning)*, which are representative of the period when painting was breaking through into the realms of subjectivity. The museum also possesses major works by Feuerbach, Von Marées and Böcklin. An entire room is devoted to Menzel. Realists whose works are on display include Wilhelm Leibl, whose famous painting *Three Women in Church* can be found hanging here.

There is a dazzling display of work by Max Liebermann *(Women Repairing Nets)*, Lovis Corinth and Edvard Munch *(Madonna)*. The section on the Classical Modern artists is dominated by the works of Max Beckmann and Oscar Kokoschka, as well as the members of the **Brücke** and **Blauer Reiter** groups (Kirchner, Nolde, Marc) Paul Klee's enchanting painting *Goldfish* is also on display in this part of the museum. A room is given over to the works of Joseph Beuys.

★ **Museum für Kunst und Gewerbe (Museum of Decorative Arts) (HY M²)** ⊘ – Thousands of arts and crafts exhibits are displayed chronologically in this museum. Among the most fascinating are the medieval statuary, gold and silver plate (Reliquary of St George by Berndt Notke), sumptuous Renaissance furniture and fine examples of north German clockmaking as well as delicate 18C porcelain. There is a generous display of ornaments, furniture and artworks from the Jugendstil *(qv)*, and an interesting section of antiquities. Note also the departments of Chinese, Japanese and Islamic art, the hall of mirrors from the Budge-Palais, and collections on graphics, photography and design.

★ **Museum für Hamburgische Geschichte (Historical Museum) (EYZ M³)** ⊘ – Here the visitor can browse over models of Hamburg in days gone by, and a brilliant scale model of the city's present railway system. There is a huge department devoted to the port and navigation on the Elbe, including more than 100 model ships, among them a cutaway section of a 1901 steamer and the impressive 1722 *Wappen von Hamburg*.

★★THE PORT (HAFEN) (EZ)

Apart from the tower of St. Michaeliskirche, the best **viewpoint★** from which to see the port as a whole is the Stintfang (**EZ**) – a raised terrace below the youth hostel.

A few statistics – The Hamburg docks comprise 60 basins and more than 68km - 42 miles of quays, in addition to a great number of mooring buoys. Thanks to a relatively small tidefall (3m - 10ft average), no locks are necessary in the basins accessible to ocean-going traffic able to navigate the Elbe (displacing up to 110 000 tons and drawing no more than 13.5m - 44ft). The port's reputation relies on a speedy turn-around and on the wide variety of equipment, warehousing, transport and offloading machinery available for every kind of cargo. Three hundred and forty shipping lines call regularly (about 650 departures a month) to transport merchandise to 1 000 ports all over the world.

Boat trip around the port (Hafenrundfahrt) ⊙ – *Boats leave from landing stage no 2 in the St Pauli district (St Pauli-Landungsbrücken)* (**EZ**).
The visitor will be astonished by the sheer size of the dockyards – 5 separate shipbuilders, 26 floating docks – and by the extraordinary activity on either side of the Elbe, where every type of vessel is constructed: tankers, lighters, tugs, cargo ships, containers, refrigerator craft and pleasure boats as well as police and customs launches. Motor ferries ply back and forth all day long, transporting south bank workers back to the city during the rush hour. Before 10am on Sundays and public holidays, do not leave the St. Pauli quays without visiting the lively Fischmarkt.

CITY OUTSKIRTS

★ **Postmuseum (Postal Museum)** (**FY M⁴**) ⊙ – This museum, in Heinrich-von-Stephan-Platz, named after the Prussian director-general who inaugurated the World Confederation of Postal Services, outlines the evolution of mail transport and dispatches from the 16C to the present day. It has a particularly fine collection of **transmitting equipment**, concentrating especially on the pioneer period of long-distance communications. There are many examples of early telegraphic equipment, telephones invented by Bell and Siemens, instrument panels with warning lights, exchange keyboards, fax machines and radio installations.
Some of the modern instruments are displayed in working order and may be tried out by visitors to the museum.

★ **Fernsehturm (Television Tower)** (**EX**) ⊙ – A slender steel and concrete plinth whose highest aerials are almost 280m - 919ft from the ground, the tower soars above the Planten un Blomen park to the west of the Alster. There is an observation platform at the top and, at a height of 132m - 433ft above ground level, a revolving panoramic restaurant affording a fine **view★★** of the entire city (one complete revolution takes 55min).

★ **Erholungspark Planten un Blomen** (**EFX**) ⊙ – Part of a green belt replacing the old fortifications which ran in an arc between the Elbe and the Alster to the west and north of the town, this park was laid out in 1936. Its geometrically arranged gardens are used as a proving ground for new species of flowers and trees. An artifical cascade tumbles into the main pool (Großer Parksee), where after dark the fountains act as background to a Son et Lumière performance (Wasserlicht-konzert). Nearby are the city conference centre (Congreß Centrum) and the Hamburg Plaza hotel.

★ **Hamburgisches Museum für Völkerkunde (Ethnographic Museum)** (**M⁵**) ⊙ – *Rothenbaumchaussee 64* (**FX**).
The collections in this museum – remarkable in their variety and rarity – are directly due to the commercial relations between this Hanseatic town and the rest of the world, Hamburg having been the departure point at the turn of the century for explorers' expeditions to Oceania and elsewhere. Well represented here are the civilizations of Europe, Asia (including the former Soviet Union and Turkey), Africa (Benin bronzes and cult objects from what is now Zaire), the Americas and the Pacific isles.
The **Golden Room** (Goldkammer), on the ground floor, has an exhibition of pre-Colombian jewellery. On the first floor, note the wand puppets used in shadow theatres from Bali and Java, a gallery of **Oceanian Masks★**, and the **Boat Hall★** (Bootshalle), which is devoted to Polynesian canoes and other craft. Symbolic figures decorate a fine **Maori Meeting Hall** from New Zealand, which is on the same floor.

★★ **Tierpark Hagenbeck (Zoo)** ⊙ – *Leave by the Grindelallee* (**FX**).
Founded in 1907 in the Stellingen suburb, the zoological gardens maintain a century-old tradition of capturing, breeding, selling and training wild animals for circuses. 2 500 creatures of 365 species from five continents live in relative freedom in 25ha - 62 acres of grassland, woods and artificial rocks. In recent years the zoo has saved from extinction the onager, a rare species of Persian wild ass.

EXCURSIONS

Altona; Klein Flottbek; Wedel – *22km - 14 miles – allow 1/2 day.*

★★**Altonaer Museum in Hamburg – Norddeutsches Landesmuseum** (Altona and North German Museum) ☉ – *Leave on the Reeperbahn* (**EZ 70**).

Art, culture and day-to-day life in Schleswig-Holstein, the lower Elbe valley and along the North and Baltic Sea coasts are illustrated here. Note the exceptional collection of **ships' figureheads** from the 18-19C. The reconstructed interiors of farmers' cottages and a room containing traditional farmers' costumes are also interesting. A thatched cottage from the Vierlande, a fruit- and flower-producing region southeast of Hamburg, has been transformed into a small restaurant for the museum's visitors.

Altonaer Balkon (Altona Balcony) – From a terrace south of Altona's town hall, there is a **view**★ of the confluence of the two branches of the Elbe which marks the limit of Hamburg's industrial and port zone. The amount of shipping which passes each hour is astonishing.

Follow the **Elbchaussee**★, a spacious avenue bordered by great houses and superb properties developed since the beginning of the 19C by the grand Hamburg shipowning and trading dynasties.

At Klein Flottbek turn right and drive along the Baron-Voght-Straße as far as Route 50.

Jenisch-Haus ☉ – A fine landscaped park planted with exotic trees surrounds this pleasant neo-Classical villa built between 1831 and 1834. The luxuriously furnished rooms illustrate the style of German bourgeois interiors from the late Renaissance to the beginning of the Jugendstil period. Note the splendid marquetry flooring of the ground floor state rooms, and the Danish style furniture upstairs manufactured in Altona.

Ernst-Barlach-Haus ☉ – *Baron-Voght-Straße 50A Jenischpark.*

"Terpsichore" ship's figurehead

Altonaer Museum in Hamburg - Norddeutsches Landesmuseum

This house, set up thanks to the donation of Hamburg tobacco tycoon Hermann Reemstma, contains an exceptional collection of sculptures, prints and drawings by local artist Ernst Barlach, born in Wedel near Hamburg. There is a particularly impressive display of sculptures in wood, including some powerfully expressive works such as *The Frieze of Listeners*, the figure of *Moses*, and the group of *Three Men Brandishing a Sword*.

Continue along the Elbchaussee, then head for Wedel after driving through the pleasant suburban resort of Blankenese.

Wedel – *Follow the Willkomm-Höft signposts to the café-restaurant beside the Elbe known as the "Schulauer Fährhaus".*

Above the terrace is a saluting base for passing ships (Schiffsbegrüßungsanlage). The ceremony – which many people come to watch – involves running up the flag and then playing the national anthem of the country of origin of every single vessel sailing upstream or downstream past the base.

There is an **Ernst-Barlach-Museum** ☉ in the house where the artist was born *(Mühlenstraße 1)* which displays drawings and lithographs as well as fine bronzes, among them the impressive *Old Men Dancing*. The works on display here are a particularly good illustration of the artist's interest in exploring literary motifs and his creative working out of his personal dramas.

Schloß Ahrensburg ☉ – *23km - 15 miles to the northeast. Leave Hamburg by B25, the Lübeck road.*

The white bulk of this moated castle is framed by the green, leafy banks of the Hunnau. Built, like Schloß Glücksburg *(qv)*, by Peter Rantzau, it comprises three main blocks flanked by corner towers surmounted by lantern towers. Scrolled gables framed by obelisks decorate the castle, which was the last true Renaissance creation to be built in Schleswig-Holstein (1595).

The interior recalls the family of Count Heinrich Carl Schimmelmann, who bought the castle in 1759 and refurbished it. Note the stairwell, the oak-panelled dining room, and the Emkendorf Room with its elegant Louis XVI furnishings.

HAMELN ★

HAMELIN – Niedersachsen – Population 58 000
Michelin map 417 J 12
Town plan in the current Michelin Red Guide Deutschland

Built on the east bank of the Weser, Hamelin glories in fine old houses, of which the most typical belong to the **Weser Renaissance** (late 16-early 17C) period *(qv)*. The style is distinguished architecturally by ram's-horn scrollwork and pinnacled gables. Other characteristics include delicately worked stone bands encircling the building, forward projecting pavilions (Utlucht) treated as smaller extensions of the main façade, and large, well-developed lucarnes (Zwerchhäuser) with decorated gables at the base of the roof.

Hamelin is also a town with a special place in European folklore; it is the home of the celebrated ratcatcher immortalized by Goethe, and by Robert Browning as the Pied Piper in English. In the summer, a dramatic version of the legend is performed each Sunday at noon on the terrace of the Hochzeitshaus. As souvenirs, toys or sweets, the rats are still to be seen in many of Hamelin's shop windows.

The Pied Piper of Hamelin – In 1284, a mysterious man in multicoloured clothes promised the townspeople that, for a substantial reward, he would free Hamelin from a plague of rats and mice. He played his pipe, and all the rodents emerged to follow him to the banks of the Weser, where they drowned.

But the reward was not forthcoming, so the piper returned on Sunday, when everyone was at church, and played again in revenge. This time it was the children who emerged from their houses. There were 130 of them, and they too followed him, never to be seen again. Only two escaped; one was dumb, the other blind.

The historical version of the tale is that overpopulation in the 13C led to a troop of young people being sent by the authorities to colonize far-away lands to the east.

SIGHTS

★ **Rattenfängerhaus (The Ratcatcher's House)** – It is a large, well-proportioned building dating from 1603. The symmetrical decoration of the façade involves differently sculpted bands of stonework, further adorned with carved busts and masks. Typical Weser scrolls and pinnacles enrich the gable.

★ **Hochzeitshaus (Marriage House)** – The building, constructed between 1610 and 1617, acted as a reception centre for burghers' weddings. Three elegant gables break the horizontals of the façade, themselves emphasized by cornices and lateral bands of stonework.

Demptersches Haus – *In the market place*. An outstanding building, dating from 1607, noteworthy especially for its fine Weser Renaissance projecting pavilion (Utlucht).

Stiftsherrenhaus (Canons' House) – *Osterstraße 8*.
Another remarkable house, this one half-timbered and built in 1558. The sculpted consoles represent biblical figures.

Haus Lücking – *Wendenstraße 8*. This is a rich, half-timbered house of 1639 with a rounded doorway centred in a rectangular recess.

Rattenkrug – *Bäckerstraße 16*. A projecting pavilion (Utlucht) and a tall gable of no less than five floors distinguish this 1568 building.

Münster (Collegiate Church) – From the public gardens to the south, the church appears to cower beneath the protection of the massive polygonal tower over the transept – once part of a 12C Romanesque basilica which was transformed a century later into the existing Gothic hall-church. Inside, the layout of the columns and their capitals, checkered or carved with palm leaves, draws attention once more to the raised transept.

EXCURSIONS

★ **Hämelschenburg** – *11km - 7 miles to the south*.
The **Schloß★** ⊙, which boasts both a moat and a lagoon, was built in the shape of a horse-shoe between 1588 and 1616. It is one of the masterpieces of the Weser Renaissance style.
The wing overlooking the road is the most ornate, with typical alternations of smooth and embossed stone bands, an oriel immediately above the moat, and four decorative gables. Weapons, trophies, paintings and furniture are on view in the interior.

Fischbeck – *7km - 3 3/4 miles to the northwest*.
The **abbey** ⊙ here was officially recognized by Otto I in the year 955 (photocopies of the original documents can be seen in the church). It is still used as a home for elderly Protestant women. The church itself dates from the 12C. It was equipped in the 19C with partitioned boxes, which allowed the noblewomen to take part in the services. The **crypt** is in a pure Romanesque style, with each column topped by a capital embellished with a different motif. Left of the chancel is a moving Ecce Homo in sculpted wood; to the right of it hangs the famous 16C **Fischbeck tapestry** illustrating the foundation of the abbey. The cloister, in its present state, dates from the 13C and 14C.

HANN. MÜNDEN★★

Niedersachsen – Population 28 000
Michelin map 417/418 L 12
Town plan in the current Michelin Red Guide Deutschland

The town of Hann. Münden, or Hannoversch Münden, with its numerous **half-timbered houses★★**, lies where the Fulda and the Werra converge to flow on as the Weser. The most interesting buildings are to be found in the streets between the town hall and the Werra.

★ **Rathaus (Town Hall)** – The main façade of this building is a typical Weser Renaissance design *(qv)*, its gables adorned with scrollwork, pyramids and statues.

St. Blasiikirche – Modified into a Gothic hall in the late 15C, this church with its steep slate roof is overlooked by a hexagonal tower. Inside, the south aisle contains the tomb of Wilhelm of Brunswick (d 1503), and there is an epitaph to his son in the northern part of the chancel. In the north aisle: a 14C baptismal font.

EXCURSION

★ **Upper Weser Valley** – *67km - 42 miles – allow 2 hours.*
From Hann. Münden to Bad Karlshafen, the Weser twists through a heavily wooded valley. In this otherwise deserted stretch of country, French Huguenot refugees gathered together in the 18C by the Landgraves of Hessen founded a number of villages baptised with such symbolically pious names as Gottstreu (Fidelity to the Creator) and Gewissensruh (Conscience in Repose). The valley is still without industry or railway.

Wahlsburg-Lippoldsberg – The old abbey church of Lippoldsberg (Ehemalige Klosterkirche St. Georg und Maria) was one of the first vaulted Romanesque churches erected in northern Germany.

Take the ferry across to the other side of the river.

Gewissensruh – Visit the tiny church (1779) here. Note the French inscriptions on the houses.

Bad Karlshafen – The town was founded in 1699 by the Landgrave Karl of Hessen and peopled with French refugees. It lies around a shipping basin at the confluence of the Weser and the Diemel.
A regular plan and uniform building design lend the place something of a monumental air. There is a small **Huguenot Museum** ⊙ (Deutsches Hugenottenmuseum, Hafenplatz 9).

Fürstenberg – Since 1747, world-famous porcelain has been created at the castle-factory here. Particularly fine pieces can be admired at the **porcelain museum** ⊙, along with an explanation of the manufacturing techniques (video film).

Höxter – Renaissance and Baroque unite in the gay, colour-washed houses of this town, with their decorated wooden side walls and roofs of pink sandstone tiles. The most picturesque and pretty line the **Westerbachstraße**. In St. Kilianskirche, there is an outstanding **Renaissance pulpit★** (1597) adorned with rare alabaster motifs.

Corvey – The only part of the original Carolingian **abbey church** that remains is the impressive Westwerk *(qv)*. The lower parts can be traced back to the 9C. Above the pre-nave entrance is a square church, two storeys high, into which opened a gallery (the Johannischor) reserved for the Emperor. The history of Corvey is outlined in a **museum** at the castle.

HANNOVER

HANOVER – Niedersachsen – Population 510 000
Michelin map 415/416/418 I 13
Plan of the conurbation in the current Michelin Red Guide Deutschland
and also on Michelin map 415

Hanover, capital of Lower Saxony, is one of the main economic centres of northern Germany. Its two annual international fairs, held in special pavilions southeast of the town, stimulate an enormous amount of business.
The city centre has been rebuilt to allow free movement of traffic and there is a pedestrian shopping area near the station. On the periphery are residential zones, waterways (Maschsee), and a green belt started as long ago as the 17C with the creation of the famous Herrenhausen gardens. There is a good view over the whole district from the dome of the **Rathaus** (**Z R**) ⊙.

HISTORICAL NOTES

The House of Hanover – The principality of Hanover fell in the 17C to a branch of the House of Brunswick and Lüneburg. The Court moved to Hanover. The transformation of Herrenhausen began. And, under the aegis of the cultured Princess Sophia, a period commenced in which literature and the arts flourished. Handel, who composed his first operas in Hamburg, was frequently invited to give concerts. The philosopher Leibniz arrived in 1676 to take up the position of Court Librarian, a post he held for forty years. In 1692 the principality became the Electorate of Brunswick and Lüneburg, the ninth in Germany.

From the Hanoverian Court to the Court of St James – The marriage in 1658 of the Duke Ernst-Augustus with the Palatine Princess Sophia, grand-daughter of the Stuart King James I, had given the Hanoverian succession a claim on the throne of England.
In 1714 the Elector Georg-Ludwig, son of Princess Sophia, did indeed find himself heir to the crown and became George I of England. The Court left Hanover and Herrenhausen. It was not to return until 1837, when the union of Hanover and England under a single sovereign was abrogated because the Salic Law (forbidding the accession of women to the throne) applied in Hanover. Victoria therefore became Queen of England, while in Hanover it was her uncle Ernst-Augustus who succeeded. Installing his Court in Hanover, the new monarch set about restoring the town to its former glory. But the year 1866 saw the fall of the House of Hanover and the annexation of the kingdom by Prussia.

★★HERRENHÄUSER GÄRTEN (HERRENHAUSEN GARDENS)
Leave by the Leibnizufer (Y) time: 1 1/2 hours

This beautiful 17C development, in the northwestern part of the city, comprises four separate and quite different gardens: the Großer Garten, the Berggarten, the Georgengarten and the Welfengarten. They are linked by an avenue of lime trees, the Herrenhäuser Allee, laid out in 1726 *(drivers take the Nienburger Straße)*.

★★**Großer Garten** – Creation of the garden started in 1666. Between 1680 and 1710 Princess Sophia took it over, transformed it, and enlarged it for – as she wrote more than once – "that garden is my very life". The oldest part is a formal French pleasure garden divided into flower borders punctuated by statues of allegorical figures and Roman gods. On one side is an open-air theatre, on the other a maze. At the southern end a mosaic of clipped hedges is cut by pathways between ornamental ponds. The powerful central fountain jets a plume of water no less than 82m - 269ft into the air (as a comparison, Nelson's Column, in London, is 170ft high).

HANNOVER

M¹ Kestner-Museum
M² Niedersächsisches Landesmuseum
M³ Historisches Museum
R Rathaus

In the southeastern corner of the garden is the small **Wilhelm-Busch-Museum** ☉, which is devoted to the local poet, illustrator and humorist (1832-1908) considered to be the originator of the strip cartoon . Busch's "Max und Moritz" was very popular among 19C German youth.

Berggarten – The greenhouses of this botanical garden display cactus plants and other succulents, as well as 2 500 varieties of orchid and flora native to the Canary Islands. At the far end of the garden's principal walk is the mausoleum of the Royal House of Hanover.

ADDITIONAL SIGHTS

Marktkirche (Y) – A four-gabled tower crowned by a sharp pinnacle presides over this church, rebuilt after 1945 in the style of the 14C original. An interesting contrast to the restored Gothic style are the modern bronze doors by Gerhard Marcks, depicting scenes from recent German history. Inside, note the 15C sculpted polychrome **reredos★★** at the high altar, which represents the Passion. Also noteworthy are the stained glass windows (14C) in the choir and the 15C baptismal font in bronze.

★ **Kestner-Museum (Z M¹)** ☉ – This valuable collection was established by Charlotte Kestner, better known, thanks to Goethe, as Charlotte Buff. On the ground floor there is a fine collection of antique coins (Greek, Roman and pre-Islamic Persian) as well as European numismatic examples from the 16C to the 20C. Five thousand years of history are recalled on the second floor, where there is a splendid exhibition of antiquities from Egypt (magnificent head of Amenophis IV-Akhenaton) and ancient Rome (glassware and bronzes). European decorative art is amply represented on the first floor, where German porcelain and faience is on display along with interesting silverware and ceramics embellished in the Jugendstil fashion. Do not miss the 12C head-reliquary – said to be that of John the Baptist – a masterpiece of goldsmithing.

★ **Niedersächsisches Landesmuseum (Museum of Lower Saxony) (Z M²)** ☉ – This huge regional museum has a special **prehistoric section★** (Urgeschichtliche Abteilung) which illustrates the evolution of primitive civilizations in northwest Germany. In the Fine Arts section an important **picture gallery** (Niedersächsische Landesgalerie) exhibits works ranging from medieval times to the present day. Primitives from Italy and Lower Saxony (Master Bertram; the Master of the Golden Table) are followed by German Renaissance artists (Holbein; Cranach) and Italian painters from the 16C to the 18C (Botticelli; Pontorno; Tiepolo; Piazetta). Flemish and Dutch work of the 17C is emblazoned with such names as Rubens, Van Dyck, Jan Brueghel, Kalf and the Ruysdaels.

German artists of the 19 and 20C are represented by C D Friedrich, F von Lenbach, the Impressionists Liebermann, Slevogt and Corinth, and Paula Becker-Modersohn of the Worpswede School. French painters exhibited include Poussin, Lorrain, Corot, Courbet and the Impressionists Monet, Renoir, Sisley and Pissarro. The **Department of Sculpture** displays works ranging from the Middle Ages, through the Renaissance (Riemenschneider), to such "moderns" as Rodin, Degas and Maillol.

★ **Sprengel-Museum (Z)** ☉ – Not far from the Maschsee, a stabile by Calder indicates the entrance to the museum, which concentrates on art of the 20C. Among the Cubists who experimented with form and volume are Picasso (*Three Women* - 1908), Léger (*The Village* - 1912), and the sculptor Henri Laurens (*Head of a Young Girl* - 1920). Expressionism, starting with Edvard Munch *(qv) (Half-Nude)*, developed in intensity with Karl Schmidt-Rottluff *(Four Bathers on the Beach)*, Otto Mueller *(Lovers)* and Ernst Ludwig Kirchner of the Brücke movement, as well as members of the Blauer Reiter movement, whose research into different uses of colour is remarkable in the works shown here. They include Kandinsky's *Diagonal*, Jawlensky's *Turandot II*, Macke's *Nude With Coral Necklace*, a fascinating *Floral Myth* by Paul Klee, and *Horse with Eagle* by Marc. In a similar vein are Nolde *(Flowers and Clouds)*, Rohlfs *(Birch Forest)*, Kokoschka and Feininger. A key position in reserved for the portraits of Beckmann *(Woman with a Bouquet of Carnations)*. Research in the Surrealist direction is represented by the pictures of Max Ernst *(Fascinating Cypress)*, by Salvador Dalí and above all by Kurt Schwitters, Hanoverian by birth and the author of many different kinds of work (*Merz-Bau*). Contemporary tendencies have their spokesmen in Tapiès, Dubuffet, Lindner and W Baumeister.

Historisches Museum (Y M³) ☉ – One section of this museum illustrates the history of Lower Saxony, and Hanover in particular, together with mementoes of the Hanoverian Royal House and a collection of carriages and harness (note the sumptuous golden coupé of the Prince of Wales, dating from 1783). Beautiful chests and cabinets from Lower Saxony are on view in the Ethnology section, as well as peasant interiors reconstructed with faience tiles and inlaid panelling.

Zoologischer Garten (Zoological Garden) ☉ – *Adenauerallee 3. Leave by the Schiffgraben* **(Y)**.
The most attractive section is that devoted to the antelopes, kangaroos and giraffes.

HARZ★★

The wooded heights of the Harz form the northern foothills of those mountains of central Europe resulting from the Hercynian upthrust in the Primary Era. Standing at the southern extremity of the vast Germano-Polish plain and almost entirely covered in forests, they break the moisture-laden winds sweeping across from the west to create a hilly region plentifully supplied with watercourses. Numerous dams have transformed the Harz into an exceptional reservoir supplying the nearby areas.

The highest point of the range, the Brocken (alt 1 142m - 3 747ft), site of the legendary Witches' Sabbath *(see Introduction)*, attracts a great number of walkers to its windswept slopes. The Harzquerbahn, a narrow-gauge railway with steam locomotives, penetrates the region from north to south, from Wernigerode to Nordhausen. This provides – especially between Wernigerode and the resort of Eisfelder Talmühle, but also from Schierke to the Brocken – an excellent way of exploring the heart of the eastern Harz.

☐ THE UPPER HARZ *81km - 50 miles – allow 1/2 day*

This itinerary follows an admirable road network, passing through huge tracts of rolling country with rounded hills covered in conifers.

★★Goslar – *See GOSLAR.*

Clausthal-Zellerfeld – This is the former mining capital of the Harz. At Zellerfeld, there is the **Upper Harz Mine Museum** (Oberharzer Bergwerksmuseum) ⊘ which illustrates the different mining techniques (once for gold and silver, later for lead, zinc and barium oxide) used until the last mine closed down in 1931.

At Clausthal, in the Hindenburgplatz, the **Pfarrkirche zum Heiligen Geist**, built in 1642, is one of the largest wooden churches in the whole of Europe. Note the majestic positioning of the galleries and the light falling obliquely from windows placed just below the panelled vaulting.

Okertalsperre (Oker Dam) – From the top of the barrage there is a fine **view** over the widely dispersed waters of the reservoir.

St. Andreasberg – The road leads first to an **old silver mine** (Silberbergwerk Samson) ⊘ at the bottom of the valley. This was closed in 1910 but has been reopened for tourists.

The Fahrkunst, a machine of ingenious simplicity which sent down and brought back the miners, can be seen at work. The device comprises two poles set side by side, each with steps cut into it, and a steady backwards and forwards movement. All the miner had to do was mark time with a foot on each pole.

Braunlage – Station on the Brocken railway. An important tourist resort, high up on a plateau overlooked by the wooded slopes of the **Wurmberg** (971m - 3 186ft).

★ **Schierke** – Station on the Brocken railway. A magnificent site here: a holiday centre from which many footpaths and ramblers' routes start – most of them leading towards the summit of the **Brocken.**

★ **Wernigerode** – *See WERNIGERODE.*

② **THE EASTERN HARZ** *89km - 55 miles – allow 1/2 day*

In this part of the Harz, the forests have a greater proportion of deciduous trees. Even if it is on a smaller scale, the landscape is at times more spectacular.

★ **Wernigerode** – *See WERNIGERODE.*

Rübeland – In this area, where the chief activity is the exploitation of limestone, tourists enjoy exploring the many caves and grottoes formed by the erosion of the rock. In **Hermann's Grotto** (Hermannshöhle) ⊙, note particularly the Chamber of Crystals and the small pool stocked with "cave fish" (Grottenolmen) – blind creatures, living out their whole lives in darkness.
Continue via Blankenburg and Thale to reach the Bode valley.

★★ **Bodetal** – The river here has gouged a passage as best it could through a maze of rock masses and now flows along the foot of impressive cliffs. The most spectacular site, without doubt, is the **Roßtrappe**★★ (The Charger's Hoofmark).
This is ten minutes' walk from the parking place. From the lookout point, which juts out dizzyingly above the river far below, there is an incredible **view**★★★ of the sheer cliffs, the stream tumbling between crags at the foot of the chasm, and the distant woods. The place owes its name to a legend, according to which a horse ridden by a princess being chased by a giant pushed so hard while readying itself to spring across the gulf, that it left an imprint in the rock.
Following the course of the river, the scenic stretch of road twists and turns through the rugged forest landscape as far as the junction with Route 81. The beauty of the scenery and the frequent blind spots as the road winds through the undulating country side all impose a reduced speed on drivers.

HEIDELBERG★★

Baden-Württemberg – Population 132 000
Michelin map 417 R 10
Plan of the conurbation in the current Michelin Red Guide Deutschland

Heidelberg, since 1386 seat of Germany's most famous university, lies on the banks of the Neckar river. It was here, in the early years of the 19C, that the poets Brentano, Eichendorff and Von Arnim united their talents to form the foundation of Germany's Romantic movement. Today, the city owes its liveliness to the presence of 27 000 students and innumerable foreign tourists, Anglo-Saxons in particular.
From the quays on the right bank of the Neckar, on either side of the picturesque bridge, the **Alte Brücke** or Karl-Theodor Brücke (**Y**), there are splendid **views**★★ of the castle ruins, their red sandstone ramparts distinct against the green of the forest, and of the old town clustered around the Heilig-Geist-Kirche.
Further superb views of the castle and the city can be seen from the **Philosophenweg** (Philosophers' Walk) (**Y**) – reached by crossing the Alte Brücke and climbing the **Schlangenweg** (**Y**) *(steep steps).*

HISTORICAL NOTES

The Rhineland Palatinate, of which Heidelberg was the political centre, owes its name to the title "palatines" given to the highest officers in the Holy Roman Empire who were in the sovereign's confidence. These functions and dignities disappeared in the 14C, except in the hereditary family ruling a group of territories whose appropriate centre was the confluence if the Neckar with the Rhine. Through the wise government of these palatine-electors (Kurfürsten), the **Electoral Palatinate** (Kurpfalz) became one of the most advanced states of Europe.

The "Orléans War" (1688-97) – In the 16C, the electors, who had become Protestant, were continually reinforcing and embellishing their castle at Heidelberg. The Elector Karl-Ludwig restored his states in an exemplary manner after the Thirty Years War. In the hope of ensuring peace in the Rhineland and extending the influence of his house he married his daughter Liselotte **(Elisabeth-Charlotte)** to Duke Philip of Orléans, brother of Louis XIV.

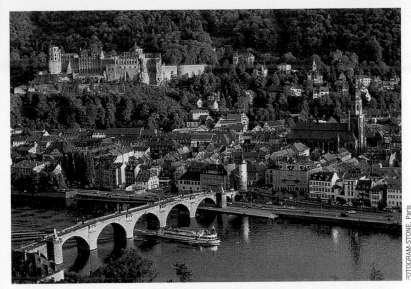

Heidelberg castle and the Neckar

The **Palatine Princess** did not pass unnoticed at the Court of France. Saint-Simon in his *Memoirs* returns frequently to her loud voice, her endless chatter and her intractable dislike of Mme de Maintenon. When the son of Karl-Ludwig died without an heir in 1685, the marriage alliance, which was invoked by Louis XIV to assert his claim to the territories on the left bank of the Rhine, proved disastrous to the Palatinate and to Heidelberg. The town was laid waste and the castle sacked in the brutal campaign of 1689. Total disaster followed in 1693, when the town was completely destroyed by fire. This catastrophe led to the rebuilding of the town in an uninspired Baroque style on the same foundations and with no thoroughfares. Before long the electors abandoned the ruined castle, turning their attention to their residences at Mannheim and Schwetzingen.

★★★SCHLOSS (CASTLE) *Cars approach via the Neue Schloßstraße* (Z).

The route marked on the plan leads to the **Rondell** promontory, once the site of a battery of cannons and now a **viewpoint★** looking out over the town, the Neckar valley and the Rhineland plain. After this comes the **Dicker Turm** (Great Tower), and then the **Elisabethentor**, a gate which Friedrich V had built in a single night in 1615, as a surprise for his wife Elizabeth Stuart, daughter of James I of England.

The castle's southeast corner is formed by the **Gesprengter Turm** (Shattered Tower). A mine laid by French sappers in 1693 gutted one side of the edifice and destroyed the gun emplacements radiating from a solid central core.

The **gardens★** were laid out in terraces under Friedrich V, after an enormous amount of earthworks lasting from 1616 to 1619. The east face of the castle, with its three towers (from right to left: the Glockenturm, the Apothekerturm, the Gesprengter Turm), is visible from the Scheffel terrace.

The courtyard and buildings

The courtyard is on the far side of a fortified bridge guarded by the **Torturm**. Immediately on the right is the fine Gothic hall of the **Brunnenhalle** (Well Wing), whose granite Roman columns came from Charlemagne's palace at Ingelheim, near Mainz.

Library (Bibliotheksbau) (6) – This Gothic building, set well back from the castle's west wing, is able thus to receive light from windows on all four sides. At one time it housed the personal library, art collections and treasure of the princely family. The loggia is charming.

★★ **Friedrich Wing (Friedrichsbau) (10)** – The façade design of this wing, with its two festooned gables, retains in its columns the classical orders of antiquity – Doric, Ionic and Corinthian – rediscovered during the Renaissance. But the composition of pilasters and cornices, creating contrasts of light and shade, presages already the subsequent taste for the Baroque. The **statues** (copies) represent the ancestors of Friedrich IV, who added the wing, among them princes of the house of Wittelsbach.

The rear of the building, the sole decorated wall directly facing the town, can best be seen from the **Great terrace** (Altan). Looking down on the roofs of Old Heidelberg, this is approached via a vaulted passageway to the right of the palace.

Hall of Mirrors Wing (Gläserner Saalbau) (**8**) – Only a shell remains of this building, which retains, nevertheless, a series of tiered galleries in the Italian Renaissance manner.

Otto-Heinrich Wing (Ottheinrichsbau) (**9**) – This palace was built by the Elector Otto-Heinrich, one of the most enlightened rulers of the Renaissance. During the three years of his reign (1556-1559), the sovereign opened the Palatinate wide to innovative ideas, notably on religious and artistic matters. The wing inaugurated the fruitful late Renaissance period in German architecture.

Horizontals predominate in the composition of the façade. In line with contemporary taste, the ornamentation combines biblical and mythological symbols. The famous sculptor Alexander Colin of Mechelen collaborated in the design of the entrance, which is in the form of a triumphal arch displaying the Elector's armorial bearings: the Palatinate lion and the heraldic lozenges of the House of Wittelsbach framing the globe surmounted by a cross symbolizing the Empire.

Interior ⊙

Two architectural models allow a comparison between the castle as it is today and as it was in the 17C. So far as the Renaissance decoration of the Friedrich Wing is concerned, this is largely due to a felicitous restoration (c1900). Statues originally ornamenting the façades can be seen in the corridors. Baroque features were added to the chapel around 1720.

★ **Großes Faß (Great Vat)** – This colossal cask, with a capacity of 221 726 litres - 48 780 gallons, was installed in the reign of Charles Theodore at the end of the 18C. Wine can be drawn from it, with the aid of a pump, in the royal banqueting hall (in the Ladies' Wing). The platform above the vat is large enough for dancing as well as wine tasting. The guardian of this Bacchic extravagance – today an idol of local folklore – was the dwarf court jester **Perkeo**, celebrated himself for the astonishing amount he could drink. The memory of Perkeo lives on in a wooden figurine and in the ingenious "surprise" clock he invented.

HEIDELBERG CASTLE

End of Feudal Period (and subsequent alterations)
1) Apothekerturm (14C) - **2**) Glockenturm (14C) - **3**) Gesprengter Turm (15C)
Gothic-Renaissance Transitional Period (Ludwig V - 1508-1544)
4) Dicker Turm (1533) - **5**) Ladies' Wing - **6**) Library - **7**) Torturm
Renaissance
8) Hall of Mirrors Wing (1549) - **9**) Otto-Heinrich Wing (1566)
Renaissance-Baroque Transitional Period
10) Friedrich Wing (Friedrich IV - 1592-1610), and below, Great terrace (Altan)
11) English Wing (Friedrich V - 1610-1632)

HEIDELBERG

A	Buchausstellung der Universitätobibliothek	**F**	Jesuitenkirche
B	Studentenkarzer	**M¹**	Deutsches Apothekenmuseum
E	Heilig-Geist-Kirche	**M²**	Kurpfälzisches Museum
		N	Haus zum Ritter

★ **Deutsches Apothekenmuseum (German Pharmaceutical Museum)** (**Z M¹**) ☉ – *Entrance beneath the steps leading to the Otto-Heinrich Wing.*
Interesting 18C and 19C apothecaries' equipment. Collection of contemporary chemists' prescriptions. An alchemist's laboratory, complete with instruments, has been reconstituted in the Apothekerturm.
There is an excellent **view**★ of the castle from the **Molkenkur** (**Z**) restaurant, reached via the Molkenkurweg or by funicular railway. The restaurant is built on the site of an ancient fortification.

ADDITIONAL SIGHTS

★ **Buchausstellung der Universitätsbibliothek (University Library)** (**Z A**) ☉ – Valuable collections of books, manuscripts and miniatures are on display here in the exhibition gallery. Note especially the **Manesse Manuscript** (Manessische Liederhandschrift), an early 14C anthology collecting songs by 140 different poets in Old High German. The manuscript, which includes 137 full-page masterpieces of illumination, is considered a jewel of medieval literary and graphic art. Another important work, compiled almost a century later, is the **Mirror of the Saxons** (Sachsenspiegel), Germany's oldest legal work, still in use in several regions (Anhalt and Thuringia) as recently as 1900.
Also to be found in the Library is **Des Knaben Wunderhorn** *(The Child with the Magic Horn)*, published in Heidelberg in 1805 by Achim von Arnim and Clemens Brentano – a compendium of popular songs marking the incursion of demotic poetry into German literature.

★ **Kurpfälzisches Museum (Electoral Palatinate Museum)** (**Z M²**) ☉ – *Hauptstraße 97.*
The galleries consecrated to the history of the Palatinate exhibit a cast of the jaw of the prehistoric "Heidelberg Man" (500 000 BC). The department of German Primitives displays the **Altarpiece of the Twelve Apostles**★★ (1509 – Windsheimer Zwölfbotenaltar) by Tilman Riemenschneider *(qv)*. The collection **Works from the Romantic Period**★★ is devoted essentially to the iconography of the town and castle.

★ **Haus zum Ritter (The Knight's House)** (**Z N**) – This magnificent bourgeois mansion owes its name to a bust of St George in knightly armour which adorns the rich, scrolled pediment. Built in 1592 for the Huguenot merchant Charles Bélier, it was the only late Renaissance masterpiece to be spared the devastations of 1689-1693.

Studentenkarzer (Students' Gaol) (**Z B**) ☉ – From 1712 to 1914, students who were too rowdy or obtrusive ran the risk of incarceration here. Many of them left on the walls inscriptions, outlines darkened with soot, or coats of arms as a reminder to future generations of what they considered a particularly estimable episode in their career.

Heilig-Geist-Kirche (YZ E) – The church is an example of the Late Gothic style. As in earlier times, covered stalls hug the walls between buttresses. The nave and chancel are of the "hall" type *(qv)*, though galleries above the aisles reduce the height on either side. The well-lit **chancel** was formerly the sepulchre of the Palatine Electors, but since the destruction wrought during the Orléans War in 1693 only the tomb of Ruprecht III and his wife remains.

Jesuitenkirche (Z F) – This Baroque church was built at the beginning of the 18C from plans drawn up by the Heidelberg architect J A Breunig. The main façade, based on the Gesù Church in Rome, was the work of the Palatinate court architect F W Rabaliatti (1716-1782).

The luminous triple nave is supported by robust pillars whose capitals are decorated with Rococo stuccowork.

The **Museum of Sacred and Liturgical Art** ⊙, which is reached through this church, houses religious artefacts (madonnas, altar crosses, liturgical objects). In the museum treasury are examples (chalices, monstrances) of the goldsmith's and silversmith's art.

EXCURSIONS

Schwetzingen – *10km - 6.2 miles to the west via the Friedrich-Ebert-Anlage (Z).*
Gourmets flock to this town on the Rhine plain during the asparagus season, while music lovers come here for the festivals held in May and June.

The **Schloß★** ⊙, destroyed dring the Orléans War, was rebuilt in 1700-1717 as a Baroque palace complex with three wings. The most splendid period of its history occurred under Prince Elector Carl Theodor, who spent every summer here with his wife Elisabeth Augusta from 1742 to 1778.

In 1803, the palace passed to the House of Baden. About 40 of the palace rooms are open to the public. One set of apartments has been restored in the style of the 19C, while the rooms on the first floor are resplendently fitted as they would have been around 1775.

The charming **Rokokotheater** ⊙, built in the mid-18C by Lorraine architect Nicolas de Pigage (1723-1796), is open during the summer. During the Schwetzingen festival, it makes a lovely tranquil setting for concerts.

★★**Schloßgarten** ⊙ – This 72ha - 178acre park was laid out stage by stage and is undoubtedly one of the finest examples of an 18C park in Europe. The French garden, with its rigorously geometric design (circular parterre with fountains along the central axis), is also the work of Nicolas de Pigage. A little later, the English style gardens were landscaped by Friedrich Ludwig Sckell, with streams, ponds and trees. The Late Rococo taste for mock ancient buildings gave rise to a number of little temples and artificial ruins dotted around the grounds.

Königstuhl ⊙ – *5km - 3 miles to the southeast, via the Neue Schloßstraße, the Molkenkurweg, and then the Gaisberger Weg; or take the funicular (stops: Stadt - near the Kornmarkt (Z), Schloß, Molkenkur, Königstuhl).*
From the television tower on the summit (568m - 1 864ft) there is a fine **panorama** of the Neckar valley, from the Odenwald to the plain of the Rhine.

HELGOLAND★★

Schleswig-Holstein
Michelin map 415 D 7

Attracted by the idea of a short sea cruise, thousands of tourists each year head for the red sandstone cliffs of the island of Helgoland, just 70km - 43 miles out from the estuary of the Elbe. English territory for many years, the island was exchanged for Zanzibar in 1890.

A fantastic rock – Undermined for centuries by the sea, the island now covers an area of less than 1km² - 1/2sq mile. In 1947, in accordance with the Potsdam Agreement, German military installations, including a submarine base, were totally destroyed by British sappers using 6 000 tons of high explosive.

Helgoland was returned to Germany in 1952, since when – thanks to a complete reconstruction of twin built-up areas divided by the form of the cliff (Unterland and Oberland) – it has once more become a tourist centre. An aquarium, an ornithological observatory and a marine biology station make the site of great scientific interest. The island has many attractions to offer the visitor: cliff walks, sea bathing from the lonely but sheltered sands of Düne Beach, even tax-free chocolates, cigarettes and spirits.

Access ⊙ – There is a daily car ferry service from Bremerhaven and Cuxhaven (passengers only), or a train-bus-boat linkup operated by the Sectouristik company from the main railway station (Hauptbahnhof) in Hamburg. A day excursion allows approximately four hours on the island.

Bad HERSFELD ★

Hessen — Population 30 000
Michelin map 417/418 N 13

The spa of Bad Hersfeld, noted for its mineral waters, is set in one of the craggiest, most convoluted parts of the Hesse forest. In the months of July and August, the town enjoys an additional popularity due to the Drama Festival (Bad Hersfelder Festspiele) staged in the majestic abbey ruins.

★ **Stiftsruine (Abbey Church Ruins)** ⊘ — The remains of the abbey, destroyed by French troops in 1761, reveal the imposing proportions of its church, which was more than 100m - 328ft long. The original building, which dated from the Ottonian period *(qv)* was designed with an expanded transept forming a single uncluttered chamber. In the 11C and 12C, while retaining the general plan, the church was modified in the Romanesque style, with two chancels. The western apse, constructed on a rectangular base and flanked by a single Romanesque tower, is impressive, particularly when viewed from inside.

The Katharinenturm (1120), also in the Romanesque style, stands in an isolated position northeast of the church. Once part of the abbey complex, it houses the 900-year-old monastery bell.

Old Quarter — The blunt tower of the parish church emerges from a picturesque huddle of half-timbered burghers' houses near the market place (Marktplatz). Note especially the sacristan's house (Küsterhaus, 1480) and the Baroque residence of the pastor (Pfarrhaus, 1714), with its beautiful entrance.

Rathaus (Town Hall) — This Gothic building, modified at the end of the 16C, is surmounted now by gables in the style of the Weser Renaissance. From the forecourt, there is a good **view**★ of the church.

EXCURSION

Rotenburg an der Fulda — *21km - 12 miles to the north.*
Situated in a steep, narrow section of the Fulda valley, Rotenburg has preserved its old-world charm. From the bridge spanning the river, the view of stone and half-timbered houses clustered against the cliff that drops sheer into the river here is quite breathtaking. The town hall boasts a Renaissance doorway and a Rococo staircase. The castle, now a School of Finance, recalls the period when Rotenburg was the official residence of the Landgraves of Hesse.

Coming soon...
the Michelin Green Guide Berlin

HILDESHEIM ★

Niedersachsen — Population 105 000
Michelin map 416/417/418 J 13
Plan of the conurbation in the Michelin Red Guide Deutschland

Louis the Pious founded a bishopric in 815, from which the town of Hildesheim evolved. As the capital of the Romanesque art which flowered in Germany during the Ottonian period, the town flourished under Bishops Bernward (993-1022) and Godehard (1022-1038). From the mid-13C to the 16C, feuds broke out repeatedly between the town's citizens and the bishops, who exerted their influence in a wide range of matters. Capricious turns of fate all too frequently prevented the town developing as it might, but over the centuries it managed to preserve its beautiful medieval buildings, until these were destroyed in an Allied Forces air attack in March 1945. After concerted efforts, the historical market square was rebuilt.

Hildesheim, which is linked by a secondary canal to the Mittellandkanal (which cuts across north Germany west to east from the Dortmund-Ems Kanal through Hannover to the river Elbe), has developed its economy largely in ecologically-friendly industries.

The thousand-year-old Rose Tree

As the legend goes, Louis I the Pious, exhausted after a day's hunting, hid his personal reliquary in a rose bush before he lay down to sleep. When he awoke the following morning, the precious casket was nowhere to be found. Interpreting this as a sign from Heaven, he founded a chapel — and subsequently a bishopric — on the spot, around which Hildesheim grew up.

In the winter of 1945, the famous rose tree — although apparently incinerated in an air raid — burst suddenly into flower. The town has likewise been re-born.

HILDESHEIM

A	Antoniuskapelle	**E**	Tempelhaus	**M¹**	Pelizaeus Museum
B	St. Andreaskirche	**F**	Heiligkreuzkirche		und Roemer Museum

SIGHTS

★ **Marktplatz** (**Y**) – The historical market square has been restored in an exemplary fashion. Visitors are greeted by the sight of buildings spanning eight centuries of architectural styles.

Rathaus – The east side of the square is lined with buildings in the Gothic style predominant between 1246 and 1290. Over the years, the Rathaus underwent numerous modifications and extensions, with the result that it clearly reflects three different periods of construction in three distinct sections. It was rebuilt in a simplified form of the original. *There is carillon daily at 12 noon, 1pm and 5pm.*

Tempelhaus – This unusual, Oriental-looking building from 1320-1330 stands on the south side of the Marktplatz. The crow-stepped gable and two round turrets are probably 16C additions. The most distinctive feature is the ornate **Renaissance oriel**★ dating from 1591, on which the parable of the Prodigal Son is depicted.

The nearby **Wedekindhaus** has bay windows projecting from ground level up to the roof gable, a typical feature of the Renaissance architecture of Lower Saxony. The half-timbered building dates from 1598. Note the beautiful carved decoration. Not far off stands the **Lüntzelhaus** (1755), which now houses a local savings bank, and the 14C Gothic **Rolandstift** with a Baroque porch (*c*1730).

The Bakers' and Butchers' Guild Houses occupy the west side of the square. The original **Bäckeramtshaus** dated from 1451 but, like the impressive **Knochenhaueramtshaus**★ (1529) next door, it is a faithful reproduction. The Knochenhaueramtshaus is deservedly well-known as the "most beautiful half-timbered house in the world". This eight-storey building is the pride of the local citizens. The five upper floors house the **local historical collections** of the Roemer-Museum.

The **Rokokohaus** on the north side of the square stands between the **Städtschänke**, a local restaurant, and the Weavers' Guild House (**Wollenwebergildehaus**).

★ **Dom (Cathedral)** (**Z**) ⊙ – The present building is a reconstruction, based on the original plans of an 11C Romanesque basilica, with later side chapels faithfully reproduced in the Gothic style and the dome above the transept modelled on the cupola added in the 18C. The interior retains the simplicity of the original. The alternate use of a single pillar and two columns in the nave is typical of the architectural school of Old Saxony.

Fine **works of art**★ can be seen in the cathedral. A huge chandelier dating from the 11C hangs above the transept crossing. On the north side, the last chapel contains a rare carved baptismal font (13C) supported by four figures representing the rivers of Paradise. In the south transept, an 11C bronze column depicting the life of Christ is displayed.

The two-storey Romanesque **cloister**★ abuts the eastern extremity of the cathedral. The legendary **rose** is trained along the outer wall of the apse.

Scenes from the Old and the New Testament are illustrated in the panels of **Bishop Bernward's bronze doors** beneath the west front porch – superb examples of early Romanesque sculpture.

Close to the cathedral, a magnificent Renaissance **rood-screen**★ can be seen in the **Antoniuskapelle** (**Z A**).

★ **Museums** (**Z M¹**) ⊙ – The **Pelizaeus-Museum** houses one of the richest collections of Egyptian antiquities in Germany. Worth special attention: the chapel containing the coffin-tomb of the royal officer Uhemka; funerary monuments of the Ancient Empire (dating back to the 3rd millenium BC), including the famous statues of Prince Hem On and the scribe Heti.

The **Roemer-Museum** exhibits an interesting collection of Chinese porcelain.

★ **St. Michaeliskirche** (**Y**) – Dating from the beginning of the 11C, this basilica is typical of Ottonian architecture in Old Saxony, with its double chancel and its alternation of pillars and columns. Note also the 13C **painted ceiling** depicting the Tree of Jesse in the nave, the two-tier galleries in the transepts, and the simplicity of the cushion capitals – again characteristic of Lower Saxony. Of the original decoration, an **Angel Screen** remains to the right of the west chancel *(on your left as you enter)*. Above is a balustrade embellished with 13 angels.

★ **St. Godehardikirche** (**Z**) – This 12C church has an elegant silhouette marked by the slender spires crowning its three towers.

St. Andreaskirche (**Z B**) – Built at the end of the 14C, this church is all that remains of the medieval quarter it once dominated. Huge Gothic windows pierce the impressive façade★. The tower, rising with its spire to a height of 118m - 367ft, is constructed on an asymmetrical base in the form of a trapezoid.

The Brühl (**Z**) – Spared by the ravages of war, this quarter is typical of old Hildesheim. Note the Wernersches Haus dating from 1606 in the lower part of the district.

Heiligkreuzkirche (**Z F**) – Behind the Baroque façade of this building hides an early (11C) Romanesque church originally refashioned from a fortified gateway. Gothic, Baroque and Ottonian elements jostle each other within.

St. Mauritius-Kirche – *Leave by the Bergsteinweg* (**Z**).
This 11C church, with its 12C cloister, lies in the Moritzberg quarter, on the west side of Hildesheim. The interior has had Baroque features added to it.

HOHENLOHER LAND

Baden-Württemberg
Michelin map 419 S 13

Separating the heights of the Swabian forest from the Tauber valley, the Hohenlohe plain remains a profoundly rural area traversed by the valleys of the Jagst and the Kocher – the former swift-running and tortuous, the latter more serene. Numerous castles along the way recall the German Renaissance period.

THE JAGST VALLEY

① From Bad Wimpfen to Schwäbisch-Hall

114km - 71 miles – about 4 hours

The route follows the sinuous course of the Jagst, along whose lush banks orchards, and sometimes vineyards, flourish.

★★ **Bad Wimpfen** – *See Bad WIMPFEN.*

Neudenau – Old houses with wooden-walled gables overlook the elegant and gracious **Marktplatz**.

Schöntal – The whole town lies within the precincts of an ancient Cistercian **abbey** ⊙. The 1727 **hall-church**★ is built in the Baroque style, although the soaring flight of free-standing pillars suggests a certain Gothic spirit. Four rare alabaster **altarpieces**★★ (17C) stand against the pillars nearest the transept crossing. Among the old abbey buildings, the abbot's antechamber, or **Orders Room**★ (Ordensaal) is especially noteworthy for its cladding of small panels painted to represent some 300 different costumes worn by the various religious orders.

Jagstberg – The village, sprawling over the crest of the valley's western slope, is dominated by a **church** (Pfarrkirche St. Burkhard) built at the beginning of the 17C to which Baroque features were added in 1765 by the stucco worker Joseph Hell.

The route passes close by the famous wooden bridge of Unterregenbach.

Langenburg – This fortified town has been built along a crest encircled at its base by a bend in the river and crowned by the **castle** ⊙ of the Hohenlohe family. The **inner courtyard**★, kernel of the original 15C fort which was enlarged in the 17C and again in the 18C, is framed by tiered galleries and overlooked by scrolled pediments. Many souvenirs of the House of Hohenlohe can be viewed within.

★★**Schwäbisch-Hall** – *See SCHWÄBISCH-HALL.*

② From Schwäbisch-Hall to Jagsthausen
73km - 45 miles – about 3 hours

★ **Hohenlohe Open-Air Museum** – *See SCHWÄBISCH-HALL: Excursions.*

Waldenburg – Situated on a spur projecting from the low ranges of the Swabian forest, this fortified town enabled the Hohenlohes to command the plain below. There are three distinct fortifications separated by moats.

The road passes through the woods of the Waldenburger Berge before continuing downhill towards Neuenstein.

Neuenstein – Massively constructed, the 16-17C **castle** ⊙ here is built with scrollworked Renaissance gables. A visit to the town gives the impression of day-to-day life in a small German court, in this case that of the Hohenlohes. A precious goblet fashioned in the form of a stag, richly encrusted furniture, ivories and glassware are among the curiosities on view.

Öhringen – The late 15C **church**★ serves as a necropolis for the House of Hohenlohe. Enter through the Gothic hall-church's cloister and note in the chancel a monument to Philip of Hohenlohe (d 1609), son-in-law of William of Orange. Scenes from the Netherlands War of Independence are illustrated in relief at the base of the statue. The **Altarpiece of St Margaret**★ (Margarethen-Altar) in the large north chapel is a delicate late 15C work.

The final section of the route follows the Kocher valley before coming to Jagsthausen.

Burg HOHENZOLLERN*

Baden-Württemberg
Michelin map 419 V 10 - Local map under SCHWÄBISCHE ALB

Built on a hill separated from the main massif of the Swabian Jura, Hohenzollern Castle, tall and bristling with turrets, looks from whichever side you see it like some fortress out of a fairytale. The site★★★, even more than the castle itself, is impressive enough to justify its fame.

The Cradle of the Hohenzollerns – The dynasty goes back to the Counts of Zollern, originally overlords of the Hechingen region, and subsequently divided into several different branches. In 1415, the Hohenzollerns of Franconia became Margraves – and thus Elector-Princes – of Brandenburg. In 1618 they succeeded to the Duchy of Prussia. In the 18C, under the rule of the Hohenzollerns, the kingdom of Prussia became a leading power in Europe. It was a Hohenzollern, Wilhelm I, who was placed at the head of the German Empire, founded in 1871 at the instigation of Prussia. But less than half a century later, military defeat in the First World War and the revolution which followed it put an end to the domination of the Hohenzollern dynasty: on 9 November 1918, Kaiser Wilhelm II was forced to abdicate.

Castle ⊙ – A fortified ramp built in the form of a spiral leads to the courtyard. The castle as it is today was reconstructed from the original plans between 1850 and 1867 by the Prussian architects Von Prittwitz and Stüler. All that remains of the ancient fortress built by the Counts of Zollern is the Roman Catholic Chapel of **St Michael** (Michaeliskapelle), whose stained glass windows are said to be the oldest in southern Germany. The neo-Gothic **Protestant Chapel**, in the north wing of the castle, has contained since 1952 – when they were moved there from Potsdam – the tombs of the Soldier-King and of Frederick the Great. Mementoes of the latter (uniforms, decorations, snuffboxes, flutes) can be seen in the collections of the castle treasury (Schatzkammer).

Before leaving the castle, make a tour of the ramparts *(start on the left, after the drawbridge)* and enjoy the **panorama** of the Swabian Jura and the Upper Neckar valley below.

HUSUM

Schleswig-Holstein – Population 20 000
Michelin map 415 C 11

The birthplace of the writer Theodor Storm (1817-1888), who wrote several of his principal works here, is a small fishing port which also serves as a terminal for boats plying between the mainland and the Halligen Isles *(see below)*.

★ **Nissenhaus-Nordfriesisches Museum (North Frisian Museum)** ⊙ – *Herzog-Adolf-Straße 25.*
The ground floor display illustrates the different types of German coastal landscape (Geest, Marsch, Polder, etc.), as well as the life and culture of its inhabitants. Natural catastrophes (the cataclysms – "Manndränken" – of 1362 and 1634, the high tide of 1962) are evoked in exhaustive detail, as are the construction of dykes and the reclamation of land by Polders. A **dyke** made of wood (Stackdeich), restored after archaeological excavations, illustrates the technique of containment in the Middle Ages. Modern methods are illustrated by a model of the Eider dam *(see below)*. On the floor above, there is an exhibition of Frisian paintings (landscapes and scenes of everyday life).

EXCURSIONS

★ **The Halligen Isles** – These numerous flat islets, created, altered, submerged or once more re-formed over the centuries by the play of the tides, are scattered through the shallows off the coast of Schleswig-Holstein. The archipelago comprises a total population of around 400, mainly farmers and fishermen, who live in thatched cottages built on what are called **Warften** (hillocks of habitation). The seals, and an infinite variety of sea birds, are protected by law. On Langeness, the largest isle, salt is farmed. A tour of the Halligens *(field-glasses recommended)* is well worthwhile.

★ **Nolde Museum at Seebüll** ⊙ – *56 km - 35 miles to the north.*
Known under the pseudonym of Nolde, the painter Emil Nansen (1867-1956) built himself a house of his own design in the solitude of the Seebüll marshes, between 1927 and 1937. Each year now, a different selection is displayed there of the works of Nolde – one of the most significant masters of German Expressionism. **The Life of Christ**, a series of nine canvases, is on permanent exhibition.
The psychic anxiety and religious emotion of the artist is expressed in thick masses of colour, aggressive and incandescent, which totally destroy any sense of form.

Friedrichstadt – *15km - 9 miles to the south.*
Dutch refugees, hounded from their country for religious reasons and given sanctuary here by Duke Friedrich III of Holstein, founded this locality in 1621 and bestowed on it the name of their protector. The settlement – a rectilinear grid of tree-shaded canals criss-crossed by streets of identical houses with scrolled or curvilinear gables – seems never to have changed since then. A calm and attractive retreat.

★ Eidersperrwerk (Eider Dam) – *35km - 22 miles to the south.*
Skirting a bird sanctuary, the road arrives at the mouth of the Eider river, closed off by a dam constructed between 1967 and 1972, after the catastrophic tidal wave of 1962. The five colossal steel sluice gates remain open when meteorological conditions are normal, permitting the customary rise and fall of tides. But they are closed when storms or abnormally high tides are threatened, preventing the sea from surging up the Eider to invade the low-lying country inland.

IDAR-OBERSTEIN

Rheinland-Pfalz – Population 38 000
Michelin map 417 Q 5

Twin towns here form a single built-up area – picturesque Oberstein lying along the foot of a gorge carved by the river Nahe, Idar spread out around a tributary beyond. The abundance in earlier times of nearby agate, jasper and amethyst deposits has left Idar-Oberstein a centre for the cutting and polishing of precious stones.

★ Felsenkirche – *Return trip 1/2 hour on foot. Access via a stairway (214 steps) rising from the Oberstein Marktplatz.*
Framed by a rock overhang in the cliff 60m - 197ft above the river, this church, restored several times, is worth a visit for the high-altar **reredos** (beginning of the 15C) alone. The scenes of the Passion represented depict with a ferocious realism, the hatred, the suffering and the annihilation involved.

★★ Deutsches Edelsteinmuseum (German Museum of Precious Stones) ⊘ – *At Idar, in the Börse (Diamond Exchange), Hauptstraße.*
The gems, cut and uncut, in every known variety, are classified according to their geographical origin, their cultural importance or their industrial use. Note the dental instruments in agate.

Idar-Oberstein – Deutsches Edelsteinmuseum

Deutsches Edelstein Museum

Museum Idar-Oberstein ⊘ – *At Oberstein, in the Marktplatz (at the foot of the Felsenkirche stairway).*
Collections of minerals and precious stones, notably "Landschaftsachate" – paper-thin flakes of agate exhibiting in transparency the appearance of phantasmagoric landscapes; also fluorescent stones and crystals.

Burgruinen – *At Oberstein.*
Castle ruins with a view of the Nahe valley.

Weiherschleife (Old Stonecutting Centre) ⊘ – *On the outskirts of Idar.*
The different stages in the facetting and polishing of gems can be seen. Skilled craftsmen still work in traditional fashion here, face down before sanded grindstones powered by a water-wheel.

EXCURSIONS

The Hunsrück – *Excursion 141km - 88 miles – allow about 5 hours. Leave Idar-Oberstein to the northwest by Route 422.*
The Hunsrück forms the southern rim of the Rhenish schist massif *(see Introduction).* It is a region of low mountains and game-stocked forests, gashed by deep and steep-sided valleys.

Erbeskopf – Topping 818m - 2 660ft, this is the highest summit of the massif. From the wooden tower, there is a panoramic view over the undulating, wooded countryside.

After Thalfang, the **Hunsrückhöhenstraße★** going northward offers fine views of the valleys, the forest-covered hills and numerous villages with ancient houses roofed by slabs of schist. The road passes the Stumpfer Turm, an old Roman watchtower.

Kirchberg – Perched on a hillside, this village retains many pretty half-timbered houses, especially around the Marktplatz. St. Michaelskirche dates back to the pre-Romanesque era, although the present building was constructed in the 15C.

Simmern – The farming centre of the Hunsrück. Tombstones from the Renaissance period can be seen beneath the vaults of the church of St. Stephan (15C). Behind the church, explore the old town.

Ravengiersburg – Hidden away at the bottom of a valley, this village boasts a Romanesque church built on top of a spur. The imposing west front has a sculptured cornice and a miniature gallery. Above the porch: Christ in Majesty.

Dhaun – The castle here is built on a remarkable **site★** on top of a sheer rock outcrop. On the esplanade, behind the statue, a staircase leads down to the gun positions.

The road on the final section of the excursion follows the valley of the Nahe before returning to Idar-Oberstein.

INGOLSTADT

Bayern – Population 100 000
Michelin map 419/420 T 18
Town plan in the current Michelin Red Guide Deutschland

Once famous for its university, Ingolstadt became in the 19C one of the most powerful strongholds in Europe.

Today the town owes its economic prosperity to a privileged geographic position which puts it at the heart of a rich agricultural area and at the same time at the junction of three important oil pipelines.

★ Maria-de-Victoria-Kirche – This plain, single nave chapel was transformed in 1732 by the Asam brothers *(qv)*. The huge ceiling fresco (490m² - 5 200sq ft) illustrates the spreading of the Faith, through the intercession of the Virgin, to the four quarters of the earth. The perspective effect is astonishing.

The high altar, with a particularly rich canopy, is adorned by four statues representing Medicine, Theology, Law and Philosophy.

Liebfrauenmünster – The interior of this church is in the form of an extended Gothic hall. It was built in the 15C, and the fine **reredos★** of the high altar (1572) is a transitional work linking the Gothic with the Renaissance. The Virgin, patron saint of Bavaria, appears in the central panel in the form of a cloaked Madonna.

★ Bayerisches Armeemuseum (Bavarian Army Museum) ⊘ – Installed in the huge chambers of a 15C fortress (Herzogschloß), the rich collections of this museum trace the military history of Bavaria from the 14C to the present day. Numerous firearms illustrate the evolution of weaponry; an enormous diorama (17 000 model soldiers) stages the battle of Leuthen, which saw the victory of Friedrich II over the Austrians in 1757.

Kreuztor – This hexagonal, battlemented keep with six pointed turrets at the angles of the walls is the finest relic of the town's 14C and 15C fortifications.

EXCURSION

Neuburg an der Donau – *23km - 14 miles to the west.*
This small Renaissance Baroque town is built on a limestone ridge above the south bank of the river.

The **castle**, constructed between 1530 and 1545 by the Palatine Count Otto-Heinrich, comprises a courtyard surrounded by a two-tier gallery, in the style of the early German Renaissance. The east wing, with its two towers, dates from 1665-68.

The courtyard's western façade is decorated with murals representing scenes from the Old Testament. The arched gateway leads also to the **chapel**, which is embellished with frescoes (1543).

There is a **museum** (Schloßmuseum) ⊘ in the east wing, where neolithic remains, examples of sacred art, and exhibits charting the history of the princely House of Pfalz-Neuburg may be viewed.

West of the castle is the **Hofkirche**, which was built at the end of the Renaissance (1607-1627). The richly decorated **stucco ceiling★** dates from the Counter-Reformation. The Baroque **reredos★** (1752-1754) is the work of J A Breitenauer, to whom the pulpit is also attributed.

JENA

Thüringen — Population 105 000
Michelin map 418 N 18

Northeast of the forest of Thuringia, midway along the course of the Saale, the town has developed steadily ever since the foundation of its university in 1588. From then on, numerous scientists and intellectuals such as the philologist Wilhelm von Humboldt, his brother Alexander, a geographer, Goethe and Schiller, contributed to Jena's importance.

Optics — In the middle of the 19C, Carl Zeiss and Ernst Abbe, both members of the university, established an optical industry developed from their invention, the microscope. Since then the **Zeiss** works have acquired a worldwide reputation in the domain of optics and precision instruments.
The tower of the university, 120m - 394ft high, dominates the town.

SIGHTS

Johannistor — *Johannisplatz.*
Together with the Pulverturm (on the other side of the square), this gate is all that remains of the town's 14C fortifications.

Stadtmuseum Göhre ⊙ — *Am Markt.*
This local museum is housed in one of the town's most beautiful buildings, built around 1500. The four floors illustrate the history of Jena since its foundation. The collection includes some beautiful items of art and cultural history.

Stadtkirche St. Michaelis — *Am Kirchplatz.*
This ancient collegiate church of the Cistercians was completely transformed in the Gothic mode in the 15C. Note, on the south side, the canopied porch.

Goethe-Gedenkstätte (Goethe Museum) ⊙ — *Fürstengraben 26.*
The famous writer always said that it was in Jena that he found the tranquillity essential for literary creation. The house in which he lived when he was in the town contains numerous mementoes of the poet.

Schiller-Gedenkstätte (Schiller Museum) ⊙ — *Schillergäßchen 2.*
A collection of the poet's personal memorabilia is on view in the house he lived in between 1797 and 1802.

★ **Zeiss-Planetarium** ⊙ — *Am Planetarium 3.*
Built next to the botanical gardens by the Zeiss firm, this scientific spectacle permits visitors to voyage through the cosmos via the artful manipulation and movement of planets and the stellar systems. Varied laser and multivisual show.

★ **Optisches Museum der Carl-Zeiss-Stiftung** ⊙ — *Carl-Zeiss-Platz.*
Carl Zeiss started making microscopes in 1847. In collaboration with the physicist Ernst Abbe and the chemist Otto Schott, he laid the foundation stone for the construction of precision optical instruments. Part of the exhibition is dedicated to his work. The collection of optical and other precision instruments is impressive. There is an extensive collection of spectacles. The historical Zeiss workshop dating from 1866 is reproduced.

KARLSRUHE ★

Baden-Württemberg — Population 270 000
Michelin map 419 S 9

Karlsruhe is one of the "new towns" designed on a geometric plan in the 18C by the princely building enthusiasts of southern Germany. After the devastations of 1689 and the destruction of his family seat at Durlach, the Margrave of Baden decided to build a castle a little further west, among the trees of the Hartwald, his favourite hunting ground. The idea, put into operation in 1715 with the construction of an octagonal tower, was for the castle to be the hub of a network of radiating streets (hunting rides to the north, fan-shaped development for a future town to the south). This "town fan" was eventually fully realized in the 19C, when Karlsruhe became the capital of the Grand Duchy of Baden (1806).
The architect **Friedrich Weinbrenner** (1766-1826), a native of the town, was responsible for its neo-Classical aspect. From this period dates the **Marktplatz**, along with the town hall (Rathaus), the Protestant church (Evangelische Stadtkirche), and the modest pyramid of the founder's mausoleum. The Kaiserstraße *(pedestrian precinct)*, today the city's commercial centre, was also designed by Weinbrenner. Cutting through the "fan" on an east-west axis, it follows the course of the old road from Durlach to the Rhine.
The former seat of the Grand Dukes today houses Germany's supreme courts (Court of Appeal and the Constitutional Court), together with the country's oldest School of Technology (1825). Among the eminent graduates of the latter are Hertz, who discovered electromagnetic waves, and Carl Benz *(qv)*, the motorcar pioneer. Karlsruhe is also the birthplace of the Baron Drais, inventor in 1817 of a vehicle — ancestor of the bicycle — known as the Draisienne.

KARLSRUHE

M   Badisches Landesmuseum   M²   Museum am Friedrichsplatz

SIGHTS

★ Staatliche Kunsthalle (Fine Arts Museum) ⊙ – The building, erected between 1838 and 1846, houses a remarkable collection of **German Primitives★** (Gemälde Altdeutscher Meister). Among them the focal point in the Grünewald Room is a terrifying Crucifixion by the painter of the same name.

The golden age of Flemish and Dutch painting is represented by Rubens, Jordaens and Rembrandt *(Self-Portrait)*. Still-life pictures by Chardin highlight a collection of 17C and 18C French paintings.

There is a selection of **works by Hans Toma★**, who occupies a special place in German painting of the 19C. *Children's Dance and Rain on the Black Forest* are among the best-known canvases by this regional artist.

The adjacent **Orangery** houses a representative collection of Classical Modern and contemporary art. Paintings by German Expressionists (*Deer in the Forest* by Franz Marc), artists of the Brücke group, artists who were influenced by Cubism (Léger, Delaunay), but also the *Hurricane* by Max Ernst and *The Seven Deadly Sins* by Otto Dix, stand alongside sculptures by Barlach, Lehmbruck and Henry Moore. The contemporary artists with work on display include Arnulf Rainer, Gerhard Richter and Tapiès.

★ Schloß – Of the original castle building, only the tall octagonal tower that marks the centre of the city's radiating road system now remains. It was the grand-ducal residence up to 1918. Today it houses the **Badisches Landesmuseum★** (Baden Regional Museum) (**M**) ⊙, where the visitor may view a sizeable collection of Egyptian, Greek and Roman antiquities; and examples of local folk art and craftwork from the Middle Ages to 1900. The Zähringersaal is dedicated to the history of the Baden Dynasty (note the beautiful furnishings). The famous **Turkish trophies** of the Margrave Ludwig Wilhelm, who was known as "Louis the Turk" (1677-1707) are particularly worthy of note.

There is a wonderful view from the **tower** ⊙ over Karlsruhe as far as the Northern Black Forest, the Kraich region and the Palatinate mountains.

From the castle park – which gives way, in the north, to a vast wooded area – there is access to the **Botanical Gardens** (Botanischer Garten) ⊙, where the **greenhouses★** (Gewächshäuser) offer a magnificent display of cactuses.

KASSEL★

Hessen — Population 197 000
Michelin map 417/418 M 12

Once the seat of the Landgraves, today the economic, administrative and cultural capital of North Hessen, Kassel is situated on the banks of the Fulda river *(boat trips from Fuldabrücke)* (**Z**), in the heart of a hilly, lush and wooded countryside. To the west, at the foot of the Habichtswald heights, Wilhelmshöhe palace and its park overlook the town. A natural spring at Wilhelmshöhe feeds the **Kurhessen thermal baths** (**X**).

Famous for its musical and dramatic activities, Kassel is nevertheless known best of all for the **Documenta**, an international exhibition of contemporary art which has been held every four or five years since 1955. The main centre for this event is the **Fredericianum** (**Z**), a pre-classical building in the vast Friedrichsplatz designed by Simon Louis du Ry to be both museum and library for the Landgrave Frederick III.

An industrial tradition — The Landgrave Karl of Hessen (1670-1730) welcomed a large influx of Huguenots into his province — industrious folk who soon started work-shops and factories all over the region. Subsequently he encouraged the research into steam power initiated by **Denis Papin**, who lived in Kassel from 1695 to 1707 after he had been granted a professorial chair at Marburg University. In 1690, the inventor designed a prototype steam engine, and in 1706 he perfected a high-pressure steam pump.

The Brothers Grimm — **Jakob** (1785-1863) and **Wilhelm Grimm** (1786-1859) lived in Kassel from 1805 to 1830, both employed as Court Librarians. Through their shared work on literature and linguistics (a German basic grammar, the first volume of a German language dictionary) they can be considered the inaugurators of the science of German philology. Fascinated by legends and folklore, the brothers collected from all over the province a wealth of stories which they published between 1812 and 1822 under the general title of *Kinder und Hausmärchen* (Stories for Children and the Home, in English simply: *Grimms' Fairy Tales*).

★★WILHELMSHÖHE (X) *time: half a day*

★★ Park — *West of the town.*
The landscaping of this huge 350ha - 865 acre park was started in 1701 under the Landgrave Karl. It was based on a design by the Italian architect Guerniero. The Baroque-style park, in which almost 800 different species of trees grow, was transformed in the second half of the 18C into English-style gardens, complete with temples, pavilions, grottoes and artificial ruins. The ruins of **Löwenburg** (**A**), a fantasy castle built between 1793 and 1801, is an excellent example of the taste for sentimental romanticism current in that period (note inside the furnishings and the valuable collection of arms and armour).

At the highest point of the park stands **Hercules★** (Herkules), emblem of the city of Kassel. This gigantic statue is a copy (1717) of the Farnese Hercules at the National Archaeological Museum in Naples. It is 72m - 236ft high (the Nelson monument in London's Trafalgar Square measures 52m - 170ft). In the Wilhelmshöhe park, the figure is placed on top of a pyramid, itself standing on a huge eight-sided pavilion, the Oktogon. From the base of the statue, there is a very fine **view★★** over the park and the castle to Kassel.

Below the Oktogon is the great **Water Staircase** (Kaskadentreppe) — an enormous **cascade★** with huge amounts of water falling in a sequence of steps to the Neptune Pool, before continuing past the rocks of the Steinhöfer waterfall, beneath the Devil's Bridge and along an aqueduct to the Fountain Pool (very high jets) in front of the castle. The Water Staircase falls 200m - 656ft from top to bottom.

Schloß (Palace) ⊙ — This building in the classical style was completed in 1803. From 1807 to 1813, Jerome Bonaparte, the King of Westphalia, held a brilliant Court here.

The historic salons of the South Wing (**museum**), with their paintings and their Louis XV and Empire furniture, still recall the splendours of that period. Another famous guest was Napoleon III, held prisoner here after the Battle of Sedan in 1870. Today the palace houses important sections of Kassel's National Art Collection (Staatliche Kunstsammlungen) *(central entrance)*.

★ Antiquities — *Ground floor.* In the entrance hall, 5C and 6C vases evoke echoes of Classical Greece. The Roman Empire is represented by an Apollo — referred to as the Kassel Apollo — a 2C work by Phydias; by a series of busts, a sarcophagus and some urns. Statuettes of gods and sacred animals in stone and bronze complete the section as examples of ancient Egyptian art.

★★★Old Masters Gallery — The rich, world-class exhibits here are derived from collections amassed by the Landgraves.
First floor: Flemish and German Primitives and paintings from the School of Antwerp: Altdorfer's Crucifixion, a triptych by Cranach the Elder, Dürer's *Portrait of Elizabeth Tucher*, Hercules at Antioch by Hans Baldung Grien and Mor's *William I of Orange*.

A	Schloß Löwenburg		**M³**	Brüder-Grimm-Museum
M¹	Hessisches Landesmuseum		**M⁴**	Naturkundemuseum
M²	Neue Galerie			

Rembrandt's *Old Man With a Gold Chain* has pride of place among Dutch painters of the 17C.

Also displayed are *The Blessing of Jacob* (1656), a *Portrait of Saskia van Uylenburgh* (the painter's first wife), *The Holy Family at the Screen, A Winter Landscape* and various self-portraits.

Among the Flemish painters of the 17C, note Rubens (*Crowning of a Hero; Mary and the Infant Jesus as a Refuge for Sinners*), Van Dyck (*Sebastian Leerse with his Wife and Son*), and Jordaens, who pictures himself as a lutenist in *The Painter's Betrothal*.

Second floor: landscapes and scenes of rustic and bourgeois life by Jan Brueghel, Ruysdael, Metsu and Jan Steen show an extraordinary sense of observation and attention to detail.

Third floor: works by painters from Italy (Belluci, Titian, Reni), Spain (Ribera, Murillo) and France (Poussin's *Love's Victory Over the God Pan*).

In the Art Library reading-room on the first floor (Kunstbibliothek), pages from the rich **collection of prints and drawings** can be seen.

The picture gallery is currently being renovated. Whilst the work is going on, a selection of 120 masterpieces are on display in the **Fridericianum** *on Friedrichsplatz. They are shown to advantage in the high-ceilinged, light and airy rooms.*

ADDITIONAL SIGHTS

* **Karlsaue Park** (**Z**) – The most popular parts of this 18C riverside park are the steeply sloping gardens below the Schöne Aussicht terrace, and the Siebenbergen – an artificial island on the Fulda.

* **Hessisches Landesmuseum** (**Z M¹**)
⊙ – The street level is devoted to collections concerned with prehistory. On the mezzanine, the **Astronomy and Physics Room**★★ contains rare and ancient scientific instruments: a large planetary clock made in 1561 and designed by the Landgrave Wilhelm IV; a celestial globe with an astronomic clock and calendar (c1600); a small astronomic clock (late 16C) which functions on Copernicus's heliocentric theory. On the first floor is the **German Tapestry Museum**★★, where more than 600 pieces chart the evolution of wall coverings from the 18C to the 20C: wallpapers with Near- or Far-Eastern motifs, embossed leather, panoramic murals, printed papers with designs from famous workshops in Germany and France (Réveillon, Paris). The techniques of printing are also illustrated.

The second floor is concerned mainly with decorative art.

* **Neue Galerie** (**Z M²**) ⊙ – Works ranging from the 18C to modern times are on display here, particularly those by German painters. Note the series of 18C portraits by the

Panoramic mural tapestry,
Deutsches Tapetenmuseum, Kassel

Verein Deutsches Tapetenmuseum

Tischbein family, among them *The Woman in Blue* (Amalie). More classical in their approach are the mythological scenes by Nahl the Younger. The works of Liebermann, Trübner, and above all Corinth *(Walchensee Landscape, Woman with a Mask)*, are close to those of the Impressionists, while Schlemmer and Kirchner *(Café at Davos)* are veering towards Expressionism. Contemporary art is represented by the extravagant *Das Rudel* of Josef Beuys.

Brüder-Grimm-Museum (**Z M³**) ⊙ – This is housed in Schloß Bellevue. Portraits, original manuscripts, letters, drawings and illustrations evoke the life and times as well as the works of the two scholars.

Naturkundemuseum (Natural History Museum) (**Z M⁴**) ⊙ – Divided into three sections – Geology, Botany and Zoology – this museum is in the former **Ottoneum**, Germany's oldest (1606) theatre. Note the remarkable **Ratzenberger Herbarium** (late 16C), also said to be the oldest in Germany, and the late 18C **Schildbach'sche Holzbibliothek** on the second floor. This comprises a series of small boxes, each made from the wood of a different tree – and each containing an example of the corresponding leaf, flower and fruit that tree produces.

EXCURSIONS

* **Schloß Wilhelmsthal** ⊙ – *12km - 8 miles to the north by the Rasenallee* (**X**).
This Rococo palace (1743-1770), surrounded by a park in the English style, was built by François Cuvilliés. Interior decoration in the then current style, with fine panelling, elegant furniture (mother-of-pearl inlaid commode), Chinese porcelain and a gallery of beauties painted by J H Tischbein the Elder exemplify the taste of the Court.

KIEL ★

Schleswig-Holstein — Population 245 000
Michelin map 415/416 D 14
Town plan in the current Michelin Red Guide Deutschland

Kiel owes its economic development to its position at the mouth of the maritime canal linking the Baltic with the North Sea. A former naval base, the city is still known principally for its busy shipyards.

★★ **Kieler Förde (Roadstead)** – The shores of this deep inlet are brightened by a series of sheltered resorts and bathing beaches, among them Schilksee, Strande, Laboe, Heikendorf and Schönberger Strand. In the northern part of the bay, regattas have been held for more than a century, and more than 3 000 yachtsmen from all over the world congregate here each year for **Kiel Week.**

★★ **Hindenburgufer** – This promenade extends for almost two miles along the shore, with shady parks on one side and extended **views** ★ of the roadstead on the other.

Rathaus (Town Hall) ⊙ – Built between 1907 and 1911, the building is noteworthy for its 106m - 348ft tower. From the upper gallery of this, there is a splendid **view** ★ of the roadstead as far as the tall Laboe Memorial.

EXCURSIONS

★★ **Schleswig-Holsteinisches Freilichtmuseum (Schleswig-Holstein Open-Air Museum)** ⊙ – *6km - 4 miles to the south.*
Sixty rural buildings and farms typical of the country north of the Elbe are grouped here in the form of hamlets, arranged according to their geographic origin. Those from the south, half-timbered, colour-washed or embellished with skilful designs in brick, resemble – inside as well as out – the rustic houses of Lower Saxony. The brick-built farms of the north Frisian area are more austere.
A forge, a potter's workshop, an old-fashioned bakehouse, flour mills and weavers' looms are all operated by local craftsmen in traditional manner.

★ **Laboe** – *20km - 12 miles to the north.*
The memorial tower, 85m - 279ft high, offers a **wide** view of the outer part of the roadstead and, on a clear day, the Danish archipelago. Together with its underground galleries, the tower – which is built in the form of a ship's stern – constitutes the **German Naval War Memorial** ★ (Marine-Ehrenmal) ⊙. It includes a museum of navigation. Also on display is the U-995, a submarine launched in Hamburg in 1943, which operated in Norwegian waters and in the Barents Sea.

Kiel Canal (Nord-Ostsee-Kanal) – This link between the Baltic and the North Sea was inaugurated by Wilhelm II in 1895. From Kiel to Brunsbüttel, its 100km - 62-mile length is the world's busiest waterway: 46 000 vessels pass through it annually (although from the point of view of tonnage transported, it is relegated to third place). From the **Prinz-Heinrich-Brücke** *(5km - 3 miles to the north, via Holtenauer Straße and Prinz-Heinrich-Straße)* one overlooks the **Holtenau** locks, which control the junction of the canal and the Baltic. Among the structures crossing the canal, the most impressive are the **Rendsburg Railway Viaduct** ★ *(see below)*, the **Grünenthal Bridge** on Route 204 (Itzehoe-Heide), and the new bridge north of Brunsbüttel.

★ **Holstein's "Little Switzerland" (Holsteinische Schweiz)** – *51km - 32 miles – allow 2 1/2 hours.*
Between Kiel and the Bay of Lübeck (Lübecker Bucht), not far from the Baltic Sea, Holstein's "Little Switzerland" region is scattered with lakes separated by wooded hills formed from the glacial moraine. (Highest point: Bungsberg, 168m - 550ft.)
In the middle of the region, beside the biggest of the lakes (Großer Plöner See) is the town of **Plön.** From the terrace of its Renaissance castle, there is a pretty **view** ★ of the surrounding lakes. Further east, **Eutin,** birthplace of the composer Carl Maria von Weber, has retained its 17C, brick-built town centre. The moated castle (1723) is surrounded by an English-style park bordering the lake.
Malente-Gremsmühlen, a small resort built on a wooded isthmus, is a departure point for boating trips.

Rendsburg – *36km - 22 miles to the west.*
Rendsburg occupied one of the strategic points of northern Germany, where the main highway from Denmark crossed the Eider. The old town, tightly packed around its 16C town hall and the 13C Marienkirche, is built on a former island in the Eider. It is now hemmed in on either side by fortifications built in the 17C to defend the bridge. The **Neuwerk Quarter** in the south, between the Kiel Canal and the old town, is notable for its huge central esplanade (Paradeplatz), from which streets radiate out in different directions.
South of Rendsburg, the Kiel Canal can be crossed by a **railway viaduct** ★ (Eisenbahnbrücke), a **tunnel for road traffic** (Kanalbrücke) and a pedestrian footway. The viaduct is 42m - 138ft above the water, with a transporter bridge below it. The tunnel beneath the canal is 640m - 656yds long; the footway, in a second tunnel parallel with the first, is equipped with 1 278m - 1 397yds of escalators and moving walkways.

KOBLENZ★

Rheinland-Pfalz – Population 107 000
Michelin map 417 O 6 – Local map under MOSELTAL
Plan of the conurbation in the current Michelin Red Guide Deutschland

The prosperity of Koblenz (from the Latin confluentia) derives from its position at the confluence of the Rhine and the Moselle. Placed under the jurisdiction of the Archbishops of Trier, the city came under French influence immediately after the Revolution, when refugees led by the Counts of Artois and Provence, brothers of Louis XVI, fled there. But in 1794 troops of the Republic occupied the east bank of the Rhine, and four years later Koblenz became the Prefecture of the French Rhine-and-Moselle Department. Subsequently the Prefect Lezay-Marnésia decided to beautify the city, and in 1809 he gave it the impressive **Rheinanlagen** (Z), a splendid riverside promenade.

The tomb of Hoche, at Weißenturm, and the Marceau cenotaph in the French cemetery at Lützel (*north of the town plan, via the Balduinbrücke* – **Y**), evoke memories of those young generals who fell during the first coalition.

Departure point for numerous excursions on both the Rhine and the Moselle, Koblenz also offers a summer festival, when the Rhine is set ablaze with flaming torches, many open-air concerts, and the celebrated taverns in its "wine village" (Weindorf).

The old town (Altstadt) is centred on the Liebfrauenkirche.

SIGHTS

★ **Deutsches Eck** (Y) – Home to a gigantic equestrian statue of Wilhelm I, which presides over the tongue of land marking the confluence. From the gallery crowning the base of the statue *(107 steps)*, there is a fine **view** of the town, the port, the Moselle bridges and the east bank of the Rhine, overlooked by the fortress of Ehrenbreitstein.

KOBLENZ

Stiftskirche St. Kastor (Y) – This Romanesque church succeeded an earlier basilica in which the Treaty of Verdun, dividing Charlemagne's empire, was drawn up in 843. Heavy fan vaulting covers the nave and chancel. The furnishings are interesting: the tombs of two archbishops lie at the back of multicoloured Gothic bays and, in the south transept, there is a series of 16 painted wood panels, once part of a rood-screen, with a picture of St Castor *(bottom left)*.

Liebfrauenkirche (Y) – This Romanesque church, remodelled in the 13C, was given a Gothic chancel in the 15C and Baroque belfries in the 17C. The carved keystones which ornament the vaulting tracery are worth examining.

Jesuitenplatz (Y) – In the courtyard of a 17C Jesuit College, now serving as the town hall, is the "Schängelbrunnen" – a fountain evoking the mischief perpetrated by the street urchins of the city.

EXCURSIONS

★★★ **Rhine Valley** – *See RHEINTAL.*

★ **Festung Ehrenbreitstein (Citadel)** – *4 1/2 km - 3 miles. Cross the Rhine by the Pfaffendorfer Brücke (Z) then turn left.*
This strategic stronghold, commanding the confluence of the two rivers, was the possession of the Archbishops of Trier from the 10C until 1799, when it was destroyed by the French. Between 1816 and 1832 the Prussians, who had ruled the Rhineland since the Congress of Vienna (1815), constructed the powerful existing fortress.
From the terrace, there is a **view** of Koblenz, Schloß Stolzenfels *(qv)* to the south, the wooded plateau of Hunsrück and the volcanic massif of the Eifel.

★ **Kloster Maria-Laach** – *20km - 12 1/2 miles to the west.*
The vast crater lake beside which this abbey stands emphasizes the monumental air of poise and solidity characterizing the abbey buildings. The 12C abbey church is a Romanesque basilica with three naves, whose exterior is reminiscent of the cathedrals of Worms, Speyer and Mainz.
The cloister-type entrance portico, added in the early 13C, has intricately worked capitals. An unusual hexagonal baldachin – perhaps suggesting a Moorish influence – is stretched over the altar. The crypt is the oldest part of the church.

Andernach – *18km - 11 miles to the north.*
This small town on the west bank of the Rhine retains a strongly medieval atmosphere. Enter the old town through the **Rheintor**, a fortified double gateway whose oldest part dates back to the 12C, and continue to the **castle ruins** (14C and 15C), which command the southern entry to the town.
The beautiful twin-towered façade of the **parish church** (Pfarrkirche) is a fine example of the early 13C Rhineland style – a transition between the Romanesque and the Gothic.

Beer

Beer has been brewed in Germany since the beginning of the 9C. In 1516 a decree on quality (Reinheitsgebot) was passed which stated that only hops, malt, yeast and water shoud be used for brewing. This ruling still applies, and the following method is used:

Brewer's malt – obtained from barley after soaking, germination and roasting – is mixed with water and hops (which flavour the must) and boiled. Yeast is added and the must is left to ferment.

Nowadays about 1 400 breweries in Germany produce 4 000 kinds of beer, which vary greatly in taste, colour and alcohol content:
– Popular beers, such as Kölsch, Altbier, Export, Pils, Märzen and Weizenbier (beer made from wheat), are light and about 3-4° proof.
– Strong beers, or Starkbiere, such as Bockbier and Doppelbock, are rich in malt and about 5-6° proof. They tend to be lighter in the south (Munich, Stuttgart), stronger and more bitter in the Rhineland (Dortmund, Cologne), and sweeter in Berlin.
– Dark beers made with roasted malt can taste quite sugary (Rauchbier, Bockbier, Malzbier).

In restaurants and bars, beer is generally served on draught *(vom Faß)*. Those drinking lighter beers such as Pils might like to order a round in advance, as they will need to wait a while for the froth to settle!

KÖLN★★★

COLOGNE – Nordrhein-Westfalen – Population 992 000
Michelin map 417 N 4
Plan of the conurbation in the current Michelin Red Guide Deutschland
and on Michelin map 417

Cologne is the capital of the Rhineland and one of the largest cities in Germany. On the Rhine's west bank, the old town forms a semi-circle between the river and the Ring – a curving, 6km - 3 1/2 miles avenue, much of it dual carriageway, that follows the line of the city's 13C fortifications. Vestiges of these still remain at a few points, notably the **Severinstor** and **Ulrepforte** (**FX**). In the Middle Ages, 40 000 people lived within these walls, and Cologne was not only the biggest but also the most densely populated city in the whole country. At that time the two main thoroughfares were the **Hohe Straße** (**GYZ**) (north-south) and the **Schildergasse** (**GZ**) (east-west), both of them busy pedestrian precincts today. The more modern quarters, developed after the destruction of the ramparts in 1881, lie in concentric circles outside this ancient nucleus. A double **Green Belt** lends space and perspective to this outer urban area.

Many bridges link historic parts of the city with the industrial zones on the east bank of the river. It is here that the **exhibitions** and **fairs** which draw so many businessmen to Cologne are held (the Photokina, a good-housekeeping exhibition and a salon of confectionery, for example).

Cologne's principal industries are mechanical (automobiles, machine tools), pharmaceutical, chemical and petro-chemical – not forgetting the perfumery business, with its famous Eau de Cologne. The principal manufacturer of this toilet water, first elaborated in the early 18C by an Italian who settled in the city, is the cosmetic firm Muelhens KG, the old Glockengasse no 4711.

The Rhine Riverside – The most impressive view of the old city and its skyline can be found on the river's east bank, south of the Hohenzollernbrücke, at the level of Kennedy quay – or even from the Deutzer Brücke (**FV**). From these points the Rhine frontage, dominated by the bold cathedral spires and the square, steepled belfry of Groß St. Martin, is majestically attractive.

Cologne's cathedral quarter, seen from the east bank of the Rhine

HISTORICAL AND ARTISTIC NOTES

Cologne in Roman Times – Once the Roman legions had extended the Empire as far as the Rhine, General Agrippa, the coloniser of the region, allowed the Ubii, a Germanic people, to occupy (38 BC) the west bank of the river. The settlement was named the *Oppidum Ubiorum*. Then, in the year AD 50, Agrippina, the third wife of the Emperor Claudius and the mother of Nero, obtained for her birthplace the official title of Roman Colony – *Colonia Claudia Ara Agrippinensium* (CCAA). "Colonia's" first defensive walls were then built, and the town became the residence of the Governor of Lower Germania. Roman ruins still exist: in the (restored) Zeughausstraße, at the north gate of the town in front of the cathedral, and at the **Praetorium**, beneath the present town hall. From its official recognition onwards, the town flourished: it was the start of an era, rich in craftwork, trade and architecture, which did not end until the time of the Great Invasions, in the 5C.

The Holy City Beside the Rhine – Cologne's political power in the Middle Ages derived from the Church. The bishopric founded by the Emperor Constantine in the 4C was upgraded to an archbishopric by Charlemagne. Until the Battle of Worringen in 1288, the Archbishops of Cologne exercised powers that were not only spiritual but also temporal. Churches, of which the cathedral was one, monasteries and collegiates rose rapidly – more than 150 in all.

In the 13C and at the beginning of the 14C, the city became the enlightened religious, intellectual and artistic centre of the Rhine Valley. Eminent men came to preach: the Dominicans **Albertus Magnus** (the teacher of Thomas Aquinas) and **Master Eckhart**, as well as the Scottish Franciscan, **Duns Scotus**. It was the work of such religious scholars that led in 1388 to the creation of Cologne university by local lay burghers.

Trade and Commerce – Because of its favoured position on the banks of the Rhine and at the crossroads of important trade routes, Cologne soon became a power in the commercial world, imposing its own system of weights and measures over the whole of northern Germany. Such authority derived from a decree known as the **Stapelrecht** (Law of Stockage), under which all foreign merchants passing through the city were obliged to keep their goods there for at least three days, thus allowing Cologne residents a prior right to purchase. The town's first fair was held in 1360. Its elevation to the status of Free City in 1475 did no more than set an official seal on the preponderant role the burghers of Cologne had in fact been playing since the 13C.

The School of Cologne – Manuscript illumination and the decoration of altars were already blossoming local arts in Cologne at the beginning of the 14C. Painting attained its summit in the first half of the 15C, with the works of **The Master of St Veronica** and **Stefan Lochner**, a native of Meersburg. From 1450 onwards, under the influence of the Dutch schools, the artists of Cologne abandoned the idealistic mysticism of the Gothic period in favour of the more gracious realism of the Renaissance (Master of the Life of The Virgin, Master of the Reredos of St Bartholomew). This later work is characterized by a delicacy of colour and a certain suavity in the treatment of subjects.

Sculpture – Religious sculpture in Cologne reached its high point between the 14C and the 15C. The many **Madonnas** on display underline a particular sentimentality of approach: more than one can be classed in the so-called "style of tenderness" sweeping Europe around 1400 – the hinted smile, a softness of drapery, a lissom stance, these all mark the distinguishing traits of such Virgins of the Late Gothic school.

MODERN CITY

Industrialization in the second half of the 19C conferred on Cologne an expansion that was both rapid and remarkable. After the Second World War, **Konrad Adenauer** continued the process of modernization he had inaugurated while he was Mayor of the city between 1917 and 1933 – the year in which he was deposed by the Nazis. It was through the man destined to become the Federal Republic's first Chancellor *(qv)* that the university, shut down under the French occupation in 1798, was re-opened (1919); that the Deutz exhibition halls (Messehallen) was built; and that the green belts girdling the city were established. Much of the aspect of Cologne today is due to Adenauer.

War and Reconstruction – Between 1942 and 1945, continual air raids that were more than usually devastating destroyed 90% of the old town and 70% of the surrounding areas. Rebuilding of the city, under the direction of the architect **Rudolf Schwarz**, involved considerable modification of the original town plan, retaining at the same time the historic kernel at the heart of Cologne. A good example is the **Fest-und-Tanzhaus Gürzenich** (**GZ A**) – a municipal hall for fairs and balls which has been incorporated in the ruins of the church of Alt-St. Alban. The restored Gothic façade hides an ultra-modern interior. A copy (E Mataré) of **The Afflicted Parents**, by Käthe Kollwitz, is displayed in the church ruins as a memorial to the victims of war.

Roman Catholicism – Reverential, yet sumptuous and enormously popular, the **Corpus Christi Procession** ("Gottestracht") is an indication each year of the importance and vitality of the Church in Cologne. First winding around the cathedral, the procession subsequently embarks in boats plying between Mülheim and St. Kunibert (**FU**) on the Rhine. The city's many modern churches testify equally to the strength of faith today. The most influential figures in this renewal of sacred art are **Dominikus Böhm** *(qv)* and his son Gottfried.

Art and Culture – Diversity is the keyword in any consideration of cultural life in Cologne today. Apart from music and drama, the plastic arts hold pride of place: no less than 80 galleries are devoted to the exhibition of contemporary work. Every year since 1967, the city has promoted an international fair titled "Cologne Art". Beside the Schnütgen Museum, the **Josef-Haubrich-Halle** (**EV N**) mounts important permanent exhibitions.

Heinrich Böll, one of the most eminent representatives of German post-war writing and winner of the Nobel Prize for Literature in 1972, was born in Cologne – and his work, sparing neither the Church nor society, is inseparable from his Rhineland birthplace.

The Carnival – The Rhinelander's gaiety and sense of fun is evident everyday in Cologne, but it is during the carnival season that this proverbial good humour reaches its apogee. Celebrations start on the Thursday before Ash Wednesday with the **Women's Carnival**, the participants outdoing one another to disrupt everyday life in the streets and shops and offices. Two days later, clownish processions organized by the schools and the various quarters of the city start to parade. It is in these **"Veedelzöch"** (a dialect word) that the survival of Cologne's Roman past is best preserved, for the origins of the carnival can be traced back to the Roman Saturnalia.

"Rose Monday" (the day before Shrove Tuesday) is when the fun is most furious, with public dancing, fanfares, elaborately decorated floats and a cavalcade of giants, each in its own way caricaturing or parodying some aspects of current news or views.

Town Life – If a sense of humour is characteristic of the city, conviviality is not far behind in the life of Cologne. This party spirit is inseparable from the **"Kölsch"** – a word standing at the same time for the local dialect and a famous beer, brewed in the region and served in huge stemmed glasses.

There is a strong sense of neighbourhood – almost rural – unity in the relationship linking the Cologne locals with their **"Veedeln"**: the traditional quarters of the old town, each centred on a parish church, each preserving its own traditions. St. Severin is the oldest and most typical *(see below)*.

But in addition to their particular corner, all Cologne citizens appreciate that part of the old town bordering the Rhine. Remodelled in the 1980s, this is now, night and day, one of the liveliest parts of the city – especially the **Martinsviertel**, where, according to legend, the number of taverns by far surpassed the norm in medieval times.

Since the riverside highway has been diverted through tunnels between the Hohenzollern and Deutzer bridges, land has been freed for the establishment of attractive **gardens** (Rheingarten) **(GYZ)** where the inhabitants can walk or relax in calm surroundings immediately above the water. **Boat excursions** leave from this point.

The **Dance Fountain** (Tanzbrunnen), situated in the 40ha - 100-acre **Rheinpark** on the far (eastern) side of the river, continues nevertheless to be very popular. The best way to get there is to take the **cable-car** (Rheinseilbahn), which runs from Easter until the end of October from a terminal near the zoo. Leave by the Konrad-Adenauer-Ufer **(FU)**.

CATHEDRAL QUARTER (GY) *time: one day*

The heart of Cologne beats in the immediate vicinity of the central station and the **Hohenzollernbrücke** – the busiest railway bridge in the world, with a train crossing it every two minutes, day and night.

Since the 1970s, road traffic has been banished from the surroundings of the cathedral, to the west and the south, to allow construction of the new Römisch-Germanisches Museum and the Diözesan-Museum.

Once these were completed, the land between the cathedral and the river, for long used simply as a car park, was incorporated in the so-called **"Rhine-Cathedral Project"**. Since 1986 this has included the Wallraf-Richartz and Ludwig Museums, housed in a complex designed by P Busmann and G Haberer – a piece of modernistic architecture whose saw-tooth roofing blends harmoniously enough with the Gothic spires of the cathedral and the silhouette of the Gründerzeit railway station. The project also embodies, at basement level, the **Philharmonia** auditorium. From the Heinrich-Böll-Platz, where the museums are located, a series of terraces leads down to the northern part of Rheingarten.

★★★**Dom (Cathedral)** – It took more than 600 years to complete this gigantic edifice. In 1164, when Frederick Barbarossa donated **relics of the Magi** to the town of Cologne, an accelerating influx of pilgrims began, and by 1248 the need for a new and larger place of worship had become pressing. Thus began the construction of a new cathedral, the first Gothic church in the Rhineland, its original design based on those in Paris, Amiens and Reims.

By 1320 the chancel was completed. Work on the south front tower, however, was stopped in 1437 – and that on the nave and transept in 1560.

More than three centuries elapsed before the gap in the building was to be filled: it was not until 1842, when neo-Gothic fever shook Romantic Germany, that work on the original plans was resumed. In 1880 the cathedral was at last ceremoniously consecrated in the presence of the Emperor Wilhelm I.

At first, the modern visitor is overwhelmed by the sheer size of the building and the profusion of its ornate decoration. The **twin-towered western façade** marks the peak of achievement in the style known as Flamboyant Gothic. Stepped windows, embellished gables, slender buttresses, burst upwards, ever upwards, slimly in line with the tapering spires that reach a height of 157m - 515ft. The apse facing the Rhine, spined with a multitude of turrets and pinnacles is a bravura expression of architectural prowess and enthusiasm. The **bronze doors (1)** in the south transept entrance (1948-53) are by Mataré (Celestial Jerusalem above; Cologne in flames on the right).

Entering the church by the west door, one appreciates the sweep of the nave in a single glance, but until the transept is reached, the building's colossal proportions cannot truly be taken in. The nave, as far as the choir, is 144m - 472ft long, 45m - 148ft wide, and 43.5m - 143ft high. Seen from the nave, the choir appears to float at some infinite distance, while the vaulting arched far above seems to reach a height that is completely unreal.

The five Late Gothic **stained glass windows★** in the north aisle (1507-08) depict the lives of The Virgin and St Peter. The south transept houses a large Flemish polyptych of 1520 known as **The Altarpiece of the Five Moors** (**2**) (Agilolphusaltar).

The 10C **Cross of Gero★** (Gerokreuz) (**3**), a unique example of Ottonian art, hangs in the first northern chapel (Chapel of the Cross) off the ambulatory. Behind, in the Chapel of the Holy Sacrament, is **The Madonna of Milan**, a Virgin and Child in the local "tender" style.

★★★ **Dreikönigenschrein** (Shine of the Magi) – This magnificent piece of medieval work is in a glass case behind the high altar. Intricately decorated with different characters, the reliquary is in the form of a basilica with unusual dimensions (2.20m - 7ft long). It was started by the goldsmith **Nicolas of Verdun** in 1181 and completed c1220 by the master craftsmen of Cologne. The altar itself dates from 1320.

In the axial Chapel of the Three Kings (**4**), there are splendid 13C stained glass windows; the last chapel off the southern sector of the ambulatory (Marienkapelle) contains the celebrated **altarpiece★★★** painted c1440 by **Stefan Lochner** and illustrating The Adoration of the Magi (centre section). Side panels portray the patron saints of the city of Cologne: St Ursula and her Virgins on the left; St Gereon on the right.

Choir ☉ – The finely carved **choir stalls★** (Chorgestühl), the most extensive medieval example in Germany, contain 104 places. High up above the stalls, on each of the chancel walls, frescoes represent symbolically the powers of Church and State.

The 14 **statues** incorporated in the pillars of the chancel (Chorpfeilerstatuen) are of Jesus, Mary and the 12 Apostles.

★ **Treasury** (Domschatzkammer) ☉ – *Enter via the north transept.* The cathedral treasury contains gold and silver liturgical plate as well as ancient vestments, episcopal crosses and accoutrements, manuscripts, miniatures and swords of justice.

South Tower (Südturm) – A very steep stairway *(509 steps)* leads to a **platform** from which, at a height of 97m - 318ft, a splendid panorama of Cologne and the surrounding country can be enjoyed. Do not neglect the **belfry** (Glochenstube). The largest of the nine bells, **St Peter's Bell** (Petersglocke) was cast in 1923. At an overall weight of 24 tons (the clapper alone accounts for 800kg - 1 763lbs) this is the biggest swinging church bell in the world.

★★★ **Römisch-Germanisches Museum** (**M¹**) ☉ – Capital of the Roman province known as Lower Germania, Cologne enjoyed an intense prosperity between the 1C and the middle of the 5C, due largely to fruitful exchanges between the civilization of the colonizers and the Germanic culture of the Ubii. In this museum, such evidence of the period as has been from time to time discovered is on display in the new site south of the cathedral. The exhibits are presented thematically, accompanied by audiovisual commentaries.

In the basement is the **Dionysius Mosaic**, uncovered here during excavations for an air-raid bunker in 1941. The work, measuring 10.5m x 7m (34ft x 23ft) was once the floor of the dining room in a Roman villa. Against a background of geometric motifs, colourful medallions depict lively scenes from the life of Dionysius, the god of wine, pleasure and fecundity. Adjacent rooms evoke day-to-day life in Roman times through the display of pottery, games, keys, sewing materials, tombstones and an astonishing swastika mosaic.

Overlooking the Dionysian mosaic is the **Mausoleum of Lucius Poblicius**, an officer of the Roman 5th Legion who lived in retirement in Cologne. The tomb, 14.5m - 47ft high, extends over several floors. It was originally erected (*c*50 AD) on the route linking Cologne with Bonn. The harmony of the monument's proportions is particularly noticeable on the upper storeys, where the ornamentation includes both mythological and vegetal motifs.

The different levels of the museum introduce the visitor to Roman statuary as well as architecture (fortified gateway inscribed with the abbreviated Roman name for the town: CCAA). There are also examples of transport (four-wheeled chariot), port activity (piles from a Rhine bridge), coinage, Roman religion, and games. Among the colonials' domestic decorations, the **Philosophers' Mosaic** is especially noteworthy. Amazing in its geometric composition, this villa floor represents the Seven Sages of Greece. Wealthy Romans did not hesitate to order such luxuries from abroad, witness the Pompeiian-style frescoes exhibited, and features in different colours of marble imported from Egypt.

Imagination pushed to the limits of fantasy informs the precious collection of **glassware**. Note especially the unique 4C vasa **diatreta** blown several times before being decorated with an outer tracery in coloured relief and a Greek inscription in purple. Vessels in the shape of animals and 2C **bottles decorated with coils** are also on view. Roman jewellery and "barbarian" ornaments in cloisonné enamel or engraved gold are of inestimable archaeological worth.

★★★ **Wallraf-Richartz-Museum/Museum Ludwig** (**M²**) ☉ – This double museum on the banks of the Rhine boasts sixty rooms – a complex including not only the Philharmonia but also a whole series of cultural institutions: a museum of photography (Agfa Foto-Historama, *see below*), a graphics collection, the Cologne cinemathèque, and a library.

Wallraf-Richartz-Museum – *First floor.* Works by German, Italian, Flemish, Dutch and French painters from the 14C to the 19C are on display here. The very valuable **Medieval Painters of Cologne** collection, culminating with the Late Gothic work of Stefan Lochner and his contemporaries, is unique. Note in particular the **Master of St Veronica** with the early 15C triptych *The Holy Family*; the **Master of Life of the Virgin** with an Annunciation triptych and *The Vision of St Bernard* (late 15C); and **Stefan Lochner's** own **Virgin and the Rose Bush** (*c*1450) – a masterpiece which impresses not only by its use of colour, the delicacy of yellows and golds, but also by the serenity of expression on the faces.

Works by the **Italian Old Masters** Martini and Lorenzetti show the pan-European dimension of religious painting in the Middle Ages. Display panels with text and illustrations explain the techniques of medieval painting, the use of illustrative themes in those times, and the history of Cologne.

Bartholomäus Bruyn the Elder (1493-1555) was one of the rare painters who took orders for portraits from private individuals. Influenced by the mannerists of Antwerp, he was much esteemed and sought after by the patrician burghers of Cologne. Note, in this gallery, the portraits of *Gerhard Pilgrim* and *Heinrich Salsburg*.

Among the **German Old Masters** on view are Dürer *(The Fife Player* and *The Tambourine Player)* and Lucas Cranach the Elder *(Virgin and Child).* The 16C Italians are represented by Titian and Tintoretto.

The collection of **Dutch and Flemish painting of the 17C** offers such great names as Rubens *(The Holy Family* and *The Stigmata of St Francis)*, Ruysdael *(View of a River)*, Frans Hals *(The Fisherman's Daughter)* and **Rembrandt**, with the famous self-portrait in which the artist, already old, wearing a turban, regards the spectator obliquely, a smile on his lips. After this comes the section featuring 17C and 18C painters: Spanish (Murillo), Italian (Tiepolo, Bordone), and French (Boucher: *Young Girl Resting*; landscapes by Claude Lorrain).

French and German artists dominate the section devoted to the 19C. The German Romantics are represented by, among others, C D Friedrich; the Realists by the Cologne-born Wilhelm Leibl (Portrait of *H Pallenberg*). The German Impressionist school offers work by Liebermann, Corinth and Klinger. With the Romantic movement (Delacroix) as a point of departure, French painting advances via Realism (Courbet) to the Impressionists: Renoir, Monet, Sisley, Cézanne, Van Gogh *(The Railway Bridge)* and Gaugin. Sculptures by Degas and Rodin are also on display.

Museum Ludwig – First and second floor (modern classics); basement. There is an important collection of 20C art in this museum, with the **Expressionist** movement particularly well represented. Among the painters of the **Brücke** group, Kirchner is noteworthy with his *Five Women in the Street*, as are his associates Heckel and Nolde.

The **Blauer Reiter** movement is represented by Macke, Marc, Kandinsky and Jawlensky; Expressionism by **Kokoschka** and Beckmann. A separate section is reserved for art between the two World Wars: Constructivism, the Bauhaus, the New Objectivity, the Cologne Progressionists.

One of the museum's strong points is embodied in a collection of **Russian Avant-Garde Art** (1910-1930). Paintings and "spatial constructions" by Gontscharova, Larinov, Malevitz and Popova vividly convey the strength of the country's artistic renewal before the cultural freeze under Stalin.

The department devoted to the Surrealists reveals that the **Dada** movement was in fact born in Cologne, just before the First World War. Apart from oil paintings, gouaches and collages by Max Ernst (*Friend's Meeting*), who was born in Brühl, near Cologne, exhibits include work by Hans Arp, Schwitters, Miro, Dalí, Magritte and Paul Klee (with his late masterpiece *Main Roads and Minor Roads*).

French modern art is represented by Modigliani, Maillol (*The Slender Bathers*), and above all the **Cubists** Braque, Léger, Delaunay and Juan Gris. A separate room contains paintings and sculpture by **Picasso**. Arman, Klein and Saint Phalle (*Nanas*) are there to illustrate "the new realism".

Paintings by Baumeister and Nay introduce the visitor to post-war German art and the "renewal" of the 1960s, in which **Beuys** and the Group Zero played an important part. American abstract painting is well represented, particularly **Pop Art** – oriented once more towards the object - which had its heyday in the United States in the 60s. Among the museum's latest acquisitions are paintings by Baselitz and Penck, as well as truly large-scale artistic compositions such as *The Black Town* by Anne and Patrick Poirier.

Prints and Drawings – *First floor*. Drawings (by, among others, Leonardo da Vinci, Raphael, Dürer, Rembrandt), miniatures, water-colours and prints from the end of the 11C to the beginning of the 20C.

★ **Museum of Photography** (Agfa Foto-Historama) ⊘ – *Ground floor and first floor*. Compiled from various private collections (the Stengler Collection, the archives of the Agfa company, etc.), these three galleries present an overall view of 150 years of photography.

The impact of the displays derives from the juxtaposition of ancient exhibits and photographs of great historical or cultural value. Thus the history of photography can be followed through its various stages – magic lantern, daguerrotype (1839), calotype (Talbot's negative process, 1841), amateur interest, spooled film (Eastman, 1888) – to the invention of microfilm and the small, high-tech cameras of today.

★ **Diözesan-Museum (Diocesan Museum) (M³)** ⊘ – The relatively small Diocesan Museum regards itself as an art museum, and has recently moved resolutely in a new direction, by increasingly acquiring examples of contemporary art on Christian themes. The result is a vigorous interplay between old and new art.

The most famous piece is Stefan Lochner's **Virgin with Violets**, where each flower represents one of the virtues of Mary. Also on display is a priceless length of **Sassanid silk cloth** (Byzantine or Syrian, c 800), which was discovered in the Shrine of St Cunibert, a 6C Bishop of Cologne. The weaving depicts a hunting scene, deployed with unique symmetry around a central palm tree. An item from **Joseph Beuys** with a munitions chest and crucifix is particularly impressive.

★ ROMANESQUE CHURCHES

The Romanesque period in Cologne, from the mid-10C to the mid-13C, saw the construction of numerous churches. In the old town alone, 12 churches from that era are still standing, one of which now houses the Schnütgen-Museum (*see below*). The damage from the Second World War has now nearly all been repaired. Strolling through its old streets, therefore, the visitor gets a good idea of the different periods and varying styles of Rhineland Romanesque architecture. Certain concepts of religious design – the **trefoil chancel**, for instance – originated indeed in the city (*see Introduction*).

Groß St. Martin (GZ) – This church, once a monastery, is built on what was once an island in the river, opposite the Roman port. The imposing square tower, rising 84m - 276ft above the transept crossing, lends with its four octagonal turrets a fortress-like aspect to the whole. In the forecourt, on the corner in front of the hostel, note the life-size bronze statues of eminent townsmen (**Tunnes** and **Schäl**).

St. Maria im Kapitol (GZ B) – Another church which recalls a fortress. Situated on the river bank, this one too has a tall, square tower with four corner turrets above the transept crossing.

St. Maria Lyskirchen (FX) – This triple-aisle basilica was built opposite the entrance to the Rhine port (c1220). The exterior is uninteresting, but there are splendid 13C **frescoes**★★ inside. A series of 24 Biblical scenes appears among the ribbed vaulting of the central nave.

KÖLN

0   200 m

Use the map of principal sights to plan an itinerary.

198

KÖLN

A Fest-
  und Tanzhaus Gürzenich
B St. Maria im Kapitol
F St. Mariä Himmelfahrt
M¹ Römisch-Germanisches
  Museum
M² Wallraf-Richartz-Museum
  und Museum Ludwig
M³ Diözesanmuseum
M⁴ Schnütgen-Museum
M⁶ Museum
  für Angewandte Kunst

St. Georg (FX) – A flat-roofed basilica with colonnades, this church dates from the 11C. Vaults above the choir and nave are 12C. The west end, where the walls are 5m - 16ft thick, is once more reminiscent of a fortified tower.

St. Severin (FX) – The oldest Christian foundation in Cologne. There is a fine Gothic nave in the **interior★**. Note, in the two arms of the transept, paintings by the Master of St Severinus; a 13C forked Cross in the south transept; and behind the high altar, a shrine to the saint (restored in the 19C). The actual tomb of St Severinus is kept in the crypt.

St. Pantaleon (EX) – Built in the 10C, this church is an example of Ottonian art. The **rood-screen★** is Late Gothic. The 10C tomb of Archbishop Bruno of Cologne lies in the crypt.

St. Aposteln (EV K) – Pure Rhineland Romanesque, this 11C church has a trefoil chancel and transept. Outside, the 13C **apse★**, flanked by two octagonal lantern turrets, is garnished with a beautiful Romanesque gallery.

St. Gereon (EV) – *Entrance via the Christopherstraße.*
The unique design of this building is instanced by its elliptical plan and (in 1220) the addition of a decagon between the two towers. The crypt, floored with 11C mosaics, contains the coffins of St Gereon and other unknown martyrs of the Theban Legion, said to have been butchered to a man for refusing to make pagan sacrifices.
The frescoes are 13C, and the reredos above the altar Renaissance, with Gothic overtones. In the body of the church, on the north side, there is a tabernacle with bas-reliefs depicting the Last Supper (1608) as well as a fine Aubusson tapestry. A polychrome Virgin and Child stands on the south side (c1400).

St. Andreas (GY) – This Romanesque church, with a very tall octagonal lantern tower and a widely projecting west transept, was transformed by the addition of a chancel in the Gothic era. The sarcophagus of Albert the Great lies in the crypt.

St. Ursula (FU) ⊘ – In the south aisle, the **Treasury★** (Goldene Kammer) contains 14-17C reliquary busts and the 1170 Aetherius Shrine in hand-embossed copper. There are also collections of human bones arranged to spell out maxims and slogans.

St. Kunibert (FU) – The last wholly Romanesque church in Cologne. The twin towers flanking the chancel are intact. In the transept crossing, a group of over-life-size statues represents the Annunciation (1439; the folds of clothing and the gestures of the subjects suggest already an advance in the direction of realism). In a chapel on the north side of the choir, murals illustrate scenes from the life of the Virgin Mary.
The **stained glass windows★** (1230) above the choir stalls represent scenes of life at Court. Bells and clappers in the south aisle were once housed in the west tower, now in ruins.

OTHER MUSEUMS

★★ Schnütgen-Museum (**GZ M⁴**) ⊙ – The 12C former Cäcilienkirche, one of the dozen Romanesque religious edifices still standing in the city, makes a suitable site for this museum devoted to sacred art from the 6C to the 19C, but essentially concentrated on the Middle Ages.

Numerous **Madonnas in wood** illustrate the local "tender" style in statuary. **St Hieronymus and the Lion** (Erkelenz: 1460-70) is a masterpiece of Late Gothic wood carving. The Wassenberg choir stalls and a series of marble portrait statues from the cathedral (c1300-1310) are additional, important examples of work from the Gothic period. The gold altar panel (c1170) is from St. Ursula's.

A collection of medieval items in **ivory**, most of them from Byzantium, France or other parts of Germany, is of particularly fine workmanship. It includes figurines, boxes, portable altars and copies of the Gospels. **Goldsmiths' and silversmiths' work** on display (reliquaries, busts, caskets, etc.) is equally impressive. Note, too, the items in bronze made by Christians from the East.

★★ Museum für Ostasiatische Kunst (Museum of Far Eastern Art) (**EV M⁵**) ⊙ – *Universitätsstraße 100*.

Germany's oldest museum of Far Eastern art (founded in 1909), was relocated in 1977 to a modern building designed by Kunio Mayekawa (1905-1986), a student of Le Corbusier. The Japanese garden was laid out by contemporary artist Massayuke Nagare (*b*1923).

The permanent exhibition displays works of Chinese, Japanese and Korean art, from the Neolithic age to the present. The Shang dynasty (*c*13-11C BC) **bronze vessels** from China are renowned, as is the museum's vast collection of **Buddhist art** – exquisitely sculpted stone, wood and lacquer images, delicately painted cult images, and powerful Zen-related depictions of humans and nature. The collection of Chinese ceramics is particularly strong in **Celadon ware**, T'ang dynasty (610-907) three-colour tomb figures and other high-quality porcelain from later period. The museum's collection of Korean ceramics is the best in continental Europe. Paintings by Chinese literati, decorative hanging scrolls and folding **screens** from Japan, as well as the colourful Ukiyo-e prints with their everyday subjects evoke scenes from the life of a bygone age. Recent additions to the exhibition include early Chinese Buddhist and Taoist sculptures (8-12C) and a collection of Chinese furniture.

Museum für Ostasiatische Kunst, Köln, Inv.-Nr. C 73.2

Ceremonial urn,
Museum für Ostasiatische Kunst

★ Museum für Angewandte Kunst (Museum of Applied Arts) (**GYZ M⁶**) ⊙ – Here there is a general survey of the evolution of a functional aesthetic, from the craftwork of medieval artisans to post-modern design.

The Renaissance department displays splendid examples of marquetry furniture as well as **Italian majolica** from Faenza, Urbino, Genoa and Venice. The section reserved for Baroque and Rococo items contains **porcelain from Meißen** and other 18C manufactures, Dutch faience (Delft), a collection of "chinoiseries" and silver from southern Germany. Fine examples of neo-Renaissance French furniture (second half of the 19C) illustrate the emergence of "historicism", while ceramics from the France of the same period already foreshadow modernity. Among the furniture from the **Jugendstil period** *(qv)* note particularly a Viennese pear-wood desk (1914), a dining suite from Darmstadt (1910), and a semicircular work-table by Henry van de Velde (Berlin, 1901).

Kölnisches Stadtmuseum (Metropolitan Historical Museum) (**EV M⁷**) ⊙ – Cologne's eventful past is evoked here by arms and armour, pictures of battles, weights and measures, episcopal tombstones and portraits of eminent townspeople.

Rautenstrauch-Joest-Museum für Völkerkunde (Ethnographic Museum) (**FX M⁸**) ⊙ – Pride of place is given to **Thai and Khmer art** from the 8C to the 16C (bronze, terracotta and stone statues; ceramics) and to pre-Colombian civilization in South America. Among the collection of metal artefacts from **Peru** (11C-15C), note the finely engraved bowls and vases in gold.

Imhoff-Stollwerck-Museum ⊙ – *Rheinauhafen*.

This highly original museum takes as its subject that most fascinating of foodstuffs, **chocolate**. Visitors are greeted by a 3m - 10ft high chocolate fountain, which they may sample, thus setting an appropriately self-indulgent mood for the rest of the tour.

Besides various delicious end-products, the display includes interesting information on the history and production of chocolate, a miniature chocolate factory, old-fashioned chocolate-vending machines, a greenhouse full of cocoa plants, and a collection of beautiful silver and porcelain drinking vessels reflecting the fact that chocolate was once an expensive luxury drink enjoyed only by the aristocracy. The museum also recounts the history of the traditional chocolate-making firm of Stollwerck, founded in Cologne in 1839.

ADDITIONAL SIGHTS

Imhoff-Stollwerck-Museum, Köln

Chocolate-vending machine

* **Altes Rathaus (Old Town Hall) (GZ)** – There are two separate sections to this building: the main 14C Gothic block, and a pavilion in the Italian Renaissance style which forms a porch to it. In 1953, beneath the new Town Hall, excavations revealed the Roman **Praetorium** – ruins of a palace (1C - 4C) of which the central octagon, the wells and the drainage system are still recognizable.

* **Botanischer Garten Flora (Botanical Park)** ⊘ – *Leave by the Konrad-Adenauer-Ufer* (**FU**).
An enormous **hothouse** (Gewächshaus) displays a variety of tropical species. The park includes an Italian "water stairway", formal terraces in the French style, and a vast English garden.

St. Kolumba (GZ) – This 1950 work by Gottfried Böhm is built on the site of a Gothic church destroyed during the war. Note the luminosity of the chancel with its blue stained glass windows, and a 15C statue of the Virgin, saved from the ruins.

St. Peter (GZ) – The Crucifixion of St Peter, by Rubens, is displayed in the entrance. Admire also the very fine late 14C stained-glass windows.

St. Marlä Himmelfahrt (GY F) – The spirit of the Counter-Reformation which inspired the building of this Jesuit church (1618-1678) led to a singular blend of Romanesque, Gothic and Baroque styles, inside as well as outside. Among Gothic elements borrowed by the Alsatian architect Christoph Wamser are the vaulting in the nave and the windows in the entrance façade. Rich Baroque decorations (restored) adorn the pillars which support galleries above the side aisles.

St. Maria-Königin – *Access via Bonner Straße southeast of the plan* (**FX**).
This modern church of vertically laid red brick was designed by Dominikus Böhm *(qv)* in 1954. Shades of grey predominate in the **glass wall** ★ (south) illuminating the interior.

EXCURSIONS

* **Schloß Augustusburg in Brühl** ⊘ – *13km - 8 miles to the south.*
This castle, known as Augustusburg after its founder, the Elector Clement-Augustus, Archbishop of Cologne, was built between 1725 and 1768 by J K Schlaun and François de Cuvilliés. Inside, the splendid **staircase** ★ peopled by Rococo caryatids and atlantes is attributed to Balthazar Neumann *(qv)*.
The **gardens** are formal in the French manner.

* **Altenberger Dom** – *20km - 12 miles to the northeast.*
This former Cistercian abbey church (still known locally as the Bergischer Dom – cathedral of the Berg Duchy) lies in a green valley much appreciated by the city dwellers of Cologne. Today it is a "parallel church", celebrating Roman Catholic and Protestant rites alternately. Note especially the gigantic (18m x 8m - 59ft x 26ft) coloured glass canopy above the west entrance, and the **grisaille stained glass windows** in the chancel.

* **Zons** – *24km - 15 miles to the north.*
A picturesque and delightful Rhineland fortified village, with a 14C **toll-house**.

Gourmands or gourmets...
*each year the **Michelin Red Guide Deutschland** gives*
an up-to-date selection of establishments renowned for their cuisine.
German gastronomic specialities are described at the end of the Introduction.

KÖNIGSSCHLÖSSER★★★

The term Königsschlösser is generally reserved for Hohenschwangau castle and its extravagantly romantic, neo-feudal neighbour, Neuschwanstein. The other royal residences of Upper Bavaria, equally examples of Ludwig II's passion for historical reconstruction, should not however be forgotten. They include Schloß Linderhof and Schloß Herrenchiemsee *(qv)*.

HOHENSCHWANGAU★ and NEUSCHWANSTEIN★★

About 3 hours walk and sightseeing
Leave the car in the special park at Hohenschwangau.

Circle the wooded spur crowned by Hohenschwangau castle until you arrive at the shady promontory of the Pindarplatz, on the northern shore of the **Alpsee★**. At this point, there is a **lookout point** with a fine **view★** of the dark, pine-ringed waters of the lake and the Säuling escarpments above. Take the path on the right which leads to the castle.

★ **Schloß Hohenschwangau** ⊘ – This castle, constructed from the ruins of a large 12C feudal fortress, was built between 1832 and 1836 on the orders of Maximilian II of Bavaria, when he was still Prince Regent.

The neo-Gothic style, strongly influenced by the traditional English manor house, satisfied the current taste for troubadour romanticism. It was in these surroundings that the unfortunate Ludwig II dreamed away his youth.

Compared with Neuschwanstein, and despite its many infelicities – excessive repetition in the décor of the etymological swan (Schwan) motif; accumulation of inelegant objets d'art offered to the Royal Family by Bavarian communities – Hohenschwangau retains the warmth of a palace that was once lived in. The presence over many years of Queen Marie, the mother of Ludwig II, goes a long way to explain the atmosphere of relative intimity that still pervades the apartments.

Having endured the mania for over-decoration characteristic of the period – in particular the High Gothic ceilings – visitors will welcome with relief the clean lines of the maple and cherrywood Biedermeier *(qv)* furniture. The place given to Oriental art is completely compatible with the ambiance of romantic chivalry instanced by huge murals depicting heroes of medieval verse chronicles, and based on cartoons by Moritz von Schwind.

The King's admiration for Richard Wagner is evoked on the second floor, where the old music room displays correspondence between the two men, and a piano which both played. Fantasy returns with the entry to the bedchamber of Ludwig II: the ceiling is painted to resemble the night sky, and the constellations can be illuminated at will. From his window, the King could observe through a telescope the progress of work at Neuschwanstein.

Take either the bus (leave from Hotel Liesl) or the horse-drawn cart (leave from Hotel Müller) to get to Neuschwanstein. Alternatively, take the wide, steeply sloping path (1/2 hour) from the car park.

★★ **Schloß Neuschwanstein** ⊘ – Bristling with turrets and pinnacles, the cold grey granite mass of this fortress rises from a spur penetrating the eastern extremity of the Pöllat gorge. As at Hohenschwangau, it was a designer of theatrical décor and not an architect who produced the original plans, which explains the dreamlike atmosphere of the place. Building began in 1869.

A tour of the interior, where gilded panelling, heavy tapestries and acres of marble proliferate, confirms the impression of unreality. Ludwig II stayed at the castle only 170 days: it was at Neuschwanstein on 10 June 1886 that he learned from a government commission hastily despatched from Munich that he had been deposed. He died three days later *(see MUNICH)*.

The most revealing rooms are on the third floor. They include an artificial stalactite grotto with a small adjoining winter garden that recalls the Tannhäuser legend; the Great Hall, whose décor has for its theme the legend of Lohengrin (another invasion of swans); and the unfinished Throne Room, a Byzantine-Romanesque sanctuary whose apse was to have accommodated the Royal Throne.

Almost the whole of the fourth floor is taken up by the Singers' Hall (Sängersaal), which has a fine coffered ceiling and many impressive chandeliers and candelabra. The designer here was influenced by Wartburg Castle *(qv)*, the Thuringian fortress said to have been the site, in the early 13C, of the legendary poetical contest recalled in Wagner's opera *Tannhäuser*. Wartburg was later made famous by the visit of Martin Luther. Wagner, who was a guest at Hohenschwangau, never stayed at Neuschwanstein, Linderhof or Herrenchiemsee.

After the tour, visitors who still have the stamina can walk up the Pöllat gorge to the Marienbrücke, which spans the chasm *(allow an extra hour for this promenade)*. Sometimes at night Ludwig II would come to this bridge to stare down at the castle, silent, empty, and in darkness except for lights he had illuminated in the Singers' Hall.

KONSTANZ★

CONSTANCE – Baden-Württemberg – Population 75 000
Michelin map 419 X 11 – Local map under BODENSEE

A German enclave on the Swiss shore of Lake Constance and the southern bank of the Rhine, Constance occupies an agreeable **site★** opposite the narrows which separate the main body of the lake (known as the Bodensee in German) from its picturesque prolongation (Untersee). The foundation of the town, long attributed to the Roman Emperor Constantius Chlorus (292-306), played a prominent part in the Great Schism of the West (1378-1429).

Constance, Capital of Christianity – From 1414 to 1418, a Council convened in the town attempted to re-establish the unity of the Church, which had been compromised by the pretentions of three ecclesiastical dignitaries, each claiming the right to be elected to the papal throne.

After long negotiations, two of the three rival Popes, Gregory XII and John XXIII, agreed to stand down; only Benedict XIII, who had taken refuge in Spain, remained adamant about the validity of his claim.

In 1417, the election of Martin V, who was universally recognized as the true Pope, put an end temporarily to the schism.

Three years previously, the Council had summoned before it the religious reformer **Jan Hus**, Rector of the University of Prague. Hostile to German influence, Hus expounded his theses – which contested papal primacy and certain rites – was declared a heretic, and burned alive. This precursor of Protestantism was hailed as a national hero in his native Bohemia.

★ THE LAKE SHORE (SEEUFER) (Y)

The lakeside part of the town is the most attractive, with the port, shady public gardens, a casino (Spielbank), ancient defensive towers such as the Rheintorturm and the Pulverturm, and the quays – especially the Seestraße – competing for the attention of the discerning tourist. The lake itself, busy with all kinds of water traffic, offers numerous opportunities for excursions. The Untersee, with its steep, indented shores, is particularly appealing.

KONSTANZ

M' Rosgartenmuseum
R Rathaus

ADDITIONAL SIGHTS

★ **Münster** (**Y**) – Since its construction was spread over a period from the 11C to the 17C, this former cathedral lacks any artistic unity.

The **panels** (Türflugel) of the porch doors in the main façade are decorated with bas-reliefs representing scenes from the life of Christ (1470).

The 17C vaulting in the central nave rests on the arcades of the original 11C sanctuary, achieving a visual harmony that is completely Romanesque. The decoration of the organ case and the loft itself preview the Renaissance. In the north transept, a spiral staircase turret (Schnegg), finely decorated in the French Late Gothic style, leads to the Treasury.

In the crypt are four plaques of gilded copper, each from a different period (11-13C). They represent Christ in Majesty, the symbolic Eagle of St John, St Conrad and St Pelagius, patrons of the diocese. A staircase to the right of the main door leads to a tower platform from which there is a fine view over the town and the lake.

Rathaus (**Z R**) – The façade of this Renaissance building is embellished with paintings that illustrate the history of Constance. In the inner courtyard – a quiet spot in the tourist season – is an elegant 16C house between two round towers.

Rosgartenmuseum (**Z M¹**) ⊘ – This regional museum devoted to the lakeshore areas is housed in a former corporation building. It contains a famous Palaeolithic wall-carving of a reindeer as well as a copy of the 1440 Ulrich Richental Chronicle.

The latter is vividly illustrated with pictures of council meetings and daily life in Constance at that time.

Konzilgebaüde (**Z**) – *Not open to the public.*

This former warehouse, built at the end of the 14C, was used by the Conclave of 1417 which proclaimed the election of Pope Martin V. Across the road, in a garden bordering the pleasureboat harbour, is a monument to Count Zeppelin (1838-1917), the celebrated airship inventor, who was born in Constance.

EXCURSIONS

★★ **Mainau Island (Insel Mainau)** ⊘ – *7km - 4 1/2 miles. 2 hours sightseeing. Leave by* ② *on the plan.*

Tropical brushwood and exotic plants collected by the Baden princes and members of the Royal House of Sweden still flourish in this huge island park. Orange trees, hibiscus and the great trumpet-shaped blooms of daturas are living proof of the mildness of the climate. The castle, church and flower gardens are impressive.

★ **Reichenau Island (Insel Reichenau)** – *7km - 4 1/2 miles to the west. Leave by* ① *on the plan.* St Pirmin founded the first German Benedictine monastery to the east of the Rhine on Reichenau Island in 724, and the seeds which he sowed germinated into a centre for arts and science which flourished for centuries. Some quite outstanding book illuminations were produced here during the Ottonian period.

Unfortunately for visitors, there are no longer any monks here, but gardeners have transformed the 430ha-1 063 acres of the island into a fertile market garden.

However the three churches are its main attraction.

The late 9C Carolingian St. Georgskirche of **Oberzell** – remarkable for the harmonious design of its stepped elements – contains a series of **wall paintings★★** (*c*1000 AD), depicting the miracles of Jesus.

At **Mittelzell**, the chief town on the island, there is an **old abbey★** (Münster) which was built between the 8C and 12C. The robust Romanesque tower of the Westwerk *(qv)* is lightened in appearance by a decorative band of Lombard pilasters and friezes. The open oak **roof frame** of the nave of the church is particularly noteworthy, being an outstanding example of medieval workmanship. The oaks are believed to have been felled in around 1190-1210, making this possibly the oldest roof frame in Germany. There is a very beautiful sandstone Madonna in the chancel (1320). In the abbey **treasury★** there is an early 14C reliquary of St. Mark fashioned in beaten silver enriched with enamels.

The former collegiate church (Stiftskirche) of St. Peter and St. Paul (11C and 12C) stands in **Niederzell** on the western tip of the island. The wall paintings in the choir are thought to date from the beginning of the 12C. They show Christ surrounded by an almond-shaped glory, with the apostles and prophets beneath him.

Admission times and charges for the sights described are listed at the end of the Guide.

Every sight for which there are times and charges is indicated by the symbol ⊘ in the middle section of the Guide.

Bad KREUZNACH★

Rheinland-Pfalz – Population 39 800

Michelin map 417 Q 7 - Town plan in current Michelin Red Guide Deutschland

This spa, whose origins go back to Roman times, is 15km - 9 miles from the Rhine, at a place where the Nahe flows out from the mountains of the Northern Palatinate. Bad Kreuznach is celebrated both for the health-giving qualities of its mineral waters and for the wines of the Nahe region – whose qualities lie between the fresh, strong taste of the Moselle and the softer appeal of Rhine wines. The centre of the thermal resort is on **Badewörth island** – its downstream tip straddled by the **Alte Nahebrücke**, an old bridge whose piles support 15C houses which appear to defy the laws of gravity. From the **Kauzenburg** *(café-restaurant on the Schloßberg)*, there is a fine view of the town and its surroundings.

★ **Römerhalle** ⊙ – *Hüffelsheimer Straße 11*. The museum is on a former smallholding at the western end of the castle park. Items discovered during archaeological excavations in Bad Kreuznach and the surrounding district are on display. There are two exceptional exhibits, both of them 13C **mosaic floors★★**: one depicts the Sea God in his element; the other illustrates wild animals and gladiators in combat. Below, a Roman central heating system has been unearthed (hypocaust).

Nearby, a **Roman villa** has been uncovered.

EXCURSIONS

★ **Bad Münster am Stein-Ebernburg** – *By car, 4.5km - 2 3/4 miles. Leave the car near the cure centre (Kurhaus); then 1 hour Rtn on foot.*
Go into the thermal **park★** and walk through the gardens to the Nahe. On the far side of the river is the **Rheingrafenstein★★**, a 136m - 446ft rock face surmounted by the ruins of an ancient castle.

Take the ferry across and, from the Hüttental café-restaurant, climb to the panoramic platform on top.

From here, there is a fine **view★** of the Bad Münster basin and, downstream, the Rotenfels, whose sheer porphyry cliffs tower 214m - 700ft above the river.

LAHNTAL

LAHN VALLEY – Hessen and Rheinland-Pfalz

Michelin map 417 O 7-9

The winding course of the lower Lahn, with its wild scenery and steeply wooded banks, makes an effective introduction to Romantic Germany. Above its sombre waters – the river is canalized but largely deserted – the ruins of perched castles and such small towns as Weilburg and Limburg offer a rich choice of historic souvenirs.

FROM BAD EMS TO WETZLAR 89km - 55 miles – about 4 1/2 hours

Bad Ems – The Lahn valley, separating the Westerwald and the Taunus-Rhine schist massif, is rich in mineral springs, like all areas on the fringe of a volcanic region. Bad Ems, treating mainly rhino-pharyngeal affections, is one of the oldest spas in the area. In the 19C Emperor Wilhelm I of Germany was a familiar figure in the town. A flagstone (Benedettistein) bearing the date 13 July 1870 and set into the quay-promenade in the pump room between Wilhelm and the French Ambassador, Benedetti. The Emperor categorically refused the French request that the Hohenzollerns renounce "forever" their claims to the throne of Spain. A report of the meeting, distorted and then leaked by Bismarck, hastened the Franco-Prussian war of 1870.

Nassau – The small city of Nassau was the cradle of the Counts of Laurenburg, who adopted the name of Nassau in the 12C. The Orange-Nassau branch, still reigning in the Netherlands, was the House of William of Orange, King William III of England.

Kloster Arnstein – *1km - 1/2 mile by a steep uphill road from the Obernhof bridge*. The church of this former Premonstratensian monastery stands alone on a wooded spur. The Romanesque west chancel contrasts with that in the east, which is Gothic.

Balduinstein – Ruins of a castle built in 1320 by Baudouin of Luxembourg, Archbishop of Trier, to rival that of Schaumburg.

Schloß Schaumburg ⊙ – A neo-Gothic reconstitution after the English manner. There is a fine view from the tallest of the crenellated towers overlooking the valley.

Diez – Dominating the small town clustered around its ramparts, the tall mass of the 17C **Schloß Oranienstein** ⊙ contains souvenirs of the House of Orange-Nassau. The gardens open onto the valley.

★ **Limburg** – *See LIMBURG.*

Runkel – The picturesque **setting**★★ of the castle, built into the rock face, and the ancient village below it, can best be appreciated from the 15C bridge over the river.

Weilburg – Once the residence of the Counts of Nassau, this Baroque town is built on a promontory enclosed by the Lahn. Of the many different structures which comprised the Renaissance **castle** ⊙, note especially the turreted clock tower and the elegant 1573 gallery, where the twinned Ionic columns of the arcades are topped by a glazed gallery with Corinthian columns. Vaulted **rooms** on the ground floor may be visited. The **Bergbau- und Stadtmuseum** (mining and town museum) ⊙ is devoted to the Upper Lahn and to souvenirs of the princely House of Nassau.

Braunfels – The castle, seen unexpectedly after a fork in the road, has a superb and exciting feudal outline. The perimeter wall encloses the whole village.

Follow the road as far as **Wetzlar** *(qv).*

LANDSBERG AM LECH★

Bayern – Population 20 000
Michelin map 419/420 V 16

A fortified frontier town between Swabia and Bavaria in the Middle Ages, Landsberg – on the old road from Salzburg to Memmingen – prospered through trade and the levying of tolls. Fortress gates, towers and perimeter walls still preserve a most attractive medieval atmosphere as one approaches the place.

There is a fine view of the tiered **site**★ from the shady riverside promenade on the west bank of the Lech, where it meets the Karolinenbrücke *(the best place to park if the Marktplatz below is full)*.

SIGHTS

★ **Marktplatz** – Triangular in shape, this market place is surrounded by a remarkable group of gaily coloured roughcast houses. The **fountain** (Marienbrunnen), in the centre, falls into a marble basin surmounted by a statue of the Virgin Mary.

Rathaus – The façade of this building was executed *c*1720 by Dominikus Zimmermann, one of the greatest artists of the Wessobrunn School *(qv)*, who was burgomaster of Landsberg at the time. The gable of the elegant structure is ornamented with finely worked stucco. The rest of the town hall was built between 1699 and 1702.

In the far corner of the square stands the **Schmalztor**, through which the upper town can be reached. Hemmed in on all sides by old houses, the 14C tower-gate is topped by a lantern turret roofed with glazed tiles.

The Alte Bergstrasse climbs steeply to the "Bavarian Gate".

Ba/**ertor (Bavarian Gate)** – With its projecting porch flanked by turrets and sculptures, this 1425 town gateway is one of the best preserved of its period in the whole of Germany. Outside the ramparts, which continue on either side, the gateway is embellished with carved and painted coats of arms and with a Crucifixion.

LANDSHUT★

Bayern – Population 59 000
Michelin map 420 U 20
Town plan in the current Michelin Red Guide Deutschland

Landshut on the Isar, once capital of the Lower Bavaria dukedom, has kept its medieval centre practically intact.

Memories of the Ingoldstadt and Landshut branches of the House of Wittelsbach, whose members until the 16C outshone even their extravagant Munich cousins, remain very much alive in the valleyed countryside surrounding the town. Every four years, Landshut commemorates with great pomp the marriage in 1475 of the son of Duke Ludwig the Rich with Hedwige, daughter of the King of Poland *(see Calendar of events)*.

SIGHTS

★ **Martinskirche** – Designed by Master Hans von Burghausen and built of rose-coloured brick, this 14-15C church impresses above all by its outstanding elevation. The **tower**★★, square at the base, slims and becomes octagonal as it soars to a height of more than 130m - 426ft. Circle the outside of the building, which is adorned with tombstones. The five Flamboyant doorways show an early Renaissance influence.

The well-lit interior shows a splendid unity of design. Octagonal pillars, deceptively fragile in appearance, support in a single thrust vaulting which rises to 29m - 95ft. There is a delicate Virgin and Child by Leinberger (1518) on the altar in the south aisle.

★ **Altstadt** – The town's most important monuments are to be found in this wide, slightly curving main street with its arcaded 15C and 16C houses, between the Rathaus and the Martinskirche. Note especially the variety and inventiveness of the gables, which can be seen again – though perhaps to a lesser extent – in the Neustadt, which runs parallel to the Altstadt. The façades in this second street have had many Baroque features added.

Stadtresidenz (Palace) ⊘ – Two main blocks linked by narrow wings comprise this palace, which faces the town hall. The German building is on the Alstadt (18C furniture, decorations, etc); the 16C Italian Renaissance one looks onto the courtyard (large rooms with painted, coffered ceilings).

Burg Trausnitz ⊘ – Of the fortress decorated during the Renaissance with arcaded galleries, the chapel, the Gothic hall known as the Alte Dürnitz, and several rooms furnished or embellished in 16C style are open to the public. The chapel is remarkable for its Romanesque statuary. Note also the Jesters' Staircase (Narrentreppe), painted in the 16C with scenes from the Commedia dell'Arte.

From an upper loggia (Söller), there is an exceptional **view** across the roofs of the town to the spire of the Martinskirche.

LEIPZIG ★

Sachsen – Population 530 000
Michelin map 418 L 21
Plan of the conurbation in the current Michelin Red Guide Deutschland

Leipzig stands at the confluence of the Weiße Elster and Pleiße rivers. The city is famous for its trade fairs (spring and autumn) and its numerous publishing houses.

HISTORICAL NOTES

The Leipzig Fairs – The first mention of the locality historically was in the Chronicle of Bishop Thietmar of Merseburg (975-1018), who noted the death of the Bishop of Meißen in "urbs Lipzi". The township of "Lipzk" was granted a city charter *c*1165. Subsequently, a situation at the crossing of several important trade routes, plus the bestowal by the Margrave Otto the Rich of the right to levy tolls – one of the oldest feudal privileges enjoyed by burghers – established Leipzig as a commercial centre of more than local influence. From the 12C onwards, markets were held over the Easter period and on the Feast of St Michael. A third event – during the New Year celebrations – was added in 1485. The Spring and Autumn international trade fairs, symbolized by the famous "Double M", have been held since 1896.

Leipzig, the Book Town – One of the world's earliest books, the Glossa Super Apocalipsim, was printed in Leipzig in 1481 by an itinerant craftsman. The German Book Exchange was founded in 1825, and this was followed in 1912 by the German Library (Deutsche Bücherei) and the Museum of Books and Literature (Deutsches Buch und Schriftmuseum). More than 35 established publishers are based in Leipzig today, among them Göschen, Brockhaus and Reclam.

The city also enjoys a fine reputation in the musical world, thanks to the Choir of St Thomas **(Thomanerchor)**, the Gewandhaus Orchestra, and the Mendelssohn-Bartholdy National College of Music.

Science and Industry – The "Alma Mater Lipsiensis", founded in 1409, the present university, and numerous colleges of higher education testify to the importance of intellectual and scientific activity in Leipzig. The industrial basin in which the city lies is one of the most productive in the eastern part of Germany, with special emphasis on chemicals, machine tools, and the extraction of lignite.

MARKT (AY)

★ **Altes Rathaus (Former Town Hall)** (**AY**) – This long, low building with its fine Renaissance façade is crowned with gables which are pierced by windows – one of the earliest examples of an architectural style typifying town hall design during the German Renaissance. It was completed in 1556 after plans drawn up by Hieronymous Lotter, architect and burgomaster of Leipzig. Today the building houses the local history museum, the **Museum für Geschichte der Stadt Leipzig** ⊘.

While in this neighbourhood, note the interesting Baroque burghers' houses in nearby **Katharinenstraße** (**AY 18**), in particular the **Romanushaus**, which was built for the burgomaster F C Romanus between 1701 and 1704 by the architect J G Fuchs. Opposite the Naschmarkt opens the **Mädlerpassage** (**AZ 24**), immortalized by Goethe because the **Auerbachs Keller** tavern is there, where some of the scenes in Faust were set.

Thomaskirche (**AZ**) – Erected between 1212 and 1222 as a collegial for canons of the Augustinian order, this triple-aisle hall church was not given its present form until the end of the 15C. On Whit Sunday in 1539, Martin Luther gave a sermon here to inaugurate the Reformation.

The church became famous through Johann Sebastian Bach, who was cantor for 27 years and who is buried here, and through the celebrated **Thomanerchor**. Originating at the School of St Thomas, founded in 1212, this choir at first had no more than 12 singers. Today, at Vespers every Sunday, it can be heard singing Bach cantatas and motets.

Opposite the church, in the 16-17C Bosehaus, the **Johann Sebastian Bach National Research and Memorial Centre** (with a museum and the Bach archives) has been installed since 1985.

★ **Alte Börse (Former Produce Exchange)** (**AY**) – *On the Naschmarkt.*
Built between 1678 and 1687 after plans by Johann Georg Starcke, this one-time commodity market was Leipzig's first Baroque edifice. It is used today for fairs and festivals.

The statue outside (by Carl Seffner in 1903) represents **Goethe** as a student.

Nikolaikirche (**BY**) – *Nikolaistraße.*
Originally built in the Romanesque style, this church was transformed into a Gothic hall *c*1520. A double gallery surrounds the triple nave.

AUGUSTUSPLATZ (BYZ)

The 142m - 466ft-tall tower of the **university building** (**BYZ U**) dominates this wide square. The Schinkeltor, a gate designed by F Schinkel and E Rietschel in 1836, has been incorporated in the amphitheatre wing. A monument to the memory of **Leibniz** is on the south side of the university.

Ägyptisches Museum (Egyptian Museum) (**AZ M¹**) ⊙ – *Schillerstraße 6.*
Five thousand years of the Pharaohs' civilization, represented by more than 5 000 separate exhibits, are covered by the splendid collections in this museum, which is attached to the university.

Neues Gewandhaus (New Concert Hall) (**BZ**) – This superb auditorium was inaugurated in 1981. More than 1 900 enthusiasts can be seated to hear the famous Gewandhaus Orchestra. The statue of Beethoven (1902) was executed by Max Klinger. In front of the concert hall is a **fountain** (Mendebrunnen, 1886, restored).
The **Opera House** (Opernhaus) (**BY**) (1956-1960) and the swan lake (Schwanenteich) are on the north side of the square.
The **main station** (Hauptbahnhof) (**BY**), to the north of the square, is the largest railway terminus in Europe.

Grassi Museum ⊙ – *Johannisplatz. Take the Grimmaischer Steinweg* (**BZ 12**).
This complex houses three museums.
The **museum of arts and crafts** ⊙ displays European arts and crafts from the Middle Ages right up to the first half of the 20C.
The **museum of ethnography**, one of the oldest and most important in Europe, illustrates the history, culture and way of life of the peoples of Asia, Africa, America, Australia and Oceania.
There are over 1 000 instruments to admire in the **museum of musical instruments** ⊙.

SOUTHWESTERN DISTRICT

Neues Rathaus (New Town Hall) (**AZ**) – Built on the foundations of the old Pleißenburg castle, the town hall marries both Renaissance and Baroque elements with features that are more modern.

★★ **Museum der Bildenden Kunsten (Fine Arts Museum)** (**AZ**) ⊙ – Art in Europe from the Middle Ages to the present day is outlined in the important collections here.
German Primitives: *The Man of Agonies* (c1425) by **Master Francke**; *Portraits of Luther and Junker Jorg* (1521) by **Lucas Cranach the Elder**; *The Seven Ages of Woman* (1544) by Hans Baldung Grien; and works by **Cranach the Younger** and **Martin Schongauer**.
Flemish Painting: *Portrait of an Old Man* (1430-40) by **Jan van Eyck**; *Visitation* (c1434) by **Rogier van der Weyden**, *Self-Portrait* (c1655) by **Rembrandt**, *The Mulatto* (c1630) by **Frans Hals**; and works by Gerard Honthorst, Van Goyen, Van Ostade, Van Ruisdael.
Italian Painting: Cima da Conegliano, Francesco Francia, **Tintoretto** (*The Resurrection of Lazarus* - c1565).
German Painting: Anton Graff, **J F A Tischbein**, J A Koch, **C D Friedrich** (*The Ages of Life* - c1835), Carl Spitzweg, Moritz von Schwind, Arnold Böcklin (*The Island of the Dead* - c1886), Max Liebermann (*The Bottlers* - 1879), Max Klinger (*Blue Hour* - 1890) and W Leibl.
In the **Sculpture Department** there are works by, among others, Balthazar Permoser, Berthel Thorvaldsen, Auguste Rodin and Max Klinger. The museum's **collection of prints and drawings** offers a panoramic survey of graphic art that goes back as far as medieval times.

AROUND THE EXHIBITION CENTRE (MESSEGELÄNDE)
Via Windmühlenstraße (**BZ**)

Messegelände (Trade Fair Sites) – The emplacements for Leipzig's annual trade and book fairs extend from the Deutscher Platz to the Wilhelm Külz Park, in the eastern part of the city.

Völkerschlachtdenkmal (Battle of the Nations Monument) ⊙ – *Take the Johannisplatz* (**BZ**).
Inaugurated in 1913, on the hundredth anniversary of the Allied victory over the armies of Napoleon (Battle of Leipzig), this memorial took 15 years to build. Five hundred steps lead to a terrace from which the entire city and its surroundings can be seen.

St. Alexi-Gedächtniskirche – *Philipp-Rosenthal-Straße.*
Dedicated to the 22 000 Russian soldiers who fell in the above battle, this church in the old Tzarist style was built by W A Pokrowski between 1912 and 1913.

Deutsche Bücherei (German National Library) – *Deutscher Platz.*
Founded, again, in 1912, the huge library attempts to group together all known books in the German language – a collection that already comprises 7.5 million titles. On the same premises the Museum of Books and Literature is open to the public.

LEMGO ★

Nordrhein-Westfalen — Population 39 600
Michelin map 417 J 10

Flourishing trade relations with England and with Flanders in the 15C and 16C brought the Hanseatic town of Lemgo a prosperity still apparent today in its well laid out avenues of wealthy private homes.

★ OLD TOWN

From the Ostertor to the east, approach the Mittelstraße, which is the main street. Note especially the fine façades of no 17 (with wood carving on all four floors) and no 36, known as the House of Planets (Planetenhaus).

★★**Rathaus (Town Hall)** — Comprising eight buildings side by side, the civic centre of Lemgo is exceptional for its oriel windows, its arcades and its unique gables. The elegantly worked façade of the old apothecary's shop on the corner of the Marktplatz displays, on the first floor, the sculpted portraits of ten famous philosopher-physicians, from Aristotle to Paracelsus. Beneath the central arcades, brutal witchcraft trials were held in about 1670.

Bear left into the Breite Straße.

Hexenbürgermeisterhaus (House of the Witches' Burgomaster) ⊘ — Dating from 1568, this splendid patrician house has one of the finest façades in the town. Inside, a local museum (Museum für Stadt-und Rechtsgeschichte) has an exhibition of historical documents and instruments of torture used in the trials.

Marienkirche — A Renaissance organ with a finely carved case, among the oldest in Germany (1587-1613), adorns this triple-aisle Gothic church constructed at the end of the 13C and the beginning of the 14C. Admire too the baptismal font (1592), the pulpit (1644) and the Cross Triumphant (1490).

Return to the Papenstraße, following it to the right.

Nikolaikirche — Appropriately dedicated to the patron saint of merchants, the church combines features that are both Romanesque (a three-figure tympanum in the south aisle; a stone triptych in the north) and Gothic (frescoes and vault keystones). The pulpit and the font are late Renaissance (c1600).

The Papenstraße leads back to the starting point.

ADDITIONAL SIGHT

★ **Junkerhaus (Karl Junker's House)** ⊘ — *Hamelner Straße 36.*
Karl Junker (1850-1912), painter, sculptor and architect, a contemporary of the blossoming Jugendstil (qv), left in his own house a memorial to his highly personal style. His design is organized around a spiral which relies for its effect on an arcane play of movements alternately balanced and opposed. Surprise is everything in this design: the visitor's perception of Junker's sculpted and painted décor (note the pointillist medallions adorning the ceilings) is of an infinite diversity, constantly changing with each different point of view.

EXCURSION

Herford — *20km - 12 1/2 miles to the west.*
The Protestant **Johanniskirche** is garnished with fine 17C **wood carving★**, both sculpted and painted. Galleries, stalls and pulpit were all donated by different city corporations, whose shields and emblems can be recognized in the design. The chancel has interesting 15C stained glass windows.

*The diagram on the back cover shows the **Michelin Maps**
covering the country described in this **Guide**;
the chapter headings specify the appropriate map for the local area.*

LIMBURG AN DER LAHN ★

Hessen — Population 31 100
Michelin map 417 O 8
Town plan in the current Michelin Red Guide Deutschland

On the banks of the Lahn, between the Taunus heights to the south and the Westerwald to the north, this small medieval town is an excellent centre for excursions. The outline of its cathedral, at the same time lofty and compact, dominates everything else as it rises above the river.

★ CATHEDRAL (DOM) *time: 1/2 hour*

Built on a rocky spur, St. Georgsdom is in a picturesque **setting★★**. Apart from that, it is remarkable for the style of its architecture: a classic example of Gothic Transitional, which was prevalent in Germany between 1210 and 1250.

The outside remains Romanesque and closely resembles the Rhineland cathedrals *(see Introduction)*, but the interior is already Gothic, with a structure directly inspired by the cathedral of Laon, in Picardy. Here we find superimposed galleries, a triforium and clerestory windows as typical of the early Gothic period as the distinctive crochet capitals. Diagonal ribs characterize the vaulting. The transept crossing lies beneath a domed lantern tower. The original multicoloured decoration has been uncovered and restored.

From the **cemetery terrace** (Friedhofsterrasse) on the north side of the church, there is a good **view★** of the river, the old bridge, and a new motorway viaduct.

★ Diözesanmuseum (Diocesan Museum) ⊘ – *Domstraße 12.*

The 10C Byzantine reliquary-cross known as the Limburger Staurothek is the jewel of the religious art collection displayed in this restored building dating from 1544. The sheath encasing the reliquary Staff of St Peter, of the same period, derives from the School of St Egbert of Trier. Among the sculptures on view, is an admirable terracotta Lamentation of Christ, a moving work that dates from 1410.

ADDITIONAL SIGHT

Old Town (Alstadt) – Clustered around the southern part of the cathedral, the oldest part of Limburg offers a wealth of half-timbered medieval houses with festooned gables.

LINDAU IM BODENSEE★★

Bayern – Population 24 000
Michelin map 419 X 13 – Town plan in the current Michelin Red Guide Deutschland

Lindau is popular with visitors. The former Free Imperial City (1275-1802) adds to the charm of its old streets an island setting, harbour lights, and a magnificent panorama visible from the windows of all its hotels.

Lindau – im Bodensee (in the lake) and not am Bodensee (by the lake) like its neighbours Überlingen and Meersburg – boasts a number of churches with belfries crowned by an onion dome. The gabled burghers' houses in the old town testify still to the prosperity of bygone days when it was an important trading centre, particularly for commerce with Italy.

There is an almost Mediterranean quality to life in this lakeside island resort at the gates of Austria – a retro charm which can be savoured to the full during an evening stroll between the port and the Maximilianstraße.

Lindau

211

A Altes Rathaus   **M¹** Städtische Kunstsammlungen

SIGHTS

Städtische Kunstsammlungen (Municipal Museum) (Y M¹) ⊘ – Installed in the **Haus Zum Cavazzen★**, a typical example of bourgeois Baroque architecture (1729), the museum exhibits ancient documents relating to Lindau. There is a gallery of painting and sculpture.

Maximilianstraße (Z) – This, the main highway leading through the old town, is a picturesque street lined by old houses and inns. Narrow, half-timbered façades with the oriel windows characteristic of the Alpine Rhine Valley and the Vorarlberg huddle together with the stepped gables of Old Swabia (the former town hall **(A)** – **Altes Rathaus** – is a fine example of the latter style).
Turn right into the Zeppelinstraße and walk to the **Brigands' Tower** (Diebsturm), a well-known Lindau silhouette with its crown of bartizans.

Hafen (Port) (Z) – Tourists crowd the quays, many of them waiting to embark on one of the large white Bodensee pleasure boats. In the centre of the activity stands the Mangturm, a fortified 12C tower once used as a lighthouse. The present small lighthouse commands, along with a monument to the Lion of Bavaria (1856), the entrance to the roadstead. A few steps lead up to the **Römerschanze★** viewpoint – a pleasant, shady place from which to admire the Rhine Gap and the Alpine landmarks surrounding the "Bodan" (the ancient form of Bodensee).These are: Kanisfluh, the Hoher Freschen, the Drei Schwestern and (in Switzerland) Säntis and Altmann.

GERMANY: the Michelin Map Series at 1:300 000

When choosing a lunchtime or overnight stop use the above maps as all towns listed in the Red Guide Deutschland are underlined in red.

When driving into or through a town use the map as it also indicates all places with a town plan in the Red Guide Deutschland.

Common reference numbers make the transfer from map to plan easier.

Schloß LINDERHOF★★

Deep in the forest, in one of the wildest valleys of the Ammergau Alps – a region the royal hunters of the House of Bavaria reserved for their own use – Ludwig II had this small cream-coloured palace built. Designed in the style of the 18C, it served as a background, along with its Moorish pavilion and its grotto, for the romantic fancies of the young king, obsessed by oriental fables and the heroic legends of Germany. The extraordinary contrasts provided by a Rococo building surrounded by gardens and terraces inspired by the Italian Renaissance, set in the middle of a park landscaped in the English manner – the whole planted in an Alpine valley – lend the project its own peculiar charm.

TOUR ⊘ *about 2 hours*

Palace – Built between 1869 and 1879, in a style intermingling the second Italian Renaissance and the Baroque, Linderhof was intended by the king to achieve a certain intimacy. Inside, nevertheless, one finds a state bedchamber surpassing in luxury even those of Versailles, a hall of mirrors, cloth panels painted to resemble tapestries, pastels and statues of Louis XIV, Louis XV, Madame de Pompadour, Madame du Barry and others. A similarity in the sheer extravagance of these decorative excesses does however impose a particular harmony on the design as a whole.

★★**Park** – The natural slopes of the valley have been used to lay out a vista in line with the castle in which pools, cascades and terraced gardens in the style of an Italian villa have been devised. Fountains of water and the blaze of formal flower beds strike yet another bizarre note in this wooded Alpine landscape. The east-west lateral borders, on the other hand, with their beech hedges and boxwood trained in pyramids, suggest a more placid approach in the French manner.

Climb to the Temple of Venus rotunda, which closes off the perspective above an ornamental lake (a fine view, especially when the fountains play). Then descend, keeping to the right of the castle, and climb the opposite slope to reach the Moorish pavilion and the grotto. It is here that the skill of the landscape gardener, Karl von Effner, is most in evidence, with plantations of oak, maple and decorative beech placed with consummate art against a backdrop of clumps of conifers into which they gradually blend to form a sombre natural density.

Moorish Pavilion (Maurischer Kiosk) – Acquired by Ludwig II after the 1867 Exposition Universelle in Paris (which was really the world's first International Fair), this metallic structure was used by him when he wished to play the oriental potentate.

Grotto of Venus – A cavern, fashioned with the aid of artificial rocks and intended to recreate the atmosphere of the Venusberg sequence in the Wagnerian opera *Tannhäuser*, the conceit here instances once more the king's taste for theatrical effect: by the royal throne is a rock evoking the Loreley, which is set beside a lake, illuminated by the play of coloured lights, on which floats a golden skiff in the form of a huge conch shell.

Schloß Linderhof

LUDWIGSBURG ★

Baden-Württemberg — Population 81 000
Michelin map 419 T 11
Town plan in the current Michelin Red Guide Deutschland

An enormous Baroque palace built at the beginning of the 18C by a Duke of Württemberg, dreaming of another Versailles, was the start of Ludwigsburg — a town whose artificial character is emphasized by its grid of dead straight streets. Visitors today are more attracted by the park than the palace.

★ SCHLOSS (PALACE) ⊙

This monumental quadrilateral has no less than 452 rooms, 75 of them open to the public.

Tour of the Apartments — *Entrance: 1st courtyard on the right on the road from Stuttgart (access also through the park).* Inside, the "best rooms" (on the 1st floor of the New Building, facing the park), in the Empire style, are arranged to illustrate life at Court in the Baroque period. Through the Ancestors' Gallery (Ahnengalerie) and the castle's Catholic Church (Schloßkirche), decorated with lavish Italian stucco, visitors arrive at the Fürstenbau state apartments. These are in the oldest and highest part of the palace, which closes off the north side of the court.

★ **Blühendes Barock (Park)** — Green Baroque arbours and terraces clothed with an embroidery of flowers have been reconstituted in the southern part of the park, in front of the newest part of the palace. The terrain to the north and east, more broken up, has been landscaped in the English manner. Fountains have been installed.

★★**Märchengarten** (Fairy-tale Garden) — Fairy stories, legends and folk tales from Germany (the Brothers Grimm) and elsewhere (Hans Christian Andersen) are illustrated here with performances by mechanical figures, some activated by the sound of children's voices.

EXCURSIONS

Marbach am Neckar — *9km - 5 miles to the northeast.*
This small town cultivates the memory of the poet Schiller (qv), its most illustrious son. The huge **Schiller-Nationalmuseum** ⊙ rising like a castle above the valley, displays portraits, casts, engravings and manuscripts, not only of Schiller (1759-1805) but also of many other Swabian literary figures who lived between the 16C and the 20C. A visit to the writer's **birthplace** (Schiller-Geburtshaus) completes the pilgrimage.

Schloß Monrepos — *2km - 1 1/4 miles to the northwest.*
Built in 1767 on a site bordering a small lake, this gracious Rococo palace encircles a rotunda.

Markgröningen — *5km - 3 miles to the west.*
The 15C **Rathaus★** in this picturesque small town is, by virtue of its impressive size and its skilful construction, a monument to German half-timbering craftsmanship. Many wood-framed houses still exist in Markgröningen.

LUDWIGSLUST ★

Mecklenburg-Vorpommern — Population 13 500
Michelin map 416 G 18

The town was founded by Duke Friedrich von Mecklenburg, who moved his residence from Schwerin to Ludwigslust in 1764. He chose the name in honour of his father, Christian II Ludwig, who owned a hunting lodge here. The castle and the town were built at the same time, under the supervision of the court master builder Johann Joachim Busch. Only the single and two storey buildings in Schloßstraße bear witness today to the town's unity of design; the subsequent classical style of Johann Georg Barca is apparent along Kanalstraße and Schweriner Straße.

Ludwigslust cardboard décor — Although Duke Friedrich's intensive building activity had exhausted his funds, he was determined to decorate his castle in an appropriate, not to say sumptous manner, and he managed to make a virtue out of necessity. The precious and expensive materials, such as marble and fine wood, used elsewhere, were substituted at Ludwigslust by papier mâché. A modellable substance was produced from used paper, glue and water in a time-consuming process (labour was after all cheap), and after it had set, it could be ground, polished and painted. Works of art made of it were even able to withstand the weather. The Ludwigslust workshop, the first and only one throughout the whole of mainland Europe, achieved such mastery that its products (decorative strips, busts, magnificent vases, centrepieces etc.) were exported as far afield as Russia. Production stopped in 1835 through lack of demand, and the original recipe was lost. Plans are now afoot to study and if possible revive this papier mâché tradition, of which some remarkable examples can be seen in the castle.

SIGHTS

* **Schloß** ☉ – The E-shaped late Baroque building (1772-1776) already features some classical elements. Made of brick, the façade was faced with Pirnau sandstone. Three projections divide the frontage, with the portico in the centre extending over the side sections. The attic parapet which crowns the roof is still adorned with the original 18 vases and 40 statues, produced by the Bohemian sculptor Rudolph Kaplunger. The figures represent the arts, sciences and virtues, and symbolise the special interests of the Duke, so that at his request, allegories were even invented to convey hydraulics and hydrostatics !

The interior – *(Only some of the rooms are open to the public).* White and gold dominates the rooms which are decorated in the German version of the Louis XVI style, with tendrils and shells being replaced by medallions and festoons. Oil paintings above the doors show countryside and animal motifs. The furniture is original, being for the most part gifts or else having been manufactured in Ludwigslust itself.

The **Golden Room★**, a banqueting hall, which is two storeys high and contains exclusively papier mâché ornamentation, is particularly sumptous. The Venus Medici in the salon just before the gallery, made to look deceptively like marble, is in fact also made of papier mâché. The former Sala terrana facing the garden was converted into a trophy room in 1878 and is now a café.

An oval lake with a **waterfall** lies in front of the castle, with a sandstone sculpture by Rudolph Kaplunger

Papier mâché decor
at Schloß Ludwigslust

displaying two river-gods on either side of the Mecklenburg coat of arms.

* **Stadtkirche** ☉ – In accordance with the preference of the time, the castle and church lie along a single line of vision (great importance was attached to such relative position during the Baroque period). The church was built between 1765 and 1770, before the castle, and is a truly theatrical building. The exterior resembles a temple, the interior a stage décor, and surprisingly enough, the idea works extremely well. Standing in front of the castle, you can see at a distance the huge monogram of Christ, 7m - 23ft in height, which towers over the building. The porch with its six Doric Tuscan pillars supports a tympanum and a portico on which four sandstone figures depict the Evangelists. Unusually, the chancel is on the southern side and is dominated by an enormous **concave painting** depicting the Annunciation to the Shepherds. The picture is the work of the court painter Dietrich Findorff, and was completed by Johann Heinrich Suhrland. What cannot be seen, although it could of course be guessed, is the fact that it is made up of painted papier mâché panels. Another original feature, which the visitor will search for in vain, is the organ, which is hidden behind the giant painting. The richly adorned **Prince's seat**, with the court loge and the choir's rostrum above it, stands on the northern side. The ceiling, which is barrel-vaulted and coffered, is supported by two rows of columns.

* **Schloßpark** – The park covers an area of 135ha – 334acres and is one of the largest of its kind in Mecklenburg-Vorpommern. It too was originally created by Johann Joachim Busch, but was transformed in the middle of the 19C by Peter Joseph Lenné. Take a stroll around the park and you will constantly discover new points of interest, including steams, monuments, mausoleums and a limonite grotto (earth containing iron, which produces a porous stone when dried out).

The current Michelin Red Guide Deutschland offers a selection of pleasant hotels in convenient locations.

Each entry specifies the facilities available (gardens, tennis courts, swimming pool, beach facilities) and the annual opening and closing dates.

There is also a selection of establishments recommended for their cuisine - well-prepared meals at moderate prices; stars for good cooking.

LÜBECK ★★★

Schleswig-Holstein – Population 216 000
Michelin map 415 E 16
Town plan in the current Michelin Red Guide Deutschland

Girdled with canals, crowned by belfries and towers, Lübeck has retained much of its medieval character as business centre of the Hanseatic League; many of its buildings and monuments are still decorated with alternating bands of red and glazed black brick courses. Today the city remains the busiest German port on the Baltic and a focal point for shipbuilding and heavy industry.

At the head of the League – The 14C marked the summit of Lübeck's power as Hanseatic capital – the most influential town of that association of Dutch and north German cities which from the 12C to the 16C monopolized trade with Scandinavia and Russia. In the 16C, the business acumen of merchants and shipowners combined to extricate the port from a long period of decline, thanks largely to the establishment of new relations with Holland, and also with France and the Iberian countries, who sent cargoes of wine. For a long time, Dutch architecture was the preferred style for the rich burghers on the banks of the Trave.

In the 19C, Lübeck's seaport status was menaced by the Prussian port of Stettin (now Szczecin) and the opening of the Kiel canal. But the construction of a canal linking the Trave with the Elbe, plus an influx of almost 100 000 refugees in 1945, have together permitted the city to maintain its importance in present-day Germany. Among other assets it has the reputation of being the country's chief importer of the red wines of France, which are matured in the celebrated **Lübeck Cellars** beneath the river Trave.

★★★ OLD TOWN (ALTSTADT) *time: 3 hours*

Leave from the Holstentor (follow the itinerary marked on the plan)

★★ **Holstentor (Y)** – This fortified gate with its enormous twin towers was built between 1469 and 1478, before the construction of the city's perimeter wall, more as a matter of prestige than protection. The most impressively designed façade, that towards the town, has three tiers of blind arcades with ornamented ceramic friezes. The building houses the **local history museum** (Museum im Holstentor).

Petrikirche (Y A) – The triple nave of the original Romanesque church (completed c1240) was modified in the Gothic style in the first half of the 14C. A fourth aisle on the south side was added in the middle of the 15C, and then a fifth, on the north, at the beginning of the 16C. From the tower platform (*lift*), there is an aerial **view★** of the port and the town – unique in its central nucleus surrounded by a double ring of canals separated by a circle of narrow islands.

★ **Rathaus (Y R)** – Built from 1250 onwards, on two sides of the Marktplatz, the town hall is an elegant edifice in dark glazed brick raised, in accordance with municipal tradition, on a gallery of arcades. Note the high protective walls, sometimes pierced with blind arcades or by gaping round openings decorated and strengthened by slender turrets with "candle-snuffer" roofs.

The Holstentor at Lübeck

W. Kaehler, FOVEA, Paris

LÜBECK

In front of the north wing, a Renaissance superstructure in ornately carved sandstone has been added. The building at the extremity of east wing, the Neues Gemach (1440), is interesting for the heightened effect lent to it by an imaginative openwork wall.

Pass beneath the arcades to see, on the Breite Straße, a stone staircase (1594) in Dutch Renaissance style.

Continuing the circuit of the Rathaus, arrive at the foot of the north façade.

The wall here displays an impressive layout, with immense bays lined up across almost its entire height.

★★ Marienkirche (Y) – One of the finest brick-built Gothic churches in Germany. The original designers in 1250 planned a hall-type church without a transept, but the concept was changed while work was in progress. Subsequently, under the influence of French cathedral architecture, the main buttress-supported vaulting was raised to a height of 38.5m - 126ft. The 125m - 410ft spires were completed in 1350. The composer Buxtehude (1637-1707) was the church's official organist. The interior, audacious in design, has grandiose proportions. A fire, started by an air raid in 1942, exposed the original polychromatic 13C and 14C decoration. At the end of the south aisle is an elegant 14C chapel, the **Briefkapelle**, with tall lancet windows recalling the High Gothic style. The star vaulting rests on two monolithic columns of granite. Inside the south tower, two huge church bells, which were brought down during the raid, remain embedded in the ground.

The ambulatory vaulting covers in a single sweep both the radial apsidal chapels and the axial Lady Chapel, which contains an altarpiece to the Virgin made in Antwerp in 1518.

Outside the church, walk around the east end and go through the arcade of the former Town Hall Chancellery (15C and 16C) to the Mengstraße.

Buddenbrookhaus (YD) ⊙ – *4 Mengstraße.*
However attractive the concept may be, **Heinrich** and **Thomas Mann** were unfortunately not born in Buddenbrookhaus. It is however a fact that in 1841 their grandfather Johann Siegmund Mann bought the Baroque house with its beautiful façade, which was built in 1758. Thomas Mann used the house in his world-renowned book *The Buddenbrooks*, in which he described the greatness and fall of a patrician family in Lübeck.

The house is now the home of the Heinrich and Thomas Mann Centre, which is dedicated to the life and works of Lübeck's most famous sons.

★ Haus der Schiffergesellschaft (House of the Seamen's Guild) (X E) – Behind the stepped Renaissance gable, the **interior★★** (now a restaurant) still preserves the picturesque furnishings of a seamen's tavern, with rough wooden tables, copper lamps and ships' models hanging from the beams.

★ Heiligen-Geist-Hospital (Hospice of the Holy Spirit) (X) – Since the end of the 13C, the three turret-bordered gables of this almshouse have stood above the Koberg. The chapel, a large Gothic hall embellished with 13C and 14C paintings, is just outside the even bigger Great Hall of the hospice (Langes Haus).

★ Jakobikirche (X K) – The magnificent woodwork of the two **organ lofts★★** (16C and 17C) in this small Gothic hall-church is noteworthy. A chapel on the south aisle contains an altar known as the "Brömbse" (15C), with bas-reliefs of very fine workmanship. The first side chapel on the north aisle is arranged as a memorial to the shipwrecked, and displays a lifeboat from the *Pamir*, the full-rigged Lübeck training ship lost with all hands in 1957.

★ Katharinenkirche (Y) – The lower niches of the 14C façade contain modern **statues★**, the first three on the left being by Ernst Barlach *(qv)*. Inside the church, which is a museum, note, on the right side as you enter, *The Resurrection of Lazarus* by Tintoretto.

The "Höfe und Gänge" – At the corner of the church, turn left into the Glockengießerstraße, on which open the courts (Höfe), set back from the street, which are typical of Lübeck – social amenities donated in the 17C by local benefactors. Note, successively, the delightful **Füchtingshof★** (no 25 – **Y S**), with its Baroque doorway dating from 1639; the Glandorps-Gang, a simple alignment of small houses along an alley (no 41); and, from nos 49 to 51, the Glandorps-Hof.

ADDITIONAL SIGHTS

★ Burgtor (X) – This fortified gateway defended the narrow isthmus – now cut by a canal – which was once the only land approach to Lübeck. The structure is a fine example of military architecture (13-15C) with a design of superimposed tiercepoint bays.

Mengstraße (Y) – Much of the original character remains in this street, with its varied brick gables at the lower end recalling the rivalries of rich neighbours in years gone by. The two houses now occupied by the Schabbelhaus restaurant have been restored with great care.

Dom (Cathedral) (Z) – The 14C reconstruction of the chancel in the Gothic style transformed this Romanesque church. A covered entrance and a very fine porch were added to the north transept in the middle of the 13C. A gigantic Bernt Notke Crucifix (1477) stands on the rood-beam. On the left of the rood-screen is the altarpiece of the Merchants of Stecknitz (1422).

★ **St. Annen-Museum** (**Z M**[1]) ◷ – Installed in a former monastery, this museum devoted to the past history of the town has a rich department of religious sculpture, in particular works by Bernt Notke, the master sculptor of Lübeck in the 15C. Note also an altarpiece depicting the Passion, painted by Hans Memling in 1491.

Behnhaus and Drägerhaus (**XY M**[2]) ◷ – The **Behnhaus** (1780-1810) with its classic façade and beautiful interior provides a attractive setting for paintings, sculptures and commercial art from the Romantic period up to the present time. The **Drägerhaus**, formerly a merchant's meeeting place, displays works by artists up to Edvard Munch, in addition to paintings by the Lübeck artist Johann Friedrich Overbeck (1789-1869). The beautiful banqueting halls and living areas are furnished in historical style.

EXCURSION

★ **Travemünde** – *20km - 12 1/2 miles to the northeast. Plan in the current Michelin Red Guide Deutschland.*
On the Trave estuary, this resort with its casino and its pleasure beaches has become the playground of Lübeck and something of an international favourite. North of the town the low cliffs of the **Brodtener Ufer** offer wide views over the Baltic.
To the northwest is the important and popular seaside resort of **Timmendorfer Strand.**

LÜNEBURG★

Niedersachsen – Population 60 000
Michelin map 415/416 G 15

The Salt Town – The town of Lüneburg is built on a salt deposit. The prosperity of Lüneburg, from the 10C onwards, was also built on salt. In the Middle Ages it was the principal supplier of the mineral to many places, notably Scandinavia, where, because of the Baltic's low saline content, it was always in short supply. Traffic followed the **Old Salt Route**, via Lauenburg, Ratzeburg and Lübeck.
The traditional architecture of Lüneburg is distinguished by stepped and scrolled gables, cornices with rounded or tiercepoint blind arcades, and the "Tausteine" – a local twisted brick feature producing an effect like a cable stitch.

SIGHTS

★★ **Rathaus** (**Y R**) ◷ – The municipal headquarters is an assembly of different buildings dating from the 13C to the 18C. Go in through the Gothic doorway on the Ochsenmarkt. The **Great Council Chamber**★★ (Große Ratsstube), on the right of the entrance hall, is a Renaissance masterpiece (1566-1584). Panelled throughout, it is adorned with intricate wood sculptures by Albert von Soest; note the wealth of expression in the small heads rhythmically animating the frieze beneath allegorical paintings. The fine door frames also are worth attention.
The **Princes' Apartment** (Fürstensaal), on the first floor, is equally rewarding. It is Gothic, with lamps fashioned from stags' antlers and a superbly beamed and painted ceiling.
The **Hall of Justice** (Gerichtslaube), with its cradle vaulting, is decorated on walls and ceilings with paintings inspired by the etchings of Hans Burgkmair and Heinrich Aldegrever.

★ **Old Town** – The houses here are characterized by the traditional brick architecture. Typical are those lining the long, narrow square known as **Am Sande**★ (**Z**), especially no 1, the 16C **Black House** (Schwarzes Haus), which was once a brewery.
In the Große Bäckerstraße stands the **Rathsapotheke** (pharmacy) (**Y A**), which dates, with its fine twisted brick gables, from 1598. The Reitende-Diener-Straße (**Y 40**) comprises a double row of identical low houses, each embellished with medallions and, again, twisted brick cornices.
A sudden contrast is provided at no 14 Rotehahnstraße, the **Haus Roter Hahn** (**Y D**), a former convent whose three 16C gables are half-timbered in a rustic style.

St. Johanniskirche (**Z E**) – The robust **west tower** (108m - 354ft high) is deliberately inclined to counter the pressure of violent winds blowing from the west. Displacement from the vertical at the top of the tower is 2m - 6ft 6in. The tower has been refurbished several times to combat subsidence. The church itself dates from the 14C. The huge interior, with five naves and two rows of side chapels, forms a perfect square, closed at the east end by plain polygonal apses.
The most valuable item of the furnishings is the sculpted reredos of the high altar, which has painted panels depicting scenes from the lives of John the Baptist, St Cecilia, St Ursula and St George (1482). The 16C **organ**, modified several times, is one of the oldest in Germany.

LÜNEBURG

A	Rathsapotheke	**E**	St. Johanniskirche	**K**	Staatshochbauamt
D	Haus Roter Hahn	**F**	Brauhaus	**R**	Rathaus

★ **Old Port Quarter (Wasserviertel)** – From the bridge across the Ilmenau, looking downstream, there is a fine view of the old galleried houses on the west bank and, on the right, a **crane** (Alter Kran) (**Y**) dating from the 14C (restored in the 18C). A **brewery** (Brauhaus) (**Y F**) stands at the corner of the Am Werder square and the Lünertorstraße. This is a Renaissance building, its gables once more decorated with medallions and twisted brick motifs. Further on, at the corner of the Lünertorstraße and the Kaufhausstraße, is a house (Staatshochbauamt) (**Y K**) built in 1574 with remarkable rusticated half-pilasters in sandstone and a solid cornice. Beside it, note the Baroque façade (1745) of an old warehouse (Altes Kaufhaus).

EXCURSIONS

Kloster Lüne – *2km - 1 1/4 miles via ① on the plan.*
15C abbey with outstanding Gothic cloister and fountain.

Lauenburg an der Elbe – *25km - 15 1/2 miles via ① on the plan.*
A sleepy township today, Lauenburg commands a point where the ancient salt route from Lüneburg to Lübeck crossed the Elbe. The old sailors' houses lie clustered at the foot of a steep, wooded slope, at the top of which is a round clock tower, all that remains of a ruined ducal castle. The summit (Schloßberg) offers a clear view of several reaches of the Elbe. The **Elbe Navigation Museum** (Elbschiffahrtsmuseum) ☉ – in the Lower Town, at no 59 Elbstraße – relates the history of river traffic between Dresden and Hamburg with the help of models, documents, illustrated panels and even ships' engines (demonstrations).

LÜNEBURGER HEIDE

LÜNEBURG HEATH – Niedersachsen
Michelin map 415/416 G 13-15

The great expanse of Lüneburg Heath lies in an area bounded by the sweep of the Hamburg-Bremen motorway, the valley of the Aller, and the road from Brunswick to Lüneburg.

Visitors have heath pastor Wilhelm Bode (1860-1927), who initiated the transformation of the Lüneburg Heath into a nature reserve, to thank for the fact that they are able to enjoy the attraction of this formely undervalued region. To preserve the heath from the increasing advance of agriculture and foresty, a 200-sq km - 77-sq mile **nature reserve** has been created in the neighbourhood of the **Wilseder Berg**, where the flora and fauna are protected and motor cars only permitted on the main roads which cross the heath. Considerable effort is being made to preserve the rural character of Lower Saxony housing, and even outside the reserve villages on the heath have retained much of their old world charm – notably in the case of their wooden belfries, separated from the church and half hidden in plantations of trees.

TOWNS, LANDSCAPES AND SIGHTS

Bergen-Belsen – *7km - 4.3 miles southwest of Bergen.*
The **memorial** (Gedenkstätte) raised to the victims of the Bergen-Belsen concentration camp – erected in 1946 on the orders of the British Military Government – stands in solitude in a clearing on Lüneburg Heath surrounded by pines and birch trees. There is a **documentation centre** (Dokumentenhaus) at the entrance, with a permanent exhibition retracing the history of the camp.

The Monument – *From the car park, 3/4 hour Rtn on foot.* The monument is beyond the tumulus which marks the site of the mass graves. It is a simple obelisk in pale volcanic tufa, with inscriptions in 13 languages honouring the memory of those who fell victim to the Nazis' "extermination" policy.

★★ Celle – *See CELLE.*

The Heath

In the Middle Ages, the name "heath" signified the boundary of a village. Only later did it come to mean the common heather (Calluna vulgaris) which carpets the whole area with its rose-pink hue in August and September. The bell-heather (Erica tetralix) which blooms in July is also found on the heath, but it is very rare, preferring moorland and damp areas.

Although we may be tempted to think of the term heath as the epitome of a natural landscape, in reality it is manmade dwarf shrubland, one of the oldest cultivated regions of Europe. 5 000 years ago the area was covered in forest, which was uprooted by farmers. Cattle were then driven into the forest to finish off the farmers' work. Only then was the light-hungry heath able to spread. To prevent the forest taking hold again, the practices of "burning", allowing cropping by moorland sheep, or lifting turf (the heath was grubbed up using a hoe) were employed.

Flora and fauna – The **Juniper** (Juniperus communis) gives the region a quite special character. The bushes appear either individually or in groups. The heath is also home to birch, mountain ash, pine and oak, together with common gorse and broom, silver grass and matgrass, crowberries, bilberries and cranberries.

The **moorland sheep** are "living mowers". Where they are still used as such, they maintain the heath heather at an optimum height of 20cm - 8in. Both the males and the females have horns, those of the male being spectacularly coiled. They have dark heads and legs. Whilst there were a million moorland sheep on the heath around 1800, when it was much larger, there are only a few thousand head left today.

The bees are also an intrinsic feature of the heath. They frequently belong to travelling beekeepers, who bring their swarms to the heath flowers, sometimes in the baskets known as "Lüneburger Bogenstülpern".

The largest bird seen on the heath is the blackcock with its lyre-shaped tail, altough it is now virtually extinct. There are plenty of buzzards, red kites, hobbies and kestrels, not forgetting the herons and snipes in the lowlands and high moors. Autumn visitors include flocks of fieldfares.

Boulders – Large and small boulders made of granite, and in some cases porphyry, are scattered all over the heath. They came from Scandinavia as boulder clay and were left behind when the glaciers of the last ice age retreated over 18 000 years ago. The angular or sharp polished stones known in German as Windkanter were formed by corrosion.

Ebstorf – *26km - 16 miles south of Lüneburg.* Do not miss the former **Benedictine abbey** (Ehemaliges Benediktinerkloster) ⊙ in this small town, where the 14C and 15C cloister and nuns' gallery are the most impressive features among the ruins. A life-size wooden statue of St Maurice (1300) and several Romanesque and Gothic Virgins can be seen in the gallery. Visitors interested in cartography can see a reproduction **Mappa Mundi★** (Ebstorfer Weltkarte). The famous 13C original, once preserved in the abbey, was destroyed during the Second World War.

Lönsgrab – *Between Fallingbostel and Walsrode.*
The memorial tomb of the poet **Hermann Löns** (1866-1914), who celebrated the beauties of the heath with extravagant lyricism, can be seen here in a setting of junipers.

Lönsstein – *1/2 hour on foot Rtn. Midway between Baven and Müden, leave the car and climb a footpath on the left which follows a line of birch trees.*
On the crest is another monument to Herman Löns in a typical pine, heather and juniper landscape.

Suhlendorf – Windmills and watermills, both actual size and scale models, are on display in the Suhlendorf **museum** ⊙. There is also an exhibition illustrating 600 years of navigation.

★ **Undeloh** – A most charming village, with its old houses sheltered beneat huge oak trees, Undeloh is the departure point for the 4km – 2 1/2-miles trip to Wilsede, a nature reserve village which has been kept apart from the onward march of a mechanized civilization *(cars are not allowed: there is a service of horse-drawn vehicles from Undeloh).*

Walsrode – *Follow the itinerary sign: Rundgang.*
Almost five thousand birds (850 species, from all parts of the world) live in this fine 22-hectare - 54-acre **ornithological park★** ⊙, most of them in their natural habitat and at semi-liberty. Waders and web-footed birds, as well as parrots and budgerigars, are particularly well represented in the ornithological park, the largest of its kind in the world.
A historic half-timbered house (1717) contains the **German birdcage museum** (Deutsche Vogelbauermuseum), where an incredible number of birdcages are on display.

★ **Wienhausen** – *See CELLE: Excursions.*

★ **Wilseder Berg** – From the summit (there is a marker post: 169m - 554ft), a vast **panorama★** of heath and woodlands is visible. On a clear day, the spires of the Hamburg churches can be seen, 40km - 25 miles away to the north.

MAGDEBURG★★

Sachsen-Anhalt – Population 287 000
Michelin map 416/418 J 18
Town plan in the current Michelin Red Guide Deutschland

Ideally situated mid-way along the 1 100km - 683-mile course of the Elbe, on its journey from northern Bohemia to the North Sea, this town in the German heartlands was an important trade centre before the Middle Ages. Sadly, the architectural witnesses to this former glory did not survive the bombardments of 1945. Only a few ecclesiastical buildings remain, notably the cathedral – a grandiose example of Gothic evolution in Germany.

From Tilly to the Allied Bombers – It was a flourishing commercial city, converted to the Protestant faith, which fell into the hands of the **General Graf von Tilly**, head of the Catholic League, during the terrible Thirty Years War *(qv)*. The carnage inflicted by the Walloon general's troops was appalling; more than two-thirds of the population perished when the town was sacked and fired.

Slowly, Magdeburg rose again from its ruins, enjoying once more an economic and cultural boom of which the most remarkable representatives were **Otto von Guericke** (1602-1686), burgomaster and physicist famous for his experiments on vacuum, and **Georg-Philipp Telemann** (1681-1767), one of the luminaries of Baroque music, who composed about 600 overtures, not to mention many operas, oratorios and concertos.

From 1850 onwards, the city was in the throes of an industrial expansion largely based on the manufacture of machine tools and mechanical components, a situation favoured by its position at the junction of important rail links. It was thus one of the richest and economically most active towns in Germany that the Allied bomber force overflew on the night of 16 January 1945. Half an hour later, virtually nothing was left of the city centre and the Baroque façades of its ancient streets.

DOM ST. MAURITUS UND ST. KATHARINA

In the Domplatz. Entrance via the cloister.

At a time when the Roma-nesque style in Germany was losing its impetus, the construction of Magdeburg cathedral at the beginning of the 13C marked the first attempt to impose a Gothic style derived from the architectural precepts of the great French cathedrals. The decision was taken by the Archbishop Albert II following a visit to France, and several of the architects commissioned to work on the project were French.

If certain alterations which supervened at different stages of the construction denied the building as a whole a stylistic unity, Magdeburg cathedral can nevertheless be considered the first great German Gothic religious edifice, well ahead of its time.

Outside, the three levels of the east end (absidioles, ambulatory, apse) at once give an impression of power.

On the north side, the **Paradise Doorway** *(reached from inside the cathedral)* displays statues★★ of the Wise and Foolish Virgins. Dating from *c*1245, these, in common with statuary at Strasbourg, Bamberg and

Statue of Otto I and the Empress Edith in the cathedral of St. Mauritius und St. Katharina

Naumburg, mark a stage in the evolution of Gothic sculpture, which became more and more inclined towards the expression of emotional feeling.

A statue of the Emperor Otto I stands at the late 15C west door. In the cloister's west gallery, the **chapel of the fountains** (Brunnenkapelle) is remarkable for the elegance of its rib vaulting.

Interior – Slender divided pillars framed by columns of Italian porphyry distinguish the polygonal chancel. The upper gallery, built between 1232 and 1240 by Cistercian workers from Maulbronn, combines forms of great simplicity not unlike those characterizing the monastic style of Burgundy.

A 1240 modification of the original plan having suppressed the intermediate pillars, the tall nave with its wide bays admits an abundance of light to illuminate the works of art displayed.

Sculpture – A southeast transept pillar incorporates a sandstone **statue★** (*c*1240) of St Maurice, with African features. In the ambulatory, there are **bronze funerary plaques★** in memory of the Archbishops Friedrich of Wettin (d 1152) and Wichmann of Seeburg (d 1192).

Seated **statues★** said to represent Christ and the Church are more likely in fact to be Otto I and his wife, the Anglo-Saxon princess Edith. Dating from *c*1245, they are housed in a small 16-sided chapel off the north transept. In the western part of the nave there is a **bronze tomb★** of the Archbishop Ernst, which was cast in 1495 in the foundry of Peter Vischer of Nuremberg.

ADDITIONAL SIGHTS

★★ **Kloster Unser Lieben Frauen** ⊘ – *Regierungsstraße.* Founded in 1015 by Augustinian monks on the fringe of the Germanic lands – separated from the Slav countries at the time by the Elbe – this abbey (dedicated to Our Lady) was designed to participate, at least spiritually, in an eventual expansion towards the east.

The buildings, largely restored after 1945, date from the second half of the 11C and form a homogenous Romanesque ensemble with the exception of the Gothic-inspired ogive vaulting of the abbey church, which was not completed until *c*1230. Groined vaulting covers the three-aisle crypt.

On the north side of the church, the **cloister**★ remains one of the best preserved in Germany. Outside, the façade of the church comprises a squared fore-part between two round towers with lateral stairways.

Rathaus – In front of the two-storey Baroque town hall (1691-1698) stands the famous statue of **The Magdeburg Knight** (*c*1240 – copy), one of the oldest equestrian sculptures in Germany. On the left, is a monument to Otto von Guericke *(see above).*

Petriberg – North of the town hall, on the banks of the Elbe. Three churches stand on the riverside rise: the **Magdalenenkapelle**, with a single Gothic nave; **St. Petrikirche**, a Gothic hall-church with three aisles (1380-1490); and the **Wallonerkirche**, a former abbey church (1285-1366) built by a community which came from the Netherlands (thus its Walloon name).

For historical background on the country
see the Historical table and notes in the Introduction.

MAINZ★

Rheinland-Pfalz – Population 180 000
Michelin map 417 Q 8
Plan of the conurbation in the current Michelin Red Guide Deutschland

Formerly the episcopal seat of the influential Prince-Electors, Mainz – elevated in 1949 to be the capital of the Land of Rheinland-Pfalz – is ideally placed for trade. Situated at the confluence of the Rhine and the Main, the city is Germany's largest and most important wine market. It is also the site of a famous annual carnival, the gaiety and colourful buffoonery of which are televised all over the country *(see Calendar of events).* **Johannes Gutenberg** (*c*1394-1468), the father of modern printing, is the city's most prominent son.

Bird's eye view – The restaurant An der Favorite, at the highest point of the **Stadtpark** (**BY**), affords a general view of the city on either side of the Rhine.

CATHEDRAL QUARTER (Z) *time: 2 hours*

Leaving the Liebfrauenplatz, walk down the Domstraße and then left around the cathedral.

From the Leichhof square, there is a **view**★★ of the cathedral in its entirety, the west chancel and transept rising loftily, their complex ridge roofs overlooked by the lantern tower which crowns the transept crossing. Baroque as well as Gothic elements adorn the upper part of this tower, which rests on a Romanesque base showing a Lombard influence.

The adjoining square, known as the Höfchen, is extended towards the south by the Guten-bergplatz (containing Thorwaldsen's statue of the craftsman printer, a theatre and the House of German Wines) and to the northeast by the market square, embellished with a **Renaissance fountain** (Renaissance-brunnen) (**Z A**).

Enter via the doorway opening onto the market square (Marktportal).

★ **Dom (Cathedral)** – The cathedral is an enormous reconstructed Romanesque building – a basilica with two chancels, one in the west, leading off a wide transept whose crossing is illuminated by a fine Rhenish dome; one in the east of simpler architectural style.

Fixed to the massive Romanesque columns is a collection of archiepiscopal **funerary monuments**★ (Grabdenkmäler der Erzbischöfe).

Turn left into the north aisle on entering the church.

In the second chapel (**1**), there is a moving late-15C Entombment. A multicoloured Gothic funerary monument is attached to one of the main pillars (**2**).

In the east crypt, beneath the chancel, a modern **gold reliquary** (**3**) of the Saints of Mainz stands upon the altar.

A pillar (**4**) on the south side of the east chancel steps bears another Gothic funerary monument in many colours, surrounded by statuettes of St Benedict, St Catherine, St Maurice and St Clare.

A door in the south aisle leads to the **cloister★** (Kreuzgang). In addition to the tombstones, there is a bas-relief (**5**), remodelled in 1783, of the master-singer Heinrich von Meißen, known as "Frauenlob" — a man who, having sung the praises of women all his life, was finally laid to rest by the burgesses of Mainz in 1323.

Fine statues adorn the doorway (**6**) of the former chapter house (Kapitelsaal), built in the 15C in an elegant Rhineland style. Cross the transept below the west chancel steps and go into the opposite arm, where there is a fine 1328 baptismal font in pewter (**7**), ornamented with delicately worked figures. Beyond, a Romanesque doorway (**8**) leads to the

Gotthardkapelle, built in the same style with a square plan and a two-storey elevation.

★★ Gutenberg-Museum (Z M¹) ☉ — The visitor to this museum is reminded how, over the centuries, men of taste and discrimination have nurtured the art of the printed word, regarding it as one of the most precious treasures of civilization, to be guarded and passed on as a sacred trust as its usage developed and spread.

Gutenberg's original hand press is in the basement of the building, along with reconstructions of early print-shops. On the first floor, along with incunabula and ancient presses, there is a collection of editions published between the 16C and the 19C. The museum's prize exhibit, the world-famous **Gutenberg Bible★★★** (1452-55), with 42 lines to the page, is on display in a second floor strong room. This three volume work in Latin is the earliest complete book printed using movable type to have survived in the West. It is sometimes known as the Mazarin Bible, as the first documented copy was kept in the Paris library of Cardinal Mazarin.

Polychromatic wood engravings and printed works from China, Japan and Korea can be seen in the Far East Department on the third floor.

The Gutenberg Bible, Mainz

MAINZ

A	Renaissancebrunnen		
D	Jupitersäule	**M²**	Römisch-Germanisches Museum
M¹	Gutenbergmuseum	**M³**	Landesmuseum Mainz

ADDITIONAL SIGHTS

★ **Römisch-Germanisches Zentralmuseum** (Romano-German Museum) (**BV M²**) ⊙ – Installed in the one-time Electors' Palace (15-17C), this museum unites collections dealing with the Mediterranean civilizations, prehistory and the Barbarians.

★ **Landesmuseum Mainz** (**Z M³**) ⊙ – The Department of Antiquities traces Rhineland civilization, and especially that of Mainz, from prehistoric times onwards. On display here too is Jupiter's Column (Jupitersäule), the most precious relic of the Roman colonization of Germany. A copy stands in the Deutschaus-Platz (**BV D**).

Schillerplatz and Schillerstraße (Z) – The Baroque mansions in this square and street now house (after restoration) the ministries of the Rheinland-Pfalz. In the centre of the Schillerplatz, a fountain is decorated with scenes illustrating the carnival.

Old Town (Altstadt) (BYZ) – Off the Augustinerstraße, the chief thoroughfare of the old quarter, which is virtually intact, opens the picturesque Kirschgarten square, lined with pretty half-timbered houses. The Kapuzinerstraße (note several houses with sandstone door frames and Rococo panels) leads to the church of St. Ignaz.

Ignazkirche (BY) – A somewhat theatrical 16C group of the **Crucifixion ★** (Kreuzigungsgruppe), by Hans Backoffen, stands outside the church, on the left.

Stephanskirche (ABY) – All that remains of this late 13C church, severely damaged in 1945, are the outside walls and Gothic pillars. The east chancel nevertheless has been garnished with a remarkable series of modern **stained glass windows ★★**. These, by the artist Marc Chagall, illustrate themes from the Old and New Testaments. Built against the south wall is a **cloister ★** of which the architecture, especially the vaulting, expresses all the virtuosity of Late Gothic design.

MANNHEIM

Baden-Württemberg – Population 305 000
Michelin map 417/419 R 9
Plan of the conurbation in the current Michelin Red Guide Deutschland

Mannheim, at the confluence of the Rhine and the Neckar, is the second largest river port in Europe *(motorboat trips around the port area start from the Kurpfalzbrücke, the bridge spanning the Neckar)*. The town, founded in 1606 by the Palatine Elector Friedrich IV, was conceived as a fortified residential enclave. Conforming to a rigid plan, the centre comprises a checkerboard of 144 identical blocks **(Quadratstadt)**, each identified only by a letter and number according to its coordinates on the city plan. Local enthusiasm for the arts – especially the theatre, where the works of Schiller were first performed – soon made Mannheim a cultural as well as a trade centre.

SIGHTS

★★ Städtische Kunsthalle (Fine Arts Museum) (DZ M¹) ☉ – Installed in a Jugendstil building designed by H Billing in 1907, the museum concentrates on works of the 19C and 20C. Statues by Rodin, Lehmbruck, Barlach, Brancusi, Giacometti and Moore occupy the ground floor. On the floor above are paintings by the French Impressionists, notably Manet's famous *Execution of the Emperor Maximilian* and Cézanne's *The Pipe Smoker*. Works by Corot, Monet and Pissarro are also on display. Slevogt and Corinth represent the German "Secessionist" movement. Expressionist paintings include Heckel's *Woman Sleeping*, Kokoschka's **View of Amsterdam**, and work by Beckmann and the Belgian Ensor. Post-1945 art and New Objectivity works are in a separate department.

★ Museum für Kunst-, Stadt- und Theatergeschichte im Reiß-Museum (CY M²) ☉ – In the Arsenal (Zeughaus, built 1777-1779).
Municipal history and the decorative arts have pride of place here, but note the 17C Dutch paintings and 18C porcelain. Writing desks (mainly 18C Baden work) and a collection of 19C bicycles are also worth seeing.

★ Museum für Archäologie und Völkerkunde (Museum of Archaeology and Ethnology) (CY M³) ☉ – In a new building opposite the Arsenal.
The archaeological collections here came from the Antiquarium founded in 1763 by the Prince-Elector Karl-Theodor. They include objects from archaeological digs, stone commemorative monuments from Roman provinces and Greek and Etruscan vases dating from the Mycenean epoch to the 3C AD. The ethnological exhibits concern mainly Indian and Pacific civilizations.

Schloß (CZ) ☉ – The building of this Baroque palace, the biggest in all of Germany (400 rooms, 2 000 windows), lasted from 1720 to 1760. Restored after heavy damage sustained in the Second World War, the main body of the palace is now occupied by departments of the university. Two wings at right-angles to the central block enclose an enormous main courtyard. The palace church terminates the right wing, the former palace library the left.
From the state staircase inside, there is a view down the entire perspective of the Kurpfalzstraße, the street that bisects the chessboard centre from one end to the other, as far as the River Neckar.
The painted ceilings have been restored after the original work of Cosmas Damian Asam *(qv)*. The same artist was responsible for the ceiling of the church (Schloßkirche) and the frescoes in the **Knights' Hall** (Rittersaal). The most interesting apartment is the green and rose **Rococo library** in the university wing, which is embellished with stucco-work, panelling and camaïeu (monochrome) paintings.

MANNHEIM

M¹ Städtische Kunsthalle
M² Museum für Stadtgeschichte Im Reiß-Museum
M³ Museum für Archäologie und Völkerkunde
M⁴ Museumsschiff Mannheim

Jesuitenkirche (CZ) – Founded at the same time as the palace (building in fact lasted from 1733 to 1769), this massive edifice is said to be the biggest Baroque church of the Upper Rhine. The façade is classical with the three orders superimposed. The well-lit interior, faced with stucco-marble, is a little cold. **The Silver Virgin with her Crown of Light** (Silbermadonna im Strahlenkranz), in the northern aisle, is the work of the Augsburg silversmith J I Saler (1747).

Museumsschiff Mannheim (Boat Museum) (DY M⁴) ⊘ – This museum is installed in the paddlesteamer *Mainz*, which was built in 1929 and is now moored beneath the Kurpfalzbrücke, on the Neckar.
The engine room and galley are well worth a visit. Many models are on display, along with river charts, photographs and equipment illustrating the history of navigation on the Rhine and Neckar.

★ **Landesmuseum für Technik und Arbeit (Regional Museum of Industrial Techniques)** ⊘ – *At Museumsstraße 1* (**DZ**).
Two hundred and fifty years of industrial development in southwest Germany are retraced in this modernistic building, which impresses with the elegance, lightness and transparence of its architecture. Over 81 000sq ft of floor space, the museum, which was opened in 1990, examines the relationship between industrialisation and the evolution of society, together with innumerable demonstrations of the techniques involved (weaving, papermaking, printing, steam locomotives, etc.).

Carnival time

The Crazy Days (Tolle Tage) leading up to Ash Wednesday are the occasion for a series of boisterous, fun-loving carnivals throughout Germany. Parades, processions, decorated floats, street parties, painted faces and fancy dress are all part of the fun.

MARBURG★

Hessen — Population 75 000
Michelin map 417 N 10
Town plan in the current Michelin Red Guide Deutschland

Marburg was once one of the great pilgrimage centres of the West, crowds being drawn to the town by the relics of St Elizabeth of Hungary. Since the Reformation, and still maintaining the magnificent Gothic cathedral dedicated to the Saint, Marburg has become through its university a centre of Protestant scholarship and theology.

Wandering through twisting medieval alleys that climb through the old quarters massed around the castle hill, the visitor is still likely to meet country folk in traditional peasant costume — especially on the Wednesday and Saturday market days.

St Elizabeth (1207-31) — Princess Elizabeth, daughter of the King of Hungary and the intended bride of the Landgrave Ludwig of Thuringia, was brought to the Thuringian court at Wartburg castle at the age of four. Early in her life she became known for her kindness to the unfortunate, and there are many stories concerning the ruses she employed to help them. In 1227 her husband Ludwig died of the plague, and Elizabeth resolved to withdraw from the world. She installed herself below Marburg castle in a house adjoining the hospital for incurables, of which she took charge. She died of exhaustion at the age of 24. Canonized four years later (1235), she was to have her remains exhumed the following year to be immortalized in the superb Gothic church built by the members of the Teutonic Order *(qv)* to receive them.

In 1527 her descendant, the **Landgrave Philip the Magnanimous**, converted publicly to Protestantism and decided once and for all to abolish the cult of relics. Personally forcing the shrine, he had his ancestor's bones removed and buried in a nearby cemetery.

★★OLD MARBURG and the ELISABETHKIRCHE *time: 2 hours*

★★**Elisabethkirche (BY)** ⊙ — The first truly Gothic church in Germany, this was built between 1235 and 1283. Its regional character derives from the stylistic unity of the chancel and transepts, each terminating in an apse, and from its three aisles of equal height — making it in fact the first hall-church *(qv)*. Transverse roof timbers covering the side aisles are typically Hessian. The towers, surmounted by stone spires, rest on massive buttresses.

Enter through the main doorway.

The chapel beneath the tower immediately on the left contains the tomb of Field-Marshal von Hindenburg (1847-1934).

Nave — Note the following works:

1) A statue of St Elizabeth (c1470) wearing an elegant court gown.

2) An openwork Gothic rood with finely decorated consoles; on the altar *(nave side)*, a modern Crucifix by Ernst Barlach.

Chancel and transepts — A collection of exceptional **works of art★★★**:

3) Altarpiece of the Virgin; 1360 Pietà in the predella.

4) Tomb of St Elizabeth (after 1250). The 14C bas-relief on the sarcophagus represents the Saint's burial.

5) The remains of frescoes visible in the niches date from the 14C and 15C. On the right, a scene evoking St Elizabeth's charitable activities (the Landgrave sees in his imagination the Saviour, in a bed in which Elizabeth placed a sick man); the formal exhumation of 1236.

6) St Elizabeth's Shrine★★ (Elisabethschrein) in the old sacristy. This masterpiece of the goldsmith's art was completed by craftsmen from the Rhineland c1250. Scenes from the Saint's life enrich the casket's sloping panels.

7) St Elizabeth's Window. Assembled from a collection of 13C medallions, this illustrates the charitable works of the Saint.

8) Above the former priest's seat, a statue of St Elizabeth as the personification of Charity (the work, dating from 1510, is attributed to Ludwig Juppe, one of the most illustrious Marburg artists).

9) "The Landgraves' Chancel" *(in fact the south transept)*. Necropolis of the Landgraves of Hessen descended from St Elizabeth.

Leaving the church, climb up into the old town by way of the Steinweg — an unusual ramp with three different levels, which continues as the Neustadt and then the Wettergasse. Banners of the various student societies are draped from the windows of the houses in June and July.

Turn right into the Marktgasse.

MARBURG

B   Haus von
　　　 Friedrich-Karl von Savigny

M   Marburger Universitätsmuseum
　　　 für Bildende Kunst

R   Rathaus

★ **Marktplatz (AY)** – Only the upper part, the Obermarkt, has retained its ancient half-timbered houses. Particularly outstanding examples among them include nos 14 and 21, dating from 1560, and no 23.

The market fountain, dedicated to St George who is depicted vanquishing the dragon, is a popular student's meeting place.

Rathaus (AY R) – A Gothic building built in 1524. Above a door in the staircase tower is a fine carving by Ludwig Juppe, representing Elizabeth bearing her coat of arms of the House of Hessen-Thuringia. A mechanical cock crows the hours from an animated clock.

Past the Gothic ossuary (Karner), the Nikolaistraße now leads to the forecourt of the Marienkirche (late 13C), from which there is a fine view over the roofs of the old town to the valley beyond. Past the church façade, at the top of a steep slope, there is a glimpse of the castle above.

At the end of the esplanade, a passage leads down to the Kugelkirche, a fine small church in the Late Gothic (end of the 15C) style. Climbing again, the route leads past the Kalbstor fortified gate at the top of the Kugelgasse, turns right into the Ritterstraße, and finally passes above the Marienkirche to rejoin the Marktplatz. In the Ritterstraße, at no 15 (**B**), is the house which belonged to the famous legal historian Friedrich Karl von Savigny (1779-1861), one of the founders of the "historical school" of the study of law.

ADDITIONAL SIGHTS

★ **Schloß (AY)** ⊙ – From the 13C to the 17C, the castle was the home of the Landgraves of Hessen, descendants of St Elizabeth and Ludwig. From the terrace beside the first entrance esplanade on the south side, there is a view along the Lahn valley to the Taunus heights.

Passing through the historic buildings on top of the spur, the visitor sees the Landgrave's study, a small Gothic chapel with a ceramic floor, and the Gothic Knights' Hall with its double nave, all of them dating from the 13C and 14C.

The **Regional and Art History Museum★** (Museum für Kulturgeschichte), housed in the 15C Wilhelmsbau wing, displays among other things precious artefacts from the Elisabethkirche (fragments of stained glass, 15C tapestries depicting the story of the Prodigal Son etc.). There is also an exhibition of medieval shields.

There is a pleasant walk through the park at the foot of the buttress.

Marburger Universitätsmuseum für Bildende Kunst (Fine Arts Museum) (BZ M) ⊙ – German paintings from the 16C to the present day are on view here.

Kloster MAULBRONN★★

Baden-Württemberg
Michelin map 419 S 10

This was one of the earliest Cistercian foundations in Germany, an enormous abbey complex, very well preserved, with all its outbuildings and dependencies enclosed within a perimeter wall. The school established here since the Reformation (1556) has seen the flowering of such diverse literary and philosophical talents as those of Hölderlin and Hermann Hesse.

★★ABBEY ⊘ time: 3/4 hour

The abbey was founded in 1147. Embracing the Protestant faith at the time of the Reformation, the abbey escaped any Baroque transformations. It has been inscribed on Unesco's World Heritage List.

★ **Abbey Church** – This was consecrated in 1178.
The early 13C Paradise Porch (**1**) is the first German example of the Romanesque-Gothic transition.
Inside, the fan vaulting of the nave and south aisle, which was not added until the 15C, spoils the homogeneity of the original Romanesque design. The ten-bay nave is separated into two sections – one for the monks, the other for the lay brothers – by a Romanesque rood-screen (**2**) of exceptionally pure line, which is topped by a dog-tooth frieze. A large Crucifix (1473) stands before the screen. The chapels off the transept are all that remain of an earlier church. Note a beautiful 14C Virgin to the left of the high altar (**3**).

KLOSTER MAULBRONN
0   50 m

/ KARLSRUHE

STUTTGART /

▲▲ **Cloister (Kreuzgang)** and **Monastery Buildings (Klosterbauten)** – A stroll through the galleries and adjoining rooms unites the pleasures of ancient stones with the poetry of the cloister garden.
The south gallery, running between the church and the close, is designed with slender columns grouped in clusters, a feature noticeable also in the church porch and the monks' refectory.
Opening off the east gallery are the chapter house, whose 14C groined vaulting springs from central pillars, and the parlatory (**A**), which has fan vaulting.
The early 13C monks' refectory is flanked by the calefactory (**B**) and the kitchens (**C**). The massively built refectory seems crushed beneath the early Gothic vaulting with its heavy ribs, despite the fact that this rests on ringed columns that are quite tall. Opposite the entrance door, a charming **lavabo★★** (Brunnenkapelle, c1350) with quadri-lobed blind arcades juts out into the cloister garden.
The west gallery leads to the (restored) lay brothers' refectory, where groined vaulting arches low over the two aisles (**D**), and to the store-room (**E**). The store-room vaulting is square-ribbed.

A number of touring programmes is given on pp 7-9
Plan a trip with the help of the map of principal sights on pp 4-6.

MECKLENBURGISCHE SEENPLATTE★★★

The Mecklenburg lake district lies in the area between the Elbe-Lübeck canal and the Ucker march. It was formed during the last ice age, when glaciers pushed up the terminal moraine into mounds and the glacial tongues produced depressions, troughs and basins. This unique region contains over 1 000 lakes, most of which are linked via natural or artificially created canals, making it a paradise for water sports enthusiasts. The area has not yet been particularly developed as a tourist attraction and marketed in the same way as the lakes of Upper Bavaria. It hasn't yet been taken over by motorboats. Only a very few lakes have shore roads, and car drivers only get the odd magical glimpse across the shining expanse of water. It is almost as if the lakes are hiding, despite the fact that most are quite large.

The principal lakes, from west to east, are:

Schweriner See, with the provincial capital **Schwerin★** *(qv)* on its banks;

Krakower See, where the Mecklenburg regional poet Fritz Reuter dreamt of paradise;

Plauer See, the third largest lake in Mecklenburg-Vorpommern, with the town of Plau on its eastern banks, and which, together with the Müritz, forms the heart of the Mecklenburg lake district;

North of these lie the **Malchiner See** and the **Kummerower See** in **Mecklenburg's "Switzerland"** with the town of **Malchin** (the interior of the brick basilica of St. Maria and St. Johannes is sumptuously decorated);

The **Müritz**, the second largest lake in Germany, 115km^2 - 44sq miles in size. The name comes from the Slavonic word *"morcze"* meaning small sea. The town of **Waren**, the main tourist centre, lies on its northern shores. In addition to the two parish churches of St. Georg and St. Maria, the Old and New Town Halls and the Löwenapotheke (pharmacy) draw the eye. **Röbel** is developing into a pretty port, with its attractive boathouses on the shores of the lake.

Lakeside houses on piles, Müritzsee

Klaus Thiele

★ **Müritz-Nationalpark** ⊘ – This national park is 310km^2 - 120sq miles in size, and includes the eastern bank of the Müritz and the area to the east of the lake. Although woodland accounts for two thirds of the park, it comprises 12% water and 8% moorland. When it was part of Eastern Germany, 25 000ha - 61 780 acres were reserved as a state hunting reserve, but the park is truly the domain of ramblers and cyclists. Visitors should only "arm" themselves with a pair of field glasses, and may be lucky enough to observe the rare **osprey** (on the road from Federow to Speck). Curiously enough, this bird likes to nest in high voltage pylons *(it is absolutely forbidden to stop close to the eyries)*. The **sea eagle**, Germany's heraldic bird, which can range over an area of 10 to 50km^2 – 5 to 20sq miles, can be found at the fish pools at Boek. **White storks** breed in Kargow, and even the **black stork** and the **crane** nest in the national park. Beech are in their natural habitat here, and pines abound in the dry earth. The fenwood and marshwood on the eastern banks of the Müritz comprise alder, birch and ash. Due to the extreme diversity of the flora and fauna (150 nesting birds and 700 different plant types), the **guided nature walks** ⊘ are heartily recommended.

MEISSEN *

Sachsen – Population 36 000
Michelin map 418 M 24

To understand the development of Meissen, only 15km - 9 miles northwest of Dresden, the foundation of the town has to be placed in the military and historical context of the campaigns waged against the Slav tribes east of the Elbe and the Saale by King Heinrich I. In 929, he fortified a height commanding a strategic ford crossing the Elbe. The fortress was built on a rocky plateau where a tributary, the Triebisch, precipitated itself into the main river. And the town grew up around the foot of the castle hill from the 12C. Since the 18C, of course, Meissen has been famous worldwide for its porcelain.

THE PORCELAIN OF SAXONY

It was in the reign of Augustus the Strong *(qv)* that the alchemist **Johann Friedrich Böttger** (1682-1719) revealed that he had discovered the formula for creating the white hard-paste porcelain until then made only in China. The formula is based on kaolin (china clay), large quantities of which could be – and still are – mined only a short distance northwest of Meissen. Böttger made the discovery in 1708, although he did not reveal the secret until 29 March 1709. A year later, Augustus, Elector of Saxony and King of Poland, founded the Royal Saxon Porcelain Manufactory, which he installed in the castle – an isolated, well-guarded site well suited to the protection of secrets. Böttger, who had until then produced only hard red stoneware, was its first director.

The Motifs – Initially, the lavish decoration imitated Chinese and Japanese models. The period of plant designs, red and green dragons, a yellow lion, flowers, birds and mythical creatures dates from the directorship of Böttger's successor, Johann Gregorius Höroldt (1720-1755), who was responsible for the factory's first flush of prosperity (Old Saxony). It was Höroldt who produced the famous **"Blue Onion"** (Zwiebelmuster) tableware design, based on the use of cobalt, which was to become one of the most celebrated glazed designs in the world. Innumerable elegant services, along with individual vases, pots, giant animals and "conversation pieces", were also created by Johann Joachim Kändler (1706-1775). The Ceramic Mark distinguishing Meissen Porcelain is a pair of crossed swords in blue.

* **Staatliche Porzellanmanufaktur (National Porcelain Factory)** ⊙ – In 1865, the studios and workshops of the Meissen factory were transferred from the castle (Albrechtsburg), where they had been for more than 150 years, to a site in the Triebisch valley.
  Today the history of the industry is retraced here via a large number of superb exhibits. In a demonstration workshop, the preparation of paste and the processes of painting, fabrication and firing can be observed.

OLD MEISSEN

Markt – The Late Gothic Town Hall (1472-1478) is surrounded by burghers' houses in both Gothic and Renaissance styles.

Frauenkirche – This three-aisle Late Gothic hall-church with its fine star-vaulting dates from the late 15C. The bells of the carillon are made of Meissen porcelain.

BURGBERG

The castle, the cathedral and its subsidiary buildings are all grouped on this hill which was the original site of the town.

* **Albrechtsburg** ⊙ – Arnold von Westfalen, one of the most esteemed architects of late medieval times, was commissioned to build this castle in 1471 by the Margrave Albert. The finished work is considered to be one of the finest civic examples of the Late Gothic style. The **spiral staircase** (Großer Wendelstein) adorning the façade is a model of its kind. Although the castle housed the porcelain factory from 1710 to 1865, most of the exhibits on view in the elegant, frescoed apartments are purely historical or concerned with other types of art – principally German painting of the 16C.

* **Dom (Cathedral)** – Another Gothic hall with a transept and three naves, this church was built from 1260 onwards on the remains of a Romanesque sanctuary and not completed until the end of the 15C. Early 16C sketches for bronze **funerary plaques** * in the Dukes' Chapel (Fürstenkapelle) are said to be due in part to Albrecht Dürer and Lucas Cranach the Elder, and came from the famous Peter Vischer studio in Nuremberg. In front of the rood screen, sculpted between 1260 and 1270 in Naumburg, is the **Lay Brothers' Altar** * (Laienaltar), which is again due to Cranach the Elder. The **Benefactors' Statues** ** (Stifterfiguren) in the chancel, from the same studio, represent the Emperor Otto I and his second wife, the Empress Adelaide. In style, they are reminiscent of the statues in the chancel of Naumburg cathedral.
  The cathedral square (Domplatz) is surrounded by **monastic buildings**. The Dean's residence, at no 5, dates from 1526; next door at no 6 is the Canons' House (1728); and the Priory (c1500) is at no 7.

MEMMINGEN

Bayern — Population 38 000
Michelin map 419 W 14
Town plan in the current Michelin Red Guide Deutschland

Medieval gateways crowned with "helmet" roofs and traces of earlier fortifications still survive in Memmingen, a former imperial town in the Allgäu Pre-Alps.

Old Town — This lies on either side of the stream canalized through the city centre. Its character is exemplified by such ancient buildings as the **Siebendächerhaus** (or House with Seven Roofs), once the tanners' headquarters. Interesting buildings also surround the Marktplatz: the **Steuerhaus** (1495), with its ground floor opened by arcades; the 1589 **Rathaus**, which was remodelled in the Rococo style in 1765. The design of this is unusual, with three oriel windows on different floors, each with an onion dome.

Martinskirche — Gothic in origin, this church had its chancel elegantly modified at the end of the 15C. Inside, the **choir stalls★** (Chorgestühl), dating from 1507, are intricately carved with figures of the prophets, sibyls and church benefactors.

Kreuzherrenkirche — *On the Hallhof square.* The final octagon on the 1617 belfry surpasses the town's other towers in the refinement of its decoration.

Bad MERGENTHEIM★

Baden-Württemberg — Population 21 000
Michelin map 419 R 13

Lying in the valley of the Tauber, the old town of Bad Mergentheim, chosen as a base for the Knights of the Teutonic Order in the 16C, owes its popularity today to its position on the "Romantic Road" *(qv)*, its castle, and its spa.

Deutschordensschloß (Castle of the Teutonic Order) ⊙ — The Order was founded as a Germanic hospitaller community in the Holy Land and became a religious order in 1190 after the collapse of the Kingdom of Jerusalem. Eight years later, the military wing was added. When the Knights returned home they fought against the Slavs and took part in the conquest of Prussia and the Baltic states.

In 1525, the Grand Master of the Order, a Hohenzollern, followed the advice of Luther and suppressed the religious side of the organization, converting the community's patrimony into a principality which became the cradle of the state of Prussia. Those Knights who remained faithful Catholics grouped themselves under the see of Mergentheim. This ambivalent situation continued until 1809, when the Order was dispossessed by Napoleon. Today, greatly reduced in power, the Order has resumed existence as a religious and charitable body, with the Grand Master a cleric.

The castle, built in 1565, was modified c1780. The armorial bearings of the Order are displayed above the main entrance, which was lavishly decorated in the 17C. The corner towers in the inner courtyard are furnished with Renaissance spiral stairways. Beside the local historic museum is a museum devoted to the Teutonic Order itself. The castle **park** was landscaped in the English manner in the late 18C.

EXCURSIONS

Stuppach — *6km - 3 1/2 miles on the Schwäbisch Hall road.*
The **parish church** ⊙ of this village now boasts the central panel of the celebrated altarpiece from the Chapel of Our Lady of the Snow in Aschaffenburg *(qv)*. The panel, known as the **Stuppacher Madonna★★** (1519), depicts a Virgin and Child and was the work of Matthias Grünewald.

Teutonic Order

This military and religious order was a major protagonist in the dramas of eastern Europe during the Middle Ages. It went through several stages of development, as a glance at the list of locations where it set up its headquarters reveals:
— its original base was in Acre, Palestine ('Akko, Israel) during the Third Crusade. The Order was originally known as the Hospital of St Mary of the German House in Jerusalem,and adopted a military religious rule like that of the Knights Templar, wearing a white tunic with a black cross.
— having shifted the sphere of its activity to eastern Europe, under the leadership of Grand Master Hermann von Salza, the Order finally set up headquarters at Marienburg, Prussia (Malbork, Poland). This was the hub of its feudal rule over the territory it had conquered in Prussia, Pomerania, the Baltic states and Germany (14-15C).
— having lost its Prussian territory, the Order transferred its headquarters to Bad Mergentheim, Germany (16-19C).
— at the end of the Napoleonic Wars, a considerably weakened Teutonic Order was re-established as a religious order in Vienna, Austria, with a function strictly limited to charitable works.

MERSEBURG

Sachsen-Anhalt — Population 50 000
Michelin map 418 L 19

An episcopal town since the end of the 10C and seat of the Dukes of Saxe-Merseburg from 1685 to 1738, Merseburg has enjoyed a substantial industrial development during the present century. Symbolizing the commercial success of this small town is the gigantic Buna petro-chemical complex (synthetic rubbers, hydro-carbon derivatives), which was built in 1936 a little way to the south. The most interesting historic monuments, the cathedral and the castle, stand on a hill (Domberg) overlooking the Saale river.

SIGHTS

★★ **Dom (Cathedral)** – Three separate styles can be distinguished in this church. The crypt testifies to the Romanesque origins of the earliest structure; the porch, transept, apse and chancel owe their early Gothic character to remodelling carried out in the first half of the 13C; and the three-aisle nave, originally Romanesque, was transformed between 1500 and 1517 into the purest of High Gothic, with reticulated vaulting and slender octagonal pillars.

The **pulpit★** (1514-1526) is richly carved in a fashion distinctively Late Gothic. The bronze **funerary plaque★** plaque of King Rudolph of Swabia (d 1080), which is in the choir, is remarkable for the elegance of its workmanship.

Schloß (Castle)– This building, frequently modified, embodies a variety of styles: Late Gothic in the east wing; Renaissance in the north and west wings; and Baroque on the upper part of the west wing.

Every year
the Michelin Red Guide Deutschland
presents a wealth of up-to-date information in a compact
form. It is the ideal companion for a holiday,
a long weekend or a business trip.

MINDEN

Nordrhein-Westfalen — Population 78 000
Michelin map 417 J 10
Town plan in the current Michelin Red Guide Deutschland

An important junction at the Porta Westfalica gap, the last point on the Weser before the river, the road and the railway branch out across the north German plain, Minden has long been a key crossroads on Europe's trade routes.

SIGHTS

★ **Dom (Cathedral)** The Romanesque **Westwerk★★** *(qv)* is beautiful. It is preceded by a porch and fretted with delicate blind arcades, above which rises the great wall of the belfry.

The interior is notable for the rounded Westphalian-style vaulting which covers the transept, and for the chancel's tiered Romanesque blind arcades in the Rhineland tradition. A copy of the celebrated Minden Cross hangs on the left-hand pillar of the transept crossing (the original is in the cathedral treasury). An altarpiece by a Westphalian master representing the Crucifixion (1480) is in the chancel. The Frieze of the Apostles (*c*1250), now in the south transept, once crowned the cathedral rood-screen.

★ **Domschatzkammer (Cathedral Treasury)** ⊙ – *On the right-hand side of the Westwerk, beneath the arcades.*

Aside from the **Minden Cross★★** masterpiece (a Crucifix dating from the second half of the 11C), a very fine Virgin in Majesty (the Silberne Madonna, *c*1230-40) is on display along with a beautifully worked gold reliquary dating from 1070. Episcopal awards and liturgical items (13C-18C) are on view in glass cases.

Mindener Museum für Geschichte, Landes- und Volkskunde (Local History Museum) ⊙ – *Ritterstrasse 23-31.*

Apart from prehistoric and archaeological departments, this museum offers a fine selection of traditional regional costumes, interiors in the Biedermeier style, and reconstituted craft workshops and studios (shoemakers, photographers, leatherworkers, cobblers, etc.). In the department of military history there is a diorama model of the battle of Minden in 1759, when the English, allied with the Prussians, beat the French during the Seven Years War.

By way of the Marienstraße, drive out of town in the direction of Bremen. Soon after the bridge over the canal, turn right and continue around the dock basin after crossing the Great Lock. There is a visitors' car park after the bridge.

★★ **Schachtschleuse (Great Lock)** – This engineering marvel, 85m - 280ft long and 10m - 33ft wide, lowers or raises shipping between the canal and the Weser, 14m - 46ft below. A small museum explains the operation of the Weser basin, the management of its course and the current work on the Mittelland-Kanal.

Return to the car and continue around the port. After the exit from a tunnel beneath the canal, it is possible to climb, on foot, up the embankment and reach the aqueduct towpath.

★ **Wasserstraßenkreuz** – It is always a spectacular sight when waterways cross, but here it is especially interesting. The Mittelland canal crosses a navigable river, the Weser, so that there are occasions when ships cross their paths on both stretches of water. The 375m - 410yd aqueduct has enabled canal traffic to treat the 211km - 131 miles separating Münster from Hannover as a single reach, obviating the necessity of any more locks.

Return to Minden via the Werftstraße.

EXCURSION

Porta Westfalica – *Tour of 28km - 17 miles. Leave Minden via the Portastraße,* ④ *on the town plan. At Barkhausen, take a right turn towards the Kaiser-Wilhelm-Denkmal.*

Kaiser-Wilhelm-Denkmal – There is a fine view of the Weser Gap from the foot of this enormous statue, raised to the memory of the Emperor Wilhelm I in 1896.

Return to Barkhausen, take Route 61 on the right and cross the Weser in the direction of the Porta Westfalica. Follow the signs: Fernsehturm.

Fernsehturm (Television Tower) ⊙ – Built on the site of the former Bismarckturm, the tower has 129 steps which lead to a viewing platform. The panorama visible from this terrace embraces the Porta Westfalica gap with its intense road and rail traffic, the Wilhelm I monument, the town of Minden and the north German plain. The horizon is blocked on the east by the Wesergebirge, and towards the south by the Lippisches Bergland.

Return to Minden via Route 482.

Information in this Guide is based on data provided at the time of going to press.
Improved facilities and changes in the cost of living make subsequent alterations inevitable.

MÖNCHENGLADBACH

Nordrhein-Westfalen – Population 260 000
Michelin map 417 M 3
Town plan in the current Michelin Red Guide Deutschland

A Benedictine abbey founded in 974 was at the origin of this thriving industrial town. The oldest part, bordered on the south by the late Gothic Roman Catholic parish church, **Hauptpfarrkirche St. Mariä Himmelfahrt**, lies around the **Alter Markt**, behind which are the cathedral and the ancient abbey buildings. The former Prelate's residence, dating from the 17C, is well preserved and serves today as the town hall. To the southwest of the old market, stepped alleys and cobbled streets lead down to the park through a quarter where there are still traces of the old medieval fortifications, notably the **Dicker Turm** (Great Tower).

SIGHTS

Städtisches Museum Abteiberg (Municipal Museum) ⊙ – *At no 27 Abteistraße.*
The use of space and light in this modern building, with its complex, overlapping and interlinked storeys, makes it an ideal site for the exhibition of 20C art. Expressionism is represented by Pechstein, Kirchner, Heckel and Rohlfs; Constructivism by Willi Baumeister. But above all it is the post-1950 avant-garde who predominate: Pien, Mack and Uecker of the Group Zero, Warhol's and Palermo's Pop Art, and exponents of Op Art, the New Realism, Conceptual Art and Process Art (many exhibits by Beuys and sculptures by Richard Serra).

Städtisches Museum Abteiberg

Mönchengladbach – Städtisches Museum Abteiberg

Münster St. Vitus – The former abbey church, a marriage of the Gothic and the Romanesque, overlooks the southern flank of the hill (Abteiberg). The powerful three-tower ensemble of the Westwerk *(qv)* dates from 1180-1183, while the three aisles of the long nave, with their quadripartite vaulting supported on massive pillars, were constructed between 1228 and 1239. The Gothic chancel (1256-1277) was designed by Master Gerhard, the chief architect of Cologne cathedral. The oldest part of this particular building is the great Romanesque **crypt-hall** (c1100) which lies beneath the choir. A Romanesque baptismal stone remains in the Apostles' chapel. The **treasury** (Schatzkammer) is reached through the northern part of the cloister.

Schloß Rheydt ⊙ – *Leave the town centre southwards via Theodor-Heuss-Straße and then take a left turn into the Breite Straße-Ritterstraße.*
A moated Renaissance castle, Rheydt was originally built with four wings, of which only two survive. Inside, a **museum** displays arts and crafts from the 16C to the 18C, along with archaeological collections relating to the history of Mönchengladbach and a department illustrating the development of weaving.

EXCURSION

***Schloß Dyck** ⊙ – *9km - 5 miles to the east.*
The buildings of this small 17C castle are arranged around a square central courtyard with a tower surmounted by an onion dome at each corner. The ground floor rooms inside are embellished with magnificent Chinese hangings originally ordered by the Empress Maria-Theresa of Austria. There is a remarkable **arms collection** (from the workshops of armourers employed by the Counts of Dyck).
A 40ha - 100-acre park invites the visitor to stroll among plantations of many rare species of bushes and trees.

*When driving in German towns use the plans
in the **Michelin Red Guide Deutschland**
which are updated each year to show
– through-routes and by-passes
– new roads and one-way systems
– car parks*

MONSCHAU★★

Nordrhein-Westfalen – Population 12 000
Michelin map 417 O 2

From a **belvedere★★** lay-by on Route 258, coming from Aachen, there is a superb view of this ancient Eifel village, with its tall, narrow, slate-roofed houses huddled together at one end of a winding gorge carved from the rock by the Rur river.

SIGHTS

Village centre – The **half-timbered façades★★** (Fachwerkhäuser) of the old buildings overlook the stream and crowd the twisting streets.
Leaving the market place via the Unterer Mühlenberg slope, on the right of the Kaular café, turn right again along the Knieberg and climb to the chapel (Friedhofkapelle) which lies beyond the cemetery. From here, again, there is a good **view★** of the town, the castle, and the ruins of the Haller watchtower.
The oldest part of Monschau is in the Kirchstraße quarter (note especially the period house at no 33, which is faced with slate).

Haus Troistorff – *Laufenstraße 18.*
A solid, well-preserved house built by a linen merchant in 1783.

Rotes Haus (Red House) – Originally inhabited by a rich draper, this 1762 building retains its full 18C **interior decor★**, which forms part of the **local museum** ☉ now installed there. Note the magnificent carved oak staircase.

EXCURSION

The North Eifel Lakes – *85km - 53 miles – allow 1/2 day.*
Still on Route 258, leave Monschau. The road rises rapidly, and after 1 mile there is yet another **lookout point★** from which a bird's-eye view of the village can be enjoyed. From Imgenbroich onwards, particularly between Strauch and Schmidt, there are attractive glimpses, on the right, of the Rur lake region. Leaving Schmidt, the Nideggen ruin lies straight ahead.

Nideggen – Until the 15C the rose-coloured sandstone **castle** ☉ – a true "eagle's eyrie" site – was the residence of the Counts and Dukes of Jülich, after which it fell into disuse. From the 12C keep (partially restored and turned into a **museum** – Burgenmuseum – devoted to the castles and fortresses of the Eifel), there are fine **views★** to the south of the Rur valley cutting into the Eifel plateau, and of the Aachen basin to the north. The restored 12C church has a Romanesque chancel with frescoes.

★ **Rur Dam** (Rurtalsperre) – In a wild stretch of country, the reservoir here, known also as the "Stausee Schwammenauel", forms with the Urft reservoir to the south the largest stretch of water in the Eifel. **Motorboat services** operate on each of them.
The road crosses the dam to enter the Kermeter forest. From Einruhr, the route skirts the southern end of the Rursee, which is overlooked from a viewpoint laid out at the top of the hill beyond.

MOSELTAL★★★

MOSELLE VALLEY – Rheinland-Pfalz
Michelin map 417 Q 3 - O 6

The wide, peaceful curves of the River Moselle flow between two massifs of Rhineland schist, the Eifel to the west and the Hunsrück to the east. Most of the steep slopes are planted with wonderful vines, producing dry white wines largely from Riesling stock. Here the schistous subsoil plays a vital part in the maturing of the grapes, the decomposed rock absorbing heat during the day and breathing it out at night among the vines. The harvest is late and sometimes continues until the Feast of St Nicholas (6 December).
The wines are light, sometimes pungent, but with an extremely delicate bouquet. The further north the vines are planted, the more acid the wine becomes.
The river, canalized from Thionville onwards, comprises twelve separate sectors, the locks beside each dam taking barges of up to 1 500 tons, or towed convoys of 3 200 tons. On this navigable part of the Moselle **river cruises** ☉ between Trier and Koblenz are available.

FROM TRIER TO KOBLENZ *195km - 121 miles – one day*

★★**Trier** – *See TRIER.*

Neumagen-Dhron – This town is known for its Roman discoveries, which have been transported to the Rhine Museum at Trier. A copy of the famous *Wine Ship* can be seen beside the chapel opposite the Weinhaus café.

★ Bernkastel-Kues – *See BERNKASTEL-KUES.*

One magnificent vineyard follows another on this route. Note the oversize sundials Sonnenuhrer) fixed here and there to bare rock outcrops, which have given their names to some of the better-known vintages (Wehlen and Zeltingen, for instance).

The road passes through many villages typical of this wine-gro-wing region: **Ürzig, Kröv, Enkirch** an **Pünderich** among them.

From Enkirch, make a 5km - 3 mile detour to **Starkenburg**. From the terrace there, there is a splendid **view★** over the river's lazy Mont-Royal meanders.

3km - 1 3/4 miles after the bridge at **Zell**, which offers a fine perspective of the riverside houses lining the bank on the far side of the water, take the left turn in the direction of Marienburg.

Marienburg – The old convent here stood in an exceptional **setting★★** overlooking the narrowest stretch of land enclosed by the river bend at Zell. From the restaurant terrace and the wooden tower *(follow the footpath: 3/4 hour Rtn)*, there are impressive **views★★** of the various curves in the course of the river, and the vineyards on either side.

Bellstein – This tiny fortified town, whose last squire was the Chancellor Metternich, is huddled at the foot of a huge church and an enormous castle. From the ruins of the **castle** ⊘ *(1/2 hour Rtn on foot, from the Liesenich road)* there is, again, a splendid **view★** of the ever-curving valley.

Cochem – Leave the car on the outskirts and follow the river bank to discover one of the most celebrated **sites★★** of the Rhineland: towering above the river, the castle crowns a conical hill entirely covered with vines.

Of the original **castle** (Reichsburg) ⊘ *(1/2 hour on foot Rtn, from the Marktplatz)*, only the keep and the foundations of the walls remained after the destructions of 1689 – but the ruins were rebuilt in 14C style during the 19C, bristling with turrets and pinnacles. The **interior** has been refurnished in an opulent "feudal" manner.

Cochem

Moselle wines are made from the Riesling grape stock, and are typically fruity with a hint of acidity.

Treis-Karden – The church of St. Kastor, in the Karden quarter, exemplifies a transitional style halfway between Rhineland Romanesque (the "dwarf gallery" in the apse) and Gothic (ribbed vaulting).

Inside, there is a 1420 high-altarpiece in carved wood representing the Three Magi and, in the chapel on the left-hand side of the chancel, a small wooden shrine to St Castor in the Gothic style (1490).

★★ Burg Eltz ⊙ – *10km - 6 miles from Hatzenport, plus 1/2 hour on foot or 5 min by bus.*

From the promontory at the first hairpin bend after the car park, there is an awe-inspiring view looking down on this romantic **site**: the fortress, bristling with towers and turrets, pinnacles and spires, rises majestically above the trees at the far end of the wild Eltz valley. There are period furnishings inside, as well as weapons and armour.

Returning to the main road, the visitor soon sees the twin-tower silhouette of Thurant Castle on the east bank of the river. At **Kobern-Gondorf**, not long before the final twist in the river, the road passes right through an enormous restored 15-17C castle – one of two overlooking this stylish small town and blending remarkably well with the landscape. The upper castle, a plain square keep, adjoins the polygonal Romanesque Chapel of St Matthias.

★ Koblenz – *See KOBLENZ.*

*Book well in advance as it may be difficult
to find accommodation during the season.*

MÜHLHAUSEN★

Thüringen – Population 43 000
Michelin map 418 M 15

The name of Mühlhausen figures in a manuscript dated as early as 775. Established as a Free City of the Holy Roman Empire in 1180, the town was incorporated in the Hanseatic League from 1418 onwards. Its prosperity was based on a trade in leatherwork, beer and cotton goods.

Mühlhausen had a more historic role to play in the 16C when **Thomas Müntzer**, a local preacher, fomented a peasant rising against the feudal overlords. He was beheaded in the town's main square once the insurrection was put down (1525).

Spared the fate of so many German towns at the end of the Second World War, Mühlhausen today still conserves the flavour of its restoration after the terrible fire which ravaged it in 1689. The houses in the best state of preservation are to be seen along the **Herrenstraße**, the **Holzstraße**, and in the quarter around **Allerheiligenkirche**, by the Steinweg.

SIGHTS

★ Town Walls (Stadtmauer) – Built in the 13C, this peripheral fortification is still largely intact, the passageway crowning its ramparts turned into a promenade. Start the tour at the Frauentor, at the end of the Herrenstrasse.

★ Marienkirche – Apart from Erfurt cathedral, this is the largest church in Thuringia. Its tower reaches a height of 86m - 282ft. The 14C exterior is notable for the exuberance of its decoration: gargoyles, statues, cornices, pinnacles and gables rival each other in the elegance and inventiveness of their design. Oddly placed on the south porch balustrade are the statues of the Emperor Karl IV and his wife. Fashioned between 1360 and 1380, these came from the Parler studios in Prague.

Inside the church, with its five aisles, the **folding altarpieces★** are finely crafted, especially the one depicting the life of St Nicholas and that relating to the Crowning of the Virgin. The latter, dating from 1530, betrays in its treatment of faces the strong influence of Lucas Cranach the Elder. On the western pillars of the transept crossing, note The Adoration of the Magi (early 16C): the treatment of draperies and the bearing of the figures already hints at the Renaissance.

Thomas Müntzer, who preached in this church, lived nearby, at no 1 Herrenstraße.

Rathaus (Town Hall) – *Ratsstraße.*

This comprises blocks built at different times between the 14C and the 19C. The main block (16C) houses the former prison, a wine cellar (Ratsstube), and the local council chamber.

Blasiuskirche – *Johann-Sebastian-Bach-Platz.*

In 1707 and 1708, Bach was organist at this church, which was built between 1235 and 1260 and transformed into a three-aisle Gothic hall in the first half of the 14C. Worth seeing: the mid-14C stained glass windows in the choir; the Late Gothic central reredos, executed by craftsmen from Erfurt.

MÜNCHEN★★★

MUNICH – Bayern – Population 1 300 000
Michelin map 419/420 V 18
Plan of the conurbation in the current Michelin Red Guide Deutschland

The Bavarian capital, one of the largest, most important cities in Germany, lies not far from the Alps. Munich is not only a first-class cultural centre but also the most flourishing economic zone in the southern part of the country. Especially in recent years, the development of high-tech industries allied to the production of automobiles, locomotives, rubber, chemicals and machine tools has enormously increased the commercial influence of the town. Nor have such trades as printing, publishing and craftwork been ignored: exhibitions such as the International Crafts Fair (Handwerkmesse) attract almost 2 400 exhibitors each year, and the products of Munich's Breweries are known worldwide.

The choice of Munich as seat of the European Patents Office (opened in 1980) recognizes the city's illustrious scientific past, resounding with such famous names as Fraunhofer, Liebig, Ohm and Sauerbruch.

Among writers working in Munich were Lion Feuchtwanger, Thomas Mann, Frank Wedekind and Ludwig Thoma – the last two also being collaborators in the production of the satirical weekly Simplicissimus. It is however in the absurd, surrealistic logic of the comedian Karl Valentin that the spirit of Munich most popularly expresses itself.

With the foundation of the review Jugend in 1896, the city became the centre of the Jugendstil movement *(qv)*; and then, after the Blauer Reiter *(qv)* exhibition in 1911, one of the meccas of modern art.

Munich's cultural wealth, its special atmosphere – a blend of gaiety, tolerance and respect for tradition – and the beauty of the surrounding countryside have combined to make it one of the most appreciated German cities.

General view of Munich

HISTORICAL NOTES

The foundation of the town – A small village founded in the 9C near a Benedictine abbey identified itself by taking the name of the monks – in German Mönch, in Old High German Muniche. Ever since, the town's emblem has been a little monk (Münchner Kindl). In 1156 the Emperor Frederick Barbarossa ceded a part of Bavaria to Henry the Lion, Duke of Saxony. Two years later, the Duke decided to take for himself the salt trade taxes formerly levied by the Bishop of Freising, and to this end destroyed the bridge, warehouse and customs building set up six miles from the town. He then built a new bridge over which traders had to pass, forcing all commercial transactions into the town. The stratagem, subsequently legalized by Barbarossa, proved to be the beginning of a long and flourishing history for Munich, which until then had been no more than a cluster of unimportant houses.

The Rise of the Wittelsbachs – In 1180 Henry the Lion was stripped of his titles and banished from his lands in southern Germany. Barbarossa replaced him with the Palatine Count Otto von Wittelsbach, and from then on that house became closely linked with Bavaria. In 1225 Munich became the ducal seat. In 1314 one of the Dukes, Ludwig the Bavarian, became King of Germany, and then Emperor (1328). After the demise of the Wittelsbachs of Landshut in 1503, Munich was created the sole capital of the Bavarian Duchy, rivalling as a trade centre both Augsburg and Nuremberg.

In 1623, Duke Maximilian I exercised the function of Prince-Elector and made the town, during the turbulence of the Thirty Years War, the bastion of German Catholicism.

During the 17C and 18C, religious and civil architecture sprang up everywhere: the Theatinerkirche, Nymphenburg castle, the Heiliggeistkirche, the Asam brothers' church and the ducal theatre (Residenztheater) among them. The ramparts were demolished and replaced by spacious, well-laid-out gardens, the finest of them in the English style.

The Kings of Bavaria – It was under the enlightened rulers of the 19C that Munich reached its artistic zenith. **Max Joseph** (1799-1825), who had at first remained neutral in the conflict opposing Napoleon and the European coalition, finally took sides with the latter – a ploy which rewarded him in 1806 with the crown of Bavaria under the name of **Maximilian I**. Despite the Napoleonic wars, in which large numbers of Bavarian troops were involved, Munich continued to flourish, embellished now with monuments in the classical style, such as the Palace of Prince Karl and the buildings of the Karolinenplatz and the Brienner Straße.

Maximilian's son, **Ludwig I** (1825-48), a great admirer of classical antiquity, welcomed to his court the best of Europe's architects, painters and sculptors. In his desire to make his capital the most beautiful in Europe, he enriched the city with the Alte and the Neue Pinakothek, the university, the Glyptothek and the Propylaea. He cut a swathe through the old town with the construction of the Ludwigstraße and greatly enlarged the ducal residence. But in 1848, faced with a rebel movement provoked by the scandal of his liaison with the Spanish dancer Lola Montez, he was obliged to abdicate in favour of his son, Maximilian. A younger son, Otto, had already become King of Greece (1832).

Maximilian II (1848-1864) continued the artistic traditions of his father, founding in 1855 the Bavarian National Museum.

In the history of the Wittelsbach dynasty, a special place must be reserved for **Ludwig II** (1864-1886). This tormented romantic, a passionate admirer of Wagner, succeeded to the throne at the age of 18. Beloved by his subjects, he was nevertheless restless and unpredictable, a young man a prey to extreme depression – especially in the face of political setbacks. After his disastrous choice of an alliance with Austria (their combined armies were beaten by the Prussians at Sadowa in 1866), he switched sides a year later and supported the proclamation of Prussia's Wilhelm I as Emperor of all Germany. But the young ruler, craving solitude and living in a fantasy world, largely withdrew from his court and built himself the three extravagant and isolated castles of Neuschwanstein, Linderhof and Herrenchiemsee. Mentally unstable, Ludwig II (whose tragic life has been the subject of books and films) was deposed in 1886 and confined to Schloß Berg, on the shores of Starnberg lake. He was found drowned there shortly afterwards.

In the absence of a direct heir – and in face of the fact that the younger brother Otto, the King of Greece, was also mentally deranged – the son of Ludwig I, **Prince Luitpold**, assumed the Regency. An able and inventive man, always open to new ideas, the Regent improved the Bavarian capital with a zoological garden, an ethnographic museum, a new town hall, the German Museum and the impressive avenue named after him, the Prinzregentenstraße. His son, crowned as **Ludwig III** (1912-1918), was the last King of Bavaria: under pressure from a workers' revolutionary movement after the defeat of Germany in the First World War, he was forced to abdicate.

In between two wars – The months following the cessation of hostilities were turbulent with strife, nowhere more so than Munich. In February 1919 Kurt Eisner, the social democrat Bavarian President, was assassinated. A month earlier, Adolf Hitler's **German Workers' party** had been formed and its aims announced by the leader at the Munich Hofbräuhaus. Meanwhile, a republican **Council of State** had been proclaimed, only to be annihilated by Imperial troops in May of the same year.

In 1923, Hitler and Ludendorff fomented a popular uprising, but it was unsuccessful, the party was dissolved and Hitler imprisoned. Released before the sentence had run its term, he reorganized the group as the National Socialist (Nazi) Party. After he had become Chancellor, it was Munich that Hitler chose in 1938 for the notorious meeting with Chamberlain, Daladier and Mussolini at which the annexation by Germany of the Sudetenland was agreed.

LIFE IN MUNICH

The most animated part of the town is concentrated in the pedestrian precincts of the Neuhauser Straße and the Kaufingerstraße, between the Karlsplatz (or "Stachus") and the Marienplatz. The most elegant shops, however, are to be found along the Maffeistraße, the Pacellistraße, the Maximilianstraße and the Brienner Straße. Beneath the colonnades of the Hofgartenstraße are the art galleries, and most of the antique dealers congregate near the Maximilianplatz, in the Ottostraße. The Schwabing quarter (via the Ludwigstraße **KLY**) deployed around the Leopoldstraße, enjoyed its hour of glory as the city's artistic and intellectual hub at the turn of the century – but with its boutiques, its pavement cafés and its nightspots remains one of the most brilliant and lively after-dark centres in Germany.

Munich Food – Local specialities include the white sausages known as Weißwurst, roast knuckle of pork (Schweinshaxe) and Leberkäs, a meat and offal pâté which can be bought in slices, hot, from most of the butchers any time after 11am. Customarily these dishes are accompanied by Semmelknödel, a bread-based dumpling. At the beer festivals, a favourite offering is Steckerlfisch (small fish grilled on a skewer). White radishes (Radi), bretzels and Munich Salzstangen (small salt rolls) are often served with beer.

Beer – Five million hectolitres - 110 000 000 gallons of beer are brewed in Munich every year, most of it being drunk in the brasseries, taverns and beergardens of the town itself. There is a season of strong beers, starting in March. The names of these more alcoholic drinks ("Which at least" – as the local people say – "help us to get through Lent!") are distinguished by the suffix "-ator". The arrival of the month of May is celebrated by the drinking of Maibock.

Holidays and Feast Days – The term Fasching is the Munich name for a carnival traditional throughout western Germany and the southwest (where it is known as Fastnacht). This festival in honour of Shrovetide, just before Lent, is a period of unbridled and uninhibited public merriment, frequently involving masked costume balls, both indoors and outdoors.

Munich beer tankard

Cherville/FOTOGRAM-STONE, Paris

The origins of the famous early autumn **Oktoberfest**, which is held on the **Theresenwiese** (via the Mozartstraße **JZ**) goes back to the official engagement of the heir to the throne, Prince Ludwig, and Princess Theresa in 1810. Almost 7 million visitors flock to Munich each year for this gigantic public fair, for which the local breweries produce a special drink, the Wiesnbier, delivered in the old style by horse-drawn drays. Under canvas marquees and in stands ranged around the base of a huge statue representing Bavaria, nearly 5 million tankards of this beer are handed out during the festivities. The party is complemented by roasts of poultry and beef (two entire oxen are cooked on a spit each day). The Oktoberfest goes on for 16 days. **Corpus Christi** (Fronleichnam) is the most important religious holiday of the year. An immense procession winds its way through beflagged streets garlanded with branches of young birch trees, the vast crowd preceded by the clergy and members of the religious orders, Roman Catholic personalities, Catholic student organizations and representatives of the various city guilds.

OLD TOWN (ALTSTADT) *allow one day*

The tour indicated starts at the Karlstor.

Richard-Strauss-Brunnen (KZ A) – Bas-reliefs on the central column of this fountain illustrate scenes from the opera Salome, which the famous Munich composer wrote in 1905.

Michaelskirche (KYZ B) – This Jesuit sanctuary was built between 1583 and 1597 on the model of the society's Roman church (Gesù). Each tier of the Renaissance façade is decorated with pilasters; the niches contain statues of those Bavarian sovereigns most devoted to the Roman Catholic cause. Between the two entrances, St Michael vanquishes the dragon.

The single nave – which inspired many builders of the Vorarlberg Baroque school – is covered by a colossal cradle vault resting on massive pillars abutting the walls. The tomb of Eugène de Beauharnais is in the north transept. Thirty of the Wittelsbach princes, including Ludwig II of Bavaria, are buried in the **crypt** (Fürstengruft).

* **Deutsches Jagd- und Fischereimuseum** (German Hunting and Fishing Museum) (**KZ M¹**)
  ⊘ – The museum, housed in a disused Augustinian church (1618-1621), displays on three different levels a splendid collection of ancient and modern arms, trophies (including the skeleton of a giant Irish stag from the Stone Age), paintings and drawings of hunting scenes, and stuffed animals. Different species of freshwater fish, stuffed and mounted, are shown in their separate groups against a diorama.

* **Frauenkirche (KZ)** – The architect of this vast Late Gothic hall-church (1468-1488) was **Jörg von Halspach**, who also designed the old town hall. The exterior of the church, in dark red brick, is extremely sober; only the side entrances and tombstones built into the walls break the monotony of the tall façades. The onion domes, which since 1525 have crowned the two towers at the west end (99 and 100m - 325 and 328ft), have become the symbol of the city.

MÜNCHEN

A	Richard-Strauß Brunnen	K	Weinstadel
B	Michaelskirche	M¹	Deutsches Jagd-
D	Altes Rathaus		und Fischereimuseum
E	Peterskirche	M²	Glyptothek
F	Heiliggeistkirche	M³	Antiken-Sammlungen

Interior – In striking contrast to the exterior, the nave, a dazzling white, impresses at once with its simplicity and its height. Eleven pairs of powerful octagonal pillars support the reticulated vaulting. Seen from the entrance, the perspective of these columns forms a continuous line, effectively hiding the aisles.

Furnishing and works of art blend the old and the new. Thus the 24 carved wood busts representing the Apostles, the Saints and the Prophets, attributed to the late 15C sculptor **Erasmus Grasser**, are placed immediately above the modern **choir stalls**. The axial chapel in the apse contains a fine Robed Madonna, and that to the south, the old Chapel of the Holy Sacrament, a 15C altarpiece (a Crucifixion and scenes from the life of Christ). The original stained glass windows (medallion of the Annunciation, 1392) have been restored to the north chapel, the chapel of the Baptism of Christ, which is also furnished with a 1510 **altarpiece**. The central panel of this, which illustrates Christ's baptism, is by **Michael Pacher**, a native of Salzburg, while the lateral panels are the work of **Jan Polack**, the greatest Munich painter of the Gothic period.

K — SCHWABING / INGOLSTADT — **L**

NEUE PINAKOTHEK

Schellingstr.

Universität

U 221

Monopteros

Theresienstr.

Amalienstr.

ALTE PINAKOTHEK

Gabelsbergerstr.

ENGLISCHER GARTEN

Karolinenpl.

Brienner

Von-der-Tann-Str.

Oskar-von-Miller-Ring

Ludwig straße

Schönfeldstr.

Königin straße

102

M

127

Ottostr.

Odeonspl.

PRINZ-CARL PALAIS

M⁶

Stuck-Villa

PASSAU

Wittelsbacher Brunnen

Odeonspl.

HOFGARTEN

RESIDENZ

50

224   170

M⁵

151

Maxburg

FRAUENKIRCHE

Marstallpl.

Lehel

214

Karl-Scharnagl-Ring

202

WASSERBURG / PASSAU

M¹

Kaufingerstr.

MARIENPL.

R

N

Maximilianstr.

165

Hofbräuhaus

M

119

ASAM KIRCHE

Rosental

M⁷

Tal

Herrnstr.

Thomas-Wimmer-Ring

Isartor

Westenriederstr.

Frauenstr.

Rumford straße

Thierschstr.

Sendlinger

REGENSBURG

162

Müllerstr.

Reichenbach str.

Gärtnerpl.

Kohlstr.

Ludwigsbr.

4

79

KULTURZENTRUM

Fraunhoferstr.

Klenze str.

Baader str.

Erhardt str.

DEUTSCHES MUSEUM

Rosenheimer Str.

ROSENHEIM

231

Reichenbachbr.

Eduard-Schmid-Str.

Schweigerstr.

Cornelius str.

Zeppelinstr.

Hoch-

0   200 m

K — TIERPARK HELLABRUNN — **L** — Bavaria-Filmstadt

M⁴ Städtische Galerie
   Im Lenbachhaus

M⁵ Bayerisches
   Nationalmuseum

M⁶ Staatsgalerie moderner Kunst

M⁷ Münchner
   Stadtmuseum

N Alter Hof

Q Viktualienmarkt

R Neues Rathaus

S Feldherrnhalle

V Theatinerkirche

Y Erzbischäfliches
   Palais

Z Portia Palais

A staircase to the left of the choir leads to the **Bishops' and Princes' Crypt** (Bischofs- und Fürstengruft), with the burial vaults of certain Cardinals of Munich and Wittelsbach princelings. A lavishly-built early 17C mausoleum dedicated to the Bavarian Emperor Ludwig (1287-1347) stands in the south aisle.

In the **south tower**, there is now a lift taking visitors to the platform, from which there is a fine **view★** of the town.

★ **Marienplatz** (**KZ**) – This square is the heart of Munich. In the centre rises the **Mariensäule**, a column erected by the Prince-Elector Maximilian in 1638. The north side is occupied by the neo-Gothic **Neues Rathaus** (1867-1908) (**R**), whose **carillon** (Glockenspiel) installed in the tower's oriel window, is a favourite tourist attraction. When the mechanism is activated *(at 11am, noon and 5pm)*, brightly coloured figures in enamelled copper emerge and enact the Dance of the Coopers (Schäfflertanz *below*) and the Tournament which accompanied royal weddings in the 16C *(above)*.

From the town hall tower (85m - 279ft: *lift*) there is another lovely **view** of the city. The façade of the **Altes Rathaus** (**D**), with its stepped gables and bell turrets, occupies the eastern side of the square.

Peterskirche (**KZ E**) – Baroque vaulting remodelled this 13C, three-aisle Gothic church in the 17C and 18C. The centre section of the enormous high altar is occupied by an Erasmus Grasser statue of St Peter (1492). Slightly lower down, the flanking figures representing the four Fathers of the Church were sculpted by Egid Quirin Asam in 1732. The church's 1386 bell tower is affectionately nicknamed "Old Pete" by the people of Munich. Visitors braving the climb to the top *(294 steps)* are rewarded with a splendid view.

Food Market (**Viktualienmarkt**) (**KZ Q**) – The permanent daily market and an adjoining beergarden *(the open-air beergarden operates only during the summer months)* make this square one of the city's liveliest. Two fountains recall the famous comedian Karl Valentin and his partner Liesl Karlstadt.

Heiliggeistkirche (**KZ F**) – Another Gothic original which paid later tribute to the local taste for the Baroque, this hall-church was completely transformed between 1723 and 1730. The façade however is neo-Baroque, and dates only from 1885. The painting above the **high altar** is by U Loth (1661), and the two angels with large wings in front of the altar pillars are the work of J G Greiff (1730). The mid-15C Virgin in the north aisle, said to be by Hammerthal, was once in the Benedictine abbey at Tegernsee.

Cross the Talstraße, take the passage beneath the old town hall, and turn right into the Burgstraße.

Weinstadel (**KZ K**) – *At no 5 Burgstraße.*
The oldest house (1552) in Munich, in days gone by the municipal office of the Clerk of the Court. The façade is decorated in trompe l'oeil. The fine doorway has a basket-handle arch.

At no 10 in the Burgstraße, take the vaulted passageway to reach the Ledererstraße, then cross diagonally (left) into the Orlandostraße.

Hofbräuhaus (**KZ**) – The best-known of the famous Munich beer halls stands on the Platzl and dates from 1589. The present building was constructed at the end of the 19C, the original brewery having already been transferred to the east bank of the Isar through lack of space. Every day, in this great temple of beer, perspiring waiters serve 100 hectolitres (17 500 pints) of beer in one-litre (1 3/4 pints) tankards (Maßkrug). In many of the rooms and in the shaded courtyard, orchestras add to the festive atmosphere with renditions of popular songs – frequently with additional help from the drinking public. The huge vaulted **Bierschwemme**, on the ground floor, where the odours of strong tobacco mingle with those of sausages and beer, is the rowdiest part of the building. Customarily there is a police presence to ensure that high spirits do not degenerate into brawls.

At the far end of the square, turn left into the Pfisterstraße.

Alter Hof (**Old Castle**) (**KZ N**) – This building, a quadrilateral opening onto an inner courtyard, was the official Wittelsbach residence from 1253 to 1474. The south wing has an elegant tower with half-timbered corbelling (late 15C). The courtyard with its fountain is charming.

The Hofgraben leads to the Max-Joseph-Platz, enclosed on the north and east by the imposing mass of the palace.

★ **Residenz** (**Palace**) (**KY**) – In 1385, the Wittelsbachs started the building of this new royal palace (Neuveste) which, with the passing of time, expanded into a complex that grew ever more vast. Work was well advanced in the Renaissance period (Antiquarium, Kaiserhof, the Residenzstraße façade) and the subsequent classical era (Festsaalbau, Königsbau).

P. Tetrel/EXPLORER, Paris

Water ewer from the Palace Treasury

★ **Schatzkammer** (Treasury) ⊙ – The magnificent exhibits here – crowns, diadems, illuminated prayerbooks, ciboria, cameos, reliquaries, etc – are enticingly set out. On no account miss the superb chased cross executed at the beginning of the 11C for Queen Gisela of Hungary, or that dazzling example of the goldsmith's art showing St George slaying the dragon (1590).

Note, too, a marvellous ivory crucifix, swords with diamond – and ruby – encrusted pommels, vases and plates in jasper, agate and lapis lazuli, exotic works of art from Turkey, Persia and Mexico.

Residenzmuseum ⊙ – *(Successive morning and afternoon guided tours are necessary if nothing is to be missed).*

Morning Tour – A room embellished with marvellous gilded stuccoes houses the Wittelsbach **Ancestors' Gallery**, where Charlemagne has the place of honour. The enormous **Antiquarium** (1570), the oldest part of the palace, impresses with its painted ceilings and innumerable Roman busts. The **State Rooms** (Die Reichen Zimmer – 1730-1737), decorated by Effner and Cuvilliés, illustrate in great style the French version of the Rococo.

Afternoon Tour – Masterpieces from the workshops of Meissen, Nymphenburg and Sèvres ("Bird Service" of 1759) are on display in the **Porcelain Rooms**. The 17C **Hofkapelle** (Court chapel) has a fine compartmented ceiling. On the first floor is the **Reliquary Room** (Reliquienkammer), where the gems of the Wittelsbach chapel treasure are on view (note the outstanding Passion shrine) as well as various examples of 16C and 18C gold and silver plate.

⁂ **Altes Residenztheater** ⊙ – This enchanting Rococo theatre was built by Cuvilliés between 1751 and 1753, with four tiers of Court boxes, each different from the others in design and decoration. The Prince-Elector's box, in the centre, is set apart by the elegance and richness of its hangings and the fine decorations in marble and stucco. The harmonization of colours in red, gold and ivory is particularly beautiful.

Bayerisches Nationaltheater – Built between 1811 and 1818, the Bavarian national theatre was endowed with one of the largest stages in the world, on a par with the Scala in Milan or the Viennese Opera. The five-tier auditorium can seat 2 100 spectators.

Odeonsplatz (KY) – A fine square dominated on the west by the lofty silhouette of the Theatinerkirche. To the south, the **Feldherrnhalle (S)** portico, erected in the 19C by F von Gärtner in imitation of the Loggia dei Lanzi in Florence, closes the long perspective of the Ludwigstraße. The far (northern) end of this splendid avenue leads in a straight line to a triumphal arch.

Theatinerkirche (KY V) – A fine example of Baroque ecclesiastical architecture, this church was built between 1663 and 1688, first under the direction of the Italian Barelli and later by Zuccalli, who came from Graubünden. The façade was added a century afterwards, by Cuvilliés.

Inside, the dome of this very tall building, which rises to a height of 71m - 233ft, emphasizes a grandiose impression of space. The stuccowork is particularly rich, the Italian stuccodore having paid especial attention to the smaller load-bearing arches and the pendentives. The wreathed double colonnade of the monumental high altar is also very generously embellished. The dark wood of the pulpit, designed in 1681 by Faistenberger, makes a striking contrast with the whites and greys in the nave and elsewhere. More princes from the Wittelsbach dynasty are buried in the crypt beneath the chancel.

From the Salvatorstraße turn into the Kardinal-Faulhaber-Straße.

Erzbischöfliches Palais (Episcopal Palace) (KY Y) – *At no 7 Kardinal-Faulhaber-Straße.* An elegant building, one of the masterpieces by the Rococo architect **Cuvilliés**, constructed between 1733 and 1737.

Palais Porcia (KY Z) – *No 12 Kardinal-Faulhaber-Straße.*
This mansion, originally designed by Zuccalli in 1694, was transformed in the Rococo style by Cuvilliés in 1735. The façade, in tones of pink and grey pargetting, is charming.

Regain the Marienplatz via the Maffaistraße and Weinstraße.

ALTE PINAKOTHEK QUARTER (KY)

***Alte Pinakothek** ☉ – This colossal building (the word Pinakothek means art gallery) was destined to house the collections of paintings amassed by the House of Wittelsbach from the beginning of the 16C onwards. It was built between 1826 and 1836 by the architect Leo von Klenze, in the Venetian Renaissance style. The collection was started by Duke Wilhelm IV, who commissioned historical scenes from the most eminent painters of his time, Altdorfer and Burgkmair. The Duke's great grandson, the Elector Maximilian I, continued the tradition by founding a home for the collection, the Kammergalerie, in the 17C. And this, under King Ludwig I, developed into the finest exhibition of art in the whole of Europe. The Alte Pinakothek, which houses the masterpieces of European painters from the 14C to the 18C, closed in 1994 for a period of around 3 years for renovation work. However, visitors can still see the treasures, since 300 of the 800 paintings formerly exhibited can still be seen in the **Neue Pinakothek**. In fact this hiatus does have a distinctly positive side to it. A prime selection of paintings from the 14C to the early 20C can now be seen under one roof, and in addition, the new chronological hanging order (the paintings were formerly hung by schools) bring whole new perspectives, challenging the visitor to make comparisons and new discoveries. A highly successful temporary arrangement! The following description of the Neue Pinakothek takes account of the new hanging order.

* **Neue Pinakothek** (**KY**) ☉ – The postmodernist style building, completed in 1981 and faced with light sandstone, was designed by Alexander von Brancas. It replaces the building erected under Ludwig I, which had to be demolished due to serious war damage. The Neue Pinakothek is dedicated to 19C art, but for the past three years it has also been exhibiting a selection of the paintings from the **Alte Pinakothek** *(galleries 1 to 13)* in addition to its own treasures *(galleries 11 and 14 to 22)*.

Gallery 1 – Works by Filippo Lippi, Dirk Bouts. Columba altarpiece, an extraordinarily beautiful triptych by **Rogier van der Weyden**, which he painted in 1460 for St. Columba in Cologne. Bartholomäus altarpiece by the master of the same name.

Gallery 2 – The *Lamentation of Christ* by Botticelli, *Virgin Mary in Glory* by Ghirlandaio, masterly Altarpiece of the Fathers of the Church by **Michael Pacher**.

Room 2a – From the first half of the 15C, *Saint Veronica* by the master of the same name, also representatives of the gentle style of the Cologne school of painting such as **Stefan Lochner**, who has several paintings on show. Works by Giotto di Bondone, Memling, Schongauer.

Room 3a – These are mainly old German masters. Works by Albrecht Dürer, Hans Baldung Grien (portrait of the Count Palatine Philipp); a highly detailed *Susanna Bathing* by **Albrecht Altdorfer**, a master of the Danube school.

Gallery 3 – We encounter Altdorfer again here. In the *Battle of Alexander* he has painted countless people with incredible accuracy. In addition to works by Grünewald (Saint Erasmus and Saint Mauritius), Holbein and Cranach, the main feature is without doubt the famous *Four Apostles* by **Albrecht Dürer**, whilst just as famous is his *Self-Portrait* from 1500, which shows him as a bearded young man of 28.

Gallery 4 – *Madonna Tempi* and *Madonna della Tenda* by **Raphael**, *Virgin and Child* by **Leonardo da Vinci**. Works by Lorenzo di Credi, Perugino, Lorenzo Lotto.

Room 4a – In addition to **Andrea Mantegna's** *Mucius Scaevola*, paintings by Francesco Francia, Basaiti, da Messina.

Gallery 5 – Here we can admire works by **Anthony van Dyck**: *Susanna Bathing* and *Rest during the Flight into Egypt*, in which Titian's influence can be seen. There are several masterpieces by **Titian** himself, including *Madonna and Child* and *The Crowning with Thorns*, a late work. There are three works by **Tintoretto**.

Room 5a – German paintings from the 16C and 17C. In addition to Hans Rottenhammer, who was clearly influenced by Tintoretto, and Georg Flegel, who tended towards the Dutch tradition of painting, the exhibits include some small format idyllic landscapes by **Adam Elsheimer** (Flight to Egypt).

Gallery 6 – Dedicated to the Brueghel family of painters. The *Land of Milk and Honey* by **Pieter Bruegel the Elder**, the painter of famous landscapes and country scenes, has an almost surrealistic feel. Also included are the *Large Fish Market* by his son **Jan Brueghel the Elder** and *Bouquet of Flowers* by **Jan Brueghel the Younger**, which is a copy of a work by his father.

Gallery 7 – Rubens gallery. The extraordinary talent of **Peter Paul Rubens** is evident from such diverse works as the anguished *Massacre of the Innocents at Bethlehem*, to *Hélène Fourment in her Wedding Dress*, and *Self-Portrait with Isabella Brant under a Honeysuckle Bower*.

Gallery 8 – Rubens once again with the *Descent into Hell*, his contemporary from Antwerp **Jakob Jordaens** with *The Satyr and the Peasant* and works by **Anthony van Dyck**.

Gallery 9 – **Claude Lorrain, Nicolas Poussin**. The principal attractions are the sentimental pictures of children by **Murillo**: *The Little Fruit Seller*, *The Grape and Watermelon Eater*.

Gallery 10 – 17C Dutch painting. **Frans Hals**, *Portait of Willem van Heythuysen*, but above all the Passion by **Rembrandt**.

Rooms 10a and 11a – More 17C Dutch painters, with some small genre scenes and country paintings and still life pictures: Pieter Claesz, Gerard Dou, Adriaen Brouwer.

Gallery 11 – Tender hues triumph in the portraits and landscapes of **Thomas Gainsborough**. Also works by **Joshua Reynolds, Anton Graff, François Boucher** with a portrait of *Madame Pompadour*.

Gallery 12 (corridor) – Several paintings by Francisco Goya.

Gallery 13 – This gallery houses large paintings: *The Ascension of the Virgin Mary* by Guido Reni, the shining *Adoration of the Magi* by Tiepolo, *The Fall of the Rebel Angels* by Peter Paul Rubens.

Room 13a – Early German Romantics, with works by Johann Georg Dillis, Wilhelm von Kobell, Carl Rottmann.

Gallery 14 – The *Portrait of Johann Wolfgang von Goethe* by Joseph Karl Stieler, Karl Blechen's heroic landscapes, highly symbolic nature paintings by **Caspar David Friedrich** (Sudetes Mountains landscape).

Room 14a – Painters from the Dresden school: Carl Gustav Carus, Georg Friedrich Kersting and of course more Caspar David Friedrich.

Gallery 15 – Reserved for the German painters inspired by Roman antiquity, such as Arnold Böcklin, Anselm von Feuerbach, Hans von Marées, who used mythological motifs and classical tradition.

Gallery 16 – Nazarenes, Classicists and paintings by Friedrich Overbeck, Friedrich Wilhelm von Schadow, Joseph Anton Koch.

Gallery 17 – The eye is drawn here to idyllic Biedermeier scenes: Ferdinand Georg Waldmüller, **Carl Spitzweg** *(The Picnic, The Poor Poet)*. Examples of early Realism include works by **Adolph von Menzel** *(The Berlin-Potsdam Railway)*.

Gallery 18 – French late Romantics and Realists: Géricault, Gustave Courbet *(Landscape with River and Bridge)*, Honoré Daumier *(The Drama)*, **Camille Corot, Eugène Delacroix**.

Gallery 19 – Paintings by the famous French Impressionists, such as **Edouard Manet** *(Barque)*, hang in this gallery. *Breakfast in the Studio* dates from his Pre-Impressionist period. Also included are **Claude Monet's** *Bridge at Argenteuil* and **Edgar Degas'** *Woman Ironing*.

Gallery 20 – More French Impressionists and Post-Impressionists. **Paul Cézanne** with a self-portrait and a *Still Life with Chest-of-Drawers*. *The Weaver*, an early work by **Van Gogh** from his sombre realistic phase. *View over Arles* and *The Plain at Auvers* were painted during the last few years of his life. Paintings by **Gauguin** include *Breton Peasants, Birth*. The exhibition includes a bronze by **Rodin**, *Crouching Figure*.

Gallery 21 – German Impressionists: **Max Slevogt** *(Garden Corner in Neukastel)*, **Max Liebermann** *(Bathing Youth)*, **Lovis Corinth**.

Room 21a – Here we have **Wilhelm Leibl** and his contemporaries. Works by Leibl include the *Portrait of Mina Gedon* and the *Portrait of Lina Kirchdorfer* which was painted under the influence of Manet.

Gallery 22 – **Symbolism** and **Jugendstil** (Art Nouveau) works, for example a portrait of a woman by **Gustav Klimt**, and *Disappointed* by Ferdinand Holder. Marble bust by Max Klinger.

Room 22 – Franz von Stuck painted *The Sin* in 1893, and *Neptune's Horses* by Walter Crane was produced in 1892.

★ **Glyptothek (JY M²)** ☉ – One thousand years of Greek and Roman sculpture are gathered together under the roof of this museum, built with its classical porch and Ionic colonnade, by the architect **Leo von Klenze** (1816-1830). The **Tenea Apollo**, with his handsome, smiling face, is typical of the Kouros – those large naked figures, half human, half divine, who spread through Greece in the 6C BC *(Gallery I)*. The **Barberini Faun** *(Gallery II)*, which appears sated with drink and half asleep, dates from the Hellenistic epoque (c 220 BC). The Classical period is represented by Roman copies of ancient Greek statues and funerary stones (5C and 4C BC): here the **bas-relief by Mnesarete** displays a magisterial harmony of proportion, and the sculptor's handling of the draperies swathing Irene, the Goddess of Peace, is equally fine *(Gallery V)*.

Note too, in the original works from the east and west pediments of the Temple of Aphaia on the island of Aegina, which were sculpted from Paros marble, how finely detailed is the shaping of the warriors' musculature. These statues *(Galleries VII-IX)* date from the end of the Archaic era (500-480 BC).

Finally *(Galleries X to XIII)*, the visitor can judge to what state of virtuosity the Romans had brought the arts of portraiture and the decoration of sarcophagi.

★ **Antiken-Sammlungen (Collection of Antiquities)** (JY M³) ⊙ – *Opposite the Glyptothek.*
A building by G F Ziebland (1838-48) which, with its Corinthian colonnade, forms an architectural counterpart to the sculpture museum across the road.

An important display of **ceramics** on the ground floor traces the evolution of pottery and the painting of vases in Greece, which reached its zenith during the 6C and 5C BC. Geometric decoration was succeeded by the representation of black figures on a red background – illustrated by an amphora and a goblet by the painter Exekias. The amphora depicts Ajax carrying the body of Achilles; Dionysius decorates the goblet, in a boat escorted by dolphins *(Gallery II, showcases 10 and 12)*. The transition towards the use of red figures against a background of varnished black can be seen on another amphora, where a single subject – Hercules' banquet in the presence of Athena – is treated in the two styles *(Gallery III, showcase 6)*.

Certain vases (loutrophora and lecythus on a white ground) were destined for funerary worship; others – such as the elegant canthare (drinking vessel in the shape of a female head) – for domestic use *(Gallery II, showcase 7 – 540 BC)*.

Bronzes on the first floor (ceremonial vessels, engraved plaques, statuettes), and particularly the **Etruscan jewellery** in the basement *(Galleries VII and X)* testify to the enormous craftsmanship enjoyed by these workers in metal: necklaces, fibula, rings, in filigree or with granulations, rival each other in the delicacy and elegance of their execution.

★ **Städtische Galerie im Lenbachhaus (Lenbach Collections)** (JY M⁴) ⊙ – Built between 1883 and 1889 in the style of a Florentine villa, the house containing the Lenbach collections is devoted mainly to the works of **Munich painters of the 19C**. Among these are the landscapes of E B Morgenstern *(Starnberg Lake)* and portraits by F A von Kaulbach and F von Defregger. There is also a set of powerful **portraits** by Franz von Lenbach himself *(King Ludwig I, Bismarck, Wagner)*.

But the gallery's international reputation is built above all on the avant-garde **Blauer Reiter collection** *(qv)*. Born in the tumultuous period just before the First World War, the movement is represented by its founder members, Kandinsky, Marc *(Blue Horse)* and Kubin, as well as by paintings from the hands of Jawlensky, Klee and Macke. Contemporary art is also displayed in the Lenbach villa.

★★★DEUTSCHES MUSEUM (LZ) ⊙

Allow at least half a day

Founded in 1903, this museum – one of the most important in the world for scientific and technical matters – is built on an isle in the Isar (Museumsinsel). It traces the history of science and technology from the beginning of time to the present day.

Apart from a large number of original items and reconstructions, most of them of great value, the exhibits comprise dioramas, synoptic tables, scale models and examples of working apparatus. In line with the expressed wish of the museum's founder, the Bavarian electrification pioneer **Oskar von Miller**, the display system is pedagogic: the visitor is there to inquire, to touch, and to discover. Thus there are innumerable **working models** and workshop and laboratory **demonstrations** to explain the relevant techniques in a way that even a beginner can understand. Such physics experiments as Faraday's Cage and Foucault's Pendulum, for example, are reproduced. And there are regular performances illustrating such manufacturing processes as papermaking, glassblowing, smelting and the fabrication of tiles. Some of the demonstrations are accompanied by a commentary on film.

A library endowed with 900 000 different volumes is associated with the museum, as well as privately donated collections and archives including documents, plans, maps, blueprints and drawings.

In view of the huge scope of subjects covered, visitors are advised to choose a particular theme to follow. There are some 18 000 exhibits displayed over an area of 55 000m² - 592 000sq ft. A brochure in English and a plan of the museum's layout are obtainable at the entrance.

Ground Floor – Natural resources (including oil); metallurgy; machine tools; machines powered by different types of energy (wind, water, steam); applications of electrical current; bicycles and barouches; civil engineering (roads, bridges, tunnels, railways, canals, etc.). In the **Railway Hall**, there are famous steam engines, including the 1912 S-3/6 which powered the Bavarian Express, and the first electric locomotive *(Werner von Siemens, 1879)*. The **Aeronautical Section** (Modern Division) exhibits early jet planes, including the Messerschmitt Me-262, the first jet fighter made on a production line, helicopters, gliders and vertical take-off machines.

An Elbe sailing ship (1880) and an Italian steam tug (1932) stand at the entrance to the Navigation Department *(continued in the basement)*.

Basement – Among many other displays, the **Navigation Section** highlights naval construction, warships (including U-1, the first German submarine, built in 1906), methods of navigation, fishing techniques, and the sphere of Jacques Piccard's 1958 bathyscaphe.

A section on **mining** details the working of a coal mine, the extraction of salt, and the treatment of ores. There is a model salt mine.

The **Automobile Department** shows an 1885 carriage with a Benz motor, an 1891 steam-driven Serpollet, luxury cars of the 1920s and 1930s (Daimler, Opel, Horsch, Bugatti), utility vehicles, racing cars (1936 Auto-Union Grand Prix Type-C), an assembly line, and motorcycles. Note the 1885 Daimler-Maybach (a replica, built in 1906).

First Floor – The most interesting section here is perhaps **Aeronautics**. Gliders built by the engineer Lilienthal (c1885), the pioneer of this form of flight, can be seen. Also a **1917 Fokker Dr. I Triplane**, of the type made famous by Baron von Richthofen's "circus" in the First World War (a replica including parts from the original). Note also the Wright Brothers' Type-A Standard (USA, 1909), a Blériot Type XI (1909), a Junkers F-13 (the first true air-liner, 1919), and the legendary Junkers Ju-52 (built under licence in France, 1947). Military aircraft of the 1930s and 1940s are on show, including the Messerschmitt Bf-109.

From this most recent gallery devoted to aeronautics, there is direct access *(by escalator)* to the second floor section on space flights. Technologies from the earliest attempts at rocketry (Hitler's V2, code-named A4) to the current Spacelab are illustrated.

Department of Physics – Physical laws and their application: optics, mechanics, electronics, thermology, nuclear physics; chemistry: alchemy, Liebig's laboratory, pharmacy, biochemistry; techniques of information; musical instruments.

Second Floor – Manufacture of glass and ceramics (beautiful 17C earthenware stove from the Thurgau area in Switzerland); paper printing; photography (Daguerre's apparatus, 1839); textile processes (Jacquard's 1860 loom).

Third Floor – Weights and measures; climatic forecasts; agriculture (dairy farming, flour milling, breweries); data processing and computer science, robotics and microelectronics. Access to the **fourth floor** observatory *(it is necessary to book a visit in advance).*

Fifth Floor – Astronomy (celestial globes, sundials, astrolabes, quadrants, etc.).

Sixth Floor – Planetarium.

ENGLISCHER GARTEN QUARTER

* **Englischer Garten (English Garden) (LY)** – Not far from the city centre, this park, with its broad sweeps of tree-bordered lawn, its streams and its lake, was designed in the late 18C by **Friedrich Ludwig von Sckell** and the British-American scientist **Sir Benjamin Thompson**, Count von Rumford. It is particularly popular in summer, when an open-air beergarden seating 7 000 people is open near the **Chinese Tower** (Chinesischer Turm). From the **Monopteros**, a circular temple built on a knoll by Leo von Klenze, there is a fine view of the belfries in Munich's old town.

** **Bayerisches Nationalmuseum (Bavarian National Museum) (LY M⁵)** ⊘ – Maximilian II created this museum in 1885 with the aim of preserving Bavaria's artistic heritage. The 47 rooms on the ground floor offer a survey of Bavarian **arts and crafts** from the Great Invasions (5C and 6C) to the 19C, including silver and gold plate and religious statuary, tapestry, furniture, altarpieces and stained glass windows.

The Italian Renaissance is evoked in other sections by jewellery, costumes, bronzes, glazed earthenware, and pewter work.

On the first floor, ceramics and porcelain are exhibited, along with gold, silver and glassware. Everyday crafts – including a collection of Christmas cribs – are illustrated in the basement.

Staatsgalerie moderner Kunst (Modern Art Collection) (LY M⁶) ⊘ – In the west wing of the Haus der Kunst, built between 1933 and 1937 in the heavy, pompous "National Socialist" style.

The ground floor concentrates on "classic" modern art: Matisse, Picasso, Braque, Léger and Juan Gris represent Cubism and Fauvism; Kirchner *(Interior)*, Schmidt-Rottluff, Marc, Kandinsky and Beckmann (remarkable self-portrait of 1943) the different tendencies of German Expressionism. Examples of the Blauer Reiter and Die Brücke *(qv)* movements are shown with paintings from the Bauhaus (Feininger's *Halle Church*). Surrealism is present with Ernst, Miró, de Chirico and Dali; sculpture with Lehmbruch, Barlach, Giacometti and Mario Marini. The upper floor is reserved for late 20C art (Abstract Expressionism, Pop Art, Photorealism, Group Zero, CoBrA and Vasarely).

NYMPHENBURG

0 ____ 200 m

★★ NYMPHENBURG *time: half a day*

6km - 3 3/4 miles from the city centre, leaving Munich by the Marsstraße (JY). Plan of the conurbation in the current Michelin Red Guide Deutschland

The oldest part of the palace, once the summer residence of the Bavarian sovereigns, is the five-storey central pavilion, built by Barelli between 1664 and 1674 in the style of an Italian palazzo. The Prince-Elector Max Emmanuel, who reigned from 1679 to 1726, added two lateral pavilions on either side which were linked to the main building by arcaded galleries. At the same time he remodelled the central block, accentuating the verticals by the addition of pilasters. His successors, Karl-Albrecht (1726-1745) and Max III Josef (1745-1777), then constructed a semicircle of outbuildings and dependencies, which underlined the castle's resemblance to Versailles.

From 1701 onwards, the surrounding park too was enlarged under the direction of Carbonet and Girard, the pupils of Le Nôtre. The formal French gardens date from this period, as do the various park pavilions: Pagodenburg (1719), Badenburg (1721), Magdalenenklause (1728) and Amalienburg (1739).

★ **Palace** ⊘ – The splendid **banqueting hall**, a symphony of white, gold and pale green, was richly adorned with coloured stuccowork and frescoes by Johann Baptist Zimmermann and his son Franz. A musicians' gallery is placed beneath the high windows looking out over the park.

The rooms in the north wing of the central block – antechamber, bedroom, study – are panelled, with tapestry hangings and paintings displayed. Beyond this the north pavilion contains views of the castle and park in the early 18C.

The most fascinating room in the main block's south wing is the one devoted to a collection of **Chinese lacquer**. In the south pavilion, the apartments of Queen Carolina contain the famous **Gallery of Beauties** conceived by Ludwig I. Commissioned by the King to immortalize the most beautiful women of the epoch, these paintings were executed by the portraitist Josef Stieler (1781-1858).

★ **Park** – *See itinerary on Nymphenburg map.*
Most of the park can be seen from the top of the steps in front of the palace's main entrance. Below the steps, beyond the formal rectilinear flower gardens lined with white marble urns and the statues of gods, the Grand Canal, which ends in a waterfall, flows straight as an arrow away into the distance.

★★ **Amalienburg** ⊘ – This charming little hunting lodge by **Cuvilliés** is one of his most accomplished designs – a model for the many Rococo country pavilions which so delighted the Courts of 18C Germany. The simplicity and sobriety of the exterior is in vivid contrast with the extraordinary richness of the interior. Beyond the curious Kennel – a panelled central room surrounded by the quarters of hunting dogs – are the Blue Room and a beautiful bedchamber, with silver woodwork on a background of lemon yellow.

In the centre of the building is the **Hall of Mirrors** rotunda. Here the combination of blue walls and ceiling, silver stucco and wood-framed glass forms a marvellous ensemble. A Hunting Room, the Pheasant Room, and kitchens whose walls are tiled with blue Delft complete this masterpiece of Bavarian Rococo.

Badenburg – A luxurious heated swimming-pool, with a ceiling decorated by mythological motifs, is the centrepiece of this 18C bath-house. A dressing room, and an antechamber serving as games and rest room are also included in the pavilion.

Pagodenburg – The 18C taste for exoticism and the Far East is exemplified in the design of this octagonal tea-house. A drawing-room, a Chinese room and a boudoir occupy the first floor.

Magdalenenklause – A "hermitage" or folly built in the then popular style of "artificial ruins", this pavilion is dedicated to St Mary Magdalene.

Marstallmuseum und Porzellansammlung (Carriage Museum and Porcelain Collection) (M) ☉ – The museum is housed in the castle's former stables. Besides superb 18C and 19C harnesses, broughams, coaches, carts, sledges and sedan chairs used by the Wittelsbachs are on display. Note especially the coronation coach of the Emperor Karl VII, and the state coach and personal sleigh of Ludwig II, all of them equipped with quite incredible luxury.

Above the old stables, a series of rooms exhibits the **Bäuml Collection of Nymphenburg Porcelain**. Painted figurines by Franz Anton Bustelli, master modellist of the factory between 1754 and 1763, are particularly fine. The **reproductions in porcelain★** – miniature copies in extraordinary detail of paintings in the Alte Pinakothek – were commissioned by Ludwig I.

Naturkundemuseum „Mensch und Natur" ("Man and Nature" Natural History Museum) – *In the north wing of Nymphenburg palace.*
Despite a relatively restricted exhibition space ($2\,500m^2$ – $26\,910sq\,ft$), this museum contains an interesting and vividly illustrated account of the story of the Earth and the evolution of life upon it. Tableaux, films and electronic displays reconstruct the animal and plant kingdoms for museum visitors, within an ecological context. The museum, founded in 1990, has been designed particularly with younger visitors in mind.

★★ **Botanischer Garten (Botanical Gardens)** ☉ – Reputed to be among the finest and most richly stocked in Europe. A stroll through the Schmuckhof *(opposite the main building)*, the Spring Garden and the Rosery, past masses of rhododendrons shaded by pines and around the Alpine Garden by the Great Lake is not only a feast for the eyes but a horticultural lesson in itself. There are marvellous orchids among the tropical and subtropical species flowering in the greenhouses.

ADDITIONAL SIGHTS

Propyläen (Propylaea) (JY) – This imposing gateway by Leo von Klenze (1784-1864) was completed two years before the Munich architect died. Inspired by the Propylaea of the Acropolis, it stands on the west side of the Königsplatz (which is thus flanked on three sides by monuments in the classical style). The frieze represents the war of liberation against the Turks; Otto I of Wittelsbach, King of Greece from 1832 to 1862, is commemorated in a statue on the pediment above the Doric colonnade.

Museum Villa Stuck ☉ – *Leave by the Prinzregentenstraße (LY).*
Professor at the Munich Academy of Fine Arts from 1895 and one of the founding members of the Munich Secession, **Franz Stuck (1863-1928)** built this Jugendstil villa with an Italian influence after his own plans. The interior of the house is magnificent: it was Stuck himself who made the furniture, the panelling, the bas-reliefs and coffered ceilings, and some of the sculpture. Note also the famous canvases by the artist, including *The Guardian of Paradise* and *The Sin*. The museum also hosts temporary exhibitions.

★ **Münchner Stadtmuseum (City Historical Museum) (KZ M⁷)** ☉ – *In the stables of the old Arsenal.*
A collection of arms and armour is among the exhibits recalling the history of Munich. Do not on any account miss the **Moorish Dancers★★** (Moriskentänzer), ten carved wooden figures painted and gilded in 1480 by **Erasmus Grasser** *(ground floor)*. **Specialized collections** consecrated to the marionette theatre, the cinema, musical instruments, photography and brewing are also on view.

★ **Asamkirche (St. Johannes Nepomuk) (KZ)** – The church, built in 1733, is always referred to locally under the name of the men who constructed it, the Asam Brothers: Cosmas Damian Asam, who specialized in the painting of frescoes, and Egid Quirin Asam, sculptor and stucco-worker. The church's remarkable unity of style is due to the fact that the two brothers drew up the plans themselves, and both executed and supervised every stage of the work.

The design of the interior is strikingly harmonious. A curved gallery links the choir, the nave and the organ loft; above, supported on pillars, a second gallery is adorned with stuccowork and statues of angels or cherubim. The frescoed ceiling, lit by windows concealed behind mouldings, depicts episodes in the life of St John of Nepomuk.

Wittelsbacher Brunnen (Wittelsbach Fountain) (KY) – *Between the Lenbachplatz and the Maximiliansplatz.*
Adolf von Hildebrand *(qv)* built this neo-Baroque fountain in 1895 to mark the completion of a water canalization programme which provided the city with clean drinking water.

EXCURSIONS

Olympiapark ⊙ – *5km - 3 miles from the centre, via the Dachauer Straße (JY).*
Munich was host to the XX Olympic Games in 1972. The many swimming-pools, gymnasia, training fields and tracks, as well as an open-air theatre, a cycling circuit and an artificial lake which remain on the site are used today as a leisure centre by the people of Munich. The 1968 **Olympiaturm** (television tower) is no less than 290m - 951ft high. At the 190m - 623ft level *(lift)*, there is a terrace with **panorama★★★**, which offers an exceptional view over the city to the Bavarian Alps.

BMW-Museum ⊙ – *At Petuelring 130. 5km - 3 miles to the north, via the Schleißheimer Straße (JY) and the Lerchenauer Straße.*
This strange silver building shaped like a cup lies at the foot of the administration tower – which in no way detracts from the futuristic effect by being built in the form of four linked cylinders. The guided tour, which progresses in a spiral, retraces the history of the famous firm founded in 1916 and specialized in the construction of motorcycles and cars (Dixie-Roadster, 1929; R-32, 1923) – and, since the Second World War, of high-performance sports models and luxury automobiles.

★ **Tierpark Hellabrunn (Hellabrunn Zoological Gardens)** ⊙ – *6km - 3 1/2 miles from the city centre, leaving via the Wittelsbacherstraße (KZ). Plan of the conurbation in the current Michelin Red Guide Deutschland.*
Munich's zoo, laid out in 1911 on the east bank of the Isar, is at the same time a nature reserve. Its 5 000 inhabitants live in their natural habitat. See particularly the Elephant House (1913), the monkey reserve and the huge free-flight aviary, where the visitors are not separated from the birds.

★ **Bavaria-Filmstadt Geiselgasteig (Bavaria Film Studios)** ⊙ – *10km - 6 miles from the centre via the Hochstraße (LZ), the Grünewalderstraße and the Geiselgasteigstraße. Plan as above.*
The first film shot in these studios was made in 1919. Since then, the Bavaria Film Studios can pride themselves on a long line of successes in the great tradition of the cinema, including such famous features as *Cabaret, The Boat* and *Neverending Story.*
Once through the gates, the visitor is immediately backstage behind the cameras, free to ease himself into a space capsule, lower himself into a submarine, or sit astride a dragon. There are demonstrations of trick photography and special effects.

★ **Schloß Schleißheim** ⊙ – *15km - 9 miles to the north. Leave by the Schleißheimer Straße (JY).*
The so-called "new" castle (Neues Schloß), which was built between 1701 and 1727, extends majestically for 330m - 1 083ft in geometric precision with the strictly formal gardens laid out in long perspective by the Frenchmen Carbonet and Girard *(qv)*. The great staircase leads to the first floor State Apartments: a huge banqueting hall in dazzling white, and a Hall of Victory, adorned with paintings of battle scenes, gleaming with gold stucco. The princely apartments and galleries, now hung with 16C and 17C Dutch and Flemish paintings, are open to the public. On the ground floor, a second series of galleries has been opened beyond the music room.

Dachau Concentration Camp – *19km - 12 miles to the northwest.*
Nazi Germany's first concentration camp was organized near the pleasant, terraced town of Dachau on the orders of Heinrich Himmler in 1933. Originally designed for the detention of German political opponents of the Nazi regime, the camp was soon flooded by tens of thousands of deportees, the majority of them Jews of diverse nationalities. More than 32 000 died there – without counting the 6 000 Russian prisoners-of-war shot dead on the nearby SS firing range. The system was described by Joseph Rovan, one of the few who escaped from the camp, as "implacable, perverted, an organization that was totally murderous, a marvellous machine for the debasement and de-humanizing of man".

Ruins, Commemorative Monuments, Museum ⊙ – *Follow the signposting "KZ - Gedenkstätte".* A Jewish memorial, a Protestant commemorative sanctuary and a Catholic expiatory chapel in the form of an open tower have been built within the precincts of the old camp. The huts were razed, but two, complete with their interior layout, have been reconstructed. On the Appelplatz (roll-call square), where prisoners were forced to muster morning and evening whatever the weather, a monument has been erected by the International Community. Behind, outside the camp perimeter, is a Carmelite convent with a chapel which may be visited.

The Museum, which outlines the punitive penal system established there by the Nazis, is housed in the former camp administration buildings. Land surrounding the cremation ovens, outside the camp, has been turned into a park-necropolis. The bodies of other victims have been buried in the cemeteries of Dachau (Waldfriedhof) and Leitenberg, 2km - 1 1/4 miles to the northeast.

★ **Ammersee** – *Round tour of 116km - 72 miles – allow 4 hours.*
Lying at an altitude of 533m - 1 749ft, this lake of glacial origin is cradled in a pretty landscape of wooded hills. Swimming, sailing and **boat trips** can be enjoyed at small resorts such as Diessen and Herrsching. Enthusiasts of the Rococo style must not miss a visit to the abbey church at Andechs.

Follow the western lake shore to reach Dießen.

Dießen – The **church**★ (Stiftskirche) was built between 1732 and 1739 to replace a former monastery collegiate. The architect was J M Fischer, one of the most celebrated of the Upper Bavarian Baroque school. The delicacy of the white, gold and rose-pink stucco, the remarkable painting of the dome, the nave vaulting and the side altars contrasts vividly with the slightly theatrical character of the high altar, which was designed by François Cuvilliés.

The climb from Fischen to Andechs offers fine views of the lake.

★ **Andechs** – Crowning the Heiliger Berg ("holy hill"), this **Benedictine abbey** overlooks the Ammersee by more than 200m - 656ft. Its **church**★★ ☉, erected on a Gothic base, was remodelled as a Rococo building between 1751 and 1755. The architect J B Zimmermann (1680-1758), then at the height of his powers as a mature artist, was responsible both for the frescoes and the stuccowork. An elegant gallery, its balustrade decorated with painted panels evoking the history of the abbey, surrounds the main body of the church. The treatment of the vault frescoes, in various shades of pastel, shows an exceptional talent in the handling of colour.
A brewery, installed in the abbey outbuildings, produces an annual 70 000hl - 1 540 000 gallons of a very high quality beer.

Return to Munich via Hersching and Seefeld.

MÜNSTER★★

Nordrhein-Westfalen — Population 252 000
Michelin map 417 K 6
Local map under MÜNSTERLÄNDER WASSERBURGEN
Plan of the conurbation in the current Michelin Red Guide Deutschland

Münster, the historical capital of Westphalia, where the local lords used to stay in winter, lies in the middle of a wooded plain studded with castles and manor houses. The city, one of Germany's most important university centres, has been carefully restored to give full value to its many Gothic and Renaissance façades.

The Peace of Westphalia – This treaty, signed on 24 October 1648, ended the Thirty Years War. During the five years of negotiations, the Emperor shuttled between the plenipotentiaries of the Protestant states in Osnabrück *(qv)* and those from the Catholic states in Münster, where the documents were finally agreed. As a result, much of Germany was carved up, to the detriment of Imperial prestige. The treaty recognized or confirmed the cession to France of Alsace and the bishoprics of Metz, Toul and Verdun, guaranteed the independence of Switzerland and the Netherlands, and favoured the development of Prussia. Three religious faiths were recognized, the Calvinists receiving the same rights as the Lutherans.

SIGHTS

★★ **Dom (Cathedral)** (Y) – A squat building with two towers, two chancels and two transepts, this church is in the transitional style typical of Westphalia in the 13C.
Entering via the 16C south porch, the visitor sees that the inner door is surrounded by 13C statues and overlooked by a Christ in Judgement. A 16C statue of St Paul, patron saint of the cathedral, looks down from the pier.

Visit the interior anti-clockwise.

The wide central nave and its bays lie beneath rounded vaulting. The side aisles are very low. In the ambulatory there is a 1540 **astronomic clock**★ in which the hours are struck by metal figurines wielding hammers. The spectators' gallery, high up in the church, was painted by Tom Ring the Elder.
The Chapel of the Holy Sacrament, left of the entrance to the cloister, is **richly furnished**★ (note especially an 18C silver tabernacle, made by a craftsman in Augsburg). The cloister entrance is reached through the north transept crossing.

★★ **Treasury** (Domkammer) (**M²**) ☉ – *Off the cloister.* This is a modern building, blending perfectly with the structure of the cathedral, to which it is indirectly attached by the cloister.

MÜNSTER

M¹ Westfälisches Landesmuseum für Kunst und Kulturgeschichte	**M²** Domkammer
	R Rathaus

On the ground floor, fourteen 15C reliquary-busts of the prophets in copper and silver, the 11C head-reliquary of St Paul, together with a 13C Virgin – both of them in chased gold – surround the **Processional Cross** of the Chapter. And this, due to superimposed openings adjusted on the three levels, becomes the focal point of the whole treasure house. In the basement there is a fine collection of liturgical vestments (copes, stoles, chasubles), particularly from the 17C and 18C, and ritual items. In the centre stands a portable altar (12C) hung with a cloth embroidered in pearls.

Noteworthy on the first floor, amidst a collection of Gothic and Baroque statuary, is the 1520 **Altarpiece of St John**.

★ **Landesmuseum für Kunst und Kulturgeschichte (Fine Arts Museum) (YZ M¹)** ☉ – The medieval art of Westphalia lives on, thanks to the Gothic statuary of the cathedral and churches of Münster, a series of stained-glass windows in this museum, and the sculptures of Johann and Heinrich Brabender. There is a remarkable collection of **altarpieces**★★ by Konrad von Soest, Koerbecke and the Masters of Liesborn and Schöppingen. Flemish influence is noticeable in the works of the Tom Ring family (Ludger Tom Ring's painting was a precursor of the still-life). Interesting portraits of Luther and his wife are by Lucas Cranach. The Thirty Years War in Westphalia is evoked in one department; another exhibits 20C art.

★ **Prinzipalmarkt (YZ)** – Running in a semicircle to the east of the cathedral, this is the busiest – and at the same time the most historic – street in town. The elegant, gabled Renaissance houses, starkly restored in a style shorn of ornament, were once the homes of rich burghers. Under the arcades, attractive shops compete for space with restaurants and beer halls. The northern end of the street opens into the Bogenstraße, a wide space equally inviting for window-shoppers and strollers (the statue halfway up, a pedlar with his basket, is known as the Kiepernkerl).

Rathaus (YZ R) – The late 14C gabled façade of the town hall, with pinnacles and fine stone window tracery, is one of the most impressive examples of Gothic civic architecture.

★ **Friedenssaal** (Peace Hall) ⊘ – A former council chamber, named after the treaty. The Gothic and Renaissance woodwork is original and intact. At the far end, symbolic scenes hide the archive compartments. Behind the councillors' bench, the fine panelling is carved with niches containing figures, and there is a frieze in which the heads of eminent burghers can be distinguished. The paintings show rulers of the treaty's signatory countries: the Emperor Ferdinand III, Philip IV of Spain, the young Louis XIV of France, and their delegates. Note the beautiful 1520 wrought iron chandelier.

★ **Residenzschloß** (Y) – Once the Prince-Bishops' residence, this Baroque palace is now part of the university. The red brick of the elegant three-part façade is variegated with sandstone facings which enliven any monotony of style. At the back, surrounded by water, lies a park (Schloßgarten) with an adjoining botanical garden. This green space is continued south of the castle by the Rampart Walk (Wallpromenade), from which there is a view of the Aasee lake.

Lambertikirche (Y) – Groined vaulting over the centre nave and star vaults above the side aisles distinguish this Gothic hall-church. Its elegant perforated **spire★** (99m - 325ft), built in the 19C, crowns a tower from which hang three iron cages. It was in these that the bodies of the three Anabaptist leaders (chiefs of a sect advocating baptism for adults only) were exhibited after the movement was crushed in 1536.
By the chevet of the church is a fine guild-house with a gable end (1588).

Ludgerikirche (Z) – Modern stained glass windows (1961) illustrating the life of Jesus have been added to the well-lit chancel.

Erbdrostenhof (Z) – This palace, dating from 1757, was built with a majestic concave façade and a triangular forecourt.

★ **Westfälisches Museum für Naturkunde (Westphalian Museum of Natural Science)** ⊘ – *Sentruper Straße 285. Entrance signposted from the Hüfferstraße* (Y).
Departments of geology, palaeontology, mineralogy, botany and zoology, all beautifully laid out, offer a huge, panoramic survey of our environment and its evolution. Note especially the collection of naturalized birds. The highlight of the palaeontology department is the largest **ammonite★** ever found in the world. The displays in the **planetarium★** provide an excellent introduction to astronomy.

Mühlenhof-Freilichtmuseum (Open-Air Windmill Museum) ⊘ – *Signposted from the Hüfferstraße* (Y), *south of the Residenzschloß gardens.*
In a peaceful setting on the shores of the Aasee, a 1748 windmill and a large farm dating from 1619 are surrounded by such traditional rural features as a forge, a Westphalian chapel, different kinds of barn, a bread oven, a local well, etc.

EXCURSIONS

Telgte – *12km - 7 1/2 miles to the east on Route 51.*
A Marian pilgrimage worships a 1370 Pietà housed in an octagonal Baroque chapel in this small town. The local museum ("Heimathaus Münsterland") ⊘ nearby displays a folk art masterpiece on cloth, the **Lenten Veil★** (Hungertuch – 1623), which measures no less than 32m² - 344sq ft.

Freckenhorst – *26km - 16 miles to the east on Route 51.*
The **Collegiate Church★** (Stiftskirche) with its fortified façade, is a fine example of pre-Romanesque German architecture *(see Introduction)*. Note the magnificent **baptismal font★** in the north aisle, inscribed with the date of the church's consecration (1129). On a tomb in the crypt is the recumbent statue of Geva, the church's founder.
Fine twinned columns support the remaining (west and south) galleries of the cloister.

Ostenfelde – *36km - 22 miles to the east on Route 51.*
The graceful **Vornholz Castle★** (1666) stands in a rolling landscape forested with ancient oaks. Built on two islets, its tall, roofed main block flanked by two wings, this is a typical Münsterland "water castle" (Münsterländer Wasserburg – *see below*).

MÜNSTERLÄNDER WASSERBURGEN ★

WATER CASTLES OF MÜNSTERLAND – Nordrhein-Westfalen
Michelin map 417 K 3-8

The charming **Wasserburgen** ⊘ – literally "water castles" – are to be found all over the Münster region. Witness to the incessant fighting between rival nobles in order to protect their territories, they are built on the sites of temporary encampments set up by the Teutons. They first appeared in the 12C in the form of wooden strongholds erected on artificial hills ("Motten") which were protected at the base by a surrounding stockade or defensive wall and a moat full of water. The invention of firearms at the beginning of the 16C made this system of defence precarious, and it was replaced, little by little, with proper fortifications isolated still more by moats or lagoons.

MÜNSTERLÄNDER WASSERBURGEN

Many of these fortresses spread over two islands, joined by a bridge. The first isle, or "Vorburg", would be used for the outbuildings; the second, or "Hauptburg" for the dwelling. Subsequently, two separate influences could be detected in their design: that of the Weser Renaissance *(qv)* from the east, and that of the Dutch architectural school coming from the west. Their defensive character became less distinct over the centuries, and especially after the Thirty Years War (1618-1648). After that, virtual palaces set in formal gardens began to appear. In the 18C, a taste for the Baroque manifested itself in the treatment of façades and gateways. Such water-surrounded castles, situated in pleasant landscapes, fascinate still with their old-world charm. Descriptions of several of them are given below.

★ **Anholt** ⊙ – Surrounded by extensive English-style parkland, this moated castle (12-17C) is built around a square inner courtyard. Inside, note the Great Staircase in oak, the Knights' Room with its portrait gallery, a reception room adorned with Flemish tapestries, the Japanese and Chinese porcelains, and a second gallery displaying paintings mainly by the Dutch Old Masters.

Gemen ⊙ – The towers, battlements and buildings of this **castle** (15C, remodelled in the 17C) are grouped on a fortified islet which arises from beautiful, shaded stretches of water. The original keep was later crowned with a Baroque roof. Today, the castle is a youth centre.

★ **Hülshoff** ⊙ – The massive square towers of the outbuildings (first island) complement a **manor house** (second island) constructed in 1545. The brick and stonework manor is distinguished by gable ends and a turret with cupola and lantern. A neo-Gothic chapel was added in 1870. The poetess Annette von Droste-Hülshoff was born here in 1797 (small museum).

★ **Lembeck** ⊙ – The approach to this castle is impressive – a long perspective of driveway punctuated by a series of Baroque gateways and flanked by the arched entrances to various parts of the central complex. The monumental edifice spread over two islands today was built at the end of the 17C on the site of a 14C fortress. Huge towers with Baroque roofs stand at every corner. A few salons inside can be visited. The biggest (Großer Saal) is embellished with fine panelling and stuccowork.

Raesfeld – Picturesque 17C brick outbuildings, including a small church, still surround this castle. The main block (1643-1658), reduced to two wings, is joined to a tower whose spire and onion dome together are as tall as the tower itself.

★ **Vischering** ⊙ – The two parts of the **castle** are on two separate islands, surrounded by a high wall in a setting that is truly delightful. The semicircular "Hauptburg" was built by the Bishop of Münster in 1271. Subsequent modifications (addition of a central tower in 1550, and an overhang on the south side in 1620) have not noticeably altered the characteristically blunt, stocky silhouette.
Carved chests and cupboards are among the furniture of the period on display in the interior. Note the handsome chimneypieces framed in faience and, in the main hall, the impressive beams.
Not far from Vischering, 8km - 5 miles southeast of Lündinghausen, is the impressive 18C water castle of **Nordkirchen**, known as "Westphalia's miniature Versailles". This beautiful palace also houses a school of finance.

★ **Vornholz** – *See MÜNSTER: Excursions.*

Festivals and carnivals.
Germany's most important religious festivals and carnivals
are listed in the Calendar of events,
in the Practical Information section at the end of the Guide.

Sachsen-Anhalt – Population 34 000
Michelin map 418 M 19

In the Middle Ages, this town built at the intersection of several trade routes was so important that its annual fair rivalled that of Leipzig. Seat of a bishopric since 1028, Naumburg retains as evidence of its former prosperity and religious rôle a magnificent cathedral.

★★DOM ST. PETER UND PAUL
(CATHEDRAL)
Access by the Domstraße

This two-chancel church is a perfect example of the architectural evolution from Late Romanesque to Early Gothic. The nave and the east chancel were built in the former style at the beginning of the 13C. Ten years later, the western section was completed by a chancel already displaying certain Early Gothic features. The east chancel, under which there is still a Romanesque crypt, was itself transformed into a Gothic structure in the 14C.

Benefactors' statues,
Naumburg cathedral

West Chancel – The Master of Naumburg, sculptor of the celebrated **statues of benefactors★★★** deployed around the choir, undoubtedly took medieval sculpture in Germany to the summit of its glory. The individual personification of these figures, the profundity of their expressions, the overall impression of seriousness all add up to an exceptional effect of humanity and grandeur. The best known are those of the founders of the town, Margrave Ekkehardt and his wife Uta *(centre, right)*. The rood screen bears a series of haut-relief scenes representing the Passion, which were executed by the same studio.

ADDITIONAL SIGHTS

★ **St. Wenzel** – The proportions of this Late Gothic church are extraordinary: the nave, for instance, built between 1517 and 1523, is 11m long by 33m wide (36ft x 108ft). The 18C organ, which was played by Johann Sebastian Bach, is the work of Zacharias Hildebrand. There are two fine paintings by Cranach the Elder: *The Adoration of the Magi*, facing the choir, in which the artist himself is represented on the right (1522); and, on the right side of the choir, *The Blessing of the Children* (1529). In this painting, Katharina von Bora, the wife of Luther, is shown surrounded by her sons and daughters.

Markt – The town hall, a Late Gothic building erected between 1517 and 1528, has six gables. It stands in the middle of a cluster of 16C and 17C houses.

For a pleasant stroll in town
look for the pedestrian streets marked on the town plans.

Römische Villa in NENNIG★

Saarland
Michelin map 417 R 3 – 3km - 1 3/4 miles southeast of Remich

The foundations of this immense Roman villa ⊙ were excavated in 1852. Built on a splendid site overlooking the Moselle Valley in the 2C or 3C AD, the façade was no less than 120m - 394ft long.
The superb reception hall **mosaic★★**, in a fine state of preservation, measures 16m x 10m (52ft x 33ft). It comprises eight cartouches, framed by intricate geometric designs, illustrating gladiatorial combats between men and beasts in the arena of the Trier amphitheatre.

NEUBRANDENBURG

Mecklenburg-Vorpommern – Population 88 000
Michelin map 416 F 23

The town is not as new as its name suggests, since it was founded in 1248 at the behest of Margrave Johann von Brandenburg, its name serving to distinguish it from the previously existing town of Brandenburg. Built on an almost circular ground plan, criss-crossed by a grid-like network of streets, the town has retained its original layout. Its later development took place outside the town walls. When eighty percent of the old town was destroyed in 1945, the fortifications with their four unique gates were quite remarkably spared from damage, making them a principal point of attraction to the tourist, in conjunction with the Tollensesee close by.

SIGHTS

★★ Fortifications – Fifty years after the town was founded, it became obvious that huge defences were needed to protect it. Consequently, work was started on a 2 300m - 11/2 miles long town wall, over 7m - 23 ft in height, 1.40m - 4.6ft wide at the base and 0.60m - 1.8ft at the top. Boulders from the vicinity were used to build the wall, capped by several rows of bricks. Four gates ware incorporated into the wall, and these were closed every evening and only opened in return for payment. These remained the only access to the town right up to the middle of the 19C when a fifth opening was made to provide access to the station.

The gates are all of the same design. The main gate is inside the wall, and is connected with an outer gate via keep walls. Each gate constitutes an individual fortification. The outer gates were secured with portcullises. As if this weren't enough to secure the town, a semicircular battle tower with 4m - 13ft thick walls, the Zingel or circular wall, was erected 19m - 62ft away from the outer gate.

So that the town could be safely defended, 3-4 floor bastions, known as **Wiekhäuser**, were built into the town wall every 30m - 98ft. There were 53 of them in the 16C, 26 of which have been reconstructed. All the able-bodied citizens were called upon to maintain the Wiekhäuser, whilst defence of the gates was the duty of the four principal guilds: Bakers, Wool Weavers, Shoemakers and Blacksmiths.

"The Maids" – Nine terracotta sculpted female figures, all with long, stiffly pleated skirts, from beneath which their feet peep out, stand on the top of the Stargarder Tor, with their backs against the town wall. On the Neues Tor there are eight of them. No-one knows their connection with the gates. One historian may see them as the clever and foolish virgins of the Bible story, whilst another may interpret them as "Worshipping Figures", since their arms are help up in an attitude of prayer. They cannot be there to welcome visitors, since they are on the inside of the gates. They have managed to keep their secret, and so continue to fascinate.

Friedländer Tor – *Facing northeast.* This is the oldest gate, built just after 1300. The gate is 19m - 62ft high. On the outside it is possible to see the transition from the Romantic to the Gothic period, whilst the town side, built later, is entirely Gothic. The houses of the former keeper of the circular defence wall, the gate recorder and the tax collector are incorporated into the 48m - 157ft long wall between the main gate and the outer gate.

Stargarder Tor – *Facing south.* Built during the first half of the 14C. The body of the tower and the gable ends form a unit in which the perpen-dicular is emphasised by the nine terracotta figures. The outer gate is especially sumptuously decorated.

Treptower Tor – *Facing west.* Built before 1400. At 32m - 105ft, the highest of the gatetowers. Both the main gate and the outer gate are sumptuously decorated with brick tracery. On this High Gothic masterpiece, the out-side is for the first time more highly decorated than the inside, an expression of the town's desire to appear imposing.

Neues Tor – *Facing east.* Built after 1550. The Late Gothic structure features no fresh influences, but instead combines the decorative elements of the other three gates. The outer gate no longer exists.

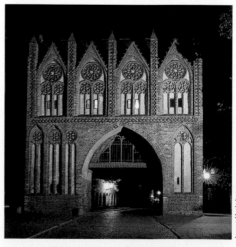

Neubrandenburg – Stargarder Tor

Jürgen Henkelmann

Fangelturm – *Facing northwest.* Of the two towers which provided reinforcement to the fortifications, only the 19m - 62ft high Fangelturm remains. It is 6.5m - 21.3ft in diameter with 2.3m - 7.5ft thick walls. The spire was added in 1845.

Marienkirche – The brick church, whose naves are of equal height and which was built at the end of the 13C, was seriously damaged in 1945. Nevertheless the eastern gable with its tracery is still impressive. The church is being renovated into a concert hall.

Johanniskirche ⊙ – The former 13C to 14C church of the Franciscan monastery is surprising due to its lack of symmetry, having only a single side aisle. The paintings with their plant motifs were produced in the 19C. The **Baroque altar** with its extravagant woodcarving depicts the crucifixion. The **Renaissance pulpit★** supported by a figure of Moses, which dates from 1598, is particularly worthy of note. It is made of limestone and displays alabaster reliefs (Christ, the Evangelists).

EXCURSIONS

Tollensee – This lake, which is 10.4km - 6.5 miles in length and almost 3km - 2 miles wide, lies to the south of the town, in the middle of an extremely attractive terminal moraine landscape. The western bank slopes steeply up to Brodaer woods.

★ **Feldberger Seenlandschaft** – *75km - 47 mile round trip.*
The road leads via **Burg Stargard**, whose castle ruins dominate their surroundings, to the town of **Woldegk** with its 5 windmills, to the south west of which lies a lovely hilly lake region. It is home to the rare old world otter, and also to the sea eagle, osprey and lesser spotted eagle. Woods, meadows, moors and lakes alternate attractively between Fürstenwerder and Feldberg. The former house of the writer **Hans Fallada** ("If you ever eat from a tin bowl") in **Carwitz**, which stands in an idyllic lakeside location, is now a memorial.

Neustrelitz – *27km - 17 miles to the south.*
The former residence of the Dukes of Mecklenburg Strelitz still bears witness today to their proud past. Visitors can admire the **Schloßpark★** with its graceful buildings and monuments, which was laid out in the 19C as an English country garden, the Orangerie with is remarkable Pompeii style **paintings★**, the Baroque **town church** (1768-1778) and the classical **Rathaus** which dates from 1841.

NÖRDLINGEN★

Bayern – Population 19 700
Michelin map 419/420 T 15
Town plan in the current Michelin Red Guide Deutschland

Lying along the Romantic Road, the fortified, former Imperial Town of Nördlingen was founded in the middle of the Ries Basin *(qv)* in the 2C BC. Its development throughout the centuries has been by concentric extension, witnessed by the street pattern and the ring of fortifications. Occupying an important position at the gates of the Bavarian Plateau, Nördlingen saw the armies of the French subdue the Austrians in 1796 and 1800.

SIGHTS

★ **St. Georgskirche** – *Am Obstmarkt.*
This late 15C hall-church, built in volcanic stone, is surmounted by a majestic, flamboyantly decorated tower 89m - 292ft high. Fan vaulting covers the interior in splendid style. The late 15C pulpit is reached via a corbelled staircase. At the high altar, the original Friedrich Herlin reredos (now in the local museum) has been replaced by a Baroque altarpiece, although the Crucifixion group and the statues of St George and **Mary Magdalene★** by Herlin still remain. Note the expression of the Saviour, moving in its sweetness and humility.

★ **Stadtmauer (Town Walls)** – The wall is reinforced by fortified gateways and watchtowers, the most elegant of which (Reisturm, Löpsinger Tor, Deininger Tor) are capped by helmet roofs. A walk around the parapet from the Berger Tor to the Alte Bastei and the Reimlinger Tor is recommended.

★ **Stadtmuseum (Local Museum)** ⊙ – The panels from the original altarpiece at St. Georgskirche were painted by Herlin, who was born in Nördlingen, between 1462 and 1477. Dedicated to the patron saint, the works display an extraordinary freshness of colour, particularly that representing women benefactors at prayer.

★ **Rieskrater-Museum** ⊙ – *Nest to the Stadtmuseum.*
The Nördlingen Giant Crater was formed approximately 15 million years ago when a **meteorite** hit the earth. Just imagine it – a giant stone sphere, 1km - 1/2 mile in diameter, leaves its orbit between Mars and Jupiter and hits the earth at a speed of

70 000km - 44 000 miles per hour, penetrating up to 1km - 1/2 mile into the rock! The energy of 250 000 Hiroshima atom bombs is released, and a wave of pressure and heat extinguishes all life within a range of 100 km - 62 miles. The heat generated by the impact is so great that the meteorite evaporates. A crater 14km - 9 miles in diameter is formed, which eventually extends to 25km - 16 miles due to all the rock that subsequently falls in. The crater, which was orginally 4km - 2.5 miles deep, is gradually filled in over the course of millions of years.

The Rieskrater-Museum, which is housed in a carefully restored 15C barn, attempts to give the general public an understanding of this scarcely imaginable phenomenon. An ambitious venture, which succeeds admirably using modern didactic methods (a slide show and videos to watch, stone to touch). There is even a lump of moon rock, which is on permanent loan to the museum from NASA.

EXCURSION

★ **Neresheim Abbey** – *19km - 12 miles to the southwest.*
The huge white buildings of the Benedictine abbey stand out in the largely undeveloped landscape east of the Swabian Jura. The abbey church (Klosterkirche), started in 1745 under the direction of Balthazar Neumann *(qv)*, was the last work of the great Baroque architect. Inside, the decorations painted in 1755 by Martin Knoller, admirably spaced, complement the exceptional size of the building.

NÜRBURGRING ★

Rheinland-Pfalz
Michelin map 417 O 4 – Local map under EIFEL

This motor-racing track, laid out over a stretch of wooded, undulating country, has taken the name of the Nürburg ruin *(see EIFEL)*, which stands inside its northern loop. The new circuit, opened in 1984, is used for such prestigious events as the World Championship for Sports Prototypes and the Nürburgring 24-hour Race for Touring Cars. The 4 1/2km - 3-mile lap includes 14 corners, with a height differential of 56m - 184ft. Aside from competitions and practice sessions, the circuits are open for normal use *(apply at the Information Bureau B258)*. The old northern loop is 20km - 12 miles long.

★ **Rennsportmuseum (Motor Racing Museum)** ⊙ – Many different models, some of them unique examples, recall the great days of motor sport and of the Ring. Note in particular a **Bugatti Type 35A** (1925), one of the cars responsible for the success of this famous make; a 1934 **K3 MG** with splendid lines; a **Mercedes-Benz W-196** single-seat Grand Prix racer capable of 171 mph (1954); and more recent Formula 1 types such as the Ferrari B3 (1973) and the 1976 McLaren M-23.
In the upstairs gallery, motor-cycling history starts off with the Belgian **FN** (1910), equipped with a shaft drive of which this company was the pioneer, and also a belt-driven **Stehermaschine-Anzani** of the same period. Dozens of other exhibits remind the spectator of the great variety of European production this century, before so many different makes disappeared.

NÜRNBERG

NUREMBERG – Bayern – Population 478 000
Michelin map 419/420 R 17
Plan of the conurbation in the current Michelin Red Guide Deutschland

Before the Second World War, Nuremberg was one of the most beautiful medieval cities in Germany. Whole blocks of half-timbered burgher's houses with embellished gables made a setting so typically "Germanic" that the city was chosen by the Nazi party for its huge annual rallies each September. Some of the buidings used for the rallies still stand in Luitpoldhain park in the southeast suburbs. It was in this "ideological capital" of the Reich that the notorious anti-semitic laws were promulgated in 1935; and it was here that the Allies held the war crimes trials when the fighting was over.

Today, with many of those medieval quarters completely destroyed, the old bronzecaster's and gold-beaters' town, together with its neighbour Fürth, is one of the main industrial centres of southern Germany. Machine tools, tractors, electrical and electronic apparatus, motorcycles, typewriters and toys are among its principal manufacturing products. Gastronomically, the Franconian capital offers a number of specialities: carp, either fried or poached in wine; Bratwurst (small grilled sausages); and **Lebkuchen** – fragrant gingerbread sold in attractive coloured boxes.

From the last Friday in November to the end of December the market place is occupied by the famous Christmas market, known locally as the **Christkindlesmarkt** (Christ-child Market). A wide choice of Christmas tree decorations and gifts are on offer.

The Golden Age – It was in the 15C and 16C that the fame of Nuremberg was at its height. At the crossroads of main trade routes and a shop window for Franconian craftsmanship, the city at that time rivalled Augsburg in importance. Nor was its renown purely commercial; literature and the arts and sciences flourished. The first German science university was founded in Nuremberg in 1526. At the same time the local humanist Willibald Pirkheimer (1470-1530) was translating texts from Latin and Greek. From 1510 onwards the locksmith Peter Henlein manufactured fob watches. In the world of art, the audacious sculptors **Veit Stoß** (c1445-1533) and **Adam Krafft** (c1460-1508); the talented bronze-caster **Peter Vischer the Elder** (1460-1529); **Michael Wolgemut** (1434-1519), the painter of altarpieces – and above all his pupil **Albrecht Dürer** – all profoundly influenced the German scene with their works.

Finally, the Nuremberg **Mastersingers** *(qv)* brought new life to German poetic form.

★★★GERMANISCHES NATIONALMUSEUM (JZ) ☉

Time: half a day

We recommend that you study the plan in the entrance hall to enable you to find your way around the extensive and varied areas.

The museum, which was founded in 1852, houses the largest collection of art and culture in the German-speaking world, with 1.2 million exhibits. 20 000 of its principal items are on permanent display. The heart of the truly massive and abundant museum is a former Carthusian monastery dating from the 14C. In 1993 it was extended across the Kartäusergasse into a generous museum complex. The Israeli artist Dani Karavan has reinterpreted the street itself, which is fully integrated into the complex, as a **street of human rights**.

The central section is the **picture gallery**, with works by **Albrecht Dürer** (*Portrait of Michael Wolgemut, Emperor Charles the Great in his Coronation Robes*), Hans Baldung Grien, Hans Holbein the Elder, Albrecht Altdorfer, Lukas Cranach the Elder *(Portrait of Martin Luther, Venus with Cupid the Honey Thief)*. Works by Veit Stoß *(The Archangel Raphael and The Young Tobias)*, Tilman Riemenschneider *(The Lamentation of Christ)* and Ignaz Günther are especially outstanding within the **sculpture collection**.

Many types of **decorative arts** are represented, including glass, ceramics, furniture and textiles. The gold and silversmith's work shoudt not be missed. The collection includes a notable quantity of medieval religious art treasures.

The **folk art collection** is impressive, with its many traditional costumes, rural household effects and exhibition areas featuring rooms decorated in rustic style. Not only children find the toys and doll's houses section (including one dating from 1693) fascinating. The collection of ancient musical instruments, with the largest collection in the world of old pianos, is extremely varied and extensive.

The most noteworthy of the very many scientific instruments is the so-called **Behaim terrestrial globe**, dating from 1492 to 1493, which is the oldest surviving depiction of the earth in globe form. In addition to the prehistoric and ancient collection, the museum also boasts a collection of historical **arms and hunting pieces** and a medical history collection, which includes complete sets of apothecary's equipment and medical and pharmaceutical instruments. Further exhibits includes examples of work produced by the trades and guilds.

There is an extensive *graphic section* with 300 000 exhibits, including miniatures, freehand drawings and printed graphics. The *coin room* contains 60 000 coins and around 20 000 medals, together with seal and coinage stamps.

The Germanisches Nationalmuseum complex also houses the **Industrial Museum**, which is linked with the Bavarian Industrial Institute. Its exhibits include examples of craftsmanship, commercial art and design dating from Antiquity right up to the 20C.

OLD TOWN *time: half a day*

⌁ **Dürerhaus (Dürer's House)** (JY) ☉ – This (restored) 15C burgher's house with jutting eaves lies at the base of the fortifications. Dürer bought it in 1509 and lived here until his death in 1528. The interior, soberly furnished, gives some idea of the life of the artist. Apart from eight sculptures in wood on the second floor, the works on view are copies.

Burg (Castle) (JY) ☉ – Symbol of the city, the castle stands proudly on a sandstone outcrop a little way to the north. The original **castle of the Burgraves** (Burggrafenburg), almost completely destroyed in 1420, had been completed in the 12C by the part known as the **Kaiserburg**; its appearance today dates from the 15C and 16C. From the outside terrace or the **Sinwellturm**, a 30m - 98ft high keep, there is an exceptional **view★** of the steeply sloped roofs and belfries of the old town. In an adjoining courtyard, the well *(under cover inside the building)* is impressive with its 53m - 174ft depth.

Among the dependencies, note particularly the two-storey Romanesque **Palatine Chapel**, which has a special Imperial Gallery from which the Emperor could survey his court assembled below.

* **Stadtbefestigung (Fortifications)** – Completed in the mid-15C, these have – uniquely for a large town in Germany – remained practically intact. They comprised an inner and an outer ring (Zwingermauer), the ramparts of the former with a covered parapet walk. A wide dry moat (in which today modern avenues run) lay outside the latter. No less than 67 defensive towers still exist. Among them are the four **Great Towers**, dating from the 16C and protected by colossal shells of cannon-proof masonry, sometimes 6m - 20ft thick (Frauentor – **KZ**, Spittlertor – **HZ**, Neutor – **JY**, Laufertor – **KY**).

The most interesting sector lies between the Kaiserburg and the Spittlertor *(west side)*. An instructive half-hour **walk** starts from the castle gardens (Burggarten) *(outside, below the Kaiserburg)*. From the ramparts it is possible to reach the watch path, which can be followed as far as the Neutorzwinger. Continue inside the ramparts. The Pegnitz river is crossed via a suspension footbridge beside the fortifications, before the promenade is concluded, once more on the outside (there is an attractive view of the castle from this point).

Stadtmuseum Fembohaus (Fembo Municipal Museum) (JY M²) – The museum is housed in a sandstone Renaissance mansion with a scrolled gable embellished by cornucopiae and obelisks. It is concerned with the history of Nuremberg, and in particular the homelife of the town's gentry between the 16C and the 19C.

* **Sebalduskirche (JY)** – A church with two chancels, built in the 13C and 14C. The sobriety of the west front, which is plain, with two Romanesque doorways framing the projecting chancel, is in vivid contrast with the huge Gothic east chancel, intricately worked and adorned with statues and pinnacles. Inside, the Romanesque and transitional Gothic western section (central and side aisles) is easily distinguished from the radiating High Gothic style of the east chancel and its ambulatory.

C   Schöner Brunnen
E   Frauenkirche

Works of Art ★★:

1) St Peter Altarpiece (1485), painted on a gold background in the Wolgemut studio.
2) Richly decorated bronze baptismal font (Gothic, c1430), including a hearth – the oldest work cast in bronze in Nuremberg.
3) St Catherine (1310).
4) St Sebald (1390).
5) The Emperor Heinrich II (1350).
6) The Virgin Mary in Glory (1420).
7) St Sebald's tomb. The Gothic shrine is part of a bronze display shelf by Peter Vischer (1519), supported by dolphins and snails and adorned with a host of statuettes. On the side panels, St Sebald is represented, and the artist himself in working clothes.
8) A Crucifixion group (1520) by Veit Stoß.

F Heilig-Geist-Spital	**M³** Spielzeugmuseum
M² Stadtmuseum Fembohaus	**M¹** Verkehrsmuseum

9) From the studio of the same artist: (above) Christ Transfigured and Mater Dolorosa (wood); (below) The Last Supper, The Mount of Olives and Christ Taken Prisoner (bas-relief in stone). Both groups date from 1499.

10) The Bearing of the Cross, by Adam Krafft (1506).

11) (Outside the church) Funerary monument of the Schreyer family: the Passion and The Resurrection, by Adam Krafft.

A fine series of **stained glass windows** (14C and 15C) illuminate the east chancel.

★ **Schöner Brunnen (Beautiful Fountain)** (**JY C**) – This 14C Gothic fountain in the old market place is one of the best-known sights of Nuremberg. Comprising 40 separate figures arranged in the form of a pyramid, the structure is 19m - 62ft high. At the top, Moses is surrounded by the prophets; around the base are the seven Electors and a series of nine Old Testament and medieval heroes: three forefathers, three Jews and three Christians. The figures decorating the fountain today are copies.

★ **Frauenkirche** (**JY E**) – A Gothic church on the east side of the market, built on the site of a destroyed synagogue, this sanctuary was erected during the reign of the Emperor Karl IV and served as a court chapel (1352-1361). The gable, with its pinnacles, niches and small oriel window, was designed by Adam Krafft (early 16C).

Dating from the same period, the clock above the balcony attracts visitors each day at noon, when a series of jacks appear to strike the hour. These colourful metal figures (Männleinlaufen) represent the seven Electors coming to swear allegiance to the Emperor after the enactment of the Golden Bull (qv) in Nuremberg in 1356.

The roof above the main body of the church, which is almost square in plan, is supported by four massive columns. On the north wall of the building is Adam Krafft's **Peringsdorffer Epitaph** (a robed Madonna), which dates from 1498. The **Tucher Altar** in the chancel, garnished with human figures, is a masterpiece of the Nuremberg school of painting: the triptych (c1440) depicts the Crucifixion, the Annunciation and the Resurrection.

Spielzeugmuseum (Toy Museum) (JY M³) ⊙ – *Karlstraße 13-15*. The museum, housed in a 17C burgher's house, illustrates the important role played by Bavaria, and Nuremberg in particular, in the intricate skills of miniaturism. Dolls'-houses, tin soldiers, clockwork toys, and model cars, railways and aeroplanes here will delight children and adults alike.

Heilig-Geist-Spital (Hospital) (JKY F) – This 14-15C building, spread over two wide arches, spans a branch of the Pegnitz. Its graceful corbelled tower, and the oriel window embellishing the façade, can be seen from the Museumsbrücke. The central courtyard *(reached from an islet upstream)*, with its wooden galleries above wide sandstone arches, recalls a rich patrician's mansion of times gone by.

Banks of the Pegnitz – Parts of the old city still standing can be seen from here. Those crossing the Maxbrücke (**JY 90**) enjoy an attractive **view** of the ancient, half-timbered wine hall (Weinstadel) and its flanking tower, together with the Henkersteg covered footbridge.

★ **Lorenzkirche (JZ)** – A magnificent rose window enlivens the west face of this 13-14C Gothic church. The impressive hall-type chancel was added in the 15C. Inside *(enter via the south door)*, once in the nave, the visitor is compelled by two outstanding works of art: the 1420 rood-beam Crucifix, with delicate medallions fashioned from its outer ends; and Veit Stoß's **Annunciation**★★ (Engelsgruß, 1517-18), which is suspended from the chancel vaulting. Marvellously sculpted in wood, the Virgin Mary and the Angel appear to float in the interior of a circular space surrounded by six medallions depicting the other Joys of the Virgin after the Annunciation.

Left of the high altar, a Gothic **ciborium**★★ by Krafft (1493-95) rises to the level of the vaulting. In the lower part, the sculptor himself is represented supporting the balustrade.

The ambulatory is lit by superb stained glass windows from the workshop of the Alsatian Peter Hemmel of Andlau, notably that representing the Tree of Jesse (1487, *second on the right, starting from the central window*).

Verkehrsmuseum (Transport Museum) (JZ M⁴) ⊙ – The chief attraction in the **Railway Department**★ is the replica of the very first German train, drawn by an Adler locomotive, which linked Nuremberg and Fürth in 1835. There are a great many scale models. Note also the **postal section**, where there is a fine collection of postage stamps. On the far side of the Sandstraße, all kinds of railroad vehicles, ancient and modern, are on display in a special hall.

EXCURSIONS

Hersbrucker Alb – *Round tour of 109km - 68 miles – allow half a day. Leave on the Sulzbacherstraße (**KY**), then take the motorway A9 in the direction of Bayreuth, leaving at the Plech exit.*

★ **Neuhaus an der Pegnitz** – This charming locality comes suddenly into view after a bend in the road, with the tall tower of Burg Veldenstein dominating the town.

Continue following the course of the Pegnitz in the direction of Hersbruck. The valley is steeply enclosed, overlooked here and there by tall, pointed crags.

Hersbruck – A busy, bustling town, situated at a point where the valley of the Pegnitz opens out. Continue *(direction Happurg)* to the river bridge, from which, looking back, there is a fine view of the Wassertor fortified gate and the huddled roofs of the ancient quarter.

Return to Nuremberg, taking road no B 14.

Erlangen – *17km - 10 1/2 miles to the north.*
This residential town of the Baroque period, with its rows of uniform houses, was one of the places where the French Huguenots settled. The Protestant church marks the centre of the quarter built for them. Sharing with Nuremberg the functions of a university city, Erlangen was the birthplace of the physicist **Georg Ohm** (1789-1854), who formulated the law relating to the resistance of electrical circuits. In an early 18C **English garden** behind the castle stands the strange **Fountain of the Huguenots**, built by the French in 1706 as a gesture of thanks to their protector, the Margrave of Bayreuth.

OBERSTDORF★★

Bayern – Population 11 000
Michelin map 419/420 X 14

The proximity of the Allgäu chain, one of the most popular with mountaineers, has led to the formation of a climbing school at Oberstdorf. Within easy reach are the Mädelegabel (2 645m - 8 676ft), the Hochvogel (2 593m - 8 505ft) and the Nebelhorn.

★★ **Nebelhorn** ⊙ – *1 1/2 hours Rtn, of which 30 minutes are by cable car and chairlift.* From the summit at 2 224m - 7 295ft, there is a splendid **panorama★★** extending from the Zugspitze (qv) in the east to the Säntis (the Swizz Appenzell Alps) in the west. In clear weather, beyond the bold outlines of the Allgäu itself, even the snows of the Bernese Oberland can be seen.

EXCURSIONS

★★ **Breitachklamm** ⊙ – *6.5km - 4 miles to the southwest, plus a one and a half hour walk Rtn. (Recommended also in winter, when fantastic "curtains" of ice are formed.)* In the lower gorge, galleries lead down to a cutting with sheer, polished walls, where the turbulent mountain stream has carved a course 100m - 300ft deep into the bedrock. At the foot of this path it is possible to turn back and re-mount by the long series of stairways that lead to the upper gorge (which is, however, less impressive). To return to Oberstdorf without a car, leave the gorge path at the top of these stairways. Walkers will then arrive at the Walserschanze, on the Kleinwalsertal road, from which there is a frequent bus service to the resort.

★ **The Kleinwalsertal** – *17km - 10 1/2 miles – allow 1/2 hour.* The name identifies a high valley of the Breitach river, a mountain area some 100km² - 38sq miles in size, which was settled in the 13C by the **Walsers** – emigrants of Germanic origin from the Upper Valais. Cut off from the rest of the Vorarlberg by the peaks of the Allgäu, the Walsers found themselves Austrian subjects when national frontiers were established in 1453, although such culture and traditions as they had were oriented exclusively towards Germany.
In 1891 the area was granted a special status whereby, still under Austrian sovereignty, it was nevertheless economically regarded as part of Germany.
Today the Kleinwalsertal has Austrian police, German customs, a German postal service but Austrian stamps, and the only legal tender is the German mark. Until a modern road was built in 1930, the valley remained isolated and the Walsers, like other hardy pioneers, retained a reputation of grim individualism and dourness of character – traits still reflected in the sombre buildings of their scattered homesteads. Having passed through the resorts of **Riezlern** and **Hirschegg**, tourists can turn down the steep hill at the entrance to **Mittelberg** that leads to the hamlet of Bödmen, which is interesting for its traditional Valaisian chalets.

ODENWALD★

Bayern and Hessen
Michelin map 417 R 10-11

A popular excursion for the inhabitants of big cities nearby, this huge natural park lies between the Rhine, the Main and the Neckar, undulating and rural to the west, forested and with steeper hills east of the Mömling river.

EXCURSION FROM MILTENBERG

92km - 57 miles – allow 4 hours

★ **Miltenberg** – A remarkable row of half-timbered houses lines the main street leading to the **Marktplatz★**. This small town is overlooked by the wooded heights bordering the final curve of the Main.

★ **Eulbach Park** ⊙ – A romantic place, with ruins, Roman remains, a lake – and an adjoining reserve where European wild oxen (bison) can be seen.

Michelstadt – Ancient houses, a flowered 16C fountain, and the town hall **façade★**, topped by a very steep roof flanked by two oriel windows, combine to form a striking ensemble in the market place. Follow the road beside the town hall and turn right into the Einhardtspforte alley: the **Odenwald-Museum** ⊙ (rural activity, craftwork) is housed in a fine group of half-timbered buildings, the former **municipal cellars** (Städtische Kellerei) around an ancient courtyard.

Leave Michelstadt to the south in the direction of Erback. Shortly after Hetzbach, turn left to Kailbach and Amorbach. The road winds through the hills and wooded valleys.

★ **Amorbach** – On the eastern slopes of the Odenwald, Amorbach is dominated by two pairs of belfries, those with red stone courses belonging to the former **abbey church**★ (Abteikirche) ⊙.
This was built between 1742 and 1747, respecting the plan of the Romanesque building which preceded it. Even the old towers were left, the architect simply adding a Rococo sandstone façade. Note the **chancel grilles**★, the Rococo pulpit and the 1782 organ.
The abbey **library**★ has rich Baroque decorations (1789-99). The neo-Classic ornamentation in the **Green Room**★ is a rare feature for a German abbey.

OLDENBURG

Niedersachsen – Population 145 000
Michelin map 415 G 8
Town plan in the current Michelin Red Guide Deutschland

Oldenburg is a widespread, open town chiefly concerned with agricultural shows and the processing of foodstuffs produced in the fertile hinterland where market-gardening, horticulture, cattle raising and horse breeding predominate. The river port is linked to the North Sea by the Hunte, a tributary of the Weser, and to the Netherlands by a coastal canal (Küstenkanal). From the Lappan (tower) in the north to the Lambertikirche in the south, a pedestrian zone now follows the plan of the medieval city centre.

★ **Schloßgarten (Castle Park)** – A mild, moist coastal climate has encouraged in this landscaped garden the growth of magnificent trees and shrubs such as rhododendrons and tulip trees. From the weeping willows on the lake shore there is an attractive view of the towers of the Lambertikirche.

Landesmuseum für Kunst und Kulturgeschichte (Regional Art and History Museum) ⊙
– The museum, housed in the former seat of the counts and grand dukes of Oldenburg, was built in the 17C and remodelled in the 18C and again the 19C.
Rembrandt's *Angel in the House of Tobias* is among the Old Masters in the state rooms on the first floor. There is also a pleasant series of **small pictures** *(Idylls)* by Johann Heinrich Wilhelm Tischbein (1751-1825), the most prominent painter of this name thanks to *Goethe in the Roman Countryside*, which hangs in the Städel Museum, Frankfurt *(qv)*.
On the top floor are reconstructions: fine 16C and 18C peasant interiors from northern Germany; a late 18C pharmacy.

★ **Stadtmuseum Oldenburg** ⊙ – Interesting here are rooms from the villas Francksen (1877) and Jürgens (1863), furnished and decorated in the fashionable styles of the 19C and early 20C.

Augusteum ⊙ – *Elisabethstraße 1.*
Works by painters from the Worpswede colony *(qv)* are on show here along with such German Expressionists as Erich Heckel. Among the Surrealists, note Franz Radziwill – who classes himself as a "symbolic realist".

Landesmuseum, Oldenburg

Staatliches Museum für Naturkunde und Vorgeschichte (Natural History Museum) ⊙
– *Damm 40-44.*
An interesting survey of the fauna found in North Germany's most typical regions:
mammals, fish, birds and environment; plant civilizations, forest and marsh eco-
systems. There is a model of a sea-wall organization to protect the low-lying coastal
regions from high tides. In the prehistoric department 2 400-year-old bodies found
preserved in the peat (Moorleichen) always attract attention.

EXCURSIONS

Cloppenburg – *31km · 19 miles to the south.*
In this town the **Museumsdorf★** ⊙ comprises 15ha · 37 acres of farms, peasant houses
and craft workshops in local style laid out around a church and a pond. In the **squire's
house** (Burg Arkenstede) is a most attractive collection of furniture and decorative
objects.

★ **Steindenkmäler von Visbek (Megalithic Monuments)** – *38km · 24 miles to the south.*
In this group collectively known as "The Intended", the **Bride** (Visbeker Braut) is a
collection of granite blocks arranged in a rectangular pattern in a clearing that
measures 80m x 7m (262ft x 23ft).
The **Groom** (Visbeker Bräutigam) comprises a dolmen, considered as a sacrificial altar
(Opfertisch), and, again, an alignment of 80 blocks in a rectangle 108m x 10m
(354ft x 33ft). At the western extremity of the site a funerary chamber recalls – it is
thought – the dwellings of this period. The site is 30 minutes' walk, there and back,
from the Engelmannsbäke inn.

OSNABRÜCK

Niedersachsen – Population 150 000
Michelin map 415 J 8
Town plan in the current Michelin Red Guide Deutschland

Lying between the Teutoburger Wald and the Wiehengebirge heights, Osnabrück
developed around two separate centres: in the 9C the Old Town spread from the ancient
market and the episcopal quarter; and from the 11C onwards, a New Town proliferated
around the Johanniskirche. When they united within a single city wall (c1300), Osnabrück
became an important commercial centre.
The all-important linen trade has now been supplanted by metallurgy (automobile
coachwork; cables) and paper mills.

Before the Peace in 1648 – Preliminaries to the Peace of Westphalia started in
Osnabrück between the Emperor and the Protestant belligerents (Sweden and the
Lutheran Princes of Germany). On the other side, the Roman Catholic powers negotiated
with the Emperor in Münster. News of the treaties' final signature was announced in
Osnabrück on 25 October 1648 to a crowd, at first incredulous and then bursting into a
spontaneous hymn of thanksgiving.

SIGHTS

Rathaus ⊙ – This early 16C building had to be restored after the Second World War,
but still retains its Gothic look beneath a wide pavilion roof. The peace of 1648 was
announced from its steps. The statue of Charlemagne, above the entrance, is
surrounded by the effigies of eight other Emperors and Kings.

★ **Friedenssaal** (The Peace Chamber) – The hall in which the peace talks were held is
adorned with portraits of the heads of state and their delegates. The floor and ceiling
have been rebuilt; the carved wooden seats and the chandelier are authentic and date
from 1554. Among the gold plate in the **Treasury** is the priceless 14C Kaiserpokal
(imperial goblet).

Marienkirche – A 14C Gothic hall-church which, with its elegant transverse gables,
closes off the northern end of the Marktplatz. Its most interesting work of art is the
early 16C **Altarpiece of the Passion★**, originally from Antwerp.

Dom St. Peter – The squat outline of this 13C Transitional Gothic church is
distinguished by large towers differing both in shape and size. The north face
boasts a fine Romanesque embellishment of blind arcades and cornices. The
interior is equally unusual, with a flat chevet and squared-off ambulatory. The
chapels leading off this contain a few works of art, notably a 15C Pietà and a 16C
stone Crucifixion.
The ogive vaulting in the nave is rounded; from the triumphal arch hangs an early 13C
Crucifix. There is a good view of the two towers from the asymmetrical cloister,
entered via the south aisle.

Johanniskirche – This Gothic hall-church, again dating from the 13C, served as a parish church for the New Town. Every architectural and decorative effect has systematically been reduced to the basic minimum. The dark wood **altarpiece** (high altar: scenes of the Passion) was carved in 1512. Outside, the long, narrow cloister once served as a burial place.

EXCURSIONS

★ **Tecklenburg** – *23km - 14 miles to the southwest. About 30 minutes. Leave the car in the park at the entrance to the town.*
Famous for its half-timbered houses and its position on the crest of the Teutoburger Wald, this is a very popular small town. Make for the main square and then head west, through the Legge gateway, to the oldest part, at the foot of the **castle**. Of this, nothing remains but a monumental Renaissance gateway and a lookout tower.

OTTOBEUREN★★★

Bayern – Population 7 300
Michelin map 419/420 W 14

Ottobeuren abbey, the jewel of German Baroque, stands in a small town surrounded by pleasant, hilly country, with the dramatic outline of the Allgäu in the background.

The Climax of the Baroque Style – Founded in 764, the Benedictine abbey prospered from the start, when its patron, Charlemagne, granted it extensive rights. The early 16C saw one of the first printing presses working here. Soon afterwards, a school was established whose fame spread far beyond Bavaria.
In the 18C the abbey was totally transformed into a Baroque style mingling the influences of Salzburg (rounded transept arms), the Vorarlberg school (dividing columns) and Rome (domes). In 1748, Johann Michael Fischer, the great architect of southern Germany, put the finishing touches on what was to be his masterpiece. But in the realms of Rococo decoration, the names of Johann Jakob Zeiller and his cousin Franz Anton Zeiller must be associated with his (for the frescoes), and also that of Johann Michael Feuchtmayer (stuccowork and statues). Under their direction, a number of German and Italian artists helped with the church's interior ornamentation.
Secularized in 1802, the abbey was re-established as a priory in 1834 and regained its former status in the Benedictine Order in 1918.

TOUR *time: 1/2 hour*

★★★**Klosterkirche (Abbey Church)**
⊙ – The squat outside appearance of the church *(illustration p 27)* offers no clue to its actual size. The towers are 82m - 272ft high; the length of the nave is 90m - 295ft; and the transept is no less than 60m - 200ft wide. It is in fact an enormous building, with an overall length outside of 480m - 1 575ft. The secret of course lies in its perfect proportions (and it is here that the theory of certain German art critics can be tested: that the exterior of a Baroque church has no intrinsic value, but serves only to reflect in its arrangement of masses the powerful influences of the interior).
Once inside *(photograph see over)*, the visitor is struck by the luminosity of the nave: this astonishing church, in defiance of tradition, being oriented north-south, the light effects are often unexpected – particularly when the sun's rays slant low, in early morning and evening.

Interior view of Ottobeuren abbey church

CESA, Marburg

270

The colours are harmonious. Half-tones of rose, amber, violet and ochre predominate, while the vault frescoes adopt warmer tints. In the chancel, relatively shadowed, more sombre shades complement gold ornamentation and the patina of natural wood.

Transept Crossing (Vierung) – The transept – being angled of course east-west – could in fact be a church in itself. Every architectural element derives from the flattened central dome. Johann Michael Fischer has even furnished the crossing piers with cut-off corners. Noteworthy here are the altars of St Michael, patron of the Ottobeuren region and of the Empire; of the Saintly Guardian Angels; of St Joseph and of St John the Baptist. But the most interesting works are the pulpit and, opposite, a group above the font representing the baptism of Christ himself, the work of the sculptor Johann Joseph Christian. Paving designed by Johann Jakob Zeiller is based on the motifs of the cross, the circle and the star. Zeiller also painted the grandiose composition embellishing the interior of the cupola, The Miracle of Pentecost.

Chancel (Chor) – At the entrance, the small altar of the Holy Sacrament is surmounted by a much venerated 12C Saviour, surrounded by stars symbolizing the sovereignty of the universe.

The high altar glorifies the Holy Trinity. At the foot of the reredos columns are statues of St Peter and St Paul; of St Ulrich, Bishop of Augsburg and patron saint of Swabia; and of St Konrad, Bishop and patron saint of the nearby diocese of Constance.

The walnut **choir stalls**★★ (1764) form, with the organ loft, a lovely composition. The backs of the stalls are decorated with gilded limewood bas-reliefs by Johann Joseph Christian depicting Biblical scenes and events in the life of St Benedict.

Karl Joseph Riepp (1710-1775), a pupil of Silbermann who worked for a long time in Burgundy (churches at Dijon, Beaune and Besançon), built the chancel **organ**★★ (1766). The instrument's musical and decorative properties, already impressive, were supplemented in 1957 by a new "Marienorgel", installed in the same loft.

Klostergebäude (Abbey Buildings) ⊘ – These were constructed between 1711 and 1731. They include an abbatial palace (Prälatur), with the usual state apartments and an Emperor's Hall, together with such luxuries as a theatre and a magnificent library.

PADERBORN

Nordrhein-Westfalen – Population 123 000
Michelin map 417 K 10
Town plan in the current Michelin Red Guide Deutschland

This old Hanseatic town, an important stage on the commercial and strategic route linking Flanders and Saxony, was one of the first episcopal sees of Westphalia (895). Almost one hundred years before, in 799, it was the site of a meeting between Charlemagne and Pope Leo III which sealed the union between the papacy and the western Empire. Each year in July, the town commemorates the transfer in 836 from Le Mans, France, to Paderborn of the relics of St Liborius, who later became the town's patron saint.

SIGHTS

★ **Dom (Cathedral)** – A massive tower, pierced with many Romanesque bays, overlooks the church, most of which dates from the 13C.

The entrance porch (Paradiesportal) is on the north side, where the doors are flanked by statues of bishops and saints (among them St Julian, the first Bishop of Le Mans), with the Virgin (c1250) above on the pier.

The 13C interior, modelled on Poitiers cathedral, demonstrates the evolution from Romanesque (in the western part of the huge hall) to Gothic (in the east). Off the north chancel is a small atrium with three equal aisles and some arches dating back to the year 1000. The crypt, reached from the transept, houses the relics of St Liborius.

Cloister (entrance via the atrium) – Note the funerary chapel of the Westphalian Counts, with a graceful Gothic altarpiece (1517), and the amusing "Three Hares Window". The animals, visible from the outside only, each have a pair of ears and yet there are only three ears in all.

Bartholomäuskapelle – A small Romanesque hall-chapel, built apart, a little way north of the main structure, by Byzantine masons in 1017. The slender columns with ornate capitals in Late Corinthian style support a domed vaulting.

Diözesanmuseum ⊘ – The attractive interior is the setting for this important collection of religious art from the 10C to 20C. The fine **Virgin of Bishop Imad**★ (1050) is outstanding. Also on display are two small portable altars of Roger von Helmarshausen (c1100), and the 1627 St Liborius shrine.

Rathaus – A monumental 1616 building with three gables, of which the ram's-horn scrollwork (Late Renaissance) recalls the Weser style of architecture (qv).

Paderquellen (The Pader Springs) – Below the cathedral, more than 200 springs bubble from the ground, merging to form streams strong enough to turn a water-wheel, before flowing into the Pader river.

PASSAU★★

Bayern − Population 50 000
Michelin map 420 U 24

Passau, a frontier town between Bavaria and Austria and known as the Town of the Three Rivers, lies in a marvellous **setting**★★ at the junction of the Inn, the Danube (Donau) and the small river Ilz. The old town, with its Baroque churches and patrician houses, lies crowded onto the narrow tongue of land separating the Inn and the Danube. Northwards, on the far bank of the Danube, rises the wooded bluff on which the Oberhaus fortress is built.

Passau's cultural and economic influence on eastern Bavaria was reinforced in 1978, when a new university was opened. In summertime, the European Weeks attract a large number of music − and theatre − lovers.

A Powerful Bishopric − The see was founded in the 8C by St Boniface, the English-born "Apostle of Germany" *(qv)*. By the end of the 10C it had become so powerful that it rivalled that of Salzburg. In 1217 the bishops were created by Princes of the Empire. Until the 15C the diocese was so huge that it encompassed the entire Danube valley in Austria, even including Vienna.

A commercial base − The arrival of the Inn waters at Passau almost doubles the flow volume of the Danube; from there on it becomes a really big river. From the Middle Ages, river trade played an important role in the town's prosperity, including such essentials as cereals, wine and salt, for which the Passau merchants enjoyed the "right of storage". Business with Bohemia, which was conducted via the valley of the Ilz, was also important. Today, when barges can go upriver as far as Kelheim, the "town of three rivers" also offers excursions, cruises and passenger traffic to Vienna and Budapest.

SIGHTS

Veste Oberhaus (Fortress) (**B**) − Work on this imposing citadel, which served the bishops as a refuge against continuous rebellions by the burghers, started in 1219. It is linked with the **Veste Niederhaus** by a fortified road along the spit of land separating the Danube and the Ilz. From the belvedere marked Zur Aussicht, near the car park − or from the top of a tower inside the compound *(142 steps)* − there are magnificent **views**★★ over the rocky promontory dividing the Inn from the Danube, with the town's churches and houses jumbled close together upon it. Some of the houses, following a former Inn valley tradition, have ridge roofs behind façades − masking the many sloping angles from street level.

The history of the town and its craftwork, folk art, and religious past are traced in a small **museum** (**B M¹**) which also displays paintings of the Danube School *(qv)*.

Dom St. Stephan (**B**) − Apart from the east chancel and the transept, the original Late Gothic cathedral was destroyed by fire in the 17C. Once rebuilt, the greater part of it was in the Baroque style. The majestic west front is so severe in concept that the late 19C addition to the two towers of a final, octagonal stage seems almost frivolous.

The huge interior is overloaded with frescoes and stuccowork. There are four **lateral chapels** with fine paintings by the Austrian artist J M Rottmayr (1654-1730). The first on the south side shows *The Beheading of John the Baptist*. Opposite is *The Conversion of St Paul*. In the two remaining chapels are *St Sebastian Succoured by St Irene (north)* and *The Martyrdom of St Agnes (south)*.

The pulpit, lavishly decorated with figures, is a Viennese work (1722-26). Henselmann's modern (1953) high altar represents the stoning of St Stephen (figures in silvered poplar wood). The organ, rebuilt in 1928 with 17 388 pipes and 231 registers, is the largest in the world.

From the Residenzplatz, visitors can admire the Cathedral's **east end**★★, a remarkable Late Gothic work (1407-1530) whose slender outline is emphasized by the domed belfry which tops the transept cupola.

Residenzplatz (**B**) − The square is bordered on the south by the bishops' **New Residence** (**A**), which dates from the beginning of the neo-Classical period. The surrounding streets are still lined with many old houses above arcades, with corbelling and concealed Inn valley ridge roofs.

Rathausplatz (**B**) − One of the town's most picturesque squares. The painted façade of the **Rathaus** (**D**) dates from the 14C; the building's tower was built in the late 18C.

★ **Glasmuseum** (**B M²**) ⊘ − Glassware from Bohemia, Bavaria and Austria, from the late 18C to the 1930s, makes up most of this fine collection. The most important display comes from **Bohemia** (Biedermeier, Historicism, Jugendstil); coloured glass, vases, pots and figurines attest to the great skill of the Bohemian glassblowers.

St. Michaels-Kirche (B) – This 17C church built by the Jesuits overlooks the north bank of the Inn. The over-rich gilding and stuccowork date from *c*1720. A reredos painted by Carlone hides the squared-off chevet.

★ **Dreiflußeckspaziergang (Three Rivers Walk)** (B) – *From St. Michaels-Kirche, go down to the Inn quayside.*
The fast, at times almost torrential, river runs at the foot of the **Schaiblingsturm** (1481), which was once part of Passau's defence system. At the confluence, the green current of the Inn can be seen running alongside the brown Danube waters for a long time before they mingle. From the Danube bank, on the far side of the promontory, there is a fine **viewpoint**, looking across the river at the wooded, rocky height of the Oberhaus fortress.

EXCURSIONS

★ **Dreisesselberg** – *48km - 30 miles to the northeast.*
The drive to this curious group of granitic rocks, eroded into flat, saucer-like shapes, runs through some of the wildest forest regions of Bohemia. The inn at the foot of the formation is soon reached from the road. Green triangles bordered with white waymark the path leading to the lowest rock outcrop. From there, steps rise to the **Hochstein** (1 332m - 4 370ft). The viewpoint at the summit affords a splendid **panorama**★ which reveals the immensity of this Bohemian forest.

Osterhofen Church – *36km - 22 miles to the northeast. Leave Passau by 6 on the town plan.*
Three great names of the Bavarian Baroque style have vent here the fulness of their talent: Johann Michael Fischer for the architecture and the Asam brothers for the decoration. The alternation of the convex lines of the balustrades and concave lines of the pilasters as well as the almost total absence of right angles gives many contours to the buildings. Note in particular the monumental high altar with its wreathed columns and its angels with enraptured smiles surrounding a radiant almond-shaped glory.

Danube School

The German painters working in the Danube valley in the 16C were among the first to depict landscape for its own sake. The best masters of this so-called school were Albrecht Altdorfer, Lucas Cranach the Elder, Wolf Huber and Jörg Breu the Elder.

PFALZ AM RHEIN★

RHINELAND PALATINATE – Rheinland-Pfalz
Michelin map 417/419 S 7 - R 9

The Palatinate mountains are a continuation of the northern Vosges, with a similar forested aspect broken up by escarpments of red sandstone.

The **Pfälzer Wald**, densely wooded and sparsely inhabited, is a huge natural park in the northern part of the massif much favoured by walkers; further south lies the broken country of the **Wasgau**, where tree-clad heights crowned by ruins or rock outcrops overlook the valley clearings which shelter the villages.

The Wines of the Palatinate – The most extensive wine-growing region of the country, the Palatinate produces almost one-third of Germany's total output: a long reach of suitable country, calcareous, protected, facing the sun, stretches along the foot of the **Haardt** – the steep eastern flank of the massif overlooking the Rhine.

The highest point of the Haardt is the Kalmit, at 673m - 2 208ft. The strip below being almost flat, vines can be cultivated in the traditional way on low cordons. This permits late-harvested grapes to ripen more and produce fruity wines of fairly high alcoholic content, the most appreciated being the whites. The most famous vintages come from the villages of Bad Dürkheim, Forst, Deidesheim and Wachenheim. The itinerary suggested below follows part of the celebrated Deutsche Weinstraße (German Wine Road), which begins at Schweigen, on the French frontier, and ends at Bockenheim, west of Worms.

FROM WORMS TO BAD BERGZABERN

158 km - 98 miles – allow one day

South of **Worms★** *(qv)*, cultivation of the Rhine plain becomes progressively devoted to the vine. Soon, the steep barrier of the Haardt appears in the distance.

Freinsheim – A large wine town, encircled by ramparts. The town hall, beside a 15C church, occupies an elegant Baroque house with an overhanging roof that protects an outside staircase.

The road continues through vineyards, past pretty villages.

Bad Dürkheim – Sheltered by the Pfälzer Wald, this thermal cure town enjoys a mild climate in which fig, almond and chestnut trees in the **Spa Park** flower early. A couple of miles west *(via the Schillerstraße and the Luitpoldweg)* are the ruins of Limburg abbey. From here there are picturesque views – to the east across the vineyards of the Rhine plain; westwards along the Isenach valley to the Hardenburg ruins.

Deidesheim – One of the most typical and prosperous towns on the German Wine Road with its smart market place, bordered by half-timbered and patrician houses.
The traditional goat auction, which takes place in historical costumes on the steps of the town hall (16C), is held every year on Whit Tuesday.

★ **Neustadt an der Weinstraße** – Narrow, picturesque lanes in this small town surround a pretty market place with a 16C town hall. The **old town**★ is attractive.

Hambacher Schloß ⊙ – *On the outskirts of Hambach.*
The ruins of this old fortress are famous in Germany because it was here, in 1832, that militant patriots demanding a more liberal approach raised for the first time the black, red and gold flag adopted as the German national emblem in 1919, and again in 1949. Fine view over the vines.

★ **The Kalmit** – *8km - 5 miles, leaving from Maikammer, then 15 min on foot Rtn.*
There is a viewpoint at the summit. From the Kalmithaus terrace, a splendid **panorama**★ of the Rhine plain and, in the east, Speyer cathedral. Return to the Wine Road through the charming village of St. Martin.

Schloß Ludwigshöhe ⊙ – *2km - 1 mile from Edenkoben.*
Built by Ludwig I of Bavaria in the "Italian villa" style, this castle now houses a gallery devoted to the works of the German painter Max Slevogt (1868-1932, qv). A chairlift carries sightseers to the Rietburg (550m - 1 804ft), departure point for forest walks.
The return journey in the chair lift affords superb views over the vine-covered slopes.

★ **Burg Trifels** ⊙ – *7km - 4 1/2 miles from Annweiler, plus 1 1/2 hour walking and sightseeing.*
On a superb site crowning the summit of a bluff in the Wasgau, rebuilt in 1937 in the style of the Romanesque palaces of the Hohenstaufens, this is one of the castles in Germany most steeped in history. It was once an imperial residence housing the crown jewels and the royal treasury – a fact lending credence to the poetic tradition that once it also contained the Holy Grail. Whilst Richard the Lionheart was returning from the Third Crusade in 1193, he was held prisoner here by Henry VI. The oldest part of the castle is built into the rock. From the chapel tower (Kappelenturm) there is a **panoramic view**★ over the Wasgau region.
Along with two neighbouring summits, the Anebos and the Scharfenberg, the Trifels forms a triple peak, which can best be seen from the Bundesstraße 10 (coming from the Annweiler suburb of Sarnstall) shortly before the junction with the Bundesstraße 48. The **view** of the three mountain peaks is best when they are outlined against a dawn sky as the sun rises.

Dahn – The **ruins**★ (Burgruinen) of three separate castles – Altdahn, Grafendahn and Tanstein – lie within the same perimeter wall here. Among the ruins, there remain troglodytic halls shored up by monolithic columns, and two ancient towers. Once more, there are fine **views**★ of the Wasgau.
Winding through a landscape scattered with rock outcrops, the road arrives at Bad Bergzabern.

Rhine-Main-Danube Canal

Ever since Roman times emperors, kings, engineers and visionaries have dreamed of linking the Rhine and Danube waterways. Charlemagne began the great enterprise, hence the name Charlemagne's Ditch (Fossa Carolina). Bavaria's Ludwig I made another attempt when he built the Ludwig Canal. However it was bargeloads of 20C dignitaries who were the first to cross the watershed between the Rhine and the Danube on 25 September 1992.
The 177km - 110 mile-canal with its hundreds of locks takes the barges up and down the 245m - 800ft climb. 12 centuries after it was originally conceived the idea of a waterway linking Europe from the North Sea to the Black Sea has become a reality.

Only a few miles west of Berlin, Potsdam was chosen at the beginning of the 17C as the official residence of the Electors of Brandenburg because of its ideal setting – a natural wooded site dotted with lakes and crisscrossed by canals and arms of the Havel river. Sacked by Swedish troops during the Thirty Years War (qv), the town was revived by Friedrich Wilhelm I. After the Revocation of the Edict of Nantes, many French Huguenots emigrated to Potsdam, amongst them merchants and craftsmen who contributed to the subsequent economic development of the area.

A Prussian Versailles – Under the rule of Friedrich Wilhelm, "the King-Sergeant" (1713-1740), Potsdam became an administrative centre and above all a garrison town (to the extent that at one time three-quarters of the population were military).

The King's son, Frederick the Great (Friedrich II: 1740-1786), was on the contrary a patron of the arts and man of letters. Most of the prestigious monuments for which the city is famous today were due to him, notably Sanssouci and the Neues Palais. Frederick, as eloquent in French as in his own language, welcomed many eminent Frenchmen to his Court, among them Voltaire, who lived in Potsdam for three years.

In 1991, 205 years after his death, the remains of Frederick the Great were reinterred in the crypt of his beloved palace of Sanssouci in Potsdam.

The Potsdam Conference – The treaty defining the role of the victors in the occupation and future of Germany after the Second World War was signed here at Cecilienhof Palace on 2 August 1945 by the leaders of the Allied powers (Churchill – subsequently Attlee – Truman and Stalin).

★★★ SANSSOUCI PALACE AND PARK

Follow the itinerary suggested on the map.

Designed by Peter Joseph Lenné (1789-1866), the most talented landscape gardener in Prussia, the 300ha - 740-acre park contains several hundred different species of tree. The various palaces and pavilions occupying it were all built between 1744 and 1860. This huge complex marrying architecture with the landscape is undoubtedly the best example of its kind in Germany. Wandering here and there it is easy to understand why Frederick the Great, turning his back momentarily on affairs of state, took such delight coming here to steep himself in the arts, especially music. In fact, Sanssouci has become his final resting place. His body was brought from Burg Hohenzollern in 1991 and interred in a vault above the terraces of the palace. His father, Friedrich Wilhelm I, is buried in a mausoleum in the Friedenskirche near the Marly gardens.

Schloß Sanssouci, Potsdam

Jogschies/EXPLORER, Paris

Neptungrotte (Neptune's Grotto) – Laid out according to plans drawn up by Knobelsdorff *(qv)* between 1751 and 1757, the grotto houses a statue of the sea god.

★ **Bildergalerie (Paintings Gallery)** ⊙ – This is the oldest museum in Germany. It was built between 1755 and 1763. Amidst the pretentious Rococo décor of the great rooms it is possible to admire the works of the Italian schools (Bassano, Tintoretto and Caravaggio), the French (Simon Vouet and Van Loo), and the Flemish (Van Dyck, Rubens and Terbrugghen).

★★★ **Schloß Sanssouci** ⊙ – *There may be a wait, because only a limited number of visitors are allowed in at once.*

It is impossible to remain unmoved by the progressive appearance of this majestic façade as one climbs the great staircase rising through the tiers of terraces before it. The original idea of the architect (Knobelsdorff again) was for the façade, adorned with 36 atlantes, to encompass the entire terrace area. But the king preferred a generous proportion of space which indeed became one of his favourite places to relax in. On the far side of the palace the state entrance is flanked by an elegant semicircular colonnade.

Interior – A walk through these rooms reveals the enormous skill and artistry in the Rococo mode of the craftsmen who decorated them.

Ante-chamber – Grey and gold, the decoration here is elegant and sober. The ceiling was painted by Harper in 1746.

Small Gallery – Paintings by Nicolas Lancret (1690-1743) and Jean-Baptiste Pater (1695-1736), both of them followers of Watteau. On the chimneypiece, busts of Frederick and his brother Henry.

Library – A relatively small room in the form of a rotunda. Decorations in cedarwood and gilded bronze.

Bedchamber and Study of Frederick the Great – Portraits of the royal family as well as the King's table and the armchair in which he died.

Concert Hall – A painting by Menzel represents the King playing the flute. The décor here is rocaille, with Pesne murals on the theme of Ovid's *Metamorphoses*.

Reception Hall – Paintings by Coypel and Van Loo. Ceiling *(Zephyr and Flora)* by Pesne.

Hall of Marble – Beneath the cupola there is a Bernini bust of Richelieu, also statues of Apollo and Venus by François Gaspard Adam (1710-1761), who introduced French taste to the Potsdam Court. The decoration, in marbles from Carrara and Silesia, is superb.

Four Guest Rooms – The fourth was Voltaire's, from 1750 to 1753. There is a replica of the great writer's bust by Jean Antoine Houdon (1741-1828).

Neue Kammern (New Rooms) ⊙ – Designed in 1747 by Knobelsdorff in the form of an orangery, this block was in fact transformed into the palace guest house.
Outside, the Sicilian gardens were designed in the Renaissance style by Lenné.

★ **Orangerie** – Built in the style of an Italian Renaissance palace between 1851 and 1860, the orangery today houses the archives of the State of Potsdam.

★★ **Neues Palais** ⊙ – This imposing – and in fact rather pompous – building was ordered by Frederick the Great to demonstrate that the economic power of Prussia remained intact after the arduous Seven Years War. Some 400 rooms behind a frontage of almost 700ft, together with over-lavish decorations and a superabundance of sculpture, themselves alone testify to the over-ambitious nature of the project – which was nevertheless completed in a relatively short time, from 1763 to 1769. The style of architecture, an unrestrained Baroque, today seems both heavy and over-mannered, very far from the elegant simplicity of Sanssouci.

Behind the palace, the so-called Communs, or outbuildings and servants' quarters, take the form of small pavilions linked by a curved colonnade (1766-69).

Interior – *The number and nature of rooms open to visitors being subject to variations, what follows below is restricted to the most popular examples.*

Ground floor

Grotto – Sea-shells and minerals contribute to the exuberant décor of this fantasy room. The ceiling fresco, *Venus and the Graces*, is by J G Niedlich.

Marble Gallery – Red jasper and white Carrara marble decorate the floor and walls of this hall. The allegorical frescoes on the ceiling, based on the hours of the day, are by C B Rode, a pupil of Pesne.

Red Damask Room – The eight canvases depicting members of the royal family were executed by Pesne when he was the official Court Painter. Note especially *Frederick II as Crown Prince*.

Oval Office – A barrel-vaulted room with a magnificent parquet floor. The marquetry, in floral motifs, was laid by the Spindler Brothers.

First floor

Marble Room – The stone floor is an elegant grey-blue, enhanced by discreet gilding. Statues in the same stone represent the Electors of Brandenburg. The ceiling fresco, by Van Loo (1769), depicts *Ganymede and Hebe on Olympus*.

Upper Gallery – This is neo-Classical in style, with stuccowork antique heads on plinths. Seventeenth-century Italian paintings include Giordano's *Judgement of Paris* and *The Suicide of Lucretia by Reni*.

Theatre – Designed as part of the palace's south wing, this is a fine example of Germany's Late Rococo style (1766-1768). The auditorium is encompassed by two galleries supported by gilded Hermes.

★ **Schloß Charlottenhof** – Designed by Karl-Friedrich Schinkel (1781-1841), this was built in the Classical style between 1826 and 1829. Visitors can see, among other things, the bedchamber and office of Alexander von Humboldt.

Römische Bäder (Roman Baths) – Serving as outbuildings and an ablutions centre for the Court gardeners, these too were based on plans by Schinkel.

★★ **Chinesisches Teehaus (Chinese Tea-House)** – A circular pavilion decorated with gilded statues, this structure arose from the "Sino-mania" so popular in 18C Germany. There is an exhibition of Chinese porcelain inside.

ADDITIONAL SIGHTS

Brandenburger Tor – *Luisenplatz*. A monumental gateway in the form of a triumphal arch, Roman style, built in the Baroque fashion in 1770.

★ **Wasserwerk (Hydraulic Waterworks)** ⊙ – *Take the Schopenhauerstraße, and then, on the right, the Breite Straße.*
Installed in a most unusual building imitating a mosque, complete with minarets, this pumping station (1841-42) supplies water to the fountains, pools and cascades in Sans-Souci Park. The ingenious machinery can be seen at work.

★ **Marstall (Old Stables)** – *Breite Straße*. Dating from 1675 and modified by Knobelsdorff in 1746. Groups of horse-trainers decorate the attics.

★★ **Nikolaikirche** – Built on the site of an old Baroque church destroyed by fire in 1795, this is a perfect example of German Classicism as conceived by Schinkel. Construction of the squared nave and preceding porch was completed in 1837. The cupola was added two years later.

* **Holländisches Viertel (Dutch Quarter)** – It is on each side of the **Mittelstraße** that one can still see these gabled houses in varying colours, built by the Dutch architect Boumann around 1740 for Netherlands artisans working in Potsdam.

* **Schloß Cecilienhof** ☉ – *Leave the northern part of the old town via the Nauener Tor.*
  Designed as a residence for the heir to the throne and his familiy, this was built on the model of an English timber-framed manor house.
  Museum – Visitors can see the workrooms used by the members of the Allied delegations and the conference hall where the Potsdam Agreements were signed (2 August 1945).
  The **New Park** (Neuer Garten), surrounded by lakes, is embellished with a number of different follies: an obelisk, a pyramid, an **orangery** (1790) and the **Marble Temple** (an imitation of an antique ruin dating from 1787-91).

EXCURSIONS

Brandenburg – *38km - 24 miles to the west.*
It was in the 14C that this small town in the heart of the Havelland (an area of scattered lakes fed by the Havel river) began to prosper, mainly through the cloth trade. The **Dom St. Peter und Paul★**, founded in 1165 and remodelled in the 14C, is furnished with several Gothic altarpieces. In the two-aisle crypt there is a mausoleum in memory of the clergy murdered during the Nazi regime.
Rich exterior decoration distinguishes the 15C **St. Katharinenkirche**, which boasts a polygonal chancel. The ambulatory (in the process of restoration) is a typical example of brick-built Gothic.

Kloster Lehnin (Abbey) ☉ – *28km - 17 miles to the southwest.*
Brick-built again, this three-aisle basilica, founded in 1180 by the Cistercian Order, has all the hallmarks of Early Gothic. Worth seeing: a Triumphal Cross dating from 1225 and the funerary stone of the Margrave Otto IV.

QUEDLINBURG ★

Sachsen-Anhalt – Population 28 000
Michelin 418 K 17

Nestling at the foot of a rock pinnacle crowned by a castle and an abbey church, the picturesque half-timbered houses and narrow, winding streets of Quedlinburg form a picture that corresponds to everyone's idea of a 17C German town. The old town, in which no less than 770 houses are classified as historical monuments, has been inscribed on Unesco's World Heritage List.

The Abbesses of Quedlinburg – A convent for the daughters of the nobility was founded on this height by Otto I around AD 930. Thanks to certain privileges, and to the lands with which it was endowed, the religious community prospered to the extent that Quedlinburg was chosen as a residence by the Saxon kings, and six Diets, or Councils of State were convened there.

★ OLD TOWN

* **Markt** – The early 17C Renaissance **Rathaus**, a two-storey building flanked by a gateway showing the town's armorial bearings, borders the northern side of the market place. On the left of the façade is a statue of Roland (*c*1420). Houses built in the 17C and 18C line the other three sides of the square.

* **Old Streets** – Circle the St. Benediktkirche via the Marktstraße and the Kornmarkt to explore the cobbled lanes behind the Rathaus, then return to the Markt along the Breitstraße, which has several picturesque alleyways opening off it. On the far side of the square, stroll to the hill that leads up to the castle by way of the Wordgasse, the Hohe Straße and the Blasiistraßse.

Klopstock-Haus ☉ – The poet Friedrich Gottlieb Klopstock was born in 1724 in this late 16C house (No 12) on one side of the charming **Schloßbergplatz★**. Drawing on sources close to the German psyche, inspired by ancient Teutonic myths, he composed a saga glorifying the hero Arminius *(qv)*, but he is best known for the huge religious epic, *Messias (The Messiah)*, said to be inspired by Milton's *Paradise Lost*. Various rooms in the house recall his life and his work.

Feininger-Galerie ☉ – *Behind the Klopstock Museum, entry at No 5A, Finkenherd.*
This small gallery houses an interesting collection of drawings and water-colours by the Expressionist painter Lyonel Feininger (1871-1956). Born in New York City, Feininger trained in France and Germany, where he exhibited with the Blauer Reiter group in 1913. After the First World War he joined the staff of the Bauhaus.

Interior of St. Servatius, Quedlinburg

★ SCHLOSSBERG

The ramp leading up to the castle ends in a wide terrace with a fine general **view**★ of the town.

★★**Stiftskirche St. Servatius** – On the site of the original 9C church, the present basilica, in the form of a Latin cross, was started in 1070 and consecrated in 1129. The **capitals**★ and friezes above the central nave were sculpted by craftsmen brought especially from northern Italy. Beneath the chancel, the **crypt**★★ is divided by three aisles with diagonal rib vaulting decorated by **frescoes**★ depicting scenes from the Bible. Note the sarcophagi of King Heinrich I and his wife Matilda, interred here in the 10C, and the funerary stones of abbesses. The **treasury**★★ (Domschatz) – manuscripts, 10C **Gospel**, and, above all, the **Quedlinburg Knotted Carpet**★ – is kept in the sacristy.

Schloß – Construction of the castle building, which formed part of the abbey, extended from the late 16C to the middle of the 17C. The irregularity of the floor plan was imposed on the architects by the nature of the rocky base onto which the castle was built.
In the **Schloßmuseum**★ ⊘, 16C and 17C paintings from the Flemish and Italian schools are on display. The Abbess's Reception Room, a Throne Room and the Princes' Hall (mid-18C) can be visited.

EXCURSION

Gernrode – *7km - 4 1/2 miles to the south.*
Here, the **collegiate church of St. Cyriacus**★, built at the end of the 10C, was designed with the three-aisle nave and flat ceiling characteristic of the Ottonian basilica. The crypt was excavated and the west chancel added at the beginning of the 12C. A late 12C baptismal font in the Romanesque style, together with the funerary plaque of the Margrave Gero, one of the convent founders, can be seen in the crypt. Upstairs, in the south aisle, is the **Holy Sepulchre group**★, a handsome and rare example of Ottonian sculpture.

RASTATT★

Baden-Württemberg – Population 40 000
Michelin map 419 T 8
Town plan in the current Michelin Red Guide Deutschland

Rastatt has never regained the prestige it enjoyed at the beginning of the 18C, when it was ruled by the **Margrave Ludwig of Baden** (1665-1707), known as **Ludwig the Turk** *(see KARLSRUHE)*. Faced by the threat of an invasion arising from the political ambitions of Louis XIV, the gallant captain abandoned the ruins of Baden-Baden and turned Rastatt into a stronghold, at the same time building a castle that was in line with his own ambitions. The town is connected with two treaties between France and the Holy Roman Empire. The first, in 1714, ended the War of the Spanish Succession. The second in fact came to nothing: the congress discussing the enforcement of the Peace of Campo Formio, inaugurated in 1797, came to a tragic end two years later when two of the French plenipotentiaries were assassinated.

Schloß ⊙ – Ludwig the Turk's enormous red sandstone palace was designed by D E Rossi, the architect to the Viennese court. It was built between 1698 and 1707, and was only just completed when Ludwig died. The three wings of the castle, based on Italian models, enclose a vast state courtyard on the town side.

Royal Apartments – The nucleus of the central block is the tall, sumptuous **Hall of Ancestors** (Ahnensaal), with the column capitals decorated will stucco figures representing Turkish prisoners. The Margrave's apartments are in the south wing, those of his wife in the north. Both are richly embellished with frescoes and stuccowork. The **Collection of Porcelain** (Porzellankabinett) is worth seeing.

★ **Schloßkirche** – *Enter from the Lyzeumstraße*. This Baroque church constructed between 1720 and 1723 by the architect M L Rohrer is attached to the north wing of the castle. The centrepiece of the magnificently decorated interior is the high altar, the colums of which have been hollowed and can be illuminated from inside. The legend of the Holy Cross is represented in the ceiling paintings.

Wehrgeschichtliches Museum (Military Museum) ⊙ – *On the ground floor of the main block (south side)*. German military history from the end of the Middle Ages up to 1815 is displayed here. The exhibits include weapons, uniforms and pictures. The research collection of **military uniforms and equipment up to 1945** is housed at 1 Karstraße.

Freiheitsmuseum (Liberty Museum) – *Also on the ground floor of the main block, but on the north side*. The displays here evoke the history of the 19C German Liberation Movement. The exhibition is oriented around the struggles arising from the 1849 Constitution of the Empire (the Baden War).

EXCURSION

★★ **Schloß Favorite** ⊙ – *5km - 3 miles to the southeast.*
This marvellous Baroque palace was built between 1710 and 1712 for the Margravine Sybilla Augusta, widow of Ludwig the Turk. The architect was again Rohrer, who had designed the church attached to her old apartments in the Rastatt palace. He coated the outside of this much smaller building with an unusual matrix of roughcast gravel and granite chips. The **interior**★★★ is particularly fine: floors of brilliant **scagliola** (stucco imitating encrusted marble), shiny as glass; mirror decorations; mosaics; chinoiserie. Note especially the **Florentine Room**, embellished with miniatures; the **Mirror Study**; Sybilla Augusta's apartments; sumptuous kitchen quarters with pottery from Frankfurt, Delft and Strasbourg; and a collection of Meißen, Nymphenburg and Chelsea porcelain.

Staatl. Liegenschaftsamt, Karlsruhe

Detail from the Florentine Room,
Schloß Favorite, Rastatt

RATZEBURG★

Schleswig-Holstein – Population 12 000
Michelin map 415/416 E 16

The island town of Ratzeburg is built attractively in the middle of a **lake**★, the biggest of many in the morainal hills between the Elbe and Lübeck. The tower *(129 steps)* rising from the woods on the eastern shore of the lake *(access via the Hindenburghöhe avenue)* provides the best **view**★ of the town dominated by the squat outline of its cathedral.

★ **Dom (Cathedral)** – Brick-built and Romanesque in style, this 12C construction lies in a stretch of parkland on the northern point of the island. Outside, note the lavish gable decorations of the south porch, remodelled as a chapel. The entrance now is through doors beneath the tower. Above the high altar is an altarpiece in the form of a triptych, illustrating the **Crucifixion**★ (1430), on the superb central shrine. Beautiful ecclesiastic vestments embroidered with gold thread may be seen in a chapel off the north aisle.

Ernst-Barlach-Museum ⊙ – *At No 3 Barlachplatz, in the town centre, beside the Peterskirche.*
The sculptor, artist, graphic designer and author Ernst Barlach (1870-1938), one of the leading exponents of German Expressionism, spent part of his youth in Ratzeburg and was buried here at his own request (suburban cemetery, Schweriner/Seedorfer Straße).
The 25 original bronze sculptures on display include *The Singer, The Flautist* and *The Reader.* There are also lithographs, drawings and woodcuts to be seen. The exhibition includes examples both of the artist's early work and from his years in Güstrow.

EXCURSION

Mölln – *11km - 7 miles to the southwest.*
A stage on the old Salt Road, this small town is famous for the memory of **Till Eulenspiegel** *(qv),* whose tombstone is at the foot of the **St Nicholas' church tower** (13C and 15C). A statue of the celebrated jester, who died at Mölln in 1350, adorns the fountain in the market below. There are many lakes in the wooded countryside around Mölln (Seenlandschaft), the most popular of which is the romantic **Schmalsee★**, easily reached on foot from the Kurhaus Waldhalle.

RAVENSBRÜCK
Brandenburg
Michelin map 416 G 23 – 1km - 1/2 mile north of Fürstenberg

Built in 1938 on the shores of Schwedtsee lake, Ravensbrück soon became Nazi Germany's largest camp for the detention of women: 132 000 women and children from 23 different countries were deported here. Conditions of work and the harshness of the imprisonment were so terrible that the camp had the highest mortality rate of any in Europe, with more than 90 000 deaths.

Nationale Mahn- und Gedenkstätte Ravensbrück (Memorial) ⊙ – Laid out even in the cells in which the deportees were herded, the **camp museum** evokes with horrifying realism the life (and death) of the victims. On the ground floor of the main block, evidence from more than 20 countries from which deportees were taken is exposed. Nearby, the execution passageway and the original crematory death ovens are on view. At the lakeside, there is a monument in memory of the victims.

RAVENSBURG
Baden-Württemberg – Population 45 000
Michelin map 419 W 12

Ravensburg remains to this day an ancient Swabian town, bristling with many towers, still sheltering behind a well-preserved rectangular city wall. The road from Wangen passes beneath the Obertor, a gateway with stepped gables *(see below).* At the end of the Marktstraße is a block of old buildings comprising the Rathaus and the Blaserturm, a square clock-tower with a polygonal coping and lantern.

The Mehlsack ("Sack of Flour") – In order to overlook and spy on the activities of the constables of Veitsburg, on a nearby hill, the burghers of Ravensburg erected this grey stone **tower**, which rises to a height of 50m - 164ft. Looking out over the city wall from the top *(240 steps),* the view extends as far as the church at Weingarten.

Liebfrauenkirche – A 14C building which has been completely modernized. It is worth visiting for its best-known work of art, which is exposed on an altar in the south aisle. This is a copy of **The Ravensburg Madonna★★**, a moving 15C sculpture of the Virgin Mary in a mantle (the original is in the Dahlem Museum in Berlin).

EXCURSION

★ Wangen im Allgäu – *23km - 14 miles to the east.*
Lying within sight of the first crests of the Allgäu Alps, this small Swabian town has been built with its colourful houses arranged in a simple cruciform plan, the two main streets crossing at right angles in the **Marktplatz★**. The Herrenstraße, running as it were from side to side, is lined with attractive houses, many with decorative shop signs. At the far end is the Ravensburgertor (or Frauentor), a square gateway of which the 17C coping, confined by engaged turrets, is topped by an elegant ribbed roof. Perpendicular to this street, the other main thoroughfare ends at St. Martinstor. Painted outside like the Ravensburgertor, this entrance is crowned with a pyramidal roof, beneath which very finely worked gargoyles jut out.

REGENSBURG★★

Bayern – Population 128 000
Michelin map 420 S 20
Plan of the conurbation in the current Michelin Red Guide Deutschland

Regensburg, originally a Celtic colony (Radasbona), later became a Roman garrison town *(Castra Regina)* guarding the natural frontier of the Danube at its most northerly point. Some evidence of Roman occupation remains (Porta Praetoria). The town was converted to Christianity by St Emmerammus in the 7C, and St Boniface founded a bishopric there in 739, making it a centre for religious life in the Middle Ages, a role reflected by the extraordinary density of religious buildings in the city centre. As the seat of the Bavarian dukes (6-13C), the town developed into an important trading post, and in 1245 it was made a Free Imperial City. The wealth and ambition of local merchants was manifested in the Italian style **towers** (Goldener Turm, Baumburger Turm) they had built all over town between the 12C and 14C. A 14C fortified gateway, the **Ostentor**, is all that remains of the medieval fortifications.

Nowadays Regensburg is the economic and, not least thanks to its university, the cultural hub of eastern Bavaria.

The City of Diets – Once a Free Imperial City, Regensburg was privileged on occasion to be the seat of plenary sessions of the Royal Diet (Reichstag), which was charged with responsibility for the internal peace and external security of the immense and confused federation of states forming the Holy Roman Empire. From 1663 to 1806, date of the Empire's dissolution by Napoleon *(qv)*, the city was the seat of a **Permanent Diet** – the first indication of a continuing, overall German government.

OLD QUARTER

Time: half a day, follow the itinerary suggested on the town plan below

★ **Dom St. Peter** (E) – Based on the design of certain French cathedrals, this pillared Gothic church has three naves and a non-projecting transept. Building began in 1250 and the major part of the work was completed by 1525, but the spires were not added until the 19C. The **Donkey Tower** (Eselsturm), above the northern part of the transept, is all that remains of the original Romanesque sanctuary built on this site. The **west front**, richly decorated, is the work of a local family of sculptors named Roritzer. The main entrance, flanked by two neo-Gothic towers, is unusual, with a triangular, jutting porch. St Peter can be seen on the pier, and there are beautiful statues in the niches – particularly the meeting of the Virgin and St Elizabeth.

Go inside via the south porch.

The huge Late Gothic interior measures: 85m long and 32m high (279ft long and 105ft high). On each side of the nave, the aisles are encircled by a gallery, that on the south side being supported by fine carved consoles. Two masterpieces of local Gothic statuary – the Archangel Gabriel, and Mary at the Annunciation, by the Master of Erminold (c1280) – stand in front of the west transept pillars. The three chancel windows are adorned with beautiful 14C **stained glass★★**.

Treasury (Domschatz) ⊙ – *In the south wing of the former bishops' residence (Bischofshof), entrance via the courtyard.* Liturgical items from the 11C to the 18C – vestments, chalices, monstrances, reliquaries – are on display here. Among the rarest and finest, note the Ottocar Cross (c1430), a Venetian reliquary chest in the form of a tiny house (c1430), and the Schaumberg Altar (1534-40), in the Zwölf-Boten-Kapelle.

Cloister (Kreuzgang) ⊙ – *Access through the cathedral garden.* This is divided by a central gallery paved with tombstones. On the right is the Romanesque **Allerheiligenkapelle**, on the walls of which are traces of ancient frescoes. Another gallery leads to the Alter Dom – the old 11C **Stefanskirche**, with its empty saint's confessional altar pierced by small openings.

★ **Diözesanmuseum St. Ulrich** (E) ⊘ – The museum is installed in the **Ulrichskirche**, an early Gothic galleried church (*c*1225-1240) decorated with 1 571 murals. Among other exhibits, visitors can see antique bishops' crosses (including the 12C Cross of St Emmerammus), fine medieval reliquaries, gold and silver plate, and religious paintings such as *The Legend of St Severinus* (a gift from the Regensburg Wool Merchants' Guild in 1456).

Taking the covered passageway that links the Herzogshof (Ducal Palace) with the massive quadrilateral of the Römerturm (Roman tower), visitors arrive at a wide, paved square, the **Alter Kornmarkt★**, where a grain market used to be held.

★ **Alte Kapelle** (E) – Originally Carolingian, this chapel was completely transformed in the Rococo style in the 18C. The two double oratories in the chancel, the splendid reredos, the painted ceiling and the gilded stuccowork executed by a Master of Wessobrunn combine to form a harmonious ensemble admirably set off by the light penetrating the tall windows.

Kassianskirche (E) – *Enter by the west door.*
A Romanesque basilica with pillars and later (18C) Rococo decoration. On the left of the main doorway, a Gothic bas-relief represents the Visitation. On an altar in the south aisle is a Schöne Maria (Lovely Mary) sculpture by Hans Leinberger, the Master of Landshut (1520).

Hinter der Grieb (D) – In this ancient alleyway with its old burghers' houses, the visitor is transported back to the Middle Ages. From the far end, there is a fine view of one of the cathedral spires.

★ **Haidplatz** (D) – A square surrounded by historic buildings, among which (at No 7) is an inn, **Zum Goldenen Kreuz**, with a grey stone tower and façade, and a crenellated pediment. In the centre of the square is the 1656 **Justitiabrunnen** (Fountain of Justice).

* **Altes Rathaus** (D) – The eight-storey tower of the old town hall dates from c1250. The Gothic western section (Reichssaalbau) was built c1360. The façade includes a gabled doorway and a pedestal supporting a charming oriel window which lights the Imperial Hall (Reichssaal).

Reichtagsmuseum ☉ – The centrepiece of this museum is the splendid Gothic hall, where the "Permanent Diet" used to meet. In the same building the Reichsstädtisches Kollegium houses an exhibition tracing the history of all the Regensburg Diets.
On the ground floor, the interrogation room (Fragestatt) and the dungeons are also open to the public.

Fischmarkt (Fish Market) (D) – The market operates every morning. Note St George's Fountain (Georgsbrunnen, also known as Fischbrunnen) which dates from c1600.

Steinerne Brücke (Stone Bridge) (E) – Built between 1135 and 1146, this 310m - 1 017ft bridge rests on no less than 16 arches. From the middle, there is a fine **view★** of the old town, its medieval roofs dominated by the cathedral's spires. In the foreground is the 14C **Brückenturm** gateway, flanked, on the left, by the huge roof of the **Salzstadel** (early 17C salt loft). Beside this building, on the quayside, is the **Historische Wurstküche**, the oldest cooked sausage kitchen in Germany.

Porta Praetoria (E) – Near the Alter Dom *(see above)*, a little way south of the Danube, this arch and corner tower are all that remains of the old Roman fortified gateway that was once the northern entrance to Regensburg.

Niedermünster (E) – A Romanesque basilica with two towers that was originally the church of a convent of nuns. The interior was remodelled in the Baroque style in the 17C and 18C. The stuccowork is good. The tomb of St Erhard, surmounted by an altar and baldachin (c1330), is in the north aisle.

ADDITIONAL SIGHTS

* **St. Emmeram** (D) – This was once the abbey church of an 8C Benedictine monastery. A Gothic gateway on the Emmeramsplatz leads to a close from which visitors pass through the huge Romanesque **porch** (12C) to the double doors at the church entrance. The 11C **sculptures** by these doors (Jesus Christ, St Emmerammus and Dionysius) are among the oldest in Germany.
The original Romanesque aspect of the church was lost when the Asam brothers introduced a Baroque decorative scheme. Light from the clerestory windows highlights the ceiling's frescoes and stuccowork. Among the numerous tombs is the **tombstone of Queen Hemma★** (c1280), by the north wall, depicting the queen with an expression of profound sadness.

Schloß Thurn und Taxis (D) ☉ – The Thurn and Taxis family – which until 1867 had the monopoly of German postal services – owns the St. Emmeram abbey buildings. The great Gothic cloister and the Abbot's halls, as well as the refectory and (separately) a **transport museum** ☉ (Marstallmuseum) (**D M²**) are open to the public.

* **Städtisches Museum** (E M¹) ☉ – A former Minorite monastery, now deconsecrated, houses this museum, which traces the cultural and artistic history of Regensburg and eastern Bavaria from the Stone Age to the present day. In the 13C building's **Roman section** is the town's "Act of Foundation" – a stone slab 8m - 26ft long on which an inscription recalls the implantation of the Roman garrison in AD 179. On the second floor there is an exhibition of paintings by **Albrecht Altdorfer** and other masters of the Danube School.

Schottenkirche St. Jakob (C) – This sanctuary church was built at the beginning of the 12C for Irish monks. The Romanesque **main entrance★** (north side) is famous for its statuary: on the tympanum, Christ is between St John and St James; above, on the frieze, the Saviour and the Apostles are flanked by Adam and Eve.

Dominikanerkirche (C) – A building that is bare to the point of severity – but nevertheless one of the oldest of all Gothic churches in Germany.

EXCURSIONS

* **Walhalla** ☉ – *11km - 7 miles to the east. Leave Regensburg by the Steinerne Brücke.* Built between 1830 and 1842 by Ludwig I of Bavaria, this Doric temple – which seems strangely out of place in the Danube valley – was intended to honour all the great men in German history (In Nordic mythology, Walhalla is the final resting place for the souls of heroes). Inside the memorial are 121 busts of famous soldiers, artists, scientists, etc., and, beneath a gallery, 64 plaques of older or lesser-known heroes.
From the peristyle there is a good view of the river bend above which the temple is built, the ruins of Schloß Donaustauf, and the distant spires of Regensburg cathedral.

★ **Befreiungshalle** (Liberation Monument) ⊙ – *32km - 20 miles to the southwest just outside Kelheim.*
The liberation is that of Germany from Napoleonic rule. It was, again, Ludwig I who conceived the idea of a memorial while returning from a visit to Greece in 1836. It takes the form of a huge rotunda, which was built between 1842 and 1863. The central hall is supported by 18 buttresses, each bearing an allegorical statue representing a Germanic people.
The coping, which partly hides the cupola roof, is adorned with trophies. Inside, 34 victory tableaux form a homogenous ring. From the outside gallery *(staircase)*, there is a fine view of the Altmühl valley.

★ **Kloster Weltenburg** (Abbey) ⊙ – *30km - 18 1/2 miles to the southwest.*
Cosmas Damian Asam *(qv)* built this abbey church in 1718, with an ante-nave – or narthex – and a nave proper, both of them oval. The attention is drawn immediately to a statue of St George, theatrically illuminated in the central arch of the reredos by light from a hidden source. Visible through an aperture in the lower dome is a trompe l'œil Asam composition in the upper dome on the theme of the Church Triumphant.

Bad REICHENHALL★

Bayern – Population 18 500
Michelin map 420 W 22
Town plan in the current Michelin Red Guide Deutschland

Built where the last of the Saalach gorges finally opens out, Bad Reichenhall is the city of salt. The cures at the Spa are mainly for people with respiratory trouble. This thermal establishment extends for just over a mile along the busiest section of the **Ludwigstraße**, the main street linking the St. Zeno-Kirche with the bridge over the Saalach river.
The town has produced domestic salt since Celtic times. The success of the industry is based on the fact that the concentration of the mineral (a maximum of 24%) is the highest in Europe – and the fact that the salt derives from abundant springs, not from rock brine as at Berchtesgaden or the mines of the Salzkammergut.
Until 1958 the waters were piped through a 79km - 49-mile conduit (Soleleitung) to extraction and refining plants at Traunstein and Rosenheim; today, together with brine from Berchtesgaden, they are treated in new saline works at Bad Reichenhall itself.

St. Zeno-Kirche – *On the street that cuts across the northern part of the town.*
This late 12C church (remodelled in the 16C and later decorated in the Baroque style) corresponds on the north side of the Alps to the well-known Romanesque church dedicated to the same saint in Verona. Lombard influence can be seen in the design and decoration of the main doorway, with its archstones of alternating shades and slender outside columns resting on couched lions. On the tympanum, a Virgin and Child are depicted between St Rupert, first Bishop of Salzburg, and the patron saint himself, invoked in the Alps against flooding.

Bad Reichenhaller Salzmuseum ⊙ – Ludwig I of Bavaria had this salt-working plant built in 1834 in the so-called "Troubadour" style in vogue at that time. Entering the huge machine-room, where two immense paddle-wheels operate the pumps, visitors could imagine themselves part of a mid-19C steel engraving in *The Illustrated London News*. Beyond this, caverns and galleries with marble cladding lead to different catchment areas where some of the archaic equipment still works – for example the 103m - 113yd transmission shaft which, thanks to five separate joints, actuates the pump at the Karl-Theodor spring.

Schloß RHEINSBERG★

Brandenburg
Michelin map 416 G 22

The castle, in its idyllic location on Grienerick lake, is inseparably linked with Kurt Tucholsky and his charming novella *Rheinsberg – A picturebook for lovers*, and above all also with Friedrich II, or **Frederick the Great**, although he only lived here for 4 years. These were however the 4 best years of his life. In retrospect he reflected "I have always been dogged with bad luck, the only place where I was happy was Rheinsberg". He had serious differences of opinion with his father, which led to an attempted flight to England (1730) and the execution of his friend Katte. His imprisonment, which was ordered by his father, ended when Frederick agreed to become engaged to Elisabeth-Christine of Brunswick. As a result, Friedrich Wilhelm I purchased the estate of Rheinsberg for his son in 1734 and furnished him with sufficient funds for converting the old 16C moated castle.

Schloß RHEINSBERG

The building director of the Mark of Brandenburg, Johann Gottfried Kemmeter designed the Baroque structure with three wings. The Crown Prince and Georg Wenzeslaus von Knobelsdorff, who took over direction of the site in 1737, were also involved in the planning. It was here that the young Frederick, in the company of his friends and in conflict with the philosophical ideas of his time, came to the conclusion that the Prince should be the "chief servant of his country". It was here too that his correspondence with Voltaire began, which lasted until the latter's death in 1778. In Rheinsberg, the master builder Knobelsdorff, the painter Antoine Pesne and the sculptor Friedrich Christian Glume created a style which was subsequently to reach its zenith in the Rococo of Frederick the Great at Charlottenburg and Sanssouci.

From 1752 to 1802, the castle was used as a residence by Prince Heinrich, Frederick's brother, who was not much liked by him. However Frederick was indulgent towards Heinrich, and apparently only once admoninished him with the words "I cannot believe that you are serious in what you say. There is no doubt that neither you nor I are responsible for current events, and only when we have done everything in our power will our own conscience and the people grant us justice". During Prince Heinrich's time, under the management of Georg Friedrich Boumann the Younger, the corner buildings on the town side were built, an obelisk was erected in honour of the Prussian Generals in the Seven Years War and the Baroque garden was redesigned as a "natural landscape".

After the Second World War the castle was used as a sanatorium. Its complete restoration will take some considerable time, but already around 20 rooms can be visited.

Schloß ⊘ – The Corps de Logis or main structure, the central projection of which was the work of Knobelsdorff, is reached via a bridge. It is enclosed by a roof parapet, which bears 4 statues, allegories of Rhetoric, Music, Painting and Sculpture. The colonnaded side wings end in round towers.

Interior – The hall of mirrors, the Bacchus room and the anterooms with their remarkable ceiling paintings by Antoine Pesne are open to visitors. There are a large number of paintings, including a portrait of the Marquise de Sabran by Elisabeth Vigée-Lebrun, in the red room in Princess Amalie's quarters. The so-called Ferdinand apartment was designed in 1767 based on plans by Carl Gotthard Langhans. The same artist was responsible for the shell room in Prince Heinrich's quarters. The castle also houses the **Kurt-Tucholsky memorial**.

Schloß Rheinsberg.

Jürgen Henkelmann

Park – The garden dates back essentially to plans by Knobelsdorff and Johann Samuel Sello, and took account of Frederick the Great's particular interest in garden culture. The aim was to combine kitchen and pleasure gardens. The geometrical grid layout of paths was retained under Prince Heinrich, who had the park extended over onto the other side of lake Grienerick (this side gives an attractive view of the castle). Most of the varied garden archi-tecture from the Crown Prince's time remains, for example the sphinx steps, and the park gate with the figures of Flora and Pomona.

Kurt Tucholsky (1890-1935), poet, short story writer and critic, also wrote witty satirical essays, directed in particular at German nationalism and militarism. Much of his poetry was immortalised as German cabaret songs. Tucholsky left Germany in 1924, and eventually settled in Sweden. He was stripped of his German nationality and his work was banned by the Nazis in 1933; Tucholsky committed suicide in 1935.

The river, 1 320km - 820 miles long, flows through four different countries and has often been a source of controversy between neighbours below Basle, for instance, no town has ever completely settled both sides of the stream. At the same time it has always been a unique highway for the exchange of commercial, intellectual, artistic and religious ideas, a vital artery of the West.

Shipping companies today organize many **excursions and Rhine cruises**, especially from Cologne, Koblenz and Rüdesheim or Bingen.

The Rhine Legends – There is not, along the whole length of the river, a castle, an island, even a rock without its tale of chivalry or legend. Lohengrin, the Knight of the Swan, appeared at the foot of the castle of Kleve (Cleves); Roland escaped from Roncesvalles to arrive too late before the island of Nonnenworth, where his fiancée, inconsolable at the rumour of his death, had taken the veil (Roland in despair withdrew to the neighbouring castle of Rolandsbogen); at the **Loreley**, the Rock of Lore, a beautiful enchantress bewitched boatmen with her song, leading their vessels to disaster.

The outstanding legend associated with the Rhine however is the story of the Nibelungen, an inexhaustible source of inspiration from which Wagner borrowed both names and ideas for his opera tetralogy *The Ring (qv)*. Inspired by Germanic and Scandinavian myths, the **Song of the Nibelungen** was probably composed towards the end of the 12C. It tells of the splendours of the 5C Burgundian Court at Worms, and of the passions scouring the hearts of its heroes, known also under the name of Nibelungen.

Brunhilde, the wife of the Burgundian king Gunther, learns from her arch-rival, the latter's sister Kriemhild, that it was not Gunther, but Kriemhild's husband Siegfried who had won her in the trial of strength which her suitors had had to fight to win her hand. Siegfried had however secretly been in love with Kriemhild all along.

Proud Brunhilde swears revenge. She persuades a fellow-conspirator, Gunther's henchman Hagen (so the story goes), to murder Siegfried during a hunting party and then throw into the Rhine the Burgundian treasure which had been Siegfried's wedding present to Kriemhild. This is to stop Kriemhild using the treasure to pay someone to avenge Siegfried in turn.

Kriemhild has to wait 13 years for her revenge. Then, having in the mean time married Attila, the King of the Huns, she invites her three brothers and Hagen to a royal banquet at Etzelburg, in Hungary. But the feast turns out to be an ambush, which turns into a general massacre. Hagen, decapitated by Kriemhild with Siegfried's sword, takes the secret of the treasure's whereabouts with him to the grave.

Burg Gutenfels and the fortified isle of Pfalz on the Rhine

From the Alps to the North Sea – At the beginning of its journey to the north, the Rhine is a typical Alpine river, with little water in the winter and a full flood in summer when the snows melt. Lake Constance (Bodensee), through which the Rhine flows, and the lakes of the Swiss plateau which drain into its tributary, the Aar, help to moderate this irregularity.

Reception of the Neckar at Mannheim and the Main at Frankfurt, each with a more regular flow, tend to even out that of the main stream, and the process is completed with the arrival of the Moselle at Koblenz.

After the exit from Lake Constance, rock outcrops from the Black Forest and the foot-hills of the Jura impede the force of the current and produce the famous Rhine Falls *(see the Michelin Green Guide Switzerland)*.

Further downstream, limestone strata result in rapids (Laufen). These obstacles, although they inhibit the use of shipping, do allow the installation of powerful hydro-electric projects.

At Basle, the Rhine abruptly changes direction, veering north to follow and fertilize the subsidence fault separating the Vosges and the Black Forest. In Alsace, a canal draws off some of the excess water, but after Breisach this is fed only from power station dams.

From Bingen to Neuwied, north of Koblenz, the Rhine cuts its way through the Rhineland schist massif, where the hard rock – especially the quartzites exposed in the neighbourhood of the Loreley – can foment dangerous whirlpools. This so-called **"romantic" stretch** of river valley, with its alternation of vineyards, woods and impressive escarpments, punctuated by ruins perched on rock spurs, is the most picturesque part of what is known as the Rhine Gorge. Later, having passed through the industrial region around Duisburg, the river turns west and curls slowly across the plain towards the sea.

An Exceptional Shipping Lane – The traditional strings of Rhine barges, displacing anything from 1 000 to 2 000 tons each as they are towed, have been supplanted latterly by self-powered "auto-barges" and convoys towed or pushed by tugs which can comprise anything up to six 2 000- or 3 000-ton freight carriers.

Recent work carried out on the more difficult reaches upstream from St Goar have guaranteed shipping a uniform navigation channel 120m - 394ft wide.

Today, the Rhine, navigable over the 850km - 528 miles between Rotterdam and Rheinfelden (upstream from Basle), handles an annual traffic of 265 million tons. Linked both to Rotterdam and to Antwerp, it boasts also in Duisburg-Ruhrort the world's largest river port (18 million tons annually).

Next in order of importance, on the river's German sector, are Cologne-Godorf, Karlsruhe, Ludwigshafen and Mannheim.

★★THE LORELEY

From Rüdesheim to Koblenz *75km - 47 miles – about 4 hours*

This route, following the Rhine's east bank, passes through the wildest and steepest part of the valley, with splendid views of the castles and fortresses on the far side of the river. After **Rüdesheim★** *(qv)*, the road runs at the foot of terraced vineyards overlooked by the ruins of Burg Ehrenfels, built by the Archbishops of Mainz at the same time as the Mäuseturm, a tower on the opposite bank to supervise the collection of tolls from shipping on the river. After Assmannshausen, silhouetted high up on the west bank, the castles of Rheinstein, Reichenstein and Sooneck appear one after the other. The crenellated tower of Fürstenberg, on the wooded slopes facing Lorch, marks the start of a more open stretch. And then the vineyards and towers of Bacharach slide into view. After that comes the fortified isle of Pfalz.

★ Pfalz bei Kaub (Pfalzgrafenstein) ☉ – The massive five-sided keep of this **toll fortress** rises from the centre of the river, encircled by a turreted fortified wall.

Kaub – One of the outstanding landmarks in the valley, this village dominated by the restored ruins of Gutenfels is worth exploring on foot by way of the picturesque main street, the Metzgerstraße.

Before a sharp, almost right-angled bend in the river, admire the **setting★★** of the towers of Oberwesel as they succeed one another at the foot of the Schönburg, on the far side of the water. The sharp bend, veering northeast and then northwest, leads to the most untamed stretch on this part of the Rhine.

★★★The Loreley – This legendary spur, towering 132m - 433ft above the rock-strewn river, has become the symbol of the Romantic Rhine and has a very special place in German literature. Heine's poem, *I Know Not Whence Cometh My Sadness*, set to music by Silcher, is traditionally played aboard ship when the promontory appears around a curve in the valley.

From St. Goarshausen, just beyond the famous rock, take the road signposted Loreley-Burgenstraße and drive up to the Hotel Auf der Loreley. From the car park, walk *(1/4 hour Rtn)* to the **Loreley viewpoint★★**. There are impressive **views★★** plunging down into the "romantic gorge" from several accessible spurs here.

St. Goarshausen – The town, strung out along the river bank (which makes a very pleasant walk), is dominated by the **Katz** (Cat) stronghold *(not open to the public)*, said to have been built to neutralize the **Maus** (Mouse), a little further downstream.

Wellmich – In the church of this small riverside town, there are traces (restored) of 15C wall paintings. Note: in the nave, the Crucifixion and the Last Judgement; in the Gothic chancel, the Legend of St Mary the Egyptian.

The Rival Brothers – *At Kamp-Bornhofen, turn right towards Dahlheim, and then right again at the sign "Zu den Burgen".*

The hill slopes become wild again. Beyond Kestert there is a fine **panorama**★★; from the ruins of the **Liebenstein** fortress, **Sterrenberg** and the valley below can be admired (the two castles are traditionally linked to an ancient legend concerning two rival brothers).

From Boppard onwards, where the Rhine swings lazily into a huge double loop, dense cultivation of vines appears and the landscape becomes less wild. Soon the fortress of Marksburg emerges on its promontory (At Braubach, take the road to Nastätten).

★ **Marksburg** – The castle ⊙, the only one in the whole Rhine valley never to have been destroyed, is built on a **site**★★ above the river that is almost aerial. Particularly notable are the fortress's great battery, a medieval garden with more than 170 different species of plant, and a collection of armour ranging from 600 BC to the 15C.

Lahneck – *3km - 2 miles from Lahnstein, near the confluence of the Rhine and the Lahn.*

The ruins of this **fortress** ⊙,

originally built in the 13C to protect neighbouring silver mines, were reconstructed in neo-Gothic style in the 19C. From the keep there is a view of the junction of the two rivers and the troubadour castle of Stolzenfels, on the far side of the Rhine.
Soon afterwards, the road arrives on the outskirts of Koblenz.

★★★THE RHINE CASTLES

② From Koblenz to Bingen *63km - 39 miles – allow a whole day*

This itinerary in effect retraces the previous one, in the opposite direction, on the other side of the river. Soon after leaving Koblenz, Lahneck comes into view again, with its tower overlooking the river confluence. Above, on the right, is Stolzenfels.

Stolzenfels – This enormous **castle** ⊙ was reconstructed, with its many crenellations, by Friedrich-Wilhelm IV in 1842. The style is now neo-Gothic, inspired by certain English manor houses. The sumptuous **interior**★ is arranged as a museum.
From the slope against which Stolzenfels is built, the terrace offers a view of Koblenz and the citadel of Ehrenbreitstein.

Rhens – A town of pretty colour-washed houses with half-timbered facades. The old town hall juts out into the main street.

Gedeonseck ⊙ – *1 hour Rtn, including 20min on a chair lift.*
Southwards, there is a superb **view★** of the great convex loop of the Rhine as it flows around the Boppard curve.

Boppard – A residential town where several small valleys meet. The **Rheinallee** makes a particularly pleasant riverside walk. Near the quay, the Gothic Carmelite church with its single tower still has its 15C choir stalls, and a very fine Renaissance funerary monument depicting the Eternal Father receiving the dead Christ.
The beginning of the "romantic" Rhine Gorge is marked by the two Rival Brothers fortresses *(see above)* on the opposite slopes. After Hirzenach, the Cat and Mouse towers are visible, standing above St. Goarshausen.

St. Goar – The village, clinging to the hillside at the foot of the impressive **Burg Rheinfels★★** ⊙, commands with St. Goarshausen the Loreley passage. The river here, obstructed and narrowed by the legendary rock, swirls and eddies dangerously as it races through the defile. Rheinfels, which threw back the assaults of Louis XIV, was until it fell to the French in 1797 the most powerful fortress in the whole valley. It is worth climbing to the top of the clock tower to get an overall view of the turbulent Rhine, the Cat and Mouse castles, and the maze of towers, gates, courts and casemates comprising the Rheinfels complex.
The banks of the river remain steep and heavily wooded until Oberwesel.

Oberwesel – South of the town, the Gothic **Liebfrauenkirche★** has a fine high-altarpiece, one of the oldest in Germany (early 14C), a Gothic rood-screen and, in the north aisle, a most unusual 1510 triptych illustrating the 15 cataclysms presaging the end of the world.
From the terrace of **Schönberg castle★**, a little further on, there is a view of Kaub, on the far side of the river, and the fortified isle of Pfalz. Schönberg is in fact a block of three forts sheltered by a common – and impressive – defense wall.
Pfalz, with the Gutenfels ruins perched on the heights far above it, is an astonishing sight: a massive stone ship, anchored in the middle of the fast-running river.

★ **Bacharach** – Once the property of the Counts of the Palatinate, Bacharach – a town of vineyards and ancient towers, relics of medieval fortifications – is one of the most popular resorts in the Rhine valley. The houses in the **Marktplatz** and the **Oberstraße**, wooden-walled and decked with flowers, are a delight. One of the last Romanesque naves built in Germany can be seen in the **Peterskirche**, although its four-stage elevation (arcades, galleries, triforium and clerestory windows) sound already a pre-echo of French Gothic. The ruins of the Gothic **Wernerkapelle** are nearby.
The ruined towers of Nollig and Fürstenberg mark the end of the valley's most grandiose stretch; from here onwards it is less winding, the river running between the steep eastern bank, topped by a few vines, and the cliffs on the opposite shore.
The road on this side passes below castles whose sites are ever more audacious, from Sooneck to Reichenstein and finally Rheinstein.

Sooneck ⊙ – This **fortress** is much restored and tiered to suit the terrain with a maze of staircases, platforms and terraced gardens beneath the turrets.

Reichenstein – Well-situated at the mouth of a rural valley, this neo-feudal **castle** ⊙ has a fine collection of arms and hunting trophies.

Rheinstein ⊙ – The **castle** is perched on a perpendicular rock spur, in a commanding position above the Rhine. From the foremost watchtower there is a **bird's-eye view★★** of the valley.
Once past the **Mäuseturm**, balanced on its tiny islet in the middle of the river, the valley widens out and the east bank becomes covered with terraced vines.

Bingen – Founded by the Romans at the confluence of the Rhine and the Nahe (Castel Bingium), this small river port today serves chiefly the wine-growing hinterland.

Burg Klopp, an ancient stronghold built by the Bishops of Mainz, has been razed to the ground more than once – in particular by the troops of Louis XIV in 1689, during the "Orléans War". Today it houses the town council, from the terrace of which there is a fine **view★** of the Binger Loch, between Hunsrück and the hills of the Rheingau, upstream from the Niederwald monument on the outskirts of Rüdesheim.

Respect the life of the countryside
Drive carefully on country roads
Protect wildlife, plants and trees

ROMANTISCHE STRASSE★★

Baden-Württemberg and Bayern
Michelin maps 419 folds 6-38/420 folds 17-42

From the Main valley to the foot of the Bavarian Alps, by way of peaceful valleys and an idyllic, rolling countryside, the "Romantic Road" itinerary recalls at every stage of its course some aspect of the past that could only belong to the history of Germany. One after the other, the tourist experiences evocations of life in the great medieval cities (Rothenburg, Nördlingen and Dinkelsbühl), the religious sensibility of artists like Tilman Riemenschneider *(qv)*, the prestige of German chivalry (Bad Mergentheim), the sumptuously Baroque character of the old episcopal courts and such imperial towns as Würzburg and Augsburg.

FROM WÜRZBURG TO ROTHENBURG o.d.T.

100km - 62 miles – about 4 hours

Leaving **Würzburg★★** *(qv)*, the B 27 winds down towards the valley of the Tauber, which it reaches at Tauberbischofsheim.

★ **Bad Mergentheim** – *See Bad MERGENTHEIM.*

Weikersheim – Once the seat of the Hohenlohe Princes, this small town has retained its 18C architectural unity, especially noticeable in the layout of the market, built in a semicircle on the palace side to provide a splendid vista.
The **castle** ⊙ was built between 1580 and 1680 on the banks of the Tauber, in a sober style divorced from Baroque influences. Two hundred years of decorative art (1550 to 1750 approximately) are illustrated by the remarkable collection of **furniture★★**. The magnificent **Knights' Hall★★** (Rittersaal), completed in 1603, is typical of the transition between the Renaissance style and the Baroque. Note the sculptured figures above the monumental doorway of emperors and empresses. The perspective of formal gardens (1710), peopled with statues in caricature in the style favoured by the Franconian courts of the period, ends in a charming perforated orangery.
The picturesque section of the run, in the narrow part of the Tauber valley, begins above the attractive town of Bieberehren. The road rises and falls over slopes covered at times by natural woodland, at times by orchards, above the willow-fringed river banks. Occasionally the stream forms a loop to feed a sawmill or watermill. This countryside is at its loveliest in springtime.

Creglingen – The isolated **Herrgottskirche** – about one mile along the road to Blaufelden – contains the precious **Altarpiece of the Virgin Mary★★** sculpted by Tilman Riemenschneider. The theme of the Assumption in the central motif has permitted the artist to translate all his own sensitivity into the attitude and expression of the Madonna.

Detwang – In the church at Detwang another Riemenschneider **altarpiece★** portrays the Crucifixion.

★★★ **Rothenburg ob der Tauber** – *See ROTHENBURG OB DER TAUBER.*

FROM ROTHENBURG o.d.T. TO DONAUWÖRTH

105km - 65 miles – about 5 hours

Feuchtwangen – A small town with an attractive market place surrounded by pretty houses and overlooked by a parish church housing another **Altarpiece of the Virgin** – this time the work of Albrecht Dürer's teacher, Michael Wolgemut. Near the café Am Kreuzgang there is a Romanesque **cloister**. Installed in a 17C peasant house is a **Museum of Franconian Folklore** (Heimatmuseum) displaying fine rustic furniture with regional pottery and costumes.

★ **Dinkelsbühl** – Ramparts and watch-towers still surround this medieval town which wakes up every year in mid-July with a colourful children's festival (Kinderzeche) commemorating the relief of Dinkelsbühl in the Thirty Years War *(see the Calendar of events)*.
The **Georgskirche★** has retained its Romanesque tower. The interior, a Gothic hall-church *(illustration p 26)*, is a remarkable sight, with all three naves decorated with skilfully designed fan vaulting. Among the town's many ancient buildings, note the **Deutsches Haus★** *(Am Weinmarkt)*, and its richly decorated Renaissance façade, as well as the **Hezelhof** *(Segringer Straße 7)*, remarkable for the long, two-tiered balconies hung with flowers that overlook its inner courtyard.

The undulating landscape of the Feuchtwangen-Dinkelsbühl region is supplanted, after Nördlingen, by the bleak wastes of the **Ries Basin**. This practically treeless depression amid the heights of the Swabian Jura forms a symmetrical bowl 20km - 12 1/2 miles across and a regular 200m - 656ft deep, which is thought by some geologists to have been caused millions of years ago by the fall of a gigantic meteorite.

Wallerstein – From the summit of the rock, reached by a pathway and then steps cut in the strata, there is a vast panorama over the Ries Basin *(access via the Fürstlicher Keller).*

★ **Nördlingen** – *See NÖRDLINGEN.*

Schloß Harburg ⊙ – A large fortified castle whose buildings, considerably enlarged and remodelled in the 18C, look down on the picturesque houses of a village tightly packed along the banks of the Wörnitz. On display are extensive **collections**★ of sculpture, ivory, enamel, tapestry and gold and silver plate.

Kaisheim – The former Cistercian **abbey church** (Zisterzienserkloster) was built at the end of the 14C in the full flower of the Gothic era. Around the chancel, very pure in style, is a 12-sided **ambulatory**★ with ogive vaulting, divided into two galleries. *(To visit, apply at the presbytery.)* The abbey itself is now used as a prison.

The valley of the Wörnitz, commanded by Schloß Harburg, peters out after a final, narrow, twisting section, allowing the Ries to connect with the Danube valley.

Donauwörth – On a hillside running steeply down to the Danube, the town is dominated by the **Heiligkreuzkirche**. The large 1720 Baroque building, with its concave interior galleries, is decorated with Wessobrunn stuccowork *(qv).*

FROM DONAUWÖRTH TO FÜSSEN

148km - 92 miles – about 1 day

This drive along the ancient Via Claudia, one of the main arteries of the old Holy Roman Empire, owes its interest less to the route (which follows the Lech valley, by now largely widened) than to the historical souvenirs evoked by the sites on the way. These include **Augsburg**★★ *(qv),* **Landsberg** *(qv),* the **Königsschlösser**★★★ *(qv)* and (at the price of a small detour) the **Wieskirche**★★ *(qv).*

ROSTOCK★

Mecklenburg-Vorpommern – Population 252 000
Michelin 416 D 20 – Town plan in the current Michelin Red Guide Deutschland

Rostock, with its widespread port installations, shipyards and huge fishing fleet, was until re-unification East Germany's only major sea outlet to the Baltic and the rest of the world. In order to get some idea of the scope of maritime activity in this city of half a million people, a **boat trip** ⊙ around the International Port is strongly recommended.

A Busy (and coveted) Port – A particularly choice situation on the wide Warnow estuary favoured the development of Rostock from the earliest days: by the beginning of the 13C, the town was already a member of the Hanseatic League, was minting its own money and was in the process of asserting its independence from the Princes of Mecklenburg. In 1419, Rostock founded the first Baltic university, which earned it the nickname of "Light of the North". Such a position and such a reputation soon excited the envy of powerful and covetous neighbours. The Danes and then the Swedes occupied the city during the Thirty Years War (1618-1648), returning for a second time while the Nordic countries were struggling for supremacy in the war raging from 1700 to 1721. Nor was the port spared during the Napoleonic Wars; it was occupied by French troops until 1813.

SIGHTS

★ **Marienkirche** – *Am Ziegenmarkt.*
The building as it is today – an imposing basilica in the form of a cross – results from a transformation in the second half of the 15C of a hall-church built in the previous century. It is one of the biggest churches in northern Germany.
The massive tower, lightened by pierced sections, was not completed until the end of the 18C. From the top there is a **panorama**★ of the city and the dock area.
Inside the church, the overriding impression is one of height, of verticality. Note especially the 1472 **astronomic clock**★★ (its face was remodelled in 1643), which comprises a calendar valid until the year 2017. The delicately worked bronze **baptismal font**★, decorated with scenes from the life of Christ, is supported by the figures of four men. The Baroque organ dates from 1770.

Rathaus (Town Hall) – *Neuer Markt.*
This is composed of three 13-14C gabled houses topped by a brick-built arcaded gallery supporting seven towers. In front of the block is a Baroque façade added in 1727. Across the square stand some fine gabled houses.

★ **Schiffahrtsmuseum (Navigational Museum)** ⊙ – *At the corner of the August-Bebel-Straße and the Richard-Wagner-Straße.*
Models, paintings and navigational instruments chart the history of maritime activity from the time of the Vikings to the present day. Note in particular the full-size reconstruction of a tramp steamer bridge, and a model of the present international port.

Kröpeliner-Straße – This pedestrian precinct, crossing the old city from the Rathaus to the Kröpeliner Tor, has become the town's shop-window and commercial centre. It is bordered by the familiar gabled houses dating from Baroque and Renaissance times. At No 82, the brick façade of the old (late 15C) Heilig-Geist-Spital presbytery is distinguished from the other buildings by a stepped gable.

★ **Kröpeliner Tor** – The 14C brick gate, six floors high, closes off the western end of the Kröpeliner-Straße. The interior has been turned into a **museum** evoking the history of the town (Stadtgeschichtliches Museum).

★ **Kulturhistorisches Museum (Historical Museum)** ⊘ – Collections of paintings and sacred art are displayed in this former Cistercian convent joined to the Heilig-Kreuz-Kirche – a brick-built, triple-aisle hall-church dating from the late 13C. On the late 15C **Altarpiece of the Three Kings★**, the background gives a good idea of Rostock in the Middle Ages.

EXCURSIONS

★ **Warnemünde** – *11km - 6 miles to the northwest.*
This one-time fishing village, "bought" by the town from the Prince of Mecklenburg in 1323, has become Rostock's most popular holiday beach. From the ferry terminal, services run to Denmark.

Bad Doberan – *15km - 9 miles to the west.*
The town developed aroud a Cistercian monastery founded in 1771. The little health resort is characterised by its Classicistic architecture, with buildings which were erected between 1800 and 1825 for the visitors of the Baltic spa town of Heiligendamm. At the time, Bad Doberan was the summer residence of the Mecklenburg court.
The principal sight is the **Münster★★** ⊘ of the former Cistercian monastery, which was built between 1294 and 1368 and is one of the most beautiful examples of the North German brick Gothic style. In accordance with the architecture of the Order, a mighty window decorates the towerless western façade. Flemish style chapels radiate out from the chancel with its ambulatory. The only decoration is this building, whose clear lines are so characteristic of the Cistercian order, is the clover leaf arched friezes made of black glazed stone under the roof.

Interior – Brick also dominates here, toned down by the colourful painted triforium between the archway and the clerestory. Ogive vaulting covers the three naves of the basilica, which radiates harmonic slenderness. The sumptuous decor reflects the church's significance as the place of burial of the Mecklenburg dukes. The **high altar★**, a filigree Lübeck wood carving dating from the year 1310, shows Old and New Testament scenes. The **rood altar** dating from 1370 and the mighty **triumphal cross★** which is part of it (depicted as the Tree of Life) have Christ on one side (for the lay-brothers) and Mary on the other (for the monks). The Late Gothic needle-shaped oak **tabernacle★**, which must be the oldest in Germany, originates from the same period. The **candelabra of Our Lady** features a charming Madonna with a crescent moon (symbolising chastity) in a glory; this outstanding work dates from the year 1290. Two side aisle windows with 14C Gothic **stained glass** are worthy of note.

Tombs of the Mecklenburg ducal house stand in the chapels around the chancel.

Heiligendamm – *21km - 13 miles to the west.*
A magnificent avenue of lime trees leads from Bad Doberan to the Baltic resorts of Heiligendamm and Kuhlungsborn, which are also accessible on the comfortable narrow gauge railway "Molli". Heiligendamm, the first German seaside resort, was founded in 1793 bu the Mecklenburg Duke Friedrich Franz I. The beautiful spa town architecture, such as the Classical spa house which dates from 1814-1816, and very many elegant buildings in Prof.-Vogel-Straße, bear witness to the resort's distinguished past.

★ **Kühlungsborn** – *30km - 19 miles to the west.*
Both a spa and a seaside resort, Kühlungsborn owes to its extensive pinewoods and a beach several miles long its position as one of the busiest holiday centres on the Baltic coast.

★ **Fischland, Darß and Zingst** – *To the northeast of Rostock.*
The peninsular chain of Fischland-Darß-Zingst in an attractive natural area in which woods, salt marshes, moorland and broad stretches of water alternate. The narrow tongue of land extends northwards and eastwards parallel to the mainland, separated from it by a lagoon (flat bays) in which brackish water from the Baltic and freshwater from the rivers leading down to it mingle. The artists' village of **Ahrenshoop** in the slightly hilly **Fischland** is a very popular Baltic resort. The holly tree is especially characteristic of the Ahrenshoop woods. **Darß and Zingst** form part of the National Park of the West Pomeranian lagoon area. The **sea eagle** nests here, and during the spring and autumn, whole colonies of cranes can be seen. The quiet charm of the salt marshes with their typical flora, such as samphire and sea asters, bewitch many a visitor. The contemplative nature of the little villages and seaside resorts with their reed-covered houses and cottages makes them especially attractive.

ROTHENBURG OB DER TAUBER★★★

Bayern — Population 11 000
Michelin map 419/420 R 14
Town plan in the current Michelin Red Guide Deutschland

One of the oldest towns on the Romantic Road *(qv)*, Rothenburg overlooks from its rocky crag four ox-bow bends in the Tauber river. As well as being old, the town is both picturesque and unspoiled. Once behind the ramparts in the car-less central enclave, the visitor faced with Rothenburg's ancient houses, street signs, fountains and narrow, cobbled lanes seems all at once in some kind of time-warp plunged back into the middle of the 16C.

HISTORICAL NOTES

The Burggarten spur, whose steep-sided promontory is enclosed within the tightest of the ox-bow curves, was a strongpoint, according to tradition, as far back as the time of King Pharamund. What is certain is that, from the 12C onwards, two castles — the first imperial, the second belonging to a count — stood successively on this rock platform so ideally placed to command the winding valley below. At first the town itself was small; the outline of its earliest circle of fortifications can be seen, with two towers (Markusturm and Weißerturm), in the arc formed by the Judengasse and the Alter Stadtgraben.

In the 13C the town spread out... then lost both its castles, destroyed in an earthquake in 1356. From then on the ambition of the local Rothenburg worthies inclined more and more towards the building, and then the embellishment, of such public works as might enhance their own importance: the Rathaus, the Jakobskirche, the long line of merchants' houses, with their impressive gables, on the Herrngasse.

But Rothenburg, now won over to the Protestant side, failed to recover from the recession and economic stagnation engendered by the rigours of the Thirty Years War *(qv)*. Reduced to the status of an obscure regional market, too poor even to rebuild its houses in line with the prevailing taste, the town vegetated ingloriously throughout the 17C and 18C, unable to expand beyond its own walls. In the 19C however this very antique-ness became an asset: strict preservation orders were placed on the steep-roofed houses with their tall gables, inherited from the Gothic period; no staircase turrets or corner oriels could be dismantled. Tourists of today, therefore, are granted a genuine glimpse into the past.

They will notice that half-timbering above a stone base or foundation is the general building rule, although roughcast or pebbledash usually hides the beams. In the Spital quarter, nevertheless, the woodwork of many lovely old houses remains exposed.

A Long Drink (Meistertrunk) – During the Thirty Years War, the Protestant Rothenburg fell to the Imperial army commanded by General Tilly *(qv)*. Tilly decided to raze the place to the ground. All pleas for mercy having been rejected, the Burgomaster as a last resort offered the victorious general a goblet of the very best local wine...and the miracle occured. His heart warmed by generosity, Tilly offered a way out. He would spare the town if some eminent local could empty in a single draught a hanap (a 6-pint tankard) of the same wine. A man named Nusch, a former Burgomaster, succeeded in this exploit and Rothenburg was saved (the after-effects on the courageous drinker are not recorded).

Every year now, on the three days of the Pentecost (Whitsun) weekend and certain other occasions, the population of Rothenburg takes part in a huge fête which is in effect a reconstitution of this event *(see Calendar of events)*.

★★★OLD TOWN (ALTSTADT) *time: 3 1/2 hours*

Starting at the Marktplatz, follow the itinerary marked on the town plan.

★ Rathaus (Town Hall) – The Gothic part, its gable topped by a 60m - 197ft belfry, is 14C, while that facing the Marktplatz, with its octagonal staircase tower, is a Renaissance work, completed by an 18C portico. Visitors can inspect various state or council chambers, or climb the tower for a **view★** of the fortified town. North of the Marktplatz is the gable of an ancient inn, the Ratstrinkstube, on which the figures of an animated clock re-enact mechanically *(at 11am, noon, 1pm, 2pm, 3pm, 9pm and 10pm)* the famous legend of the Long Drink.

Baumeisterhaus – The steps on the gables of this Renaissance house serve as pedestals for dragon motifs. Statues on the first floor represent the seven cardinal virtues, those on the second the seven deadly sins.

Mittelalterliches Kriminalmuseum (Museum of Medieval Justice) ☉ – Medieval attitudes towards crime and dissidence are reflected in this museum installed in the former headquarters of the Knights of the Order of St John of Jerusalem. Law books, seals, engravings, along with instruments of torture, punishment and execution are exhibited on four different floors. Among the most typical are a spiked chair used in witchcraft trials, iron-collared yokes, and "masks of shame".

Plönlein – A picturesque corner formed by the bifurcation of two streets, one level, one descending — but both ending at the same fortified gateway.

Leave the town by the Koboldzell gate, on the right, turn sharp right again, and follow the path circling the spur some way below the ramparts.

In the valley below, there is a remarkable arched, two-storey, **fortified bridge** (Doppelbrücke) which crosses the Tauber. Return to the Old Town via the Burggarten.

Burggarten – All that remains of the double fortress erected on this promontory is a chapel, the Blasiuskapelle, which has been turned into a war memorial, and a fortified gateway, the Burgtor. The area is now a public garden with views of the river, the two-tier bridge, the Topplerschlößchen (a riverside tower oddly topped by apartments) and, some way to the north, the village of Detwang.

Herrngasse – The mansions of formerly well-known personages line this busy commercial street. Those interested should look into some of the courtyards, for instance No 15 (**A**), where the half-timbered gallery rests on embossed wooden pillars.

St. Jakobskirche – Building of the Gothic church's east chancel started in the mid-14C. The foundation of the west chancel is penetrated by a vaulted passageway that leads to the Klingengasse. This chancel also houses the most precious work of art: Tilman Riemenschneider's **"Holy Blood" altarpiece**★★ (1504).
The composition of the main scene, the Last Supper, is original. Judas is shown from behind, facing Christ. The expressions are tense and perplexed, except for that of Jesus, which is full of compassion.
The east chancel overlooks a square on which stands the 1593 Renaissance building of the former college (Gymnasium).
Return to the Marktplatz.

297

ADDITIONAL SIGHTS

* **Spital (Hospital)** – A picturesque group of buildings, mostly 16C and 17C, built on the southern extremity of the plateau known locally as the Kappenzipfel (peak of the cap).
  There are works of art in the Gothic chapel and, in the middle of the courtyard, the Hegereiterhäuschen – a graceful pavilion with a pointed roof and turrets.
  From the hospital courtyards, the **Kalkturm** viewpoint can be reached (also accessible from outside), with its **view**★ over the town centre and the watch-path linking the Stöberleinsturm and the Sauturm.

* **Stadtmauer (The Ramparts)** – Constructed in the 13C and 14C, these ramparts, complete with gates and towers, are still in a state of perfect preservation. Long stretches are open to the public. Near the hospital, the southern entry to the town is defended by the **Spitaltor**★, a massive 16C bastion enclosing two inner courtyards, both oval.

  Wolfgangskirche – North of the Klingentor. A curious late 15C Gothic church, fortified and incorporated into the barbican doubling the defences of the gateway. The casemates and the parapet walk can still be viewed.

  Franziscanerkirche – The rood-screen, as well as walls and columns in this church, is decorated with fine 15C and 16C sculptures. Note also, on the left above a funerary niche, the Creglingen Madonna (1400).

  Reichsstadtmuseum ⊙ – A Dominican monastery from 1258 to 1544, this building is now a local museum showing, among other collections in its spacious, oak-beamed rooms, the Rothenburg Stations of the Cross (1494). Perhaps the most fascinating exhibit is the original hanap drained by ex-Burgomaster Nusch in front of General Tilly *(see above)*. The tankard's design depicts the Emperor and the seven Electors. It was made in 1616.

ROTTWEIL★

Baden-Württemberg – Population 24 000
Michelin map 419 V 9

Rottweil is a small, pleasant, fortified town on a spur circled by a bend in the Upper Neckar. The site, between the Swabian Jura and the Black Forest, is attractive. At carnival-time, Rottweil is renowned for its spectacular fools' procession (Narrensprung) *(photograph p 383)*.

SIGHTS

Leave the car in the carpark on the corner of Kriegsdammstraße and Nägelesgrabenstraße, and make your way on foot to the Schwarzes Tor, the gateway to the upper town.

Hauptstraße – From this street, dropping abruptly towards the river, the visitor can see what the old city must have looked like – between the old houses with their three-sided oriel windows, there is an appealing **view**★ of the distant Swabian Jura.

Heiligkreuzmünster – *On the left, past the Rathaus.*
A Gothic church remodelled in the 16C. Use the south entrance (the porch is neo-Gothic). Many **altarpieces**★ are displayed in the side chapels.
Outside, on the Münsterplatz esplanade, stands the Georgsbrunnen, a Gothic fountain ornamented with three charming sculpted groups: The Virgin, St George, St Catherine.

Go through the Pfarrgasse, left along Schulgasse and then onto Kriegsdamm.

Dominikanermuseum ⊙ – The museum owes its name to a Dominican monastery which was founded on this site in 1266. Of the monastery buildings, only the Baroque church remains. The architecturally attractive museum, which was built in 1992, exhibits the most important local finds dating from Roman times. The beautiful **Orpheus Mosaic**★ from the 2C AD, which is composed of 570 000 small stones, is well worth seeing. In addition the museum houses a high quality collection of **Swabian sculptures**★ from the 14C to 16C with works by famous artists (Multscher, Michel Erhart).

Take the Lorenzgasse to the Lorenzkapelle.

Lorenzkapelle – This former cemetery chapel was built in 1580, and now houses a collection of **Rottweil stonemasonry**. It displays the best work produced by the Rottweil stonemason's lodge in late medieval Swabia.

Turn left, and take the Hauptstraße back to the town's central crossroads.

Kapellenkirche – The **tower**★ of this Gothic church, Baroque on the inside, is a splendid example of the Flamboyant style. The square base, quartered with graceful staircase turrets, supports on the façade an unusual pierced loggia. The upper part of the tower, in two octagonal tiers, is lit by windows with a fine tracery of stonework. The three entrances retain their original Gothic carvings: the Last Judgement (west face) and the Knight's Betrothal (right corner turret) are outstanding.

EXCURSION

★ **Dreifaltigkeitsberg (Trinity Hill)** – *20km - 12 1/2 miles to the southeast.*
A minor road leads up to the pilgrimage church here from Spaichingen, on the edge of the Swabian Jura. From the top of the hill a wide **panorama**★ includes the Baar Depression and, a dark line in the distance, the sombre outline of the Black Forest.

RÜDESHEIM AM RHEIN★

Hessen – Population 9 600
Michelin map 417 Q 7 – Local map under RHEINTAL

The wine town of Rüdesheim lies at the southern end of the Rhine Gorge – where the river, deflected westwards through the Rheingau vineyards by the Taunus massif, decides to turn north again. Here at the Bingen Gap, gateway to the "Romantic Rhine", Rüdesheim has become the most popular tourist centre in the whole valley: the narrow streets, including the famous **Drosselgasse**, are crammed with visitors, attracted by the wine bars offering a taste of the celebrated local Riesling. There are also distilleries to be visited and cellars where sparkling wine can be drunk.

Brömserburg – Residence-cum-refuge for the Bishops of Mainz until the 13C, this stronghold passed into the hands of the Knights of Rüdesheim, and then became a meeting place for brigands. It was re-taken in 1281 by Archbishop Wernherr. Today, it is arranged as a **wine museum**. The outstanding exhibits are 21 old wine presses and a collection of amphorae (vases, jars, bins for storage or transport of wine).

EXCURSIONS

Niederwald Monument – *Access by road (2km - 1 mile) or by cable car (terminal on the Oberstraße: 20min Rtn).*
Built (1877-83) to commemorate the re-establishment of the German Empire in 1871, the monument comprises a statue of Germania (which alone weighs 32 tons) on a plinth with bronze bas-reliefs showing Bismarck, the Emperor Wilhelm I, the German Princes and their armies. From the terrace there is a **view** of the vineyards, Bingen, and the confluence of the Rhine and Nahe. The heights of the Palatinate are visible in the distance.

★ **The Rheingau** – *23km - 14 miles – allow 2 hours.*
A southern exposure allows successful cultivation of vines high up on the foothills of the Taunus. Before passing through these vineyards to reach Eberbach abbey, the road passes the picturesque villages of Geisenheim, Winkel and Hattenheim.

★★ **Kloster Eberbach** ⊙ – The former Cistercian abbey, the only sister foundation of Clairvaux in Germany apart from Himmerod in the Eifel, lies in a charming valley in absolute isolation. The abbey still emanates the peace and invitation to contemplation sought by its founders. In 1135, whilst St. Bernard was still alive, the Cistercian monks from Burgundy came here and laid the foundation stone for one of the best kept medieval monasterial establishments in Germany.
The **abbey church** was built in two stages, in 1145-1160 and 1170-1186. It is a Roman cross vaulted basilica with three naves, and its lack of decoration is characteristic of Cistercian architecture. Gothic chapels with beautiful tracery windows were built on the south side around the 1310-1340. A number of remarkable tombs dating from the 14C to the 18C bear witness to the church's significance as a burial place.
The individual abbey buildings are grouped around the **cloister**, which was built in the middle of the 13C and 14C. Only the portal remains of the **monks' refectory** which was built before 1186. Rebuilt in 1720, the room is impressive, with a magnificent stucco ceiling by Daniel Schenk from Mainz (1738)
The lay brothers' refectory contains a collection of mighty **wine presses**★★, documenting the wine producing tradition of the abbey which has endured for over 800 years. The oldest press dates from the year 1668.
The **monks' dormitory**, which is around 85m - 279ft long and which dates back mainly to the period around 1250/1270, is remarkable. The double-naved ribbed vaulted room was built with a slightly rising floor, and the columns were shortened accordingly, so that it appears longer than it is. The **chapter house** was built prior to 1186. A particularly beautiful star-ribbed vault from the year 1345 should not be missed. The stylised plant decoration dates back to 1500.

The abbey was secularised in 1803 and became a wine-growing property. Today it is the provincial winery of Hesse.

Kiedrich – The 15C **church** in this wine-growers' market town is still furnished in its original, rare Flamboyant form: the early 16C carved **pews★** and choir stalls are still adorned with polychromatic embellishment; they still have their Gothic inscriptions. The 14C **Kiedrich Madonna★**, beneath the rood-screen, shows French influence.

Eltville – Built beside the Rhine, the castle here was the residence of the Prince-Electors of Mainz in the 14C and 15C. Living quarters in the tower can still be viewed. In the Church of St Peter and St Paul *(Rosengasse 5)*, there is a very fine baptistry from the Mainz studio of Hans Backhoffen, with the symbols of the Four Apostles worked into the base.

RÜGEN★

Mecklenburg-Vorpommern

Michelin 416 C 23-24

Joined to the mainland by a long bridge (2.5km - 1 1/4 miles) straddling the straits opposite the town of **Stralsund★** *(qv)*, Rügen is Germany's largest island. In a total area of 926km² - 358sq miles, the Baltic island offers a surprising variety of scenery. In the west, as the straits widen towards the open sea, the coastline is indented, following the irregular contours of many inlets. Chalk cliffs and sandy beaches in the east attract summer crowds; the wooded southern shores face the wide, shallow waters of the Greifswalder Bodden (Gulf); and to the north Rügen is cut almost in two by the deep, extraordinarily jagged penetration of the Jasmunder Bodden – which is practically an inland sea.

MAIN SIGHTS

★ **Putbus** – The "white town" in the southeast of the island was founded in 1810 by Prince William Malte of Putbus, in imitation of Bad Doberan, as a royal seat and bathing resort. Although the princely castle was demolished in 1960, the Classical town has miraculously remained. A surprising harmonious picture of a homogenous whole, such as is rarely found in Germany, greets the visitor. It is not without justification that Putbus is known as "the pearl of Rügen".

★ **Circus** – The round circus, from which the roads radiate in a star shape, is surrounded by eaves-fronted houses, many with Classical ornamentation. Finished in dazzling white, they stand out from the green of the oaks. The 21m - 69ft high obelisk, which bears the Prince's crown on the top, stands in the centre of the circus.

★ **Theatre** – *Alleestraße*. The building was erected between 1819-1821 by the Berlin architect Steinmeyer (a student of Schinkel). The portico is made up of four Tuscan columns. Above the entrance, a blue stucco frieze, depicting Apollo and the Muses, stands out from the bright white of the building. The theatre is famous for its acoustics.

★ **Schloßpark** – The 75ha - 185 acre Schloßpark with its **orangery** (converted in 1853 by Friedrich August Stüler), **royal stables** and **parish church**, is laid out in the style of an English landscape garden.

★ **Jagdschloß Granitz** ⊘ – *South of Binz.*
In 1837 Prince William Malte I of Putbus had a hunting castle, the most important secular building on the island, built in the neo-Gothic Tudor style on the 107m - 351ft high Tempelberg, the highest point in Eastern Rügen. The four crenellated corner towers of the square castle rise up in the middle of Granitz woods. A 38m - 125ft high viewing tower was built in the inner courtyard in 1844, based on plans by Karl Friedrich Schinkel. The viewing **spiral staircase** (recommended as a subject for amateur photographers). From the top, the view of Rügen island is breathtaking. The rooms inside the castle are open to the public.

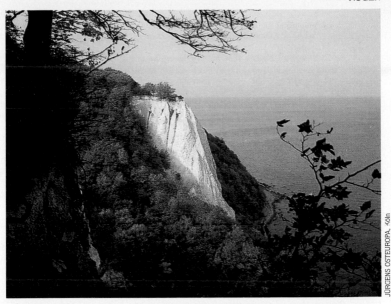

The Stubbenkammer, Rügen

* **Bathing resorts** – These are all in the southwest of the island. **Binz**, **Sellin**, **Baabe** and **Göhren** await the visitor with their inviting sandy beaches, beautiful seaside resort architecture and a woodland backdrop.
They can be reached in the "Racing Roland", a little train that connects Putbus to Göhren (via Granitz).

Saßnitz – Ferries to Scandinavia leave from this port. There are very beautiful beech forests in the north.

** **Stubbenkammer** – The **Königstuhl**, a 117m - 384ft high cliff, towers over the impressive chalk bluff which projects out into the sea. If you are lucky enough to visit on a sunny day you will see the breathtaking sight of the white cliff, surrounded by green foliage, shining brightly above the deep blue sea. It would be idyllic, if it weren't for the many visitors.

* **Kap Arkona** – Kap Arkona, with its 50m - 164ft high chalk cliffs, is the northernmost point of the island. The **old lighthouse** ⊙, a square three storeyed brick building on a granite base, was built in 1826-1829 based on plans by Karl Friedrich Schinkel. There is a wonderful **view**** from here right across to the neighbouring island of **Hiddensee**, where Gerhard Hauptmann lived for many years. Not far from the lighthouse, an embankment reminds us of the Jaromarsburg fortification, which was built there by the Slavs, but was destroyed by the Danes in 1168.

RUHRGEBIET

RUHR BASIN – Nordrhein-Westfalen
Michelin 417 L 4 - M 9, enlarged inset folds 1-2
Town plans in the current Michelin Red Guide Deutschland

Europe's largest single industrial centre, the Ruhr Basin (1 930 square miles) lies between three rivers: the Ruhr, the Rhine and the Lippe. The total population of the area is over five million, and almost 700 000 of these work in industry. But the Ruhr no longer merits its "Black Country" image, and today less than 2/5 of this workforce is employed by the mines and steelworks once characteristic of the Basin. The implantation of light industries, and an extensive "green belt" policy followed after the massive destructions of the Second World War, mean that a motorist today can cross certain sections of the region without seeing a single blast furnace or factory.

MINES, INDUSTRIES, LANDSCAPES

The Ruhr coal reserves are exceptionally well situated: seams run straight with few faults and little folding, dropping gently from south to north as they increase in thickness. All types of coal are present, from anthracite and slack to gas-bearing lodes. But since its beginnings in the 18C, the mining industry has moved its sites constantly towards the north. The original opencast outcrops in the Ruhr valley were abandoned long ago.

Richer deposits occur between the Ruhr and the Emscher, but in the century between 1850 and the beginning of the 1960s, no mine ever had to be sunk deeper than 400m - 1 312ft. Even here, however, rusting pitheads and deserted buildings testify to the large number of workings now shut down.

It is in the "new basin", a little further north, between the Emscher and the Lippe, that mining activity is concentrated today. Late 20C rationalization demands restriction of production to the most prolific source with the most efficient equipment, and since 1969 the existing Ruhr companies have been regrouped into a single development organization, the Ruhrkohle AG. Now, with a coalfield extending as far as Münster, with ultra-modern installations, fewer shafts and pits sometimes as much as half a mile deep, the exploitation yield has risen to 4 1/2 tons per day per man employed.

Costs nevertheless remain high: Ruhr coal is too expensive, competitive neither with the imported product nor with rival forms of energy. The mining industry is in recession and the workforce contracts every year. Two definitive changes have resulted from this situation, one geographical, the other social. Each also depends upon two factors – the production of steel and heavy industry – inseparable from the use of coal and relatively affected in the same way today. Resettlement plans and environmental imperatives have thus combined to make profound changes in these aspects of the Ruhr.

INDUSTRIAL REORGANIZATION

In the southern zone, as mining moved north, the old ironworks have given way to the scattered introduction of metal workshops and the small, clean installations of modern light industry. These Ruhr valley hillsides – the Bergisches Land – half industrial, half forested, without being idyllic nevertheless make a welcome stopping place.

In the middle zone – a 50km - 30 mile stretch between Duisburg and Dortmund – the prewar concentration of steelworks, factories, mines and industrial towns had by 1950 produced an urban sprawl of such density that all traces of agriculture, market towns and rural life had long been submerged. Yet even here, following a plan put into operation in 1968, seven north-south green belts, lakes, parks, airy workers' resettlement developments and re-established woodland areas have wrought astonishing changes in the landscape.

With heavy foreign competition in the fields of metallurgy and steel, the industrial face of the Ruhr turns increasingly towards chemicals, electronics, textiles, glassware, petro-chemical derivatives and the manufacture of automobiles.

But the process is not complete: the establishment of "clean" new industrial patterns remains the prime concern of the Ruhr's economic policy. Efforts already made in the direction of town planning (green spaces, restriction of traffic flow), of education (the new university at Bochum), of new technology and the defence of the environment, demonstrate the scope of the reconversion envisaged. Together with intense activity in the field of culture and a publicity campaign presenting the Ruhr Basin as "Germany's Rising Star" it is hoped this will erase the "Black Country" image of the Ruhr once and for all.

MUSEUMS OF THE RUHR AND THE BERGISCHES LAND
(A SELECTION)

Technical Museums

★★Deutsches Bergbau-Museum (German Mining Museum) ⊙ – At **Bochum** *(plan of the conurbation in the current Michelin Red Guide Deutschland).*

Founded in 1930, this museum is on the site of the old Germania mine (recognizable by its 68m - 223ft pithead frame). Over more than 100 000sq ft of floorspace it gives a complete picture of mining from antiquity to the present day. Models, reconstructions, graphics and original equipment cover every aspect of extraction, along with such techniques as drilling, ventilation and the use of explosives. Fifty feet underground, more than a mile of abandoned workings have been restored to illustrate various methods of coalface extraction and transport.

Deutsches Bergbau-Museum

Bochum – Deutsches Bergbau-Museum

★★Westfälisches Freilichtmuseum (Open-Air Technical Museum) ⊙ – At **Hagen-Selbecke**, *in the valley of Mäckingerbachtal. From Hagen (plan of the conurbation in the current Michelin Red Guide Deutschland), leave by ④ on the town plan. At Eilpe, turn right in the Breckerfeld-Halver direction and continue for just over a mile to Selbecke. From the museum car park (Museumsparkplatz), on the left of the road, 15min on foot.*

Along one and a half miles of this valley, more than 70 installations or buildings have been reconstructed to illustrate the evolution of crafts and techniques in Westphalian industry. Traditional metalwork displays (at the foot of the valley) include giant iron and copper hammers activated by water from artificial lakes. A half-timbered 18C house has been turned into a **Blacksmith Museum** with a working forge. There are also examples of James Nasmyth's steam hammer (c1840) and the zinc rolling mill of Hoesch (1841), both of which marked the start of true industrialization.

Higher up the valley an 18C papermill houses a **Printing Museum**. Finally there is a whole village of traditional craftsmen, where not only saddlers and smiths and ropemakers and dyers, but also bakers and brewers ply their trade.

★Eisenbahnmuseum (Railway Museum) ⊙ – At **Bochum-Dahlhausen**, *halfway between Essen and Bochum (C. Otto-Straße 191).*

Founded by a society of railway enthusiasts, this museum is installed in a disused station and rolling-stock repair shop on the north bank of the Ruhr. Equipment dating from 1914 (an engine house, a turntable, a hydraulic crane) is for the most part still in mint condition. More than 100 machines that ran on rails retrace the evolution of this form of transport from the beginnings to the end of the steam era. The highlights of the collection are 15 steam locomotives, the oldest of which is a Prussian T-3 of 1882. A postal locomotive built by AEG in 1913 marks the start of electrification. Railcars, hand-operated gangers' trucks, many types of wagon and a rail-or-road motorbus can also be seen.

★★Historische Sammlung Krupp in the Villa Hügel – *See ESSEN.*

★Klingenmuseum (Blade Museum) ⊙ – At **Solingen-Gräfrath.**

Known the world over for its knives and its scissors, Solingen is the centre of fine metalwork in Germany. The museum traces the history of side arms (magnificent dress swords), surgical instruments, razors and table cutlery.

Museum für Frühindustrialisierung (Early Industrialization Museum) ⊙ – *At* **Wuppertal-Barmen.**

Housed in a disused factory, this museum traces the economic and social history of the Wupper valley since the middle of the 18C.

Brauerei Museum (Brewery Museum) – *See DORTMUND.*

Fine Arts Museums

★ **Museum Folkwang** – *See ESSEN.*

★★ **Ikonenmuseum (Icon Museum)** ⊘ – *At* **Recklinghausen**, *Kirchplatz.*
The marvellous specimens exhibited here are arranged by theme: the Holy Trinity and
the Celestial Hierarchy (a theme rich in symbolism); the Virgin Mary; the Saints and
their Days (a splendid calendar of all the religious feasts). To these must be added a
collection of iconostases (screens separating the sanctuary from the rest of the church).

★ **Von der Heydt-Museum** ⊘ – *At* **Wuppertal-Elberfeld.**
This museum, housed in a former town hall built between 1827 and 1842 and
extensively remodelled in 1990, has an interesting collection of paintings: Flemish and
Dutch from the 16C and 17C; French and German from the 19C to the present day.
Sculptures from the 19C and 20C are also on display. Works by local painter Hans von
Marées (1837-1887) feature prominently. The cafeteria was designed by Buren.

Karl-Ernst-Osthaus-Museum ⊘ – *At* Hagen *(plan of the conurbation in the current
Michelin Red Guide Deutschland), Hochstraße 73.*
Housed in a building designed by Henry van de Velde in the Jugendstil *(qv)*, this
displays for the most part the paintings and drawings of the artist Christian Rohlfs
(1849-1938), German 20C art and Jugendstil decorative arts.

Kunstsammlungen Museum Bochum ⊘ – *At* **Bochum**, *Kortumstraße 147, opposite
the park.*
The collections in this spacious, airy modern building concentrate mainly on
contemporary art from Eastern Europe.

Ostwall-Museum – *See DORTMUND.*

Oberes SAALETAL★

SAALE VALLEY – Thüringen
Michelin 418 N 18 - O 19

Rising on high ground at the eastern extremity of the Thüringer Wald *(qv)*, the River Saale
flows 427km - 265 miles to the north before joining the Elbe upstream from Magdeburg.
Its winding course forms a natural link between such towns as Jena and Halle,
masterpieces of sacred architecture like Merseburg and Naumburg, and the innumerable
castles – Heidecksburg, Weißenfels, Dornburg – built on its banks.
The itinerary suggested below heads south through a countryside of woods and fields and
small market towns to an attractive upland region dotted with lakes, in a corner formed
by the old East- and West-German demarcation line and the Czech frontier.

FROM RUDOLSTADT TO SAALBURG

61km - 38 miles – allow 4 hours

Rudolstadt – Once the seat of the Princes of Schwarzburg-Rudolstadt, this town is
dominated by the fine silhouette of **Schloß Heidecksburg★** ⊘, which dates from 1737.
Several **rooms★★** magnificently decorated in the Rococo style are open to the public.

Saalfeld – In medieval times, Saalfeld was among the most important towns in
Thuringia, thanks to local silver and copper mines and a position on the main trade
route to Bohemia which assured its commercial prosperity.
The Renaissance **Rathaus** in the Marktplatz is designed around a façade that centres
on a staircase tower with two oriel windows. On the other side of the square, the
Stadtmarktapotheke (pharmacy) is one of the rare Romanesque (restored) buildings
in the area. The **Johanniskirche** displays a late 14C Last Judgement above its main
entrance. Several altarpieces from a Saalfeld studio (late 15C) can be seen in the
Thüringer Heimatmuseum ⊘, which has been installed in a former Franciscan abbey.

★ **Feengrotten (Fairy Grottoes)** ⊘ – *1km - 1/2 mile southeast of Saalfeld on Route No 281.*
Stalactites, stalagmites, concretions and petrifications... such near-magical
subterranean décor can be found in the abandoned galleries of this disused mine.

Leave Saalfeld on Route No 85. Cross the Saale at the Hohenwarte dam.

The artificial lake at **Hohenwarte** (Hohenwarte-Talsperre) curves for half a dozen miles,
in a series of wide arcs magnificently incorporated into the existing landscape.
Woodland scenery alternates with crops as the road crosses the plateau.

*Via Drognitz and Remptendorf, the suggested route arrives at the Bleiloch reservoir.
Driving across the dam, sightseers regain the river's east bank.*

This reservoir, 29km - 18 miles long, with an enormous volume of water retained, is
the largest of the five artificial lakes between Blankenstein and Saalfeld.

Saalburg – Now a lakeside town, Saalburg lost part of its outskirts when first the valley
was flooded. Remains of the 16C fortifications, however, can still be seen.

SAARBRÜCKEN*

Saarland — Population 200 000
Michelin map 417 S 5

The capital of the Saarland was first mentioned in the record books in 999, altough it dates back to Celtic and Roman times. During the 1C, the Romans built a vicus (small market town) at a river crossing of the Saar, crossroads of the Metz to Worms road and the link between Trier and Strasbourg. They also built a stone bridge over the river, which was to be used right up to the Middle Ages. The medieval settlement was the seat of the Counts of Saarbrücken. In 1321 it was given the status of a town, together with St. Johann on the north bank of the Saar. It came to the house of Nassau by marriage in 1381.

Baroque Saarbrücken – In 1738 Count Wilhelm Heinrich von Nassau (1741-1788) summoned the master builder **Friedrich Joachim Stengel**, who originally came from Zerbst, to the court in Saarbrücken. A time of intensive and fruitful building activity began, and the city's architecture today owes its character to the large number of buildings that have been preserved. The castle, the Ludwigskirche, the collegiate church in St. Johann, all originate from this period. Under the influence of Palladio, Stengel created impressive works in a Classical late Baroque style. Alt-Saarbrücken was therefore to gradually take on a new aspect, from 1752, as the seat of the court.

During the 19C, industrialisation along the Saar brought Saarbrücken economic growth, change and prosperity, but also monostructure. In 1909 (Alt-)Saarbrücken, St. Johann and Malstatt-Burbach joined together to become the city of Saarbrücken, following the incorporation of St. Arnual in 1896. Although it was seriously damaged during the Second World War, the city has developed into a regional metropolis, especially since 1950, when it became the capital of the 11th German province and completed the secession of the Saarland from France. It has since taken full advantage of its border situation.

Saarbrücken, full of the joys of living – People from the Saarland in general, and those from Saarbrücken in particular, are extremely convivial and enjoy celebrations. They will find any excuse to celebrate. You only have to visit the St. Johann market in the old city to see what we mean. Ludwig Harig, a well known Saarland writer, once said: "People from Saarbrücken iron out differences, they can lead the wolves to the lambs", which sums up the Saarlanders' flexible and tolerant mentality extremely well.

ALT-SAARBRÜCKEN (ON THE SOUTH BANK OF THE SAAR)

Schloß – The medieval fortress was succeeded at the beginning of the 17C by a Renaissance castle, which was demolished in 1738 to make way for a Baroque castle designed by the court architect Friedrich Joachim Stengel. Wars and conversion work left deep marks, so that reconstruction was necessary in 1982 and the new design was entrusted to **Gottfried Böhm**. The classical three-winged structure was renovated and the central façade was determinedly given a modern look, becoming a glass building through which the light floods. The banqueting hall is a successful symbiosis of glass and colour (the attentive visitor will not fail to miss three painted doves and a snake with a rose in its mouth, although Böhm has hidden them well).

The **Saar historical museum** ⊙, a glass and steel construction and a further creation of Gottfried Böhm, adjoins the right wing of the castle. Its permanent exhibition "Ten years, not a thousand" deals with National Socialism in the Saar region. Another important exhibition shows development since the post-war era and during the fifties, up to the point at which the Saarland became part of Germany.

Schloßplatz – A darkly paved central strip, in reality an invisible memorial, leads to the castle. The artist **Jochen Gerz** and students of the Saarland Academy of Art carved out all the names of the Jewish cemeteries known in Germany in 1933, on the underside of 2 146 stones. These were relaid with the inscription facing downwards. The **pump room** on the left should be seen, according to Gottfried Böhm, as a derivation from the Baroque guardhouses. It enlivens the extremely simple Schloßplatz.

Museum für Vor- und Frühgeschichte ⊙ – *First building on the left in Schloßplatz.* Housed in the former district parliament house, a neo-Baroque building. Inside there is a remarkable cast iron bannister from a Saarbrücken wealthy middle-class house, the Bodesch Palais (25 Altneugasse), created by court blacksmith Höer. On the ground floor, finds mainly from Roman times can be admired. The central feature of the museum is however the **Celtic princess's grave**★★ from Reinheim on the 1st floor, which dates back to 400 BC. The find is considered one of the most important in Central Europe from the early Celtic period. The princess's jewellery and the tomb furnishings, which include a gilded bronze pitcher, are wonderfully well preserved.

A further building by Stengel, the old town hall, or **Altes Rathaus**, with its clocktower and its imperial roof (1748-1750) stands at the western end of the Schloßplatz. The Saarbrücken city coat of arms is visible on the gable end. The **Abenteuermuseum** (Museum of Adventure) ⊙ housed on the upper storey contributes to an understanding of foreign peoples and foreign countries.

The **Erbprinzenpalais** stands on the southern side of the Schloßplatz, a building converted by Stengel for the hereditary prince Ludwig von Nassau between 1760 and 1766 from three older houses and adapted to the style of the castle, with a triaxial central projection and a mansard roof. It has been used for many purposes since the French Revolution, for example as the seat of the Prussian mountain authority, the mining administration or police headquarters, and today the offices of municipal institutions.

Schloßkirche – *Am Schloßberg.*
The church was built at the end of the 15C and reconstructed in late Gothic style in 1683 after a serious fire, seriously damaged during the Second World War and rebuilt again in 1956-1958.
Twenty six glass paintings by **Georg Meistermann** must be admired, together with Baroque **tombstones** of the graves of Nassau-Saarbrücken, including that of Wilhelm Heinrich and his wife from the year 1772 (in the tower), created by the court sculptor Johann Philipp Mihm.

★★ **Ludwigsplatz and Ludwigskirche** – This is Stengel's masterpiece, one of the most beautiful and uniform late Baroque complexes in Germany, erected between 1762 and 1775.

Ludwigsplatz – The square is bordered in the north, south and west by eight palaces of various sizes. All with three storeys and mansard roofs, they illustrate the transition from the late Baroque to the neo-Classical style. Their white and silver-grey colouring enhances the effect of the Ludwigskirche, which is built in yellow and red sandstone in the centre of the square. The long building (front elevation) on the western side is the former orphanage. The Minister-President also has his offices in Ludwigsplatz.

Ludwigskirche ⊘ – A successful restoration project has allowed this unique Baroque Protestant church to radiate its former glory once again. The east and west ends of this building in the shape of a cross are slightly shorter and polygonal. The east end exhibits a degree of splendour which is quite unusual in a Protestant church, with elaborate window frame and statues of the Evangelists by Franziskus Bingh in the splays either side of the projecting building. A stone roof balustrade with further statues by Bingh (now copies), representing figures from the Old and New Testaments, runs around the church.
The **interior**, with its restrained elegance, forms a contrast to the sumptuous iconological exterior. The extremely light and airy impression is enhanced by the light delicate colouring of the stucco ornamentation. Of the original four galleries, only those in the east and west ends (choirs) have so far been reconstructed. They are supported by canephori, which symbolise worldly and spiritual power (east end) and the sacraments, the sermon, the vocal and instrumental church music (they support the organ). The golden shining eye of God, a frequent image of the Baroque and Enlightenment age, watches in the central dome, which is supported by four pillars.
The **Friedenskirche** built by Stengel, completes the harmonious impression of this beautiful ensemble beyond the eastern side of Ludwigsplatz.

Ludwigskirche and Ludwigsplatz, Saarbrücken

Marion Worm/Amt für Öffentlichkeitsarbeit

ST. JOHANN

★ **St. Johanner Markt** – The old city around the market is the true heart of Saarbrücken. The focal point is the beautiful market fountain, with its obelisk and cast iron railing, which was built in 1759-1760. Life pulses in the crooked streets and the numerous bistros (France is very close by). No 22, the seat of the former freemasons' lodge with its beautiful wooden door is worthy of note. No 19 is said to feature the oldest window in the old city, dating from 1668.

★ **Basilika St. Johann** ⊙ – Built by the princely master builder Stengel between 1754 and 1758, and consecrated to St John the Baptist and St. Ludwig, this church with its onion tower and lantern is another jewel of the late Baroque period. The tympanum over the main doorway shows the Synagogue and the Church. The balconies were built in 1789 by Heinrich Heidehoff, and are supported by six oak beams surrounded by artificial marble. The four confessionals, which date back to original plans by Stengel and already hint at the Louis XVI style, are noteworthy. The paintings in the medaillons show King David, Saint Mary Magdalene, Peter and Dismas (the penitent thief). The pulpit is original and its shell-shaped niches show the four Evangelists and Christ as a teacher. The side altars are copies (from the church of St. Nicolas in French Sarreguemines). However the figures of the Saints, which were produced by Wunnibald Wagner, are originals.

The mirrored ceiling above the high altar (original) shows the rose motif which also appears elsewhere in the church, as a symbol of discretion, but also as the coat of arms of the town of St. Johann.

A **Pietà** of beautiful quality stands in the right hand chapel of the chancel. It dates from the first half of the 15C, and has been restored in colour.

ADDITIONAL SIGHTS

Saarland-Museum – Alte Sammlung ⊙ – *1 Karlstraße (opposite the Moderne Galerie).*

Paintings and decorative arts (including a remarkable Renaissance cabinet from Limburg monastery) from southwest Germany and Lorraine from the Middle Ages up to early modern times. There is an extensive collection of ceramics and procelain.

Moderne Galerie ⊙ – *Bismarckstraße, on the banks of the Saar.*

20C art (paintings, sculptures, graphic art). The main emphasis is on German Impressionism and above all **Expressionism★**. There are major works by artists of international stature, such as Picasso, Léger, Tapiès, Beuys, Polke.

★ **Stiftskirche St. Arnual** – *In the district of St. Arnual, via Talstraße and Saargemünder Straße.*

The Gothic church was erected between the end of the 13C and the early 14C, and was given a Baroque domed roof in 1746, based on plans by Stengel. It was named after Bishop Arnuald von Metz, who lived in the 7C. The cross-shaped three naved vaulted basilica which incorporates the west tower and the projecting porch is one of the most important religious buildings in southwest Germany, a transitional building of French Gothic design in the east, but restrained by influence from Trier.

Having been the burial place of the Dukes of Nassau-Saarbrücken since the 15C, the church houses fifty **tombs★★** dating from the 13C to the 18C, some of which are masterly and are decorated in colour. The tomb of **Elisabeth von Lothringen** (who died in 1446 and won a name for herself as a translator and writer of medieval prose) is to be found in the chancel. The northern wall of the chancel features the larger than life-sized Renaissance grave of **Count Philipp von Nassau-Saarbrücken** (who died in 1621) with his mother Anna Maria von Hesse and his sisters Dorothea and Luise Juliane. In the northern transept, note the altar tomb of **Count Johann III** (who died in 1472), in full armour, with his two wives Johanna von Heinsberg and Elisabeth von Württemberg, a work of considerable artistic merit. Above it stands the wall tomb of Count **Johann Ludwig** (who died in 1545) with his two sons. The octagonal **font★** (15C) made of red sandstone shows the Ecce Homo motif and an angel with the instruments of the Passion.

Deutsch-Französischer Garten – *Deutschmühlental, towards Forbach.*

A park (50ha - 124 acres in size) with a Lilliputian world straight out of Gulliver's Travels, chairlift and Europe's largest water organ beckons visitors to promenade outside the gates of Saarbrücken.

EXCURSIONS

Schloßberghöhlen ⊙ – *In Homburg, 20km - 12 miles to the east via the A6 motorway.*

The largest coloured sandstone caves in Europe are manmade. Mile long corridors, 2km - 1 mile of which can be visited, extend over 12 levels. The caves were built between the 11C and 17C and were mainly used for defence purposes. They served as munitions and food stores, and during the Second World War they were used as air raid shelters. At a constant temperature of 10°C - 50°F, the humidity is between 80 and 90%. Ventilation is natural.

The stone out of which the caves are hollowed is a sediment brought about by wind and sea deposits during the Triassic period (230-160 million years ago). The beautiful yellowish red sandstone gives the underground world unexpected colour.

Römermuseum Schwarzenacker ⊙ – *2km - 1 mile to the east of Homburg, via the B 423.*

The Roman settlement of Schwarzenacker was apparently as large as the medieval town of Worms. It was founded at around the time of the birth of Christ and was destroyed by the Alemanni in 275 AD. The excavations uncovered roads, buildings and also many examples of diffrent skills. The house of an optician and a columned house with a cellar have been reconstructed and are graphic examples of Roman architecture. The finds are exhibited in a Baroque house, the Edelhof, from where a Baroque garden leads to the open-air museum.

Unteres SAARTAL

SAAR VALLEY – Rheinland-Pfalz and Saarland
Michelin map 417 Q 3 - R 3

Between Mettlach and Konz, the River Saar cuts its way through the crystalline Hunsrück Massif, the resistance of which reduces the valley to a winding defile at times visible only from the top of its steeply sloping sides.

FROM METTLACH TO TRIER

57km - 35 miles – about 2 hours

Mettlach – The Baroque, red sandstone façade of the old abbey – now the offices of a ceramics factory – rises above the trees bordering the road leading uphill towards Merzig. Downstream, in a public park nearby, stands the Alter Turm, a ruined octagonal funerary chapel dating from the 10C.

★★ Cloef – *7km - 4 miles west of Mettlach then 15min on foot Rtn.*

From a viewpoint high above the river, there is a view of the Montclair Loop, a hairpin curve enclosing a long, densely-wooded promontory.

Return to Mettlach.

From Mettlach to Saarburg, the road runs at the foot of the valley, forested on the lower slopes, with tall escarpments above. Vines appear as the valley widens.

Saarburg – The setting of this small town is typical of the valley's final section, with terraced vineyards now on every side. There is an attractive view of the town from a knoll crowned with the ruins of a 10C castle. In the old quarter, near the Markt, a 20m - 66ft cascade plunges between houses built on the rock.

After Konz, where the Saar joins the Moselle, follow the river to Trier.

★★ Trier – *See TRIER.*

German wines

Since legislation passed in 1971 and 1982, German wines can be divided into four categories:

(Deutscher) Tafelwein – table wine with no clearly defined region of origin, which may in fact be a blending of other Common Market wines or of purely German ones

Landwein – medium quality wine which carries a general indication of origin (eg Pfälzer Landwein) and can only be made from officially approved grapes; it must have at least 55° "Öchslegrade" and be dry or medium dry

Qualitätswein bestimmter Anbaugebiete – wine of superior quality which carries an official control number and originates from one of the officially recognised regions (Gebiet), eg Moselle, Baden, Rhine

Qualitätswein mit Prädikat – strictly regulated wine of prime quality, grown and made in a clearly defined and limited area or vineyard and generally carrying one of the following descriptions: *Kabinett* (a perfect reserve wine), *Spätlese* (wine from late harvest grapes), *Auslese* (wine from specially selected grapes), *Beerenauslese* and *Trockenbeerenauslese* (sweet wines), *Eiswein* (wine produced from grapes harvested after a minimum -7°C frost).

SÄCHSISCHE SCHWEIZ★★★

SWISS SAXONY – Sachsen
Michelin map 418 N 26

Lying between Dresden and the Czech frontier, the region known as Swiss Saxony is one of Germany's most popular – and most spectacular – natural wonders. It is an area of sheer sandstone cliffs, of table-shaped outcrops and isolated pillars, of deep gorges gouged from the rock and fantastically shaped formations through which the upper reaches of the Elbe flow in wide curves.

This huge depression can be explored by road, following the itinerary suggested below, or from the river, taking one of the "Weiße Flotte" boats plying between Dresden and Bad Schandau.

The Bastei viewpoint, Swiss Saxony

Geological Formation – The Elbe sandstone massif (Elbsandsteingebirge) resulted from the raising up – and subsequent decomposition – in the Tertiary Era of sedimentary limestones originally laid down over the Primary bedrock.

Vertical faulting of the horizontal sandstone beds, followed by the action of erosion, then produced over the millenia the flat-topped maze of fantasy formations through which the river today winds its way.

ROUND TOUR FROM DRESDEN

78km - 49 miles – 1 day

★★★ **Dresden** – *See DRESDEN.*

Leave the city to the east by the Pillnitzer Landstraße (V) on the town plan inset on Michelin map 418.

★ **Schloß Pillnitz** – *See DRESDEN: Excursions.*

★★★ **Bastei** – This magnificent viewpoint perched 200m - 656ft above the Elbe crowns a bleak spine commanding a lunar landscape carved from the rock. The superb **view★★** takes in the greater part of Swiss Saxony.

From the hotel nearby, a footpath leads to **Felsenburn Neurathen**, a fortress which is reached via a natural bridge spanning a deep ravine. Below the castle, an open-air theatre quarried from the rock can be seen.

★ **Bad Schandau** – Apart from being the main tourist centre of the region, Bad Schandau is also a spa renowned for the properties of its iron-rich waters, which have been exploited since 1730. At the exit from the town, in the direction of Schmilka, a lift and a footpath lead to the Ostrauer Scheibe, from which there is a superb **view★** of the Schrammsteine – a chaotic rock massif much favoured by amateur mountaineers.

The **Kirnitzsch valley★** (Kirnitzschtal), which can be followed by mountain railway, is hemmed in by steep cliffs.

Cross the Elbe at Bad Schandau and turn right along the south bank of the Elbe towards Königstein fortress.

★★ Festung Königstein – The great sweep of the Elbe here is overlooked by the 415km - 1 362ft Lilienstein on the east bank, and the Königstein (360m - 1 181ft) on the west. The formidable fortress crowning the latter was built between the 13C and the 16C, strengthened and enlarged in the 17C and 18C, and served several times as a refuge for the Court of Saxony. Prisoners held there had very little chance of escaping. Among the most famous internees were Böttger, the inventor of hard-paste porcelain *(see MEISSEN)*; August Bebel, founder with Karl Liebknecht of the Social Democrat party in 1869; and the Second World War French General Giraud. (Giraud was one of the few who did get away, a celebrated escape accomplished with the help of a rope tied to the bars of a loophole in the castle's outer wall.) From the old rampart walk, which follows the edge of the Erzegebirge, there are splendid **views★★** of the Lausitz foothills and the distant mountains of Bohemia.

★ Barockgarten Großsedlitz ☉ – This **Baroque pleasure ground** was partly laid out by Pöppelmann *(qv)* in the French style in 1719. It is still possible to see the Orangery, the Stille Musik – a double-flight stairway surrounding an ornamental pool – and statues of mythological Greek heroes sculpted by Kirchner and Thoma.

Continue the itinerary and return to Dresden on road no 172.

Bad SÄCKINGEN★

Baden-Württemberg – Population 16 000
Michelin map 419 X 7

A small town on the fringe of the Black Forest and beside the Rhine – where the river forms the frontier with Switzerland. Much of the lay architecture shows Swiss influence.

★ Fridolinsmünster – Named after the missionary who converted the Alemanni in the 6C, this 14C Gothic church is an example of how Baroque features were sometimes added to another architectural style – arcades of Gothic arches passing directly into groined vaulting; lowered vaults to make an easier decorating surface; tall windows transformed into rounded bays. The decoration includes fine stucco-work from the School of Wessobrunn *(qv)*.
The church treasury contains the Shrine of St Fridolin (magnificent 18C work from Augsburg, in the form of a carriage chest).

★ Rheinbrücke (Rhine Bridge) – Built to span the Rhine at the end of the 16C, this roofed bridge constructed of wood is the oldest of its kind still standing in the world.
Restricted today to pedestrians and cyclists, the structure rests on pillars of stone.

EXCURSION

Waldshut – *26km - 16 miles to the west.*
Halfway up a wooded, semicircular slope rising from a curve in the Rhine, this small town retains its two fortified gateways and its **Kaiserstraße** – a street whose ordered lines are broken by houses with overhanging eaves in the manner of Bernese peasant homes.

Abtei SALEM★

Baden-Württemberg
Michelin map 419 W 11

This Cistercian abbey, founded in 1137, was at its most influential under the Abbot Anselm II (1746-1778), the builder of Birnau (qv).
Part of the buildings are now occupied by a private school started by the educationist Dr Kurt Hahn and attended before the Second World War by Britain's Duke of Edinburg (Dr Hahn later emigrated to Scotland and founded Gordonstoun).

★ **Münster** ⊙ – The former abbey church was constructed between 1299 and 1414. Outside, the extreme severity of the Gothic façade is relieved by slender bays lightening the east and west gables.
Inside, the design is typical Cistercian Gothic, with a large chancel and flattened chevet, soaring vaults and side aisles supporting the nave through walls abutting on wide arcades.

★ **Schloß** ⊙ – The abbey buildings were remodelled in the Baroque style at the beginning of the 18C. Visitors can follow the evolution of the stuccowork entrusted to artists of the Wessobrunn School (qv) over a whole century.

Oratory (Betsaal) – Wessobrunn stucco still adorns the ceiling of this former summer refectory.

Library – Another superb ceiling, this time with basket-handle vaulting.

Emperors' Hall (Kaisersaal) – Completed in 1708, this was the first great State Hall in the Baroque style inaugurated in a German abbey. Statues of Emperors and medallions of Popes comprise the sculpted decoration.

Abbots' Apartments (Prälatenquartier) – Note among these discreetly charming rooms the green Rococo study (1764) with its swan motif – the emblem of Abbot Anselm II.

Untertor-Haus (Lower Gatehouse) – Between the pilasters of this strikingly elegant Baroque entrance, the decorative window lintels have a different design on each storey.

Feuerwehr-Museum – 500 years of the history of the fire brigade is brought to life here, with equipment from around the world.

ST. BLASIEN★

Baden-Württemberg – Population 4 400
Michelin map 419 W 8

The majestic domed church dedicated to St Blaise comes suddenly into view at the far end of a wooded valley in the Hotzenwald, in the southern part of the Black Forest. It stands in the grounds of a medieval monastery founded in 835 by a brotherhood of hermit monks who ranged all over the southern part of Germany. Although the air is bracing, the town – popular with holiday-makers – distils an air of great tranquillity.

★★ **Dom** – The Baroque church, following a plan favoured in that epoque, is built within a rectangle of old abbey buildings. The French architect, Pierre-Michel d'Ixnard (1726-1795), graced it with a central cupola, behind a peristyle, which rises 64m - 210ft from the ground. After St Peter's, Rome, and Les Invalides in Paris, this is the third largest dome in Europe. Within it, lit by deeply embrasured windows, is a false cupola. Despite the fact that it appears to rest on the columns of the central rotunda, this is in fact suspended from the true dome. The chancel, which has cradle vaulting, lies behind the high altar.

EXCURSIONS

The Hochkopf Massif – 45km - 28 miles to the west – 3 hours. Drive, via Todtmoos, to the Pass of Weißenbachsattel.

Hochkopf – 1 hour Rtn on foot. From the car park, on the right side of the road, a footpath leads to the lookout tower, from which there are superb **views**★★ of the barren peaks of the Belchen and the Feldberg, to the west, and – on clear days – the Alps to the southeast.

★ **Bernau** – In a lush pastural valley, the fine Bernau farms, hugging the fertile ground, are grouped in picturesque hamlets.
At Bernau-Dorf, the Rathaus houses an **exhibition** of paintings by the local artist **Hans Thoma** – notably landscapes of the Black Forest executed with great sensitivity.

The Valley of the Alb (Albtal) – 30km - 18 1/2 miles to the south – 1 hour.
The road runs high above the Alb Gorges, alternating sections along the edge of the cliffs with tunnels through the rock, before it rejoins the Rhine at Albbruck.

SAUERLAND ★
Nordrhein-Westfalen
Michelin map 417 M 6-8

The Sauerland, which forms the hinterland to the Ruhr Basin, is the most mountainous, if not actually the highest part, of the Rhineland Schist Massif.
It is crowned by the **Langenberg** (843m - 2 766ft), near Niedersfeld, which is already in effect a transitional area linking the Sauerland with the Waldeck heights.
Numerous artificial lakes in the region supply water and hydro-electric energy to the industrial towns of the Ruhr, serving also as centres for water sports. The Upper Sauerland, especially the Rothaargebirge, a range covered by forests of beech and fir, is very popular with tourists.

FROM SOEST TO BAD BERLEBURG
181km - 112 miles – allow one day

★ **Soest** – *See SOEST.*

★ **Möhnesee** – *See SOEST: Excursions.*

Arnsberg – The old town is built on a spur enclosed by a bend in the Ruhr river, rising in tiers above the waterside. To the north, a clock tower commands the approach to the **Schloßberg** ruins (good view); to the south lies the former abbey quarter, where a superb Rococo gate, the Hirschberger Tor, still stands.

Beyond Arnsberg, the road skirts the right bank of the Sorpesee reservoir *(water sports)*, then crosses the Lennegebirge massif. There are many attractive viewpoints, particularly near the pass. On the far side of Finnentrop, the Bigge valley is punctuated by a number of rock-strewn passages.

★ **Attahöhle (Grotto)** ⊘ – *On the right-hand side of the road, just before Attendorn.*
This strange cavern eroded from the limestone extends for no less than 3km - 1 3/4 miles into the bedrock. Apart from a multitude of stalactites and stalagmites, curious stone "draperies" are visible, some of them translucent.

Attendorn – The reputation of Attendorn was at its height in the Middle Ages, as witness the splendid 14C **town hall** (Historisches Rathaus) with its stepped gable, the open, arcaded hall of the old covered market (Alter Markt), and the **Sauerland cathedral** (Sauerländer Dom). This Gothic hall-church has magnificent 14C interior decorations. Southeast of Attendorn, on the other side of the Bigge, is **Burg Schnellenberg**, which dates, in its present form, largely from the 17C.

Biggetalsperre – This dam, in service since 1964, forms with the Lister barrage – which has flooded an adjacent valley – the largest reservoir in Westphalia.

About 2km - 1 mile before Olpe, fork left on Route B 55. Soon after Bilstein, on a small mountain road, take a right turn in the direction of the Hohe Bracht.

Hohe Bracht – (584m - 1 916ft). From the viewing tower (620m - 2 034ft), there is a fine panorama, including the hummocked Rothaargebirge massif as far as Kahler Asten.

After crossing the rural landscape of the Lenne valley, the route passes **Grafschaft** and **Oberkirchen**, two villages with pretty half-timbered houses, and then the country becomes wilder and more hilly. Beyond **Nordenau**, a typical Upper Sauerland village where the houses are roofed with slate, is the ski station of Altastenberg. Finally, on the far side of an open upland plateau with splendid views all around, the road arrives at Kahler Asten.

Kahler Asten – At 841m – 2 759ft, this is the highest point of the Rothaargebirge. From the lookout tower, as might be expected, there is a superb **view** all around. To the northeast is the spa and winter sports centre of Winterberg.

Slate quarries flank the road back down, which is twisty but well-made. There are many attractive views towards the south.

Bad Berleburg – The slate cladding which faces the houses lends this mountain village an air that is both sober and dignified. From the upper levels there is a good view of the 16-18C **castle**.

SCHLESWIG ★

Schleswig-Holstein – Population 26 000
Michelin map 415 C 12
Town plan in the current Michelin Red Guide Deutschland

Schleswig, an old maritime town of white houses, was built on low-lying banks at the inner end of an arm of the sea, the **Schlei**, which penetrates the coast for 43km - 27 miles. From the car park on Route B 76, there is an attractive **view**★ of the old town below the cathedral, on the far side of the water.

The Vikings – Merchants were settled on the south bank of the Schlei at the beginning of the 9C. Their favoured position at the crossroads of the old north-south road to Jutland and the east-west route used to transport light loads from the Baltic to the North Sea soon made the settlement an important North European trade centre.

A century later, Vikings from Sweden invaded the region. They renamed the area **Haithabu** ("the town in the heather") and encircled it with a vast defence system of which the **semi-circular retrenchment** beside the Haddebyer Noor *(access by ② on the town plan)* remains today.

Near this lagoon, stones with runic carvings such as the **Busdorfer Runenstein** (access via the Busdorfer Straße) are visible at another archaeological site. There are further Viking remains at Gottorf castle.

In the 11C, the townspeople of Haithabu, seeking better defences against Scandinavian marauders, crossed to the north bank of the Schlei to found the town of Schleswig.

★★★THE NYDAM BOAT (NYDAM-BOOT) ⊙ *time: 1/2 hour*

This oak-hulled long ship with its fine lines is the oldest Germanic vessel of any size that has ever been discovered. Dating from about the 4C, it was excavated in 1863 from the Nydam marshes, on Danish territory. Displayed in the Archäologisches Landesmuseum, the ship is 23m long by 3m wide (75ft by 10ft). It was powered by 36 oarsmen.

Other discoveries preserved for centuries in the peat, can be seen in the museum. They include weapons, footwear, the remains of clothing – mostly leather – and even human bodies.

ADDITIONAL SIGHTS

Schloß Gottorf ⊙ – Two large museums devoted to the Schleswig-Holstein Land are housed in this 16-18C castle, once the seat of the Holstein-Gottorf ducal family, which in 1762 became the Imperial House of the Tsars of Russia. The **Schleswig-Holsteinisches Landesmuseum**★★ has representative collections of local art, crafts and handiwork.

Note especially the Gothic Hall (sacred art of the Middle Ages), the galleries exhibiting furniture, and the **Renaissance Chapel**★★, complete with ducal loggia. The **Archäologisches Landesmuseum**★ *(see also above)* offers a systematic presentation of the area's prehistory, from Neolithic times to the era of the Vikings.

★ **Dom St. Peter** – Thanks to its graceful spire, this brick-built Gothic hall-church can be seen from far off. Enter by the south (St Peter's) doorway, which is of stone, with a carved tympanum dating from 1170. The most remarkable work of art is the 1521 **Bordesholm Altarpiece**★★, which can be seen in the chancel. Northwest of the transept lies the 14C **cloister**, with stylized vine-leaf motifs painted on the vaulting.

The Holm – This is an old sailors' and fishermen's quarter. The low houses crowd around a quiet square, the **Friedhofsplatz**★, which contains a cemetery and a chapel.

SCHLESWIG

Wikinger Museum Haithabu (Viking Museum) ⊙ – *Access via Route B 76, direction Kiel.*

This annexe to the ArchäologischesLandesmuseum is near the Haddebyer Noor lagoon, next to the old Viking site *(see above)*, whose history it traces. A large number of objects unearthed in various digs (jewels, weapons, tools and domestic implements) are on display, along with graphics and models of the Viking settlement. The galleries are very well laid out, with a wealth of information on the life and times of the Haithabu inhabitants. In the **Boat Hall★** (Schiffshalle) there is a Viking longship, partly reconstituted from contemporary fragments dredged up in the ancient port site.

EXCURSIONS

Eckernförde – *23km - 14 miles to the east, again via Route B 76.*
The town lies at the inner end of the Eckernförder Bucht, a deep, wide inlet penetrated by the waters of the Baltic. It is a picturesque fishing port which existed already in the 12C (a document dating from that period mentions "fishermen's community"). Eckernförde is the home of a Holsteiner delicacy known as Kieler Sprotten (smoked fish).

The **Nikolaikirche**, a sober triple-aisle brick church, stands in the market place. The **interior★**, supported by four massive columns, is lavishly decorated. The early Baroque **altarpiece** (1640) is said to be the most accomplished work of the wood carver Hans Gudewerdt the Younger, whose father sculpted the Renaissance pulpit with its Biblical scenes. The bronze **baptismal font** in the middle of the church, also richly decorated, dates from 1588. On either side of the west tower are the tombs of the nobility (17C), and the **Sintflutbild** – a large oil painting dating from 1632 which recalls floods, plagues and the horror of the Thirty Years War.

SCHWÄBISCHE ALB★
SWABIAN JURA – Baden-Württemberg
Michelin map 419 V 10 - T 15/420 U 13 - T 15

The high limestone plateaux of the Swabian Jura, watershed between the Rhine (Neckar Basin) and the Danube, lie between the Black Forest and the crystalline massifs of Bohemia and form in effect the "roof" of southern Germany. The highest point is at Lemberg (1 015m - 3 330ft). From this summit, the Jura drop no less than 400m - 1 312ft to the Neckar Basin in the northwest.
Mountain outcrops detached from the main block form natural fortresses, and some have been chosen as castle sites by familes subsequently to enjoy great glory and dynastic fame (the Hohenstaufens, the Hohenzollerns).

An ingenious population – As in many mountainous regions, the length and harshness of the winters have resulted in the formation of numerous small family businesses or cottage industries. In the 19C, through the philanthropic activities of pastors, schoolteachers and modest inventors, the whole northern fringe of the massif became covered with workshops, studios and small factories turning out toys, precision instruments, musical accessories, clothing, etc.

★ ① FROM KIRCHHEIM UNTER TECK TO BURG HOHENZOLLERN *125km - 78 miles – allow one day*

Kirchheim unter Teck – The pinnacled tower of the half-timbered **Rathaus** overlooks the main crossroads. The building dates from 1724.

Holzmaden – Follow the arrows leading to the **Urwelt-Museum Hauff★** ⊙: an astonishing assembly of saurian fossil skeletons immured in the local schists and dating back almost 160 million years.

Burgruine Reußenstein (Castle ruins) – *Round tour 20min on foot.*
Make for the edge of the escarpment to appreciate to the full the **setting★★** of Reußenstein as it dominates the coomb of Neidlingen. From the lookout point built into the castle ruins, there is a **view★** of the whole narrow valley and, beyond it, the plain of Teck.

After Wiesensteig (half-timbered houses), the route follows one section of the "Schwäbische Albstraße", which is marked by blue-green indication arrows.

Bad Urach – A pretty town, enclosed deep in the Erms valley, with half-timbered houses clustered round a central Marktplatz.

Uracher Wasserfall (Urach Falls) – *1/4 hour on foot Rtn. Leave the car in the park marked "Aussicht 350m".*
Impressive **view★** of the valley and the waterfall (flow reduced in summer).

314

Schloß Lichtenstein ⊙ – Built on a rock spur protected by a natural cleft, Lichtenstein was completely re-designed and decorated in the "troubadour" style in 1842. Before crossing the entrance bridge, turn right and make for two viewpoints: one overlooks the Echaz valley, the other the castle itself.

Bärenhöhle ⊙ – The biggest cavern in this "Bear Grotto" contains well-preserved stalactites and stalagmites.

At Onstmettingen, follow the signs "Nädelehaus" and "Raichberg".

★ **Raichberg** – *1/2 hour on foot Rtn.*
Leave the car at the hotel and walk past a brown stone tower, across the fields to the lip of the plateau. From here there is a fine **view**★ of the downward sweep of the Jura and, two miles away, Burg Hohenzollern *(qv)*.

Return to Burg Hohenzollern via Tannheim and Hechingen.

★ ② THE HEUBERG PLATEAU AND THE DANUBE GAP

From Hohenzollern to Sigmaringen

89km - 55 miles – allow half a day

★ **Burg Hohenzollern** – *See Burg HOHENZOLLERN.*

★ **Lochenstein** – *1/2 hour on foot Rtn.*
Leave the car at the saddle (Lochenpaß) and climb to the summit (altitude 963m - 3 160ft) of the Lochenstein, which is surmounted by a Cross. From here there is a **view**★ of the Balingen-Hechingen Depression, and still – away in the distance – Hohenzollern castle.
Beyond the pass, the road sweeps downhill in tight curves and then crosses the bare, rolling uplands of the Großer Heuberg plateau.

★ **Knopfmacherfelsen** – Below the car park, make your way to a viewpoint from which there is a **view**★ of the Danube valley as far as Beuron abbey and, on the right, Schloß Bronnen.

Kloster Beuron ☉ – A flourishing Benedictine congregation at Beuron contributed greatly to the revival of monastic life, the liturgy and the use of the Gregorian chant in Germany. The Gnadenkapelle, abutting the Baroque abbey church, is treated in the "Beuron style" – derived from a late 19C school of sacred art much influenced by Byzantium.

Burg Wildenstein – *7km - 4 1/4 miles from Beuron via Leibertingen.*
This small citadel commanding the Danube was designed with two moats and a forward defence system on the plateau side comprising two towers linked by a long wall.
Below Beuron, the road follows the **Danube valley**★ past the rocky fortresses of Wildenstein and Werenwag on the way to Sigmaringen *(qv)*. Approaching the town, the cliffs give way to curious rock needles which form a fantastic ensemble between Thiergarten and Gutenstein.

★ **Sigmaringen** – *See SIGMARINGEN.*

SCHWÄBISCH GMÜND
Baden-Württemberg – Population 60 000
Michelin map 419 T 13
Town plan in the current Michelin Red Guide Deutschland

Traditionally, Schwäbisch Gmünd is a centre for the working of precious metals, and its silverware is seen on many German tables. The town is a good excursion centre, since it is near the **Kaiserberge** (Imperial Mountains), whose three conical peaks, the Hohenstaufen, Hohenrechberg and Stuifen, are clearly visible and characteristic of that part of the Swabian Jura.

★ **Heiligkreuzmünster** – The cathedral was built in the 14C by Heinrich Parler, a Swabian master whose descendants designed cathedrals as far apart as Prague, Vienna and Milan. Surprisingly, it has no towers. The pinnacles, balustrades and exterior tracery are Flamboyant Gothic. The architect skilfully worked the decoration into a grid over the west gable, and both chancel doors are sculpted beneath porches which were once also fully decorated. The two-tier chevet is gracefully conceived.
The interior is a perfect hall, the chancel – which has a similar layout to the nave – profiting from more intricately worked ribbed vaulting. The early Renaissance choir stalls and radiating chapels are rich in statuary: note especially, in the axial chapel, an early 15C Holy Sepulchre watched over by the three Marys. The Baptismal Chapel contains the Tree of Jesse (1520), composed of 40 sculpted figurines.

Marktplatz – A huge square whose Baroque character is emphasized by the prosperous-looking houses surrounding it and a twin-statue fountain dedicated to the Virgin Mary. Several half-timbered buildings, the hospital and the Gräth (old town hall) nevertheless recall the medieval existence of the town.

EXCURSIONS

★ **Hohenstaufen** – *14km - 8 1/2 miles to the southwest, plus 30 mn on foot Rtn.*
From the two churches at the top of the town, a shady footpath leads to the summit at 684m - 2 244ft. Nothing remains of the castle, the one-time seat of the royal Hohenstaufens, but the climb is worthwhile for the **panorama**★ of the two remaining Kaiserberge and, on the horizon, the Swabian Jura. *(The car should be left on the village's central esplanade.)*

★ **Hohenrechberg** – *12km - 7 1/2 miles, plus 1 hour on foot Rtn.*
The castle ruins, again, command a vast horizon. Visitors can stroll around the ancient rampart walk or, higher up, walk around the ruined walls whose crests have been converted into a walkway. In the foreground is the massive cone of Hofenstaufen.

*The **Michelin Red Guide Deutschland***
which is revised annually
gives a selection of establishments offering
– carefully prepared meals at reasonable prices
– simple meals at moderate prices
– prices including or excluding service
– car parking

SCHWÄBISCH HALL★★

Baden-Württemberg – Population 31 500
Michelin map 419 S 13 – Local map under HOHENLOHER LAND
Town plan in the current Michelin Red Guide Deutschland

This old town, built in tiers up the steep flank of the Kocher valley, grew up around salt springs known as far back as Celtic times. In the Middle Ages, it was famous for the Imperial silver coins, the Häller or Heller, minted there.

From the Mauerstraße (the quay on the west bank), at the level of the Löwenbrauerei (brewery), there is a fine **general view**★★ of the old town, with its roofs stepped one above the other at the foot of the Michaelskirche, and the imposing 1527 **Büchsenhaus** or Neubau (the former arsenal). Below, the arms of the river are spanned by attractive roofed wooden bridges. Still in the old town opposite, the two parallel streets of the **Obere-** and the **Untere-Herrngasse**, linked by stone stairways, are bordered by several 15C and 16C half-timbered houses.

★★MARKTPLATZ *time: 3/4 hour*

Laid out on a slope, this square is dominated by the monumental stone steps of the Michaelskirche (where actors, during a festival from June to August each year, perform a repertory of the world's theatre classics). In the square itself, only a characteristic alignment of half-timbered gables on the south side – spared by the great fire of 1728 – remains to remind us of what the town must have looked like in the early 18C.

★ **Rathaus** – An elegant building in the Late Baroque style.

Marktbrunnen – Dating from 1509, the fountain stands against a decorative wall adorned with statues of Samson, St Michael and St George. The rectangular design, unusual in a Gothic work, includes the old pillory post.

Michaelskirche – The church's position at the top of 53 steps is impressive. The octagonal porch, opening beneath a Romanesque tower with a Renaissance top, has a statue of its patron saint in front of its central pillar. The **interior**★, originally Romanesque also, was transformed into a Gothic hall-church in the 15C. The Flamboyant chancel was added in the 16C.

ADDITIONAL SIGHTS

Hällisch-Fränkisches Museum (Regional Museum) ⊙ – This historical museum is in a tall Romanesque tower ten storeys high, which was once inhabited. The collections include mementoes of the region's past in general, and that of the town in particular (as an industrial salt centre, as a mint, etc.). Several rooms are devoted to Württemberg-Franconian regional art.

Gräterhaus – This beautiful half-timbered house, so exquisitely decorated, stands in the town's northern suburb. It dates from 1605.

Henkersbrücke – There is an attractive view from this bridge of the mass of half-timbered buildings of the Ilge quarter, and their reflection in the waters of the Kocher. The **view** is perhaps even better from the junction of the street named Am Spitalbach and the Salinenstraße quay, from which the east end of the old church of St. Johann can also be seen.

EXCURSIONS

★ **Groß Comburg** – *3km - 2 miles to the south.*
The church of this old fortified **abbey** ⊙ still has its three Romanesque towers. The rest of the building was reconstructed in 1715, the interior taking the form of a Baroque hall. Along with those of Aachen and Hildesheim, the church's chandelier is one of the most precious in the West. Dating from 1130 and designed in the shape of a crown, the **chandelier**★★★ (Radleuchter) is made of iron, subsequently copper-plated and then gilded. In front of the high altar is an **antependium**★ of the same period, made of gilded beaten copper representing Christ among the Apostles. The framework supporting this is treated with cloisonné enamel and filigree work.

★ **Hohenloher Freilandmuseum (Hohenlohe Open-Air Museum)** ⊙ – *At Wackershofen, 5km - 3 miles to the northwest – local map under HOHENLOHER LAND.*
Over thirty buildings from the 16C to the 19C, which originally stood in different locations, have been reconstructed here and faithfully recapture the rural life of this area from the mid-16C to the end of the 19C. There is an exhibition of furniture and agricultural implements.

The Hohenlohe – *See HOHENLOHER LAND.*

SCHWARZWALD★★★

The Black Forest, stretching for 170km - 106 miles from Karlsruhe to Basle, is separated from the Vosges by the subsided plain of the Rhine. The two ranges, facing one another across this consequence of the Alpine Fold, have much in common. Each is densely wooded; each rises from a crystalline base in the south, sloping gently towards the north, where the massif is covered by limestone beds; both drop steeply in the direction of the Rhine, less abruptly on the far side of the crests − to the Swabian plateaux of the Upper Neckar in one case, to the plateau of Lorraine on the other. Even the highest points of each range correspond: the Feldberg at 1 493m and the Grand Ballon at 1 424m (4 899ft and 4 674ft respectively).

Unlike the Vosges, however, the Black Forest − the larger and denser of the two massifs − displays no marked north-south line of crests, and no coherent east-west arrangement of passes.

The economy of the region has always been linked to the **forest**, wood being practically the sole construction material and the base of all crafts. The trunks of trees, often 50m - 165ft long, were floated away as far as the Netherlands, where they were much in demand by boat-builders. **Clock-making**, symbolized by the famous cuckoo clock, remains a fruitful activity.

Fruit farms and **vineyards** are cultivated on the foothills along the western limits of the forest.

Northern Black Forest − Drained by the Murg, the Nagold and the two Enz rivers, this sandstone area is almost entirely covered by conifers. The contrast, within a few miles, between the upper parts of the Grinde moors and the orchards and vineyards flourishing south of Baden-Baden, is remarkable.

Central Black Forest − The main axis of this region follows the valleys of the Kinzig and the Gutach − a gap through which the main road and rail arteries cut diagonally towards the Upper Danube and Lake Constance. The patchiness of the infertile sandstone topsoil is reflected in the forest's separation into groves, distanced by fields and pastureland. South of the Elz and Berg valleys, the Upper Black Forest, notably in the Feldberg region, forms a landscape that is almost Alpine in character.

Southern Black Forest − Gashed by the racing watercourses of the Wehra, the Alb and the Schlücht, the land drops progressively towards the Rhine. The climate, favourable to mountain cures, has led to the establishment of health resorts in the region.

★★★SCHWARZWALD-HOCHSTRASSE (CREST ROAD)

① From Baden-Baden to Freudenstadt

80km - 50 miles − about 4 hours

Amply provided with viewpoints and car parks, the Black Forest crest road, or Hochstraße, runs past many winter ski slopes with ski-lifts. Much of the route is at heights approaching 1 000m - 3 280ft.

★★ **Baden-Baden** − *See BADEN-BADEN.*

Mummelsee − This small, dark glaciation lake is at the foot of the **Hornisgrinde** (1 163m - 3 816ft), the highest point of the Northern Black Forest.

At Ruhestein, the itinerary leaves the Hochstraße temporarily to plunge towards the **Allerheiligen valley**★ and then climb back from Oppenau towards Zuflucht by way of an extremely steep mountain road.

★ **Allerheiligen** − The ruins of a late 13C church, built for a Premonstratensian monastery, add a romantic touch to this lonely dell. The vaulted porch and the walls of the transept are still standing, together with a polygonal Gothic chapel leading off them. A footpath leads from the ruins to the celebrated waterfall.

★ **Allerheiligen-Wasserfälle** − *3/4 hour on foot Rtn from the car park at the foot of the falls (2km - 1 1/4 miles beyond the abbey ruins).*

A steep, stepped path climbs beside the torrent between rock walls overhung by huge trees.

From Zuflucht to Kniebis, the route crosses an upland plateau, most of it marshy moorland typical of the Grinde.

★ **Freudenstadt** − At the crossing of several routes, the town, built in the 17C by order of the Duke of Württemberg, was destroyed by fire in 1945. Rebuilt since the war, it now follows a checkerboard plan centred on the **Marktplatz**★, a huge square surrounded by houses with arcades.

The 17C **church** (Stadtkirche) is oddly placed: its two naves, arranged at right-angles, form one corner of the Marktplatz. The pulpit, supported by the four evangelists, and the carved 12C **lectern**★★, come from Alpirsbach, the most important Romanesque church in the Black Forest.

Black Forest landscape

J. Ducarge/TOP, Paris

★★CENTRAL BLACK FOREST

② From Freudenstadt to Freiburg *152km - 94 miles – one day*

The itinerary follows the foot of the Kinzig and Elt valleys, passing through a number of busy villages before reaching the Upper Black Forest at Kandel.

★ **Alpirsbach** – The church, joined to the old **Benedictine abbey**★ buildings, has a 12C apse with unusual lines: the Romanesque lower floor supports a Gothic chancel in which the buttresses do not reach the floor but stand on free columns. Inside, at the apse's lower level, a hollowed-out niche – the central one out of three – bears traces of 12C **wall paintings**: Christ in Glory between the Chosen and the Damned on the vaulting; The Crucifixion on the hemispherical surface. In the **cloisters** *(ring for the caretaker)*, the vault tracery and the bays, much restored, are in the Gothic Flamboyant style.

Gutach – The skills of the people of the Black Forest in matters of rural building, craftwork and agriculture are celebrated in the admirable **Freilichtmuseum Vogtsbauernhof**★★ (Black Forest Open-Air Museum) ⊙ in the Gutach valley. The Vogts-bauern farm, still in its original (1570) state, is surrounded by half a dozen reconstituted farmhouses with their outbuildings. At the **Hotzenwaldhaus** , replicas of a cowshed and interior furnishings are confined to an inner gallery to protect them from the weather. The **Hippenseppenhof** farm represents the commonest type, especially those found in the wilder upland valleys; its position on the slope allows farm carts direct access to the hayloft. There is no trouble identifying the **Vogtsbauernhof** itself: the central portion is stone-built. Inside, note the timber roof framework, with the load-bearing beams set horizontally. Crafts connected with forest life are on display on the ground floor of the **Lorenzerhof** farm.

The road leading through the Landwassereck pass offers a number of fine **views**★ over the undulating landscapes of the Central Black Forest. Upstream from Oberprechtal, the beautiful cascades of the Elz border the route.

★ **Triberg** – This centre of the clockmaking industry is also a favourite health resort. The **Waterfall Walk**★ *(1 hour on foot Rtn)* follows the Gutach rapids in a natural setting of boulders and tall trees. The **Schwarzwald Museum** ⊙ specializes in the exhibition of traditional costumes and local craftwork: watch and clockmaking, ceramics, wood veneers, etc. The church of **Maria in den Tannen** (Our Lady of the Firs), one of the most popular pilgrims' sanctuaries in the Black Forest, displays carved and painted Baroque **furnishings**★ in an exuberant style that is wholly rustic.

Furtwangen – Cases and movements from all over the world, selected for their value, their artistic character or the ingeniousness of their conception are on display at the **Deutsches Uhrenmuseum**★ ⊙ in this small clock-making town. Also on view are fantasy clocks, cuckoos, singing birds, wooden clocks and a reconstruction of a period watchmaker's workshop.

From the town it is only 6km - 3 3/4 miles to the **source of the Breg** *(signposts "Katzensteig-Martinskapelle" and then "Donauquelle")*. The Breg, one of the rivers flowing into the Danube which lies furthest from its mouth, rises here at a height of 1 078m – 3 537ft. The source of the Danube itself is located at Donaueschingen.

Soon after leaving Furtwangen, turn right for **Hexenloch**. Pass through a deep, steeply wooded gorge enlivened by many waterfalls. Between St. Märgen and St. Peter, the twists and turns of the road allow plenty of clear **views★★** of the Central Black Forest.

★ **St. Peter** – A Baroque church attached to the huge **abbey** (1727) is the burial place of the Dukes of Zähringen, the founders of Freiburg-im-Breisgau (statues by the great sculptor J A Feuchtmayer).

The extravagance of the Late Rococo style is exemplified in the high altar and the ceiling paintings. The elegant (restored) Baroque **library★** ⊙ is decorated with delicate stuccowork.

* **Kandel** – From the viewing table here *(1/2 hour Rtn on foot)* there is a splendid **panorama★** taking in the Vosges, the Feldberg, the Belchen, and the isolated Kaiserstuhl massif.

* **Waldkirch** – Lovely 18C houses, once part of the chapter of canons, surround the former collegiate church of St. Margaretha in a tranquil, shady quarter of this small industrial town.

★★★UPPER BLACK FOREST

③ Round tour leaving Freiburg-im-Breisgau
142km - 88 miles – one day

This circuit, mountainous in the first part, passes the three principal summits of the Black Forest (Schauinsland, Belchen and Feldberg), and then the two best-known lakes (Schluchsee and Titisee) in the massif.

* **Schauinsland** – The mountain road, extremely twisty, leads to the upper teleferic station. From the car park, climb to the top of the viewing tower *(91 steps)* after following the signs "Rundweg" and "Schauinsland Gipfel" *(1/2 hour Rtn on foot)*. The lookout point offers a **view★** across upland meadows to the Feldberg.
Follow the road now for 1km – half a mile, and take the right-hand fork towards Stohen, and the Münstertal. Winding down through the meadows, the route finally plunges once more into the forest. At Wiedener Eck, turn right towards the Belchen.

* **★★Belchen** – *From the end of the road, walk (1/2 hour Rtn) to the viewing table on the summit.*
This rounded mountain with its steep, bare flanks, dominates the Wiesenthal and the valleys which, like the Münstertal, interlace the western fringe of the Black Forest. When visibility is good, it makes a magnificent **observation point★★★** from which to see the Rhine plain, the rounded heights of the High Vosges, and the Alps from Säntis to Mont Blanc. The Belchen summit is at a height of 1 414m - 4 637ft.

* **The Falls of Todtnau** – *1 1/2km - about 1 mile from Todtnau.*
Climbing through a wooded combe, a footpath leads *(1 hour Rtn)* to an impressive series of cascades.

* **★★Feldberg** – A chairlift conveys sightseers to the Seebuck (1 448m - 4 750ft), which is crowned by the Bismarck monument. From here there is a **view★** of the symmetrically perfect, circular bowl of the Feldsee, a small lake at the bottom of a glaciated circus or amphitheatre. It is possible to reach the Feldberg summit at 1 493m - 4 897ft (1 1/2 hours Rtn), to enjoy, again, a vast **panorama★★** stretching as far as the Alps.

* **Schluchsee** – This lake, quite small to start with, has become – thanks to a dam – the most immense stretch of water in the Black Forest.
The Titisee is reached via Lenzkirch. During the final part of the descent, the road overlooks the lake.

* **★★Titisee** – This pretty lake, formed by a moraine barrier, is at the junction of several tourist routes. Because of its position, it has developed both into a health centre (Titisee-Neustadt and **Hinterzarten★**) and a departure point for many Black Forest excursions. The return to Freiburg *(qv)* is through the **Höllental★** ("The Vale of Hell"), which – except perhaps in the Hirschsprung Gorge – does nothing to justify its nickname.

SCHWERIN ★

Mecklenburg-Vorpommern – Population 130 000
Michelin map 416 F 18 – Town plan in Michelin Red Guide Deutschland

Magnificently situated in a landscape of lakes and forests, Schwerin renewed its links with an administrative past by becoming a Land capital in 1990. The origins of the town go back to the 11C, when the Slavs built a fortress on what is now an island – Schloßinsel. It was not long, however, before they were expelled by Henry the Lion, the Duke of Saxony *(qv)*, who used the emplacement as a base for the construction of the first German town east of the Elbe. For almost five centuries after that (1358-1918), Schwerin was capital of the Duchy of Mecklenburg.

★★SCHLOSSINSEL *time: 2 hours*

The island, and the two bridges linking it with the town, separate the smaller Burgsee from the 21km - 13 mile stretch of Schwerin Lake.

* **Schloß** ⊙ – Built between 1845 and 1857 in the neo-Renaissance style – with elements borrowed from the Gothic and the Baroque – this is one of the most important civic constructions of 19C Germany. From the outside, it recalls the Château of Chambord on the Loire, by which in fact the architects Demmler and Stüler were inspired.

The rooms inside are lavishly decorated, with particularly fine floors. Note especially the **Throne Room**★ (Thronsaal), the Ancestors' Gallery (Ahnengalerie) and the Smoking Room (Rauchzimmer).

★ **Schloßkapelle** – This is much older; it was built between 1560 and 1563. The Renaissance galleries and vaulting rest on Tuscan columns.

★ **Schloßgarten** – Created in the mid-18C, this formal Baroque garden is organized around canals in the form of a cross and rectilinear walks. It is peopled with statues (copies) by Balthazar Permoser *(qv)*.

ADDITIONAL SIGHTS

★ **Staatliches Museum (National Museum)** ⊘ – *Werderstraße*.
Important Flemish and Dutch paintings of the 17C (Brueghel, Brouwer, Jordaens and Van Ruysdael) are on display in this museum, a neo-Classic block built between 1877 and 1882 beside an old public garden (Alter Garten) near the theatre. The outside is adorned with Italian Renaissance decorations.
A department of 18C and 19C European painting houses works by Houdon, Pesne, Friedrich, Liebermann, Corinth, etc.
Relics of Slav settlements established in the region in the Stone Age are on view in a Prehistoric section.

Markt – Four late 17C half-timbered houses with gables have been preserved next to the Town Hall. On the north side of the square, the so-called **New Building** (Neues Gebäude) was erected between 1783 and 1785 in the Classic style, with Doric columns and attics, to be used as a Chamber of Commerce.

★ **Dom (Cathedral)** – Brick-built in the Gothic style during the 14C and 15C, the church contains several works of art worth a visit. They include a Gothic altarpiece (from a Lübeck workshop, c1480); a number of 14C funerary plaques; and, in the Chapel of the Assumption, frescoes dating from c1335.

SIGMARINGEN★

Baden-Württemberg – Population 15 000
Michelin map 419 V 11 – Local map under SCHWÄBISCHE ALB

The strong defensive position of Sigmaringen – a rocky spur rising from the valley at the mouth of the Upper Danube Gap – made the town an ideal choice as minor capital of the principality ruled by the Swabian (Catholic) branch of the Hohenzollerns *(qv)*. The castle rises in traditional style from the edge of the cliff, but the only feudal parts remaining are the site and its general appearance: all the buildings and their interior decoration are pastiches of different styles.

★ **The Castle and its Annexes** ⊘ – *Time: 1 hour*.
The approach ramp starts at the highest point reached by the road cutting across the land enclosed by the loop of the Danube *(leave the car in front of the Stadthalle, the Rathaus, or the fortified gateway to the castle)*.

Schloß (Castle) – The State Apartments adorned in 16C style with coffered ceilings and tapestries (Royal Bedchamber, Ancestral Hall, etc.) will be of most interest to those versed in the history of European royalty. Fine **collection of arms and armour**.

Church – Luminous with Rococo stuccowork, the church clings to the castle rock. A shrine in a transept chapel on the left contains the Cradle of St Fidelio of Sigmaringen (1577-1622), first Capuchin martyr, Patron of the Order and local patron saint.

Museums – On view here are paintings (Swabian Primitives) and an exhibition of means of transport (Marstallmuseum).

SOEST★

Nordrhein-Westfalen – Population 43 000
Michelin map 417 L 8 – Local map under SAUERLAND

Traditionally the agricultural market for the Westphalian Plain, Soest today looks much as it must have done in medieval times. The old ramparts still enclose a spider's-web of houses, gardens and narrow, twisting lanes that lend the place an almost village-like air. One of the most remarkable half-timbered buildings is the twin-gabled hotel, **Im Wilden Mann (Y A)**, in the Markt. Another, decorated with motifs in colour, is the **Haus zur Rose (Z C)**, at the corner of the Marktstraße and the Rosenstraße. The well-preserved **Osthofentor** (East Gate) **(Y)**, with its fine Gothic embellishments, formed part of later 16C fortifications. The past history of the town can be traced in the **Burghofmuseum (Z M¹)**. **Pumpernickel**, the black rye bread baked for 24 hours which is found on so many German breakfast tables, is made in Soest.

SOEST

A	Gasthaus Im Wilden Mann	
C	Haus zur Rose	
D	Nikolaikapelle	
M¹	Burghofmuseum	

SIGHTS

★ **Patroklidom** (**Z**) – The interest in this massive 11C and 12C Romanesque building lies entirely in the **Westwerk**★★ *(qv)* and its perfectly balanced square **tower**★★ austerely decorated with blind arcades and blind rose windows. The two tiers of arcades lightening the upper part of the tower are matched by two more at the base, the lower of which is furnished with very delicate small columns. The Romanesque frescoes in the apse of the north transept are original, having survived the Second World War. The others were restored to Romanesque designs in 1950. A fine 15C Crucifix stands on the altar. Parts of the original furnishings salvaged from the war damage can be seen in the Treasury.

Nikolaikapelle (**Z D**) – In the chancel of this two-aisle chapel is the **St Nicholas Altarpiece**★, painted on a gold background in about 1400 by Conrad von Soest *(qv)*, a great name in Westphalian art. St Nicholas is shown as the patron of merchants and mariners.

★ **Wiesenkirche** (**Y**) – Length, width and height are virtually identical in the nave of this beautifully lit 14C Gothic hall-church. A late 14C Virgin and Child can be seen at the pier of the south doorway.
The 1520 **stained glass window of the Last Supper**, above the north doorway, gave the artist the chance to advertise some local specialities: boar's head, ham, pitchers of beer and small loaves of rye bread can be recognized on the table. The most important work of art in the church is the 1525 **Aldegrever Altarpiece**★ – the Virgin Mary between St Anthony and St Agatha, bathed in a halo of light – in the south apsidal chapel.

Hohnekirche (Y) – This bizarre, squat church of Romanesque origin was built with a flat chancel and dissymmetric apsidal chapels out of line with the main block. It was converted into a hall-church in the 13C. The whole interior, walls, vaults and roofing included, is covered with frescoes. In the chancel, the **Dance of the Angels** (c1280) depicts the Virgin in Majesty surrounded by a ring of 16 angels with stylized wings in the form of flames.

A **funerary niche** (Grabnische) with 13C frescoes faces the south entrance; on the left, half hidden by three short, thick columns, is the baptistry with its Romanesque font.

EXCURSIONS

* **Möhnesee** – *11km - 7 miles to the south. Leave by 3 on the town plan.*
This artificial lake on the northern edge of the Sauerland is 10km - 6 1/2 miles long. The dam retaining the reservoir is 650m - over 700 yards across and almost 40m - 131ft high. To the north, the lakeshore is open to tourists and those practising water sports. The south bank, on the other hand, which is well forested, is a nature reserve harbouring many species of birds, some of them very rare.

* **The Sauerland** – *See SAUERLAND.*

SPEYER *

Rheinland-Pfalz – Population 46 000
Michelin map 417/419 S 9 – Local map under PFALZ AM RHEIN
Town plan in the current Michelin Red Guide Deutschland

The old imperial City, on an elbow of the river in the Upper Rhine Plain, can be recognized from far off by the silhouette of its belfries. Because of its exposed situation, however, few of the town's historic monuments have resisted the tides of war. As the seat of the Diet *(see Historical Notes)* and the Imperial Council, Speyer was annihilated by the troops of Louis XIV in 1689. Some idea of its past, nevertheless, may be gained from the group of buildings formed by the Emperors' Cathedral, the houses on the Maximilianstraße and the Altpörtel, a tall tower that was once the town's main gateway.

The "Protestants" – The Edict of Worms *(qv)*, in fact never enacted, was confirmed by the Diet of Speyer in 1529. The Lutheran states then made a solemn protest against the Diet's decisions, from which derives the label "protestant" to identify partisans of the Reformation. The fact is commemorated in the existence of a neo-Gothic church, the Gedächtniskirche, built early this century on the Bartholomäus-Weltz-Platz.

SIGHTS

** **Dom (Cathedral)** ⊙ – This fine building, founded by Konrad II in 1030 and remodelled at the end of the 11C, is a Romanesque basilica with four towers and two domes.

Exterior – There is an interesting **view**** of the east end from the garden approach to the 13C **Heidentürmchen** (Pagan Tower). An elegant dwarf gallery circles the nave and transept just below the roof. The finely carved capitals display a wide variety of motifs on the garden side of the apse. On the lower part of one of the blind arcades, in the centre, a worn 11C relief depicting the Kingdom of Peace can be distinguished. The window arches of the east transept show Lombard influence and – especially on the south side – a lavish deco-ration of palm leaves and scrollwork. Similar motifs are repeated on the cornice below the roof.

CESA, Marburg

The east end, Speyer cathedral

In the gardens south of the cathedral is the **Ölberg** (1502-1512), once the centre of the cloisters. A large stone trough – the **Domnapf** – stands in the forecourt. In days gone by, each time a bishop was enthroned, it was filled with wine and anyone who wished to could drink until he dropped.

Interior – The most impressive way to enter is via the door in the west face (rebuilt in the mid-19C). On the right of the porch is a statue of Rudolph of Habsburg. The huge, well-lit nave has groined vaulting with prominent transverse arches. The half columns engaged in the main pillars are cut by rings and capitals with acanthus leaves.

The sobriety of the side aisles, also with groined vaulting, is remarkable. There is a good view of the building's harmonious proportions from the top of the south aisle stairway.

The raised **transept**★★ is a masterpiece of unity and balance. Note particularly, above the transept crossing, the octagonal cupola on squinches with its small lantern tower. The lack of texture and ornamentation on the walls emphasizes the natural decorative character of the architecture itself. The **Chapel of the Holy Sacrament** (Afrakapelle) *(on the left, before the north transept)* houses two 15C bas-reliefs: the Bearing of the Cross and the Annunciation. Opposite, before the south transept, eight groined vaults surround a two-tier central rotunda in which are the **baptistry** (Chapel of St Emmerammus) and, above, a chapel dedicated to St Catherine.

★★★**Crypt** ⊘ – This is the finest and largest Romanesque crypt in Germany. Beneath the chancel and the transept, whose crossing above is marked by four columns with splendid cushion capitals, Romanesque groined vaulting spreads out like a net supported by transverse arches of alternately pink and white sandstone.

Four Holy Roman Emperors and four German Kings are buried in the impressive **Royal Vault**. The 13C tombstone of Rudolph of Habsburg stands guard at the entrance.

★ **Judenbad (Jewish Baths)** – *Access via the Judengasse, southwest of the cathedral (signposted).*

Ritual ablutions were performed here. The building (Judenhof), in the centre of the medieval Jewish quarter, was erected in the 12C, probably by workmen engaged in the construction of the cathedral.

A stairway with double doors leads down to the first chamber, which has groined vaulting and, on the left, an anteroom for changing. A second, semicircular staircase then descends to the level of the water-table, where the actual bath is situated.

Dreifaltigkeitskirche – *In the Große Himmelsgasse.*

The **interior**★ of this enormous Baroque church (1701-1717) is surrounded by a two-storey gallery with a balustrade adorned by paintings. The wooden capped vaulting is painted too.

Historisches Museum der Pfalz (Palatinate Museum) ⊘ – In Gallery 4 on the ground floor of this museum is the celebrated **Golden Hat**★ of Schifferstadt, the rarest, most valuable item in the Prehistoric Department. In the shape of a cone, this solid gold religious cult object dates from the 12C BC.

Focal points of the museum are the Roman, medieval and modern departments. The sumptuous collection of art and decorative arts from the 16C to the 19C, which includes some beautiful Frankenthal porcelain, should not be missed.

Cathedral treasury (Domschatzkammer) – *In both the basement storeys of the new building.* There is no doubt that the tomb furnishings of the Emperors and Kings from the vault of the cathedral are the main points of attraction, for example the funerary crown of Konrad II, the first Salian Emperor, the Imperial orb of Heinrich III, the crown of the Canossa penance of Heinrich IV. A little piece of German history is brought to light. There are some magnificent liturgical robes and articles.

Weinmuseum – The museum presents two thousand years of wine history. The showpiece is the **Roman wine**★, which is the oldest still liquid wine in the world, in its aphora-like bottle. It was found in Palatinate in a Roman stone sarcophagus dating from the 3C AD. There is sumptuous collection of decorated barrels, and imposing wine presses dating from the 16C and 18C.

The vineyards of Germany cover 104 000 ha - 257 000 acres and 13 regions: Ahr, Mittelrhein, Mosel-Saar-Ruwer, Nahe, Rheingau, Rheinhessen, Hessische Bergstraße, Franken (Franconia), Rheinpfalz (Rhineland Palatinate), Württemberg, Baden, Elbe valley (Dresden-Meißen), Saale and Unstrut (Naumburg-Feyburg).

White wines represent about 80% of German production. A variety of grape stocks is used from region to region, including: fruity, slightly acidic **Riesling** (Mittelrhein, Mosel-Saar-Ruwer, Rheingau, Baden – where it is known as Klingelberger); potent, fruity **Silvaner** (Franken, Rheinhessen, Nahe, Rheinpfalz); lively, potent **Müller-Thurgau** (Franken, Rheinhessen, Baden, Nahe, Elbe valley, Saale, Unstrut); delicate **Weißburgunder** (Baden, Elbe valley, Saale, Unstrut); spicy **Traminer** and **Gewürztraminer** (Baden, Elbe valley).

SPREEWALD★★

A network of more than 300 waterways criss-crosses this lush countryside – site of an ancient forest swamp painstakingly cleared and drained – lending it the appearance of a "Venice in the Woods". The region's special interest lies also in its **Sorbian minority**, descendants of western Slav people who settled in the Lausitz area of Germany after the migrations of the 6C, who remain fiercely proud of their language, traditions and culture today *(see the Serbski Muzej at Bautzen)*.

Basically agricultural, the Spreewald specialises in the cultivation of cucumbers and horseradish.

Barge Trip (Kahnfahrt) ⊙ – *At Lübbenau, leave the main road opposite the railway station and take Maxim-Gorki-Straße to one of the car parks near the landing stage.* From here, boat-men/guides organize excursions aboard flat-bottomed craft which ferry passengers to the heart of a leafy paradise shaped by man into a limitless garden. Only the ripple of water, the singing of birds and the quacking of ducks break the silence.

A stop at **Lehde★**, a tiny lagoon village with a population of 150 which boasts almost as many islands as houses, allows sightseers to visit the **Open-Air Museum** (Freilandmuseum Lehde). Here, three early 19C farms, complete with living quarters and outbuildings, display rustic furniture, agricultural implements and fishing gear, along with a generous selection of livestock native to the area.

Visitors preferring to make these discoveries on foot can choose between three different footpaths starting from Lübbenau: one leading towards Lehde *(time: 1 hour Rtn)*, another to Wotschofska and a third to Leipe *(time: 3 hours Rtn)*.

STADE

Turned into a strongpoint when it was under Swedish rule from 1648 to 1712, this old Hanseatic town linked to the Elbe by a navigable channel has retained part of its original fortifications and its water-filled moats.

Alter Hafen (Old Port) – Traditionally handling wood on the ancient Hanseatic route, the winding basin is now almost deserted, leaving only a nostalgic stretch of still water bordered by rusting iron. An idea of how it must have looked in the 17C is nevertheless provided by the fine houses, meticulously restored, which stand on either side.

★ **Schwedenspeicher-Museum** ⊙ – *Am Wasser West.*
Built between 1692 and 1705 on one of the quays, this brick granary now houses a museum illustrating the town's commercial history and its old system of defences. There is also a prehistoric department exhibiting four magnificent **bronze wheels★** (*c*700 BC) from a funerary carriage, as well as antique jewellery, weapons and pots. Not far from the museum *(at Wasser West No 7)*, the Kaufmann Collection, housed in a handsome building, displays paintings of the Worpswede School *(qv)*. The artists include Fritz Mackensen, Otto Modersohn (*Marsh, Barns and Silver Birches*, 1896), Paula Modersohn-Becker (*Peasant Woman with Red Scarf*, 1900) and Fritz Overbeck (*Flooding in the Marsh*, 1903).

St. Cosmae und Damianikirche – The Baroque spire of this 13-15C church, complete with onion bulb, rises above a picturesque old quarter where the wooden houses are bricked in between the beams. Inside, the fine 17C furnishings (organ, pulpit, copper chandeliers) are intact. The wrought iron grillework (1670) is imaginative.

EXCURSION

★ **Altes Land** – *Round tour of 51km - 32 miles to the southeast – about 2 hours. Roads narrow, twisting and cobbled. Take the main Hamburg road for Buxtehude.* Between Stade and Buxtehude, the flat land beside the Elbe is a countryside of apple and cherry orchards, enchanting in the spring when the blossoms are out. Leave Buxtehude via the Jork road, which runs northwards beside the winding Este embankment. After the pretty village of Estebrügge, turn left in Königreich towards **Jork★**. Drive through to see, right at the far end, a series of thatched **farmhouses★** (Bauernhäuser) with decorative brickwork embellishing the gables in mosaic designs. At Mittelkirchen, stay on the east bank of the canal, crossing further downstream at the Steinkirchen weighbridge. Return to Stade via Grünendeich (splendid view of the Elbe from the top of the embankment).

STENDAL

Sachsen-Anhalt — Population 50 000
Michelin map 416/418 I 19

Founded c1160 by the Margrave Albrecht the Bear, Stendal soon developed into an important trade centre. The town was a member of the Hanseatic League from 1359 to 1518, and until the middle of the 16C remained the most influential in the Brandenburg March. The ravages of the Thirty Years War, however finally dealt it a death blow. Several monuments typical of Gothic brick architecture can still be seen from its period of prosperity still.

Stendal was the birthplace of **Johann Joachim Winckelmann** (1717-1768), considered to be the inaugurator of a scientific approach to archaeology. One of his admirers, the French novelist **Henri Beyle** (1783-1842) adopted as a pseudonym the name of the town (with a slightly different spelling: Stendhal).

SIGHTS

Rathaus — *On the Markt.*
The oldest part of the town hall, in exposed brick, dates from the beginning of the 15C. The gables are stepped. Added at the end of that century, the main wing was later remodelled in Renaissance style. On the square stands a copy of the statue of Roland destroyed by a hurricane in 1972.

Marienkirche — *Behind the Markt.*
A triple-aisle hall-church, this was built between 1435 and 1477. The chancel, surrounded by an ambulatory, is separated from the nave by a delicately worked partition. The high altar (Crowning and Death of the Virgin) is in the Flamboyant Gothic style.

★ **Dom St. Nikolaus** — The former Augustinian monks' church was supplanted in the 15C by a cathedral of much larger size, the square ground-plan recalling the hall-churches of Lower Saxony, in particular St. Johanniskirche in Lüneburg *(qv)*. The **stained glass windows★** (1420-1460) are remarkable. Note especially those in the chancel, which, because of the amount of wall they replace, suggest a huge conservatory.

★ **Uenglinger Tor (Uenglingen Gate)** — *Northwest of the old town.*
Dating from c1380, this is one of the most interesting fortified medieval gateways in the region. From the outside, the two lower storeys present an aspect that is purely defensive, while the upper part — added in the 15C — is much more decorative.

EXCURSIONS

★ **Tangermünde** — *10km - 6 miles to the southeast.*
Situated (as the name suggests) where the waters of the Tanger river join those of the Elbe, Tangermünde's history closely follows the history of Stendal. The small town, still enclosed within its late 14C ramparts, is crossed by two parallel streets, bordered by half-timbered houses with finely worked doorways. The brick-built 1430 **Rathaus★** has a three-gable façade garnished with a superb lacework of carved decorations.
The town's ancient gateways retain their monumental aspect, particularly the Neustadter TorH, an imposing circular tower on the south side.

Havelberg — *46km - 29 miles to the north; cross the Elbe at Tangermünde.*
Overlooking this small, pretty town on the banks of the Havel river the **cathedral of St. Marion★** ⊘ was founded at the end of the 12C but almost entirely rebuilt in the Gothic style between 1279 and 1330. The sculpturing of the chancel partition and the rood-screen **panels★★** (c1400) is greatly to be admired. Illustrating scenes from the life of Jesus, these were probably the work of craftsmen from the Parler studio in Prague. Note also three **sandstone candelabra** and a **Triumphal Cross** (c1300). The early Gothic cloister dates from the 13C.

STRALSUND★

Mecklenburg-Vorpommern — Population 70 000
Michelin map 416 D 23 — Local map under RÜGEN

Separated from the island of Rügen *(qv)* by a narrow sea channel and surrounded by lakes, the Baltic town of Stralsund has developed since the earliest times as a centre of maritime navigation and long-distance trade. Its Gothic brick buildings, inspired by those of Lübeck, its more powerful neighbour, are among the best-known in northern Germany.

A Coveted City — From the moment of its foundation by Prince Jaromir of Rügen in 1209, Stralsund was subjected to assaults from envious neighbours: from Lübeck, from Denmark, from Sweden and even Holland they came with their troops to seize this port, so admirably situated. Protected by its massive rampart belt, the town was able during the Thirty Years War to beat off the forces of the all-conquering Imperial General Albrecht von Wallenstein. Subsequently taken — several times — by Sweden, it returned to Prussian rule after the Napoleonic Wars. Today, Stralsund's prosperity depends mainly on its shipyards and its fishing fleet.

SIGHTS

★ **Rathaus (Town Hall)** – *Alter Markt.*
Built in the 13C and 14C, this splendid edifice comprises two separate, parallel blocks. The magnificent **north façade★**, crowned by a pediment with openwork gables – again, inspired by the Rathaus in Lübeck *(qv)* – was added *c*1450. The ground floor arcades open onto a covered market hall. From this a passageway leads to the west porch of the Nikolaikirche. Among the old houses bordering the market place, the **Wulflammhaus** (No 5), brick-built in the mid-15C, is noteworthy for its odd three-storey gable pierced by small windows.

★ **Nikolaikirche** – *Alter Markt.*
Modelled on the Marienkirche of Lübeck *(qv)*, this 13-14C hall-church has seen its central nave raised and its single tower replaced by a powerful façade with two towers. The relatively low ambulatory at the east end is dominated by solid buttresses.

Inside, there is a striking contrast between the modest height of the side aisles, flanked by low chapels, and the spectacular, soaring nave. Certain columns and several chapels still have late Gothic frescoes.

Among the altarpieces, note the stone group figuring St Anne (*c*1290) and the central reredos, made at the beginning of the 18C based on designs by Andreas Schlüter.

★ **Deutsches Museum für Meerkunde und Fischerei (Oceanographic Museum and Aquarium)** ⊙ – *Mönchstraße.*
Buildings which once belonged to a former abbey (the Katharinenkloster) have been transformed into galleries devoted to the Baltic Sea – its flora, its fauna, the exploitation and refinement of salt, etc –

Deutsches Museum für Meereskunde und Fischerei

and to the fishing industry. Among the aquaria installed in the old church crypt is a huge 50 000-litre (11 000-gallon) tank stocked with tropical species.

Kulturhistorisches Museum (Historical Museum) ⊙ – *Mönchstraße.*
Sacred art from the Middle Ages, gold and silver plate from the isle of Hiddensee (Rügen), and the history of Stralsund itself are among the diverse exhibits displayed here.

★ **Marienkirche** – *Neuer Markt.*
Apart from the impressive 104m - 340ft west tower, which was added between 1416 and 1478, this church was built towards the end of the 14C. Its originality lies in the fact that the flying buttresses of the chancel are concealed below the roof. The interior of the west tower comprises a central portion flanked by side aisles, in the manner of a transept.

Stadtbefestigung (Ramparts) – The sections on the west side of the town are in the best condition, between the Kniepertor and the Kütertor, beside the lake.

STRAUBING

Bayern – Population 40 600
Michelin map 420 T 21

Embraced by a loop of the Danube, this small market-town in the Gäuboden – the "granary of Bavaria" – remains faithful to its agricultural traditions.

★ **Stadtplatz** – In the centre of the huge main square stands an original 13C tower crowned by five pointed turrets, the remains of an old town hall. The tower lends a final flourish to a vista which begins with the gabled houses of the Theresienplatz, continuing with a beautiful Renaissance fountain and the Dreifaltigkeitssäule (Column of the Trinity), adorned with swirling statuary. The whole is an elegant reminder that Austria is not far off.

Jakobskirche – Just off the Stadtplatz, this large brick hall-church was built in the 15C. The ribless vaulting of interpenetrating ovals above the nave is supported on round, slender pillars. Unusual in this part of Bavaria is an almost total lack of Baroque decoration.

The panels of the high altar reredos, bought in 1590 from a church in Nuremberg, frame some 16C statuary. Note particularly the figure of the Virgin, in the middle, and – at the far left – Mary Magdalene. In the first chapel north of the axial chapel is the admirable tomb of Ulrich Kastenmayer (1430), his effigy costumed as a magistrate of the town. The features and expression are of a poignant realism.

The church pulpit dates from 1753.

St. Peter – *1 1/2km - 1 mile. Leave the town in the direction of the Danube by Route 20 (signposted Cham). Turn right before the bridge. St. Peter's is the second church.*

The old burial ground surrounding the Romanesque church contains many crosses made of wrought iron, of which the town was once a manufacturing centre. Ask the caretaker to open the Chapel of the Dance of Death (Totentanz-kapelle) and the Chapel of **Agnes Bernauer**, a touching and popular folk heroine in Germany.

Agnes, a young commoner from Augsburg, was secretly married to her love, the son of a Duke of Bavaria. But she fell victim to the spite of her father-in-law, who had her condemned for witchcraft and thrown into the Danube in 1435.

EXCURSIONS

The Abbeys of the Danube – *Round trip of 46km - 29 miles, downstream, on the north bank of the river. Allow 2 1/2 hours.*

Oberalteich – *1km - 1/2 mile south of Furth.* Founded by Count Friedrich von Bogen, Bailiff of Regensburg cathedral *c*1100, this Benedictine monastery church was transformed between 1622 and 1630 into a hall-church with five aisles. Note especially the hanging staircase that leads to the gallery, a technical feat at that time, and the Rococo tabernacle with its furiously busy embellishments, realized by Matthias Obermayer in 1759.

Metten – *4km - 2 1/2 miles northwest of Deggendorf.*
The onion-domed towers of the **Benedictine abbey** ⊙ of Metten rise at the lower fringe of the Bavarian Forest *(qv)*. The church, whose foundations are pre-Romanesque, was remodelled in the Gothic era but was given its final facelift between 1720 and 1729. Tall windows illuminate the frescoes on the cradle vaulting. The high-altarpiece, a work due to Cosmas Damian Asam, represents St Michael slaughtering the dragon. It is possible to visit the old abbey **library★**, decorated in Baroque style by F J Holzinger from 1706 to 1720. There are no less than 160 000 volumes on the shelves, among them one of the first Bibles to be translated into German (1477) and the original Nuremberg Chronicle (1493).

Niederalteich – *14km - 9 miles southeast of Deggendorf.*
The present **abbey church★** is the result of a Baroque remodelling of the original Gothic hall-church, of which nothing but the nave columns were re-used. The chancel was again rebuilt in 1726 with flattened vaulting. The upper parts of the aisles are interrupted by galleries oddly pierced by lantern-windows which afford an astonishing view of the vaulting.

*From here it is possible to reach the church at **Osterhofen**, on the south bank of the Danube (10km - 6 miles – see PASSAU: Excursions).*

STUTTGART★

Baden-Württemberg – Population 559 000
Michelin map 419 T 11
Plan of the conurbation in the current Michelin Red Guide Deutschland and on map 419

The capital of the Baden-Württemberg Land lies in a depression surrounded by wooded hills opening in the northeast onto the Neckar. The site itself is undulating, with an encircling belt of trees separating the city centre from extensive suburbs. The finest overall **view★** of Stuttgart is from the upper platform of the **Fernsehturm** (television tower) (*access via the Hohenheimer Straße* – **LZ**), which soars 400m - 1 312ft above the woods on the southern side of town.

The name of the city, originally **Stutengarten**, derives from a 10C seigniorial stud farm which flourished in the region, the German word "Stute" meaning "mare". By the 14C, the town which had grown up there was significant enough to be protected by fortified walls and had become the seat of the Counts of Württemberg. Soon, supplanting such older burgs as Cannstatt, Waiblingen and Esslingen, which were equally part of the Hohenstaufen heritage, it became also the home of the Dukes and Kings of the realm.

Two Automobile Pioneers – An engineer who lived in Bad Cannstatt, **Gottfried Daimler** (1834-1900) pioneered the adaptation of the internal combustion engine to the powering of vehicles. Collaborating with the brilliant designer Wilhelm Maybach, he developed a vertical motor which was patented in 1883.

Unlike Daimler, **Carl Benz** (1844-1929) was less concerned with the actual invention of a new motor than with its universal application. Born and educated at Karlsruhe, he envisaged an entire motor vehicle, which he elaborated himself in every detail at Mannheim. Soon he was able to start manufacturing in series and put his cars on the market. In 1899 he sold his 2000th vehicle and thus became the world's leading automobile manufacturer. Then, in 1901, Daimler's company marketed a model baptized **Mercedes**, after the daughter of its most important foreign agent. The name was to make a fortune. And since the two firms amalgamated in 1926 Mercedes-Benz has been synonymous with luxury cars built to a high standard of excellence and technical prowess. Today, above the roofs of the city, the night sky over Stuttgart blazes with the illuminated three-point-star within a circle that is the firm's world-famous trademark.

Urban Landscape – The former appearance of the city can only be found today on the **Schillerplatz** (**KLY**), which is flanked by the Stiftskirche (collegiate church) and the Altes Schloß (Old Castle). The **statue of Schiller** in the centre of the square is the work of the Danish sculptor Thorwaldsen (1839).

In front of the **Neues Schloß** (New Palace) (**LY**) is the wide **Schloßplatz** (**LY 72**), off which a tree-lined avenue leads through the castle gardens to **Rosenstein-Park** *(access via the Heilbronner Straße* – **LY**) in the north. The Neues Schloß was built between 1746 and 1807 after a design by L Retti. It is now the home of regional ministerial departments. Modern Stuttgart's business centre is based on the Königstraße (**KLY**), in the pedestrian zone.

CENTRAL SIGHTS

★★ **Linden-Museum** (**KY M¹**) ⊙ – This museum consecrated to fine arts and folk arts worldwide dates back to the foundation of the Württemberg Commercial Geography Society in 1884. The exhibits, beautifully presented, fall under six main headings: America; the Pacific *(ground floor)*; Africa; the Middle-East *(first floor)*; Southern and Eastern Asia *(second floor)*. Both ancient and modern civilizations are illustrated, and the accompanying explanations examine present-day problems of development.

America – There is a display of **ancient Peruvian ceramics**, including an interesting collection of vessels decorated with human figures, and examples of fine workmanship in silver and gold (note the death-mask in gold leaf, dating from *c*400 AD). The section on **North-American Indians** (Apache, Pawnee, Crow, Cree, Dakota, etc.) is perhaps the most fascinating. A rich variety of weapons, jewels, clothing and everyday objects provides a comprehensive illustration of tribal life as it once was.

Hunting and cooking implements, as well as a 19C kayak, a selection of toys, and clothing made from furs and skins give the visitor an idea of existence among the Eskimos.

The Pacific – Here the interest is concentrated on the inhabitants of **New Guinea** and neighbouring isles in the **Papuan archipelago** (New Britain, New Ireland) where the indigenous culture is centred on belief in spirits and the cult of ancestors.

Africa – Reconstitution of a typical North Nigerian market is the first thing to meet the eye in this department. Gold body ornaments from Ghana and bronze reliefs from Benin (Southern Nigeria) are examples of superb craftmanship. The traditions of African tribal life and its superstitions are evoked in fantasy **masks** representing, among animist deities, crocodiles, sawfish and sharks. Replicas of a royal palace and an army post (Cameroon) exemplify forms of political and military organization.

The Middle-East – Visitors to this department pass through an oriental **bazaar** with its potters, dyers, tinsmiths and jewel workers before being presented with different aspects of Islamic culture and beliefs. These include a mosque, the Koran, ornaments and ceramics, the tomb of a 12C Ghaznavide dignitary, even dervishes. Note also the varied examples of fine Arab cloth, splendid beaten metalwork ranging from the 11C to the 14C, and an exhibition of Persian arms (17C to 19C).

The Far East – Initially, visitors to this department pass through a Japanese tea-house, a lacquer workshop and a traditional Japanese room (reconstructions). The Chinese sections give pride of place to porcelain and ceramics, including ancient ceramics used in funeral rites with human and animal motifs. One of the finest examples of Chinese pictorial art is a 12-panel folding screen decorated with scenes representing the Festival of Fishing (Ch'ing dynasty, 1707).

STUTTGART

A	Stiftskirche	
M¹	Linden-Museum	
M²	Staatsgalerie	
M³	Wüttembergisches Landesmuseum	
M⁴	Galerie der Stadt Stuttgart	
M⁵	Museum am Löwentor	
M⁶	Mercedes-Benz-Museum	

Southern Asia – Tibet is represented by bronze figurines, ritual instruments and replicas of ceremonial vestments and an altar used by the Dalai Lama.

An atmosphere of magic bathes the galleries showing examples of the Chinese shadow theatre and marionettes from Bali and Java. Bronze statues of the divinities (including Shiva, king of the dance) preside over the section devoted to Hindu India, and there are temple bas-reliefs in stone on display as well as religious items relating to the more rustic cultures (open-air altars from Rajasthan; an 18C ritual plough in silver from northern India).

* **Staatsgalerie (Art Gallery) (LY M)** ☉ – Painting from medieval times to the Impressionists is on show here. Note especially the **Old Masters Section**★★, in which Swabian painting from the 14C to the 16C is pre-eminent. One of the masterpieces exhibited is the **Herrenberg Altar** of Jerg Ratgeb (1519), which portrays – from left to right – the Last Supper, the Martyrization Of Jesus, the Crucifixion and the Resurrection. Fourteenth-century Venetians and Florentines dominate an excellent collection of Italian painters. Among the Dutch Old Masters are Hans Memling *(Bethsheba Bathing)*, Rembrandt *(St Paul In Prison)*, Jacob van Ruisdael and Rubens.

An annexe (opened in 1984) designed by the British architect James Stirling houses the Department of **Modern Art**. Among the

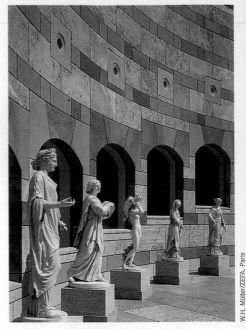

Neue Staatsgalerie, Stuttgart

W.H. Müller/ZEFA, Paris

"modern classics" on display are works by the Fauvists and French Cubists (Matisse, Braque, Juan Gris), the German Expressionists (a fine selection of Kokoschka paintings), the artists of New Objectivity or Verism (Dix, Grosz) and artists of the Bauhaus School *(qv)*. A special place is reserved for the work of **Willi Baumeister** (1889-1955) and **Oskar Schlemmer** (1888-1843) of the Bauhaus, both natives of Stuttgart. Schlemmer's famous six-figure Triadic Ballet is on view, as well as certain enormous sketches for murals (the finished works, painted in 1929, were victims of the Nazi crusade against the so-called "degenerate art"). Another highlight of this museum is a collection of 12 **Picasso** works covering every period of his working life. Among them is the world-famous sculpture group in wood, **The Bathers**.

The section on contemporary art covers the half century since the Second World War, starting with Dubuffet and Giacometti and ending with the latest works of Baselitz and Kiefer, by way of American Pop Art (Warhol, Segal), Italy's Arte Povera and the "installations" of Beuys.

Altes Schloß (Old Castle) (LY) – Four wings flanked by round towers comprise this building, most of which dates from the 16C. The **Renaissance Courtyard**★ is surrounded by three floors of arcaded galleries. The interior now houses the **Württembergisches Landesmuseum**★ **(M³)** ☉.

On the ground floor and the mezzanine, the exhibits include rare tapestries, craftwork in ceramics, glass and silver tableware (from the 14C to the 19C), and clothes worn by the nobility (especially in the 18C). Ancient history and prehistory are also represented on the first floor, while the second contains an extremely interesting collection of **religious statuary**★★. Note above all the eight Scenes of the Passion (in the central octagon) executed by the sculptor Jörg Syrlin in 1515 for the church at Zwiefalten *(qv)*.

Funerary objects (weapons, jewels and household items) can be seen in the section devoted to the Franks and the Alemanni, which is also on the second floor, and gives some idea of the civilization of these peoples between the 5C and the 8C.

There is a fine collection of musical instruments and clocks on the third floor, which also houses a numismatic gallery.

The Treasury Tower *(Kunstkammerturm – entrance on the ground floor or second floor)* contains items from the "Ducal Chamber of Arts and Marvels" (Herzogliche Kunst-und-Wunderkammer) which range from the 15C to the 18C. They include the crown jewels of the Kings of Württemberg (19C).

Stiftskirche (KY A) – The most impressive part of this church, built in the middle of the 15C, is the west tower belfry porch with superimposed polygonal copings (1490-1531). When the church was restored after the war damage of 1945, the nave and former aisles were combined into a single hall covered with panelled vaulting. A large funerary **monument**★, a memorial to the Dukes of Württemberg, stands in the chancel. Commissioned by Duke Ludwig III, this was executed by the sculptor S Schlör c1580. Eleven armoured figurines representing ancestors of the Duke are standing in front of a décor of Renaissance arcades.

Galerie der Stadt Stuttgart (City Gallery) (LY M⁴) ⊙ — Between-the-wars painting (1918-1939) figures prominently in this museum. Note particularly the **work★** of Neue Sachlichkeit artist **Otto Dix**, famous for the ferocity of his criticism of modern society and its depravities, and his disgust at the horrors of war. Typical of his approach are the Big City *(Großstadt)* triptych and the anti-war picture *Grabenkrieg*. Young Stuttgart artists of the 1980s are represented, and so too are the local painters Hölzel, Schlemmer and Baumeister *(see above)*.

ADDITIONAL SIGHTS

★ **Wilhelma Park and Zoo** — *Leave by the Heilbronner Straße* (**LY**). *The approach to the zoo is signalled by a herd of painted elephants trooping across the road on the side of a bridge.*
This botanical and zoological garden laid out more than a century ago is furnished with hothouses displaying many fascinating tropical plants and a celebrated exhibition of orchids. Worth seeing also: the aquarium and a terrarium.

Staatliches Museum für Naturkunde (National Museum of Natural Sciences) ⊙ — *In Rosenstein-Park.*
There is a Zoology Department in the museum in **Schloß Rosenstein** which features a collection of stuffed creatures (especially mammals and birds) from all over the world, displayed in their natural habitat. The most imposing exhibit is a 13m - 43ft northern whale, reconstituted around a genuine skeleton.
The department consecrated to the origins of Planet Earth is now installed in the new **Museum am Löwentor ∧** (**LY M⁵**) ⊙ — a collection of spacious modern galleries in the same park. Here, through a fine assembly of Baden-Württemberg fossils, beautifully displayed, 600 million years of world history can be skimmed over. Fossil birds, fish, reptiles, tortoises and even dinosaurs can be seen. There are also actual skeletons of large prehistoric mammals, excavated bones, and a section dealing with man in the glacial period in different parts of the museum.

★ **Höhenpark Killesberg** ⊙ — *Leave by Heilbronner Straße* (**LY**).
A little way to the west of the Rosenstein, this park is a continuation of the green belt encircling the inner city. Laid out on a height to the north of the centre, it integrates perfectly with the undulating terrain. Terraced cascades, fountains and brilliantly coloured flowerbeds invite the visitor to relax and admire, and there is a **miniature train** on which a tour of the whole park can be made.
A panoramic view of Stuttgart can be enjoyed from a lookout tower at the highest point (Aussichtsturm).

★ **Kurpark Bad Cannstatt** (Spa Park) — *Leave by the Cannstatter Straße* (**LY**).
The old town of Bad Cannstatt, now the city's largest residential suburb, has retained its function as a spa. The 18 thermal springs – feeding a fountain and three swimming-pools – have made the place, after Budapest, Europe's second largest producer of mineral water. The park (Kurpark) is attractive. Once a year, in late September/early October it hosts a funfair as part of the Cannstatter Volksfest.

★ **Mercedes-Benz-Museum** ⊙ — *Leave by the Schillerstraße* (**LY M⁶**). *At 136 Mercedesstraße, in a block of the company's main factory, located at Stuttgart-Untertürkheim.*
Nearly 100 vintage and veteran motor cars are on show here, the models ranging from the earliest to the most recent, as well as video films tracing the history of engines and cars, especially at Daimler-Benz. The racing car collection testifies to the success of Mercedes worldwide until 1955. Engines powering aircraft, airships (Zeppelin) and rail-cars complete the exhibition.

A 1927 Mercedes Sportwagen "S" (Mercedes-Benz Museum, Stuttgart)

INTER NATIONES, Born

EXCURSIONS

* **Schloß Solitude** ⊙ – *Leave by the Rotebühlstraße* **KZ**).
The former summer residence of the Württemberg Court stands on the edge of a plateau about five miles from the city centre, west of the Botnang suburb. Flanked by lateral wings, the castle is centred on an oval pavilion with a cupola, the whole being majestically raised on a base of open arcades. Around this, the lower outbuildings lie in an immense arc. The design was by the French Court architect, La Guépière, who supervised construction between 1764 and 1769. A certain restraint, tempering the sumptuousness of the concept, can be traced to the architect's admiration for the buildings of ancient Greece.
Inside, the decorations of the central rotunda (Weißer Saal) and the small marble room are in the neo-Classical tradition. The other apartments, which are panelled, are French Rococo. One of the more bizarre items on view is the desk used by Friedrich I of Württemberg – largely hollowed out because of the obesity of its owner, so cruelly ridiculed by Napoleon.

* **Schwäbisches Brauereimuseum (Swabian Brewery Museum)** ⊙ – *At 12 Robert-Koch-Straße, Stuttgart-Vaihingen.*
Five thousand years of beer-making are traced in this museum. Objects discovered in Mesopotamian and Ancient Egyptian digs (some of them reproductions) prove that, even in the mists of antiquity, appreciation of this liquid with a base of hops and barley was not confined to Europe. The principles and techniques of brewing are explained in the lower basement. Well-chosen instruments and plants illustrate the different stages in the making of beer (malting, crushing, wort preparation, fermentation, filtering, bottling, etc.).

* **Porsche-Museum** ⊙ – *Leave on Heilbronner Straße* (**LY**), *in the direction of the motorway. Before the motorway, take the exit signposted Zuffenhausen-Industriegebiet, and then turn right into the Porschestraße. Stop at No 42.*
In 1934, the engineer Ferdinand Porsche (1875-1951), already distinguished by his work at Daimler-Benz, produced a design for the famous "people's car" – the Volkswagen. His prototype evolved into the celebrated "Beetle". Porsche himself, from 1948 onwards, devoted himself to a sports model bearing his own name, which was developed from the original VW chassis and engine and subsequently manufactured at Zuffenhausen. In one of the factory buildings 30 different Porsches are now on show, along with a display of high-performance engines.

* **Tiefenbronn** – *38km - 24 miles to the west.*
The Gothic **church** (Pfarrkirche) in this village houses the well-known **Lucas Moser altarpiece**★★ (1431) in its south aisle. On the outside of the panels, the artist has illustrated, in a unified of style, the legend of Mary Magdalene: on the tympanum is the Feast at Bethany; in the centre, the crossing of the Mediterranean from Palestine to Provence by Martha, Lazarus, Maximinus and Cedonius, then the homeless saints staying in Marseille and Mary Magdalene appearing before the town governor in a dream and, finally, Mary Magdalene's last communion.

SWABIAN JURA★
See SCHWÄBISCHE ALB

SWISS SAXONY★★★
See SÄCHSISCHE SCHWEIZ

SYLT★★
Schleswig-Holstein
Michelin map 415 B 8

The Frisian island of Sylt, the most northerly point of German territory, extends in a north-south direction for 40km - 25 miles, although in parts it is less than 500 yards across. Despite the reduced area of this long, narrow isle, however, the landscape is varied. Around Kampen, Westerland and Morsum, the agricultural aspect of the countryside testifies to its rich Geest *(qv)* origins. This is increased in area to the southeast by Marschen reclaimed from the sea.
On the west side, facing the open sea, an immense beach of fine sand runs for miles. Passing beneath low red cliffs (Rotes Kliff) between Kampen and Wenningstedt, this superb strand finally joins a continuous belt of dunes south of Westerland. The island as a whole is a holiday paradise where sea, sand, sun and the magnificent northern light reign supreme. There are a number of official naturist reserves on the coast.

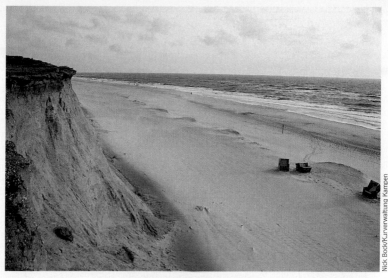

Sylt – Red cliffs at Kampen

Speed should be reduced while driving along the island roads and through built-up areas. Motor traffic is regulated in certain places.

Access by rail ☉ – Train-car ferries depart from Niebüll and cross the arm of sea separating Sylt from the mainland via the Hindenburgdamm causeway.

Access by car-ferry ☉ – There is a seaborne car ferry service between Havneby *(on the Danish island of Römö - accessible by road)* and List, on the northern tip of Sylt.

★★**Westerland** – This is the most important seaside resort in the whole of Germany, meeting place for the elegant and fashionable, with a lively, popular casino. The 1 1/2-miles seafront promenade (Kurpromenade) is always busy – and when the tide is high, the sea hurls itself with relentless force against its foundations.

The therapeutic virtues of saltwater treatment have recently regained popularity, and in Westerland now there is a huge cure establishment specializing in marine and mud baths (Kurmittelhaus).

Keitum – This is the exact opposite of animated Westerland – and old, peaceful Frisian village with thatched roofs half hidden among trees and plantations of lilac. Behind the Louise-Schröder-Heim institution, a path leads to a low coastal bluff (Keitumer Kliff), a pleasant, shady **site**★ where visitors can sit and admire a view in which the horizon is lost in a limitless expanse of sea, sand, mudflats, and the sky above the low mainland shore beyond.

For a quiet place to stay
*consult the annual **Michelin Red Guide Deutschland***
which gives a choice of pleasant hotels.

THÜRINGER WALD★★

Forest of THURINGIA – Thüringen
Michelin map 418 N 14 - O 16

Much in the same way as the Harz *(qv)*, the Forest of Thuringia is a wooded massif, orientated northwest-southeast, with an average height of 1 000m - 3 300ft. Long known as "the green heart of Germany", the massif is scattered with charming villages whose inhabitants still retain their traditional skills and craftsmanship. A wealth of tourist amenities, particularly at Oberhof, and the development of several resorts have made the region popular with a large number of ramblers and summer holidaymakers.

Granite, gneiss and porphyry formations underlie the central nucleus of the forest, while the foothills are composed mainly of sandstone and limestone sedimentary deposits.

Flora and fauna – The forest covering practically the whole area is largely beech, pine and fir. Marshy plateaux have developed in some of the higher reaches, and there is moorland on the approaches to some crests. Among the larger varieties of game, stags, roe deer and wild boar are abundant.

THÜRINGER HOCHSTRASSE (FOREST HIGH ROAD)

From Eisenach to Ilmenau *110km - 68 miles – 1 day*

This fascinating forest road mainly follows the Rennsteig, a ramblers' path 160km - 100 miles long which keeps to the highest parts of the forest and includes such major summits as the Großer Inselsberg (916m - 3 005ft) and the Großer Beerberg (982m - 3 222ft).

Leave **Eisenach★** *(qv) in the direction of Gotha.*

Großer Inselsberg *– 1 hour Rtn on foot.*
The **panorama★★** extending from the summit takes in the greater part of the forest.

★ **Marienglashöhle** ☉ – Crystalline gypsum is extracted from this natural cavity. The use of this mineral in the decoration of church altars has led to the grotto's unusual name (Marienglas = Glass of Mary).

The road cuts across the Rennsteig and twists between the Regenberg (727m - 2 385ft) and the Spießberg (749m - 2 457ft), offering numerous possibilities for sightseeing and walks, especially in the direction of **Ebertswiese**, a zone of marsh and meadows. Steinbach is overlooked by the Hallenburg ruins. The road continues towards Oberhof via the Kanzlergrund, a valley with wide stretches of grass and meadowland.

★ **Oberhof** – At 800m - 2 625ft altitude, this town is the most important leisure centre and winter sports station in the Forest of Thuringia.
In the **Rennsteiggarten**, a botanical park specializing in Alpines and the flora of Central European heights, more than 4 000 varieties of plant can be seen.

Ohratalsperre (Dam) *– Follow Route 247 to the large car park.*
The reservoir dammed by this barrage, the surface of which extends over 88ha - 218 acres, supplies water to Weimar, Jena, Gotha and the Thuringian capital, Erfurt.

Leaving Oberhof in the direction of Schmücke, the country road winds once again sinuously between the Großer Beerberg (982m - 3 222ft) and the Schneekopf (978m - 3 209ft). From the hotel car park at Schmücke, there is a fine viewpoint looking out over the valley. The 944m - 3 097ft Finsterberg is visible on the left.

Ilmenau – This locality on the northern fringe of the Forest of Thuringia has always been associated with Goethe, who is said to have been particularly fond of its natural beauties. There is a plaque in his memory on the wall of the town's municipal headquarters (Amtshaus, in the Marktplatz), which has been transformed into a Goethe museum, and another in the Gabelbach hunting lodge. A pathway baptised "**In Goethe's Footsteps**" (Auf Goethes Spuren) links the places associated with the great writer.

Bad TÖLZ

Bayern – Population 13 600
Michelin map 419/420 W 18

Bad Tölz is really two towns: on one side of the Isar is a modern spa, reputed for the healing qualities of its iodized water (at 41.5mg per litre, the richest in Germany); and facing it across the Alpine torrent is the picturesque old town, with its monuments to the Baroque and medieval eras.

* **Marktstraße** – Much of the character of this street derives from its wide curve and steep slope, bordered by multicoloured façades beneath overhanging eaves.

Kalvarienberg (Calvary Hill) – At the top of the Kalvarienberg pathway, which is flanked by the Stations of the Cross, a small chapel (1743) is dedicated to St Leonard, whose powers are still widely revered among the peasants of Bavaria and Austria. In this part of the country his intercession is sought not only for the deliverance of prisoners (note the chain surrounding the chapel), but also for the protection of horses. The saint's anniversary, November 6, is celebrated each year by a parade of rustic wagons and carts, colourfully decorated and drawn by teams of brilliantly harnessed horses *(see Calendar of events)*.

EXCURSIONS

Benediktbeuern ⊙ – *15km - 9 miles to the southwest.*
Built on the lower slopes of the Bavarian Alps foothills, this imposing complex dating from AD 739 is the oldest Benedictine abbey in Upper Bavaria. The **abbey church** ⊙ as it is now was remodelled between 1681 and 1686. On those parts of the cradle vaulting left free of stuccowork, Georg Asam – father of the famous Asam Brothers *(qv)* – painted the first complete cycle of frescoes dating from the beginning of the Bavarian Baroque period: the Birth, Baptism, Transfiguration and Resurrection of the Saviour, the Descent of the Holy Spirit and the Last Judgement.
Elegant frescoes and finely worked stucco make the **Anastasiakapelle★** (1751-53), a chapel a little to the north of the church, one of the most charming examples of Rococo art. The designer, J M Fischer, and the craftsmen who carried out the work for him, were commissioned a few years later to repeat their artistry at Ottobeuren *(qv)*.

* **Walchensee** – *40km - 25 miles to the southwest.*
Framed by dense woods, this deep blue reservoir-lake is one of the beauties of the Bavarian Alps. Its waters serve the power station on the Kochelsee, some 200m - 600ft lower down. A chairlift rises to the Fahrenberg, from which a path leads in 30 minutes to the summit of the **Herzogstand** (1 731m - 5 679ft). From the observation deck, there is a superb **all-round view★★** taking in the Walchensee, the Kochelsee, the Karwendel massif and the rock wall of the Wetterstein, which culminates in the Zugspitze.

TRIER★★

Rheinland-Pfalz – Population 99 000
Michelin map 417 Q 3 – Local map under MOSELTAL
Town plan in the current Michelin Red Guide Deutschland

This venerable episcopal city, whose ecclesiastical Electors ruled as far north as Koblenz, is the first German town reached by the Moselle and an important winegrowing centre. It can be regarded as the capital of Ancient Rome in Germany – a situation emphasized by the richness and variety of the works of art that remain.
The philosopher and economist Karl Marx (1818-1883) was born in Trier.

A SECOND ROME

Trier became the meeting point very early on for the Celtic, Germanic and Latin cultures which evolved to form Western civilization.
After the conquest of the Treveri, a Celtic tribe from the eastern part of Gaul, the Roman Emperor Augustus founded on their territory the town of **Augusta Treverorum** (*c*15 BC), which soon became a centre of intense economic, cultural and intellectual activity, continuing to develop until the invasion of Germanic tribes in AD 274. Essentially a civic and residential settlment, the town fell before the onslaught.
Later, however, when Diocletian reorganized the Roman Empire, Trier was retaken and became capital of the western territories (Gaul, Spain, Germania and Britain). As the town regained its former eminence, the Emperor Constantine (306-337) surrounded it with a defensive wall within which magnificent buildings were erected. In this second period of prosperity, Trier was given the status of imperial residence.
In the year 313, the Edict of Milan put an end to the persecution of Christians, and a year later the See of Trier, the oldest in Germany, was created. But towards the end of the 4C, renewed pressure from the Germanic tribes became so strong that the imperial residence was transferred to Milan and the prefecture to Arles. In 470, Trier finally fell into the hands of the Franks. During the Middle Ages, the Archbishops of Trier wielded a great deal of power as Prince-Electors.

OLD TOWN *time: one day*

★★Porta Nigra (DX) ⊙ – This magnificent four-storey structure – originally the northern entrance to the walled town – dates from the 2C and is the most important Roman relic on German soil. Its name derives from the dark patina forming over the centuries on the sandstone blocks used in its construction. The stones are fitted together without mortar, held only here and there with iron crampons. The gateway was designed for military use: the double arcade of the central block, flanked by two massive towers, leads to an inner court where only the upper arcades are pierced – and assailants forcing the outer gates would find themselves exposed here to attack from all sides.

The Porta Nigra at Trier

In the 11C, the fortified gateway was transformed into a church on two levels, dedicated to St Simeon. The Romanesque apse can still be seen on the east side, and there are traces of additional alterations – Rococo decoration, for example – in the upper galleries (on the inner courtyard side). It was Napoleon who ordered the monument to be restored to its original form in 1804. There is a fine view from the tower terrace.

Städtisches Museum (DX M²) ⊙ – This municipal museum is installed in a Romanesque convent, the **Simeonsstift**, built beside the Porta Nigra at the same time as the church (11C). The history of Trier is illustrated with models, paintings, engravings, maps and sculptures, among them the original figures surrounding the fountain in the market place (the Four Virtues and St Peter, late 16C). Above the arcades, the old **cloister** has been transformed into a lapidary museum.

★ Dreikönigenhaus (House of the Three Kings) (DX K) – This early Gothic town house (*c*1230), with its arched windows, recalls the Italianate towers of the patricians of Regensburg *(qv)*.

★ Hauptmarkt (DX) – One of the finest old squares in Germany. In the middle is the **Market Cross★** (Marktkreuz), erected in the year 958 when the town was granted the right to hold a market. The **fountain**, with its painted figures, dates from the late 16C. Standing by the Cross (which was restored in the 18C), the visitor can see fifteen centuries of history encapsulated in the monuments around the square. To the north is the Porta Nigra, to the east the Romanesque cathedral, to the south the Gothic **Gangolfkirche**, whose early 16C tower was once used as a lookout post.

Picturesque half-timbered houses, both Renaissance and Baroque, stand on the west side. The **Steipe (D)**, a medieval (15C) municipal building with a steep, tall roof, is elegantly built over an open gallery. Beside it, the 17C **Rotes Haus** (Red House) **(E)**, bears the proud inscription: "There was life in Trier for 1 300 years before Rome even existed".

Frankenturm (CX) – A heavily-built Romanesque tower (*c*1100) with small windows.

★ Dom (Cathedral) (DX) – Seen from its forecourt (Domfreihof), Trier cathedral looks more like a fortress than a church. A rounded apse projects from a massive, austere façade which, with its squat, square towers, is a fine example of early Romanesque architecture.

From the north side, different stages in the construction are evident. A flattened gable and rectangular plan distinguish the 4C Roman heart of the building. West of this central block is the 11C Romanesque section; east of it the polygonal chancel, which is furnished with a dwarf gallery and dates from the 12C *(see Introduction)*. Unfortunately, a Baroque axial chapel crowned by a dome was added to this in the 18C.

Entering the cathedral from the forecourt, note near the main door the fallen section (Domstein) of a Roman column which supported part of the former church. Inside, the decoration is principally Baroque and includes some interesting altarpieces. In the west chancel *(on the left of the entrance)* there is a Gothic funerary monument of the Archbishop and Prince-Elector Baldwin of Luxembourg. A splendid **tympanum★** in the south aisle depicts Christ between the Virgin Mary and St Peter. Another Madonna, a graceful 16C example, stands in the stuccoed chapel on the right of the chancel.

TRIER

B	Schatzkammer der Stadtbibliothek
D	Die Steipe
E	Roth Haus
K	Dreikönigenhaus
M¹	Bischöfliches Museum
M²	Städtisches Museum Simeonsstift

★ Treasury (Domschatz) ☉ – Silver and gold plate (portable altar of St Andrew, richly enamelled), valuable ivories, and magnificently illuminated Gospels are on view here, in the domed axial chapel.

Cloister (Kreuzgang) – From the Gothic cloister, there is a good **view★** of the cathedral and the Liebfrauenkirche. In the northeast corner is the 15C Malberg Madonna.

★ Liebfrauenkirche (Church of Our Lady) (DX) – One of the earliest Gothic sanctuaries in Germany (1235-1260), this church was directly inspired by one in Champagne, with the ground plan in the form of a Greek cross. There are thus four apsidal chapels, between each pair of which two smaller, three-sided chapels have been interposed, giving the whole church the highly original form of a rose with 12 petals.

The **tympanum** over the west porch shows St Mary Enthroned, the Annunciation, the Adoration of the Magi, the Massacre of the Innocents and the Presentation in the Temple. The Coronation of the Virgin is represented at the north entrance.

The interior has an incomparable elegance, enhanced by rings of foliage carved around each column, by the finesse of the public gallery, and the richness of the high central vaulting. There is a fine 17C **funerary monument★** (north chapel) to Metternich's personal canon.

★ Bischöfliches Dom- und Diözesanmuseum (Episcopal Museum) (DY M¹) ☉ – The most interesting exhibits here are the frescoes (Deckenmalerei, 4C) of the Palace of Constantine, discovered beneath the cathedral. It is supposed that they represent St Helen, the Emperor's mother, and his wife Fausta. The colours are extraordinarily fresh and the technique highly skilled.

The first floor of the museum is reserved for sacred art (note the original statues which once adorned the west face of the Liebfrauenkirche).

Basilika (DY) – Once the main hall of the building, this "Aula Palatina" is all that remains of the imperial palace built by Constantine *c*310. Remodelled and altered many times, it was finally restored to its original form in the 19C and early 20C. The basilica is used today as a Protestant church. The interior, restrained in decoration, nevertheless overwhelms with its sheer size.

Ehem. Kurfürstliches Schloß (DY) – Only the north and east wings remain of the former Renaissance electoral castle, on which building was begun in 1615. The Rococo wings were built between 1756 and 1762, based on plans by the court master builder Johannes Seitz. His virtuosity (he was a student of Balthasar Neumann) is expressed in a magnificent **staircase**, one of the most beautiful creations of its kind in Germany. The south façade with its gentle colouring looks out over the **palace gardens★**, laid out in the French style with ponds, flower borders and Baroque statues.

★★ Rheinisches Landesmuseum (Rhineland Museum) (DY) ☉ – At street level, a Department of Prehistory and a section on Roman antiquities are particularly interesting.

Palaeolithic Age: Stone Age implements, ceramics and weapons; objects found in Bronze Age tombs; jewels set in gold from Iron Age sepulchres.

Roman Period: marvellous mosaics; bronze statuettes; sculptures and bas-reliefs (including a school scene and one depicting the payment of farm rent). Among the sculpture discovered at Neumagen *(see MOSELTAL)* is the representation of a ship sailing down the Moselle loaded with wine . Included in this **Neumagen Ship** carving is the figure of "the jolly sailor" – a mariner with a broad grin who has passed into the folklore of the Moselle. Regional ceramics and jewels and glassware found in Frankish tombs are also on display.

★★ Kaiserthermen (Imperial Roman Baths) (DY) ☉ – Among the largest in the Roman empire, these baths date from the time of Constantine, but appear never to have been used. The construction of the rounded walls – alternate layers of brick and rubble – is typically Roman. The window openings are wide and arched. Inside, the hot water caldarium is preceded by a tepidarium (warm water baths), a frigidarium (cold) and a gymnasium for physical exercises. The two floors below ground where the heating and circulating plant were installed are particularly interesting to see.

★★ Schatzkammer der Stadtbibliothek (Municipal Library Treasury) (DY B) ☉ – Fascinating exhibits are on view here. The collection includes rare ancient manuscripts, beautifully illuminated (medieval Bibles, homilies, fables, etc.); examples of the earliest books to be illustrated (Gospels, teaching manuals, legal volumes); and many old documents, treaties, letters of credit and safe conduct passes.

Karl-Marx-Haus (CY) ☉ – *Brückenstraße 10.*
The birthplace of the socialist theoretician has been turned into a museum. Letters, manuscripts, first edition of Communist Manifesto, etc.

ADDITIONAL SIGHTS

★ Pfarrkirche St. Paulin – *Access via Thebäerstraße* **(DX)**.
Tall windows illuminate the single nave of this church designed by Balthazar Neumann *(qv)* and completed in 1754. The martyrdom of the Saint and members of the Theban Legion in AD 268 is illustrated in paintings on the ceiling, Rococo stucco decorates the vaulting.

Barbarathermen (CY) ☉ – 2C Roman baths, used for several centuries, now in ruins.

Amphitheater (Roman Amphitheatre) (DY) ☉ – Once seating 20 000 spectators, this arena was used as a quarry in the Middle Ages, and became so damaged by the 18C that vines were grown on the terraces. The cellars below ground house theatrical equipment.

St. Matthias – *Access via Saarstraße* **(CY)**.
A 12C pillared Romanesque basilica, now a Benedictine convent church housing the St Matthias reliquary shrine. Apart from Romanesque, the façade shows traces of Baroque and neo-Classical influence.

Weißhaus – Restaurant with a terrace giving a good **view** of the west bank of the Moselle and Trier on the opposite bank.

Take the cable railway from the Zurlauben stop, or drive there, crossing the river over the Kaiser-Wilhelm-Brücke and then taking Bitburger Straße and the Stückradweg.

The Michelin Green Guide France
aims to make touring more enjoyable
by suggesting several touring programmes
which are easily adapted to personal taste. ·

TÜBINGEN★★

Baden-Württemberg – Population 78 000
Michelin map 419 U 11 – Local map under SCHWÄBISCHE ALB
Plan of the conurbation in the current Michelin Red Guide Deutschland

Built on the banks of the Neckar and overlooked by Schloß Hohentübingen, this ancient medieval city boasts a university, founded in 1477, which has schooled – among many others – such poets as Hölderlin, Mörike and Uhland, the philosophers Hegel and Schelling, scholars like Kepler and theologians of the status of Melanchthon.

Today, with its animated student life, its steep and narrow streets rising between old houses from a pleasant riverside setting, Tübingen remains one of the most attractive towns in southern Germany.

From **Eberhardsbrücke** (**Z**), there is a fine **view**★ upstream of the Neckar, bordered by weeping willows, with time-worn roofs and the outline of the Hölderlin tower emerging through the greenery. On the left, the **Platanenallee**★★ (**Z**) – an avenue of plane trees on a man-made island – is a delightful place for a waterfront stroll, especially in summer when the river at night is alive with lantern-lit boats and student songs echo beneath the lights of the old town.

SIGHTS

★ **Am Markt** (**Y**) – An old square, very animated on market days (Mondays, Wednesdays and Fridays). In the centre, a Renaissance fountain and statue of Neptune.

★ **Rathaus** (**Y R**) – The outside decoration of this 15C building dates from 1876. The astronomic clock on the façade (1511) is the work of Stöfler.

Stiftskirche (**Y**) ⊙ – A Gothic hall-church built in the 15C. The rood-screen and the canopied **pulpit**★ are in the Flamboyant style. The chancel is in fact the burial place of the Princes of Württemberg. Note the funerary monument of Eberhard the Bearded, original founder of the university, and the Renaissance **tombs**★★ of Duke Ludwig and his wife, adorned with fine alabaster relief work.

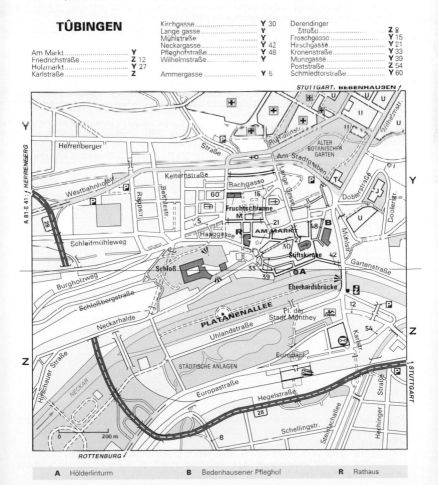

A Hölderlinturm   B Bedenhausener Pfleghof   R Rathaus

Tübingen

From the top of the church tower, there is an interesting **view**★ of the river, the castle promontory and, in the distance, the Swabian Jura.

Schloß (**YZ**) – The present edifice was built on mid-11C foundations during the Renaissance. It now houses several Departments of the university. In the cellars are prison cells and a 1548 vat which held no less than 850hl - 18 700 gallons of wine.

From the bastion terraces there are, again, good views of the Neckar and the old town.

Hölderlinturm (**Z A**) ⊘ – *Bursagasse 6.*

Once part of the fortifications, this tower was turned into a dwelling house and inhabited by Hölderlin (1770-1843). Now a museum, it displays many souvenirs of the poet.

Bebenhausener Pfleghof (Bebenhausen Hospital) (**Y B**) – Once the tithe barn of Bebenhausen abbey *(see below)*, this building dates from the 15C. Jutting from the tall, steep roof is a three-storey dormer through the windows of which the grain was passed into the lofts.

Fruchtschranne (**Y**) – Designed as the ducal granary, this wood-walled 15C building has a most unusual roof, since it boasts four storeys, each with mansards.

EXCURSION

★ **Kloster Bebenhausen** – *6km - 3 1/2 miles to the north via the Wilhelm-straße* (**Y**).

This ancient Cistercian monastery, founded in 1180 in the solitude of Schönbuch forest, is an interesting example of Romano-Gothic architecture in Germany. Built to the classic Cistercian plan, but much restored, the abbey church still shows traces of Romanesque design.

The **cloister**, in the Flamboyant style, has splendid fan vaulting. Facing the lavabo is the summer refectory; to the west the winter one is now a small museum.

ÜBERLINGEN ★

Baden-Württemberg – Population 19 600
Michelin map 419 W 11 – Local map under BODENSEE

This ancient Empire outpost on the shores of Lake Constance *(qv)* has become a popular summer resort because of its exceptionally mild climate and the opportunities it affords for water sports.

West of the town there is a pleasant **moat walk**★ (Stadtbefestigungsanlagen) (**A**) which leads to the lakeside **Seepromenade** (**AB**). The town stands on the northern shore of the lake's Überlingersee arm.

ÜBERLINGEN

M Städtisches Museum
R Rathaus

SIGHTS

Münsterplatz (**B**) – The square lies between the Gothic cathedral, the north façade of the town hall, and the Renaissance municipal chancellery (Alte Kanzlei).

★ **Münster** (**B**) – The cathedral, or minster, has an enormous central portion with five aisles covered by Gothic fan vaulting. A graceful Swabian work of 1510, the Virgin of the Crescent Moon, stands in the St Elizabeth chapel off the south aisle.

★ **Rathaus (Town Hall)** (**B R**) – *Enter through the turret on the right and walk up to the first floor.* The **council chamber**★ (Ratssaal) ⊙ is decorated with great finesse in the Gothic manner: panelled walls embellished with projecting arches; ribbed, and slightly rounded, wooden ceiling; a series of 15C statuettes.

★ **Städtisches Museum** (**B M**) ⊙ – Among the exhibits, housed in a late 15C mansion, is a collection of cribs (Krippen): 18C wood carvings in the folk tradition, representing, scenes from the life of Jesus in miniature.

EXCURSION

★ **Salem Abbey** – *11km - 7 miles to the east. See Abtei SALEM.*

ULM★★

Baden-Württemberg – Population 110 000
Michelin map 419/420 U 13

The commercial importance of Ulm derives from its situation, at the point where the great Stuttgart-Munich highway, newly descended from the Swabian Jura, crosses a Danube swollen from the inflow of waters from the Iller. If the ancient proverb "the money of Ulm governs the world" no longer applies, local industries, mechanical and electrical, still thrive. The Nobel Prize physicist Albert Einstein was born in Ulm in 1879.

★★ **General View** – A walk along the **Jahnufer** (the south bank of the Danube) (**Z**) opens a fine view of gabled houses crowning the ramparts on the far side of the river, of the Metzgerturm (Butchers' Tower) and the cathedral.

★★★ **MÜNSTER** (**CATHEDRAL**) (**Y**) *time: 45 minutes (not counting ascent of the spire)*

At a total height of 161m - 528ft, Ulm cathedral spire is the tallest in the world. It appears to arrow the entire Gothic building skywards in its slender trajectory. The church's sweeping vertical lines, added to the lightness of the pierced masonry, are wholly admirable. Although the foundation stone was laid in 1377, the two towers and the spire were not erected until 1890. A beautiful porch with three arcades and a very fine profile precedes the double Renaissance entrance doors (at the pier, an expressive 1429 statue, *Man In Sorrow*, by Hans Multscher).

Interior – The upswept nave, with sharply pointed arches, is emphasized in its soaring flight by the absence of a transept, which also concentrates attention on the chancel. The pillars of the central nave support a series of graceful early 15C consoles. The pulpit is surmounted by a splendid wooden luffer-board dating from 1510, and above this is what appears to be a second pulpit in the Flamboyant style. This is intended for the Holy Spirit, the invisible preacher. The ciborium, left of the chancel entrance, is in the same style, and so are the four side aisles with fine fan vaulting.

ULM

A Fischkasten	**M¹** Ulmer Museum
M² Brotmuseum	**R** Rathaus

***Choir Stalls** (Chorgestühl) – A marvellous example of wood carving, executed by Jörg Syrlin the Elder between 1469 and 1474, faces two series of personages, from the Bible and from pagan antiquity, one opposite the other. Men are grouped on the left, women on the right, the upper gables being devoted to the Church's apostles and martyrs, and the high backs of the stalls to Old Testament figures.

The most expressive sculptures are carved from the sides of the stalls and include sibyls on the right, busts of Greek and Latin philosophers and writers (Pythagoras, Cicero, etc.) on the left. Behind the altar, Syrlin's magnificent triple throne for the priest completes the ensemble. (The sculptor and his wife head the ranks nearest the nave.)

Ascent of the spire – *(768 steps)*. From the tower platform or the bulb of the spire, the all-round **panorama★★** includes the town, the Danube, the plateaux of the Swabian Jura and the Alps.

Ulm cathedral choir stalls: a sibyl

ADDITIONAL SIGHTS

★ **Fischerviertel (Fishermen's Quarter)** ( ) – Start from the Fischerplätzle, a small square shaded in summer by a lime tree. Take an alley on the left that spans a culvert. The picturesque building here, the **Schiefes Haus**, has subsided over a tanners' canal in a curious way.

Follow the itinerary as far as the Metzgerturm (Butchers' Tower), and then return.

★ **Ulmer Museum** (**M¹**) ⊘ – The Fine Arts Department of this museum, housed in a mansion that once belonged to a local dignitary, is the most interesting. Among works by the Masters of Ulm, note a reliquary bust by Syrling the Elder, a Virgin and Child by Daniel Mauch, the *Portrait of Eitel Besserer* by Martin Schaffner and Hans Multscher's Bilhafingen Madonna. Picasso, Klee and Kandinsky represent the 20C.

Rathaus (Town Hall) (**R**) – An elegant Gothic and Renaissance building with pierced gables and painted façades, richly decorated in trompe l'oeil. An astronomic clock adorns the fine west façade.

The **Fischkasten** (**A**) in the nearby Marktplatz is a fountain whose spiral stem was fashioned by Jörg Syrlin the Elder in 1482.

Heilig-Geist-Kirche – *To the southwest, via the Römerstrasse* ( ). This modern church, distinguished by its bell-tower in the form of a pointing finger, stands on a fine panoramic site above the town.

Brotmuseum (Bread Museum) (**M²**) ⊘ – This quite special museum has found a worthy setting in the Salzstadel in Ulm, an extremely attractive building dating from the year 1592. 6 000 years of cultural and social history connected with bread are represented here, and the links between this basic nutrient and religion, tradition and politics are emphasised. A wide range of equipment shows how bread is made from grain.

EXCURSIONS

Kloster Wiblingen (Abbey) ⊘ – *5km - 3 miles to the south, via the Wiblinger Straße* ( ). Although its foundation dates back to the 11C, the final touches were not put to this abbey until the 18C. As at Vierzehnheiligen, more than a third of the abbey church's floor plan is occupied by the transept, where pilgrims worshipped relics of the Holy Rood. The flattened domes of this Baroque building could give visitors the impression of being crushed, but this is compensated for by the illusion of height provided by the painter Januarius Zick in the frescoes which cover them. The abbey **library★**, completed in 1760, is one of the finest examples of the Rococo in Swabia.

The main interest lies in a gallery, supported by 32 columns, which projects into the centre of the room and at each end. The rhythmically placed columns, painted alternately pink and blue, combine with the large false relief fresco on the ceiling to create an ensemble rich in colour and movement.

★ **Blaubeuren** – *18km - 11 miles to the west. Leave by 5 on the town plan.*
Follow the signposts Blautopf-Hochaltar, in this village of the Swabian Jura renowned for its fine setting among the rocks, then leave the car near the monumental abbey entrance.

Blautopf – 15 minutes on foot Rtn. This deep blue pool was formed by a natural embankment of glacial origin. The shady approaches have been laid out as walks.

Old Benedictine Abbey – *Time: 1/2 h. Follow the "Hochaltar" signs.* The premises include a picturesque group of ancient wood-walled buildings. In the chancel of the old **abbey church** (Klosterkirche) ⊘ is the celebrated **Blaubeuren Altarpiece★★** (Hochaltar), a collective work created by the principal studios of Ulm in the 15C. The themes treated are the Passion, the life of John the Baptist, and the Virgin among the Saints.

USEDOM★

Mecklenburg-Vorpommern
Michelin map 416 D 25 - E 26

Usedom is Germany's easternmost island and at 445km² - 172sq miles it is the largest after Rügen. The eastern part of the island, with the town of Świnoujście, covering around one fifth of the total area, belongs to Poland. Usedom displays a wonderfully unspoilt natural landscape, alternating between moors, inland seas, forest, dunes, sandy beaches, with steep cliffs here and there. The flat northwest contrasts with the hilly southeast part, which likes to be known as Usedom's Switzerland. The island is part of the Usedom-Oderhaff nature reserve. Its extremely irregular outline can best be compared with a wide-open crocodile's jaw. At the narrowest point, at Koserow, the island is barely 200m - 220yds wide. Its main industry is tourism, since the elegant bathing resorts on the Baltic coast developed after 1820. At the turn of the 19-20C it became known as "Berlin's bathtub", since it was mainly the residents of the capital who came here to relax and recuperate. Notable bathing resort architecture from this period remains, and has been carefully restored everywhere.

Wolgast – *On the mainland.*

One point of access to Usedom is in the south at Zecherin, and the other lies in the north-west, from Wolgast over the Peene river. The parish church, **Pfarr-kirche St. Petri** ⊙ in the birthplace of the Romantic painter Philipp Otto Runge, with its formidable octangular tower, dating back to the year 1370, is a must for visitors. Its undecorated exterior contrasts with its sumptuous interior. There are wall paintings from the 15C and 16C, a danse macabre cycle,

which was painted around 1700 by Caspar Sigmund Köppe based on a woodcut by Hans Holbein the Younger, and a Renaissance gravestone.

Krummin – *To the east of Wolgast.*

The most beautiful **avenue of lime trees★** (Lindenallee) in Usedom leads to the right off the main 111 road, down to the little fishing village which lies on the Krummin cove.

The surfaced road is only just two kilometres long, but it is quite marvellous. The rounded canopy formed by the leaves overhead gives one the impression of being in a high Gothic cathedral. It gives the visitor pause for thought and soothes many a troubled breast.

Hist.-techn. Informationszentrum Peenemünde ⊙ – The army test establishment of Peenemünde, the development site of the V2 rockets, which cost thousands their lives during the Second World War, but which signalled the beginning of modern space travel, was built right in the north of the island in 1936. This double-edged sword is described and explained in a video presentation.

The "Taille" Usedoms – At the narrowest point or waist of the island, the white sandy beaches of the resorts of **Zinnowitz, Koserow, Kölpinsee** and **Ückeritz** stretch out, interrupted from time by the steep cliff.

★ **Bansin, Heringsdorf, Ahlbeck** – These "three sisters" in the southeast of the island, are linked by a 10km - 6 mile long beach promenade. During the 19C these were fashionable resorts, the rendezvous of the aristocracy and the wealthy. The many imposing villas and hotels, which have happily stood the test of time and make these resorts so attractive, bear witness to the past.

Pier, Ahlbeck

Despite its rather ordinary name, **Heringsdorf** was an extraordinarily fashionable resort, and Emperor Wilhelm II was a regular visitor. He resided in the Villa Staudt *(6 Delbrückstraße)*, which still stands today. **Ahlbeck** is justifiably proud of its attractive historical pier★, which was built in 1898. A restaurant was added in 1902, and with its white walls, red roof and the four green-roofed corner towers, it is one of the most favoured photographic subjects on the island.

Mellenthin – *Northeast of the town of Usedom, 2km - 1 mile to the north of the B 110.*

This little-visited village radiates peace, and with its Renaissance castle, it forms a rural idyll. The three winged building surrounded by a moat is unadorned, whilst a colourfully mounted Renaissance fireplace from the year 1613 in the entrance hall is quite magnificent. The 14C **village church** in the centre of a cemetery full of 600 year old oak trees is urgently in need of restoration, but it is still a little pearl with its **interior decoration**★ dating from the 17C. The painted Baroque gallery from 1755 in particular radiates fresh and simple belief. The offertory dates from 1125.

Wallfahrtskirche VIERZEHNHEILIGEN ★★

Bayern

Michelin map 418/420 P 17

This pilgrimage church dedicated to the fourteen Saints of Intercession stands on an open hillside in the Upper Main Valley, opposite Kloster Banz *(qv)*. The bold concepts of Balthazar Neumann, master of the Baroque, are evident in the interior.

The Pilgrimage – In 1445 and 1446, a herdsman on this hillside was blessed with a number of visions, the last of them identified as the Christ Child among the "Fourteen Intercessors". The cult of this pious band, actively fostered by German Dominicans and Cistercians, must be seen in the context of mysticism prevailing at the beginning of the 15C, when "visions" were frequent (the "voices" heard by Joan of Arc – born 1412 – were those of St Catherine and St Margaret, themselves part of this intercessionary group). This devotion to the holy intercessors remained alive for many years among local people, attracting crowds of pilgrims to a chapel which was to be superseded, in the 18C, by a sumptuous Rococo church.

TOUR *about 1/2 hour*

The façade of the church, built between 1743 and 1772 in handsome ochre stone, is framed by domed towers unusually tall for a Baroque building. The design of the façade itself is admirably vigorous, with jutting cornices to emphasize the tiered arrangement of pilasters and columns and the sinuous lines of the convex front. In accordance with the taste of the time – Rococo rather than purely Baroque – these elements do not simply constitute a covering, as at Ottobeuren *(qv)*, but form an embellishment in its own right. The four rows of windows, small at mezzanine or attic level, wide and spacious elsewhere, together with a broken pediment crowned with statues, are reminiscent of the castles of the period. The statues, once gilded, represent Jesus Christ between Faith and Charity.

Interior – *Illustration p 27*. The interior arrangement is organized as a succession of three oval bays framed by colonnades and covered by low inner domes. The true centre of the church is the bay containing the altar to the Saints of Intercession – to the detriment of the transept crossing, which is invaded by the bay's colonnade. Circular domes, again, cover the transepts. Such geometric subtleties create an overall perspective concentrating the worshippers' view relentlessly on a central focal point – an ideal haunting 18C architects wearied of the endless succession of rectangular bays. Many visitors will be surprised by the restraint and elegance of the church's Rococo interior decoration. Outstanding are the colour combinations of the painting inside the domes, the lightness of the stuccowork, the richesse of the gold outlines defining the woodwork of the galleries, and the grace of putti surmounting confessionals and cornice.

★★ **Altar to the Fourteen Saints of Intercession** (Nothelfer-Altar) – A Rococo pyramid with a pierced baldachin, where every line is nevertheless convex or concave, this remarkable work was executed by stucco-workers of the Wessobrunn School *(qv)* in 1764. It stands on the spot where the herdsman's visions are said to have occurred.

The Altar Statues

Balustrade: 1) St Dionysius - **2)** St Blaise - **3)** St Erasmus - **4)** St Cyriacus (delivery from the Devil at the final hour).

Altar Niches: 5) St Catherine, patron saint of the learned, of students and girls wishing to get married (the model of Christian wisdom). - **6)** St Barbara, patron saint of miners, artillerymen and prisoners (the grace of a noble death).

Buttresses: 7) St Achatius (the agonies of death).
- **8**) St Giles, the only intercessor not to suffer
martyrdom (to obtain the grace of a true
confession). - **9**) St Eustace (converted by the
vision of a stag with a Cross between its antlers).
- **10**) St Christopher, patron saint of travellers.

On top of the baldachin: 11) St Guy (epilepsy). - **12**)
St Margaret (intercession for the forgiveness of
sins). - **13**) St George, patron saint of peasants
and their possessions - **14**) St Pantaleon.

Those who enjoy seeing – or photographing –
unusual views should climb the slopes above the
church. Before long, Banz abbey comes into view
on the far side of the valley, framed by the
Vierzehnheiligen towers, in line with – and apparently resting on – the ridgepole of the
church roof.

WALDECKER BERGLAND★

Hessen
Michelin map 417 M 10-11

This small stretch of country on either side of the River Eder lived under the rule of the
Waldeck Princes and was half forgotten by the world until 1918. Today its deep forests,
the magnificent lake retained by the Eder dam, and the spa resort of Bad Wildungen make
it one of the most popular tourist areas of central Germany.

ROUND TOUR STARTING FROM BAD WILDUNGEN

145km - 90 miles – allow 1 day

Bad Wildungen – The most impressive bathing installations of this spa follow
one another on either side of the Brunnenallee, through the Kurpark and as far as
the horse-shoe buildings of the George-Viktor spring – the busiest centre of this
picturesque region.
In the old town, the **Evangelical Church** (Evangelische Stadtkirche) contains an altarpiece
said to be one of the earliest milestones in German painting: the **Wildunger Altar★★**,
which dates from 1403.
Embellishing the high altar, these scenes from the life and Passion of Christ are notable
for their profundity and for the stylized elongation of the idealized figures.

★ **Waldeck** – Rising above
the steep, wooded shores
of the artificial lake, the
castle seat of the Waldeck
Princes, abandoned in the
17C, is now part hotel,
part museum. From the
terrace there is a fine **view★**
of the lake, curving away
out of sight between the
wooded heights. The **Burgmuseum** ⊙ galleries evoke
the history of the House of
Waldeck. The castle boasts
a Witches' Tower (Hexen-
turm) with three prison
cells, one be-low the other.
The Eder dam, completed in
1914, retains 200 million
m³ - 44 000 million gallons
of water. In 1943, during
the Second World War, a
specialized raid by the RAF
breached the dam with a
single 4-ton bomb, blowing
a gap in the stonework 70m
- 77 yards wide and 22m -
72ft high, resulting in
catastrophic floods.

*Drive to Arolsen via Nieder-
Werbe, Sachsenhausen,
Freienhagen and Landau.*

Arolsen – Formerly the residence of the Waldeck Princes, this is a small town whose symmetrical plan testifies to its aristocratic origins.

The **Schloß** ⊙, its design inspired by the Château de Versailles, was built between 1714 and 1728, although the interior decoration was to continue until the beginning of the 19C. The apartments, adorned with stuccowork and painted ceilings (1715-1719), are gained via a vestibule and double staircase. Together with the Baroque Garden Chamber (Gartensaal) and the Great Hall (Großer Saal), these complete the state rooms.

Korbach – The present town was formed by joining together two fortified settlements: Alstadt (built around the church of St. Kilian – without a tower) and Neustadt (built around the church of St. Nicolai – a tower with a spire). Many old half-timbered houses have been preserved. **St. Kilian's** is a Gothic hall-church wider than it is long, a particularity showing Westphalian influence. There is a fine group of statues at the south door: the Virgin Mary stands against the pier, while the Last Judgement is depicted on the tympanum.

Frankenberg an der Eder – The upper town contains impressive wooden houses dating from the 16C, especially around the two central squares, the Obermarkt and Untermarkt. The latter is noteworthy for the **Rathaus★**, bristling with turrets. On the crest behind stands the 13-14C Liebfrauenkirche, with the **Lady Chapel** (Marienkapelle) abutting on the south transept. The chapel is Gothic, built with an asymmetric polygonal floor plan. It contains a stone altarpiece, now lacking its statues but with a rare decorative perfection.

★ **Haina** – The **church** of the former Cistercian abbey, built here in the heart of the woods, is a huge, rather plain Gothic hall. The flat east end, the small columns in the nave broken halfway up by historiated consoles, and the six transept chapels are Romanesque.

The cloister, however, shows both Romanesque and Gothic features (note the Romanesque "Lamb of God" entrance).

The road passes through the beechwoods and plantations of oak forming the Kellerwald forest massif before regaining the outskirts of Bad Wildungen.

WALDSASSEN ★

Bayern – Population 8 000
Michelin map 420 P 20

Like its neighbours, Selb and Weiden, Waldsassen owes its prosperity to the glass and ceramics industry. The three towns lie between the Fichtelgebirge and the Oberpfälzer Wald, in a forested region east of Bayreuth that was once a glacial moraine.

★ **Stiftsbasilika** – Completed in 1704, mainly on plans drawn up by Georg Dientzenhofer, this building is distinguished by its unusual length (83m - 272ft) and a chancel occupying more than one third of the floor space – a feature recalling the design of Cistercian churches.

The aisles and galleries form two storeys of chapels which communicate vertically by apertures in the vaulting. The decoration is particularly lavish: the stuccowork is by G B Carlone; the **choir stalls★** are by local craftsmen, and so is the red and black marble high altar, with its sculpted reredos (the Annunciation) incorporating a tabernacle in the form of a gilded globe.

On the pillars of the transept crossing are imposing statues of the four Fathers of the Church. The whole effects is that of an early example attempting to adapt Italian Baroque to German taste.

★★ **Bibliothek** ⊙ – This library is something very special. The visitor will be spellbound with admiration before the carved woodwork framing the shelves, decorating the balustrade and, above all, forming the ten life-size statues supporting the gallery. Karl Stilp and Andreas Witt, the local artists who created these masterpieces, brought a profound realism, touched with wry humour, to their task.

The ten figures symbolize, with wit and truth, the different guilds involved in the production of a book. They include, among others, the rag sorter who provides the raw materials, the shepherd who delivers the animal skins to the bookbinder, the bookseller who distributes the finished work. The stance and characterization of each one is remarkable – and each face, according to the viewpoint of the observer, can show opposing expressions. Thus the oriental bookseller (2nd statue on the left of the entrance) presents a noble profile on one side, and features twisted by illness and cunning on the other. The butcher, brandishing a knife, leers maliciously in the direction of his neighbour, the shepherd. The strangest figure is that of the critic (2nd on the left side of the end door): his hands are tied, and a bird of prey, emerging from his head, has seized him by the nose – the inference being that the character has a sharp wit but is nevertheless a prisoner of his pride.

Completed in 1726, this library is one of the finest flowers of lay Baroque art.

EXCURSION

★ Kappel Church – *6.5km - 4 miles to the north.*
Isolated in a pastoral **setting★★**, this church dedicated to the Holy Trinity is within sight of the Cheb Basin in the Czech Republic. It was built in 1689 by Georg Dientzenhofer in the shape of a trefoil rotunda punctuated by three towers. Inside, three apses, each dedicated to one of the three characters forming the Trinity, radiate from a central triangular bay with three columns. Three altar niches have been hollowed out from each apse.

*Use **Michelin** Maps with **Michelin** Guides.*

WASSERBURG AM INN
Bayern – Population 10 500
Michelin map 420 V 20

Wasserburg owes its existence to its site, on a rise encircled by a loop of the River Inn, and its name to a castle built there by the Wittelsbachs. River navigation and the trade in salt contributed to the town's rapid development in the Middle Ages. Coming from the south, the bridge over the river affords an attractive **view★** of the old town, with the tall facades of the quayside houses reflected in the water. The mixture of flat roofs, stepped gables and ridged roofs behind copings give Wasserburg the half-German, half-Italian look typical of the Inn and Salzach valleys.

SIGHTS

Marienplatz – Bordered by arcaded houses, this main square is closed off by the tall, stepped gable of a **Rathaus** decorated with paintings in which religious subjects alternate with armorial bearings. The façade has Renaissance windows. On the first floor, next to the banqueting hall, there is a **room** with painted panels and walls covered by 16C woodwork beneath carved beams of the same period. On the opposite side of the square, the lovely **Patrizierhaus Kern** displays an outstanding façade with two-storey oriel windows, paintings, and richly ornamented stuccowork by Johann Baptist Zimmermann.

Pfarrkirche St. Jakob – The church is crowned by a tall, square tower. The interior, in the Gothic style, contains a carved wood pulpit dating from 1638.

★ Heimatmuseum ⊙ – The four floors of this huge Gothic building house many different displays. Note Bavaria's oldest postal sleigh *(ground floor)*, exhibitions of furniture *(first and second floors)*, and the craft workshops on the third floor. Examples of religious art from the 15C to the 18C can be seen behind the building in a gallery housed in the former stable block.

EXCURSION

Rott am Inn – *15km - 9 1/2 miles to the south.*
Of the former Benedictine abbey founded in the 11C, only an interesting **church**, to which a number of Baroque features were added in the 18C, remain in Rott today. The remodelling was carried out by Johann Michael Fischer (architect), Franz Xavier Feuchtmayer and Jakob Rauch (stuccowork), Matthäus Günther (frescoes) and Ignaz Günther (sculpture). Together, they achieved a quite remarkable visual harmony.

WEIMAR★★
Thüringen – Population 62 000
Michelin map 418 N 18

To most non-Germans, the name of Weimar recalls the ill-fated republic which existed uneasily between the end of the First World War and the Hitler years. But the town's claim to a place in European history rests unshakably on an extraordinary flowering of intellectual talent which has grown steadily over the centuries. Early in its existence it attracted personalities as diverse as Luther, the painter Cranach, Bach, Wieland, Schiller and Liszt. The one genius whose traces it is impossible to escape in Weimar, however, is that greatest of German classicists, Johann Wolfgang von Goethe.

Weimar has been chosen as the European City of Culture for 1999.

THE "GERMAN ATHENS"

The first historical mention of Weimar occurs in a document dated 975. By 1348 the town had been granted an urban charter, and in 1547 it became the capital of the Duchy of Saxe-Weimar. From this time onwards dates the formidable cultural expansion which made the town the true spiritual capital of Germany.

The Intellectual and Cultural Centre – Weimar's hour of glory coincided with the succession, in 1758, of the Duchess Anna Amalia. It was during her reign that the town's intellectual reputation grew, largely because of **Goethe** (1749-1832). He had first been summoned to the Court at the age of 26 by the Grand Duke Carl August, son of Amalia. In the small provincial capital – at that time numbering no more than 5 000 inhabitants – he was appointed Minister and raised to peerage, and he created the greater part of his work, including Faust. His influence was enormous. For more than 25 years he directed the Weimar Theatre, which soon became accepted as the German National Theatre, renowned for its staging of international classics.

This was the result of a fruitful collaboration with Friedrich von Schiller *(see below)*, who moved permanently to Weimar in 1799. The work produced by these two friends, along with the writings of the theologian **Johann Gottfried Herder** (1776-1803), a disciple of Kant, raised Weimar's literary reputation to the point where the town was considered "the home of German classicism". In the **Goethe-Schiller Archives** *(Jener Straße)*, which are among the most important literary collections in the country, several posthumous works are conserved, together with letters from almost 1 000 personalities worldwide.

Goethe and Schiller, Weimar

Art and Music in Weimar – It was in Weimar that Lucas Cranach the Elder worked – from 1552 until his death a year later – on his final masterpiece: the altarpiece triptych for the local church of St. Peter and St. Paul *(see Stadtkirche below)*. Johann Sebastian Bach was organist and choirmaster there from 1708 to 1717. In 1848 Franz Liszt in his turn became choirmaster and surrounded himself with the artistic elite of the period. It was Liszt who was the driving force behind the creation of Weimar's famous school of music, which still bears his name today.

In 1860, an establishment was founded which left an indelible mark on 20C German painting. This was the School of Fine Arts – later to be transformed into the College of Architecture. It was under the influence of such celebrated graduates as Arnold Böcklin (1827-1901) that painters spearheading the contemporary avant-garde movement developed what is known as "the Weimar School".

The Weimar Republic (1919-33) – The constitution of the Weimar Republic was set up by the German National Assembly under Hitler *(see Historical table and notes in Introduction)*, and it sat at that time in the Weimar National Theatre.

HISTORIC CENTRE

Lucas-Cranach-Haus – *Marktplatz.*
The famous painter spent the last year of his life in this Renaissance house (1549) with scrolled gables. His studio was on the 3rd floor. The **Rathaus**, opposite, was built c1500 but heavily remodelled in the middle of the 19C.

Platz der Demokratie – The equestrian statue of the Grand Duke Carl August of Saxe-Weimar-Eisenach (1757-1828), executed by Adolf von Donndorf, stands in this square. On the south side, the former palace (1757-1774) is occupied by the **Franz Liszt Hochschule für Musik.**
The 16-18C **Grünes Schloß** today houses the **Central Library of German Classics**. It contains medieval manuscripts, very early printed works, rare documents dating from the 16C and 17C, and above all original, priceless 18C volumes. For many years now, the museum has been collecting manuscripts, publications and translations relating to the "Age of Enlightenment" (Aufklärung) – Kant, Locke, Leibnitz, etc.
To the west of the square stand the 16C **Rotes Schloß**, with a Renaissance doorway, and the Baroque **Gelbes Schloß** (18C).

Haus der Frau von Stein – *Ackerwand 25.*
Goethe met Charlotte von Stein, lady-in-waiting to the Duchess Anna Amalia, in November 1775. The first ten years of his stay in Weimar were profoundly influenced by his feeling for her. The house was remodelled in 1776 to his own design.

★★★**Goethehaus** ⊙ – *Frauenplan.*
The dramatist-politician lived in this Baroque mansion for more than 20 years, from 1809 until his death in 1832. The interior is for the most part the way he left it. The living-rooms, workroom and library (5 400 volumes) can all be visited. An annexe has been turned into a museum which gives an idea of his personality, his poetical works and his scientific researches.

★★**Schillerhaus** ⊙ – *Schillerstraße 12.*
The writer moved here in 1802 to be nearer to his great friend Goethe. It was here that *William Tell* and *The Bride of Messina* were written. The **Schiller Museum** offers a rundown on his life and his work.

Follow the Schillerstraße as far as the Theaterplatz.

Deutsches Nationaltheater – The present structure, which dates from 1907, was built on the site of a 1779 Baroque building. It was in this old theatre that Schiller's great plays were staged and directed by Goethe; it was here, in 1850, that the first performance of Richard Wagner's Lohengrin was given. And it is in front of the present-day building that the **statues**★★ of Goethe and Schiller, sculpted in 1857 by Ernst Rietschel, are to be found.

Wittumspalais ⊙ – After the death of her husband the Duchess Anna Amalia moved to this 1767 Baroque palace with two wings; it was here that she organized the famous salons of which Goethe, Schiller, Herder and Wieland were so important a part. Today, the **Wieland Museum** illustrates the lifework of "the German Voltaire" – fervent supporter of German classicism, translator and spokesman for the Aufklärung.

Stadtkirche – *Am Herderplatz.*
This triple-nave Gothic hall church *(see Art and Music in Weimar above)* was built between 1498 and 1500 and much remodelled in the Baroque style between 1735 and 1745. It is also known as the **Herderkirche**, in memory of the sermons preached there by the philosopher, who is buried in the church. The famous **Cranach Triptych**★★, started by Lucas Cranach the Elder and finished by his son in 1555, represents the Crucifixion on its central panel. This is surrounded by scenes from the Old and New Testmanent. On the right, Luther and Cranach the Elder himself appear.

Stadtschloß ⊙ – This complex with four separate wings dates from the 15C to the 20C and has frequently been enlarged, most notably by C W Coudray, N Grohmann and N F Thouret. One of the additions to its eastern part is a classical peristyle.
Established in the castle apartments is the **Stiftung Weimarer Klassik** (Foundation for Weimar Classicism), and with this there is also the **Staatliche Kunstsammlungen** (National Art Collection). This comprises numismatics, prints and – perhaps of wider interest – galleries of paintings. Here, visitors can see: Thuringian altarpieces of the Flamboyant Gothic period; an important **Cranach collection**★★ *(Sybil of Cleves, Portrait of Luther)*; Flemish and Italian paintings; and work by Hans Baldung Grien, Albrecht Dürer and Bartholomäus Bruyn the Elder. The Weimar School (Von Schwind and Rohlfs) and contemporary German artists (Max Beckmann, Max Liebermann) are also represented. In the southwestern wing of the complex is the castle tower (1729-1732) with its Baroque cupola, and the 1545 (renovated) keep.

ILM PARK

"Weimar is in fact a park in which they happened to build a town." This approving comment was written by Adolf Stahr in 1851 – and indeed today Weimar is still a city of green spaces, indissolubly linked with its riverside park. From the palace of Tiefurt to the Belvedere, there is a single stretch of greenery centered on the gardens laid out on each side of the Ilm. There was no intention of restraining nature – said Goethe, planning the English-style landscaping – but simply of guiding and at the same time respecting her. The gardens are only a few yards from the city centre.

★★**Goethes Gartenhaus** – Augustus the Strong made a present of this summer residence to Goethe, and the great man liked it so much that he lived there permanently from 1776 to 1782. It remained his favourite retreat until the end of his life.
Among his works there is even a short poem recording his delight in the place.

> *"It is an unpretentious*
> *Small house beneath a tall roof.*
> *Everyone who came there*
> *Felt light-hearted;*
> *Trees I had planted grew strong and green,*
> *And the spirit as well*
> *Thrived on this blessed ground."*

It was in this house that Goethe wrote *Wilhelm Meister's Theatrical Mission*, important parts of *Iphigenia*, early drafts of *Egmont* and *Torquato Tasso*.

Facing it is the **Borkenhauschen**, Augustus's own favourite retreat. Ten minutes walk away is the **Römisches Haus**, a classical building (1791-1797) conceived by Goethe for the Grand Duke.

Cross the park now in the direction of the Belvederer Allee.

Liszt-Haus ⊙ – *Belvederer Allee.*
In this one-time gardeners' lodge at the entrance to the park it is possible to visit the apartments lived in by the composer during his second stay in Weimar, from 1869 to 1886.

The Geschwister-Scholl-Straße leads to the old cemetery (Alter Friedhof).

Fürstengruft – This is central focus of the ancient cemetery and was built in 1825-1827 by C W Coudray as the burial place of the princely family. In addition to Duke Wilhelm IV and Archduke Carl August, the two princes of poetry **Goethe** and **Schiller** found their last resting place here. The **Russian Orthodox Church** nearby was built between 1859 and 1862 specially for Maria Pavlova, Grand Duchess and daughter-in-law of Augustus.

EXCURSIONS

Schloß Tiefurt ⊙ – *2km - 1 mile to the east.*
The former summer residence (18C) of the Duchess Amalia is surrounded by English-style gardens. Both palace and gardens were frequently the scene of the literary gatherings she loved. Goethe, the Humboldt brothers and the other members of her cultural coterie were welcome guests. The apartments, in the neo-Classical style, evoke the classical era of Weimar.

Schloß Belvedere ⊙ – *4km - 2 1/2 miles to the southeast.*
This is one of the most delightful – and the most artistically successful – stately homes of Thuringia. Comprising a large central block flanked by two low wings, the mansion is completed by four outbuildings and an orangery harbouring a **collection of carriages and barouches.**
The grounds, originally formal in the Baroque style, were redesigned and laid out as an English garden between 1814 and 1840.

Buchenwald – *8 km - 5 miles to the west.*
Only a few miles from Weimar, cradle of Humanism and first capital (1918) of a democratic Germany, the beechwoods of the Ettersberg hid for eight years one of the largest concentration camps of the Hitler regime.

Between Beeches and Wolves – Established in July 1937 for the internment of Germans who opposed the Nazi ethos, the camp was quick to take the Jews and Gypsies persecuted by the National Socialists – and then, as the invasion of Europe expanded, victims from the occupied countries. A total of almost 300 000 human beings, including innumerable children, took the road that led to Buchenwald; for 65 000 of them, it was a one-way trip.
Despite conditions of unbelievable hardship and a merciless system of surveillance, the camp was liberated, on 11 April 1945, by the inmates themselves. The novel, *Naked Among Wolves*, by Bruno Apitz, remains the most striking testimony to this sinister chapter of German history.

Buchenwald Memorial Centre (Gedenkstätte) ⊙ – *Map and descriptive brochure at entrance.*
The Information Centre shows a film tracing the history of the camp.
A tour of the camp starts at the gatehouse, which still retains above the entrance the chilling slogan: **"Jedem das Seine"** ("You get what you deserve").
The position of each hut is marked out on the ground; at the far end, on the right, is the building which was used for storing the inmates' possessions and effects, now transformed into a museum. Outside the camp, a road leads to the quarry where excessively rigorous working conditions resulted in a particularly high death rate among those sent there. Nearly 20 000 Buchenwald prisoners were transferred to a camp named **Dora** *(see local map under HARZ)*, for forced labour in an underground factory developing secret weapons. The nature of their work meant that none of them ever saw daylight again.

Special camp 2 – From 1945 to 1950, the Soviet occupation force set up a special camp here, in which Nazi criminals and officials, and also arbitrarily arrested individuals, were interned. According to Soviet sources, over 7 000 people died in this camp.

Memorial (Mahnmal der Gedenkstätte Buchenwald) – *1km - 1/2 mile in the direction of Weimar.* From the entrance, the Steles' Way leads to the Avenue of Nations, which links three mass graves. From the last of these, Liberty Avenue brings you to the memorial bell tower, in front of which is the statuary group of *Eleven Buchenwald Prisoners*, by Fritz Cremer.

On a marvellous site at the foot of the Harz Mountains, with many of its narrow streets bordered by old, half-timbered houses still intact, Wernigerode is one of the most delightful small towns in this region and an ideal starting point for exploration of the massif.

SIGHTS

★★ **Rathaus (Town Hall)** – *Am Marktplatz.*
Considered to be one of the finest half-timbered buildings in Germany, this municipal treasure dates from the first half of the 16C. Its splendid façade includes superimposed oriel windows surmounted by slender spires. Note the double staircase and the carved wood features representing town aldermen.

★★ **Half-timbered Houses (Fachwerkhäuser)** – The most picturesque group is on the **Breite Straße**, as it leaves the Marktplatz – several rows of town houses built by the rich burghers of Wernigerode in the 16C, 17C and 18C. The wooden sections and joists are often decorated with masks or carved patterns – as for instance on the 1674 house at No 72 known as the "Krummelsches Haus".
An exploration of the lanes between the Breite Straße and the castle hill to the south is also worthwhile. The houses here are smaller but full of charm. At the highest part of the Kochstraße (No 43) is the tiniest house of all, which is only 3m - 10ft wide.

Pfarrkirche St. Johannis – *Take the Breite Straße and then, on the left, the Grüne Straße.*
This late 15C, triple-aisle Gothic hall church has a four-panel altarpiece in carved wood dating from 1425. It represents the Virgin with angels.

Schloß – Extensively remodelled in the late 19C, the castle is in a magnificent position overlooking the town. The main apartments have been organized as a **museum** ⊙, outlining the origins and development of feudalism, with a selection of craftwork and sacred art of the time.

EXCURSION

★★ **Harz Mountains** – *See HARZ.*

WERTHEIM★

Baden-Württemberg – Population 21 700
Michelin maps 417 Q 12

Wertheim lies at the foot of a mighty fortress. This beautiful location, together with the well preserved architecture of the town, contribute to the attraction of this small town to painters. Pretty, half-timbered houses, mainly from the 16C, border its twisting, narrow streets.

Marktplatz – Amongst the half-timbered houses around the market place, the 16C **Zobelhaus** is especially worth seeing. The "**angels' well**" (Engelsbrunnen) which dates from the Renaissance period, stands at the end of the square next to the collegiate church. The sandstone draw well, which was built in 1574, is decorated with figures which depict the citizens of Wertheim and the planets of Mercury, Mars, Jupiter, Saturn and Venus. It is crowned by two angels.
The **Grafschaftsmuseum** is not far away in the Rathausgasse. It is housed in the old town hall, a building dating from the 16C. The stair tower with its **double spiral staircase** (1540) is especially noteworthy. Opposite the museum stands the **Haus der Vier Gekronten** (house of the four crowned heads), a particularly beautiful half-timbered structure from the second half of the 16C.

Stiftskirche – The Gothic building erected between 1384 and 1445 has been kept unadorned, with the exception of the oriel-type "little chancel" (next to the north porch). This makes the sumptuous sculpture on the 40 or so **tombs**★★ inside all the more impressive. They were erected from 1407, when the church was selected as the burial place of the Counts of Wertheim. The tombs in the chancel, including the **Isenburg gravestone** *(on the left)*, the **Eberstein tomb** *(in the centre)* and the **Stohberg gravestone**, are of particular importance. The free-standing tomb known as the "Bedstead" stands alone in the centre of the chancel, and was created in 1618 by Michael Kern for Count Ludwig III zu Löwenstein (who died in 1611) and Countess Anna zu Stolberg.

Burg – A well-fortified castle was created over the centuries, from a fortress built in the 13C. It was however destroyed during the Thirty Years War by the Emperor's troops. The outer fortress gate was extended into an archive library.
From the castle ruins, the visitor looks down on the town, the confluence of the rivers and the wooded heights of Spessart (to the north) and the Odenwald (west).

EXCURSIONS

Ehemaliges Kloster Bronnbach ⊘ – *10km - 6 miles to the south.*
The late 12C **church★** here has retained its original Romanesque design and, in particular, the groined vaulting above the nave. This was specially conceived to enable tall, deeply pierced windows to be installed, so providing much brighter lighting than was customary in the period. From the Gothic cloister, with its triple-arched windows, there is a good view of the church's south wall, and the tiered roofs above it.

WESSOBRUNN★

Bayern – Population 1 740
Michelin map 419/420 W 17 – 10km - 6 miles northwest of Weilheim

This locality in Upper Bavaria is known for the famous **Wessobrunn Prayer** (Wessobrunner Gebet), one of the oldest known documents in the German language. The 9C manuscript, in a Bavarian dialect of Old High German, is kept in the Munich Civic Library (Staatsbibliothek).

School of Wessobrunn – In the 17C and 18C, Wessobrunn produced a series of architects and artists of multiple talents who, according to the needs of construction projects or the dictates of their own inspiration, were able at will to exchange the compass for the paintbrush or the tools of the stucco worker. Working in a corporate and family framework known as the Wessobrunn School, these artists of Baroque genius, who were in no way specialists, beautified churches and civic buildings all over Bavaria, Swabia and the Tyrol. The names of the **Feuchtmayer** and **Schmuzer** families stand out brilliantly within the group, though the most celebrated is perhaps **Dominikus Zimmermann**, who was responsible for the church at Wies *(qv)*.

Ehemalige Benediktinerabtei (Former Benedictine Abbey) ⊘ – The history of the abbey goes back to the 8C. After its secularization in 1803, the mother church was destroyed and only the 13C clock tower with its saddleback roof remains today.
On the first floor of the old monastic block is the magnificent **Princes' Gallery★** (Fürstengang), a 17C masterpiece due to the Wessobrunn School, whose versatility is exemplified in the long hall where painted medallions adorn a vaulted roof covered in stucco-work mingling acanthus leaves, the heads of cherubim and other motifs.

WETZLAR

Hessen – Population 52 000
Michelin map 417 O 9
Town plan in the current Michelin Red Guide Deutschland

Until the beginning of the 19C, Wetzlar was a town of lawyers, the seat of one of the law courts of the Holy Roman Empire. Today it is famous for the manufacture of optical and photographic equipment (Leitz). The small format (35mm) film was invented here by the engineer Oscar Barnack in 1924.
The cathedral quarter and three ancient squares, the **Eisenmarkt**, the **Kornmarkt** and the **Schillerplatz**, still bear witness to the town's illustrious past.

SIGHTS

Dom (Collegiate Church) – Of the original 12C Romanesque building, only the north tower of the façade – a sombre construction of dark sandstone and basalt – remains today. Of the subsequent Gothic façade, again, only one Flamboyant 14C tower was completed (in the south). Since this particular stage of the work seems to have been interrupted, the central doorway (whose embellishment, the Coronation of the Virgin, was finished) opens onto nothing.
The sandstone of the south tower is red, in contrast both with the north tower and the light stone in which nave and chancel were eventually finished in 13C Gothic style. Despite its rather bizarre outside appearance, however, the church has two interesting works inside: an ensemble of Gothic frescoes in the south transept; and a fine 14C Pietà in the first chapel off the south aisle.

Stadt-und Industrie Museum ⊘ – The buildings of the former Teutonic Order foundation serve as the backdrop for this museum. Both the history of the town and the signifiance of industry in the Wetzlar area are emphasised. The beautiful furniture from the 17C and 18C is impressive.

Lottehaus ⊘ – Lotte was Charlotte Buff, the diplomat's fiancée to whom the young Goethe was passionately attracted. The affair – which ended tragically with the suicide of the diplomat – was immortalized by Goethe in *The Sufferings of Young Werther*, one of the first novels ever to be presented in the form of letters. In this house, which was the young woman's birthplace, glass cases of souvenirs, furniture and other mementoes recall the personality of the heroine.

First editions of *Werther*, and copies of translations in 30 different languages underline the enormous success of the novel (which Napoleon claimed to have read seven times, one after the other).

Sammlung Dr. Irmgard von Lemmers-Danforth ☉ – *Kornblumengasse 1.*
The rooms of a fine 18C house have been transformed into examples of the Renaissance and Baroque styles in Italy, France, Holland and Germany. Paintings, furniture, clocks, jewellery and work by goldsmiths and silversmiths can be admired.

Reichskammergerichtsmuseum (Tribunal Museum) ☉ – *Hofstatt 19.*
The history of the Holy Roman Empire court in Wetzlar (1693-1806) is evoked by ancient law books, court documents and verdicts, and the portraits of personalities concerned with these trials.

EXCURSIONS

Burg Greifenstein – *17km - 11 miles to the northwest.*
This castle was built in the 12C, on a rise overlooking the road from Frankfurt to Cologne – an important trade route in need of protection in the Middle Ages. One of the fortress bastions houses a collection of bells, the oldest of which dates from the 11C.

★ **Münzenberg** – *28km - 17 1/2 miles to the southeast.*
Together with those of Gelnhausen and Büdingen *(qv)*, this **feudal stronghold** formed a defensive line destined to protect the Wetterau – an open depression between the Taunus and Vogelsberg massifs. The whole of the depression is visible from the top of the east tower. The ruins are very well preserved, with the outer wall and its bastions emerging from the surrounding greenery. Between the two keeps, fine examples of Romanesque interior decoration can be seen in the living quarters.

★ **Arnsburg** – *30km - 18 1/2 miles to the southeast.*
The early Gothic chapter house of this one-time **abbey** is still standing; the abbey **church**★, entirely in ruins, was built to the Cistercian plan, with a flat chevet. The remains of massive columns with Romanesque capitals can be seen in the old transept crossing.

WIESBADEN★

Hessen – Population 267 000
Michelin map 417 P 8
Town plan in the current Michelin Red Guide Deutschland

Lying at the foot of the Taunus mountains and favoured by the mild climate of the Rhine valley, the capital city of Hessen has great variety to offer visitors. The refined atmosphere of a spa town, the flair of an elegant city, its proximity to the Rhine region, its attractive surroundings, all serve to contribute to its special attraction.

First mentioned during the 9C as "Wisibada" (spa in the meadows), the city was owned from the 13C on by the house of Nassau, and from 1806 it became the seat of government of the newly founded duchy of Nassau. For a time the city blossomed and enjoyed an upturn in its economy, which is evident from the generous layout of the roads and in the spa quarter built by Christian Zais in the Classical style. During the time of the Emperor William II, when the Emperor brought his court to Wiesbaden every summer, new quarters with elegant villas and new roads were built, for example the Wilhelmstraße and the Ringstraßen, which still afford visitors an insight into the city's original style.

The "world spa town" – Even the Romans were aware of the benefits of the 26 hot sodium chloride springs (46° to 66°C - 115° to 150°F), and Plinius noted with surprise that the water from the springs stayed warm for three days. The middle of the 19C saw the start of Wiesbaden's heyday as a spa town, when it became a rendezvous for the crowned heads and higher nobility of the world. Nowadays the spa business has a different clientèle, although it is still booming. Equipped to the standards of a modern health resort, Wiebaden has achieved an excellent reputation as a spa for sufferers of rheumatism.

OLD TOWN

Schloß ☉ – The former residence of the Dukes of Nassau was built between 1837 and 1841 in the unadorned Classical style. The main entrance lies on the diagonal and is emphasised by a rotunda. Today the palace is the seat of the Hessen provincial parliament.

Altes Rathaus (Old Town Hall) – The oldest building in the city, whose ground floor has been kept in late Renaissance style, it was built in 1609-1610, whilst the upper storey in the Romantic Historicising style originates from the year 1828.

Neues Rathaus (New Town Hall) – Georg Hauberisser, the architect of the Munich town hall, erected this building in the German Renaissance style, divided by oriels and projecting bays, in 1886-1887. It is somewhat free of adornment, but is impressive due to the considerable use of sandstone and the beautiful proportions on the ground floor and in the central part.

Marktkirche – This first brick built church in the Nassau region was erected in the middle of the 19C. Its architect, Carl Boos, copied the Friedrich-Werder church in Berlin which was created by Schinkel. *Carillon rung daily at 9 am, noon and 5 pm.*

SPA QUARTER

Kaiser-Friedrich-Bad – *38-42 Langgasse.*
The Jugendstil *(qv)* building built at the beginning of the 20C cost 3 million Gold Marks. The late Jugendstil frescoes in the entrance hall are worth seeing, as is the Roman-Irish steam bath with its majolica glazed tiles manufactured in Darmstadt and Karlsruhe.

Kochbrunnen – This fountain is made up of 15 springs. Its hot salty water contains iron, as is easy to tell from the reddish scale deposit on the granite fountain basin. Amongst Roman women the reddish powder was highly regarded, as they used it to colour their hair red. The octangular **Kochbrunnen temple** dates from 1854.

★ **Kurhaus (Spa-house)** – A lawn as flat as a bowling green, flanked on either side by the hydro and the theatre colonnades and by lofty plane trees, planted at the beginning of the 19C, leads up to what is, according to Emperor Wilhelm II, "the most beautiful spa-house in the world".
The spa-house itself was built in 1907. The inscription "Aquis Mattiacis" refers to the springs and the Germanic Mattiaker tribe who settled here in Roman times. The sumptuous interior decoration was restored to its original state in 1987. Although visitors don't get to see the magnificent rooms, unless they are attending an event or trying their luck in the casino which is located in the left wing, they should at least have a look in the **foyer**, in order to get a glimpse of the splendid décor.

Staatstheater – The impressive Renaissance style building, built in 1892-1894, lies to the south of the theatre colonnade. The taste for lavish decoration which existed at the turn of the century is evident in its **foyer**, redolent of the Rococo, with a double flight of outdoor stairs.

★ **Kurpark und Kuranlagen (Spa park and grounds)** – A vast park, laid out in 1852, extends eastwards behind the spa-house. Sonnenberger Straße *(to the north)* and Parkstraße *(to the south)* feature magnificent villas dating from the Gründerzeit *(qv)*.

FROM WILHELMSTRASSE TO THE NEROBERG

Museum Wiesbaden – This museum is in fact made up of three separate museums: the **natural sciences collection**, the **collection of Nassau antiquities** and finally the **art collections**, which proudly boast the largest **Jawlensky collection** ★ in the world. The artist lived in Wiesbaden from 1921 up his death in 1941. The exhibition includes significant works from the 16C and 17C as well as classical modern paintings. Wiesbaden's main street, the **Wilhelmstraße**, is flanked on one side by elegant shops and on the other by the "Warmer Damm" park, which leads to the Staatstheater.

Taunusstraße, which leads to the Nerotal park, will make the heart of every lover of antiques beat faster, since a large number of antique dealers have set up shop here.

Whilst walking through the **Nerotal**, a beautiful park with ponds, it is impossible not to admire the magnificent Gründerzeit villas along the Wilhelminenstraße.

Griechische Kapelle, Wiesbaden

357

★ **Nerobergbahn** ☉ – The cable rack railway, which still runs as well and safely today as it did when it was built in 1888, is a very special monument to technical achievement. It leads up the Neroberg, Wiesbaden's local mountain, 245m - 804ft in height. Driven with water ballast (a 7 000l - 1 540gal tank), the car moving down into the valley pulls up the car going up the mountain. When it arrives at the bottom, the water is pumped back up to the top to be reused. It couldn't be more environmentally friendly!

Griechische Kapelle ☉ – *Photograph previous page.* Although its name implies that it is Greek, this is in reality a Russian chapel. It was built by Duke Adolf von Nassau in 1845-1855 for his wife Elisabeth, a Russian grand duchess, who died at the tender age of 19. It includes a central building with five gilded cupolas, which overlook the whole of the city. The marble tomb was created by Emil Alexander Hopfgarten, a copy of Rauch's tomb of Queen Luise in Berlin-Charlottenburg.

EXCURSION

★ **Schloß Biebrich** – *South of the city on the banks of the Rhine.*
The uniformity of the horseshoe-shaped building, the residence of the Princes and Dukes of Nassau, is deceptive, since several master builders, in particular Maximilian von Welsch and Friedrich Joachim Stengel, the creator of the castle at Saarbrücken (Saarbrücken belonged to Nassau at the time), built this Baroque palace, whose long pink and white façade faces the Rhine, between 1700 and 1744. The round central building with the roof balustrade and the roof parapet figures is an architectural success. The palace chapel, whose vault has plaster of Paris decoration by C M Pozzi, is located on the ground floor. The cupola of the round banqueting hall above it rests on eight marble pillars. The so-called winter building (the northwest wing) contains Baroque and Classical plaster of Paris decoration. Schloß Briebrich is used by the Hessen government to hold official receptions.

The **castle park**, originally laid out as Baroque style gardens, was converted into an English garden in 1817-1823 by Friedrich Ludwig von Sckell. The 35ha - 86acre park, home to the Moosburg (Moss Castle), an artificial castle ruin (1805-1816), is a popular destination for an excursion.

WIESKIRCHE★★

WIES CHURCH – Bayern

Michelin map 419/420 W 16 – Local map under Deutsche ALPENSTRASSE

A masterpiece of Bavarian Rococo, the Wieskirche stands amid the forests, meadows and peat bogs whose gentle undulations characterize the final slopes of the Ammergau Alps between the Lech and the Ammer.

The Architect – It was **Dominikus Zimmermann** (1685-1766), one of the most gifted members of the **Wessobrunn School** *(qv)*, who was entrusted with the task of building this pilgrimage church "in der Wies" (in the meadow), and dedicated to Jesus Scourged. Aided by his brother Johann Baptist, a painter at the Bavarian court, Zimmermann started the work in 1746, soon after he finished Steinhausen *(qv)*, and completed it in 1754. Indeed, much of the church was based on the Steinhausen design: the focal point, as in the earlier edifice, was an oval cupola, which lent itself to painted decorations and emphasized the Rococo approach.

Zimmermann was so pleased with the result, which he considered the most successful of all his works, that he spent the last ten years of his life in a small house near the church.

The Church ☉ – A certain sobriety in the exterior leaves the visitor unprepared for the splendour and magnificence of the oval bay and the long, narrow chancel which prolongs it. Gilded stucco, wood carvings and vividly coloured frescoes stand out from the whitewashed walls, while the richly glowing effect is enhanced by an abundance of light entering through windows whose elaborate design is typical of the architect – an essential feature of the whole, both inside and out.

It is in fact this same finesse in the adaptation of detail to the global effect that strengthens the balance between architecture and ornamentation and achieves that visual harmony for which the Wieskirche is renowned. The lower parts of the interior, for example – the walls and paired pillars defining the ambulatory in the usual manner of pilgrimage churches – are deliberately sparsely decorated because they symbolize, in the mind of the designer, the earth. The upper reaches, on the other hand, symbolizing the heavens, vibrate with a profusion of paintings, stucco and gilded work. The immense **cupola fresco** represents the Second Coming, the Gates of Paradise (still closed) and the Court of the Last Judgement with the throne of the Judge himself yet to be occupied.

The decoration of the choir is unparalleled: columns, balustrades, statues, gilded stuccoes and frescoes combine to form a symphony of colour. The wide reredos painting is of Christ Made Man. The richness and delicacy of the lavish ornamentation adorning the organ loft and pulpit mark the high point of the Rococo style in southern Germany.

Bad WIMPFEN★★

Baden-Württemberg – Population 6 000
Michelin map 417/419 S 11 – Local map under HOHENLOHER LAND

Imperial residence of the Hohenstaufens in the 13C, this small fortified town, with its network of narrow streets lined with half-timbered houses, is built on a rise overlooking the River Neckar.

Along the foot of the hill extend the Ludwigshalle salt works, whose product once brought prosperity to the whole surrounding region, and especially the built-up area of Bad Wimpfen im Tal, which grew up around an old collegiate church.

★★BAD WIMPFEN AM BERG (UPPER TOWN) *time: 1 1/2 hours*

Follow the itinerary on the town plan, starting at the Marktplatz.

Kaiserpfalz (Remains of the Imperial Palace) – Standing on its own behind the Rathaus is the **Blauer Turm** (Blue Tower) (**A**), whose "neo-feudal" top dates only from the 19C. From the top of the tower – occupied today as in medieval times by a watchman – there is a panoramic view of the town and the Neckar valley. A little further on is the Romanesque **Steinhaus** (**B**), with its 16C stepped gable, where there is a museum tracing the history of Bad Wimpfen since the Roman occupation.

Eight steps down from the Steinhaus terrace, on the right at the foot of the wall, note the twin-columned Romanesque arcading through which light entered the gallery of the old palace. The decorative intricacy of the arcades demonstrates the building talents of the Hohenstaufens, under whose rule Romanesque civic architecture reached its peak.

Continue to follow the wall as far as a flight of steps, on the right, which leads to the tip of the spur on which the town is built, at the foot of the **Roter Turm** (Red Tower) (**C**), the fortress's final defensive point.

Return to the town centre, descending to pass beneath the **Hohenstaufentor** (**D**), which was the castle's main entrance in medieval times, and join the Klostergasse.

Old Streets – In the Klostergasse, which has considerable rustic charm, there are a number of half-timbered houses standing in their own gardens. On the left are the former spa bath-houses, recognizable by their outside galleries. To explore more of the town's old streets, return to the Langgasse crossroads and take a narrow alley on the right which leads to the **Hauptstraße**. At No 45 is the courtyard of a former hospital (Spitalhof), one of the oldest buildings in Wimpfen. Return along the Hauptstraße, with its many picturesque, finely worked signs, and pass the beautiful 1576 Eagle Fountain (Adlerbrunnen) (**K**) before regaining the Marktplatz via the Salzgasse.

A Blauer Turm	**C** Roter Turm	**K** Adlerbrunnen
B Steinhaus	**D** Hohenstaufentor	

BAD WIMPFEN IM TAL
(LOWER TOWN)

Stiftskirche St. Peter und St. Paul – This Gothic parish church has retained from an earlier Romanesque building a Westwerk *(qv)* which is strikingly crude. The **cloister★★** (Kreuzgang) ⊙ shows the Gothic style slowly evolving towards an aridity of design, though the late 13C east gallery is an example of the period at its best: a true

Bad Wimpfen am Berg

Nach Foto R. Schuler

purity of line informs the sculpted decor and the tri- and quadrilobed windows. The north gallery (*c*1350), already more angular in design, marks the transition to the style of the west gallery, which is even more austere, heralding the sober forms of the Renaissance.

EXCURSIONS

★ **Auto- und Technikmuseum (Automobile and Technical Museum)** ⊙ – *At* **Sinsheim**, *25km - 15 1/2 miles to the west.*
Mechanical vehicles of many types are brought together in this collection. In the first building are impressive early 20C tractors, steam locomotives, luxury motor cars (Bugatti, Mercedes), and a replica of the first hang-glider to be commercially marketed, the Lilienthal, which dates from the late 19C.
A second building exhibits a collection of mainly military material (tanks, motorized artillery, aeroplanes).

★ **The Neckar Valley (Neckartal)** – *Round tour of 74km - 46 miles – about 4 hours.*
Downstream from Bad Wimpfen, the Neckar, cutting once more through the sandstone massif of the Odenwald *(qv)*, runs through an area of wooded hills, many of them crowned by castles. Linked now with the great flow of navigation on the Rhine, river traffic is heavy.

★ **Burg Guttenberg** ⊙ – A massive defence wall protects this castle on the side facing the mountain. Inside, there are unusual **collections of objets d'art★** and a series of archives. Note especially the odd 18C "Library-Herbarium", in which the plants are encased in 92 pseudo "books" made of wood. A 15C altarpiece, The Virgin Mary in her Cloak, is on display. There is a fine view of the river from the keep.

Burg Hornberg ⊙ – *1.5km - about 1 mile outside Neckarzimmern.*
Crowning a hill planted with vines, this castle – now partly in ruins – can be recognized from far away by its cylindrical keep. In the part now turned into a **museum**, note the body armour of Götz von Berlichingen, who died here in 1562. This knight, popularised in German folkore as a Robin Hood figure, was immortalised in a play by Goethe. From the high keep, the **view★** extends a long way down the valley.

In the village of Hirschhorn am Neckar, turn right towards Beerfelden, then right again to reach the entrance to Hirschhorn castle.

★ **Hirschhorn am Neckar** – The castle stands on a fortified spur. From the tower *(121 steps, a difficult climb)* the **view★** extends over the meander and wooded slopes of the Neckar valley.

Neckarsteinach – Four castles dominate this site.

Dilsberg – *4.5km - 3 miles from Neckarsteinach.* Follow the Signposts "Burgruine" to reach the ruined castle. From the tower *(97 steps)* there is another **panorama★** over the winding river Neckar.
The best way to arrive in **Heidelburg** is by the east bank road, which leads straight to the castle.

Jagst Valley (Jagsttal) – *See HOHENLOHER LAND.*

Neckarsulm – *10km - 6 miles to the southeast.*
The castle once belonged to the Teutonic Order. Today the castle houses the **German Cycle and Motorcycle Museum** (Deutsches Zweiradmuseum, NSU-Museum) ⊙. Nearby is the NSU motor factory which produced the first bicycles in Germany.

WISMAR★

Meckenburg-Vorpommern – Population 55 000
Michelin map 415/416 E 18

Wismar dates back to the year 1226. It enjoyed its heyday for a time as a Hanseatic city, relying principally on trade with the main countries in Europe. The brewery trade (Wismar was known for its excellent beer) and wool weaving were further sources of wealth. Its downfall came with the Thirty Years War. The peace of Osnabrück meant that the town came under Swedish rule in 1648, under which it remained until 1803. Industrial operations only started up at the end of the 19C, and the town revived again as merchant shipping grew in importance.

During the last few decades, shipbuilding, merchant shipping and fishing have determined the fate of the town. On the threshold of the 21C, Wismar will have to move in a new direction. Tourism will play a decisive role, since the town has a large number of old gabled houses and other admirable buildings.

SIGHTS

Remarkable houses can be discovered everywhere in the old town. They are either noticeable because they have been renovated, or are still eking out their humble existence. With a little imagination, the visitor will be able to picture what a treasure Wismar once was and promises to become again.

★ **Marktplatz** – Of considerable size (10 000m² - 107 600sq ft), it is dominated in the north by the white silhouette of the Classical **Rathaus**, which dates from 1817 to 1819. The gabled houses belong to a number of different epochs, and each of them records a chapter of architectural and art history. On the eastern side, the oldest wealthy middle-class house in the town, a red brick building, known as the "Old Swede" and built around 1380, catches the eye. On its right stands the Reuterhaus, where the works of the Mecklenburg writer Fritz Reuter were published and on its left, a house with charming Jugendstil ornamentation. On the southeastern side of the market place an artistic pavilion, the **waterworks★**, draws the eye. It was built in 1580-1602 in the Dutch Renaissance style and served to supply the town with water for centuries.

Marienkirchturm – Only the 80m - 262ft high tower remains of the mighty Marienkirche which was built during the first half of the 13C and destroyed during the Second World War. *(Carillon at midday, 3pm and 7pm.)* The brick built **archdeaconry** at the corner of Marienkirchhof and Sargmacherstraße dates from 1450.

Fürstenhof – *To the west of the Marienkirchturm.*
The building, which was erected in two phases, is thought to be the northernmost Renaissance castle in Europe. The more recent, long section in particular, built in 1553-1554 by Gabriel von Aken and Valentin von Lyra, is impressive with the ornaments on the pilaster and friezes. Those facing the road represent the Trojan wars, and those facing the courtyard represent the parable of the Prodigal Son. The gateway and window frames are sumptuously decorated.

Wismar harbour

St. Georgen-Kirche – The Late Gothic brick church (begun in 1290 and ended during the 15C) was seriously damaged during the Second World War. Extensive restoration work should help to restore it to its former splendour and dignity by the turn of the century.

Grube – The "Grube" is a watercourse laid in 1255, where washing was done right up into the 20C. It is the only artificial stream of its kind still existing in Germany. After careful renovation, the streets which flank it could become one of the most picturesque corners of Wismar.

★ **Schabbellhaus** – The sumptuously decorated red brick building in the Dutch Renaissance style, which stands on the corner of Schweinsbrücke and Frische Grube, was erected between 1569 and 1571 by the Dutch master builder Philipp Brandin for Hinrich Schabell. It bears witness to the wealth of the owner, a respected merchant and mayor of the town (his gravestone is in the Nikolaikirche). The house is on two floors, but the four storey gable end pointing towards the Grube adds a certain cachet. The house is home to a **museum of local history** ⊙.

★ **Nikolaikirche** ⊙ – Beyond the Grube looms the dark mass of this, the highest brick church in the world, after the Marienkirche in Lübeck. The basilica was built between 1381 and 1487. Arched buttresses over the side aisles support the considerable pressure and at the same time alleviate the austere appearance of the building. The southern gable with its glazed figures is attractive. The interior is impressive with its sumptuous décor, with some valuable pieces from both the other destroyed churches contributing to the decorations. The **Altar der Krämergilde** ★ (Grocers' Guild Altarpiece), a hinged, panelled altarpiece in a later softer style, erected in 1430, is especially noteworthy. The figures on the central panel, the Virgin Mary, the Archangel Michael and St. Mauritius, exude a strong, expressive sensivity. A bronze font cast in 1335 depicts the Life of Christ, the Last Judgement and the Wise and Foolish Virgins. The "Devil's railing" around the font originates from the 16C. The Triumphal Cross group (15C) is captivating, thanks to the quality of the crucifix. The frescoes in the side halls of the tower, including an immense St Christopher, date from the period around 1450.

Alter Hafen (Old Port) – From the Grube and the idyllic street "Am Lohberg", just a few steps lead to the port, at the end of which stands an unadorned Baroque building, the Baumhaus (tree house). Here the port used to be locked by the lock keeper at fixed times with a tree trunk. The function of the two "Swedish heads" executed in colour is not clear. Were they intended to frighten people off? In any event, they are known to date from 1672.

EXCURSION

★ **Neukloster** – *17km - 11miles to the east of Wismar.*
The **monastery church** ⊙ of the former Cistercian convent was built around 1219-1240 under the influence of the Ratzeburg cathedral, and served in turn as a model for very many Mecklenburg churches. It is a cross-shaped, well-proportioned brick building, characterised by its excellent workmanship. The remains of late Romanesque **stained glass** ★, dating from before 1245, are of particular interest.

WITTENBERG

Sachsen-Anhalt – Population 5 000
Michelin map 418 K 21

In a pleasant situation between the wooded hills of Fläming and the Elbe, this small town is known mainly because of its connection with Martin Luther.

A Key Town in the Reformation – Summoned by the Elector Friedrich the Wise (1502) to teach philosophy in the university he had just founded, Luther was at the same time appointed the town preacher. After the celebrated public burning of a Papal Bull, Luther was forced to appear before the Imperial Diet at Worms *(qv)*. Then, installed again in Wittenberg in 1522, he was obliged to temper the excesses of his own followers, especially Thomas Müntzer *(qv)*. A year after Luther's death, in 1546 at Eisleben (qv), and eight years before he signed the Peace of Augsburg, allowing freedom of worship to the Lutherans, the Emperor Charles V seized Wittenberg and is said to have meditated over the tomb of the great Reformer.

SIGHTS

★ **Schloßkirche (Castle Church)** – *Am Schloßplatz, in the western part of the town.*
The church attached to the royal residence was burned down in 1760 and rebuilt in the Baroque style. It was on the original doors that Luther had pinned up his famous 95 Articles condemning the abuses practised by the Church (1517). The new church contains the text, which was cast in bronze in 1855. Luther's tomb, too, is in this church, as is that of Melanchthon *(see below)*, as well as the bronze epitaph to Friedrich the Wise executed in 1527 by Peter Vischer.

★ **Markt** – In front of the Late Gothic (1440) town hall stand statues of Luther (by Schadow, 1821) and of his friend and disciple Melanchthon (Drake, 1860). The square is bordered by houses with gables, that in the southwest corner having been the home of the painter Lucas Cranach the Elder from 1505 to 1547, when he was the town's mayor.

Stadtkirche – *Am Kirchplatz, east of the Markt.*
This triple-aisle Gothic (14C and 15C) church was redecorated in neo-Gothic style in the 18C. The fact that Luther preached here is celebrated in one panel of the 1547 Cranach **Reformation Altarpiece★**. Melanchthon is depicted on the left-hand panel.

Melanchthon-Haus ⊘ – *Collegienstraße 60.*
The building in which Luther's companion lived and died is a Renaissance edifice topped by a gable of particularly elegant form. A man of moderate temperament, more tolerant than Luther, the author of the Confession of Augsburg (qv) worked for most of his life trying to reconcile the different factions of the Reformation. His study, and many documents relating to his work, can be seen in this house.

★ **Lutherhalle** ⊘ – *At the far end of the Collegienstraße.*
Occupied by Luther from 1524 onwards, this house faces the courtyard of the Collegium Augusteum, the town's old university. The **Reformation Museum**, housed here since 1883, exhibits collections of antique Bibles, manuscripts, and original editions of Luther's works. One department displays a selection of fine arts from Luther's time: portraits of the Reformer, prints and paintings by Cranach the Elder, canvases by Hans Baldung Grien, etc.

EXCURSIONS

★★ **Wörlitzer Park** – *18km - 11 miles to the west. Take the car ferry across the Elbe in Coswig.*
This huge park in the English style extends over more than 100ha - 250 acres. Landscaped at the end of the 18C, it embraces lakes and several bends of the Elbe. A number of different amenities add to the pleasures of the park. **Schloß Wörlitz★** ⊘, for instance, built in the neo-Classical style, houses works by Canaletto, Pesne, Ruysdael and others. The **Gothic House** is a strange building – in fact neo-Gothic – where paintings by Cranach the Elder are on view, along with 15C and 16C stained glass from Switzerland.
A boat trip takes in all these attractions as well as the park itself, with its wealth of statues and wide variety of plants.

WOLFENBÜTTEL★★

Niedersachsen – Population 50 000
Michelin map 416/418 J 15

For three centuries, until the Court transferred to Brunswick in 1753, Wolfenbüttel was the seat of the Dukes of Brunswick and Luneburg. The precise, spacious plan of the small town, with die-straight streets linking large squares of symmetrical shape, makes it one of the most successful examples of Renaissance town planning in Germany.

SIGHTS

★ **Half-timbered Houses (Fachwerkhäuser)** (**ABYZ**) – Picturesque groups of these houses in different styles reflect the town's social structure under the Dukes. Lining the Kanzleistraße, the Reichstraße and the west end of the Harzstraße, for instance, majestic façades with overhangs on either side of the main entrance distinguish the homes of high Court officials, most of them built c1600. The corbelled upper floors of these houses are supported on brackets. The decoration of smaller houses owned by lesser dignitaries and merchants, oddly enough, is more elaborate. A single gable normally tops their wide, flat façades (Lange Herzogstraße, Brauergildenstraße, Holzmarkt, Krambuden). At No 12 Harzstraße, note the curious grimacing heads above cornices carved with Biblical inscriptions. The simpler, two-storey houses of the less well-to-do (Krumme Straße, Stobenstraße) are prettily ornamented with coloured fan designs. The corner houses with oriels which project only slightly are characteristic of Wolfenbüttel. The most harmonious single group of these half-timbered houses is to be found surrounding the main town square (Stadtmarkt).

★ **Stadtmarkt** (**AZ**) – On the north and west side of the square, the Rathaus comprises a number of buildings with splayed beams filled in by brickwork. The Weights and Measures Office has a distinctive arched doorway surmounted by King Solomon's Edict and the Wolfenbüttel coat of arms. Picturesque weather vanes creak in the wind. The philologist **Schottelius**, or Schottel, known as "the father of German grammar", lived in the square in about 1650.
A statue of Duke Augustus the Young (1635-1666) honours one of the most cultivated princes of the House of Brunswick and Lüneburg.

WOLFENBÜTTEL

Schloß (AZ) ⊙ – This is reached via an attractive narrow street bordered by arcades known as the Krambuden. Originally a 12C stronghold conquered by Henry the Lion *(qv)*, the building was the subject of many transformations before it evolved into the Baroque residence visible today, complete with several pediments and overlooked by a fine Renaissance **tower★**. In the 16C and 17C, under the rule of several ducal patrons, the castle became a centre of literature and sacred music.

The Ducal Apartments – *Access via a stairway, on the right beneath the porch.*
Rare furniture, tapestries, porcelain and valuable paintings recreate the atmosphere of court life, especially during the reigns of Duke Anton-Ulrich and Augustus-Wilhelm (early 18C). Mythological scenes, executed in marquetry with an ivory inlay, adorn the walls of the small study.

Herzog-August Bibliothek (Library) (AYZ) ⊙ – Founded in 1572 by Augustus the Young, and rebuilt at the end of the 19C, this was the largest, most important library in Europe in the 17C. Still an invaluable treasure-house for researchers and scholars, it houses today some 600 000 volumes. Among the priceless manuscripts and illuminated documents from the Middle Ages are *The Story of the Lovely Melusina*, by Jean d'Arras (1478), a rare example of the 14C *Saxon Mirror*, and the first *Helmarshausen Gospel* (12C) said to have belonged to Heinrich the Lion. These are exhibited in the Augusteer-Halle and in the room below it. On the left of the latter are two globes, terrestrial and celestial, as well as ancient maps and a portulan (marine chart) which provide interesting information on the state of geographic knowledge and the advances in cartography during the 15C, 16C and 17C. On the right *(shown in rotation)* are books illustrated by great artists of the present century.

Lessinghaus (AZ) ⊙ – Lessing, the great forerunner of German theatre, lived in Wolfenbüttel from 1770 to 1781, working as official ducal librarian and writing, among other works, Nathan the Wise. His last home was this mansarded pavilion just before the library on the north side of the esplanade. An evocation of his life and works is on view inside.
On the right of the Lessing house is the **Zeughaus** (Arsenal, 1613), a distinctive Renaissance building with projecting gables flanked by obelisks and scrolls. Note the fine rusticated west doorway.

Hauptkirche (BZ) – Built on the Kornmarkt in 1608, this Protestant church is laid out in the Gothic manner, with very tall windows and pointed vaulting, but it also has features characteristic of the Late Renaissance.

Note the lateral gables, whose pediments embellished with niches and columns boast a curiously thick decoration of twisted scrollwork. The massive tower with its Baroque roof resembles the castle tower in shape.

Trinitatiskirche (BZ) – The church, which closes off the east end of the Holzmarkt, was built in 1719. In its construction, the architects made use of an existing, twin-towered structure which was once a city gate. This explains the strangely flat silhouette of the church. Behind it, a deconsecrated burial ground has been transformed into a romantic **public garden.**

WORMS★

Rhineland-Pfalz – Population 76 000

Michelin map 417/419 R 9 – Local map under PFALZ AM RHEIN

The city of Worms was, like Speyer and Mainz, an imperial Residence on the banks of the Rhine, a town with a legendary past, a town of history and prestige. Today it extends along the river irrigating the rich soil of the Palatinate Plain vineyards. The **Liebfrauenkirche** (*leave by Remeyerhofstraße* – **B**), which stands amidst the vines in the northern suburb, has given its name to the most famous of all Hocks: Liebfraumilch. Remains (now restored) of the medieval walled town destroyed during the Thirty Years War are visible near the **Torturmplatz (B)** and the **Karolingerstraße (B 22)**.

Luther before the Diet – Everybody knows the old chestnut about Luther and the "diet of worms", bandied about to much hilarity during school history lessons. In fact this particular Diet had perhaps the most far-reaching consequences of any conference before the two world wars (see "The Reformation and the Thirty Years War: Luther"). Summoned before it by the young Charles V in 1521, after a Papal Bull condemning everything he believed in, Luther arrived in Worms "as though going to the torture chamber". He went nevertheless without hesitation, held back by the anxiety of his friends but acclaimed by enthusiastic crowds. Refusing to retract his beliefs, he was banned to the outer parts of the Empire *(see also WITTENBERG).*

WORMS					
		Petersstraße	**A** 32	Friedrich-Ebert-Str	**A** 14
		Stephansgasse	**A** 38	Heinrichstraße	**B** 16
		Wilhelm-Leuschner Str	**A** 40	Herzogenstraße	**B** 18
Adenauerring	**A** 2			Karolingerstraße	**B** 22
Am Römischen Kaiser	**A** 5	Allmendgasse	**B** 3	Mälzgasse	**B** 24
Hardtgasse	**A** 15	Bärengasse	**B** 6	Martinsgasse	**A** 26
Kämmererstraße	**A** 23	Bauhofgasse	**B** 8	Pfauenpforte	**A** 34
Ludwigsplatz	**A** 25	Fischmarkt	**A** 9	Pfauentorstraße	**A** 35
Marktplatz	**A** 30	Folzstraße	**A** 12	Remeyerhofstraße	**B** 36
Neumarkt	**A** 30	Friedrichstraße	**A** 13	Valckenbergstraße	**A** 39

B	Raschi-Haus	**M¹**	Kunsthaus Heylshof
D	Dreifaltigkeitskirche		
E	St. Martinskirche	**M²**	Städtisches Museum

★★DOM ST. PETER (A) *time: 30 min*

Worms cathedral is a Romanesque building with two apses quartered in each case by two round towers. From the outside, the **west chancel★★** of this four-towered structure, completed *c*1230, is one of the finest Romanesque creations in Germany, with its double tier of Rhineland dwarf galleries *(qv)*.

Interior – The best way to go in is through the south (Gothic) doorway. On the tympanum: the Coronation of the Virgin. A splendid Christ In Judgement is on the far side of the door, dating from the 12C. A very old sculpture in the first chapel on the south side represents Daniel in the Lions' Den.

The east chancel, with its pointed vaulting, is the oldest: the high altar is the work of Balthazar Neumann *(qv)*. Nine Imperial tombs of relatives of Emperor Konrad II are beneath the choir. The transept crossing, surmounted by a Rhineland cupola on squinches, is admirable.

The Romanesque nave, which has vine bays with diagonally ribbed vaulting, is embellished with blind arcades whose intricate carving typifies the later development of the style. The west chancel, the last to be built, is extremely elegant, with rose windows, a chequered frieze and arches added to its blind arcades.

Five **Gothic sculptures★** in the north aisle (Reliefs aus dem Leben Christi) represent the Annunciation, the Nativity, the Entombment, the Resurrection and the Tree of Jesse.

ADDITIONAL SIGHTS

Lutherdenkmal (Luther Monument) (A) – Unveiled in 1868, the monument commemorates the Reformer's appearance before the Diet. Luther himself, in the centre, is surrounded by the precursors of the Reformation: Pietro Valdo, John Wycliffe, Jan Hus and Savonarola. At the four corners are *(back)* the Reform theologians Melanchthon and Reuchlin, *(front)* the Landgrave of Hessen Philip the Magnanimous *(see MARBURG)* and the Elector of Saxony who protected Luther. Seated women symbolize the towns of Speyer, Augsburg and Magdeburg.

★ **Kunsthaus Heylshof (A M¹)** ☉ – Installed in the salons of a former town house, this museum displays **paintings★** from the 15C to the 19C. Among them are works by Rubens, Van Loo, Mignard and Knaus. Also on view are ceramics (from Winterthur, Delft and China), glassware and crystal, 300 pieces of Frankenthal porcelain, and examples of 15C and 16C stained glass windows.

★ **Judenfriedhof (Jewish Cemetery)** (A) – Worms was one of the most highly-esteemed centres of Jewish culture in Germany. This ancient burial ground, in use since the 11C, is studded with more than 2 000 steles carved in Hebrew.

Synagogue (B) – Dating also from the 11C (and rebuilt in 1961), this is the oldest synagogue in Germany. Nearby is the Mikwe (Women's Bath-house) and the **Raschi-Haus** (B B), an old Jewish school restored to exhibit archives, ceremonial items and other examples of life in the Rhineland Jewish community.

Städtisches Museum (A M²) ☉ – The historic and prehistoric exhibits are displayed in the Romanesque buildings of a former monastery. Note the collection of helmets in the Roman section. The church contains sacred art, with a lapidary museum in the cloister.

Dreifaltigkeitskirche (A D) – Only the tower and façade of the original Baroque (18C) buildings remain. The interior commemorates the Reformation.

St. Martinskirche (A E) – The Romanesque west door is flanked by eight columns with crocheted capitals. Note the decorative interlacing of vine stems and leaves on the tympanum.

EXCURSION

★ **Rhineland Palatinate** – *See PFALZ AM RHEIN.*

MICHELIN GUIDES

The Red Guides (hotels and restaurants)

Benelux – Deutschland – España Portugal – Europe – France – Great Britain and Ireland – Italia – Switzerland

The Green Guides (fine art, historic monuments, scenic routes)

Austria – Belgium and Luxembourg – Brussels – California – Canada – England: The West Country – France – Germany – Great Britain – Greece – Ireland – Italy – London – Mexico – Netherlands – New England – New York – Portugal – Quebec – Rome – Scandinavia-Finland – Scotland – Spain – Switzerland – Tuscany – Venice – Wales – Washington DC

and the collection of regional guides to France.

WÜRZBURG★★

Bayern − Population 124 000
Michelin map 417/419/420 Q 13

On the far side of the Main and below the episcopal citadel of Marienburg, the original semicircular layout of Würzburg was planned between 1650 and 1750 by three Prince-Bishops of the Schönborn family, who were also responsible for the Baroque churches of the old town and the Residenz palace.

The Master of Würzburg – This was the title bestowed on the great Flamboyant Gothic sculptor **Tilmann Riemenschneider** (1460-1531), who came to live in Würzburg in 1483 and was the town's mayor in 1520 and 1521. Riemenschneider's work was never purely decorative: his whole interest centred on human beings, whose faces, hands – even their clothes – served as vehicles to express emotion and sensitivity. A gravity that is almost melancholy distinguishes his finest work, which includes the magnificent altarpieces at Creglingen and Rothenburg, the statues in Würzburg's local museum, and the tomb of Heinrich II in Bamberg cathedral – all priceless treasures of Franconian art.

★★RESIDENZ (Z) ⊘ *guided tour: 1 hour*

This superb Baroque palace, one of the biggest in Germany, was built between 1720 and 1744 under the direction of that architect of genius, **Balthazar Neumann** (qv), supplanting the old Marienberg stronghold as the bishops' residence.
The monumental **Grand Staircase★** (Treppenhaus), which ends in a double flight and occupies the whole northern part of the vestibule, is one of Neumann's masterpieces. The huge **fresco★★** (600m² - 6 400sq ft) decorating the vaulted ceiling is by the Venetian, **Tiepolo** (1753). This gigantic work depicts the homage of the four then known continents to the Prince-Bishop Karl-Friedrich von Greiffenklau. In the White Room (Weißer Saal), between the Grand Staircase and the Imperial Hall, the stuccoes, also Italian, are the work of Antonio Bossi.
The oval **Imperial Hall★★** (Kaisersaal) is splendid. Situated on the first floor, it, too, is adorned with **frescoes by Tiepolo**. Following a fashion current in the Baroque period, the artist makes an impeccable transition, moving imperceptibly from sculpture to false relief painting.
It is also possible to visit the **Imperial Apartments** (Paradezimmer), a luxurious suite of rooms restored in all their splendor with Rococo stucco-work, tapestries and German furniture.

★★**Hofkirche** – The architectural fantasy and audacity displayed by Neumann in the royal chapel are astonishing. The complex positioning of oval arching, the pink-veined marble columns, the white and gold of false marble highlighting the warm tints of frescoes by the Court Painter Rudolf Byss – all of these combine to form a colourful composition rich in contrasts. Two more Tiepolo paintings hang above the side altars: the Assumption and the Fall of the Angels.

★**Hofgarten** – Astute use of old, stepped bastions has produced a layout of terraced gardens with majestic ramp approaches. From the eastern side, the whole 167m - 545ft of the palace façade, with its elegant central block, is visible. The stucco is the work of Johann Peter Wagner.

Fresco by Tiepolo in the Imperial Hall of Würzburg Residenz

FULDA, VEITSHÖCHHEIM

WÜRZBURG

★ **Martin-von-Wagner-Museum** ⊘ – *In the south wing.*
On the second floor there is a **painting gallery**★ exhibiting German and other European work from the 14C to the 19C. Particularly noteworthy: altar paintings by the Masters of Würzburg (14-16C) and Franconian sculpture, especially that of Riemenschneider. Dutch and Italian painters from the 16C to the 18C are well represented (Tiepolo again). On the third floor, there is a collection of **antiquities**★ displaying an interesting series of **painted Greek vases**★ (particularly from the 6C to the 4C BC). The department also exhibits Roman pottery, earthenware items, and jewellery from Ancient Egypt. Note the Greek and Roman sculpture and implements made from bronze.

ADDITIONAL SIGHTS
ON THE EAST BANK OF THE MAIN

Dom (Cathedral of St Kilian) (Z) – This basilica with columns and four towers, rebuilt in 1945, preserves its original (11-13C) silhouette, although the interior is marked by many other centuries. The Baroque stucco-work of the chancel contrasts with the high ceiling and simplicity of the Romanesque nave; the **Altar of the Apostles** in the south transept was conceived in 1967 by H Weber as a resting place for three **sandstone sculptures**★ by Riemenschneider which were created between 1502 and 1506.
Against the pillars on either of the great nave, **funerary monuments**★ to the Prince-Bishops, ranging from the 12C to the 17C, stand in proud array. Those by the 7th and 8th pillar on the north side (Rudolf von Scherenberg and Lorenz von Bibra) are also by Riemenschneider.
The **crypt**, accessible via the north transept, houses a monument (13C) to the founder of the cathedral, Archbishop Bruno. Off the north transept is the **Schönborn chapel**, built between 1721 and 1736 by Balthazar Neumann and the architect Maximilian von Welsch to take the tombs of the Prince-Bishops of that House. The 15C Gothic **cloister** abuts on the south face of the Cathedral.

Neumünster (YZ B) – The imposing Baroque **west façade** of this church (1710-1716) is attributed to Johann Dientzenhofer. The twin superimposed gables of the central section, sharply curved and richly decorated, lend power to the whole façade.
The three-aisle nave inherited from the original Romanesque building was extended at the beginning of the 18C by a huge domed bay at the western end. In niches below this cupola are a Riemenschneider Virgin and Child and a Christ in an unusual pose with arms folded below the chest (14C).

WÜRZBURG

In the west crypt is the **tomb of St Kilian**, apostle, patron of Franconia and missionary, executed in Würzburg in 689.

North of the chancel, on the left, is the entrance to the **Lusamgärtlein**, a small garden laid out on the site of a medieval cloister. It was here, so they say, that the troubadour-poet Walther von der Vogelweide *(qv)*, who died in 1231, is buried.

Marienkapelle (Y E) – This fine Gothic hall-church with its lovely upswept lines was built by the town burghers in the 14C and 15C. There is an attractive Annunciation on the tympanum of the north doorway *(c1420)*. Inside the west front is the 1502 tombstone of Konrad von Schaumberg, carved by Riemenschneider and, on the north side, a **silver Madonna** made by the Master of Augsburg, J Kilian, in 1680.

East of the chapel is the **Haus zum Falken★** (Falcon House) (**D**), with its graceful 1752 façade decorated in the Rococo style (reconstructed after the war).

★ **Alte Mainbrücke (Z)** – Built between 1473 and 1543, the bridge over the Main was adorned in the Baroque era with twelve huge sandstone statues of saints.

Rathaus (Town Hall) (YZ R) – A 13C building, once an episcopal residence. The painted façade dates from the 16C. The interior courtyard is charming. The western part, known as the **red building** (Roter Bau), is an example of the Late Renaissance (1659) architectural art. The **fountain** (Vierröhrenbrunnen) (**F**) in front of the town hall dates from 1765.

SIGHTS ON THE WEST BANK OF THE MAIN

★ **Festung Marienberg (X)** ⊙ – From 1253 to 1719, this stronghold was the home of the Prince-Bishops of Würzburg. Built on a commanding height above the west bank of the Main, the original early 13C medieval castle was transformed into a Renaissance palace by Julius Echter c1600. It was under the Schönborn bishops that it became one of the fortresses of the Empire from 1650 onwards.

Marienberg today forms a complex around a rectangular central courtyard in which stand a fine 13C **circular keep**, a circular chapel dedicated to the Virgin Mary (Marienkirche) and a Renaissance covered well that is 104m - 341ft deep. The chapel, crowned by an impressive cupola decorated with Baroque stucco-work, dates back to the early 8C (it was consecrated in 706). It houses many episcopal tombstones.

From the terrace of the **Fürstengarten** (Princes' Garden): a fine **view★** of the town.

★★ Mainfränkisches Museum (Franconian Museum of the Main) (**X M¹**) ⊙ – *The entrance is on the right in the fortress's first courtyard.*
Among the displays of local art and crafts in this former arsenal (Zeughaus, 1702-1712) is a collection of **Riemenschneider sculptures** *(Gallery 3, first floor)*.
In the splendid vaulted galleries of the **Echterbastei**, religious gold and silver plate, Gothic easel paintings and examples of Franconian folk art can be seen. In the **cellars** are old wine presses.

St. Burkard (**Z K**) – The chancel of the Romanesque-Gothic (11-15C) riverside church straddles the Uferstraße *(covered passageway)*. The bust of a Riemenschneider Madonna enlivens the south transept.

Käppele (**X**) – At the top of a monumental Way of the Cross, this well-situated pilgrim sanctuary, the work of Balthasar Neumann, comprises a central Baroque chapel with curious bulbous domes and decorations that include Matthäus Günther frescoes and Rococo stucco-work by Johann Michael Feuchtmayer.
The finest **view★★** of Würzburg and the river is from the chapel terrace, with the fortress of Marienberg rising from the vineyards in the foreground.

EXCURSIONS

★ Schloß Veitshöchheim ⊙– *7km - 4 miles to the northwest by* ⑥ *on the town plan.*
The castle, built at the end of the 17C and enlarged around 1750 after plans drawn up by Balthazar Neumann, contains splendid Rococo and Empire furniture, including gaming and billiard tables. But it was above all the **park★** that received particular attention from the Prince-Bishops, who improved it so consistently that by the end of the 18C it was an entirely Rococo creation. In the southern part, formalized in the French manner, comical statues people the shaded walks and leafy arbours, brightening avenues bordered by artistically clipped lime trees. In the middle of the great lake stands the superb **Parnassus Group** (Pegasus, the Muses and Apollo), which was carved in 1766.

★ The Main Valley Vineyards (Bocksbeutelstraße) – *Round tour of 87km - 55 miles – allow 1 day. Leave Würzburg via* ③ *on the town plan.*
It was monks at the beginning of the Middle Ages who introduced viticulture to the Franconian region of the Main – an area with a mild climate and hot, dry summers. The 4 500ha - 11 115 acres under the vine produce mainly white wines from the **Müller-Thurgau** and traditionally fruity Silvaner grape stock. Such wines adapt perfectly to the essentially rich Franconian cooking.

Sommerhausen – A small Franconian walled town. The picturesque gables of the 16C town hall and the castle overlook the main street.

Ochsenfurt – Another town still encircled by ancient **ramparts★** punctuated by gates. In the centre, many old half-timbered houses and hotels are adorned with wrought iron statuettes or signs. A clock with mechanical figurines striking the hours is an attraction at the **Neues Rathaus** (late 15C). At the southwest corner of the building is a graceful 1498 statue of the Virgin Mary. The **Andreaskirche**, built between the 13C and the 15C, is noteworthy for its interior decoration.

Frickenhausen – A fortified town dating from late medieval times. There is a beautiful Renaissance gateway with ramshorn scrollwork decorating the pediment. The town hall is Late Gothic.

Marktbreit – Here there is a fine **Renaissance ensemble★** formed by the town hall, dating from 1579, a bridge (Breitbachbrücke) and the gateway beyond it (Maintor, *c*1600). Two Baroque houses with corner oriels complete the picture.

Sulzfeld – Another fortified town. The gables of the 17C town hall are decorated with projecting scrollwork.

Pass through Kitzingen and Mainstockheim (on the east bank of the Main), and take the road for Dettelbach.

★ Dettelbach – This charming fortified market town stands on the northern slopes of the Main valley. See the Late Gothic (*c*1500) town hall and the mid-15C parish church, whose principal tower is linked by a wooden bridge to the smaller staircase tower. Northeast of the upper town is the **pilgrimage church "Maria im Sand"** (1608-1613), an interesting example of the transition between Flamboyant Gothic and a Renaissance already tainted by the Baroque. The 1623 **Renaissance doorway★** was made by Michael Kern, who was also responsible for the sandstone and alabaster **pulpit★** (1626).

From Dettelbach to Neuses am Berg, the road crosses an open plateau planted with vines, with good views of the neighbouring slopes. It then drops down again to the valley of the Main and the peaceful village of **Escherndorf**. From Escherndorf, a small ferry crosses the river to Nordheim.

★ Volkach – This delightful little wine-growing town lies on the east (outer) side of a wide oxbow curve in the Main. Of the original medieval enclave only two gates remain: the **Gaibacher Tor** and the **Sommeracher Tor**, one at each end of the main street. On one side of the Marktplatz is the **Renaissance town hall** (tourist information centre), built – with its double-flight outside stairway and corner turret – in the middle of the 16C.

The building known as the **Schelfenhaus**, a civic mansion in the Baroque style dating from c1720, is worth seeing for its interior decorations *(in the Schelfengasse, north of the market place)*.

At the northwestern limit of the town *(about 1km - half a mile, in the direction of Fahr)* stands the 15C **pilgrimage church "Maria im Weingarten"**, in the middle of vineyards covering the Kirchberg. Inside is the famous **Virgin with Rosary★** (Rosenkranzmadonna), a late work (1512-1524) of Tilmann Riemenschneider, in carved lime wood.

From the Kirchberg there is a superb **panorama** including Volkach, the vineyards and the valley of the Main.

XANTEN

Nordrhein-Westfalen – Population 16 000
Michelin map 417 L 3

Xanten, birthplace of Siegfried, hero of the Nibelungen saga *(qv)*, was originally a Roman town and honours St Victor, martyr of the Theban Legion. Traces of the medieval fortifications, such as the 1393 **Cleves Gate** (Klever Tor), can still be found.

★ **Dom (Cathedral)** – *The south doorway is being restored.*
This cathedral is one of the finest Gothic buildings in the Lower Rhineland. A Romanesque church was erected here in the 12C on the site of an earlier sanctuary founded by St Helen to house the relics of St Victor. The towers and Westwerk *(qv)* of this, damaged in the Second World War, are nevertheless still standing. The present Gothic structure was begun in 1263, although the five-aisle nave was not completed until the 16C.
The high altar, harbouring the shrine of St Victor, has a handsome reredos by Bartholomäus Bruyn the Elder (1530) which illustrates the lives of St Victor and St Helen. Heinrich Douvermann, the Master Sculptor of Kalkar, created the 1536 Altarpiece of the Virgin, with its intricately worked predella, in the south aisle. The north aisle houses the Altarpiece of St Anthony, which dates from 1500. The outer panels were painted by Derick Baegert. The Gothic **cloister** is 16C.

Cathedral Museum – *Closed for renovation.*

Regionalmuseum ⊙ Roman and Celtic discoveries from archaeological excavations nearby are exhibited on the ground floor. There is a Department of Prehistory. The first floor is reserved for temporary exhibitions.

Archäologischer Park ⊙ – North of the town, near the site of the digs, a Roman town has been reconstituted, complete with perimeter wall, amphitheatre, bath-house, etc.

ZITTAUER GEBIRGE★

Sachsen
Michelin map 418 N 27-28

This mountain range extends for 20km - 12 miles in a southeast-northwest direction, forming an abrupt barrier towering over the Zittau Basin. A favourite region for rock climbers, mountaineers and winter sports enthusiasts, it is also noted for such spas as Lückendorf, Oybin and Jonsdorf, and the trips that can be made from them. The highest peaks in the range – Lausche (793m - 2 602ft), Hochwald (749m - 2 457ft) and Jonsberg (681m - 2 234ft) – are steep phonolithic (clinkstone) cones extruded among sandstone beds. The juxtaposition of sandstone and limestone heights with the remains of volcanic and igneous eruptions is characteristic of the Zittau mountains.

ROUND TOUR STARTING FROM ZITTAU

26km - 16 miles – allow about 3 hours

Zittau – The depression in which the town lies is hemmed in by the Zittau mountains, the Lausitz range and its eastern foothills, and the region drained by the Neiße river. The town's **Marktplatz** is dominated by the **Rathaus** (1840-1845), which was built after plans originally drawn up by Karl-Friedrich Schinkel (qv) in the Italian Renaissance style.
The **Johanniskirche** (15-19C) has also been restored on the basis of plans by Schinkel. The **church of St. Peter und Paul**, once part of a Franciscan monastery, is a Flamboyant Gothic structure (15C) built on Romanesque foundations. The upper part of the tower is Baroque.

Leave Zittau and take the road signposted to Lückendorf.

The road runs through a delightful, hilly landscape dotted with woods and forests of conifers. The many sandstone outcrops recall the "Swiss Saxony" area *(see SÄCHSISCHE SCHWEIZ).*

At Lückendorf, leave the car in the parking place on the right of the road, opposite the Kurhaus "Karl Lucas".

Oybinblick – After ten minutes' walk, there is a fine view of Lückendorf and, on the far side of the frontier, the nearer reaches of the Czech Republic. Twenty-five yards past the viewpoint, bear left in the direction of Oybinblick, from where there is another splendid view of the Oybin spa and the rock masses of the Großer Wetterstein and the Kelchstein.

At the exit from Jonsdorf, there is a large car park from which there are opportunities for interesting walks and rambles towards the Steinbruchschmiede, the Waldbühne and the Carolafelsen.

West of Jonsdorf rises the bulk of the Lausche, the highest peak in the Zittau range. *Return through Jonsdorf to Zittau.*

ZUGSPITZE★★★

Bayern

Michelin map 419/420 X 16

With a summit at 2 964m - 9 724ft, the Zugspitze is the highest peak on German territory. It is the northwest pillar of the Wetterstein limestone massif, a rocky barrier enclosing the valley of the Loisach. The matchless panorama it offers, added to extensive ski slopes which can be used up to the beginning of summer in the Schneeferner corrie, have meant that the mountain is particularly well served so far as tourist arrangements are concerned. It can be reached by Gletscherbahn (cable car) from Zugspitzplatt station, the terminus of the rack-railway rising from Garmisch, or directly from the Eibsee, or again from Ehrwald with the Tyrolean Zugspitz train.

THE ASCENT ⊙ *(Be sure to wear warm clothing)*

From Garmisch-Partenkirchen – Departure from the Zugspitzbahn station or the terminus at the Eibsee *(qv)*, accessible by road from Garmisch. The whole trip lasts 75min, a 5 000-yd tunnel bored through the mountain ending the rack-railway climb to Zugspilzplatt station. As long as the snow is good (from October to May), the lower part of the corrie known as the Zugspitzplatt offers a skiable area of some 7.5km^2 - almost 3sq miles, equipped with many ski-tow installations.

From the Eibsee – *By rack-railway (see above). Cable car direct to the summit in 10 minutes.*

From the Zugspitzkamm (Austrian Tyrolese side) – *See the current Michelin Green Guide Austria.* From Ehrwald, the Tyrolean cable car (which carries 100 people) takes you from the valley station to the summit in 10 minutes.

The Zugspitze range

★★THE SUMMIT (ZUGSPITZGIPFEL)

The upper terminals of the Gletscherbahn and the Eibsee cable car are on the German side, next to the eastern peak of the mountain where a cross has been planted. After that come the "Münchner Haus" refuge and an observatory. The lookout terrace by the Gipfelbahn is at an altitude of 2 964m - 9 724ft. On the Austrian side is the upper station of the Tyrolean Zugspitzbahn. The crossing from Austria to Germany at the summit has been redesigned and revised.

The **panorama★★★** to the east reveals the forward bastions of the Kaisergebirge, the Dachstein and the Karwendel, the glacial peaks of the Hohe Tauern (Großglockner, Groß Venediger), the High Alps of the Tirol (Zillertal, then Stubai and Ötztal to the south) as well as the Ortler and the Bernina.

Nearer, towards the southwest, the mountains of the Arlberg (Silvretta, Rätikon) stand in front of the Säntis in the Appenzell Alps and, further away to the west and northwest, the Allgäu and Ammergau ranges. To the north, the Bavarian lowlands are visible, together with the Ammersee and Starnbergersee lakes.

ZWICKAU

Sachsen — Population 116 000
Michelin map 418 N 21

The geographic site of Zwickau, on the northern edge of the Erzgebirge ("the ore mountains") has played an all-important role in the town's economic development. Since 1316, mines south of the town have been exploited for copper, iron and silver, but it was above all the discovery in 1470 of richer silver-bearing lodes at Schneeberg, a few miles away, which brought prosperity to the city.

On the cultural level, Zwickau is famous as the birthplace of the composer **Robert Schumann** (11810-1856).

SIGHTS

★ **Dom St. Marien** – This three-aisle hall-church in the Flamboyant Gothic style was built between 1453 and 1565 on an earlier (13C) construction. Successive stages in the work were directed by the architects N Eichhorn, P Harlaß and C Teicher. The Baroque octagonal superstructure crowning the west tower was designed by J Marquardt (1671-1677). The austerity of the cathedral's exterior contrasts vividly with an interior bathed in light, where star-vaulting which appears to leap upwards and outwards from well-spaced slender pillars forms an audacious visual statement.

The jewel of the cathedral's interior decorations is the 1479 **high altar★★** (sometimes on display in the Städt. Museum, see below). The six painted panels of the altarpiece, depicting the life of Mary and the Passion of Christ, were executed by Michael Wolgemut of Nuremberg. Also from the School of Nuremberg is the major work of Michael Heuffner, the 1507 **Holy Sepulchre**★ (between the two south pillars of the chancel). **The Lamentation of Christ★** (1502), carved in lime wood, is by Peter Breuer, a Master of Zwickau. Paul Speck, a sculptor from Freiberg, executed the **pulpit★** and the **baptismal font** (1538).

The decorations embellishing the various parts of the entrance and the rail leading to the pulpit foreshadow already in their richness the style of the Renaissance (note for instance the terracotta medallions with portraits created by J Elsesser in 1560).

Robert-Schumann-Haus ☉ – At No 5, Hauptmarkt.

The birthplace of the composer (1810-1856) was demolished in 1955 due to its dilapidated state, and subsequently rebuilt true to the original. Schumann passed his childhood in Zwickau but left it at the age of 18 when his education was complete. At the age of 46 he died in the health resort of Endenicht (near Bonn). Many documents and articles belonging to Robert Schumann and his wife, the pianist Clara Wieck, can be seen. The historical room is decorated with original furniture. For example, visitors can admire the grand piano on which Clara performed for the first time when she was 9 years old.

Marktplatz – The Marktplatz is surrounded by burghers' houses built at various times between the 15C and the 19C. The **town hall** was restored in neo-Gothic style in 1862, although the Council Chamber (formerly the Jakobskapelle) has preserved its original Gothic lineaments.

The **Gewandhaus**, which has served as a municipal theatre since 1823, unites elements from the Late Gothic and Early Renaissance. It dates from 1525.

Städtisches Museum ☉ – At No 1, Lessingstraße.

Documentation on the history and development of Zwickau, an important collection of minerals and fossils, and sculptures and painting ranging from the 16C to the mid-20C (including, among others, the works of Peter Breuer).

ZWIEFALTEN★★

Baden-Württemberg – Population 2 300
Michelin map 419 V 12

This village, on the Danubian edge of the Swabian Jura, has a remarkable **Baroque church**. Like most Baroque edifices in this region, the building's sober exterior conceals a lavishly decorated interior.

Entering the church, which was built by Johann Michael Fischer between 1739 and 1753, the initial impression is of an extraordinary profusion of luminous colours, a richness and exuberance in the decoration and an extreme virtuosity on the part of the stucco-workers. The eye, intoxicated at first by this deluge of painting, stucco and statues, finally settles on the details: the ceiling paintings devoted to the Virgin Mary, the Feuchtmayer pulpit, the angels and cherubs, in every attitude and from every corner, addressing themselves to the pilgrims.

The choir is separated from the nave by an altar to the Virgin surrounded by superb grilles dating from 1757. The stalls are richly carved and gilded. Before leaving the church, note the most unusual confessionals built to resemble grottoes.

Interior of Zwiefalten church

EXCURSION

★★**The Baroque Churches of Upper Swabia** – *Round tour of 84km - 52 miles – allow 4 hours.*

Between Ulm and Lake Constance (Bodensee), the Upper Swabian Plateau, with its gentle hills and soft light, is scattered with beautiful Baroque churches whose fluid, low-key decorations in pastel tints harmonize perfectly with the landscape.

Obermarchtal – The old **abbey church** ⊙ in this small town, dating from 1686, was one of the first to be completed by the Vorarlberg School *(qv)*. The rigidity of the architecture – a Baroque still undeveloped – is accentuated by the heaviness of the furnishings: only the Wessobrunn *(qv)* stucco-work lightens the overall effect.

★ **Steinhausen** – Designed by Dominikus Zimmermann *(qv)*, master of the Baroque in this part of the country, the abbey church in this hamlet comprises a single nave and a small chancel, both of them oval in shape.

A crown of pillars, which supports the inner shell of the vaulting, marks the limit of a gallery circling the nave. The capitals, cornices and window embrasures, carved and coloured, are adorned with birds and insects or flowers with heavy corollas.

374

Bad Schussenried – A pleasant small town. The old abbey buildings (now a psychiatric hospital) and the **abbey church** owe their sumptuous Baroque appearance to former Premonstratensian abbots. In the church, the upper panels of the intricately decorated choir stalls (1717) are separated by 28 statuettes representing men and women who founded religious orders. The **library★** ☉ has a huge painted ceiling and a sinuous gallery and Rococo balustrade supported by twin columns. The column pedestals are embellished alternately with vivacious cherubim in burlesque costumes and effigies of Fathers of the Church.

★★ **Weingarten** – A dominant position in this town of 23 000 inhabitants is held by the abbey church, with its fine bare sandstone façade. Consecrated in 1724, the church rivals Ottobeuren as the largest Baroque sanctuary in Germany. It is 102m long and 44m wide at the transepts (335 × 144 ft). The west front, framed by two short but elegant towers, is rounded. This, with the construction of a dome on a drum with wide window openings above the transept crossing, betrays an Italian influence transmitted by way of Salzburg.

The interior vistas are amplified by openings pierced through the dividing piers in a manner typical of the Vorarlberg School. The painting and strucco-work, relatively restrained, were entrusted to the masters of the day. Scenes on the vaulting by Comas Damien Asam are full of virtuosity.

Take Bundestraße 30 to return to **Ravensburg** *(qv).*

Unesco World Heritage Sites in Germany

		Michelin map reference
Aachen	Cathedral	417 N 2
Bamberg	Cathedral	419/420 Q 16
Brühl	Schloß Augustusburg and Falkenlust	417 N 4
Goslar	Historic Town and Rammelsberg Mines	418 K 15
Hildesheim	St. Michaeliskirche and Cathedral	416/417/418 J 13
Lorsch	Abbey and Altenmunster	417 R 9
Lübeck	Hanseatic City	415 E 16
Maulbronn	Abbey	419 S 10
Messel	Pit Fossil Site	417 Q 10
Potsdam and Berlin	Palaces and Parks	416/418 I 23-24
Quedlinburg	Old Town, Abbey Church and Castle	418 K 17
Speyer	Cathedral	417/419 S 9
Trier	Roman Monuments, Cathedral and Liebfrauenkirche	417 Q 3
Völklingen	Ironworks	417 S 4
Wies	Pilgrimage Church	419/420 W 16
Würzburg	Residenz	417/419/420 Q 13

Practical
Information

Travelling to Germany

Entry Formalities – Proof of identity in the form of a valid passport, identity card or equivalent is required by foreigners entering Germany. No visa is required for visitors with a valid passport visiting Germany for up to three months from the following countries: Australia, Canada, Ireland, New Zealand, UK, USA.

Customs Regulations – Since the implementation of the single European market in 1993, there are effectively no longer any restrictions on the quantities of goods which can be purchased within the EU by private travellers from its member states. A leaflet entitles *A Guide for Travellers* is available from HM Customs, UK (or telephone ☎ 0181 346 1144 or 0171 620 1313).
Non-residents of EU member states should enquire about customs regulations at their local customs service. US residents can obtain a free publication *Know Before You Go* from the US Customs Service, PO Box 7407, Washington, DC 20044, ☎ 202-927-5580.

Medical treatment – British citizens should apply to the Department of Health and Social Security for an **E111 Form**, which entitles the holder to emergency treatment for accidents or unexpected illness in EU countries. Non-EU residents should check that their private health insurance policy covers them for travel abroad, and if necessary take out supplementary medical insurance with specific overseas coverage.

Disabled travellers – An information service for disabled travellers is provided by BAG, Eupenerstr. 5, 55131 Mainz. A guide to suitable accommodation can be obtained by writing to BAG, "Hilfe für Behinderte", Kirchfeldstr. 149, 40215 Düsseldorf, or to BVB, Alt Krautheimerstr. 17, 74238 Krautheim/Jagst. Disabled motorists should take note that a disabled car badge/sticker does not entitle them to unrestricted parking, as it does in the UK (local disabled residents are granted special parking permits only in exceptional circumstances). Apart from this, Germany is on the whole a well-equipped country for disabled visitors.

By air – Various international airline companies operate regular services to one or all of Germany's international airports (Berlin, Bremen, Dresden, Düsseldorf, Frankfurt/Main, Hamburg, Hannover, Köln/Bonn, Leipzig, München, Münster/Osnabrück, Nürnberg, Saarbrücken, Stuttgart). The international German airline Lufthansa can be contacted at 10 Old Bond Street, London, W1X 4EN, ☎ 0345 737 747, or c/o Dublin Airport, Eire, ☎ 01 844 5544, for information about flights to and in Germany.

By rail and sea – The principal travel routes by rail and sea are from:
London, Victoria Station, via Dover and Ostend (sailing: 4 hours; jetfoil: 1 hour 40min) or Sheerness and Vlissingen (sailing: 9 hours);
London, Liverpool Street Station, via Harwich and the Hook of Holland (sailing: 7-9 hours) or Hamburg (sailing: 20 hours);
London to Brussels via Folkestone and Calais (the Channel Tunnel);
Hull to Rotterdam (sailing: 13 hours).

By road – When driving to the continent the ideal ports of entry for Germany are Hamburg (from Harwich), Rotterdam (from Hull), the Hook of Holland (from Harwich), Zeebrugge (from Hull, Felixstowe and Dover) as well as Ostend (from Dover) and Calais (from Dover, or Folkestone via the Channel Tunnel). From these ports there is a wide choice of routes using motorway or national roads into Germany.

Hamburg to Berlin 289km - 180 miles.
Rotterdam to Berlin via Hanover 721km - 448 miles.
Vlissingen to Munich via Cologne, Bonn, Mainz, Stuttgart and Augsburg 895km - 556 miles.
Ostend to Munich via Regensburg 787km - 489 miles.

Travelling in Germany

By car

Documents – A valid national or international driving licence is required (enquire at your local German Tourist Office to check whether it is necessary to obtain an accompanying translation in German) and third-party insurance cover is compulsory; it is advisable to obtain an International Motor Certificate or Green Card issued by insurance companies.

Driving Regulations – Traffic in Germany drives on the **right**. Drivers in cities in which **trams** operate should be extra careful when looking to check that the road is clear before crossing tramlines. The **maximum speed** permitted in built-up areas is 50kph - 31mph. On the open road the maximum increases to 100kph - 62mph. There is no official limit on motorways (Autobahnen), but drivers are recommended not to exceed 130kph - 81mph. There is a compulsory speed limit of 80kph - 50mph on roads and motorways for vehicles with trailers. In Germany careless or reckless driving is considered a serious offence and fines can be stiff. The maximum limit for **level of alcohol** in the blood is 0.8ml/g.

German **motorways** are toll-free and are well equipped with service areas. These are usually open round the clock and provide the following facilities: petrol, spare parts and accessories, washrooms, toilets, public telephones, refreshments, accommodation and first-aid equipment.

The wearing of **seat belts** is obligatory, in the back as well as in the front of the car. Children under the age of 12, or less than 1.5m - 4ft 11in tall, are required by law to be seated and fastened in a suitable **child car seat**; failure to comply is being fined. It is necessary to carry the regulation **red emergency triangle**, warning other motorists of a breakdown or enforced roadside halt.

In Germany emergency services are always given priority and drivers should pull over to the side of the road.

Emergency telephone numbers:
Police: 110
Fire brigade: 112
Ambulance: 110 (115 in the new Federal states)

Breakdown Service – This is taken care of on main roads and motorways by the ADAC (the Auto Club Europa in the eastern part of the country). On-the-spot repairs are free, only the cost of replacement parts being charged.
ADAC, Am Westpark 8, 81373 München. ☏ 0 89/ 7 67 60, 24-hour information hotline: ☏ 0 89/ 2 22 22.
ADAC Central Breakdown Service, ☏ 01 30/ 81 92 11. The Michelin Red Guide Deutschland lists the numbers to use to contact this service in all big towns.
AVD (Automobil Club von Deutschland), Lyonerstraße 16, 60528 Frankfurt, ☏ 0 69/ 66 06-0.

Petrol – The following grades of petrol (gas) are available in Germany:
Super Plus Bleifrei: Super unleaded (98 octane)
Super verbleit: 4-star leaded
Normal Bleifrei: Standard unleaded (95 octane)
Normal verbleit: 2-star leaded (not very common)
Diesel

Car Hire – Cars may be hired only if the driver is over 23 and has had a driving licence for more than one year.
The major car hire firms (Autohansa, Avis, Europa Service, Hertz, Severin & Co, SU Inter-Rent and Sixt-Budget-Autovermietung) have offices at airports and main stations and in large towns.

Important warning signs:

Anfang	start, beginning	*Links einbiegen*	turn left
Ausfahrt	exit	*Rollsplitt*	gravel hippings
Baustelle	roadworks, site	*Stau*	hold-up, jam
Einbahnstraße	one-way street		
Ende	end	*Unfall*	accident
Einfahrt	entrance	*Umleitung*	deviation
Gefahr/gefährlich	danger	*Verengte Fahrbahn*	road narrows
LKW	heavy lorries, trucks	*Vorrang*	priority
PKW	private cars	*Vorsicht*	attention! Look out!
Rechts einbiegen	turn right		

By train

Tickets and fares – Special offer tickets (**Eurodomino** – for unlimited travel all over Germany, **German Regional Rail Pass** – 5 or 10 days of travel in a particular region within a 31 day period, Bahncards – for frequent travellers to Germany and discount fares for children, students and senior citizens) are available from your local German Rail office or travel agents (such passes should be obtained before you leave home, as they are not available in Germany). Generally speaking, children under 4 travel free and children aged 4-11 years inclusive pay half fare. Motorail bookings are also available. For further information and reservations apply to:

London – German Rail Sales, c/o DER Travel Service Ltd, 18 Conduit Street, London W1R 9TD. ☎ 0171 290 1116, Fax 0171 629 7442.

Dublin – Compass Travel, 34 Lower Abbey Street, Dublin 1, ☎ 01 874 1777.

New York – German Rail, 747 Third Avenue, New York, NY 10017, ☎ 212 308 3100.

Los Angeles – German Rail, 11933 Wilshire Bld, Los Angeles, CA 90025. ☎ 213 479 2772.

Toronto – German Rail, 1290 Bay Street, Toronto, ONT M5R 2C3. ☎ 416 968 3272.

Germany's leading transport organisation, **Deutsche Bahn** (DB) has a network of some 43 000km - 26 700 miles and provides a quick and reliable means of transport. Over 50 cities are served by the InterCity (supplement fare payable) and Inter-Regional (IR) services. The DB InterCity express (ICE) operates on certain high-speed routes (special fares payable).

General information

Money – The unit of currency in Germany is the German Mark (DM), subdivided into 100 Pfennige (Pf). At the time of writing this guide the rate of exchange was 2.21DM to £1 (1.48DM to US$1).

Credit cards (European and Japanese) are increasingly accepted throughout Germany, but it is unwise to rely entirely on them, especially in smaller towns and villages, or out-of-the-way petrol stations (it is advisable to confirm that your credit card will be accepted before making your purchase, even when there is a sign saying that credit cards are accepted). At times it may be more convenient to make a purchase in cash obtained with a Eurocard (Mastercard), Visa or American Express card. **Cash dispensers** at banks such as Citibank, Deutsche Bank and Commerzbank in large towns and cities, or at main railway stations, generally accept Visa and Eurocards.

Banks are open on weekdays from 8.30am to 12.30pm and 2-2.30pm to 4pm (often until 6pm on Thursdays). They are closed on Saturdays, Sundays and public holidays.

Post Offices – Post Offices are open Mondays to Fridays 8am to 6pm and Saturdays from 8am to 12noon. Postal rates at the time of writing this guide were: 1DM (letter up to 20g sent within the EU); 80Pf (postcards sent within the EU); 2DM (aerogrammes).

Post offices with poste restante facilities (postlagernde Sendungen) are shown on the town plans in this guide. Poste restante mail is only issued on presentation of a passport or identity card.

Telephone – Off-peak rates apply at weekends. Phonecards (Telefonkarten) for the increasingly card-operated public call-boxes can be bought from any post office.

The **international dialling code** for Germany is 49, so from the UK one would dial 00 49, followed by the local dialling code (omitting the 0) and the subscriber's number.

Telephoning from Germany overseas, dial 00 followed by the country code (UK: 44, Ireland: 353, USA and Canada: 1, Australia: 61, New Zealand: 64), then the local code (omitting the 0) and the subscriber's number.

Shops – Most shops are normally open between 9am and 6-6.30pm Mondays to Fridays and on Saturday mornings from 9am to 1-2pm. On the first Saturday in the month (Langer Samstag) shops stay open until 4-6pm (although butchers and bakers still close at 1pm). Some shops in town centres stay open until 8.30pm on Thursdays. In smaller towns and rural areas, shops are often closed on Wednesday afternoons.

Public holidays – 1 January, 6 January (in Baden-Württemberg and Bayern only), Good Friday, Easter Day, Easter Monday, 1 May, Ascension Day, Whit Sunday and Monday, Corpus Christi (in Baden-Württemberg, Bayern, Hessen, Nordrhein-Westfalen, Rheinland-Pfalz, Saarland and those new Federal states in towns with a predominantly Roman Catholic population), 15 August (in Saarland and Bayern only), 3 October (Day of German Unity), 31 October (Reformation Day celebrated in the new Federal states only), 1 November (in Baden-Württemberg, Bayern, Nordrhein-Westfalen, Rheinland-Pfalz, Saarland and those new Federal states in towns with a predominantly Roman Catholic population), Buß- und Bettag (Day of Repentance and Prayer: usually third Wednesday in November, observed in Sachsen only) and 25 and 26 December.

Accommodation

Germany offers a wide range of traditional (Hotel, Gasthof, Gasthaus) accommodation. Lists of local hotels, pensions and boarding houses can be obtained at any tourist information centre.

Hotels – The **Michelin Red Guide Deutschland** is revised annually and gives a selection of hotels and restaurants based on impartial inspectors' reports, ranging from a modest inn to the most luxurious grand hotel, or from the centrally situated modern establishment catering for the needs of today's business person to the secluded retreat.

Places listed in the Red Guide are underlined in red on the Michelin map series at a scale of 1:300 000 (maps 415, 416, 417, 418, 419 and 420).

German Hotel Reservation Service (Allgemeine Deutsche Zimmerreservierung) – Reservations in all hotels, inns and pensions can easily be made through this German reservation service.

ADZ (Allgemeine Deutsche Zimmerreservierung), Corneliusstraße 34, 60325 Frankfurt am Main, ☎ 0 69/ 74 07 67, Fax 0 69/ 75 10 56. Reservations should be made 4 or 5 weeks in advance (although this period may be reduced in urgent cases). A deposit will be required. English spoken.

HRS Hotel Reservation Service, Drususgasse 7-11, 50667 Köln, ☎ 02 21/ 2 07 70, Fax 02 21/ 2 07 76 66. Immediate reservation. English spoken.

Bed and Breakfast – The sign **Zimmer Frei** outside private houses indicates that guest rooms are available. Final prices quoted should include tax, service charges etc. The DZT (Deutsche Zentrale für Tourismus) produces a Bed and Breakfast brochure with further information (address lists) and lists of cities and towns in which bookings may be made through local tourist offices during office hours, Mondays to Fridays.

Camping and Caravanning – Numerous camp sites are available to tourists. To obtain a full list and discover the amenities offered by each site, write to:
– ADAC, Am Westpark 8, 81373 München, ☎ 0 89/ 7 67 60.
– Deutscher Camping-Club (DCC), Mandlstraße 28, 80802 München, ☎ 0 89/ 3 80 14 20.

Youth Hostels (Jugendherbergen – JH) – German houth hostels are open to all young people who are members of the German Youth Hostel Association or of another youth hostel association affiliated to the International Youth Hostel Federation. Priority is given to young people under 26. The stay may not exceed three consecutive nights at any one youth hostel. For lists of all youth hostels apply to the German National Tourist Office. To reserve in advance write to:
Deutsches Jugendherbergswerk, Hauptverband, Bismarckstraße 8, 32756 Detmold, ☎ 0 52 31/ 7 40 10.

Holiday villages, flats and bungalows – Details from the German National Tourist Office (DZT). Details of holidays "on the farm" (Urlaub auf dem Bauernhof) or in stately homes (Gast im Schloß) are also available from the DZT.

Where to eat – The current **Michelin Red Guide Deutschland** lists a large selection of restaurants in which tourists can taste for themselves the best and most original specialities of each German region (see the section headed Food and Drink in the Introduction).

Generally speaking, hotel breakfasts are substantial. Notwithstanding that familiar sinking feeling at midday can easily be assuaged at an "Imbiß", a small fast-food concern to be found everywhere, in town, on motorways or at the roadside. These offer the traditional snack of **Bratwurst** (grilled sausage), sometimes accompanied by a potato salad or chips, and usually washed down with beer (often on draught – Bier vom Faß).

One of the most delightful of German eating habits – Kaffee und Kuchen – is observed mid-afternoon in one of the many coffee houses to be found nationwide. These veritable havens for the weary traveller always smell delicious and customarily have a large selection of revitalising cakes, such as Schwarzwälder Kirschtorte (Black Forest cherry cake), unctuous Käsekuchen (cheesecake) or delicious fruit tarts. The coffee served with these pastries is always accompanied by cream (Kaffeesahne), and the pastries themselves are frequently adorned with a generous dollop of whipped cream (Schlagsahne).

The Weinstube (wine cellar or wine bar) is an agreeable place to spend an afternoon or evening, with a pleasant atmosphere, where the best wines can be bought and tasted by the glass.

*The **current Michelin Red Guide Deutschland** offers*
a selection of pleasant hotels in convenient locations.
Each entry specifies the facilities available
(gardens, tennis courts, swimming pool, beach facilities)
and the annual opening and closing dates.
There is also a selection of establishments recommended for their cuisine -
well-prepared meals at moderate prices; stars for good cooking.

Tourist information

German National Tourist Offices (DZT)

Chicago: German National Tourist Office, 104 S Michigan Avenue, Suite 600, Chicago, IL 60603-5978, ☎ 312-782-8557, Fax 312-782-3892;

London: German National Tourist Office, Nightingale House, 65 Curzon Street, London W1Y 7PE, ☎ 0171 495 3990, Fax 0171 495 6129;

Los Angeles: German National Tourist Office, 11766 Wilshire Boulevard, Suite 750, Los Angeles, CA 90071, ☎ 310-575-9799, Fax 310-575-1565;

New York: German National Tourist Office, Chanin Building, 122 East 42nd Street, 52nd floor, New York, NY 10168-0072, ☎ 212-661-7200, Fax 212-661-7174;

Sydney: German National Tourist Office, Lufthansa House, 9th floor, 143 Macquarie Street, Sydney, NSW 2000, ☎ 012-367-3890, Fax 012-367-3895;

Toronto: German National Tourist Office, 175 Bloor Street East, North Tower, 6th floor, Toronto, ONT M4W 3R8, ☎ 416-968-1570, Fax 416-968-1986.

Regional Tourist Offices in Germany

Allgäu – Bavarian Swabia: Tourismusverband Allgäu/Bayrisch-Schwaben e.V., Fuggerstraße 9, 86150 Augsburg, ☎ 08 21/ 3 33 35, Fax 08 21/ 3 83 31.

Baden-Württemberg: Landesfremdenverkehrsverband Baden-Württemberg e.V., Esslinger Straße 8, 70182 Stuttgart, ☎ 07 11/ 23 85 80, Fax 07 11/ 2 38 58 99.

Bavaria: Landesfremdenverkehrsverband Bayern e.V., Prinzregentenstraße 18, 80538 München, ☎ 0 89/ 2 12 39 70, Fax 0 89/ 29 35 82.

Berlin: Verkehrsamt Berlin, Martin-Luther-Straße 105, 10820 Berlin, ☎ 0 30/ 2 12 34, Fax 0 30/ 21 23 25 20.

Black Forest: Fremdenverkehrsverband Schwarzwald e.V., Bertoldstraße 45, Postfach 16 60, 79098 Freiburg, ☎ 07 61/ 3 13 17-18, Fax 07 61/ 3 60 21.

Brandenburg: Landesfremdenverkehrsverband Brandenburg e.V., Friedrich-Ebert-Straße 115, 14467 Potsdam, ☎ 03 31/ 29 56 32, Fax 03 31/ 29 66 83.

East Bavaria: Fremdenverkehrsverband Ostbayern e.V., Landshuter Straße 13, 93047 Regensburg, ☎ 09 41/ 58 53 90, Fax 09 41/ 5 85 39 39.

Franconia: Fremdenverkehrsverband Franken e.V., Am Plärrer 14, 90429 Nürnberg, ☎ 09 11/ 26 42 02, Fax 09 11/ 27 05 47.

Hamburg: Tourismus-Zentrale Hamburg GmbH, Burchardstraße 14, Postfach 10 22 49, 20015 Hamburg, ☎ 0 40/ 30 05 10, Fax 0 40/ 30 05 12 54.

Harz: Harzer Verkehrsverband e.V., Marktstraße 45, 38640 Goslar, ☎ 0 53 21/ 2 00 31, Fax 0 53 21/ 34 04 66.

Hessen: Hessischer Fremdenverkehrsverband e.V., Abraham-Lincoln-Straße 38-42, 65189 Wiesbaden, ☎ 06 11/ 77 88 00, Fax 06 11/ 78 80 40.

Lake Constance – Upper Swabia: Fremdenverkehrsverband Bodensee-Oberschwaben e.V., Schützenstraße 8, 78462 Konstanz, ☎ 0 75 31/ 2 22 32, Fax 0 75 31/ 1 64 43.

Lüneburg Heath: Fremdenverkehrsverband Lüneburger Heide e.V., Lünerweg 22, 21335 Lüneburg, ☎ 0 41 31/ 5 20 63, Fax 0 41 31/ 5 24 42.

Mecklenburg – West Pomerania: Landesfremdenverkehrsverband Mecklenburg-Vorpommern e.V., Hauptgeschäftsstelle, Platz der Freundschaft 1, 18059 Rostock, ☎ 03 81/ 44 84 26, Fax 03 81/ 44 84 24.

Munich – Upper Bavaria: Fremdenverkehrsverband München-Oberbayern e.V., Sonnenstraße 10, 80331 München, ☎ 0 89/ 59 73 47, Fax 0 89/ 59 31 87.

Neckar Valley and Swabia: Touristikverband Neckarland-Schwaben e.V., Lohtorstraße 21, 74072 Heilbronn, ☎ 0 71 31/ 7 85 20, Fax 0 71 31/ 78 52 30.

North Sea – Lower Saxony – Bremen: Fremdenverkehrsverband Nordsee-Niedersachsen-Bremen e.V., Bahnhofstraße 19-20, 26122 Oldenburg, ☎ 04 41/ 92 17 10, Fax 04 41/ 9 21 71 90.

Rhineland: Landesverkehrsverband Rheinland e.V., Rheinallee 69, 53173 Bonn, ☎ 02 28/ 36 29 21-22, Fax 02 28/ 36 39 29.

Rhineland Palatinate: Fremdenverkehrs- und Heilbäderverband Rheinland-Pfalz e.V., Löhrstraße 103-105, 56068 Koblenz, ☎ 02 61/ 3 10 79, Fax 02 61/ 1 83 43.

Saar: Fremdenverkehrsverband Saarland e.V., Dudweiler Straße 53, 66111 Saarbrücken, ☎ 06 81/ 3 53 76 and 3 70 88, Fax 06 81/ 3 58 41.

Sauerland: Fremdenverkehrsverband Sauerland e.V., Brückenplatz 14, Le-Puy-Str. 23d, 59872 Meschede, ☎ 02 91/ 14 75, Fax 02 91/ 14 79.

Saxony: Landesfremdenverkehrsverband Sachsen e.V., Friedrichstraße 24, 01067 Dresden, ☎ 03 51/ 4 96 97 03, Fax 03 51/ 4 96 93 06.

Saxony – Anhalt: Landesfremdenverkehrsverband Sachsen-Anhalt e.V., Trothaer Straße 9 h, 06118 Halle/Saale, ☎ 03 45/ 34 00 86, Fax 03 45/ 34 00 97.

Schleswig-Holstein: Fremdenverkehrsverband Schleswig-Holstein e.V., Niemannsweg 31, 24105 Kiel, ☎ 04 31/ 5 60 00, Fax 04 31/ 56 98 10.

Thuringia: Thüringer Landesfremdenverkehrsverband e.V., Stauffenbergallee 18a, 99085 Erfurt, ☎ 03 61/ 540 22 34, Fax 03 61/ 6 46 14 75.

Weser Valley: Fremdenverkehrsverband Weserbergland-Mittelweser e.V., Inselstraße 3, 31787 Hameln, ☎ 0 51 51/ 2 45 66, Fax 0 51 51/ 2 68 32.

Westphalia: Landesverkehrsverband Westfalen e.V., Friedensplatz 3, 44135 Dortmund, ☎ 02 31/52 75 06-07, Fax 02 31/52 45 08.

Discovering Germany

If the traditional summer holiday tour allows visitors to discover the richness and beauty of Germany under the best possible conditions (pleasant climate, plenty to see and do), there are many other ways to appreciate the warmth of German hospitality and explore the charms of this great country.

Carnival Time – The three days before Ash Wednesday unite a people traditionally calm and sober in an extended bout of boisterous merry-making, a sort of non-stop national street party. The carnival is at its liveliest in Cologne, Düsseldorf, Mainz, Munich and the towns of the Black Forest.
Cologne Carnival: details from the Verkehrsamt der Stadt Köln, Unter Fettenhennen 19, 50667 Köln, ☎ 02 21/ 2 21 33 45.
Munich Carnival: details from Fremdenverkehrsamt München, Sendlinger Straße, 80331 München, ☎ 0 89/ 2 39 11.
In the Rhineland region, the Thursday of the week preceding Ash Wednesday is known as "Fetter Donnerstag" or "Schmutziger Donnerstag", a day on which no man is safe as women seize the initiative (for example, by cutting the end off any tie seen being worn in public)!

Cruises

Rivers Rhine, Moselle, Main and Elbe – For Rhine cruises from Cologne to Mainz, and cruises on the Moselle, Main, and the Elbe from Hamburg to Dresden, relevant details can be obtained from Köln-Düsseldorfer, Frankenwerft 15, 50667 Köln, information and bookings ☎ 02 21/ 2 08 82 88, Fax 02 21/ 2 08 82 31.
At Dresden it is possible to prolong the trip as far as Prague. Ask for the dates.

North Sea – For details of cruises from Cuxhaven, or from Hamburg to Helgoland, or from Travemünde to Warnemünde/Rostock or to Rødbyhavn (Denmark), contact: Seetouristik, Postfach 26 26, 24916 Flensburg, ☎ 0 40/ 40 29 29 or 04 61/ 8 64 17, Fax 04 61/ 8 64 64.

Baltic Sea – Connections between Stralsund, Rügen, the Isle of Usedom and Poland are all operated by Die "Weiße Flotte GmbH", Fährstr. 16, 18439 Stralsund, ☎ 0 38 31/ 2 68 10, Fax 0 38 31/ 26 81 29.

Rambling – Those who long for peaceful holidays will delight in the countrywide network of footpaths and ramblers' routes, all of them clearly signposted. Whether it is a matter of a three-day hike or a simple walk around a chosen area, many maps are available to help you prepare an itinerary. KOMPASS maps and guides cover the most popular tourist regions.

Städt. Verkehrsbüro, Rottweil

The Fools Procession, Rottweil

The Spa Establishment, Baden-Baden

Spas and Hydrotherapy – Apart from the towns traditionally known for their cures (water or mud), a series of medium-altitude health resorts, and seaside thermal establishments, Germany offers a wide choice of spas specializing in what is known as the Kneipp System. Details of resorts specialising in this system can be obtained from the Kneippbund, Adolf-Scholz-Allee 6, 86825 Bad Wörishofen, ☎ 0 82 47/ 3 00 20.

The principal German spa towns include: Baden-Baden, Badenweiler, Bad Brückenau, Bad Doberan, Bad Düben, Bad Ems, Bad Homburg, Bad Kissingen, Bad Kreuznach, Bad Langensalza, Bad Orb, Bad Pyrmont, St. Peter-Ording, Bad Reichenall, Bad Tölz, Bad Vilbel, Bad Wiessee, Bad Wildbad and Bad Wildungen.

The best-known climatic health resorts are: Bayrischzell, Bad Bergzabern, Braunlage, Freudenstadt, Garmisch-Partenkirchen, Hahnenklee, Bad Herrenalb, Königstein im Taunus, Isny, Oberstdorf, Rheinsberg, Rottach-Egern, St. Blasien, Schönwald, Bad Suderode and Titisee-Neustadt.

Coastal health resorts include (North Sea coast): Borkum, Helgoland, Juist, Norderney, Wangerooge, Westerland on Sylt, and Wyk on Föhr; and (Baltic coast): Damp, Grömitz, Heiligenhafen, Scharbeutz-Haffkrug, Timmendorfer-Strand and Heiligendamm.

> Sebastian Kneipp (1821-1897), curate and then priest at Wörishofen, developed the set of treatments named after him following an illness. His cure system combines baths, an alternation of warm and cold showers and a "healthy" lifestyle, involving a strictly controlled diet, plenty of walking and herbal medication.

Details of these and other health resorts available from: Deutsche Bäderverband, Schumannstraße 111, 53113 Bonn, ☎ 02 28/ 26 20 10, Fax 02 28/ 21 55 24.

Tourist routes – Very clearly signposted, these "thematic" itineraries provide an original means of crisscrossing the country and getting to know it better. They include:

German Holiday Route (Deutsche Ferienstraße), which links the Baltic Sea (Puttgarden) with the Alps (Berchtesgaden);

German Alpine Road (Deutsche Alpenstraße – described in this guide), from Lindau to Berchtesgaden;

German Wine Road (Deutsche Weinstraße), from Bockeheim to Schweigen;

Castle Road (Burgenstraße), from Mannheim to Nuremberg;

Romantic Road (Romantische Straße), from Würzburg to Füssen;

Route of Emperors and Kings (Straße der Kaiser und Könige), from Frankfurt to Regensburg;

Fairy-tale Road (Deutsche Märchenstraße), from Hanau (east of Frankfurt) to Bremen;

Upper Swabian Baroque Route (Oberschwäbische Barockstraße), from Ulm to Weingarten;

Romanesque Road (Straße der Romanik), in Sachsen-Anhalt.

On the Michelin maps at a scale of 1:300 000, these tourist itineraries are indicated by a black dotted line running beside the road.

Winter Sports – In Germany there is a wide variety of ski resorts, all well equipped and easy to reach. Most centres also offer swimming pools and skating rinks.

RESORTS	Michelin map no and map co-ordinates		Minimum and maximum altitude (in metres) of resort	Cable cars and chair-lifts	Ski lifts	Extent (in km) of runs for downhill skiing	Extent (in km) of trails for cross-country skiing	Beds available
Allgäu/Alps								
OBERSTAUFEN	419	X 14	800/1 700	3	34	30	120	7 000
IMMENSTADT	419	X 14	730/1 750	3	12	40	67	3 750
RETTENBERG/ KRANZEGG	419	X 14	850/1 700		15	30	30	1 200
HINDELANG/ OBERJOCH	419	X 15	850/1 600	1	16	32	45	7 000
FISCHEN im ALLGÄU	419	X 14	760/1 665	5	26	50	100	5 214
OBERSTDORF	419	X 14	843/2 224	7	19	42	80	16 700
FÜSSEN	419	X 16	800/1 800	3	7	15	60	5 500
PFRONTEN	419	X 15	900/1 840	2	14	25	65	5 400
NESSELWANG	419	X 15	860/1 600	2	6	8	40	3 000
GARMISCH-PARTENKIRCHEN	419	X 17	720/2 720	15	39	73	32	10 045
BAD TÖLZ	419	W 18	700/1 237	1	4	8	75	4 400
MITTENWALD	419	X 17	920/2 244	1	7	22	40	5 835
BAD WIESSEE	420	W 19	735/1 700	2	18	15	95	14 000
GMUND	420	W 19						
KREUTH	420	X 19						
ROTTACH-EGERN	420	W 19						
TEGERNSEE	420	W 19						
SCHLIERSEE-SPITZING	420	WX 19	800/1 700	4	15	30	30	4 000
INZELL	420	W 22	700/900		5	5	40	5 500
REIT IM WINKL	420	W 21	700/1 850	3	20	50	80	4 800
RUHPOLDING	420	W 21	690/1670	4	16	35	60	6 400
BAD REICHENHALL	420	W 22	470/1 800	4	1	11	18	10 000
BERCHTESGADEN	420	X 22	540/1 800	5	24	40	57	25 200
Bavarian Forest								
BISCHOFSMAIS	420	T 23	720/1 100		5	3	60	2 500
BODENMAIS	420	S 23	600/1 456		7	0	65	4 900
GRAFENAU	420	T 24	700		2	1	65	3 000
ZWIESEL	420	S 23	560/1 456		9	10	120	3 000
Black Forest								
BAIERSBRONN	419	U 9	560/1 000		9	4	62	12 000
FELDBERG	419	W 8	900/1 493		17	42	45	4 200
FREUDENSTADT	419	U 9	700/1 000		4	2	120	6 600
HINTERZARTEN	419	W 8	900/1 200		3	2	15	3 000
SCHÖNWALD	419	V 8	950/1 150		4	2	42	3 800
St.-GEORGEN im SCHWARZWALD	419	V 9	800/1 050		5		33	1 500
TITISEE-NEUSTADT	419	W 8	850/1050		4	2	54	4 700
TODTNAU	419	W 7	660/1 388		21	40	60	4 500
TODTMOOS	419	W 8	800/1 263		4	7	27	4 000
Harz								
ALTENAU	418	K 15	420/930		5	1	30	6 500
BAD HARZBURG	418	K 15	300/900		3	2	40	4 500
BAD LAUTERBERG	418	L 15	500/700		1		42	4 000
BAD SACHSA	418	L 15	450/700		3	4	48	3 500
BRAUNLAGE	418	K 15	560/980		9	12	46	7 900
HAHNENKLEE	418	K 15	600/730		2	4	21	5 600
St-ANDREASBERG	418	K 15	600/900		9	8	42	2 700

Calendar of events

1 January

Garmisch-Partenkirchen .... New Year's Day International Ski Jump

Last 10 days in January

Berlin .... International Green Week

Sunday before Shrove Tuesday

Munich .... "München narrisch" Carnival

Shrove Monday

Cologne, Düsseldorf, Mainz ...... Rosenmontagszug: procession and street carnival

Shrove Monday and Tuesday

Rottweil .... Narrensprung Carnival: elaborate traditional costumes and expressive wooden masks; Dance of the Fools

Maundy Thursday to Easter Monday

Bautzen .... Traditional Sorbian Easter Egg Market

Mid-April to the end of June

Karlsruhe .... European Cultural Festival: theatre, music and exhibitions

30 April to 1 May

Towns in the Harz region .... Walpurgisnacht: Witches' Sabbath Festival

Marburg .... Maifeier: Students' Festival during which town and gown bury the hatchet

One Sunday a month from Easter to September

Rothenburg ob der Tauber .... Historischer Schäfertanz: Historical Shepherds' Dance

End of April to end of May

Wiesbaden .... International May Festival: theatre, music

Mid-May to mid-September every Sunday at 12 noon

Hamelin .... Rattenfängerspiel: pageant retracing the legend of the Pied Piper

Friday after Ascension

Weingarten .... Blutritt: mounted cavalcade in honour of the Holy Blood

May to June

Schwetzingen .... Music Festival

End of May to beginning of June

Dresden .... Music Festival

Whit Sunday

Schwäbisch Hall .... Kuchen und Brunnenfest: dance of the salt-workers in traditional costume

Whit Monday

Kötzting .... Pfingstritt: mounted cavalcade

Whit Tuesday

Deidesheim .... Historische Geißbockversteigerung: auctioning of a goat; period costumes; folk dancing; local fair

Last Saturday in May
Merfelder Bruch........................ Roundup of wild horses, rodeo

Whit weekend (Friday, Saturday, Sunday), 2nd Sunday in July, 1st Sunday in September
Rothenburg ob der Tauber........ Meistertrunk: performance of the legend
of the "Long Drink" (period costumes, local festival)

Corpus Christi
Munich..................................... Solemn procession through the decorated town
Cologne.................................... Procession of boats along the Rhine
Hüfingen .... Procession through flower-decked street

14 days after Whitsun, from Friday to Monday
Schwalmstadt .... Salatkirmes: Salad Fair commemorating the
introduction of the potato to the Hessen region;
traditional local costumes

Mid-June to mid-August
Schwäbisch Hall .... Open-air theatre performances

1st weekend in June and September, 2nd weekend in July
Heidelberg .... Castle illuminations; firework displays

June to August
Chorin .... Summer Music Festival
Feuchtwangen........................... Cloister Festival (theatre)
Bad Hersfeld .... Festival of Drama and Opera in the abbey ruins

Last week in June
Kiel .... Kiel Week: international sailing regatta;
local festival

End of June to mid July (every 4 years, next time: 1997)
Landshut .... Fürstenhochzeit (Landshut Royal Marriage):
historical pageant in period costume

July to August
Various places
in Schleswig-Holstein .... Schleswig-Holstein Music Festival

1st Sunday in July
Hannover................................... Archers' Festival: procession of archers

Mid July to mid-August
Pommersfelden.......................... Collegium musicum: musical concerts

Mid-July (every 4 or 5 years, next time: 1998 or 1999)
Ulm .... Fischerstechen (Fishermen's Festival)

2nd weekend in July
Speyer .... Bretzel Festival

3rd weekend in July
Dinkelsbühl............................... Kinderzeche: commemorating the saving of the
town by a deputation of children (historical costumes)

Penultimate Monday in July
Ulm .... Schwörmontag: river procession on the Danube

3rd Sunday and Monday in July
Kaufbeuren .... Tänzelfest: historical procession by schoolchildren

Last Saturday in July and 1st Sunday in August
Hitzacker................................... Music Festival

End of July to end of August
Bayreuth .... Bayreuther Festspiele: Wagner Opera Festival

August to September
Erfurt.. Festival on the cathedral steps

2nd Saturday in August

Koblenz...................................... Der Rhein in Flammen (The Rhine Ablaze): illumination of the river valley from Braubach to Koblenz

Constance .... Seenachtsfest: evening lakeside festival

2nd week in August

Furth im Wald........................... Der Drachenstich (Death of the Dragon): pageant of the legend of St George, in period costumes

Saturday after 24 August

Markgröningen .... Schäferlauf: shepherds' race (barefoot over a field of stubble)

2nd and 3rd Sunday in September

Bad Dürkheim............................ Dürkheimer Wurstmarkt: sausage fair and major wine fair

3rd Saturday in September

St. Goar...................................... Der Rhein in Flammen: illumination of the Rhine and its castles

End of September to beginning of October

Bad Cannstatt............................ Cannstatter Volksfest: popular local fair (with fairground)

Munich....................................... October Beer Festival

1st and 2nd weekend in October

Neustadt an der Weinstraße..... Weinlesefest: Wine Fair and election of the Queen of Wine

1st half of October

Frankfurt am Main .... Frankfurt Book Fair

3rd weekend in October

Donaueschingen......................... Donaueschingen Contemporary Music Festival

Last 10 days in October

Bremen .... Bremer Freimarket: largest popular fair in northern Germany

6 November (St Leonard)

Bad Tölz..................................... Leonhardifahrt: prior to a Mass in honour of St Leonard, gaily decorated horse-drawn carts process through town to the church

Sunday after 6 November

Benediktbeuern .... Leonhardifahrt: similar celebration to that at Bad Tölz

10 November

Düsseldorf.................................. Martinszug: children's torchlit procession through old town; commemorative dividing of cloak in front of Rathaus

Friday before Advent to 24 December

Nuremberg.................................. Christkindlesmarkt: Christmas market (Christmas tree decorations and gifts); seasonal performances by children

Sundays in Advent

Dresden...................................... Striezelmarkt: oldest Christmas market in Germany

24 December

Villingen-Schwenningen............. Kuhreihenblasen: concert of cowherds' horns

24 December and New Year's Eve

Berchtesgaden .... Weihnachtsschießen und Neujahrsschießen: Christmas and New Year shooting matches

Admission times and charges

As admission times and charges are subject to modification due to increases in the cost of living, the information printed below is for guidance only.

The following list details the opening times and charges (if any) and other relevant information concerning all sights in the descriptive part of this Guide accompanied by the symbol ⊙. The entries below are given in the same order as in the alphabetical section of the Guide.

Normally, especially in the case of large towns, the telephone number and/or address of the local tourist office (Fremdenverkehrsamt), indicated by the symbol ⊟, is given. Generally most efficient, these organizations are able to help passing tourists find accommodation (hotel, pension, camp site, youth hostel) as well as providing information on exhibitions, performances, guided tours and other items of interest locally.

The prices quoted apply to individual adults, but many places offer reduced rates for children, OAPs, and some a discount family ticket.

The times are those of opening and closure, but remember that some places do not admit visitors during the last hour or half hour.

NB In German alphabetical order, adopted below, ä = ae, ö = oe and ü = ue.

A

AACHEN
⊟ Friedrich-Wilhelm-Platz ☎ 02 41/ 1 80 29 60

Dom und Domschatzkammer – Open 7am to 7pm. During the reorganisation of the treasury, the major exhibits are on display in the cathedral and can be seen as part of a guided tour. 5DM. ☎ 02 41/ 4 77 09 27.

Rathaus – Open daily 10am to 1pm and 2pm to 5pm. Closed 25 December and during special exhibitions. 2DM. ☎ 02 41/ 1 80 29 60.

Couven-Museum – Open 10am to 5pm. Closed Mondays and public holidays. 2DM. ☎ 02 41/ 4 32 44 21.

Suermondt-Ludwig-Museum – Open Tuesdays, Thursdays and Fridays 11am to 7pm, Wednesdays 11am to 9pm, weekends and public holidays 11am to 5pm. Closed Mondays, 1 January, during the Carnival, 24 to 26 and 31 December. 6DM. ☎ 02 41/ 47 98 00.

Ludwig Forum für Internationale Kunst – Open Tuesdays and Thursdays 10am to 5pm, Wednesdays and Fridays 10am to 8pm, weekends 11am to 5pm. Closed Mondays and public holidays. 6DM. ☎ 02 41/ 18 07-0.

Deutsche ALPENSTRASSE

Wendelstein funicular railway – From the valley station at Brannenburg May to October hourly departures 9am to 3pm, last trip down from the mountain station at 5pm; December to April 9am to 2pm, last trip down at 4pm. Journey time: 25min. Enquire about closure during November and December. Rtn fare 38DM. ☎ 0 80 34/ 3 08-1 11.

ALTENBURG
⊟ Weibermarkt 17 ☎ 0 34 47/ 31 11 45

Schloß- und Spielkartenmuseum – Open 9am to 5pm (last admissions 30min before closing). Closed Mondays and 1 January. 2.50DM. ☎ 0 34 47/ 31 51 93.

Lindenau-Museum – Open 10am to 6pm. Closed Mondays, and from 1pm on 24 and 31 December. 3DM. ☎ 0 34 47/ 25 10.

AMORBACH
⊟ Marktplatz ☎ 0 93 73/ 47 78

See ODENWALD

ANNABERG-BUCHHOLZ

Technisches Museum Frohnauer Hammer – Guided tour daily 9am to 11.45am and 1pm to 4pm. Closed 1 January, 24, 25 and 31 December. 4DM. ☎ 0 37 33/ 2 20 00.

ANNWEILER

See PFALZ AM RHEIN

ANSBACH

Residenz – Guided tour (1 hour) April to September at 9am, 10am, 11am, 2pm, 3pm and 4pm; October to March at 10am, 11am, 2pm and 3pm. Closed Mondays, 1 January, Shrove Tuesday, 1 November, 24, 25 and 31 December. 3DM, children under 16 free. ☎ 09 81/ 31 86.

ARNSTADT

🅸 Markt 3 ☎ 0 36 28/ 20 49

See ERFURT

AROLSEN

🅸 Prof.-Klapp-Str. 14 ☎ 0 56 91/ 20 30

See WALDECKER BERGLAND

ASCHAFFENBURG

🅸 Schloßplatz 1 ☎ 0 60 21/ 39 58 00

Schloß Johannisburg: Staatsgalerie – Open April to September 9am to 11.30am and 1pm to 4.30pm; October to March 10am to 11.30am and 1pm to 3.30pm. Closed Mondays. 3.50DM. ☎ 0 60 21/ 33 04 46.

Städtisches Schloßmuseum – Open April to October 9am to 12noon and 1pm to 5pm; November to March 10am to 12noon and 1pm to 4pm. Closed Mondays, 1 January, 1 November, 24 and 25 December. 3.50DM. ☎ 0 60 21/ 33 04 46.

ATTENDORN

🅸 Kölner Str. 12a ☎ 0 27 22/ 6 42 29

See SAUERLAND

AUGSBURG

🅸 Bahnhofstr. 7 ☎ 08 21/ 50 20 70

Städtische Kunstsammlungen – Open May to September 10am to 1pm and 2pm to 5pm, weekends 11am to 1pm and 2pm to 5pm; October to April 10am to 12noon, weekends 10am to 1pm and 2pm to 4pm. Closed Mondays, Sunday before Lent, Shrove Tuesday, Good Friday, 1 May, 24, 25 and 31 December. 4DM (free on 1st Sunday of month). ☎ 08 21/ 3 24 21 71.

Maximilianmuseum – Open May to September 10am to 1pm and 2pm to 5pm, weekends 11am to 1pm and 2pm to 5pm; October to April 10am to 1pm, weekends 11am to 1pm and 2pm to 4pm. Closed on same days as Städtische Kunstsammlungen. 4DM (free on 1st Sunday in month). ☎ 08 21/ 3 24 21 71.

Mozarthaus – Open 10am to 1pm and 2pm to 5pm (October to April mornings only), weekends 11am to 1pm. 2.50DM. ☎ 08 21/ 3 24 21 96.

Staatsgalerie in der Kunsthalle – Open May to September Tuesdays to Fridays 10am to 1pm and 2pm to 5pm, weekends 11am to 1pm and 2pm to 5pm; October to April Tuesdays to Fridays 10am to 1pm, weekends 11am to 1pm and 2pm to 4pm. Closed Mondays. 4DM (free on 1st Sunday of month). ☎ 08 21/ 3 24 21 71.

AUGUSTUSBURG

🅸 Marienberger Str. 29b ☎ 03 72 91/ 65 51

See CHEMNITZ

B

BADEN-BADEN

🅸 Augustaplatz 8 ☎ 0 72 21/ 27 52 00

Neues Schloß – Guided tour (45min) May to September at 3pm (minimum group size: 10). Closed weekends and public holidays. 4DM. ☎ 0 72 21/ 2 55 93.

Römische Badruinen – Open from Good Friday to 31 October daily 10am to 12noon and 1.30pm to 4pm. 2.50DM. ☎ 0 72 21/ 27 59 40.

BADENWEILER

🅸 Ernst-Eisenlohr-Str 4 ☎ 0 76 32/ 7 21 10

Excursions

Schloß Bürgeln – Guided tour (40min) March to November Wednesdasy to Mondays at 11am, 2pm, 3pm, 4pm and 5pm. 5DM. ☎ 0 76 26/ 2 37.

BAMBERG

🛈 Geyerswörthstr 3 ☎ 09 51/ 87 11 61

Diözesanmuseum – Open 10am to 5pm. Closed Mondays, Good Friday, 24 and 25 December. 2DM. ☎ 09 51/ 502-325.

Neue Residenz – Guided tour (1 hour) April to September daily 9am to 12noon and 1.30pm to 5pm; October to March until 4pm (last admissions 30min before closing). Closed 1 January, Shrove Tuesday, 1 November, 24, 25 and 26 December. 3DM. ☎ 09 51/ 5 63 51.

E.-T.-A.-Hoffmann-Haus – Open May to October 4pm to 6pm, weekends and public holidays 10am to 12noon. Closed Mondays. 2DM.

Excursion

Schloß Pommersfelden – Guided tour (30-60min) April to October at 9am, 10am, 11am, 2pm, 3pm and 4pm. Closed Mondays. 5-7DM. ☎ 0 95 48/ 2 03.

BAUTZEN

🛈 Fleischmarkt 2 ☎ 0 35 91/ 4 20 16

Serbski Muzej (Sorbian Museum) – Open April to October daily 10am to 12.30pm and 1pm to 5pm; November to March until 4.30pm. 2DM. ☎ 0 35 91/ 4 24 03.

BAYERISCHER WALD

Großer Arber: Chairlift – Journey time: 20min Rtn. Operates 8am to 5pm. Closed November to mid-December. 10DM. ☎ 0 99 25/ 5 42.

BAYREUTH

🛈 Luitpoldplatz 9 ☎ 09 21/ 8 85 88

Markgräfliches Opernhaus – Guided tour (20min) April to September 9am to 11.30am and 1.30pm to 4.30pm; October to March 10am to 11.30am and 1.30pm to 3pm. Closed Mondays, 1 January, 24, 25 and 31 December. 2.50DM. ☎ 09 21/ 5 36 66.

Neues Schloß – Guided tour (30min) April to September 10am to 12noon and 1.20pm to 5pm; October to March 10am to 12noon and 1.30pm to 3.30pm. Closed Mondays, 1 January, Shrove Tuesday, 1 November, 24, 25 and 31 December. 2DM. ☎ 09 21/ 6 53 13.

Richard-Wagner-Museum – Open daily 9am to 5pm. Closed 1 January, Easter Day, Whit Sunday, 24 and 25 December. 3DM. ☎ 09 21/ 7 57 28 16.

Festspielhaus – Guided tour (30min) at 10am, 10.45am, 11.30am, 1.30pm, 2.15pm and 3pm. During the Wagner festival (late July to late August) guided tours in the morning only. Closed Mondays and during November. 3.50DM. ☎ 09 21/ 7 80 21.

Schloß Eremitage – Guided tour (30min) April to September 9am to 11.30am and 1pm to 4.30pm; October and March 10am to 11.30am and 1pm to 2.30pm; November to February by appointment only. Closed Mondays, Shrove Tuesday, 1 November, 24, 25 and 31 December. 2.50DM. ☎ 09 21/ 9 25 61.

Excursions

Teufelshöhle – Guided tour (45min) Easter to 1 November daily 9am to 5pm; 2 November to Easter, Tuesdays and Saturdays 10am to 12noon; 26 December to 6 January daily 1.30pm to 3.30pm. Closed 24 and 25 December. 4.50DM. ☎ 0 92 43/ 7 08 41.

Sanspareil: Burg Zwernitz – Open mid-April to mid-October 9am to 12noon and 1.20pm to 5pm. Closed Mondays. 2DM, tour of the Oriental building: 2DM.
Rock garden: open all hours and admission free. ☎ 0 92 74/ 3 30.

Kulmbach: Plassenburg – Guided tour (45min) April to September 10am to 5pm; October to March 10am to 3pm, weekends and public holidays 10am to 3.30pm. Closed Mondays, Shrove Tuesday, 1 January, 1 November, 24, 25 and 31 December. 3DM. ☎ 0 92 21/ 41 16.

Kulmbach: Zinnfigurenmuseum – Open April to September 10am to 5pm; October to March 10am to 3pm. Closed Mondays (apart from Easter and Whit Mondays), 1 January, Shrove Tuesday, 1 November, 24, 25 and 31 December. 3DM. ☎ 0 92 21/ 95 88-40.

BENEDIKTBEUERN

🛈 Prälatenstr. 5 ☎ 0 88 57/ 2 48

See Bad TÖLZ

BENSHEIM

🛈 Rodensteinstr. 19 ☎ 0 62 51/ 1 41 17

See BERGSTRASSE

BERCHTESGADEN

Schloß – Guided tour (50min) 10am to 1pm (last tour at 12noon) and 2pm to 5pm (last tour at 4pm). Closed Saturdays, Good Friday, 1 May and all Sundays and public holidays from October to Easter. 7DM. ☎ 0 86 52/ 20 85.

Salzbergwerk – Guided tour (1 hour) May to mid-October daily 8.30am to 5pm; mid-October to April Monday to Saturday 12.30pm to 3.30pm, Easter 8.30am to 5pm. Closed Good Friday and Whit Sunday. 16DM. ☎ 0 86 52/ 60 02-0.

Obersalzberg and the Kehlstein – Bus connection between Obersalzberg and Kehlstein from mid-May to mid-October (weather permitting) daily 7.40am to 5pm. 19DM for bus and lift. ☎ 0 86 52/ 96 70.

Königssee – Boat trips (round trip of about 1 hour 45min). Timetable varies with season (following details are approx.): high season (July and August) daily 7.45am to 5.30pm every 10-20min; mid-May to June and September to mid-October 8.15am to 3.45pm every 15-30min; winter 9.45am to 3.30pm every 45min. 19DM. ☎ 0 86 52/ 96 36 18.

Roßfeld-Höhenringstraße – Toll: 10DM per car.

BERGSTRASSE

Lorsch: Torhalle – Open March to October 10am to 4.30pm; November to February 10am to 3.30pm. Closed Mondays, 1 January, 25 and 31 December. 4DM. ☎ 0 62 51/ 5 14 46.

Bensheim-Auerbach: Auerbacher Schloß – Open 10am to 6pm. Closed Mondays October to March. Admission free. ☎ 0 62 51/ 1 41 17.

BERLIN

Zeughaus: German Historical Museum – Open daily 10am to 6pm. Admission free. ☎ 0 30/ 21 50 20.

Nikolaikirche: Permanent Exhibition from the Märkisches Museum – Open 10am to 6pm (last admission 30min before closing). Closed Mondays, 1 May, 3 October and 24 December. 3DM. ☎ 0 30/ 23 80 90 81.

Pergamonmuseum – Open daily 9am to 5pm. Closed Mondays, 1 January, Tuesdays after Easter and Whitsun, 24, 25 and 31 December. 4DM (admission free on Sundays and public holidays). ☎ 0 30/ 20 35 54 44.

Alte Nationalgalerie (Museumsinsel) – Same admission times as the Pergamonmuseum. 4DM (admission free on Sundays and public holidays). ☎ 0 30/ 20 35 54 44.

Bodemuseum – Same admission times as the Pergamonmuseum. 4DM (admission free on Sundays and public holidays). ☎ 0 30/ 20 35 54 44.

Altes Museum – Special opening times – ask at the information bureau in the Pergamonmuseum. 4DM. ☎ 0 30/ 20 35 54 44.

Siegessäule – Open Tuesdays to Sundays 9am to 6.30pm, Mondays 1pm to 6.30pm. 1.50DM. ☎ 0 30/ 3 91 29 61.

Zoologischer Garten – Open April to September daily 9am to 6.30pm; October to March 9am to 5pm or 5.30pm. 10DM. ☎ 0 30/ 25 40 10.

Aquarium – Open daily 9am to 6pm, last Saturday of the month until 9pm. 9DM. ☎ 0 30/ 25 40 10.

Kunstgewerbemuseum (Tiergartenstr.) – Open 9am to 5pm, weekends 10am to 5pm. Closed Mondays, 1 January, Tuesdays after Easter and Whitsun, 24, 25 and 31 December. 4DM (admission free on Sundays and public holidays). ☎ 0 30/ 2 66 29 02.

Kupferstichkabinett – Open Tuesdays to Fridays 9am to 4pm. Closed 1 January, Tuesdays after Easter and Whitsun, 24, 25 and 31 December. 4DM. ☎ 0 30/ 2 66 20 01.

Neue Nationalgalerie (Potsdamer Str.) – Open 9am to 5pm, weekends 10am to 5pm. 4DM (admission free on Sundays and public holidays). ☎ 0 30/ 2 66 26 51.

Philharmonie – Guided tour (30min) by appointment. ☎ 0 30/ 2 54 88-0.

Musical Instruments Museum – Open Tuesdays to Fridays 9am to 5pm, weekends and public holidays 10am to 5pm. Closed Mondays and certain holidays. 4DM (admission free on Sundays and public holidays). ☎ 0 30/ 25 48 1-0.

Gedenkstätte Deutscher Widerstand – Open Mondays to Fridays 9am to 6pm, weekends and public holidays 9am to 1pm. Guided tour every Sunday at 11am. Films on German Resistance every 1st Sunday in the month at 10am. Closed 1 January, 24, 25, 26 and 31 December. Admission free. ☎ 0 30/ 26 54 22 02.

Schloß Charlottenburg – Open Tuesdays to Fridays 9am to 5pm, weekends and public holidays 10am to 5pm. Apartments of Friedrich I and Sophie-Charlotte: guided tour every 50min. Closed Mondays, 1 January, Tuesdays after Easter and Whitsun, 24, 25 and 31 December. 8DM for the Charlottenburg palace complex.

Charlottenburg: Gallery of Romanticism – Same opening times as palace above. 4DM. ☎ 0 30/ 3 20 91-1.

Charlottenburg: Collection of Antiquities – Open Mondays to Thursdays 9am to 5pm, weekends 10am to 5pm. Closed Fridays, 1 January, Maundy Thursday, 24, 25 and 31 December. 4DM (admission free on Sundays and public holidays). ☎ 0 30/32 09 12 16.

Charlottenburg: Egyptian Museum and Papyrus Collection – Same admission times and charges as the Collection of Antiquities. ☎ 0 30/ 32 09 12 61.

Charlottenburg: Bröhan-Museum – Open 10am to 6pm. Closed Mondays, 24 and 31 December. 6DM. ☎ 0 30/ 3 21 40 29.

Dahlem Museums – Open Tuesdays to Fridays 9am to 5pm, weekends and public holidays 10am to 5pm. Closed Mondays, 1 January, Tuesdays after Easter and Whitsun, 24, 25 and 31 December. 4DM. ☎ 0 30/ 83 01-1.

Postmuseum Berlin – Open Mondays to Thursdays 9am to 5pm, weekends 10am to 5pm. Closed Fridays. Admission free. ☎ 0 30/ 21 71 17 17.

Museum für Verkehr und Technik – Open Tuesdays to Fridays 9am to 5.30pm, weekends 10am to 6pm. Closed Mondays, 1 May, 24, 25 and 31 December. 4 DM. ☎ 0 30/ 2 54 84-1 25.

Käthe-Kollwitz-Museum – Open Wednesdays to Mondays 11am to 6pm. Closed Tuesdays, 24 and 31 December. 6DM. ☎ 0 30/ 8 82 52 10.

Martin-Gropius-Bau: Berlin Gallery – Open 10am to 8pm. Closed Mondays, 1 May, 24 and 31 December. 6DM. ☎ 0 30/ 2 54 86-1 08.

Topographie des Terrors – Open 10am to 6pm. Admission free. ☎ 0 30/ 2 54 86-7 03.

Museum Haus am Checkpoint Charlie – Open daily 9am to 10pm. 7.50DM ☎ 0 30/ 2 51 10 31.

Märkisches Museum – Open 10am to 6pm (last admission 30min before closing). Closed Mondays, 1 May, 3 October, 24 December. 3DM. ☎ 0 30/ 23 80 90 62.

Kunstgewerbemuseum (Schloß Köpenick) – Open 9am to 5pm. Closed Mondays, 1 January, Tuesdays after Easter and Whitsun, 24 and 31 December. 4DM. ☎ 0 30/ 6 57 26 51.

Botanischer Garten – Open May to August daily 9am to 8pm; April and September until 7pm, March and October until 5pm; November to February until 4pm. The greenhouses close earlier. 4DM. ☎ 0 30/ 83 00 61 27.

Botanisches Museum – Open 10am to 5pm. Closed Mondays, 24 and 31 December. Admission free. ☎ 0 30/ 83 00 61 27.

Brücke-Museum – Open 11am to 5pm. Closed Tuesdays. 5DM. ☎ 0 30/ 8 31 20 29.

Jagdschloß Grunewald – Open April to September 10am to 6pm; March and October 10am to 5pm; November to February 10am to 4pm. Closed Mondays, Tuesdays after Easter and Whitsun, 1 May, 24, 25 and 31 December. 2.50DM. ☎ 0 30/ 8 13 35 97.

Pfaueninsel: Castle – Guided tour (30min) April to September 10am to 5pm; October 10am to 4pm. Closed Mondays, Tuesdays after Easter and Whitsun, 1 May, 24, 25 and 31 December. 3DM. ☎ 0 30/ 8 05 20 47.

Funkturm – Open daily 10am to 10.30pm. 5DM. ☎ 0 30/ 30 38-39 99.

Deutsches Rundfunk-Museum – Open Wednesdays to Mondays 10am to 5pm. Closed Tuesdays, 1 May, Ascension Day, 24, 25 and 31 December. 3DM. ☎ 0 30/3 02 81 86.

Bauhaus-Archiv, Museum für Gestaltung – Open 10am to 5pm. Closed Tuesdays, 24 and 31 December. 4DM. ☎ 0 30/ 2 54 00 20.

Gedenkstätte Plötzensee – Open March to September daily 8am to 6pm; February and October 8.30am to 5.30pm; January and November 8.30am to 4.30pm; December 8.30am to 4pm. Closed 1 January, 24, 25, 26 and 31 December. Admission free. ☎ 0 30/ 3 44 32 26.

Schloß Tegel (Humboldt-Schloß) – Guided tour (45min) May to September Mondays 10am to 12noon and 3pm to 5pm. 10DM. ☎ 0 30/ 4 34 31 56.

Spandauer Zitadelle – Open 9am to 5pm, weekends 10am to 5pm (last admission 30min before closing). Closed Mondays, 1 May and 3 October. 1.50DM. ☎ 0 30/33 91-2 00.

Excursions

Oranienburg: Gedenkstätte und Museum Sachsenhausen – Open April to September 8am to 6pm; October to March 8.30am to 4.30pm. Closed Mondays. Admission free. ☎ 0 33 01/ 80 37 16-17.

Kloster Chorin – Open April to October daily 9am to 6pm; November to March 9am to 4pm. 3DM. ☎ 03 33 66/ 3 22.

BERNKASTEL-KUES
🛈 Gestade 5 ☎ 0 65 31/ 40 23

St. Nikolaus-Hospital – Open Tuesdays to Fridays 9am to 12noon and 2pm to 6pm. Admission free. Library: guided tour (1 hour) for groups by prior appointment. 3 DM. ☎ 0 65 31/ 22 60.

BOCHUM
🛈 Hauptbahnhof ☎ 02 34/ 1 30 31

See RUHRGEBIET

BONN
🛈 Münsterstr 20 ☎ 02 28/ 77 34 66

Rheinisches Landesmuseum – Open Tuesdays, Thursdays and Fridays 9am to 5pm, Wednesdays 9am to 8pm, weekends 10am to 5pm. Closed Mondays, Weiberfastnacht (Thursday before Shrove Tuesday), Sunday before Shrove Tuesday, Shrove Tuesday, 24, 25 and 31 December. 4DM (free on 1st Sunday of the month). ☎ 02 28/ 7 29 41.

Beethovenhaus – Open April to September Mondays to Saturdays 10am to 5pm, Sundays and public holidays 10am to 1pm; October to March Mondays to Saturdays 10am to 4pm, Sundays and public holidays 10am to 1pm; Weiberfastnacht (Thursday before Shrove Tuesday), Easter Monday, Ascension Day, Whit Monday, Day of German Unity (3 October), 31 December open 10am to 1pm. Closed 1 January, Good Friday, Easter Day, 1 May, Whit Sunday, Corpus Christi, 1 November, Buß- und Bettag (a Wednesday in mid-November), 24 to 26 December. 5DM. ☎ 02 28/ 63 51 88.

Haus der Geschichte der Bundesrepublik Deutschland – Open Tuesdays to Sundays 9am to 7pm. Admission free. ☎ 02 28/ 9 16 50.

Bundeskunst- und Ausstellungshalle – Open Tuesdays to Sundays 10am to 7pm. 8DM. ☎ 02 28/ 9 17 10.

Excursions

Bad Godesberg: castle – Tower can be climbed April to October Wednesdays to Sundays 10am to 6pm. 1DM. ☎ 02 28/ 31 60 71.

Funicular to Drachenfels ruins – Operates 1 January to mid-November: May to September 9am to 8pm every half hour; January, February and November Mondays to Fridays 12noon to 5pm, weekends 11am to 6pm; March and October 10am to 6pm; April 10am to 7pm. Rtn fare: 12DM. ☎ 0 22 23/ 9 20 90.

Remagen: Friedensmuseum – Open March to November daily 10am to 5pm. 2.50DM. ☎ 0 26 42/ 2 25 72.

BRAUNSCHWEIG
🛈 Hauptbahnhof ☎ 05 31/ 27 35 50

Herzog-Anton-Ulrich-Museum – Open 10am to 5pm, Wednesdays to 8pm. Closed Mondays, Easter Day, 1 May, Whit Sunday, 24, 25 and 31 December. Admission free. ☎ 05 31/ 4 84 24 00.

Medieval Art Collection in the Burg Dankwarderode – *5min on foot*. Open 10am to 5pm. Closed Mondays, Easter Day, 1 May, Whit Sunday, 24, 25 and 31 December. Admission free. ☎ 05 31/ 4 84 24 00.

BREMEN
🛈 am Bahnhofsplatz ☎ 04 21/ 30 80 00

Boat trip round the port – Embarcation from the quay by the St. Martinikirche. Duration of trip: 1 hour 15min. Departures March to end of October daily at 11.30am, 1.30pm and 3.15pm; April to end of September, additional departures at 10am and 4.45pm. 12DM. ☎ 04 21/ 32 12 29.

Rathaus – Guided tour (30min) March to October Mondays to Saturdays at 10am, 11am and 12noon, Sundays and public holidays at 11am and 12noon. 4DM. ☎ 04 21/ 3 61 62 04.

Roseliushaus und Paula-Becker-Modersohn-Haus – Open 11am to 5pm. Closed Mondays, Good Friday, Easter Day, 1 May, Whit Sunday, 24, 25 and 31 December. 8DM. ☎ 04 21/ 3 36 50 77.

St. Martinikirche – Open mid-May to mid-September Mondays to Saturdays 10.30am to 12.30pm. Admission free. ☎ 04 21/ 32 48 35.

Kunsthalle – Open Wednesdays to Sundays 10am to 5pm, Tuesdays until 9pm. Closed Mondays. 6DM. ☎ 04 21/ 3 29 08 47.

Übersee-Museum – Open 10am to 6pm. Closed Mondays, Good Friday, Easter Day, 1 May, Whit Monday, 3 October, Buß- und Bettag (a Wednesday in November), 24, 25 and 26 December. 4DM. ☎ 04 21/ 3 61 92 01.

Focke-Museum – Open 10am to 6pm. Closed Mondays. 4 DM. ☎ 04 21/ 3 61 35 75.

BREMERHAVEN
🛈 Columbus-Center, Obere Bürger 13 ☎ 04 71/ 4 30 00

Deutsches Schiffahrtsmuseum – Open 10am to 6pm. Closed Mondays, 25 and 31 December (last admissions 30min before closing). 5DM including Freilichtmuseum. ☎ 04 71/ 4 82 07-0.

Technikmuseum U-Boot Wilhelm Bauer – Open April to October daily 10am to 6pm (last admissions 30min before closing). 2.50DM. ☎ 04 71/ 4 82 07-0.

Freilichtmuseum – Open April to September 10am to 6pm. Closed Mondays, 25 and 31 December (last admissions 30min before closing). 5DM including Deutsches Schiffahrtsmuseum. ☎ 04 71/ 4 82 07-0.

Zoo am Meer – Open May to September daily 8am to 7pm; October to April 8am to 5pm (last admissions 30min before closing). 4DM. ☎ 04 71/ 4 20 71.

Excursion

Cuxhaven: Wrackmuseum – Open April to October Tuesdays to Fridays 9am to 1pm and 3pm to 6pm, weekends and public holidays 10am to 1pm and 3pm to 6pm. Closed Mondays. 4DM. ☎ 0 47 21/ 2 33 41.

BRUCHSAL
🛈 Am alten Schloß 2 ☎ 0 72 51/ 7 27 71

Schloß – Open Tuesdays to Saturdays 9am to 5pm. Closed Mondays (apart from public holidays), 24, 25 and 31 December. 3DM. ☎ 0 72 51/ 74 26 61.

Museum Mechanischer Musikinstrumente – Guided tour (1 hour) Tuesdays 10am to 5pm, Wednesdays to Sundays 9.30am to 5pm. Closed Mondays, 24, 25 and 31 December. 5DM. ☎ 0 72 51/ 74 26 61.

Städtisches Museum – Open Tuesdays to Fridays 2pm to 5pm, weekends 9am to 1pm and 2pm to 5pm. Closed Mondays, Shrove Tuesday, 24, 25 and 31 December. Admission free. ☎ 0 72 51/ 79-2 53.

BRÜHL
🛈 Uhlstr. 3 ☎ 0 22 32/ 7 93 45

See KÖLN

BÜCKEBURG
🛈 Lange Str. 45 ☎ 0 57 22/ 20 61 81

Schloß – Guided tour (45min) daily 9am to 12noon and 1pm to 6pm (5pm in winter). Closed 1 January, 25 and 31 December. 7DM. ☎ 0 57 22/ 50 39.

Hubschraubermuseum – Open daily 9am to 5pm. 5DM. ☎ 0 57 22/ 55 33.

Kleinenbremen: Besucherbergwerk – Guided tour (1 hour 30min) April to 20 June and 29 August to October on Saturdays, Sundays and public holidays 10am to 4pm; from 23 June to 25 August on Tuesdays and Fridays as well at these times. 10DM. ☎ 05 71/ 39 94-0.

BÜDINGEN
🛈 Marktplatz 7 ☎ 0 60 42/ 88 41 37

See GELNHAUSEN

BURGHAUSEN
🛈 Rathaus, Stadtplatz 112 ☎ 0 86 77/ 24 35

Burgmuseum und Gemäldegalerie – Open April to September daily 9am to 5pm; October to March Tuesdays to Sundays 10am to 12noon and 1pm to 4pm. Closed Mondays (October to March), 1 January, Shrove Tuesday, 24, 25 and 31 December. 2DM. ☎ 0 86 77/ 46 59.

Stadtmuseum – Open May to September daily 9am to 6.30pm; mid-March to end of April and October to 1 November 10am to 4.30pm. 2.50DM. ☎ 0 86 77/ 88 74 80.

If you intend combining a tour of Germany
with a visit to one of the neighbouring countries,
remember to take the appropriate Michelin Green Guide
to Scandinavia-Finland, Netherlands, Belgium and Luxembourg, France,
Switzerland, Austria or Europe (forthcoming).

C

CELLE

🚩 Markt 6 ☎ 0 5141/ 12 12

Schloß – Guided tour (50min) April to October daily, apart from Mondays, at 10am, 11am, 12noon, 1pm, 2pm, 3pm and 4pm; November to March at 11am and 3pm. Closed 1 January, Good Friday, Buß- und Bettag (a Wednesday in November), 24, 25, 26 and 31 December. 4DM. ☎ 0 51 41/ 1 23 73.

Bomannmuseum – Open April to October daily 10am to 5pm; November to March 10am to 5pm, Sundays and public holidays 10am to 1pm. Closed Mondays, 1 January, Good Friday, Buß- und Bettag (a Wednesday in November), 24, 25, 26 and 31 December. 3 DM. ☎ 0 51 41/ 12-3 72.

Excursions

Kloster Wienhausen – Guided tour (1 hour 15min) April to mid-October at 10am, 11am, 2pm, 3pm, 4pm and 5pm, Sundays and public holidays every hour from 12noon to 5pm. 5DM. ☎ 0 51 49/ 3 57.

CHEMNITZ

🚩 Straße der Nationen 3 ☎ 03 71/ 6 20 51

Museum für Naturkunde – Open 10am to 6pm, Wednesdays until 9pm. Closed Mondays. 6DM. ☎ 03 71/ 4 88 45 51.

Städtische Kunstsammlungen – Open 10am to 6pm, Wednesdays to 9pm. Closed Mondays. 4DM. ☎ 03 71/ 4 88 44 24.

Excursions

Schloß Augustusburg: Museum für Jagdtier und Vogelkunde – Open April to September 9am to 6pm, weekends until 6.30pm; October to March 10am to 5pm, weekends until 6.30pm. Closed 25 December. 3DM. ☎ 03 72 91/ 20 67.

Schloß Augustusburg: Motorradmuseum – Open April to October 9am to 6pm, weekends until 6.30pm; November to March 10am to 5pm, weekends until 5.30pm (last admissions 30min before closing). Closed 25 December. 5DM. ☎ 03 72 91/ 2 67 or 3 40.

CHIEMSEE

Prien-Stock landing stage – Boat trips all year round. 15min trip to Herreninsel; 30min trip to Fraueninsel. Rtn fare: 9DM for Herreninsel, 10.50DM for both. ☎ 0 80 51/ 60 90.

Schloß Herrenchiemsee – Guided tour (30min) April to September daily 9am to 5pm; October to March 10am to 4pm. Closed 1 January, Shrove Tuesday, 1 November, 24, 25 and 31 December. 6DM. ☎ 0 80 51/ 30 69.

CLAUSTHAL-ZELLERFELD

🚩 Bahnhofstr. 5a ☎ 0 53 23/ 8 10 24

See HARZ

CLOPPENBURG

🚩 Mühlenstr. 20 ☎ 0 44 71/ 1 85 81

See OLDENBURG

COBURG

🚩 Herrngasse 4 ☎ 0 95 61/ 7 41 80

Fürstenbau – Guided tour (35min) April to October 9.30am to 12noon and 2pm to 4pm; November to March 2pm to 4pm. Closed Mondays and 25 December. 4DM. ☎ 0 95 61/ 9 20 88.

Kunstsammlungen – Open April to October 9.30am to 1pm and 2pm to 5pm; November to March 2pm to 5pm. Closed Mondays. 4DM. ☎ 0 95 61/ 87 90.

Schloß Ehrenburg – Guided tour (1 hour) April to September at 10am, 11am, 1.30pm, 2.30pm, 3.30pm and 4.30pm; October to March at 10am, 11am, 1.30pm, 2.30pm and 3.30pm. Closed Mondays, 1 January, Shrove Tuesday, 1 November 24, 25 and 31 December. 3DM. ☎ 0 95 61/ 80 88-0.

Schloß Rosenau – Guided tour (40min) April to September at 10am, 10.45am, 11.30am, 1.30pm, 2.15pm, 3pm, 3.45pm and 4.30pm; October to March at 10am, 10.45am, 11.30am, 1.30pm, 2.15pm, 3pm and 3.45pm. Closed Mondays, 1 January, Shrove Tuesday, 1 November, 24, 25 and 31 December. 2DM. ☎ 0 95 63/ 47 47.

COCHEM

🚩 Endertplatz ☎ 0 26 71/ 39 71

See MOSELTAL

CUXHAVEN

🚩 Lichtenbergplatz ☎ 0 47 21/ 3 60 46

See BREMERHAVEN

D

🛈 Luisen-Center, Luisenplatz 5 ☎ 0 61 51/ 13 27 80

Hessisches Landesmuseum – Open Tuesdays to Saturdays 10am to 5pm, Sundays and public holidays 11am to 5pm. Closed Mondays. 5DM. ☎ 0 61 51/ 16 57 03.

Schloß – Guided tour (1 hour) Mondays to Thursdays 10am to 1pm and 2pm to 5pm, weekends and public holidays 10am to 1pm. Closed Fridays. 3.50DM. ☎ 0 61 51/2 40 35.

Prinz-Georg-Palais – Currently closed for restoration. The porcelain collection is temporarily on display in the Staatspark Fürstenlager in Bensheim-Auerbach. Further information can be obtained from the tourist office. ☎ 0 61 51/ 13 27 80.

Jagdschloß Kranichstein – Closed for restoration. At the time of going to press, the date of reopening had not been released.

DETMOLD 🛈 Rathaus, Lange Straße ☎ 0 52 31/ 97 70

Residenzschloß – Guided tour (45min) daily at 10am, 12noon, 2pm and 5pm; October to March at 10am, 12noon and 2pm. Closed 25 December. 4DM. ☎ 0 52 31/ 2 25 07.

Westfälisches Freilichtmuseum – Open April to October 9am to 6pm (last admissions at 5pm). Closed Mondays (except public holidays). 5DM. ☎ 0 52 31/ 7 06-1 04.

Hermannsdenkmal – Open daily in summer 9am to 6.30pm, in winter 9.30am to 4pm. 2DM. ☎ 0 52 61/ 2 50 20.

Externsteine – Open April to October 9am to 7pm; the rest of the year depending on the weather. 1.50DM. ☎ 0 52 34/ 32 00.

DIEZ 🛈 Rathaus, Wilhelmstr. 63 ☎ 0 64 32/ 50 12 70

See LAHNTAL

Bad DOBERAN 🛈 Goethestr. 1 ☎ 03 82 03/ 21 54

See ROSTOCK

DONAUESCHINGEN 🛈 Karlstr. 58 ☎ 07 71/ 85 72 21

Fürstenberg-Sammlungen – Open 9am to 12noon and 1.30pm to 5pm. Closed Mondays and during November. 5DM. ☎ 07 71/ 8 65 63.

Schloß – Guided tour (1 hour) Easter to mid-October 9am to 12noon and 2pm to 5pm. Closed Tuesdays. 5DM. ☎ 07 71/ 8 65 09.

DORTMUND 🛈 am Hauptbahnhof ☎ 02 31/ 14 03 41

Westfalenpark – Open daily 7am to 11pm. 2DM. ☎ 02 31/ 5 02 61 00.

Brauerei-Museum – Open 10am to 6pm. Closed Mondays. Admission free. ☎ 02 31/ 5 41 22 89.

Museum für Kunst und Kulturgeschichte – Open 10am to 5pm. Closed Mondays, 1 January, 1 May, 24, 25 and 31 December. 4DM. ☎ 02 31/ 50-2 55 22.

Ostwall-Museum – Open 10am to 5pm. Closed Mondays, 1 May and 25 December. 4DM. ☎ 02 31/ 5 02 32 47.

DRACHENFELS 🛈 Drachenfelsstr. 11, Königswinter ☎ 0 22 44/ 88 93 25

See BONN

DRESDEN 🛈 Prager Str. 10 ☎ 03 51/ 4 95 50 25

Day-ticket for all Dresden museums (Staatliche Kunstsammlungen): 10DM.

Zwinger:

– **Gemäldegalerie Alter Meister** – Open 10am to 6pm. Closed Mondays. 7DM. ☎ 03 51/491 46 19.

– **Rüstkammer** – Open 10am to 6pm. Closed Mondays. 3DM. ☎ 03 51/ 491 46 19.

– **Porzellansammlung** – Open 10am to 6pm. Closed Thursdays. 3DM. ☎ 03 51/ 491 46 19.

– **Mathematisch-Physikalischer Salon** – Open 10am to 6pm. Closed Thursdays. 3DM. ☎ 03 51/ 4 95 13 64.

Albertinum:

– **Gemäldegalerie Neuer Meister** – Open 10am to 6pm. Closed Thursdays. 7DM. ☎ 03 51/ 491 46 19.

– **Grünes Gewölbe** – Open 10am to 6pm. Closed Thursdays. 7DM. ☎ 03 51/ 491 46 19.

Stadtmuseum – Open 10am to 6pm. Closed Fridays, 1 January, 24, 25 and 31 December. 3DM. ☏ 03 51/ 4 98 66 25.

Museum für Sächsische Volkskunst – Open 10am to 6pm. Closed Mondays. 2DM. ☏ 03 51/ 48 40-6 19.

Deutsches Hygiene-Museum – Open 9am to 5pm. Closed Mondays, 25 and 26 December. 5DM. ☏ 03 51/ 48 46-3 04.

Excursions

Schloß Moritzburg – Open April to October 10am to 5pm; March and November until 4pm; December 10am to 3pm. Closed Mondays, 25 and 31 December. 5DM. ☏ 03 52 07/ 4 39.

Schloß Pillnitz – The Bergpalais (Decorative Arts Museum) is open May to October Tuesdays to Sundays, and the Wasserpalais Wednesdays to Mondays, 9.30am to 5.30pm. 3DM. ☏ 03 51/ 3 93 25.

DÜSSELDORF
🛈 Konrad-Adenauer-Platz ☏ 02 11/ 17 20 20

Kunstmuseum – Open 10am to 6pm. Closed Mondays. 5DM. ☏ 02 11/ 8 99 24 60.

Kunstsammlung Nordrhein-Westfalen – Open 10am to 6pm. Closed Mondays, 24, 25 and 31 December. 10DM. ☏ 02 11/ 83 81-2 04.

Hetjens-Museum/Deutsches Keramik-Museum – Open Tuesdays, Thursdays, Fridays and Saturdays 2pm to 6pm, Wednesdays 2pm to 8pm and Sundays 11am to 6pm. Closed Mondays, 1 January, Shrove Tuesday, Easter Day, Whit Sunday, 1 May, 24, 25 and 31 December. 6DM. ☏ 02 11/ 8 99 42 10.

Landesmuseum Volk und Wirtschaft – Open Mondays, Tuesdays, Thursdays and Fridays 9am to 5pm, Wednesdays 9am to 8pm, and Sundays and public holidays 10am to 6pm. Closed Saturdays, 1 January, Sunday and Monday before Shrove Tuesday, Easter Day, Whit Sunday, 1 May, 24, 25 and 31 December. 2DM. ☏ 02 11/ 4 92 11 08.

Löbbecke-Museum und Aquazoo – Open daily 10am to 6pm. Closed 1 January, Monday before Shrove Tuesday, 1 May, 24, 25 and 31 December. 9DM. ☏ 02 11/8 99 61 50.

Excursions

Benrath: Schloß – Guided tour (1 hour) 11am to 6pm. Closed Mondays, 1 January, Carnival Sunday, Easter Day, 1 May, Whit Sunday, 24, 25 and 31 December. 6DM. ☏ 02 11/ 8 99 72 71.

Neandertal: Urgeschichtliches Museum – Open 10am to 5pm, Sundays 11am to 6pm. Closed Mondays. 2DM. ☏ 0 21 04/ 3 11 49.

E

EBSTORF
🛈 Rathaus, Hauptstr. 30 ☏ 0 58 22/ 24 81

See LÜNEBURGER HEIDE

EDENKOBEN
🛈 Poststr. 23 ☏ 0 63 23/ 32 34

See PFALZ AM RHEIN

EICHSTÄTT
🛈 Kardinal-Preysing-Platz 14 ☏ 0 84 21/ 79 77

Diözesanmuseum – Open April to October Tuesdays to Saturdays 9.30am to 1pm and 2pm to 5pm, Sundays and public holidays 11am to 5pm. Closed Mondays. 2.50DM. ☏ 0 84 21/ 5 02 79.

Fürstbischöfliche Residenz – Guided tour (10min) April to October Mondays to Thursdays 10am to 11am and 2pm to 3pm, Fridays 10am to 11am, weekends and public holidays 10am to 12noon and 2pm to 4pm. Closed November to Easter. Admission free. ☏ 0 84 21/ 7 02 20.

Jura-Museum – Open April to September 9am to 12noon and 1pm to 5pm; October to March 10am to 12noon and 1pm to 4pm (last admission 30min before closing). Closed Mondays, 1 January, Shrove Tuesday, 1 November, 24, 25 and 31 December. 4DM. ☏ 0 84 21/ 29 56.

Museum für Ur- und Frühgeschichte – Open April to September 9am to 12noon and 1pm to 5pm; October to March 10am to 12noon and 1pm to 4pm. Closed Mondays, 1 January, Shrove Tuesday, 1 November, 24, 25 and 31 December. 4DM. ☏ 0 84 21/ 8 94 50.

Excursions

Weißenburg: Römische Thermen – Open Palm Sunday to 1 November 10am to 12.30pm and 2pm to 5pm. Closed Mondays. 2DM. ☎ 0 91 41/ 9 07-1 24.

Weißenburg: Römermuseum – Open March to December 10am to 12.30pm and 2pm to 5pm. Closed Mondays, 24 and 25 December. 3DM. ☎ 0 91 41/ 9 07-1 24.

Ellingen: Schloß – Guided tour April to September at 9am, 10am, 11am, 1pm, 2pm, 3pm and 4pm; October to March at 10am, 11am, 2pm and 3pm. 3DM. ☎ 0 91 41/ 33 27.

EINBECK
Excursions

Alfeld: Stadtmuseum – Open 10am to 12noon and 3 to 5pm, weekends 10am to 12noon. Closed Mondays and public holidays. Admission free. ☎ 0 51 81/ 70 32 16.

EISENACH   🅱 Bahnhofstr. 3 ☎ 0 36 91/ 48 95

Schloß: Thuringian Museum – Closed for restoration. The collection of medieval art is on display in the Predigerkirche. Open 9am to 5pm. Closed Mondays. 5DM. ☎ 0 36 91/62 46 78.

Lutherhaus – Open May to September daily 9am to 1pm and 2pm to 5pm, Sundays and public holidays 2pm to 5pm. 3DM. ☎ 0 36 91/ 2 98 30.

Bachhaus – Open April to September Mondays 12noon to 5.45pm, Tuesdays to Sundays 9am to 5.45pm; October to March Mondays 1pm to 4.45pm, Tuesdays to Sundays 9am to 4.45pm. 5DM. ☎ 0 36 91/ 20 37 14.

Automobil-Ausstellungspavillon – Open daily 9am to 5pm. Closed Mondays. 2.50DM. ☎ 0 36 91/ 7 60 56.

Fritz-Reuter-und-Richard-Wagner-Museum – Open 10am to 5pm. Closed Mondays. 4DM. ☎ 0 36 91/ 20 39 71.

Wartburg – Guided tour (1 hour) May to October daily 8.30am to 5pm; November and January daily 9am to 3.30pm; February 9am to 3.30pm, weekends until 4pm; March daily 9am to 4pm; April 8.30am to 4.30pm, weekends until 5pm. 10DM. ☎ 0 36 91/ 20 30 01.

EMDEN   🅱 Alter Markt ☎ 0 49 21/ 2 00 94

Ostfriesisches Landesmuseum – Open April to September Mondays to Fridays 10am to 1pm and 3pm to 5pm, weekends 11am to 1pm (until 5pm June to August); October to March Tuesdays to Fridays 10am to 1pm and 3pm to 5pm, weekends 11am to 1pm. 5DM. ☎ 0 49 21/ 2 28 55.

Kunsthalle (Stiftung Henri Nannen) – Open Tuesdays 10am to 8pm, Wednesdays to Fridays 10am to 5pm, weekends and public holidays 11am to 5pm. Closed Mondays, 1 May and 25 December. 7DM. ☎ 0 49 21/ 2 09 95.

ERFURT   🅱 Bahnhofstr. 37 ☎ 03 61/ 5 62 62 67

Augustinerkloster – Guided tour (50min) April to October Tuesdays to Saturdays every hour 10am to 12noon and 2pm to 4pm, Sundays after Mass; November to March Tuesdays to Saturdays at 10am, 12noon and 2pm, Sundays at 10.30am. Closed Mondays. 4.50DM. ☎ 03 61/ 5 62 36 03.

Angermuseum – Open Tuesdays to Sundays 10am to 5pm (Wednesdays until 8pm). Closed Mondays, 1 January, 24 December. 3DM. ☎ 03 61/ 5 62 33 11.

Barfüßerkirche – Open Easter to end of October 10am to 1pm and 2pm to 5pm. Closed Mondays. 2DM. ☎ 03 61/ 5 62 33 11.

Excursions

Arnstadt: Museum für Stadtgeschichte und Bachgedenkstätte – Open Mondays to Fridays 8.30am to 12.30pm and 1pm to 5pm, weekends 9.30am to 5pm (last admissions 30min before closing time). Closed 1 January, 24 and 31 December. 4DM. ☎ 0 36 28/ 60 29 32.

Arnstadt: Neues Palais, Mon Plaisir Puppensammlung – Open May to mid-October 8.30am to 12noon and 1pm to 4.30pm; mid-October to April 9.30am to 4pm. Closed Mondays. 2.50DM. ☎ 0 36 28/ 60 29 32.

Gotha: Schloß Friedenstein – Open 9am to 5pm. Closed Mondays. 8DM. ☎ 0 36 21/ 5 30 36.

ESSEN

Design Zentrum Nordrhein Westfalen – Open 10am to 6pm. Closed Mondays, 1 January, 1 May, 24 and 31 December. 6DM. ☎ 02 01/ 8 20 21-0.

Museum Folkwang – Open 10am to 6pm, Thursdays until 9pm. Closed Mondays, 1 January, 1 May, 24 and 31 December. 5DM. ☎ 02 01/ 88 84 84.

Domschatzkammer – Open Tuesdays to Saturdays 10am to 5pm, Sundays and public holidays 12.30pm to 5pm. Closed Mondays, Good Friday, Easter Day, Whit Sunday, 25 December. 2DM. ☎ 02 01/ 2 20 42 06.

Villa Hügel: Krupp Collections – Open 10am to 6pm. Closed Mondays. The apartments in the great house are not open to the public during art exhibitions. ☎ 02 01/ 42 25 59.

F

FLENSBURG

🚉 Speicherlinie 40 ☎ 04 61/ 2 30 90

From Flensburg, there are **boat connections** to Glücksburg and the small neighbouring ports of the Danish Archipelago.

Städtisches Museum – Open Tuesday to Saturday 10am to 5pm, Sundays 10am to 1pm. Closed Mondays. 2DM (admission free on Sundays). ☎ 04 61/ 85 29 26.

Excursions

Glücksburg: Wasserschloß – Open May to September 10am to 5pm; October and April 10am to 4pm (apart from Mondays); November and December weekends only 10am to 3pm (but open every day 25-30 December). Closed 24 and 31 December. 6DM. ☎ 0 46 31/ 22 43.

FRANKFURT AM MAIN

🚉 Hauptbahnhof ☎ 0 69/ 21 23 88 49

Henninger Turm – Open 3pm to 11pm, Sundays and public holidays 12noon to 11pm. Lift fare: 5DM. ☎ 0 69/ 6 06 36 00.

Kaisersaal – Open 11am to 3pm. Closed Mondays. 3DM. ☎ 0 69/ 2 12-3 32 37.

Dommuseum – Open 10am to 5pm, Sundays and public holidays 11am to 5pm. Closed Mondays. 2DM. ☎ 0 69/ 28 92 29.

Historisches Museum – Open Tuesdays to Sundays 10am to 5pm, Wednesdays until 8pm. Closed Mondays and certain public holidays. 5DM (admission free Wednesdays). ☎ 0 69/ 2 12-3 55 99.

Museum für Moderne Kunst – Open Tuesdays, Thursdays, Fridays and Sundays 10am to 5pm, Wednesdays until 8pm, Saturdays 12noon to 7pm. Closed Mondays and certain public holidays. 7DM (admission free Wednesdays). ☎ 0 69/ 2 12-3 04 47.

Goethe-Haus und Goethe-Museum – Open April to September Mondays to Saturdays 9am to 6pm, Sundays and public holidays 10am to 1pm; October to March Monday to Saturday 9am to 4pm, Sundays and public holidays 10am to 1pm. Closed 1 January, Good Friday, 24, 25 and 31 December. 4DM. ☎ 0 69/ 28 28 24.

Jüdisches Museum – Open 10am to 5pm, Wednesdays until 8pm. Closed Mondays. 5DM (admission free Saturdays). ☎ 0 69/ 2 12-3 50 00.

Städelsches Kunstinstitut und Städtische Galerie – Open 10am to 5pm, Wednesdays until 8pm. Closed Mondays and certain public holidays. 8DM (admission free Wednesdays). ☎ 0 69/ 60 58 98-0.

Museum für Kunsthandwerk – Open 10am to 5pm, Wednesdays until 8pm. Closed Mondays and certain public holidays. 6DM (admission free Wednesdays). ☎ 0 69/2 12-3 40 37.

Deutsches Filmmuseum – Permanent exhibition open Tuesdays, Thursdays, Fridays and Sundays 10am to 5pm, Wednesdays until 8pm, Saturdays 2pm to 8pm. Closed Mondays. 5DM. ☎ 0 69/ 21 23 88 30.

Städtische Galerie Liebighaus – Open 10am to 5pm, Wednesdays until 8pm. Closed Mondays and certain public holidays. 5DM. ☎ 0 69/ 2 12-3 86 17.

Deutsches Postmuseum – Open 10am to 5pm. Closed Mondays and certain public holidays. Admission free. ☎ 0 69/ 60 60-0.

Deutsches Architektur-Museum – Open 10am to 5pm, Wednesdays until 8pm. Closed Mondays. 8DM. ☎ 0 69/ 2 12-3 88 44.

Museum für Völkerkunde – Open 10am to 5pm, Wednesdays until 8pm. Closed Mondays and 1 May. 4DM (admission free Wednesdays). ☎ 0 69/ 21 23 59 13.

Zoo – Open mid-March to end of September 9am to 7pm, weekends and public holidays 8am to 7pm; October to mid-March 9am to 5pm. 11DM. ☎ 0 69/ 21 23 37 35.

Naturmuseum Senckenberg – Open Mondays to Fridays 9am to 5pm, Wednesdays until 8pm, weekends and public holidays until 6pm. Closed Good Friday and 24 December. 5DM. ☎ 0 69/ 75 42-0.

Palmengarten – Open April to September 9am to 6pm; November to February until 4pm; March and October until 5pm. 7DM. ☎ 0 69/ 21 23 39 39.

Excursions

Offenbach: Deutsches Ledermuseum – Open daily 10am to 5pm. Closed 1 January, 24, 25 and 31 December. 5DM. ☎ 0 69/ 81 30 21.

Königstein im Taunus: Burgruine – Open April to September daily 9am to 7pm; October 9.30am to 4pm; November to February 9.30am to 3pm (weekends until 4pm); March 9.30am to 4.30pm. 1.50DM. ☎ 0 61 74/ 20 22 51.

Großer Feldberg: Aussichtsturm – Ascent of tower (163 steps) in summer 11am to 9pm; in winter until nightfall. Closed in bad weather. 2DM. ☎ 0 61 74/ 2 22 19.

FREIBURG

ⓘ Rotteckring 14 ☎ 07 61/ 3 68 90 90

Münster: Chancel – Open 10am to 6pm, Sundays and public holidays 1pm to 6pm. 1DM. ☎ 07 61/ 3 10 99.

Münster: Tower – Open 10am to 5pm, Sundays and public holidays 1pm to 5pm. Closed Mondays between November and April. 1.50DM. ☎ 07 61/ 3 10 99.

Augustinermuseum – Open Tuesdays to Fridays 9.30am to 5pm, weekends 10.30am to 5pm. Closed Mondays. 4DM. ☎ 07 61/ 2 01 25 31.

Schloßberg: Cable-car – From the Stadtgarten. June to September Mondays to Fridays 10.30am to 8pm, weekends 10am to 8pm; October to January daily (apart from Tuesdays) 11.30am to 6pm; March to May Mondays to Fridays 11.30am to 7pm, weekends 10am to 7pm. Closed in February. Rtn fare 5DM. ☎ 07 61/ 3 98 55.

FRIESLAND

Ostfriesische Inseln: Sea links – To **Borkum:** from Emden outer harbour (about 2 hours 30min), reservation necessary ☎ 0 49 21/ 89 07 22; to **Norderney:** from Norddeich (about 1 hour) – ☎ 0 49 31/ 1 80 20; to **Wangerooge:** from Harlesiel (about 1 hour 15min) – ☎ 0 44 64/ 14 53, to **Langeoog:** from Bensersiel (about 45min) – ☎ 0 49 72/ 69 30; to **Juist:** from Norddeich (about 1 hour 15 min) – ☎ 0 49 35/ 5 87.

Nordfriesische Inseln: Sea links to Amrum and Föhr – From Dagebüll (journey time anything from 45min to 2 hours). Places for private cars should be reserved in advance from Wyker Dampfschiffs-Reederei GmbH in Wyk on Föhr – ☎ 0 46 81/ 80 40.

FRITZLAR

ⓘ Rathaus ☎ 0 56 22/ 98 86 43

Dom – Guided tour in summer Tuesdays to Fridays 9am to 12noon and 2pm to 6pm, Saturdays 9am to 12noon, Sundays 2pm to 5pm; in winter Tuesdays to Fridays 10am to 12noon and 2pm to 4pm, Saturdays 10am to 12noon, Sundays 2pm to 4pm. 5DM. ☎ 0 56 22/ 99 99 21.

Domschatz und Dommuseum – Open May to October Mondays to Saturdays 10am to 12noon and 2pm to 5pm, Sundays 2pm to 5pm; November to April Mondays to Saturdays 10am to 12noon and 2pm and 4pm, Sundays 2pm and 4pm. 4DM. ☎ 0 56 22/ 99 99 21.

FÜRSTENBERG

ⓘ Meinbrexener Str. ☎ 0 52 71/ 51 01

See HANN. MÜNDEN

FÜSSEN

ⓘ Augsburger Torplatz 1 ☎ 0 83 62/ 70 77

Museum der Stadt Füssen (Kloster St. Mang) – Open April to October 11am to 4pm; November to March 2pm to 4pm. Closed Mondays, 24 December. 3DM. ☎ 0 83 62/ 50 53 46.

FULDA

Dommuseum – Open April to October Tuesdays to Saturdays 10am to 5.30pm, Sundays and public holidays 12.30pm to 5.30pm; November to March 10am to 12.30pm and 1.30pm to 4.30pm, Sundays and public holidays 12.30pm to 4pm. Closed during January and on Mondays, Easter Day, Whit Sunday, 25 December. 3DM. ☎ 06 61/ 8 72 07.

Schloß Fasanerie – Guided tour (1 hour) April to October 10am to 12noon and 1pm to 5pm (last admissions 4pm). Closed Mondays. 5DM. ☎ 0 51 52/ 86 03.

FURTWANGEN
🛈 Rathaus, Marktplatz 4 ☎ 0 77 23/ 93 91 11

See SCHWARZWALD

G

GARMISCH-PARTENKIRCHEN
🛈 Dr.-Richard-Strauss-Platz ☎ 0 88 21/ 18 06

Wank: Cable-car – Operates in summer 8.45am to 5pm and in winter 9am to 4.30pm. Closed April and mid-November to Christmas. Rtn fare 26DM. ☎ 0 88 21/ 7 53-3 32.

Excursion

Mittenwald: Geigenbau- und Heimatmuseum – Open Mondays to Fridays 10am to 12noon and 2pm to 5pm, weekends 10am to 12noon. Closed November to about mid-December. 2.50DM. ☎ 0 88 23/ 25 11.

GELNHAUSEN
🛈 Obermarkt ☎ 0 60 51/ 82 00 54

Kaiserpfalz – Open March to October 10am to 1pm and 2pm to 5.30pm; November to February until 4.30pm (last admissions 30min before closing). Closed Mondays, 1 January, 25 and 31 December. 2DM. ☎ 0 60 51/ 38 05.

Excursions

Büdingen: Castle – Guided tour (1 hour) mid-March to 23 December Tuesdays to Fridays at 11.30am, 2pm, 3pm and 4pm, Saturdays at 2pm, 3pm, 4pm and 5pm, Sundays and public holidays at 11.30am, 2pm, 3pm, 4pm and 5pm. Closed Mondays. 6DM. ☎ 0 60 42/ 88 92 03.

Schloß Steinau: Brüder-Grimm-Museum – Open March to October 10am to 5pm; November to February until 4pm (last admissions 30min before closing). Closed Mondays, 1 January, 24 and 31 December. 2DM. ☎ 0 66 63/ 68 43.

GLÜCKSBURG
🛈 Sandwigstr. 1a ☎ 0 46 31/ 9 21

See FLENSBURG

Bad GODESBERG
🛈 Münsterstr. 20, Bonn ☎ 02 28/ 77 34 66

See BONN

GÖRLITZ
🛈 Obermarkt 29 ☎ 0 35 81/ 40 69 99

Städtische Kunstsammlungen – Open Tuesdays and Wednesdays 10am to 1pm and 2pm to 6pm, Thursdays to Sundays until 4pm. Closed Mondays all year and Sundays May to October. 3DM. ☎ 0 35 81/ 67 14 17.

Kaisertrutz – Open May to October Tuesdays and Wednesdays 10am to 1pm and 2pm to 6pm, Thursdays to Sundays until 4pm. Closed Mondays. 2DM. ☎ 0 35 81/6 73 51.

GÖTTINGEN
🛈 Altes Rathaus, Markt 9 ☎ 05 51/ 5 40 00

Städtisches Museum – Open Tuesdays to Fridays 10am to 5pm, weekends and public holidays 10am to 1pm. Closed Mondays, 1 January, Good Friday, Easter Day, Whit Sunday, Ascension Day, Buß- und Bettag (a Wednesday in November), 25 December. 3DM. ☎ 05 51/ 4 00 28 43.

GOSLAR
🛈 Markt 7 ☎ 0 53 21/ 28 46

Huldigingssaal – Guided tour (15min) April to October daily 10am to 5pm; November to March 10am to 4pm. Closed 1 January, 24 and 25 December. 3DM. ☎ 0 53 21/ 7 04-2 41.

Siemenshaus – Open Mondays to Fridays 9am to 12noon. Prior reservation recommended. Admission free. ☎ 0 53 21/ 2 38 37.

Kaiserpfalz – Open April to October 10am to 5pm; November to March 10am to 4pm; Buß- und Bettag (a Wednesday in November), 26 and 31 December open 10am to 1pm (last admissions 30min before closing). Closed 1 January and 25 December. 3.50DM. ☎ 0 53 21/ 7 04-3 58.

Goslarer Museum – Open April to October 10am to 5pm; November to March 10am to 4pm. Closed Mondays, 1 January, 24 and 25 December. 3.50DM. ☎ 0 53 21/ 4 33 94.

Rammelsberger Bergbaumuseum – Open 10am to 5pm. 3DM. Guided tour 1 (Roeder gallery): 6DM, guided tour 2 (tour by train): 9DM. ☎ 0 53 21/ 28 91.

GOTHA
🛈 Blumenbachstr. 1 ☎ 0 36 21/ 5 40 36

See ERFURT

GREIFSWALD
🛈 Schuhhagen 22 ☎ 0 38 34/ 34 60

Marienkirche – Open mid-April to mid-May Mondays to Fridays 10am to 12noon, Sundays and public holidays 10.30am to 12noon; mid-May to end of October Mondays to Fridays 10am to 12noon and 2pm to 4pm, Saturdays 10am to 12noon, Sundays and public holidays 10.30am to 12noon. Guided tour: 1DM. ☎ 0 38 34/ 22 63.

Dom St. Nikolai – Open May to September Mondays to Fridays 10am to 4pm, Saturdays 10am to 2pm, Sundays and public holidays before or after the religious services. Ascent of the tower: 2DM. ☎ 0 38 34/ 26 27.

St. Jakobikirche – Open Mondays to Fridays 10am to 12noon and 2pm to 4pm, Saturdays 10am to 12noon.

Museum – Open Wednesdays to Sundays 10am to 6pm; July and August also open Mondays and Tuesdays. 3DM. ☎ 0 38 34/ 27 20.

Botanischer Garten – Open Mondays to Fridays 9am to 3.45pm, weekends and public holidays 1pm to 3pm (January, February, December), or 1pm to 4pm (March, April, October, November), or 1pm to 6pm (May to September). The greenhouses are closed between 12noon and 12.30pm every day all year. Donations accepted. ☎ 0 38 34/ 7 55 69.

GÜSTROW
🛈 Gleviner Str. 33 ☎ 0 38 43/ 6 10 23

Schloßmuseum – Open mid-April to mid-October 10am to 6pm; mid-October to mid-April 9am to 5pm. Closed Mondays. 5DM. ☎ 0 38 43/ 50 21.

Dom – Open June to September 10am to 12noon and 1pm to 5pm, Sundays and public holidays 2pm to 4pm; October and May 10am to 12noon and 2pm to 4pm, Sundays and public holidays 2pm to 3pm; November to March 11am to 12noon and 2pm to 3pm, Sundays and public holidays 2pm to 3pm. Closed October to May on Mondays. ☎ 0 38 43/ 6 24 33.

Pfarrkirche St. Marien – Open January to April and October to December Tuesdays to Saturdays 11am to 12noon and 2pm to 3pm, Sundays and public holidays 2pm to 3pm; May, June and September Mondays to Saturdays 10am to 12noon and 2pm to 4pm, Sundays and public holidays 2pm to 4pm; July and August Mondays to Saturdays 10am to 4pm, Sundays and public holidays 2pm to 4pm. ☎ 0 38 43/ 68 20 77.

Ernst-Barlach-Gedenkstätte – Open March to October 10am to 5pm; November to February 11am to 4pm. Closed Mondays. 3DM. ☎ 0 38 43/ 6 22 06.

H

HAGEN
🛈 Rathaus, Friedrich-Ebert-Platz ☎ 0 23 31/ 2 07 33 83

See RUHRGEBIET

HAIGERLOCH
🛈 Rathaus, Oberstadtstr. ☎ 0 74 74/ 6 97 26

Atommuseum – Open May to September daily 10am to 12noon and 2pm to 5pm; October, November, March and April weekends and public holidays only 10am to 12noon and 2pm to 5pm. Closed December to February. 2DM. ☎ 0 74 74/ 6 97-26.

HALBERSTADT

Dom St. Stephanus – Open May to October 9am to 11.30am and 12noon to 5pm, Saturdays 10am to 11.30am and 12noon to 4.30pm, Sundays 12noon to 4.30pm; November to April Saturdays 10am to 11.30am and 12noon to 4pm, Sundays 12noon to 4pm. ☎ 0 39 41/ 2 42 37.

Domschatz – Guided tour (1 hour including visit of the cathedral) May to October Mondays to Fridays at 10am, 11.30am, 2pm and 3.30pm, Saturdays at 10am and 2pm, Sundays and public holidays at 11.30am and 2.30pm; November to April Mondays to Saturdays at 10am and 2pm, Sundays and public holidays at 11.30am. 4DM. ☎ 0 39 41/ 2 42 37.

Städtisches Museum – Open Tuesdays to Fridays 9am to 5pm, weekends 10am to 5pm. Closed Mondays, 1 January and 25 December. 5DM. ☎ 0 39 41/ 2 42 16.

HALLE

Händel-Haus – Open daily 9.30am to 5.30pm, Thursdays until 7pm. Closed 1 January and 25 December. 2DM. ☎ 03 45/ 50 09 00.

Salinenmuseum – Open April to September 10am to 5pm; October to March 10am to 4pm. Closed Mondays. 1.50DM. ☎ 03 45/ 2 50 34.

Staatliche Galerie Moritzburg – Open Tuesdays 11am to 8.30pm, Wednesdays to Fridays 10am to 5.30pm, weekends 10am to 6pm. Closed Mondays, 24 and 31 December. 3DM (5DM during temporary exhibitions). ☎ 03 45/ 3 70 31.

HAMBURG

Boat trip round the Alster – Departures from the Jungfernstieg quay daily 10am to 6pm every half hour. Journey time: 50min. 13DM.

"Michel" tower platform – Ascent of the tower May to October Mondays to Saturdays 9am to 5.30pm, Sundays and public holidays 11.30am to 5.30pm; November to April Mondays to Saturdays 10am to 4pm, Sundays and public holidays 11.30am to 4pm. 4DM.

Kunsthalle – Open 10am to 6pm, Thursdays until 9pm. Closed Mondays. 6DM. ☎ 0 40/ 24 86 26 12.

Museum für Kunst und Gewerbe – Open 10am to 6pm, Thursdays until 9pm. Closed Mondays, 1 January, 1 May, 3 October, 24 and 31 December. 6DM. ☎ 0 40/ 24 86 28 28.

Museum für Hamburgische Geschichte – Open 10am to 6pm. Closed Mondays. 6DM. ☎ 0 40/ 35 04 23 60.

Boat trip around the port – During tourist season, HADAG boats offer half-hourly departures 9am to 6pm (Sundays from 8.30am). Out of season, the timetable is different, sometimes with only hourly departures. Embarcation: St. Pauli-Landungsbrücken, Brücke 2. Trip takes 1 hour. 15DM. ☎ 0 40/ 31 17 07-0.

Postmuseum – Open Tuesdays, Wednesdays and Fridays 10am to 3pm, Thursdays until 6pm. Closed Mondays, weekends and certain public holidays. Admission free. ☎ 0 40/ 35 03 77 01.

Fernsehturm – Panorama viewpoint open 10am to 11pm. Lift 6DM. ☎ 0 40/ 43 80 24.

Erholungspark "Planten un Blomen" – Illuminated fountain displays with musical accompaniment May to August at 10pm, and in September at 9pm.

Hamburgisches Museum für Völkerkunde – Open 10am to 6pm. Closed Mondays, 1 May, 24 and 31 December. 5DM. ☎ 0 40/ 44 19 55 24.

Tierpark Hagenbeck – Open daily 9am to 6pm (until 7pm during summer holidays, and until 4.30pm in winter). 18DM (including the Troparium), children: 13DM. Delphinarium 6DM, children: 4DM. ☎ 0 40/ 54 00 01 47.

Excursions

Altonaer Museum – Norddeutsches Landesmuseum – Open 10am to 6pm. Closed Mondays, 1 January, 1 May, 3 October, 24 December. 6DM. ☎ 0 40/ 38 07-5 14.

Jenisch-Haus – Open April to October 10am to 5pm; November to March 1pm to 4pm, Sundays 10am to 4pm. Closed Mondays, Easter Day, Whit Sunday, 1 May, 3 October, 24 December. 3DM. ☎ 0 40/ 38 07-4 89.

Ernst-Barlach-Haus – Open 11am to 5pm. Closed Mondays, 24 and 31 December. 3DM. ☎ 0 40/ 82 60 85.

Wedel: Ernst-Barlach-Museum – Open 10am to 12noon and 3pm to 6pm. Closed Mondays, 1 January, 24 and 25 December. 5DM. ☎ 0 41 03/ 1 51 50.

Schloß Ahrensburg – Open April to September 10am to 12.30pm and 1.30pm to 5pm, November to January until 3pm, February, March and October until 4pm. Closed Mondays, Good Friday, Buß- und Bettag (a Wednesday mid-November), and 24 December to 1 January. 5DM. ☎ 0 41 02/ 4 25 10.

HAMELN

Excursions

Hamelschenburg: Schloß – Guided tour (40min) April to October on the hour 10am to 12noon and 2pm to 5pm. Closed Mondays. 6DM. ☎ 0 51 55/ 85 39.

Fischbeck: Abbey – Guided tour (1 hour 30min) Easter to mid-October 2pm to 4pm, Mondays, Tuesdays and Fridays also 9am to 11am. Closed Mondays. 4DM. ☎ 0 51 52/ 86 03.

HANN. MÜNDEN

Bad Karlshafen: Deutsches Hugenottenmuseum – Open mid-February to 30 December 2pm to 6pm, Sundays 11am to 6pm. Closed Mondays, 24 and 25 December. 3DM. ☎ 0 56 72/ 14 10.

Fürstenberg: Porcelain Museum – Open 9am to 5pm, Sundays and public holidays 10am to 5pm. Closed Mondays. 5DM. ☎ 0 52 71/ 40 11 63.

HANNOVER

Rathaus – Access to dome (via a lift): April to October daily 10am to 1pm and 1.30pm to 5pm. 3DM. ☎ 05 11/ 1 68 53 33.

Wilhelm-Busch-Museum – Open 10am to 5pm. Closed Mondays, Good Friday, 24 and 31 December. 3DM. ☎ 05 11/ 71 40 76.

Kestner-Museum – Open Tuesdays, Thursdays and Fridays 10am to 4pm, Fridays 10am to 4pm, Wednesdays until 8pm, weekends until 6pm. Closed Mondays, 1 January, Good Friday, 1 May, Ascension Day, 24 and 31 December. 2DM. ☎ 05 11/ 1 68-21 20.

Niedersächsisches Landesmuseum – Open 10am to 5pm, Thursdays until 7pm. Closed Mondays, Tuesdays after Easter and Whitsun, 24, 25 and 31 December. Admission free. ☎ 05 11/ 98 07-5.

Sprengel-Museum – Open Tuesdays 10am to 10pm, Wednesdays to Sundays 10am to 6pm. Closed Mondays, 1 January, Good Friday, 1 May, 25 December. Admission free. Temporary exhibitions: 5-10DM. ☎ 05 11/ 1 68-38 75.

Historisches Museum – Open Tuesdays 10am to 8pm, Wednesdays to Fridays 10am to 4pm, weekends 10am to 6pm. Closed Mondays, 1 January, Good Friday, 1 May, 24, 25 and 31 December. 4DM. ☎ 05 11/ 1 68-30 52.

Zoologischer Garten – Open April to mid-September 8.30am to 6pm (last admissions 5pm); mid-September to October and February to March 9am to 5pm (last admissions 4pm); November to January 9am to 4.30pm (last admissions 4pm). 10DM. ☎ 05 11/ 28 07 40.

HARZ

Clausthal-Zellerfeld: Oberharzer Bergwerksmuseum – Open daily 9am to 5pm. 6DM. ☎ 0 53 23/ 8 25 02.

St. Andreasberg: Silberbergwerk Samson – Guided tour (1 hour) 8am to 12.30pm and 2pm to 4.30pm. Closed Sundays, 1 January, 24 December. 4.50DM. ☎ 0 55 82/ 12 49.

Rübeland: Hermannshöhle – Guided tour (45min) daily May to October 9am to 5.30pm; January to April and November and December 10am to 4pm. Closed 24 December. 7DM. ☎ 03 94 54/ 91 32.

HEIDELBERG

Schloß – Guided tour (50min) daily 9am to 5pm or 4pm (November to March). 4DM. The courtyard and the Großes Faß can be visited separately. 2DM. ☎ 0 62 21/ 53 84 14.

Deutsches Apothekenmuseum – Open mid-March to end of October daily 10am to 5pm. Closed 1 January and 25 December. 3DM. ☎ 0 62 21/ 2 58 80.

Buchausstellung der Universitätsbibliothek – Open Easter to 1 November 11am to 4pm; 2 November to Good Friday Mondays to Saturdays 10am to 7pm. Admission free. ☎ 0 62 21/ 54 23 80.

Kurpfälzisches Museum – Open 10am to 5pm, Wednesdays until 9pm. Closed Mondays. 4DM. ☎ 0 62 21/ 58 34 00.

Studentenkarzer – Open Tuesdays to Fridays 10am to 12.30pm and 2pm to 5pm, Sundays and public holidays by appointment (telephone) only. Closed Mondays. 1.50DM. ☎ 0 62 21/ 2 95 45.

Museum of Sacred and Liturgical Art – Open June to October Tuesdays to Saturdays 10am to 5pm, Sundays 1pm to 5pm; November to May Saturdays 10am to 5pm, Sundays 1pm to 5pm. Closed Mondays, 1 January, Good Friday, Easter Day, 25, 26 and 31 December. 2.50DM. ☎ 0 62 21/ 47 56 22.

Excursions

Schwetzingen: Schloß – Guided tour (1 hour) April to October 10am to 4pm; November to March Fridays at 2pm, weekends at 11am, 2pm and 3pm. Closed Mondays, 24 and 31 December. 7DM. ☎ 0 62 02/ 8 14 81.

Schwetzingen: Rokokotheater – Guided tour in July and August at 11.30am, 2pm, 3pm and 3.30pm. 2DM. ☎ 0 62 02/ 8 14 81.

Schwetzingen: Schloßgarten – Open April to September daily 9am to 8pm (last admissions 7pm); October to March 9am to 5pm (last admissions 4.30pm). 3.50DM. ☎ 0 62 02/ 8 14 81.

Königstuhl: Funicular – April to October every 10-20min 9am to 7pm. Enquire about winter timetable. Rtn fare: 7DM (from Heidelberg-Kornmarkt stop). ☎ 0 62 21/5 13-0.

HELGOLAND
🛈 Landungsbrücke ☎ 0 47 25/ 3 55

Access – March to October daily boat connections from Cuxhaven (foot passengers only). A day trip to Helgoland allows about 3 hours 30min on the island itself (departure from Cuxhaven at 10.30am, return to Cuxhaven at 6.30pm). Rtn fare May to September from Cuxhaven 55DM. There are also connections from Büsum (44DM Rtn), Bremerhaven (55DM) or Wilhelmshaven (54DM). For details of boat connections from Cuxhaven November to February, enquire at the shipping company Cassen Eils: ☎ 0 47 21/ 3 50 82.

Bad HERSFELD
🛈 Am Markt ☎ 0 66 21/ 20 12 74

Stiftsruine – Open 10am to 12.30pm and 2pm to 5pm, Saturdays 10am to 12noon and 2pm to 5pm. Closed Mondays, winter (November to February) and during the Festspiele (May to end of August). 2DM. ☎ 0 66 21/ 6 77 28.

HILDESHEIM
🛈 Am Ratsbauhof 1c ☎ 0 51 21/ 1 59 95

Dom – Open 9.30am to 5pm, Sundays 12noon to 5pm. Closed Good Friday. 0.50DM. ☎ 0 51 21/ 3 20 21.

Roemer- und Pelizaeus-Museum – Open 9am to 4.30pm. Closed Mondays, 1 January, 1 May, 24, 25 and 31 December. 3DM (admission free on Sundays). ☎ 0 51 21/ 9 36 90.

HOHENLOHER LAND

Schöntal: Abbey – Abbey church open daily 9am to 6pm. Guided tour of conventual buildings April to October daily at 11am, 3pm and 4.30pm; in winter at 11am and 3pm. 2DM. ☎ 0 79 43/ 8 94-0.

Langenburg: Castle – Guided tour (45min) daily Palm Sunday to 1 November 9am to 12noon and 1.30pm to 6pm (last admission 5.15pm). 4.50DM. ☎ 0 79 05/ 2 64.

Neuenstein: Castle – Guided tour (50min) mid-March to mid-November 9am to 12noon and 1.30pm to 6pm. Closed Mondays. 6DM. ☎ 0 79 42/ 22 09.

HOHENSCHWANGAU
🛈 Rathaus Schwangau ☎ 0 83 62/ 8 19 80

See KÖNIGSSCHLÖSSER

Burg HOHENZOLLERN

Castle – Guided tour (45min) mid-March to mid-October daily 9am to 5.30pm; mid-October to mid-March 9am to 4.30pm. Closed 24 December. 7DM. ☎ 0 74 71/ 24 28.

HUSUM
🛈 Zingel 4 ☎ 0 48 41/ 6 69 91

Nissenhaus-Nordfriesisches Museum – Open April to October daily 10am to 5pm; November to March daily except Saturdays 10am to 4pm. 5DM. ☎ 0 48 41/ 95 45.

Excursions

Seebüll: Nolde-Museum – Open March to October daily 10am to 6pm; November 10am to 5pm. 5DM. ☎ 0 46 64/ 3 64.

A number of touring programmes is given on pp 7-9

Plan a trip with the help of the map of principal sights on pp 4-6.

I – J

IDAR-OBERSTEIN
🛈 Hauptstr. 213 ☎ 0 67 81/ 6 44 21

Deutsches Edelsteinmuseum – Open May to September daily 9am to 6pm; October to April 9am to 5pm. 7DM. ☎ 0 67 81/ 48 21.

Museum Idar-Oberstein – Open daily 9am to 5.30pm. 5DM. ☎ 0 67 81/ 2 46 19.

Weiherschleife – Open 20 March to 30 October Mondays to Fridays 9am to 5pm, weekends 10am to 4pm. Admission free. ☎ 0 67 81/ 3 31 65.

INGOLSTADT
🛈 Rathaus, Rathausplatz ☎ 08 41/ 30 54 17

Bayerisches Armeemuseum – Open 8.45am to 4.30pm. Closed Mondays (except Easter and Whit Mondays), Shrove Tuesday, Good Friday, 1 November, 24, 25 and 31 December. 4DM. ☎ 08 41/ 3 50 67.

Excursions

Neuburg an der Donau: Schloßmuseum – Open 10am to 5pm. Closed Mondays, 1 January, Shrove Tuesday, 1 November, 24, 25 and 31 December. 3DM. ☎ 0 84 31/ 88 97.

JENA
🛈 Löbderstr. 9 ☎ 0 36 41/ 2 46 71

Stadtmuseum Göhre – Open 10am to 1pm and 2pm to 5pm, Wednesdays until 6pm. Closed Mondays. 5DM. ☎ 0 36 41/ 2 39 98.

Goethe-Gedenkstätte – Open mid-April to mid-October 10am to 12noon and 1pm to 4pm. Closed Mondays and Tuesdays. Admission free. ☎ 0 36 41/ 63 03 04 (Schillerhaus).

Schiller-Gedenkstätte – Open Tuesdays to Fridays 10am to 12noon and 1pm to 4pm, Saturdays 11am to 4pm. Closed Sundays and Mondays. 1DM. ☎ 0 36 41/ 63 03 04.

Zeiss Planetarium – Presentations Tuesdays to Sundays at 10am, 11am, 12noon, 3pm, 4.30pm and 8pm. Closed Mondays, 31 December and 1 January. 6DM. ☎ 0 36 41/ 2 73 15.

Optisches Museum – Open Tuesdays to Fridays 10am to 5pm, Saturdays 1pm to 4.30pm, Sundays 9.30am to 1pm. Closed Mondays and public holidays. 5DM. ☎ 0 36 41/ 5 51 06.

Tourist Information Centres
are located on the town plans by the symbol 🛈
and the telephone number and address are listed
in the **Michelin Red Guide Deutschland.**

K

Bad KARLSHAFEN
🛈 Rathaus ☎ 0 56 72/ 10 22

See HANN. MÜNDEN

KARLSRUHE
🛈 Bahnhofplatz 6 ☎ 0/ 21/ 3 55 30

Staatliche Kunsthalle – Open Tuesdays to Fridays 10am to 5pm, weekends until 6pm. Closed Mondays, Shrove Tuesday, 24 and 31 December. 5DM. ☎ 07 21/ 9 26-33 55.

Badisches Landesmuseum – Open 10am to 5pm, Wednesdays until 8pm. Closed Mondays, Shrove Tuesday, 24, 25 and 31 December. 5DM.

Schloß: tower – Open daily, except Mondays, 10am to 4pm, Wednesdays until 7pm (in winter until nightfall). 3DM. ☎ 07 21/ 9 26-65 14.

Botanischer Garten – Open daily 8am to nightfall. Admission free. The greenhouses are open Tuesdays to Fridays 9am to 4pm, weekends 9am to 12noon and 1pm to 5pm (4pm October to March). Closed 24, 25 and 31 December. Greenhouses: 2.50DM. ☎ 07 21/ 9 26 30 08.

KASSEL

🚉 Intercity-Bahnhof Wilhelmshöhe ☎ 05 61/ 3 40 54

Schloß Wilhelmshöhe – Open 10am to 5pm. Closed Mondays, 1 May, 24, 25 and 31 December. 3DM (admission free on Saturdays). At the time of going to press the Old Masters Gallery is closed. ☎ 05 61/ 9 37 77. During the period of closure a selection of the main works is on display in the Fredericianum, open 10am to 5pm. Closed on Mondays. 8DM. ☎ 05 61/ 77 00 34.

Hessisches Landesmuseum – Open 10am to 5pm. Closed Mondays, 1 May, 24, 25 and 31 December. 3DM. (admission free on Saturdays). ☎ 05 61/ 7 84 60.

Neue Galerie – Open 10am to 5pm. Closed Mondays, 1 May, 24, 25 and 31 December. 3DM (admission free on Saturdays). ☎ 05 61/ 1 52 66.

Brüder-Grimm-Museum – Open daily 10am to 5pm. Closed on certain public holidays. Admission free. ☎ 05 61/ 10 32 35.

Naturkundemuseum – Closed for restoration at the time of going to press.

Excursions

Schloß Wilhelmsthal – Guided tour (45min) March to October 10am to 4pm; November to February 10am to 3pm. Closed Mondays, 1 January, 25 and 31 December. 4DM. ☎ 0 56 74/ 68 98.

KELHEIM

🚉 Ludwigsplatz ☎ 0 94 41/ 70 12 34

See REGENSBURG

KIEL

🚉 Sophienblatt 30 ☎ 04 31/ 67 91 00

Rathaus – Open Mondays to Thursdays 6.30am to 5pm, Fridays 6.30am to 3pm. ☎ 04 31/ 6 79 10-0.

Schleswig-Holsteinisches Freilichtmuseum – Open April to October Tuesdays to Saturdays 9am to 6pm, Sundays 9am to 5pm; July to mid-September also on Mondays 9am to 6pm; November to March on Sundays and public holidays only (weather permitting) 11am to 4pm. Closed 25 December. 7DM. ☎ 04 31/ 6 55 55.

Excursions

Laboe: Marine-Ehrenmal – Open April to September daily 9am to 6pm; October and March until 5pm; November and February until 4pm. Closed 24 December. 4DM for the memorial, 2.50DM for the submarine. ☎ 0 43 43/ 87 55.

KÖLN

🚉 Am Dom ☎ 02 21/ 2 21 33 40

Dom: Choir – Open daily 7am to 7pm. Guided tour (no charge) at 10am, 11am, 2.30pm and 3.30pm.

Domschatzkammer – Guided tour (30min) April to October Mondays to Saturdays 9am to 5pm, Sundays 12.30pm to 4pm; November to March Mondays to Saturdays 9am to 4pm, Sundays 12.30pm to 4pm. Closed 1 January, Monday before Shrove Tuesday, 25 December. 2DM. ☎ 02 21/ 21 75 15.

Römisch-Germanisches Museum – Open Tuesdays to Fridays 10am to 4pm, weekends 11am to 4pm. Closed Mondays, 1 January, during the Carnival, 24, 25 and 31 December. 5DM. ☎ 02 21/ 2 21 44 38.

Wallraf-Richartz-Museum/Museum Ludwig – Open Tuesdays to Fridays 10am to 6pm, weekends 11am to 6pm. Closed Mondays, 1 January, during the Carnival, 24, 25 and 31 December. 10DM. ☎ 02 21/ 2 21 23 72.

Agfa Foto-Historama – Same admission times as the Wallraff-Richartz-Museum. 10DM. ☎ 02 21/ 2 21 24 11.

Diözesanmuseum – Open 10am to 5pm. Closed Thursdays, 24 and 31 December. Admission free. ☎ 02 21/ 2 57 76 72.

St. Ursula (Goldene Kammer) – Open 9am to 12noon and 1pm to 5pm, Sundays 3pm to 5pm. Closed Tuesdays, Maundy Thursday to Easter Day and all public holidays. 2DM. ☎ 02 21/ 13 34 00.

Schnütgen-Museum – Open Tuesday to Friday 10am to 4pm, weekends 11am to 4pm. Closed Mondays, 1 January, during the Carnival, 24, 25 and 31 December. 5DM. ☎ 02 21/ 2 21-36 20.

Museum für Ostasiatische Kunst – Details of admission times and charges not available at the time of going to press. ☎ 02 21/ 94 05 18.

Museum für Angewandte Kunst – Open Tuesdays to Fridays 11am to 5pm, weekends 12noon to 5pm. 8DM. ☎ 02 21/ 2 21-67 14.

Kölnisches Stadtmuseum – Same admission times as the Schnütgen-Museum. 5DM. ☎ 02 21/ 2 21 23 52.

Rautenstrauch-Joest-Museum für Völkerkunde – Same admission times as the Schnütgen-Museum. 5DM. ☎ 02 21/ 3 36 94-13.

Imhoff-Stollwerck-Museum – Open daily 10am to 6pm (last admission at 5pm). Closed Sunday and Monday before Shrove Tuesday, 24, 25 and 31 December, 1 January. 10DM. ☎ 02 21/ 93 18 88-11.

Botanischer Garten Flora – Open daily 8am to nightfall. Greenhouses 10am to 12 noon and 1pm to 6pm. Admission free. ☎ 02 21/ 76 43 35.

Excursions

Brühl: Schloß Augustusburg – Guided tour (50min) 9am to 12noon and 1.30pm to 4pm. Closed Mondays, and throughout December and January. 3DM. ☎ 0 22 32/ 4 24 71.

KÖNIGSSCHLÖSSER

Schloß Hohenschwangau – Guided tour (35min) April to September daily 8.30am to 5.30pm; October to March 10am to 4pm. Closed 24 December. 9DM. ☎ 0 83 62/ 8 11 27.

Schloß Neuschwanstein – Guided tour (40min) April to September daily 9am to 5.30pm; October to March 10am to 4pm. Closed 1 January, Shrove Tuesday, 1 November, 24, 25 and 31 December. 9DM. ☎ 0 83 62/ 8 10 35.

KÖNIGSTEIN im Taunus
🛈 Hauptstr. 21a ☎ 0 61 74/ 20 22 51

See FRANKFURT AM MAIN

KONSTANZ
🛈 Bahnhofplatz 13 ☎ 0 75 31/ 28 43 76

Rosgartenmuseum – Open Tuesdays and Wednesdays 10am to 5pm, Thursdays 10am to 7pm, weekends 10am to 4pm. Closed Mondays and public holidays (except Easter Day). 3DM. ☎ 0 75 31/ 90 02 46.

Excursions

Insel Mainau – 23 March to 22 October 7am to 7pm; 23 October to 20 March 9am to 5pm. Closed 24 and 25 December. 14DM. ☎ 0 75 31/ 3 03-0.

Bad KREUZNACH
🛈 Kurhausstr. 23 ☎ 06 71/ 8 36 00 50

Römerhalle – Open 10am to 5pm. Closed Mondays, 24, 25 and 31 December. 2DM. ☎ 06 71/ 8 00-2 48.

KULMBACH
🛈 Stadthalle, Sutte 2 ☎ 0 92 21/ 9 58 80

See BAYREUTH

L

LABOE
🛈 Kurverwaltung, im Meerwasserbad ☎ 0 43 43/ 73 53

See KIEL

LAHNTAL

Schloß Schaumburg – Open March to October 10am to 5pm. Closed Mondays. 5DM. ☎ 0 64 32/ 37 84.

Diez: Schloß Oranienstein – Currently closed for restoration. Contact the tourist office for further information (i Rathaus, Wilhelmstr. 63 ☎ 0 64 32/ 50 12 70.

Weilburg: Castle – Guided tour (45min) March to October 10am to 4pm; November to February 10am to 3pm. Closed Mondays, 1 January, 25 and 31 December. 4DM. ☎ 0 64 71/ 22 36.

Weilburg: Bergbau- und Stadtmuseum – Open April to October Tuesdays to Sundays 10am to 12noon and 2pm to 5pm; November to March Mondays to Fridays 10am to 12noon

LANDSHUT
🛈 Altstadt 315 ☎ 08 71/ 92 20 50

Stadtresidenz – Guided tour (45min) April to September 9am to 12noon and 1pm to 5pm; October to March until 4pm. Closed in winter on Mondays, 1 January, Shrove Tuesday, 1 November, 24 and 25 December. 3DM. ☎ 08 71/ 2 26 38.

Burg Trausnitz – Same admission times as the Stadtresidenz. 3DM. ☎ 08 71/ 2 26 38.

LANGENBURG

0 79 05/ 9 10 20

See HOHENLOHER LAND

LAUENBURG an der Elbe

🛈 Im Schloß ☎ 0 41 53/ 59 09 81

See LÜNEBURG

LEIPZIG

🛈 Sachsenplatz 1 ☎ 03 41/ 7 95 90

Museum für Geschichte der Stadt Leipzig – Open Tuesdays to Fridays 10am to 6pm, weekends 10am to 4pm. Closed Mondays, 1 January, Tuesdays after Easter and Whit Sunday, 24, 25 and 31 December. 3DM. ☎ 03 41/ 7 09 21.

Ägyptisches Museum – Open 1pm to 5pm, Sundays 10am to 1pm. Closed Mondays, 1 January, 25 December. 1DM. ☎ 03 41/ 28 21 66.

Grassi-Museum:

Museum of Arts and Crafts – Open Tuesdays to Fridays 10am to 6pm, weekends until 5pm. Closed Mondays, 24 and 31 December. 4DM (admission free Sundays). ☎ 03 41/ 2 14 20.

Museum of Ethnography – Open Tuesdays to Fridays 10am to 5.30pm, weekends until 4pm. Closed Mondays. 5DM (admission free 1st Sunday in month). ☎ 03 41/ 2 14 22 30.

Museum of Musical Instruments – Open Tuesdays to Saturdays 10am to 5pm, Sundays until 1pm. Closed Mondays, Good Friday, 3 October, 24 December. 5DM. ☎ 03 41/ 2 14 21 20.

Museum der Bildenden Künste – Open Tuesdays to Sundays 9am to 5pm, Wednesdays 1pm to 9.30pm. Closed Mondays, 1 January, 24, 25 and 31 December. 5DM (admission free Sundays). ☎ 03 41/ 2 16 99-0.

Völkerschlachtdenkmal – Open May to October daily 10am to 5pm; November to April 9am to 4pm. Closed 1 January, 24, 25 and 31 December. 3.50DM. ☎ 03 41/ 8 04 71.

LEMGO

🛈 Papenstr. 7 ☎ 0 52 61/ 21 33 47

Hexenbürgermeisterhaus – Open 10am to 12.30pm and 1.30pm to 5pm. Closed Mondays, 1 January and 25 December. 1.50DM. ☎ 0 52 61/ 21 32 76.

Junkerhaus – Open mid-March to mid-December 10am to 12.30pm and 1.30pm to 5pm. Closed Mondays. 1.50DM. ☎ 0 52 61/ 21 32 76.

LIMBURG AN DER LAHN

🛈 Hospitalstr. 2 ☎ 0 64 31/ 61 66

Diözesanmuseum – Open mid-March to mid-November Tuesdays to Saturdays 10am to 1pm and 2pm to 5pm, Sundays 11am to 5pm. Closed Mondays. 2DM. ☎ 0 64 31/ 29 54 82.

LINDAU IM BODENSEE

🛈 Am Hauptbahnhof ☎ 0 83 82/ 2 60 00

Städtische Kunstsammlungen – Open April to October 10am to 12noon and 2pm to 5pm. Closed Mondays, Easter Saturday, 1 May, Whit Sunday, Corpus Christi, and November to March. 4DM. ☎ 0 83 82/ 27 54 05.

LINDERHOF

Schloß – Guided tour (2 hours in summer, 30min in winter) April to September 9am to 12.15pm and 12.45pm to 5.30pm; October to March 10am to 12.15pm and 12.45pm to 4pm. Fountain displays on the hour. In high season, be prepared to queue for up to 3 hours. The Venus grotto and Moorish pavilion are closed in winter. 8DM in summer, 6DM in winter, admission free to park. ☎ 0 88 22/ 35 12.

LORSCH

🛈 Rathaus, Marktplatz 1 ☎ 0 62 51/ 59 67 50

See BERGSTRASSE

LUDWIGSBURG

🛈 Wilhelmstr. 10 ☎ 0 71 41/ 91 02 52

Schloß: Apartments – Guided tour (1 hour 30min) March to October 9am to 12noon and 1pm to 5pm; November to February Mondays to Fridays at 10.30am and 3pm, Saturdays at 10.30am, 2pm and 3.30pm, Sundays and public holidays at 10.30am and 1.30pm to 4pm. 8DM. ☎ 0 71 41/ 18 64 40.

Schloß: Blühendes Barock – Open March to October 8.30am to 6.30pm. 10DM. ☎ 0 71 41/ 92 42 41.

Excursions

Marbach: Schiller-Nationalmuseum – Open daily 9am to 5pm. Closed 24 and 25 December, and 31 December in the afternoon. 4DM. ☎ 0 71 44/ 84 86 01.

LUDWIGSLUST
🛈 Schloßfreiheit 8 ☎ 0 38 74/ 2 90 76

Schloß – Open April to October 10am to 6pm; November to March 10am to 5pm (last admission 30min before closing). Closed Mondays (apart from public holidays). 5DM. ☎ 0 38 74/ 2 81 14.

Stadtkirche – Open May to September 10.30am to 11.30pm and 3pm to 4.30pm, Sundays 3pm to 4.30pm; October to April from 3pm. ☎ 0 38 74/ 2 12 08.

LÜBBENAU
🛈 Ehm-Welk-Str. 15 ☎ 0 35 42/ 36 68

See SPREEWALD

LÜBECK
🛈 Markt ☎ ☎ 04 51/ 1 22 81 06

Buddenbrookhaus – Open daily 10am to 5pm. 4DM. ☎ 04 51/ 1 22 41 92.

St. Annen-Museum – Open April to September 10am to 5pm; October to March 10am to 4pm. Closed Mondays, 24, 25 and 31 December. 4DM (admission free on Fridays). ☎ 04 51/ 1 22 41 37.

Behnhaus und Drägerhaus – Same admission times as the St. Annen-Museum. 4DM. ☎ 04 51/ 1 22 41 48.

LÜNEBURG
🛈 Am Markt ☎ 0 41 31/ 3 22 00

Rathaus – Guided tour (45min) April to mid-October every hour 10am to 12noon and 2pm to 4pm; mid-October to mid-March at 10am, 11am, 2pm and 3pm. Closed Mondays. 5DM. ☎ 0 41 31/ 30 92 30.

Excursion

Lauenburg an der Elbe: Elbschiffahrtsmuseum – Open March to October daily 10am to 1pm and 2pm to 5pm; November to February Wednesdays, Fridays and weekends 10am to 1pm and 2pm to 4.30pm. Closed 1 January and 25 December. 2DM. ☎ 0 41 53/ 59 09-84.

LÜNEBURGER HEIDE

Ebstorf: Ehemaliges Benediktinerkloster – Guided tour (1 hour 30min) April to September Mondays to Saturdays 10am to 11am and 2pm to 5pm, Sundays and public holidays at 11.15am and 2pm to 6pm; 1st two weeks of October Mondays to Saturdays, 10am to 11am and 2pm to 3pm, Sundays and public holidays at 11.15am and 2pm to 3pm. Closed Good Friday and mid-October to mid-March. 5DM. ☎ 0 58 22/ 23 04.

Suhlendorf: Museum – Open 10am to 6pm. Closed Mondays and the period from 20 December to end of January. 4DM. ☎ 0 58 20/ 3 70.

Walsrode: Ornithological Park – Open March to 1 November 9am to 7pm. 16DM. ☎ 0 51 61/ 20 15.

With this Green Guide
use the Michelin Maps no 415 to 420 at a scale of 1:300 000 (1cm: 3km)
The maps provide both road and tourist information

M

MAGDEBURG
🛈 Alter Markt 12 ☎ 03 91/ 5 41 47 04

Kloster Unser Lieben Frauen – Open Tuesdays to Sundays 10am to 6pm, Thursdays until 8pm. Closed Mondays. 2DM. ☎ 03 91/ 5 41 47 22.

MAINZ
🛈 Bahnhofstr. 15 ☎ 0 61 31/ 28 62 10

Gutenberg-Museum – Open Tuesdays to Saturdays 10am to 6pm, Sundays 10am to 1pm. Closed January, Mondays and certain public holidays. 5DM (admission free on Sundays). ☎ 0 61 31/ 12 26 40.

Römisch-Germanisches Zentralmuseum – Open 10am to 6pm. Closed Mondays, 25 and 31 December. Admission free. ☎ 0 61 31/ 23 22 31.

Landesmuseum Mainz – Open Tuesdays to Sundays 10am to 5pm (Tuesdays until 8pm). Closed Mondays, 1 January, during Carnival time, Easter Day, Whit Sunday, 24, 25 and 31 December. Admission free. ☎ 0 61 31/ 23 29 55.

MANNHEIM
🛈 Kaiserring 10 ☎ 06 21/ 10 10 11

Städtische Kunsthalle – Open 10am to 5pm, Thursdays 12noon to 5pm. Closed Mondays, Shrove Tuesday and Sunday before it, Maundy Thursday, Good Friday, 1 May, 24 and 31 December. 4DM. ☎ 06 21/ 2 93-64 13.

Museum für Kunst-, Stadt- und Theatergeschichte im Reiß-Museum – Open 10am to 5pm. Closed Mondays, 1 January, Maundy Thursday, 1 May, 24 and 31 December. 4DM (admission free on Thursdays). ☎ 06 21/ 2 93 97 29.

Museum für Archäologie und Völkerkunde – Same admission times as Museum für Kunst-, Stadt- und Theatergeschichte. 4DM. ☎ 06 21/2 93 97 29.

Schloß – Open April to October Tuesdays to Sundays 10am to 12noon and 3pm to 5pm; November to March weekends 10am to 12noon and 3pm to 5pm (last admission 30min before closing). Closed Mondays, 1 January, 1 May, 25 December. 3DM. ☎ 06 21/ 2 92-28 90.

Museumsschiff Mannheim – Open Tuesdays to Fridays 9.15am to 5pm (Wednesdays until 8pm), weekends 10am to 5pm. Closed Mondays (apart from Easter and Whit Mondays), Shrove Tuesday, Good Friday, 24, 25 and 31 December. Admission free. ☎ 06 21/ 2 92-47 30.

Landesmuseum für Technik und Arbeit – Same admission times as Museumsschiff. 4DM. ☎ 06 21/ 2 92-47 30.

MARBACH
🛈 Rathaus ☎ 0 71 44/ 10 22 45

See LUDWIGSBURG

MARBURG
🛈 Neue Kasseler Str. 1 ☎ 0 64 21/ 20 12 49

Elisabethkirche – Open April to September Mondays to Fridays 9am to 6pm, Saturdays 9am to 5.30pm, Sundays 11.15am to 5.30pm; October Mondays to Saturdays 9am to 5pm, Sundays 11.15am to 5pm; November to March Mondays to Saturdays 10am to 4pm, Sundays 11.15am to 4pm. Closed 24 December. 2DM. ☎ 0 64 21/ 6 55 73.

Schloß – Open April to October 10am to 6pm; November to March 11am to 5pm. Closed Mondays (or Tuesdays, if the Monday is a public holiday), 24, 25 and 31 December. 3DM. ☎ 0 64 21/ 28 23 55.

Marburger Universitätsmuseum für Bildende Kunst – Open 11am to 1pm and 2pm to 5pm. Closed Mondays. Admission free. ☎ 0 64 21/ 28 23 55.

MAULBRONN

Abbey – Open April to October daily 8.30am to 6.30pm; November to March Tuesdays to Sundays 9.30am to 1pm and 2pm to 5pm. Closed Mondays (November to March), 24, 25 and 31 December. 6DM. ☎ 0 70 43/ 74 54.

MECKLENBURGISCHE SEENPLATTE

Müritz-Nationalpark: Nature walks – Information from ☎ 0 39 91/ 73 90.

MEISSEN
🛈 An der Frauenkirche 3 ☎ 0 35 21/ 45 44 70

Staatliche Porzellanmanufaktur – Porcelain collection open 9am to 5pm. 10DM. Showcase workshop: guided tour (30min) 9am to 5pm (last admission at 3.30pm). 10DM. Closed Mondays, 1 January, 24, 25, 26 and 31 December. ☎ 0 35 21/ 46 82 08.

Albrechtsburg – Open 10am to 6pm (last admission at 5.30pm). Closed Mondays and during January. 6DM. ☎ 0 35 21/ 4 70 70.

Bad MERGENTHEIM
🛈 Marktplatz 3 ☎ 0 79 31/ 5 71 35

Deutschordensschloß – Open Tuesdays to Fridays 2.30pm to 5.30pm, weekends and public holidays 10am to 12noon and 2.30pm to 5.30pm. Closed Mondays. 3DM. ☎ 0 79 31/ 5 22 12.

Excursions

Stuppach Parish Church: Stuppacher Madonna – Open May to October daily 9am to 5.30pm; March to April 10am to 5pm; November to February 11am to 4pm. 2DM. ☎ 0 79 31/ 26 05.

MICHELSTADT
🛈 Marktplatz 1 ☎ 0 60 61/ 7 41 46

See ODENWALD

MINDEN

Domschatzkammer – Open Tuesdays, Thursdays and weekends 10am to 12noon, Wednesdays and Fridays 3pm to 5pm. Closed Mondays. Admission free. ☎ 05 71/ 2 30 74.

Mindener Museum für Geschichte, Landes- und Volkskunde – Open Tuesdays, Wednesdays and Fridays 10am to 1pm and 2.30pm to 5pm (Thursdays until 6.30pm), Saturdays 2.30pm to 5pm, Sundays 11am to 6pm. Closed Mondays, 1 January, 1 May, Corpus Christi, 24, 25 and 31 December. Admission free. ☎ 05 71/ 8 93 16.

Excursion

Porta Westfalica: Fernsehturm – Open Easter to October daily 10am to 6pm. 1DM. ☎ 05 71/ 7 11 76.

MITTENWALD

See GARMISCH-PARTENKIRCHEN

MÖNCHENGLADBACH

Städtisches Museum Abteiberg – Open 10am to 6pm. Closed Mondays, 1 January, Easter Day, Whit Sunday, 24, 25 and 31 December. 5DM. ☎ 0 21 61/ 25 26 31.

Schloß Rheydt – Open 2pm to 8pm, Sundays 11am to 8pm. Closed Mondays, 1 January, 24, 25 and 31 December. 5DM. ☎ 0 21 66/ 92 89 00.

Excursion

Schloß Dyck – Open 10am to 6pm. 3.50DM. ☎ 0 21 82/ 40 61.

MONSCHAU

Rotes Haus: Local Museum – Open Good Friday to end of November. Admissions at 10am, 11am, 2pm, 3pm and 4pm. Closed Mondays. 4DM. ☎ 0 24 72/ 50 71.

Excursion

Burg Nideggen – Open Easter to October 10am to 5pm; November to Easter weekends only. Closed Mondays, 25 and 26 December. 3.50DM. ☎ 0 24 27/ 63 40.

MOSELTAL

River cruises along the Moselle – From May to mid-October there are connections from Koblenz to Cochem (Rtn fare 40.40DM; extra charge for hydrofoil). 2- and 3-day cruises between Frankfurt and Trier (via Koblenz) or between Trier and Cologne are available during high season. Enquire at the offices along the pier or at Köln-Düsseldorfer, Frankenwerft 15, 50667 Köln, ☎ 02 21/ 20 88-2 88.

Bellstein: Metternich Castle Ruins – Open daily 8am to 8pm. Closed 1 November to Easter. 2DM.

Cochem: Reichsburg – Guided tour (40min) 15 March to 15 November daily 9am to 5pm. 5DM. ☎ 0 26 71/ 2 55.

Burg Eltz – Guided tour (40min) April to 1 November daily 9.30am to 5.30pm. 8DM. ☎ 0 26 72/ 13 00.

MÜNCHEN

Deutsches Jagd- und Fischereimuseum – Open daily 9.30am to 5pm, Mondays and Thursdays until 9pm. Closed Shrove Tuesday, 24 and 31 December. 5DM. ☎ 0 89/ 22 05 22.

Residenz: Schatzkammer – Open 10am to 4.30pm. Closed Mondays, 1 January, Shrove Tuesday, Good Friday, Easter Day and Whit Sunday, 1 May, 1 November, 24, 25 and 31 December. 4DM. ☎ 0 89/ 2 90 67-1.

Residenzmuseum – Same admission times as Schatzkammer. 4 DM. ☎ 0 89/ 2 90 67-1.

Altes Residenztheater (Cuvilliés-Theater) – Open 2pm to 5pm. 2.50DM. ☎ 0 89/ 2 90 67-1.

Alte Pinakothek – This museum is closed for restoration work unitl 1997. The main works of art are on display in the Neue Pinakothek during this period.

Neue Pinakothek – Open 10am to 5pm, Tuesdays and Thursdays until 8pm. Closed Mondays, 24 December. 6DM (admission free on Sundays and public holidays). ☎ 0 89/ 2 38 05-1 95.

Glyptothek – Open 10am to 4.30pm, Thursdays 12noon to 8.30pm. Closed Mondays, 1 January, Good Friday, 1 May, Whit Sunday, 3 October, 24 and 25 December. 5DM (admission free on Sundays). ☎ 0 89/ 5 59 15 51.

Antiken-Sammlung – Open 10am to 4.30pm, Wednesdays 12noon to 8.30pm. Closed Mondays, Good Friday, Easter Day, 1 May, Corpus Christi, 1 November, 24 and 25 December. 5DM. ☎ 0 89/ 5 59 15 51.

Städtische Galerie im Lenbachhaus – Open 10am to 6pm. Closed Mondays, Shrove Tuesday, 24 and 31 December. 8DM. ☎ 0 89/ 23 33 20 02.

Deutsches Museum – Open daily 9am to 5pm. Closed 1 January, Shrove Tuesday, Good Friday, Easter Day, Whit Sunday, 1 May, Corpus Christi, 1 November, 24, 25 and 31 December. 8DM. ☎ 0 89/ 2 17 93 24.

Bayerisches Nationalmuseum – Open 9.30am to 5pm. Closed Mondays, Shrove Tuesday, Good Friday, 1 May, Whit Sunday, 1 November, 25 December. 5DM (admission free on Sundays). ☎ 0 89/ 2 11 24-1.

Staatsgalerie moderner Kunst – Open 10am to 5pm, Thursdays until 8pm. Closed Mondays, 1 January, Good Friday, Easter Day, Whit Sunday, 1 May, Corpus Christi, 1 November, 24 and 25 December. 5DM. ☎ 0 89/ 21 12 71 37.

Nymphenburg – Open April to September 9am to 12.30pm and 1.30pm to 5pm; October to March 10am to 12.30pm and 1.30pm to 4pm. Closed Mondays, 1 January, Shrove Tuesday, 1 November, 24, 25 and 31 December. 2.50DM. ☎ 0 89/ 17 90 80.

Amalienburg – Same admission times as Nymphenburg, however also open Mondays. 2DM. ☎ 0 89/ 17 90 80.

Marstallmuseum und Porzellansammlung – Open April to September 9am to 12noon and 1pm to 5pm; October to March 10am to 12noon and 1pm to 4pm. Closed at the same times as Nymphenburg. 2.50DM. ☎ 0 89/ 17 90 80.

Naturkundemuseum "Mensch und Natur" – Open 9am to 5pm. Closed Mondays, Shrove Tuesday, 24, 25 and 31 December. 3DM (admission free Sundays and public holidays). ☎ 0 89/ 17 64 94.

Botanischer Garten – Open daily May to August 9am to 7pm; April and September 9am to 6pm; February, March and October 9am to 5pm; January, November and December 9am to 4.30pm. The greenhouses close 30min earlier and are also closed 11.45am to 1pm. Closed 24 and 31 December. 3DM. ☎ 0 89/ 17 86 13 10.

Museum Villa Stuck – Open 10am to 5pm. Closed Mondays, 24 and 31 December. 6DM. ☎ 0 89/ 45 55 51 25.

Münchner Stadtmuseum – Open 10am to 5pm, Wednesdays until 8.30pm. Closed Mondays, Shrove Tuesday and Sunday before it, Good Friday, Easter Day, Whit Sunday, 1 May, 1 November, 24 and 25 December. 5DM. ☎ 0 89/ 23 32 23 70.

Excursions

Olympiapark – Open 8.30am to 6pm. 7DM for the whole park, 1DM for the Olympia stadium, 5DM for the lift to the top of the Olympia tower. ☎ 0 89/ 30 67 24 14.

BMW-Museum – Open daily 9am to 5pm (last admission 4pm). Closed 24 and 31 December. 4.50DM. ☎ 0 89/ 3 82-2 33 07.

Tierpark Hellabrunn – Open daily April to September 8am to 6pm; October to March 9am to 5pm. 7DM. ☎ 0 89/ 62 50 82-0.

Bavaria-Filmstadt Geiselgasteig – Guided tour (1 hour 30min) daily March to October 9am to 4pm. 12DM. ☎ 0 89/ 64 99 23 04.

Schloß Schleißheim – Open April to September 10am to 12.30pm and 1.30pm to 5pm; October to March until 4pm. Closed Mondays, 1 January, Shrove Tuesday, 24, 25 and 31 December. 2DM. ☎ 0 89/ 3 15 02 12.

Dachau Concentration Camp Memorial – Open 9am to 5pm. Closed Mondays, 24 and 31 December. Admission free. ☎ 0 81 31/ 17 41.

Andechs: Church – Open 8am to 7pm, or 6pm (in winter). Guided tour (1 hour) of the abbey church. 2DM. ☎ 0 81 52/ 3 76-0.

Domkammer – Open 10am to 12noon and 2pm to 6pm, Sundays 2pm to 6pm. Closed Mondays, Good Friday to Easter Day. 1DM. ☎ 02 51/ 4 24 71.

Westfälisches Landesmuseum für Kunst und Kulturgeschichte – Open 10am to 6pm. Closed Mondays. 5DM (admission free on Fridays). ☎ 02 51/ 59 07 20-1.

Rathaus: Friedenssaal – Open Monday to Friday 9am to 5pm, Saturdays until 4pm, Sundays 10am to 1pm. Closed 1 January and 25 December. 1.50DM. ☎ 02 51/ 4 92 27 45.

Westfälisches Museum für Naturkunde – Open 9am to 6pm. Closed Mondays, 24, 25 and 31 December. 5DM, Planetarium 5DM. ☎ 02 51/ 5 91 05.

Mühlenhof-Freilichtmuseum – Open April to October daily 10am to 6pm (last admission 5pm); November to March daily 11am to 4.30pm (last admission 4pm). 5DM. ☎ 0251/ 8 20 74.

Wasserburgen des Münsterlandes – From Münster there are bus trips to the various castles in the surrounding area April to mid-October on Saturdays. Details from the Verkehrsverein Münster GmbH, Berliner Platz 22, 48143 Münster, ☎ 02 51/ 49 20.

Excursions

Telgte: Museum Heimathaus Münsterland – Open 9.30am to 12noon and 1.30pm to 5pm (last admission 30min before closing time). Closed Mondays, 24, 25 and 31 December. Periodically closed during preparations for temporary exhibitions. Enquire in advance. 2DM. ☎ 0 25 04/ 9 31 20.

MÜNSTERLÄNDER WASSERBURGEN

Anholt: Wasserburg – Open 10am to 6pm. Closed Mondays, 24 to 26 December and New Year. Schloß: 7DM, Park: 5DM, both: 10DM. ☎ 0 28 74/ 4 53 53.

Gemen: Wasserschloß – Since the castle is an educational centre, it is not always open to the public. Enquire in advance. ☎ 0 28 61/ 92 20-0.

Hülshoff: Wasserburg – Open mid-March to mid-December daily 9.30am to 6pm. 4DM. ☎ 0 25 34/ 10 52.

Lembeck: Schloß – Guided tour (45min) March to October daily 9am to 6pm. 6DM. ☎ 0 23 69/ 71 67.

Vischering: Burg – Open April to October 10am to 12.30pm and 1.30pm to 5.30pm; November to March 10am to 12.30pm and 1.30pm to 4.30pm (last admission 30min before closing). Closed Mondays. 3DM. ☎ 0 25 91/ 36 21.

N

NENNIG

Römische Villa – Open April to September 8.30am to 12noon and 1pm to 6pm; October to March 9am to 12noon and 1pm to 4.30pm. Closed Mondays and during January. 1DM. ☎ 0 68 66/ 13 29.

NEUBRANDENBURG   🅑 Turmstr. 11 ☎ 03 95/ 5 82 22 67

Johanniskirche – Open June to September 10am to 4pm. ☎ 03 95/ 5 82 34 75.

NEUBURG an der Donau   🅑 Amalienstr. A 51 ☎ 0 84 31/ 5 52 40

See INGOLSTADT

NIDEGGEN   🅑 Rathaus, Zülpicher Str.1 ☎ 0 24 27/ 80 90

See MONSCHAU

NÖRDLINGEN   🅑 Marktplatz 2 ☎ 0 90 81/ 43 80

Stadtmuseum – Open March to October 10am to 12noon and 1.30pm to 4.30pm. Closed Mondays, 1 January, Shrove Tuesday, Good Friday, 1 May, 1 November, Buß- und Bettag (a Wednesday in November), 24-26 and 31 December. 3DM. ☎ 0 90 81/ 8 41 20.

Rieskrater-Museum – Open 10am to 12noon and 1.30pm to 4.30pm. Closed at same times as Stadtmuseum. 5DM. ☎ 0 90 81/ 8 41 43.

NÜRBURGRING

Rennsportmuseum – Open March to October daily 10am to 6pm; November to February Tuesday to Saturday 10am to 5pm. 8.50DM. ☎ 0 26 91/ 92 06 12.

NÜRNBERG

Germanisches Nationalmuseum – Open 10am to 5pm, Wednesdays until 9pm. Closed Mondays, 1 January, Shrove Tuesday, Good Friday, 1 May, 3 October, 24, 25 and 31 December. 5DM. ☎ 09 11/ 13 31-1 16.

Dürerhaus – Open March to October 10am to 5pm, Wednesdays until 9pm; November to February Tuesdays to Fridays 1pm to 5pm, Wednesdays until 9pm, weekends 10am to 5pm. During Advent, same admission times as in the summer. Closed Mondays, 1 January, Shrove Tuesday, Good Friday, 1 May, 24, 25 and 31 December. 4DM. ☎ 09 11/ 55 54 99.

Kaiserburg – Guided tour (30min) April to September daily 9am to 12noon and 12.45pm to 5pm (last admission at 4.30pm); October to March 9.30am to 12noon and 12.45pm to 4pm (last admission at 3.30pm). Closed 1 January, Shrove Tuesday, 1 November, 24, 25 and 31 December. 3DM. ☎ 09 11/ 22 57 26.

Spielzeugmuseum – Open 10am to 5pm, Wednesdays until 9pm. Closed Mondays, 1 January, Shrove Tuesday and Monday before it, 3 October, 24, 25 and 31 December. 5DM. ☎ 09 11/ 2 31-31 64.

Verkehrsmuseum – Open daily 9.30am to 5pm. Closed 1 January, Shrove Tuesday, Good Friday, Easter Day, Whit Sunday, 1 May, 3 October, Buß- und Bettag, 24 and 31 December. 5DM. ☎ 09 11/ 2 19 24 28.

OBERSTDORF

Nebelhorn: Cable-car/Chairlift – Operates 8.15am to 5pm. Closed for about 3 weeks 8 days after Easter and from November to Christmas. 31DM to the Nebelhorn mountain station, 37DM to the Nebelhorn summit. ☎ 0 83 22/ 10 92.

Excursion

Breitachklamm – Accessible 8am to 4pm (3pm in winter). Not accessible during spring, as the snow melts. 3DM. ☎ 0 83 22/ 48 87.

ODENWALD

Eulbach Park – Open all year 9am to 5pm. 5DM. ☎ 0 60 62/ 37 00.

Michelstadt: Odenwald-Museum – Open 2nd Saturday before Easter to 1 November Tuesdays to Sundays 10am to 12.30pm and 2pm to 5.30pm, similarly during Advent open Thursdays to Sundays. 2DM. ☎ 0 60 61/ 7 41 39.

Amorbach: Abteikirche – Guided tour (35min) Mondays to Saturdays every 40min 9.20am to 12noon and 1.20pm to 6pm, Sundays 11.20am to 6pm (May to September); Mondays to Saturdays 9.20am to 12noon and 1.20pm to 5.20pm, Sundays 11.20am to 5.20pm (April and October); Mondays to Saturdays 9.40am to 11.40am and 1.40pm to 5pm, Sundays 1 to 5pm (March); the rest of the year by appointment only. 4DM. ☎ 0 93 73/ 12 52.

OFFENBACH

See FRANKFURT AM MAIN

OLDENBURG

Landesmuseum für Kunst und Kulturgeschichte – Open Tuesdays to Fridays 9am to 5pm, weekends 10am to 5pm. Closed Mondays. Admission free. ☎ 04 41/ 2 20 26 00.

Stadtmuseum Oldenburg – Open Tuesdays to Fridays 9am to 5pm, Saturdays 9am to 12noon, Sundays 10am to 5pm. Closed Mondays, 24 and 31 December. Admission free. ☎ 04 41/ 2 35 28 81.

Augusteum – Same opening times as Landesmuseum. ☎ 04 41/ 2 20 26 00.

Staatliches Museum für Naturkunde und Vorgeschichte – Open Tuesdays to Thursdays 9am to 5pm, Fridays 9am to 3pm, weekends 10am to 5pm. Closed Mondays, 1 January, Good Friday, Easter Day, Whit Sunday, 1 May, 25 December. Admission free. ☎ 04 41/ 2 65 72.

Excursion

Cloppenburg: Museumsdorf – Open March to October 9am to 6pm; November to February 9am to 4pm, Sundays and public holidays 10am to 4pm. 6.50DM. ☎ 0 44 71/ 94 84-0.

OSNABRÜCK

🛈 Markt 22 ☎ 05 41/ 3 23 22 02

Rathaus – Open Mondays to Fridays 9am to 6pm, Saturdays 9am to 1pm, Sundays 10am to 1pm. Closed on certain public holidays. Admission free. ☎ 05 41/ 3 23-22 02.

OTTOBEUREN

🛈 Marktplatz 4 ☎ 0 83 32/ 68 17

Klosterkirche – Open April to October 9am to 7pm; November to March 7am to 5pm. ☎ 0 83 32/ 7 98-0.

Klostergebäude – Open Easter to October 10am to 12noon and 2pm to 5pm; November to 6 January 2pm to 4pm; 7 January to Easter Sundays only 2pm to 4pm. 2DM. ☎ 0 83 32/ 79 80.

P – Q

PADERBORN

🛈 Marienplatz 2a ☎ 0 52 51/ 2 64 61

Diözesanmuseum – Open 10am to 6pm (10am to 8pm on 1st Wednesday in month). Closed Mondays. 4DM. ☎ 0 52 51/ 12 52 16.

PASSAU

🛈 Rathausplatz 3 ☎ 08 51/ 3 34 21

Glasmuseum – Open daily 10am top 4pm; out of season 2pm to 4pm. 3DM. ☎ 08 51/ 3 50 71.

PFALZ AM RHEIN

Hambacher Schloß – Open March to November daily 9am to 6pm. 4DM. ☎ 063 22/ 9 61-3 28.

Edenkoben: Schloß "Villa Ludwigshöhe" – Guided tour (30min) April to September Tuesdays to Sundays 9am to 1pm and 2pm to 5.30pm; October to March until 4.30pm. 5DM. ☎ 0 63 23/ 31 48.

Annweiler: Burg Trifels – Open Holy Week to September daily 9am to 6pm; October to Holy Week daily 9am to 5pm (last admission 30min before closing time). Closed in December. 5DM. ☎ 0 63 46/ 84 70.

PORTA WESTFALICA

🛈 Kempstr. 4 a ☎ 05 71/ 79 12 80

See MINDEN

POTSDAM

🛈 Friedrich-Ebert-Str. 5. D ☎ 03 31/ 30 11 00

Sanssouci: Bildergalerie – Closed for restoration at the time of going to press. ☎ 03 31/96 94-2 02.

Schloß Sanssouci – Guided tour (40min) April to September daily 9am to 5pm; February, March and October 9am to 4pm; November to January 9am to 3pm. Closed 1st and 3rd Mondays of month, 24 and 31 December. 8DM. ☎ 03 31/ 96 94-2 02.

Neue Kammern – Same admission times as Schloß Sanssouci. Closed Fridays, 24 and 31 December. 5 DM. ☎ 03 31/ 96 94-2 02.

Neues Palais – Same admission times as Schloß Sanssouci. Closed 2nd and 4th Mondays of month, 24 and 31 December. 8DM. ☎ 03 31/ 96 94-2 02.

Wasserwerk – Guided tour (20min) mid-May to mid-October Wednesdays to Sundays 9am to 12noon and 1pm to 5pm; mid-October to mid-May weekends 9am to 4pm. Closed Mondays, Tuesdays, 24 and 31 December. 2DM. ☎ 03 01/ 9 69 42 48.

Schloß Cecilienhof – Open daily 9am to 5pm. Closed 2nd and 4th Mondays of month, 24 and 31 December. 5DM. ☎ 03 01/ 96 94-2 02.

Excursion

Kloster Lehnin – Open May to September Mondays to Saturdays 9am to 4.30pm, Sundays 12noon to 4pm; October to April by appointment. ☎ 0 33 82/ 76 82 11.

QUEDLINBURG

🛈 Markt 2 ☎ 0 39 46/ 28 66

Klopstock-Haus – Open May to September 10am to 6pm; October to April 9am to 5pm, weekends 10am to 5pm (last admission 30min before closing). Closed Mondays. 2.50DM. ☎ 0 39 46/ 27 30.

Feininger-Galerie – Open 10am to 12noon and 1pm to 6pm (last admission 30min before closing). Closed Mondays and 1 January. 3DM. ☎ 0 39 46/ 22 38.

Schloßmuseum – Same admission times as Klopstockhaus. 2.50DM. ☎ 0 39 46/ 27 30.

R

RASTATT

Schloß – Guided tour (45min) Tuesdays to Sundays 9.30am to 5pm. Closed Mondays (apart from public holidays). 6DM. ☎ 0 72 22/ 97 83 85.

Wehrgeschichtliches Museum – Open Tuesdays to Sundays 9.30am to 5pm. Closed Mondays (apart from public holidays), 1 January, 24, 25 and 31 December. Admission free. ☎ 0 72 22/ 3 42 44.

Schloß Favorite – Guided tour (45min) mid-March to end September 9am to 5pm; October to mid-November 9am to 4pm. Closed Mondays. 4DM. ☎ 0 72 22/ 3 42 44.

RATZEBURG

Ernst-Barlach-Museum – Open March to November 10am to 12noon and 3pm to 6pm. Closed Mondays. 2DM. ☎ 0 45 41/ 37 89.

RAVENSBRÜCK

Nationale Mahn- und Gedenkstätte Ravensbrück – Open May to September 8am to 6pm (last admission 5.30pm); October to April 8am to 5pm (last admission 4.30pm). Closed Mondays, 1 January, 24, 25 and 31 December. Admission free. ☎ 03 30 93/ 3 92 41.

RECKLINGHAUSEN

See RUHRGEBIET

REGENSBURG

Dom St. Peter: Domschatz – Open March to 1 November 10am to 5pm; December to February Fridays only 10am to 4pm. Closed Mondays, 2-30 November, 24 and 31 December. 2DM. ☎ 09 41/ 5 10 68.

Kreuzgang – Open April to October 6.30am to 6pm; November to March 6.30am to 4pm. Guided tour (1 hour 15min) May to October at 10am, 11am and 2pm, Sundays at 12noon and 2pm; November to April at 11am, Sundays at 12noon. 3DM for guided tour. ☎ 09 41/ 5 77 96.

Diözesanmuseum St. Ulrich – Open March to 1 November 10am to 5pm. Closed Mondays. 2DM. ☎ 09 41/ 5 10 68.

Reichstagsmuseum – Guided tour (1 hour) April to October Mondays to Saturdays 9.30am to 12noon and 2pm to 4pm, Sundays and public holidays from 10am; November to March Mondays to Saturdays 9.30am to 11.30am and 2pm to 4pm, Sundays and public holidays 10am to 12noon. 5DM. ☎ 09 41/ 5 07 44 12.

Schloß Thurn und Taxis – Guided tour (1 hour 15min) April to October Mondays to Fridays at 11.15am, 2pm and 3.15pm, weekends and public holidays at 10am, 11.15am, 2pm and 3.15pm; November to March weekends and public holidays only at 10am, 11.15am, 2pm and 3.15pm. Closed 24 December. 12DM. ☎ 09 41/ 50 48-1 33.

Marstallmuseum – Open April to October 11am to 5pm, weekends and public holidays from 10am; November to March guided tours only (45min) weekends at 10.30am, 11.15am, 2.30pm and 3.15pm. 4DM, or 7DM with guided tour. ☎ 09 41/ 50 48-1 33.

Städtisches Museum – Open 10am to 4pm. Closed Mondays, 1 January, Good Friday, 1 May, 1 November, 24 and 25 December. 4DM (admission free on 1st Sunday in month). ☎ 09 41/ 5 07 14 40.

Excursions

Walhalla – Open April to September daily 9am to 6pm; October until 5pm; November to March 10am to 12noon and 1pm to 4pm (last admission 15min before closing). Closed Shrove Tuesday, 24, 25 and 31 December. 2DM. ☎ 0 94 03/ 39 09.

Kelheim: Befreiungshalle – Open April to September daily 9am to 5pm; October to March 9am to 12noon and 1pm to 4pm, weekends 9am to 4pm. Closed Shrove Tuesday, 1 November, 24, 25 and 31 December. 2DM. ☎ 0 94 41/ 70 12 34.

Kloster Weltenburg – Open daily 6.15am to 8.30pm in summer, and 8am to 6pm in winter. Closed to sightseers during services. Admission free. ☎ 0 94 41/ 50 60.

Bad REICHENHALL

Bad Reichenhaller Salzmuseum – Guided tour (45min) April to October daily 10am to 11.30am and 2pm to 4pm; November to March Tuesdays and Thursdays 2pm to 4pm. 7DM. ☎ 0 86 51/ 70 02-51.

REMAGEN

See BONN

RHEINSBERG

🛈 Markt (Kavalierhaus) ☎ 03 39 31/ 20 59

Schloß – Open April to September 9.30am to 5pm; November to January 9.30am to 3.30pm; February, March and October 9.30am to 4.30pm. Closed Mondays, 24 and 31 December. 5DM. ☎ 03 39 31/ 96 94-2 02.

RHEINTAL

Pfalz bei Kaub (Pfalzgrafenstein) – Open April to September 9am to 1pm and 2pm to 6pm; October to March until 5pm. The fortress is on an island: take the ferry there from Kaub. 4DM. ☎ 0 67 74/ 2 22.

Marksburg – Guided tour (50min) Easter to October daily 10am to 5pm; November to Easter 11am to 4pm. Closed 24-31 December. 7DM. ☎ 0 26 27/ 2 06.

Burg Lahneck – Guided tour (40min) daily April to October 10am to 5pm. 5DM. ☎ 0 26 21/ 17 52 42.

Schloß Stolzenfels - Guided tour (45min) Holy Week to September 9am to 6pm; October to Palm Sunday until 5pm (last admission 45min before closing). Closed Mondays and during December. 5DM. ☎ 02 61/ 5 16 56.

Gedeonseck: Chairlift – Operates mid-June to end of August 9.30am to 6.30pm; 1st 2 weeks of June 10am to 6.30pm; May and September 10am to 6pm; April and October 10am to 5pm. Closed November to March. Rtn fare 8DM. ☎ 0 67 42/ 25 10.

St. Goar: Burg Rheinfels – Open Easter to October daily 9am to 5pm. 5DM. ☎ 0 67 41/ 3 83.

Burg Sooneck – Guided tour (30min) Holy Week to September 9am to 6pm; October to Palm Sunday until 5pm (last admission 45min before closing time). Closed Mondays and during December. 5DM. ☎ 0 67 43/ 60 64.

Burg Reichenstein – Open mid-March to mid-November daily 9am to 6pm. 6DM. ☎ 0 67 21/ 61 17.

Burg Rheinstein – Open March to November daily 9am to 6pm. 6DM. ☎ 0 67 21/ 63 77.

ROMANTISCHE STRASSE

Weikersheim – Guided tour (1hour) April to October daily 9am to 6pm; November to March 10am to 12noon and 1.30pm to 4.30pm. 5.50DM ☎ 0 79 34/ 83 64.

Harburg: Schloß – Guided tour (40min) mid-March to end of September 9am to 11.30am and 1.30pm to 5.30pm; in October until 4.30pm. Closed Mondays. 3-8DM depending on number of people. ☎ 0 90 03/ 14 46.

ROSTOCK

🛈 Schnickmannstr. 13 ☎ 03 81/ 4 59 08 60

Boat trip round port – Departures from Kabutzenhof (Rostock) or Alter Strom (Warnemünde) hourly from 10am. Time: 1 hour to 1 hour 30min. 12DM.

Schiffahrtsmuseum – Open 9am to 5pm (last tickets sold at 4.30pm). Closed Mondays, 1 January, 25 December. 4DM ☎ 03 81/ 4 92 26 97.

Kulturhistorisches Museum – Open April to September 10am to 6pm; October to March 10am to 5pm. Closed Mondays, 1 January, 24, 25 and 31 December. 4DM. ☎ 03 81/ 45 59 13.

Excursions

Bad Doberan: Münster – Open May to September Mondays to Saturdays 9am to 6pm (guided tour on Fridays at 9am); March, April and October Mondays to Saturdays 9am to 4.30pm, Sundays 12noon to 4.30pm; November to February Tuesdays to Fridays 9am to 12noon and 2pm to 4pm, Saturdays 9am to 4pm and Sundays 12noon to 4pm. Guided tour at 9am, 10am, 2pm and 3pm. 1DM, guided tour: 2DM. ☎ 03 82 03/ 27 16.

ROTHENBURG OB DER TAUBER

🛈 Rathaus ☎ 0 98 61/ 4 04 92

Mittelalterliches Kriminalmuseum – Open April to October daily 9.30am to 6pm; November, January and February 2pm to 4pm; December and March 10am to 4pm. 5DM. ☎ 0 98 61/ 53 59.

Reichsstadtmuseum – Open April to October daily 10am to 5pm; November to March 1pm to 4pm. 3DM. ☎ 0 98 61/ 4 04 58.

ROTTWEIL

🛈 Rathaus, Rathausgasse ☎ 07 41/ 49 42 80

Dominikanermuseum – Open 10am to 1pm and 2pm to 5pm. Closed Mondays. 3DM. ☎ 07 41/ 49 43 30.

See Oberes SAALETAL

RÜDESHEIM AM RHEIN

Kloster Eberbach – Open April to September daily 10am to 6pm; October to March 10am to 4pm, weekends 11am to 4pm. 1.50DM. ☎ 0 67 23/ 42 28.

RÜGEN

Jagdschloß Granitz – Open April to September 9am to 5.30pm; October 9am to 4.30pm; November to March daily, except Mondays, 9am to 4.30pm. Closed 25 December. 4 DM. ☎ 03 83 93/ 22 63.

Kap Arkona: Old Lighthouse – Guided tour 10am to 6pm, or 8pm (1 July to 1 September). Closed November to February. 3DM. ☎ 03 83 91/ 316.

RUHRGEBIET

Bochum: Deutsches Bergbau-Museum – Open Tuesdays to Fridays 8.30am to 5.30pm, weekends and public holidays 10am to 4pm. Closed Mondays, 1 January, 24 to 27 and 31 December. 6DM. ☎ 02 34/ 58 77-1 46.

Hagen-Selbecke: Westfälisches Freilichtmuseum – Open March to October 9am to 5pm. Closed Mondays, 24 and 31 December. 5DM. ☎ 0 23 31/ 78 07-44.

Bochum-Dahlhausen: Eisenbahnmuseum – Open Wednesdays and Fridays 10am to 5pm, Sundays and public holidays 10am to 12.45pm (last admission 45min before closing). Closed Mondays and Tuesdays, Thursdays and Saturdays, and from 20 December to 5 January. 5.50DM. ☎ 02 34/ 49 25 16.

Solingen-Gräfrath: Deutsches Klingenmuseum – Open 10am to 5pm, Fridays 2pm to 5pm. Closed Mondays. 5DM. ☎ 02 12/ 5 98 22.

Wuppertal-Barmen: Museum für Frühindustrialisierung – Open 10am to 1pm and 3pm to 5pm. Closed Mondays, 1 January, 1 May, 25 December. 3DM. ☎ 02 11/ 5 63-64 98.

Recklinghausen: Ikonenmuseum – Open Tuesdays to Fridays 10am to 6pm, weekends 11am to 5pm. Closed Mondays, 1 May. 5DM. ☎ 0 23 61/ 50 19 41.

Wuppertal-Elberfeld: Von der Heydt-Museum – Open 10am to 5pm, Thursdays until 9pm. Closed Mondays, 1 May, 24, 25 and 31 December. 5DM. ☎ 02 02/ 5 63-22 23.

Hagen: Karl-Ernst-Osthaus-Museum – Open 11am to 6pm (Thursdays until 10pm). Closed Mondays, 1 January, 1 May, 24, 25 and 31 December. 5DM. ☎ 0 23 31/ 2 07-31 38.

Bochum: Kunstsammlung Museum – Open Wednesdays to Fridays 12noon to 8pm, weekends and public holidays 10am to 6pm. Closed Mondays and Tuesdays. 4DM. ☎ 02 34/ 9 10 22 37.

S

Oberes SAALETAL

Rudolstadt: Heidecksburg – Guided tour (45min) May to September 10am to 6pm; October to April 10am to 5pm. Closed Mondays. 5DM. ☎ 0 36 72/ 2 21 45.

Saalfeld: Thüringer Heimatmuseum – Open March to December Tuesdays to Fridays 8am to 12noon and 1pm to 4pm, weekends 9.30am to 12noon and 1pm to 5pm; January and February Mondays to Fridays 8am to 12noon and 1pm to 4pm. 2DM. ☎ 0 36 71/ 3 50 10.

Saalfeld: Feengrotten – Guided tour (40min) February to mid-November daily 9am to 5pm. 6DM. ☎ 0 36 71/ 23 51.

SAARBRÜCKEN   🏛 Rathaus, Großherzog-Friedrich-Str. 1 ☎ 06 81/ 3 69 01

Historisches Museum Saar – Open 10am to 6pm. Closed Mondays, 24 and 31 December. Admission free. ☎ 06 81/ 5 06-5 49.

Museum für Vor- und Frühgeschichte – Open 9am to 5pm, Sundays 10am to 6pm. Closed Easter Monday, 25 December. Admission free. ☎ 06 81/ 5 84 96 34.

Banqueting hall, Schloß, Saarbrücken

Abenteuermuseum – Open Tuesdays and Wednesdays 9am to 1pm, Thursdays and Fridays 3pm to 7pm. 2DM. ☎ 06 81/ 5 17 47.

Ludwigskirche – Open Tuesdays 3pm to 5pm, Wednesdays 4pm to 6pm, Sundays 11am to 12noon. 1DM. ☎ 06 81/ 5 25 23.

Basilika St. Johann – Open 10am to 6pm. ☎ 06 81/ 3 29 64.

Saarland Museum – Open 10am to 6pm. Closed Mondays. 2DM. ☎ 06 81/ 9 96 40.

Excursions

Homburg: Schloßberghöhlen – Open 9am to 12noon and 1pm and 5pm. Closed 2 weeks in December and 1 week in January. 3DM. ☎ 0 68 41/ 20 66.

Römermuseum Schwarzenacker – Open April to November 9am to 12noon and 1pm to 5pm; December to March Wednesdays 9am to 4.30pm, weekends 12noon to 4.30pm. Closed Mondays. 3DM. ☎ 0 68 48/ 8 75.

SÄCHSISCHE SCHWEIZ

Großsedlitz: Barockgarten – Open April to September 7am to 8pm; October to March 8am to 6pm. 1DM. ☎ 0 35 29/51 92 12.

SALEM
🛈 Schloßseeallee 20 ☎ 0 75 53/ 70 11

Münster, Schloß und Feuerwehrmuseum – Guided tour (1 hour) April to October 10am to 4pm. 14DM. ☎ 0 75 53/ 8 14 37.

ST. ANDREASBERG
🛈 Am Glockenberg 12 ☎ 0 55 82/ 8 03 36

See HARZ

ST. GOAR
🛈 Heerstr. 86 ☎ 0 67 41/ 3 83

See RHEINTAL

ST. PETER
🛈 Rathaus ☎ 0 76 60/ 2 74

See SCHWARZWALD

SAUERLAND

Attendorn: Attahöhle – Daily tours in summer 9.30am to 4.30pm, in winter 10am to 4pm. 7DM. ☎ 0 27 22/ 30 41.

SCHLESWIG
🛈 Plessenstr. 7 ☎ 0 46 21/81 42 26

Nydam-Boot – In the Nydamhalle. Open March to October daily 9am to 5pm; November to February Tuesdays to Sundays 9.30am to 4pm. Closed 1 January, Buß- und Bettag (a Wednesday in November), 24, 25 and 31 December. 5DM (includes admission to Schleswig-Holsteinisches Landesmuseum in Schloß Gottorf). ☎ 0 46 21/ 8 13-3 00.

SCHLESWIG

Schloß Gottorf: Schleswig-Holsteinisches Landesmuseum und Archäologisches Landesmuseum – Same admission times as the Nydamhalle. 5DM. ☏ 0 46 21/ 8 13-3 00.

Wikingermuseum Haithabu – Open April to October daily 9am to 6pm; November to March Tuesdays to Fridays 9am to 5pm, weekends 10am to 6pm. Closed 1 January, 24 and 25 December. 4DM. ☏ 0 46 21/ 8 13-3 00.

Bad SCHUSSENRIED   🏛 Georg-Kaess-Str. 10☏ 0 75 82/ 4 01 34

See ZWIEFALTEN

SCHWÄBISCHE ALB

Holzmaden: Urwelt-Museum Hauff – Open 9am to 5pm. Closed Mondays, 1 January and 25 December. 6DM. ☏ 0 70 23/ 28 73.

Schloß Lichtenstein – Guided tour (30min) 9am to 12noon and 1pm to 5.30pm, Sundays 9am to 5.30pm. Closed December and January. 5DM. ☏ 0 71 29/ 41 02.

Bärenhöhle (Erpfingen) – Open April to October daily 8.30am to 5.30pm. 4DM. ☏ 0 71 28/ 6 96.

Kloster Beuron – The abbey church is open daily 5am to 8pm. Gregorian chants are sung at Mass at 10am on Sundays, 11.15am the rest of the week. Diaporama on the history of the abbey on Sundays at 1.30pm (May to October). Enquire at the porter's lodge of the abbey. ☏ 0 74 66/ 17-1 75.

SCHWÄBISCH HALL   🏛 Am Markt 9 ☏ 07 91/ 75 12 46

Hällisch-Fränkisches Museum – Open 10am to 5pm, Wednesdays until 8pm. Closed Mondays, Good Friday, 24, 25 and 31 December. Admission free. ☏ 07 91/ 7 51-3 60.

Excursions

Groß-Comburg: Abbey – Open mid-March to end of October Tuesday to Saturday 10am to 12noon and 1.30pm to 5pm, Sundays 1.30pm to 5pm. Closed Mondays. 2DM. ☏ 07 91/ 25 48.

Hohenloher Freilandmuseum – Open May September 9am to 6pm; April and October 10am to 5.30pm. Closed Mondays. 7DM. ☏ 07 91/ 8 40 61.

SCHWARZWALD

Gutach: Freilichtmuseum Vogtsbauernhof – Open April to Beginning of November daily 8.30am to 6pm. 6DM. ☏ 0 78 31/ 2 30.

Triberg: Schwarzwald Museum – Open May to September daily 9am to 6pm; October to April 10am to 12noon and 2pm to 5pm. Closed mid-November to mid-December. 4DM. ☏ 0 77 22/ 44 34.

Furtwangen: Deutsches Uhrenmuseum – Open April to 1 November daily 9am to 5pm; 2 November to March 10am to 5pm. 4DM. ☏ 0 77 23/ 9 20-1 17.

St. Peter: Abbey Library – Guided tour (1 hour) April to October Mondays and Wednesdays at 11am, Tuesdays and Thursdays at 2.30pm, Sundays at 11.30am; November and December Sundays at 11.30am. 5DM. ☏ 0 76 60/ 9 10 10.

SCHWERIN   🏛 Am Markt 11 ☏ 03 85/ 81 23 14

Schloß – Open mid-April to mid-October 10am to 6pm; mid-October to mid-April 10am to 5pm. Closed Mondays, 24 and 31 December. 6DM. ☏ 03 85/ 5 25 29 20.

Staatliches Museum – Open 10am to 5pm, Tuesdays until 8pm. Closed Mondays. 4DM. ☏ 03 85/ 5 92 40-0.

SCHWETZINGEN   🏛 Am Schloßplatz 2 ☏ 0 62 02/ 49 33

See HEIDELBERG

SIGMARINGEN   🏛 Schwabstr. 1 ☏ 0 75 71/ 10 62 23

Schloß – Guided tour (45min) February to November daily 8.30am to 12noon and 1pm to 5pm (last admission 30min before closing time). Closed during December and January, and on Shrove Tuesday. 6DM. ☏ 0 75 71/ 72 90.

SINSHEIM   🏛 ☏ 0 72 61/ 40 41 10

See Bad WIMPFEN

SOLINGEN-GRÄFRATH

🛈 Potsdamer Str. 41 ☎ 02 12/ 2 90 23 33

See RUHRGEBIET

SPEYER

🛈 Maximilianstr. 11 ☎ 0 62 32/ 1 43 95

Dom – Open April to October 9am to 7pm, Sundays 7am to 7pm; November to March 9am to 5pm, Sundays 7am to 7pm. Admission free. ☎ 0 62 32/ 10 22 29.

Crypt – Same admission times as Dom. ☎ 0 62 32/ 10 22 29.

Historisches Museum der Pfalz – Open 10am to 6pm, Wednesdays until 8pm. Closed Mondays, 24, 25 and 31 December. 8DM. ☎ 0 62 32/ 1 32 50.

SPREEWALD

Lübbenau: Barge trip – Embarcation in Lübbenau harbour. April to October (weather permitting) from 9am. Duration: 1 hour 30min, or 4 hours with a halt. ☎ 0 35 42/ 22 25.

STADE

🛈 Bahnhofstr. 3 ☎ 0 41 41/ 37 38

Schwedenspeicher-Museum – Open Tuesdays to Fridays 10am to 5pm, weekends until 6pm. Closed Mondays. Admission free. ☎ 0 41 41/ 32 22.

STENDAL

Excursions

Havelberg: Dom St. Marien – Open April to October 10am to 6pm, Sundays and public holidays 10.30am to 6pm; November to March 10am to 12noon and 1pm to 5pm, Sundays and public holidays 10.30am to 12noon and 1pm to 5pm. 3DM. ☎ 03 93 87/ 3 97.

STRALSUND

🛈 Ossenreyerstr. 2 ☎ 0 38 31/ 25 22 51

Deutsches Museum für Meereskunde und Fischerei – Open July and August Mondays to Thursdays 9am to 6pm, Fridays to Sundays 9am to 5pm; May to June and September to October daily 10am to 5pm; November to April Wednesdays to Sundays 10am to 5pm. 7DM. ☎ 0 38 31/ 29 51 35.

Kulturhistorisches Museum – Open 10am to 5pm (last admission 4.30pm). Closed Mondays, 1 January and 24 December. 4DM. ☎ 0 38 31/ 29 21 80.

STRAUBING

Excursions

Metten: Benedictine Abbey – Guided tour (45min) daily (apart from Easter week) at 10am and 3pm. 3DM. ☎ 09 91/ 9 10 80.

STUTTGART

🛈 Königstr. 1a ☎ 07 11/ 2 22 82 40

Linden-Museum – Open 10am to 5pm, Thursdays until 8pm. Closed Mondays. Admission free. ☎ 07 11/ 1 23-12 43.

Staatsgalerie – Open 10am to 5pm, Tuesdays and Thursdays until 8pm. Closed Mondays, 1 January, Shrove Tuesday, Good Friday, 24, 25 and 31 December. 5DM. ☎ 07 11/ 2 12-40 50.

Württembergisches Landesmuseum – Open Tuesdays 10am to 1pm, Wednesdays to Sundays 10am to 5pm. Closed Mondays, 1 January, Good Friday, 24, 25 and 31 December. 5DM. ☎ 07 11/ 2 79-34 00.

Galerie der Stadt Stuttgart – Open 11am to 6pm, Wednesdays until 8pm. Closed Mondays, 1 January, 1 May, 24, 25 and 31 December. Admission free, special exhibitions: 5DM. ☎ 07 11/ 2 16 21 88.

Staatliches Museum für Naturkunde – Open Tuesdays to Fridays 9am to 5pm, Wednesdays until 8pm, Saturdays 9am to 6pm, Sundays 10am to 6pm. Closed Mondays. 4DM. ☎ 07 11/ 8 93 60.

Museum am Löwentor – Same admission times and charges as Staatliches Museum für Naturkunde. ☎ 07 11/ 8 93 60.

Höhenpark Killesberg – Information from ☎ 07 11/ 25 89-0.

Mercedes-Benz-Museum – Open 9am to 5pm. Closed Mondays and certain public holidays. Admission free. ☎ 07 11/ 1 72 25 78.

Excursions

Schloß Solitude – Open April to October 9am to 12noon and 1.30pm to 5pm; November to March 10am to 12noon and 1.30pm to 4pm. 4DM. ☎ 07 11/ 69 66 99.

Schwäbisches Brauereimuseum – Open 10.30am to 5.30pm. Closed Mondays and public holidays. Admission free. ☎ 07 11/ 73 70-2 01.

Porsche-Museum – Open 9am to 4pm, weekends 9am to 5pm. Admission free. ☎ 07 11/ 8 27 56 85.

SYLT

Rail connection – From Niebüll: depending on season between 17 and 24 trips daily (no reservations). From 69DM for each vehicle, but passengers go free. ☎ 0 46 61/ 42 33.

Ferry connection – From Havneby (Denmark): 14 crossings per day from mid-June to end of August. Rtn fare 75-82DM per vehicle including passengers, 8DM for foot passengers. Information and reservations: ☎ 00 45/ 74 75 53 03 in Havneby (Denmark), ☎ 0 46 52/ 4 75 List (Germany) or from travel agents'.

T

TELGTE

🛈 Markt 1 ☎ 0 25 04/ 1 33 27

See MÜNSTER

THÜRINGER WALD

Marienglashöhle – Guided tour (30min) mid-April to September 9am to 5pm; October to mid-April 9am to 4pm. 6DM. ☎ 0 36 23/ 49 53.

Bad TÖLZ

Excursions

Benediktbeuern: Abbey – Guided tour 8am to 6pm, Sundays 9am to 6pm. Closed Good Friday, Christmas and New Year. Admission free. ☎ 0 88 57/ 8 80.

Benediktbeuern: Abbey Church – Open 9am to 6pm, Sundays and public holidays 11am to 6pm. Admission free.

TRIBERG

🛈 Luisenstr. 10 ☎ ☎ 0 77 22/ 95 32 30

See SCHWARZWALD

TRIER

🛈 An der Porta Nigra ☎ 06 51/ 97 80 80

Porta Nigra – Open April to September daily 9am to 6pm; January to March and October and November daily 9am to 5pm; December daily 10am to 4pm. 4DM. ☎ 06 51/ 9 78 08-0.

Städtisches Museum Simeonsstift – Open Tuesdays to Fridays 9am to 5pm, weekends 9am to 3pm, or 1pm from November to March. Closed Mondays. 3DM. ☎ 06 51/ 7 18 24 40.

Dom: Domschatz – Open April to October 10am to 12noon and 2pm to 5pm, Sundays 2pm to 5pm; November to March 10am to 12noon and 2pm to 4pm, Sundays 2pm to 4pm. 1DM. ☎ 06 51/ 71 05-3 78.

Bischöfliches Dom- und Diözesanmuseum – Open 9am to 1pm and 2pm to 5pm, Sundays 1pm to 5pm (last admission 30min before closing). Closed Mondays, 1 January, 24 to 26 December. 2DM. ☎ 06 51/ 7 10 52 55.

Rheinisches Landesmuseum – Open Mondays 10am to 4pm, Tuesdays to Fridays 9.30am to 4pm, Saturdays 9.30am to 1pm and Sundays 9am to 1pm. Closed 1 January and 25 December. Admission free. ☎ 06 51/ 4 35 88.

Kaiserthermen – Same opening times as the Porta Nigra. 4DM. ☎ 06 51/ 9 78 08-0.

Schatzkammer der Stadtbibliothek – Closed at the time of going to press. ☎ 06 51/ 7 18 24 35.

Karl-Marx-Haus – Open April to October 10am to 6pm, Mondays 1pm to 6pm; November to March 10am to 1pm and 3pm to 6pm, Mondays 3pm to 6pm. Closed between 25 December and 1 January. 3DM. ☎ 06 51/ 4 30 11.

Barbarathermen – Open April to September 9am to 1pm and 2pm to 6pm; January to March and October and November 9am to 1pm and 2pm to 5pm (last admission 30min before closing). Closed Mondays and during December. 4DM. ☎ 06 51/ 9 78 08-0.

Amphitheater – Open April to September 9am to 6pm; January to March and October and November 9am to 5pm. Closed December. 4DM. ☎ 06 51/ 9 78 08-0.

TÜBINGEN

🛈 An der Eberhardsbrücke ☎ 0 70 71/ 9 13 60

Stiftskirche – Open April to September 10.30am to 5pm, Sundays and public holidays 12noon to 5pm and during school holidays in Baden-Württemberg open daily 10am to 5pm. 2DM. ☎ 0 70 71/ 5 25 83.

Hölderlinturm – Open Tuesdays to Fridays 10am to 12noon and 3pm to 5pm, weekends and public holidays 2pm to 5pm. Closed Mondays. 3DM. ☎ 0 70 71/ 2 20 40.

U – V

ÜBERLINGEN

🚩 Landungsplatz 14 ☎ 0 75 51/ 40 41

Rathaus: Ratssaal – Open mid-April to mid-October Mondays to Fridays 9am to 12noon and 2.30pm to 5pm, Saturdays 9am to 12noon; mid-October to mid-April Mondays to Fridays 9am to 12noon and 2.30pm to 5pm. Closed Sundays and public holidays, and on Saturdays during winter. Admission free. ☎ 0 75 51/ 99 10 11.

Städtisches Museum – Open Tuesdays to Saturdays 9am to 12.30pm and 2pm to 5pm; April to October also open Sundays 10am to 3pm. Closed Mondays. 4DM. ☎ 0 75 51/ 99 10 70.

ULM

🚩 Münsterplatz ☎ 07 31/ 1 61 28 30

Ulmer Museum – Open 10am to 5pm, Thursdays until 8pm. Closed Mondays. 5DM (admission free on Fridays). ☎ 07 31/ 1 61-43 30.

Deutsches Brotmuseum – Open 10am to 5pm. Closed Mondays. 4.50DM. ☎ 07 31/ 6 99 55.

Excursions

Kloster Wiblingen – Open April to October Tuesdays to Sundays 10am to 12noon and 2pm to 5pm; November to March Tuesdays to Fridays 2pm to 4pm, weekends and public holidays 10am to 12noon and 2pm to 4pm. Closed Mondays, 24 and 25 December. 2DM. ☎ 07 31/ 1 61-28 30.

Blaubeuren: Ehemalige Klosterkirche – Open Palm Sunday to 1 November daily 9am to 6pm; 2 November until Palm Sunday Mondays to Fridays 2pm to 4pm, weekends 10am to 12noon and 2pm to 5pm. 2.50DM. ☎ 0 73 44/ 63 06.

USEDOM

Wolgast: Pfarrkirche St. Petri – Open mid-May to mid-September Mondays to Saturdays 10.30am to 12noon and 1.30pm to 3pm, Sundays 1.30pm to 3pm; mid-September to mid-May Mondays to Fridays at 11am. St. Petri tower: 3DM.

Peenemünde: Historisch-technisches Informationszentrum – Open April to October 9am to 6pm; November to March 10am to 4pm. Closed Mondays. 6DM. ☎ 03 83 71/ 2 05 73.

VEITSHÖCHHEIM

🚩 Rathaus ☎ 09 31/ 9 00 96 37

See WÜRZBURG

W

WALDECK

🚩 Altes Rathaus ☎ 0 56 23/ 53 02

See WALDECKER BERGLAND

WALDECKER BERGLAND

Waldeck: Burgmuseum – Open mid-March to October Mondays to Fridays 10am to 4pm, weekends 10am to 4.30pm. 3DM. ☎ 0 56 23/ 5 89-0.

Arolsen: Schloß – Guided tour (45min) May to September daily 10am to 4.15pm. 5DM. ☎ 0 56 91/ 30 44.

WALDSASSEN

🚩 Johannisplatz 11 ☎ 0 96 32/ 88 28

Bibliothek – Guided tour (25min) daily 10am to 11.30am (11am Sundays) and 2pm to 4.45pm. Closed Monday mornings, Maundy Thursday, Good Friday and in December until Christmas. 4DM. ☎ 0 96 32/ 92 00 25.

WALSRODE

🚩 Lange Str. 20 ☎ 0 51 61/ 20 37

See LÜNEBURGER HEIDE

WASSERBURG AM INN

🚩 Rathaus ☎ 0 80 71/ 1 05 22

Heimatmuseum – Open May to September Tuesdays to Fridays 10am to 12noon and 1pm to 4pm, weekends and public holidays 11am to 3pm; October to April Tuesdays to Fridays 1pm to 4pm, weekends and public holidays 10am to 12noon. Closed Mondays, Good Friday, 1 November, mid-December to end of January. 3DM. ☎ 0 80 71/ 1 05 42.

WEIKERSHEIM

🛈 Marktplatz ☎ 0 79 34/ 1 02 55

See ROMANTISCHE STRASSE

WEILBURG

🛈 Mauerstr. 10 ☎ 0 64 71/ 76 71

See LAHNTAL

WEIMAR

🛈 Marktstr. 10 ☎ 0 36 43/ 20 21 73

Goethehaus – Open March to October 9am to 5pm; November to February 9am to 4pm (Goethe-Museum open until 5pm). Closed Mondays, 24 and 31 December. 8DM. ☎ 0 36 43/ 54 51 02.

Schillerhaus – Open March to October 9am to 5pm; November to February 9am to 4pm (Schiller-Museum until 5pm). Closed Tuesday, 24 and 31 December. 6DM. ☎ 0 36 43/ 54 51 02.

Wittumspalais – Open March to October 9am to 12noon and 1pm to 5pm; November to February 9am to 12noon and 1pm to 4pm. Closed Mondays, 24 and 31 December. 6DM. ☎ 0 36 43/ 54 51 02.

Stadtschloß: Kunstsammlungen zu Weimar – Open 10am to 6pm. Closed Mondays. 4DM. ☎ 0 36 43/ 6 18 31.

Liszt-Haus – Open March to October 9am to 1pm and 2pm to 5pm; November to February 9am to 1pm and 2pm to 4pm. Closed Mondays, 24 and 31 December. 4DM. ☎ 0 36 43/ 54 51 02.

Excursions

Schloß Tiefurt – Open March to October Tuesdays to Sundays 9am to 1pm and 2pm to 5pm; November to February Wednesdays to Sundays 9am to 1pm and 2pm to 4pm. Closed 24 and 31 December. 6DM. ☎ 0 36 43/ 54 51 02.

Schloß Belvedere – Open March to October 10am to 6pm (possibly open during the rest of the year – ring for details). Closed Mondays. 5DM. ☎ 0 36 43/ 6 18 31.

Gedenkstätte Buchenwald – Open May to September 9.45am to 5.45pm; October to April 8.45am to 4.45pm (last admission 30min before closing). Closed Mondays, Christmas and New Year. Admission free. ☎ 0 36 43/ 4 30 20.

WEISSENBURG

🛈 Martin-Luther-Pl. 3 ☎ 0 91 41/ 90 71 24

See EICHSTÄTT

WERNIGERODE

🛈 Nikolaiplatz ☎ 0 39 43/ 3 30 35

Schloßmuseum – Open 10am to 6pm (last admission at 5pm). Closed Mondays. 6DM. ☎ 0 39 43/ 2 33 03.

WERTHEIM

Excursions

Bronnbach: Ehemaliges Kloster – Guided tour (45min) April to October daily 9.15am to 11.45am and 2pm to 5pm, Sundays and public holidays 1pm to 5pm (last admission 30min before closing). 3DM. ☎ 0 93 42/ 3 95 96.

WESSOBRUNN

Ehem. Benediktinerabtei – Guided tour (45min) Mondays to Saturdays at 10am, 3pm and 4pm, Sundays and public holidays at 3pm and 4pm. Closed Easter Day, Whit Sunday and 25 December. 2DM. ☎ 0 88 09/ 9 21 10.

WETZLAR

🛈 Domplatz 8 ☎ 0 64 41/ 9 93 38

Stadt- und Industrie Museum – Open 10am to 1pm and 2pm to 5pm. Closed Mondays, Good Friday and Buß- und Bettag (a Wednesday in November). Admission free. ☎ 0 64 41/ 9 92 69.

Lottehaus – Open 10am to 1pm and 2pm to 5pm. Closed Mondays, Good Friday and Buß- und Bettag (a Wednesday in November). Admission free. ☎ 0 64 41/ 9 92 69.

Sammlung Dr. Irmgard von Lemmers-Danforth – Guided tour (1 hour) 10am to 1pm and 2pm to 5pm. Closed Mondays, 1 January, Good Friday, 24 and 31 December. Admission free. ☎ 0 64 41/ 9 92 69.

Reichskammergerichtsmuseum – Open 10am to 1pm and 2pm to 5pm. Closed Mondays. Admission free. ☎ 0 64 41/ 9 96 12.

WIESBADEN

🏛 Rheinstr. 15 ☎ 06 11/ 1 72 97 80

Schloß – Guided tour (1 hour) on every 1st Saturday in the month at 10am. Admission free. ☎ 06 11/ 35 02 92.

Nerobergbahn – Operates May to August daily 9.30am to 7pm; April (apart from Good Friday) and September Wednesdays and Saturdays 12noon to 7pm, Sundays and public holidays 10am to 7pm; October Wednesdays, weekends and public holidays 12noon to 6pm. 3DM Rtn. ☎ 06 11/ 7 80-34 12.

Griechische Kapelle – Open April to October daily 10am to 5pm (on days with a religious service, open 10am to 3pm or 1pm to 5pm – check in advance); November to March open weekends and public holidays 11am to 4pm.1DM. ☎ 06 11/ 52 84 94.

WIESKIRCHE

Church – Open April to September 8am to 7pm; October to March until 5pm. Admission free. ☎ 0 88 62/ 5 01.

Bad WIMPFEN

🏛 Hauptstr. 45 ☎ 0 70 63/ 5 31 51

Stiftskirche: Cloister – Guided tour (1 hour) mid-April to mid-October by prior appointment. ☎ 0 70 63/ 97 04 11.

Excursions

Sinsheim: Auto- und Technikmuseum – Open daily 9am to 6pm. 13DM. ☎ 0 72 61/ 6 11 16.

Burg Guttenberg – Open March to October daily 9.30am to 5pm. 4DM. ☎ 0 62 66/ 13 73.

Burg Hornberg – Open daily. 3.50DM. ☎ 0 62 61/ 50 01.

Neckarsulm: Deutsches Zweiradmuseum, NSU-Museum – Open Mondays to Fridays 9am to 12noon and 1.30pm to 5pm, weekends 9am to 5pm. 7DM. ☎ 0 71 32/ 3 52. 71.

WISMAR

🏛 Am Markt 11 ☎ 0 38 41/ 28 29 58

Stadtgeschichtliches Museum "Schabbellhaus" – Open May to September 10am to 6pm; October to April 10am to 4.30pm. Closed Mondays, 1 January, 24 and 31 December. 2DM. ☎ 0 38 41/ 28 23 50.

Nikolaikirche – Open April to October Mondays to Fridays 11am to 1pm and 2pm to 5pm, Saturdays 11am to 5pm, Sundays 1pm to 5pm. ☎ 0 38 41/ 61 36 24.

Excursions

Neukloster: Monastery Church – Open May to September 11am to 12noon; October to April Sundays 11am to 12noon. Closed Mondays. ☎ 03 84 22/ 54 51.

WITTENBERG

🏛 Collegienstr. 29 ☎ 0 34 91/ 22 39

Melanchthon-Haus – Open May to October 10am to 6pm; November to April 9am to 5pm (last admission 30min before closing). Closed Fridays, 24, 25 and 31 December. 2DM. ☎ 0 34 91/ 32 79.

Lutherhalle – Open March to October 9am to 6pm; November to February 10am to 5pm (last admission 30min before closing). Closed Mondays, 24 and 31 December. 6DM. ☎ 0 34 91/ 26 71.

Excursions

Schloß Wörlitz – Guided tour (45min for the palace, 45min for the Gothic house) May to September on Mondays 1pm to 6pm, Tuesdays to Sundays 10am to 6pm; in April and October on Mondays 1pm to 4.30pm, Tuesdays to Sundays 10am to 4.30pm. Last admission 1 hour (palace), or 30min (Gothic house), before closing. 4DM (palace), 3.50DM (Gothic house). ☎ 03 49 05/ 2 03 91.

WÖRLITZ

🏛 Am Neuen Wall ☎ 03 49 05/ 2 16

See WITTENBERG

WOLFENBÜTTEL

🏛 Stadtmarkt 9 ☎ 0 53 31/ 8 64 87

Schloß – Open Tuesdays to Saturdays 10am to 5pm, Sundays 10am to 1pm (last admission 15min before closing). Closed Mondays. 3DM. ☎ 0 53 31/ 57 13.

Herzog-August-Bibliothek – Open daily 10am to 5pm. Closed Mondays, Good Friday, 24, 25 and 31 December. 5DM. ☎ 0 53 31/ 8 08-2 14.

Lessinghaus – Same admission times as Herzog-August-Bibliothek. 5DM. ☎ 0 53 31/ 8 08-2 14.

WOLGAST

🏛 Rathausplatz 1 ☎ 0 38 36/ 60 01 18

See USEDOM

WORMS

Kunsthaus Heylshof – Open May to October 10am to 5pm; November to April 2pm to 4pm, Sundays 10am to 12noon and 2pm to 4pm. Closed Mondays, Good Friday, 25 December. 2DM. ☎ 0 62 41/ 2 20 00.

Städtisches Museum – Open 10am to 12noon to 2pm to 5pm. Closed Mondays, 1 May, 24 December to 1 January. 3DM. ☎ 0 62 41/ 85 33 36.

WÜRZBURG

Residenz – Open April to October 9am to 5pm; November to March 10am to 4pm (last admission 30min before closing). Closed Mondays, 1 January, Shrove Tuesday, 1 November, 24, 25 and 31 December. 5DM. ☎ 09 31/ 35 51 70.

Martin-von-Wagner-Museum – Open Tuesdays to Saturdays 9.30am to 12.30pm (picture gallery) and 2pm to 5pm (antiques collection), Sundays and public holidays 9.30am to 12.30pm (picture gallery and antiques collection alternate week to week). Closed Mondays, 1 January, Good Friday, 1 May, 3 October, 1 November, 24 and 25 December. Admission free. ☎ 09 31/ 3 18 66.

Festung Marienberg – Open April to September 9am to 12.30pm and 1pm to 5pm (last admission 4.30pm); October to March 10am to 12.30pm and 1pm to 4pm (last admission 3.30pm). Closed Mondays, 1 January, Shrove Tuesday, 1 November, 24, 25 and 31 December. 3DM. ☎ 09 31/ 35 51 70.

Mainfränkisches Museum – Open April to October 10am to 5pm (last admission 4.30pm); November to March 10am to 4pm (last admission 3.30pm). Closed Mondays, 24 and 25 December. 3.50DM. ☎ 09 31/ 4 30 16.

Excursions

Schloß Veitshöchheim – Guided tour (30min) April to September 9am to 12noon and 1pm to 5pm (fountain display 1pm to 5pm). Closed Mondays. 3DM. ☎ 09 31/ 9 15 82.

WUPPERTAL

See RUHRGEBIET

X – Z

XANTEN

Regionalmuseum – Open May to September Tuesdays to Fridays 9am to 5pm, weekends and public holidays 11am to 6pm; October to April Tuesdays to Fridays 10am to 5pm, weekends and public holidays 11am to 6pm. Closed Mondays, 24, 25 and 31 December. 3DM. ☎ 0 28 01/ 37-2 38.

Archäologischer Park – Open March to November daily 9am to 6pm; December to February 10am to 4pm. 7DM. ☎ 0 28 01/ 29 99.

ZUGSPITZE

Ascent – From Garmisch-Partenkirchen (Zugspitzbahnhof) with the rack-railway every hour from 7.35am to 2.35pm (from 8.35am January to June) up to the Zugspitzplatt station. Journey time: 75min. Cable-car from here to summit leaves every half hour (journey time: 4min). Return to Garmisch leaves from Zugspitzplatt every hour. Rtn fare: 67DM (until the beginning of the skiing season), or 56DM (during skiing season).
From Eibsee, cable-car every half hour from 8.30am to 4.30pm. Journey time: 10min. Rtn fare: 67DM (until the beginning of the skiing season), or 56DM (during skiing season). ☎ 0 88 21/ 7 97-9 51.

ZWICKAU

Robert-Schumann-Haus – Open 10am to 5pm. Closed Sundays, Mondays, Good Friday, Easter Day, 24 and 31 December. 3DM. ☎ 03 75/ 2 52 69.

Städtisches Museum – Open Tuesdays to Fridays 9am to 5pm, weekends 10am to 5pm. Closed Mondays. 3DM. ☎ 03 75/ 83 45 20.

ZWIEFALTEN

Excursions

Obermarchtal: Abbey Church – Viewing by appointment only: ☎ 0 73 75/ 4 99.

Bad Schussenried: Abbey Library – Open April to October 10am to 12noon and 2pm to 5pm, Sundays from 10.15am; November to March 2pm to 4pm, Sundays and public holidays 10.15am to 12noon and 2pm to 4pm. Closed 22 December to mid-January. 2DM. ☎ 0 75 83/ 33-20 9.

Index

This index, like the other alphabetical lists in this guide, follows the normal German alphabetical order, where the vowels ä, ö, ü are classified under æ, œ and ue respectively, ß is classified under ss, and St. under Sankt (Saint).

C

437

X - Y - Z

Glossary

Abtei	abbey	*Jugendherberge, JH*	youth hostel
Ausfahrt	(motorway/highway) exit	*Kap*	cape, headland
		Kapelle	chapel
Aussicht	view	*Kirche*	church
Autobahn	motorway (highway)	*Kloster*	abbey, monastery
		Krankenhaus	hospital
Bad	spa	*Münster*	cathedral, collegiate church
Bahnhof	railway station		
Berg	mountain	*Platz*	(town) square
Botschaft	embassy	*Polizei*	police
Brücke	bridge	*Quelle*	fountain, spring
Brunnen	fountain	*Rathaus*	town hall
Burg	castle, fortress	*Residenz*	palace
Denkmal	memorial	*Sankt-, St.-*	Saint-, St-
Dom	cathedral	*Schloß*	castle, palace
Dorf	village	*Schlucht*	gorge
Einbahnstraße	one-way street	*See*	lake, reservoir
Fels	rock, cliff	*Stadt*	town, city
Fernsehturm	television tower	*Staudamm*	dam
Flughafen	airport	*Straße*	road
Fluß	river	*Tal*	valley
Fremdenverkehrsamt	tourist office	*Talsperre*	dam
Garten	garden(s)	*Thermalbad*	spa
Gebirge	mountain range	*Tierpark*	zoo
Gedenkstätte	memorial	*Turm*	tower
Gletscher	glacier	*Wache*	guardhouse, police station
Grotte	cave		
Hauptbahnhof	mainline railway station	*Wald*	forest
		Wasserfall	waterfall
Haven	port, harbour	*Zeughaus*	arsenal
Höhle	cave	*Zoll*	customs
Insel	island		

MANUFACTURE FRANÇAISE DES PNEUNATIQUES MICHELIN

Société en commandite par actions au capital de 2 000 000 000 de francs

Place des Carmes-Déchaux – 63 Clermont-Ferrand (France)

R.C.S. Clermont-Fd B 855 200 507

© Michelin et Cie, Propriétaires-Éditeurs 1996

Dépôt légal Septembre 1996 – ISBN 2-06-150402-7 – ISSN 0763-1383

Printed in the EU 08-96

Photocomposition : EURONUMÉRIQUE, Montrouge

Impression et brochage : I. F. C., Saint-Germain-du-Puy

Cover illustration by Didier WIBROTTE/Pascal VITRY

Michelin is expanding *its* English-language Green Guide collection

● California ● Canada ● Chicago
● Mexico ● New England ● New York
City ● Quebec ● Washington DC

EUROPE

Austria ● Belgium Luxembourg
Brussels ● France ● Germany
Great Britain ● Greece ● Ireland
Italy ● London ● Netherlands
● Portugal ● Rome ● Scotland
Spain ● Switzerland ● Tuscany
● England : The West Country

FRANCE

● Atlantic Coast
Auvergne Rhône Valley ● Brittany
Burgundy Jura ● Châteaux of the
Loire ● Dordogne ● Flanders Picardy
and the Paris region ● French Riviera
● Normandy ● Paris ● Pyrenees
Languedoc Tarn Gorges

*To get the most out of your vacation
use Michelin Guides and Maps.*

MICHELIN®